INTERNATIONAL HANDBOOK OF EDUCATIONAL POLICY

Springer International Handbooks of Education

VOLUME 13

A list of titles in this series can be found at the end of this volume.

International Handbook of Educational Policy

Part Two

Editors:

Nina Bascia
Ontario Institute for Studies in Education of the University of Toronto, ON, Canada

Alister Cumming
Ontario Institute for Studies in Education of the University of Toronto, ON, Canada

Amanda Datnow
University of Southern California, Los Angeles, CA, USA

Kenneth Leithwood
Ontario Institute for Studies in Education of the University of Toronto, ON, Canada

and

David Livingstone
Ontario Institute for Studies in Education of the University of Toronto, ON, Canada

 Springer

Library of Congress Cataloging-in-Publication Data is available.

ISBN 1-4020-3189-0 HB
ISBN 1-4020-3201-3 e-book

Published by Springer
PO Box 17, 3300 AA Dordrecht, The Netherlands

Sold and distributed in North, Central and South America
by Springer,
101 Philip Drive, Norwell, MA 02061, U.S.A.

In all other countries, sold and distributed
by Springer,
PO Box 322, 3300 AH Dordrecht, The Netherlands

Printed on acid-free paper

Printed and bound in Great Britain by MPG Books Limited, Bodmin, Cornwall.

TABLE OF CONTENTS

SECTION 5

WORKPLACE LEARNING

Section Editor: David Livingstone

SECTION 3

Teaching Quality

Section Editor: Nina Bascia

23

TEACHER CERTIFICATION POLICY: MULTIPLE TREATMENT INTERACTIONS ON THE BODY POLITIC

Elaine Chin* and Rose Asera†
*Cal Poly San Luis Obispo; †Carnegie Foundation for the Advancement of Teaching, USA

This chapter on teacher certification policy is written not by policy makers or analysts, but by two policy consumers who work in K-12 and higher education. Our work as educators has been affected by various policies, often without a sense of their rationale. As we read policy documents, we feel that the viewpoints of practitioners – teacher educators, school administrators, teachers – seem absent from the process of policy making. Teachers and administrators seem to be the objects of policy, but not an evident presence in its creation. From their location in schools and universities, educators frequently view policy as an arbitrary event created by someone far away; policy becomes one more obstacle, burden, or challenge to get around (see e.g., Tyack & Cuban, 1995). But it is also the case that practitioners rarely have the opportunity to examine policy critically. When the work of teachers begins and ends within the boundaries of the classroom, they may not perceive the broader contexts – historical, social, or political – in which their work takes place. Examining policy is a chance to locate the current work of teacher education in the broader landscape.

In this chapter we turn critical eyes to the case of teacher education policies in one state in the U.S. Our observation is that these policies seem fragmented, disconnected, and conflicting. Particular policies address particular problems as if they were isolated, unrelated symptoms rather than parts of a complex, interrelated educational system. Within this complex system, policies interact in unexpected ways, with unanticipated consequences. In health care, practitioners have become concerned that various drugs prescribed for different physical conditions can interact in unexpected ways. Whose responsibility is it to pay attention to the interaction of multiple treatments on the body politic?

The next section of this chapter will describe the characteristics of teacher preparation and licensure in the United States, with California as a particular case, and emphasize how it is different from teacher preparation in many other countries. That will be followed by a brief section on the literature on teacher

International Handbook of Educational Policy, 473–490
Nina Bascia, Alister Cumming, Amanda Datnow, Kenneth Leithwood and David Livingstone (eds.)
© 2005 Springer. Printed in The Netherlands.

certification and licensure, which are two different processes. While certification is an educational process ensuring that individuals preparing for a profession meet minimum standards of competence and licensure is a legal process granting individuals the right to practice a profession (Cronin, 1983), much of the current discussions around certification and licensure use the two terms interchangeably. The main body of the chapter is a critical analysis of the teacher certification policies in California. Tracing the policies from 1970 to the present, the analysis reveals the unanticipated consequences of interactions with other policies.

International Comparisons

In the United States teacher licensure is a state rather than a federal responsibility. This is in contrast to most European countries where the education system, the curriculum, and the production of teachers are all centralized national functions (Wang, Coleman, Coley, & Phelps, 2003). While each state is responsible for policy decisions about teacher licensure, in practice, there is some overlap between federal and state policies. For example, each state may choose the process for licensure, but the federal government mandates that the results – pass and failure rates of candidates – be publicly reported. In addition, national non-governmental bodies that accredit teacher education programs and the commonality of teaching standards (as exemplified by the National Board of Professional Teaching Standards) means that in fact there are broad similarities across programs and across states.

A recent study by Wang et al. (2003) highlighted a number of key differences between teacher education in the United States and other countries, particularly Australia, England, Hong Kong, Japan, Korea, Netherlands, and Singapore, where students scored well in international comparisons of mathematics and science achievement. In particular, the study noted that in other countries, more rigorous criteria are applied earlier in the process of teacher preparation. Even in countries where teacher preparation occurs in specialized institutions or colleges not affiliated with universities, entry requirements may be rigorous, including high school grades and national (high school) exit exams. In contrast, in the U.S., entry to teacher preparation programs is usually not highly competitive (the degree of rigor in entry requirements is related to the degree of selectivity of the host institution). In most states (although California is an exception), requirements for teacher certification can be completed in the course of an undergraduate degree. Entry to teacher education programs usually takes place in the second or third year of undergraduate study though completion may require a fifth year.

The U.S. and England are the only countries that require licensure exams in addition to program exams. The U.S. and U.K. are also the only countries with "alternative" routes to certification. These alternative routes to certification allow people with undergraduate degrees to be hired in teaching positions and concurrently or subsequently complete requirements for certification. In some cases, those alternative requirements are less than those required by a university-based program (Feistritzer & Chester, 2003).

Historical and Current Issues in Teacher Certification

The literature on teacher certification includes historical accounts describing the development of certification policies, debates about the value of certification in assuring the supply and quality of teachers, and descriptive studies of alternative routes to certification. Each of these literatures is instructive in laying the grounds for current discussions about certification, though none provide guidance for analyzing the policies governing certification or their effects in shaping the supply of quality teachers for K-12 schools.

Sedlak (1989) provides a concise history of certification and licensure in the United States. From the late 18th through the mid 19th century, teachers were "certified" if they could pass an examination created by a local board governing the schools. These early examinations were more concerned with moral character and physical abilities than with academic prowess. The rise of state control of certification took place during the mid 19th century with the expansion of the common school, which was driven by a concern that as many children as possible acquire rudimentary skills in arithmetic and literacy. As states gained more power in granting teaching licenses in the 1920's, they established standards for performance. Examinations came to play less of a role in determining who would be certified to teach. Instead, academic preparation in teacher preparation programs became the route to certification. By the 1930's, many states no longer based licensure decisions on test performance.

Interest in developing and using standardized national teacher examinations was renewed in the 1930s and again in the 1950s and 1970s. The National Teacher Examination was developed in 1940 by the Cooperative Testing Service, a division of the American Council on Education, in response to a comparative study of student performance on standardized tests of academic ability and subject matter knowledge. Conducted by William Learned and Ben Wood for the Carnegie Foundation for the Advancement of Teaching, the study reported that the average test score for candidates in teacher education programs was below that of all other test takers except those majoring in art, agriculture, business or secretarial studies. Because teacher education students were perceived as less academically able than other majors, teacher examinations were a tool for weeding out those whom teacher preparation programs may have passed. Despite later studies that contradict the findings of Learned and Wood (e.g., Gray et al., 1993), public opinion persists that the least academically able choose to teach. As a result, in times of teacher surplus, interest in using teacher exams for licensure increases. Most states now use a combination of examination and academic preparation in granting teaching licenses. However, the debate rages on today about which basis for licensure should prevail. This debate is reflected in much of the current literature on the value of certification in ensuring teacher quality.

Like the earlier conflict, the debate has been framed by concerns about teacher supply. Throughout the past several decades, alarms have been regularly sounded about the shortage of qualified teachers. Massive retirements of experienced teachers which have been forecasted for nearly twenty years are now coming to pass at the same time that schools are being overwhelmed by a large influx of school-aged children. Two competing camps have emerged in these debates. One side argues for the greater professionalization of teaching and the higher standards that certification is supposed to confer, while the other argues for market-driven reforms that reduce the barriers erected by current certification requirements (Zeichner, 2003). As the history of teacher certification reveals, the two sides of the professionalization and market-driven debate parallel the earlier competing viewpoints about the basis for certification. Like the earlier reformers, both camps are interested in defining how to achieve an adequate supply of highly qualified teachers and want to influence policy at national and state levels. They differ, however, in how they define the problems of supply and quality.

Proponents of the professionalization agenda argue that the quality of teachers can be enhanced by raising standards for preparation and requiring that beginning teachers demonstrate their competencies in these standards through a variety of means (National Commission on Teaching and America's Future, 1996). Traditional teacher education programs are viewed as the sites where novices can best learn the skills and knowledge needed to meet these higher standards. Quality is a function of the preparation process. Thus, the supporters of the professionalization agenda argue that higher education needs to continue to play a major role in preparing teachers (Darling-Hammond, 2000, 2002).

Market-driven reformers view quality as a function of the individuals who choose to enter teaching. They argue that there is little evidence of a link between licensure (and by extension, of the professional education underlying certification and licensure) and higher student achievement (Ballou & Podgursky, 2000). Instead, individuals' attributes determine the quality of future teachers not preparation through a teacher education program. They do insist that individuals are qualified in terms of their command of subject matter and possess the moral character required of those molding young people. Tests of subject matter knowledge and clearance on criminal background checks are seen as sufficient evidence of an individual's qualifications. Market reformers argue that self-selection is adequate to assure that only those most committed and able would be likely to choose teaching. Basic knowledge about pedagogy can be adequately assessed through examination, and that greater expertise can be learned through direct experience in classrooms or recalled from an individual's past experience as a student.

As with quality, the supply of teachers is viewed quite differently by each camp. The professionalization camp maintains that shortages are overstated. The problem is not an inadequate supply of teachers, but shortages in specific specializations or an uneven distribution of fully credentialed teachers (Darling-Hammond, Berry, Haselkorn, & Fideler, 1999). They further note that the shortage problem is particularly acute in schools that serve predominantly students in poverty, those from linguistic or cultural groups that historically have not been well served by schools (e.g., second language learners), and those living in communities unable to provide the resources needed for basic schooling (Shields, Esch, Humphrey, Young, & Gaston, 1999). Schools lacking necessary resources or who pay less than the median teacher's salary are typically found in remote rural areas or in poor urban communities. Supplying teachers for schools that are hard to staff can be rectified in part through traditional preparation programs. Proponents of the professionalization agenda propose that traditional programs provide a grounding in theories and methods that is necessary for teaching in challenging schools. Socialization through preparation programs is seen as the means to recruit and retain good teachers where they are most needed.

Market reformers see supply as constricted by the bureaucratic requirements for attaining licensure. They argue that qualified candidates, i.e., intelligent and committed people, are blocked from entering teaching because of the obstacles that traditional teacher education, certification and licensure processes present (Ballou & Podgursky, 2000; Fordham Foundation, 2003; Kanstoroom & Finn Jr., 1999). Market-driven reformers believe in "deregulating" the teacher education "industry" and allowing individual schools and districts to determine who is qualified to teach their children. Thus, an adequate supply of already credentialed teachers does not redress the supply problem; it merely provides a pool of individuals whom market reformers do not believe are adequately prepared or committed to working in the hardest to staff schools. What is needed, instead, are market incentives that will attract interested individuals from communities that schools serve or individuals who feel a strong compulsion to serve.

The policy recommendations that emerge from the current literature can be understood in terms of the underlying ideological positions staked out by each side in the debate. Alternative certification approaches straddle the line between the professionalization and market-driven agendas. They have roots in the market-driven agenda in that they were designed to attract people interested in becoming teachers who might not otherwise pursue a credential through a traditional program. As such, candidates who choose alternative routes exhibit many of the characteristics that market reformers view as desirable for future teachers. Studies of alternative certification candidates show them to be older, more racially diverse, possessing greater life experience and skills in specific subject matters that are in high demand (Dill & Stafford-Johnson, 2001; Haberman, 1996; Hutton, Lutz, & Williamson, 1990). Thus, alternative certification programs address the quality issues by recruiting individuals whose personal characteristics and experiences are viewed as quality indicators. Generally, a wider range of experience especially in technical fields is translated as deep knowledge in science and/or mathematics. Some studies have shown that deep knowledge in one's subject areas is not equivalent to the type of skills and knowledge necessary to teach that subject matter to K-12 students (see e.g., Grossman, 1989).

In some states, however, alternative certification approaches adopt or may even require more stringent requirements than traditional teacher education programs. Some programs are considered "alternative" because they require greater study in educational foundations, theory and pedagogy than that required in a traditional program. Connecticut and Maryland are two states that have implemented alternative routes to certification that require equal or higher standards for certification than found in traditional programs (Darling-Hammond, 1990). The increased time candidates spend teaching in internship-like experiences in Connecticut and Maryland's programs are designed to deepen and extend candidate's ability to apply theoretical learning to practical problems. In California, in contrast, alternative programs lower the barriers of cost and time for candidates by allowing them during their preparation programs to teach as full-time teachers of record, and thus earn a salary. But California's alternative certification candidates are required to meet the same standards of competence required by traditional teacher education programs.

Little is actually known about the effects that alternative certification programs have had upon either the supply or the quality of teachers. Evaluations of the effects that alternative programs have had in increasing the supply or quality of teachers have been mixed. As part of an internal evaluation, some alternative programs have tried to ascertain the number of teachers who are retained in the districts or schools where they were first employed as interns (Haberman, 1999; Stafford & Barrow, 1994). While these evaluation studies claim high rates of retention within the first five years of teaching, there is no way to independently verify the actual employment of graduates from these programs. The evaluation studies of teacher retention have had to rely on the efforts of program staff to track down program completers, a process fraught with difficulties.

The evidence about quality differences between alternatively and traditionally certified teachers is equally mixed. Some studies claim that alternatively prepared teachers are perceived by their administrators as more effective than traditionally prepared teachers (see e.g., Bliss, 1990; Hutton et al., 1990) while others show the opposite result (Jelmberg, 1996). However, the global ratings used to measure differences do not address how well each group actually performs. Generally, policy makers do not have a clear picture of these programs' effects because the studies cannot be compared. They use different instruments and methods. In addition, researchers are not always clear about what "alternative" means (Zeichner & Schulte, 2001).

Given the lack of clarity on the effects of teacher certification policy, we have chosen to scrutinize the policies' original legislative intent. As professionals affected by the policies, we wanted to know what problems the policies were trying to solve: were they trying to increase: quality, supply or both? Because there have been no formal evaluations of these polices, our understanding is limited to what we can glean from the unfolding of these policies over time.

Teacher Licensure Policies in California: Conflicts and Contradictions

We have chosen to aim our critical eyes at thirty-three years of teacher education policies in California and other education policies that affect teacher licensure.

California is the third largest U.S. state in terms of land mass and ranks among the five largest economies in the world. Its economic base and population are equally diverse. One can find every type of industry represented in the state, from manufacturing to large-scale agriculture to large service and high tech industries. The 2000 U.S. Census revealed that no single racial group constitutes the majority of the population. However, the diversity of the population is not equally distributed across the state. State regions possess their own unique mix of cultures, languages and economies. In many ways, the issues in California resemble those in other nations. Because of the demographics of an aging population, even countries in Europe that have had ethnically, religious, and linguistically homogenous populations are now grappling with rising immigration and face the question of how to educate the children of those who come to work in their country.

California public schools have had to accommodate fast growth in the school-age population, a large number of recent immigrant children who do not speak English, an undersupply of fully credentialed teachers, and an uneven distribution of qualified teachers. The issues facing California are on a much larger scale than those faced by other states in the U.S. California is the most populous. As recently as 2001 the state projected that in the next decade it would need 30,000 new teachers each year (McKibbin, 2003).

We have chosen to examine two landmark policies, the Ryan Act of 1970 and Senate Bill 2042, the Reform of Teacher Preparation in California, enacted in 1998, being implemented as we write this in 2003. The Ryan Act fundamentally restructured the organization of teacher licensure. It defined teacher education as strictly a post-baccalaureate activity. It established a new state agency, the California Commission on Teacher Credentialing (CCTC), and charged it with overseeing all aspects of teacher licensure, including the accreditation of teacher education programs. Accreditation is the process whereby an agency allows an institution the right to provide particular educational programs and to grant degrees to their students. It is a form of quality control over programs or institutions.

Twenty-eight years later, Senate Bill 2042 (SB 2042) shook the teacher licensure system equally hard. SB 2042 expanded the time allotted for teacher development to include the first two years of employment after completion of a teacher education program. It required that schools, the initial employers of novice teachers, play a role equal to that of teacher preparation programs in the development of a novice's professional expertise. And it aligned the curriculum of teacher education programs with the curriculum standards of K-12 schools. Under SB 2042, teacher education programs are required to prepare their candidates to be able to teach to the new academic subject matter standards defined by the state.

In these two policies, policymakers have attempted to fulfill both the needs for quality teachers and an adequate supply of them. But the good intentions behind policy are not enough: the need for strong professional teachers is often undermined by a sense of urgency to get people into classrooms *quickly*: when both quality and quantity are sought simultaneously, the two goals often compete. In addition, in defining quality, teacher certification policy often pits the importance of content knowledge against the value of pedagogical and professional knowledge. For example, as our analysis later will show, a close reading of the Ryan Act reveals an imbalance between the volume and detail of attention paid to subject content knowledge and the thin prose and limitations devoted to pedagogical preparation. Finally, because, no policy exists in isolation, policies enacted at different times and with different intentions may have unpredicted interactions.

The Ryan Act of 1970

Prior to 1970, California's teacher licensure requirements were like those of most other states. Individuals could obtain certification by completing an undergraduate program that fulfilled the state requirements for licensure in terms of subject matter preparation, professional education courses, and field experiences. That changed, however, with the passage of the Ryan Act ("Teacher Preparation and Licensing Law of 1970," 1970).

The rationale for the change can be found in part in the language of the statute stating legislative intent:

> The Legislature, recognizing the need for excellence in education and the variety and vitality of California's many educational resources, intends to set broad minimum standards and guidelines for teacher preparation and licensing to encourage both *high standards* and diversity. (emphasis added) (Teacher Preparation and Licensing Law of 1970)

The significant phrase in this statement is the reference to *high standards*. *High standards* reflect the legislature's general concern about the quality of the teachers prepared through university-based teacher education program. However, a close reading of the policy reveals that quality is defined as an increase in time and energy devoted to learning subject matter, with a consequent decrease in time spent in professional education courses and activities.

We see how quality becomes equated with subject matter knowledge when we look at the specific provisions of the Ryan Act. It changed teacher licensure by requiring all preparation programs to be post-baccalaureate rather than undergraduate. The entire undergraduate program was to be devoted to the courses related to an academic major; education and professional preparation courses and field experiences were now relegated to the post-baccalaureate program. (This focus on the academic major seems to reflect a fairly traditional range of majors. It did not in any way anticipate either interdisciplinary majors or the question of loosely related academic fields. Could a theater or film studies major teach English? Or could an accountant teach secondary mathematics? The recognized major for elementary teaching in the California State University system is called Liberal Studies and has been an amalgam of choices across the entire curriculum. The nominal attention to subject matter preparation does not take into account the distance between the K-12 and university curricula.)

The specifics in the language of the Act itself also reveal the ways that quality becomes equated with content area preparation. The law describes in considerable detail how future teachers are to demonstrate subject matter knowledge, either by undergraduate major or by examination. A considerable portion of the bill is devoted to providing details about the exams and the procedures to be used in reviewing a candidate's competencies in their subject matter major. It is notable that within the discussion of college majors, the law makes a point of stating that coursework provided by schools or departments of education *cannot be included* as part of any degree program in a major (nor can education be an undergraduate academic major). The field of teacher education is frequently criticized for the inadequate subject matter preparation of prospective teachers, but the control of subject matter preparation was taken entirely out of the hands of teacher educators.

The sections of the Act dealing with professional preparation pay little attention to the specifications of professional education courses. The article on Professional Preparation actually spends as much space and attention to limiting candidate's exposure to professional education courses as it does to outlining the requirements for this type of coursework. One might infer from this lopsided presentation in the bill that professional education courses are the least important aspects of teacher preparation. In fact, the Ryan Act imposes strict limits on the amount of time and number of units that can be allotted to professional education courses. Post-baccalaureate programs can be only one year in length and at least half of that year must be spent in a student teaching experience.

Policy Patches in the Intervening Years: 1970–1998

In the years between the Ryan Act and SB 2042, teacher certification was not a major focus of political attention. Other educational issues – curriculum, standards, and student achievement – were constant sources of controversy, never far from the public eye nor the political horizon. After 1970, fifth-year university-based teacher education became the normal preparatory practice in California. Although there were geographic shortages and topical teacher shortages (particularly in special education, mathematics and the sciences), in general the supply of teachers was considered sufficient and in some cases possibly oversupplied. As various deficits in the system were discovered, a series of targeted policy "patches" were created to cover the gaps. Two common strategies were emergency permits and intern programs, both of which allowed districts to hire individuals without teaching credentials. These two "work-arounds" have found their way into common practice, especially in urban districts.

Emergency permits. Emergency permits are not a new phenomenon. Before 1970 provisional credentials could be granted to individuals who had not completed a teacher preparation program but met minimum qualification of 60 units of college work. After the Ryan Act, the California Commission on Teacher

Credentialing (CCTC) specified that emergency "credentials" be based on at least 90 semester units of college work. For emergency permits, a district is responsible for filing the Declaration of Need for Fully Qualified Educators and must provide permit holders with orientation, guidance, and assistance including curriculum training, classroom management, and classroom instruction. Teachers on emergency permits are restricted to the district requesting the permit.

As areas of shortage were noted, various targeted policies were created to patch holes in the system, rather than systemically address the problem. For example, the 1976 Emergency Bilingual Certificate of Competence Teaching Credential was a direct response to California bilingual education legislation, which required schools to provide bilingual education to non-English speaking students in order to guarantee their equal access to education. That meant that schools needed to hire teachers who were certified in bilingual education, leading to the creation of a new emergency teaching credential. Again, specifying more detail about content area than pedagogy, the emergency bilingual certificate required a minimum of 90 college semester units, competence in the target language, three semester units or staff development in bilingual teaching method-ology, and two years teaching or employment as a paraprofessional in a bilingual classroom. A person so certified could teach any subject in a bilingual class in grade 12 and below.

The policy established by the CCTC on emergency permits strengthened requirements over time and had the intention of moving partially credentialed individuals towards full certification. In order to increase the quality of teachers serving in schools on emergency permits, in 1981, administrative regulations for teachers with emergency permits included enrollment in a degree or credential program – the individual had to complete six semester units in order to serve an additional year on an emergency permit. In 1982, California legislated that emergency permit holders must hold a baccalaureate degree and pass the California Basic Education Skills Test (CBEST). Emergency permit holders could renew their permit for up to five years before they were no longer allowed to work in schools. Each year they were required to show progress towards a full credential. In 1983 there was an initial concurrent (and probably resultant) drop in the numbers of emergency permits.

Despite the more stringent requirements, the numbers of emergency permits rose significantly during the 1990's, with sustained growth through 1995 (McClean, 1999). The number jumped considerably in 1996 with the passage of the Class Size Reduction Act (CSRA) and continued to increase until 2000 (Burke, 2003). The passage of the federal No Child Left Behind Act (NCLB) in 2002 put pressure on the state to decrease the number of teachers working on emergency permits. In a later section of this chapter, we take up the ways in which these two other policy mandates interact with the policies regarding teacher education, not least in terms of how they affect supply and demand.

Intern and pre-intern programs. Like emergency permits, internships existed as a route to certification prior to the Ryan Act. The Teacher Education Internship Act of 1967 allowed school districts to establish internship programs so that they could hire uncertified individuals as teachers in their schools. The intent of this original legislation was to create programs that joined "theory and practice as closely as possible ... during the learning period" ("Teacher Education Internship Act of 1967", 1969). The language of this act invokes the intention of strengthening teacher quality, arguing the merits of including direct classroom experience in teacher education. But by the late 1980's and early 1990's, the demand that internships met was one of quantity.

Intern teachers hold a baccalaureate degree and have been jointly recommended to a teaching position by the school district employing them and the county superintendent of schools. They must meet the same requirements for certification that the state imposes on candidates in non-internship programs. The major difference is that candidates in internship programs work as the teacher of record in the classroom; they assume all of the roles and responsibilities of a fully credentialed teacher and receive only slightly less pay. Interns are required to be enrolled in a preparation program and the school district and/or preparation program must provide support. In contrast to emergency permits, an intern credential is valid for two years and only in the district where they are hired. The school district must work with a local college or university to establish programs of study needed to advance an individual from an internship to a teaching credential.

We see the first indications of how internships would meet the urgent demand for more teachers with the passage of the 1983 Hughes-Hart Education Reform Bill. Hughes-Hart allowed districts to hire uncertified people for secondary schools if they could verify a shortage. In 1984, facing shortages in secondary math and science teachers, the Los Angeles Unified School District was given permission to develop its own internship training program. This change marked the first time that a school district was allowed full responsibility for candidate selection, training, and recommendation for licensure in the state.

The creation of a district-based teacher certification program highlights another enduring conflict that prevails in teacher licensure policy: where should teacher preparation be located – in the universities or in the schools where teachers will work? By requiring school districts and universities to work together to develop and run internship programs, the state seemed to recognize the need to involve both in teacher preparation. However, the debate has not been resolved. We see the conflict played out in the fiscal policies governing internship funding. California's internship programs are supported by state funds. Passage of Assembly Bill 1161 in 1993 set the level of funding at $2500 per intern. Programs may use these funds in any manner they wish as long as they follow the state's guidelines for allowable expenditures. But the fiscal agent for the internship monies is always the school district who partners with the university, even when the internship is housed in or run by a university. No university is allowed to be the sole fiscal agent for the internship funds. If we follow the money, it appears that school districts are given greater control over the internship preparation programs than the universities that provide the courses for certification.

The primary intent of AB 1161 was to create an alternative route to certification that would immediately put teachers in schools heavily staffed by uncredentialed ("emergency permit") individuals. Implicit in this legislation is an alternative vision of teacher quality. Internship programs were designed to attract people who might not otherwise have chosen teaching as a career. The policy-makers were most interested in attracting second career candidates, especially those retiring from a down-sized military or from high-tech fields. They assumed that second career individuals were likely to possess particularly strong content knowledge and would be high quality candidates given their experience and success in their first career. The extent to which internships have attracted well-qualified, second-career individuals has yet to be demonstrated empirically, despite claims based upon anecdotal evidence (Dill, Hayes, & Stafford-Johnson, 1999).

Inoculating Against Low Student Achievement: Class Size Reduction. The mid-to-late 1990s saw a run of policies meant to improve student learning, fueled by the booming state economy and spurred on by the poor showings of comparative academic achievement. For example in the 1995 National Assessment of Educational Progress (NAEP) scores, California fourth graders tied for last place in reading among 34 states. One such policy, Class Size Reduction (CSR) was enacted in California in 1996. Based on findings of the large scale Tennessee Project STAR (Student Teacher Achievement Ratio), California mandated limitations to the number of students (to a ratio of one teacher to 20 students) in all K-3 classrooms and in some ninth grade mathematics and language arts classes.

The policy had some positive effects and unanticipated costs to the system overall. Implementing this legislation dramatically increased the need for teachers; the pool of long-term substitute teachers were absorbed into the regular teaching force and students in credential programs were frequently hired before completion. Accompanying these trends was an increase in the number of teachers hired on emergency permits, extraordinary growth in the existing internship programs, and the creation of Pre-internship programs to equip candidates with better subject knowledge and eventually full certification. The 1997 California Pre-Intern Teaching Program (AB 351) was passed in the shadow of Class Size Reduction, a policy initiative described below that had a major impact on teacher demand. Pre-intern programs focused on providing candidates with intensive subject matter preparation. Prospective teachers in pre-intern programs have one year to complete subject matter coursework or to take the subject matter examination(s). (For elementary school pre-interns, this examination is the MSAT or Multiple Subjects Assessment for Teachers, Praxis and SSAT for single subjects.) If the candidate passes, he or she enters an internship or other professional preparation program. If the candidate does not meet the requirements in the first year, he or she is allowed only one more year on a pre-intern certificate.

The increased numbers of K-3 classes also strained resources and space in schools. Sadly, intent and effect can be different. Evaluation of the state policy noted that class size reduction was associated with declines in teacher qualifications and exacerbated the maldistribution of credentialed teachers (Behrnstedt

& Stacher, 2002). Urban districts hired more teachers without full credentials (Shields et al., 1999). Rather than improving the quality of student learning, the policy may have had the opposite or mixed effects.

SB 2042: Reform of Teacher Education Programs – Redux

By the mid-1990s, the rhetoric and logic of systemic reform were taking hold in the education system – curriculum standards were developed and put in place, and under the banner of accountability, the system attempted to align curriculum and assessment. This general overhaul of the system brought attention to teacher education. The major legislation aimed directly at teacher preparation was Senate Bill 2042, The Reform of Teacher Preparation in California ("SB 2042, Alpert Teacher credentialing," 1998). SB 2042 directed the CCTC to overhaul the requirements for teacher certification based upon newly designed standards for the teaching profession adopted by the state in 1997. SB 2042 represented a significant change in the state's approach to teacher education along a number of dimensions. The bill addressed challenges that California's schools were facing, namely the shortage of fully qualified teachers and a significant increase in numbers of students with special linguistic or learning needs. SB 2042 is a policy attempting simultaneously to strengthen professional quality and increase supply.

To address teacher shortages in California, SB 2042 reversed the state's long-standing commitment to a strictly post-baccalaureate certification route. SB 2042 encouraged the development of undergraduate education minors or "blended" programs of teacher preparation. Blended programs combine study in specific subject matters and professional preparation in teaching starting in undergraduate years. Like post-baccalaureate programs, professional preparation in blended programs can occupy no more than the equivalent of one-year of coursework and its accompanying field experiences. Most blended programs can be completed in a little more than four years; they were seen as one strategy to get people into classrooms more quickly. In addition, the bill mandates the expansion of programs that "attract qualified persons to teaching," language that supports the state's continuing commitment to developing alternative routes to certification like internship programs. We note that this locates the qualification in the individual rather than in the preparation.

Even before the enactment of the Ryan Act, teacher credentialing in California was a two-tiered process. The Ryan Act specified requirements for the first and second tier credentialing. Teachers new to California public schools (whether newly trained or as emigrants from another state where they had been licensed) obtain a preliminary (Level 1) credential which allows them to teach for five years. At the end of that time, teachers may apply for a Professional Clear (Level 2) credential. To earn a Professional Clear Credential, teachers had to prove they had engaged in certain types of professional development activities or taken courses that helped them acquire knowledge and skills in (a) teaching students who were non-native English speakers or who had special needs, and (b) to use emerging technologies like computers or other multi-media applications. Until

1985, the Professional Clear was a lifetime credential that required no recertification. Now the Clear Credential is valid for only five years. Teachers must demonstrate that they have engaged in 150 hours of professional growth activities during each five-year period in order to be recertified.

SB 2042 pushed the requirements previously part of a Clear credential into the Preliminary Credential programs. It put the onus on teacher education programs to expand their curriculum, but it did not allow for a concomitant increase in the amount of time for professional preparation. To be fair, the new standards established by SB 2042 were designed to address the pressing need for schools to educate all students, regardless of their backgrounds or abilities. It was a move to ensure that teacher preparation programs did not ignore the complexities of teaching in the growing number of multilingual, multicultural classrooms. However, in redesigning programs to meet these new standards for accreditation and licensure, many teacher educators interpreted this mandate as a challenge to do more in less time.

SB 2042 also redefined the requirements for qualifying for a Professional or Level 2 credential by mandating that beginning certified teachers participate in formal induction programs during their first two years of teaching. The inclusion of an induction period was supposed to represent a "seamless" process of teacher development. Universities and other teacher education providers have one year to prepare candidates for the preliminary credential. The districts where candidates are employed are then responsible for ensuring their teachers complete an induction program during the next two years of their career. Thus the majority of time devoted to teacher development is under the control of school districts. School districts may look to universities to help provide induction programs, but they are not required to do so. The expansion of time devoted to teacher development contained within the legislation could be read as a positive development because it acknowledges that learning to teach does not occur in just one year of a teacher preparation program. However, it could also be interpreted as a move to take control of teacher education out of the hands of higher education.

Contextual Effects on Policy Implementation

SB 2042 was enacted at a time when the state's coffers were flush with surplus money generated from the booming high-tech economy. Five years later, it is being implemented in fiscally hard times with the largest budget deficit in the state's history. With state budgets cut drastically, districts are strapped for resources. The future of class size reduction is uncertain and continuation and even need for intern programs is in doubt, even though the governor's proposed 2003–04 budget still contains a little more than $22 million dollars for the intern programs (McKibbin, 2003, personal communication). The current fiscal crisis has forced the state to reconsider all budget priorities. As of the 2004–2005 budget the state is maintaining support for the internships with a slight increase in funding, but uncertainties in the economic situation make it difficult to forecast how the employment picture will be altered and affect internship programs and intern teachers. The majority of these programs require that interns obtain employment with a participating school district before they qualify for the program and spend at least two years completing their credential. Some programs go so far as to help interns acquire positions. However, the programs are being buffeted by the economic shifts. The threatened lay-off of teachers in Spring 2003 and subsequent rehiring in Fall 2003 has muddied the situation for both program directors and intern teachers. School sites that were once predictable placements are no longer certain; many interns exist in a kind of limbo until they learn if they will be employed. Only interns in high-need specializations such as special education or those employed by districts with chronic shortages, such as Los Angeles, are still sure of present employment.

Because of the shrinking job market and the increase in numbers of fully credentialed teachers seeking jobs, the shortages that internship programs were designed to address are no longer as pressing a problem. However, shortages in the neediest schools continue to exist. The evidence is inconclusive as to whether the internship programs have helped alleviate the problem of the maldistribution of teachers in the state.

The overall intent of SB 2042 was to provide higher quality teachers by imposing more rigorous standards upon teacher education programs while also expanding the pool of candidates entering the teaching profession. While there is no inherent contradiction between simultaneously increasing quality and quantity, there are a number of ways in which current legislation makes it difficult to achieve both results. The time limits placed upon teacher education programs makes it difficult for them to provide both depth and coverage of the additional competencies new teachers must demonstrate. The demands upon school districts to carry the burden for professional development through induction programs are not matched by funding from the state to support such efforts. Nor has there been adequate time and resources given to the professional development that school systems may need to take on an educational role different from their traditional mission. The severe budget deficit that the state faces has forced it to reconsider whether participation in a formal induction program will be required. The state is now looking at the possibility of allowing teachers to earn their Level 2 credential by paying for and taking additional coursework because the state can no longer afford induction programs.

Additional avenues towards licensure that can expand the pool, like the use of "paper and pencil" tests to waive professional education or subject matter knowledge requirements, may actually lead to less control over the quality of teachers employed by school. Thus, the reforms in teacher preparation currently in place in California present both producers and employers of future teachers with a contradictory set of expectations that are nearly impossible to meet. The reforms of the 1990s reflect policy makers' continuing distrust of teacher educators while at the same time displaying a desire to improve the education of future teachers.

The state policy picture would be muddled enough if we stopped at the question of implementation of SB 2042. But the federal policy, No Child Left

Behind (NCLB), adds one more dimension of complication, particularly around the definition of quality. NCLB mandates that every classroom have a highly-qualified teacher by 2005–2006 and that all new hires in Title I (serving a high poverty population) schools be highly-qualified. The NCLB definition of quality rests on competence in the subject areas they teach. Thus the California State Board of Education has developed a conceptual plan to meet this mandate. All new elementary teachers will have to pass a rigorous state examination, and waivers from subject area majors (such as Liberal Studies) will no longer be recognized. Implementation of this federal policy also eliminates pre-internship programs and may have the same effect on recently-established blended programs as well.

Caught Between the Lines: Enacting, Interpreting, and Implementing Policy

What can two bemused educators conclude looking back over this thirty-some year policy trajectory? While multiple and extensive policies have been enacted, the central issues of teacher education remain the same. Policy has not been effective at insuring either quality or supply of teachers, and often pits one need against the other. California is still confronted with acute shortages of mathematics, science, and special education teachers, and there is still a serious maldistribution of certified teachers, with a dearth of certified teachers in urban schools serving minority and immigrant populations.

Workforce projections do not seem able to anticipate accurately major external events or their impact. The supply of teachers continues to be confounded by changes in the political and economic context. Thus the system can have unexpected deficits or gluts at a time when the longer term policy effect is moving in the other direction. Implementing a policy can require several years – time needed for the system to adjust and for individuals to traverse the new requirements. Unfortunately, the time frame for external influences can be much faster. And individuals can be caught in-between.

Class Size Reduction, for example, which was based on research findings, had systemic effects far beyond the desired personal attention of smaller classes. Class Size Reduction established in the bountiful years created an immediate increase in need. That need was filled haphazardly with emergency permits while the system geared up for higher production. The economic downturn is having the opposite effect, almost as quickly. As district budgets contract, the newest teachers are the first let go, and prospective teachers in the pipeline – many of whom responded to the rhetoric of projected need – wonder if they will be able to get teaching jobs.

Reading the policy records, we often could see good intentions and responsibility in the legislative intention. But from our current vantage point, it did not appear that the perception of the problem or the proposed solution took into consideration the complexity of the educational system. Some small scale solutions cannot be ramped up to the whole state and have the same projected effect. The policies do not acknowledge that what they have identified as the problem to be solved may be more complicated or that it may be just a symptom of a larger problem. And singular or simplistic solutions do little to resolve complicated settings.

These policies do not seem to anticipate the complexity of the educational setting – at the state, district, school, or classroom level – where the policy will influence practice. For example, SB 2042, layered more pedagogical responsibilities onto an already overstuffed year of post-baccalaureate teacher preparation. It is no wonder that many teacher educators did not respond to the increased professional spirit of the legislation with delight, but felt discontented and burdened by the additional requirements.

Perhaps it is the age of accountability we live in that makes one more absence so striking: the licensure policies we have examined do not contain criteria nor mechanisms for measuring their impact. We have no data to assess the effect or effectiveness of these policies. These policies have not been time-limited in a way that would precipitate a reassessment of the original conditions to see if the context has changed, if they have had their desired impact, or if impact has changed the context. While it is not possible to anticipate all the changes and forces on the system, it is reasonable to anticipate that things will change. Regular data collection and evaluation of impact could provide ongoing feedback to policy makers.

Medical treatment models have shifted from treating a disease or problem to acknowledging that it is the person who has the disease. Policy patches and instant remedies seemed to ignore the fact that there is a complex educational system – the body politic – and that policies affect the entire body, not just the isolated problem.

References

Ballou, D., & Podgursky, M. (2000). Reforming teacher preparation and licensing: What is the evidence? *Teachers College Record, 102*(1), 5–27.

Behrnstedt, G. W., & Stacher, B. M. (2002). *What We Have Learned About Class Size Reduction in California?* CSR Research Consortium.

Bliss, T. (1990). Alternative certification in Connecticut: Reshaping the profession. *Peabody Journal of Education, 67*(3), 35–54.

Burke, S. (2003). *2001–02 Annual report: Emergency permits and credential waivers.* Retrieved August 8, 2003, 2003, from http://www.ctc.ca.gov/reports/2001_2002_EPW.pdf

Cronin, J. M. (1983). State regulation of teacher preparation. In L. S. Shulman & G. Sykes (Eds.), *Handbook of teaching and policy* (pp. 171–191). New York: Longman.

Darling-Hammond, L. (1990). Teaching and knowledge: Policy issues posed by alternative certification for teachers. *Peabody Journal of Education, 67*(3), 123–154.

Darling-Hammond, L. (2000). Reforming teacher preparation and licensing: Debating the evidence. *Teachers College Record, 102*(1), 28–56.

Darling-Hammond, L. (2002). Research and rhetoric on teacher certification: A response to "Teacher Certification Reconsidered". *Education Policy Analysis Archives, 10*(36).

Darling-Hammond, L., Berry, B. T., Haselkorn, D., & Fideler, E. (1999). Teacher recruitment, selection, and induction; policy influences on the supply and quality of teachers. In L. Darling-Hammond & G. Sykes (Eds.), *Teaching as the learning profession* (pp. 183–232). San Francisco: Jossey-Bass.

Dill, V. S., Hayes, M. J., & Stafford-Johnson, D. (1999). Finding teachers with mature life experiences. *Kappa Delta Pi Record, 36*(1), 12–15.

Dill, V. S., & Stafford-Johnson, D. (2001). *The data is in: What works in alternative teacher certification program design.* Retrieved February 8, 2001, from http://educationnews.org/data_is_in.htm

Feistritzer, C. E., & Chester, D. T. (2003). *Alternative teacher certification: A state-by-state analysis 2003.* Washington, DC: National Center for Education Information.

Fordham Foundation (2003). *The teachers we need and how to get more of them.* Retrieved July 30, 2003, from http://www.fordhamfoundation.org/library/teacher.html

Gray, L., Cahalan, M., Hein, S., Litman, C., Severynse, J., Warren, S. et al. (1993). *New teachers in the job market: 1991 update.* Washington, DC: Office of Educational Research and Improvement.

Grossman, P. (1989). Learning to teach without teacher education. *Teachers College Record, 91*(2), 191–208.

Haberman, M. (1996). Selecting and preparing culturally competent teachers for urban schools. In J. Sikula, T. J. Buttery & E. Guyton (Eds.), *Handbook of research on teacher education: A project of the Association of Teacher Educators* (2nd ed., pp. 747–760). New York: Macmillan.

Haberman, M. (1999). Increasing the number of high-quality African American teachers in urban schools. *Journal of Instructional Psychology.*

Hutton, J. B., Lutz, F. W., & Williamson, J. L. (1990). Characteristics, attitudes, and performance of alternative certification interns. *Educational Research Quarterly, 14*(1), 38–48.

Jelmberg, J. (1996). College-based teacher education versus state-sponsored alternative programs. *Journal of Teacher Education, 47*(1), 60–66.

Kanstoroom, M., & Finn Jr., C. E. (Eds.) (1999). *Better teachers, better schools.* District of Columbia.

McClean, M. (1999). *Second annual report on the use of emergency permits and credential waivers for 1997–98.* Retrieved July 1, 2003, from http://www.ctc.ca.gov/aboutctc/agendas/may_1999/caw/cca2.html

McKibbin, M. (2003). *California teacher recruitment summit: Explorations of the best practices in teacher recruitment and preparation* (Report). Sacramento, CA: Sacramento County Office of Education.

National Commission on Teaching and America's Future (1996). *What matters most: Teaching for America's future.* New York.

SB 2042, Alpert. *Teacher credentialing, California State Senate* (1998).

Sedlak, M. W. (1989). "Let us go buy a school master": Historical perspectives on the hiring of teachers in the United States, 1750–1980. In D. Warren (Ed.), *American teachers: Histories of a profession at work* (pp. 257–290). New York: Macmillan.

Shields, P., Esch, C. E., Humphrey, D. C., Young, V. M., & Gaston, M. (1999). *The status of the teaching profession: Research findings and policy recommendations. A report to the Teaching and California's Future Task Force.* Santa Cruz, CA: The Center for the Future of Teaching and Learning.

Stafford, D., & Barrow, G. (1994). Houston's alternative certification program. *Educational Forum, 58*(2), 193–200.

Teacher Education Internship Act of 1967, Article 2.5 13221–13242 (1969).

Teacher Preparation and Licensing Law of 1970, Chapter 557 (1970).

Tyack, D., & Cuban, L. (1995). *Tinkering toward utopia: A century of public school reform.* Cambridge, MA: Harvard University Press.

Wang, A. H., Coleman, A. B., Coley, R. J., & Phelps, R. P. (2003). *Preparing teachers around the world.* Princeton, NJ: Educational Testing Service.

Zeichner, K. M. (2003). The adequacies and inadequacies of three current strategies to recruit, prepare and retain the best teachers for all students. *Teachers College Record, 105*(3), 490–519.

Zeichner, K. M., & Schulte, A. K. (2001). What we know and don't know from peer-reviewed research about alternative teacher certification programs. *Journal of Teacher Education, 52*(4), 266–282

24

RETAINING TEACHERS IN HIGH-POVERTY SCHOOLS: A POLICY FRAMEWORK[1]

Karen Hunter Quartz, Kimberly Barraza-Lyons, and Andrew Thomas
University of California, USA

Ensuring all children have a qualified teacher is a global struggle. Although the causes and contours of the problem vary from country to country, the shortage of good teachers is of wide concern throughout the world. Policies that address this shortage typically focus on supply-side solutions such as recruitment. Yet there is increasing evidence that getting more teachers into the career pipeline only scratches the surface of a complex problem. The pipe itself leaks and it does so in ways that further disadvantage high-poverty schools where the shortage is most acute. In the United States, for example, 46% of teachers leave the profession within their first five years and more of these leavers are fleeing high-poverty schools than affluent schools (Ingersoll, 2001, 2002, 2003a, 2003b). The disproportionate impact of the teacher shortage in certain schools should make these schools "high priority" targets for teacher retention policies. These schools, often termed "urban," or "hard-to-staff," are predominately schools located in cities and their immediate surroundings, although there are many high-poverty rural schools that face similar challenges. These high-priority schools are under-resourced and under-funded, often situated in low-income communities of color that serve a majority of academically low-performing children whose parents have comparatively low levels of formal schooling. Each year U.S. public schools fitting this description lose and must replace approximately one-fifth of their teaching faculty. In large urban high schools this can translate into 50 or so new hires each fall. Filling 50 positions at one school every year is indeed a challenge, but the even bigger challenge is to fill these positions with qualified teachers who will stay over the long haul and help transform these high-priority schools.

This chapter offers a policy framework for understanding and addressing the teacher shortage crisis as a crisis of retention – not inadequate supply – that is felt most acutely in high-poverty schools. Focusing on three policy arenas – teacher preparation, induction, and career advancement – this framework attempts to capture U.S. efforts to professionalize teaching in high-priority schools, efforts that will set the stage for a more stable, qualified workforce. These policy arenas contribute to a professional culture of teaching and schools

International Handbook of Educational Policy, 491–506
Nina Bascia, Alister Cumming, Amanda Datnow, Kenneth Leithwood and David Livingstone (Eds.)
© 2005 *Springer. Printed in Great Britain.*

where learning is not packaged into stages or programs but instead is viewed as a continuum that lasts throughout a teacher's career. Instead of isolating bureaucracies, schools need to become professional learning communities – hopeful sites for both students and teachers to grow and develop. With this vision in mind, we review below the policy landscape surrounding the global teacher shortage crisis and suggest what we consider the most promising response for the particular context of U.S. schools.

The Global Teacher Shortage Crisis: Defining the Problem

Each year in the United States, more teachers leave the profession than enter. In 1999, for instance, 230,000 people entered teaching, yet nearly 290,000 left (Ingersoll, 2003b). And 250,000 more teachers moved or migrated from one school to another – usually away from "hard to staff" high-priority schools. Other countries face a similar struggle. Studies sponsored by UNESCO and the Organization for Economic Cooperation and Development (OECD) report teacher attrition rates of between 5 and 30 percent around the globe. Unlike the low retention rates found in industrialized nations' urban cores, rates of retention are lowest in the rural areas of poor, less developed countries and analysis of the World Education Indicators Program reports that in participating countries, which include Argentina, Brazil, Chile, Egypt, Indonesia, Malaysia, Peru, Paraguay, the Philippines, Thailand, Tunisia, Uruguay and Zimbabwe, the demand for teachers is increasing, especially in those with the lowest levels of economic development. Moreover, economic and social instability appears to increase attrition; in countries like Liberia and the Czech Republic, for example, attrition rates reach between 20 and 30 percent (Macdonald, 1999).

Teacher attrition has serious financial, organizational, and academic implications. Recruiting and hiring teachers is a time consuming and expensive process, requiring districts to shift financial and human resources away from other programs in order to search for and hire new teachers. The financial costs of teacher turnover in one U.S. state have been estimated at between 329 million and 2.1 billion dollars annually (TSBEC, 2003). The costs of attrition extend from those largely hidden in tuition and tax support for teachers to the direct funds schools invest in induction and professional development efforts (e.g., Dianda & Quartz, 1995). High-poverty schools' higher turnover rates make the associated costs especially damaging, adding to the long list of challenges already facing these schools.

When schools are forced to devote time and energy to recruiting and preparing newly hired teachers, their overall effectiveness declines (Rosenholtz, 1985). This is an especially pressing problem for high-poverty schools that face the additional burden of repeatedly inducting new hires that are woefully under-prepared, exacerbating already low levels of school effectiveness. Organizational theorists contend that high levels of turnover also contribute to a negative working climate – making turnover both a cause and a result of school dysfunction. Tragically, this dysfunction translates into the under-achievement of low-income students most in need. The strongest predictor of student achievement is having a fully credentialed teacher in the classroom (Darling-Hammond, 2000) and research shows that student achievement in math and language is correlated with teacher subject matter expertise (Rowan et al., 1997 cited in Henke, Chen, & Geis, 2000). We also know that teachers' level of professional commitment is related to increased student achievement in math and language arts (Kushman, 1992; Rosenholtz, 1989). Conversely, teachers in schools with low-achieving students report greater levels of job dissatisfaction than those in high-performing schools and are more likely to leave their schools and the profession (Shann, 1998; Hanushek, 2001). The bottom line is that high-poverty schools struggle to both attract and retain qualified teachers and this lack of staff capability and stability helps perpetuate the cycle of under-achievement for students most in need.

Why Do Teachers Leave?

Significant research has created a fairly consistent portrait of those who leave teaching – individual characteristics that are tied to macro-level conditions. Content focus seems to matter, although the areas with highest attrition differ from country to country. In the United States, for example, secondary mathematics and science teachers, along with teachers of special and bilingual education, leave at higher rates than those in other fields, while in the UK, English, music, and physical education teachers also appear to leave at higher rates (Boe, Bobbitt, Cook, Whitener, & Weber, 1997; Macdonald, 1999). It is theorized that U.S. math and science teachers may leave because they have more career options than other teachers, and, according to one study, physical education teachers may leave simply due to the physically exhausting nature of their work. Some differences in attrition have also been noted with respect to age and gender. There does not appear to be a significant gender difference in the rate of teacher leavers, although the turnover rate – remaining in the profession, but changing schools – is highest for women in their 20s and 30s who often relocate because of their husbands' careers or leave temporarily to raise children (Boe et al., 1997; Henke et al., 2000). Both male and female teachers are more likely to leave earlier in their careers and at a younger age than their older and more experienced counterparts (Bobbitt, Leich, Whitener, & Lynch, 1994; Boe et al., 1997; Grissmer & Kirby, 1987; Stinebrickner, 1999; Theobald, 1990). Some researchers conclude that the teachers most likely to ultimately leave the profession are those considered academically superior than their retained colleagues, i.e., those with higher undergraduate GPAs and standardized test scores, those who hold advanced degrees, and those with majors or minors in subjects other than education (Darling-Hammond & Sclan, 1996; Murnane, 1991; Schlechty & Vance, 1983; Sclan, 1993; Stinebrickner, 1999). Ironically, as the call increases for highly qualified teachers, it seems to be the "best and brightest" candidates that leave earlier and in greater numbers than their less academically grounded counterparts.

In a number of U.S. and international studies, low salaries are cited as one of the primary reasons behind teachers' decision to leave (GTC, 2001; Henke et al., 2000; Ingersoll, 2003a; Murnane & Olsen, 1989; Towse, Kent, Osaki, & Kirua, 2001). With alternative careers increasingly offering significantly higher pay scales, it is often assumed that the opportunity cost of staying in teaching is, in many countries, unreasonable. Yet in some countries, South Korea, for example, relatively few teachers who leave the classroom do so in order to enter other fields (Kim & Han, 2002). In 1998, U.S. teachers ages 22–28 earned an average of $7,894 less per year than other college-educated adults of the same age. From 1994–1998, salaries for master's degree holders outside teaching increased 32%, or $17,505, while the average salary for teachers increased less than $200 (Education Week, 2000). Not surprisingly, a 1997 study by the National Center for Education Statistics found that teachers demonstrate increased professional commitment when provided higher salaries (Ingersoll & Alsalam, 1997). But increasing salaries across the board may not be a viable option to increase retention. UNESCO reports that "teachers' salaries and allowances are the largest single factor in the cost of providing education, accounting for two-thirds or more of public expenditure on education in most countries" (OECD, 2002). Additionally, Hanushek, Kain, and Rivkin (2001) estimate that school districts in the United States would have to increase urban teachers' salaries by up to 50 percent to convince them to stay.

Low salary is not the only reason teachers leave the profession. In the United States, more than half of teacher leavers report that they do so out of a desire to pursue another job or due to overall job dissatisfaction (Ingersoll, 2003b). Few teachers believe they significantly influence the establishment of curriculum at their school site, the content of their own professional development programs, how money is spent, or the hiring and evaluation of teachers at their own schools (Choy, Henke, Alt, Medrich, & Bobbitt, 1993; Henke, Choy, Chen, Geis, & Alt, 1997; Lippman, 1996). Predictably, higher attrition rates are associated with inadequate administrative support and a lack of teacher involvement in decision-making at the school site (Ingersoll & Alsalam, 1997; Shen, 1997; Weiss, 1999). All of these factors are compounded in high-poverty schools.

Public school teachers across the U.S. report having limited input into school-wide social and instructional decisions such as curricular, tracking and discipline policies (Yee, 1990; Ingersoll, 2003a). This is especially true for teachers at large, comprehensive public schools, those most often found in urban, high-poverty areas. Large urban schools tend to have highly centralized bureaucracies, resulting in hierarchical settings in which educators have a limited amount of autonomy, constraining teacher participation and stakeholder collaboration (Weiner, 2000). Teachers at large urban schools report having less influence over key workplace decisions than teachers at smaller public schools and the current push for accountability compounds this situation. The decisions over which teachers feel they have the most influence are those at the classroom-level, such as selecting concepts to teach and the strategies by which to teach them (Ingersoll, 2003a). Louis, Marks, and Kruse (1996) argue that urban teachers are more inclined to leave their schools than their suburban or rural counterparts because of the organizational design of their schools and their limited input into decisions directly affecting their classroom practices. Unfortunately, teacher dissatisfaction with the amount of control they have over their professional lives seems to be increasing (Sclan, 1993).

Prescriptions versus Professionalism: The Tension Between Short versus Long-Term Policy Responses

Faced with 50 teaching positions to fill and a pool of largely underqualified applicants, an urban high school principal must struggle with a deep tension: she must hire, orient and attempt to support new teachers, frequently with too few resources, knowing that many of them will leave in a year or two. The principal may also have to ask more experienced teachers to teach out of their subject areas and take on increased class sizes to ease the hiring demand. Further, in response to the challenge of this underqualified and transient faculty, the principal's superintendent – like many high-poverty urban district superintendents across the United States – may have mandated prescriptive "teacher proof" curricula that afford teachers little control over course content and classroom pedagogy in exchange, he hopes, for increased test scores. The tension, of course, is that such prescriptions risk sacrificing qualified and/or career-oriented teachers who experience these demands as another indicator of society's deep disrespect for what they do.

Lack of respect for teaching has a long and well-documented history in the United States that makes quick supply and demand-side prescriptions seem reasonable to some policymakers. This history recounts the feminization of the teaching workforce, its link to childcare, the commonsense notion that anyone can teach – and do so on a temporary basis – and the resultant low pay and low status (e.g., Spencer, 2000; Lortie, 1975; Tyack, 1974). Although the status of teaching differs across countries – and there are clear examples such as Japan and Ireland (Coolahan, 2003) where teachers enjoy relatively high status within their societies – low status for teaching may be the norm internationally. In 1966, for example, UNESCO and the International Labour Organisation held a Special Intergovernmental Conference on the Status of Teachers and recommended:

> [teachers' status should be] commensurate with the needs of education and assessed in the light of educational aims and objectives; it should be recognized that the proper status of teachers and due regard for the profession of teaching are of major importance for the full realization of these aims and objectives (UNESCO, 1998 as cited in Towse et al., 2002, p. 649).

More recently, in 2002, the OECD created a Directorate for Education with a mission to produce research and policy recommendations that apply to educational issues worldwide. One of their first projects sought to understand the global teacher shortage and sponsored background reports from several countries. Some of these reports speak to the issue of low teacher status. For example, Korea, where teachers have traditionally enjoyed relatively high status, has experienced a "decline of teachers' rights and image since the mid-1990s" (Kim & Han, 2002, p. 111).

The link between teaching's low status and workforce policies is clear. As Ingersoll argues: "social scientists have long characterized K-12 teaching as a lower status, easy-in/easy-out, high-turnover occupation that has relied historically on recruitment, and not retention, to solve its staffing problems" (Ingersoll, 2003, p. 18). In the United States, recruitment solutions continue to be prominent and are fueling a conservative move towards deregulation (Zeichner, 2003). Based on the assumption that anyone with subject matter expertise and good intentions can teach, peace corps-like programs such as Teach for America actively recruit college graduates to teach in high-priority schools for two years. Alternatives to teacher certification are also popular recruitment strategies and often target mid-career professionals looking for a change. Overall, these strategies eschew the value of pedagogical training and instead argue that increasing the supply of talented individuals into the teaching workforce will abate the teacher shortage. On the surface, these strategies appear to elevate the status of teaching by recruiting more competent individuals into the profession. What counts as competency in other fields or in university, however, may not translate into teaching competency, critics argue (Darling-Hammond, 2000; Zeichner, 2003). Moreover, such recruitment strategies may themselves contribute to the retention crisis. For instance, although Teach for America recruits and minimally trains college graduates as teachers, 60–100 percent of the recruits leave after their initial two-year commitment, leaving schools to once again face the economic hardships and organizational instability associated with high teacher turnover (CREDO, 2001; Ingersoll, 2003b).

In the United States, the National Commission for Teaching and America's Future (NCTAF) recently framed the key to solving the retention crisis as "finding a way for school systems to organize the work of qualified teachers so they can collaborate with their colleagues in developing strong learning communities that will sustain them as they become more accomplished teachers" (NCTAF, 2003, p. 7). This is one long-term policy response – a response that has deep roots in American education. As Zeichner (2003) describes, it is "the quest to establish a profession of teaching through the articulation of a knowledge base for teaching based on educational research and professional judgment" (p. 498). Firmly grounded in university-based teacher education programs, the most recent professionalization movement seeks to improve teacher quality by proposing higher standards for entry into teacher education programs, subject matter exams and performance-based assessments for prospective teachers, clearly articulated standards for teaching and teacher education, the accreditation of all credential-granting institutions, the establishment of state and national boards for professional standards and greater support for mentoring and professional development. Although certification requirements and examinations differ across states, professionalization proponents assert that licensing teachers based on displayed performance rather than course completion is essential for raising the status of the profession, ultimately attracting more capable candidates to teacher education programs who will then remain in teaching for long and productive careers.

Variations of this professionalization movement appear throughout the world, although as Popkewitz (1994) warns, "the Anglo-American conception of profession is not a neutral term that can be incorporated easily into other national vocabularies. It imposes an interpretive 'lens' about how occupations work" (p. 2). Teacher professionalism seems to be similarly interpreted in Australia, the United Kingdom, Canada and the United States each of which – either on a national scale or at the state or provincial level – is engaged in moves to establish clearer, more consistent eligibility requirements for teaching. On one hand, this move to heighten teacher professionalism is a hopeful and far-reaching solution to the retention crisis. It seeks to elevate the status of teachers by setting up structures and regulations that ensure a high quality of work focused by continual learning. On the other hand, advocates for deregulation warn that teacher professionalism is merely a way to protect the educational establishment, housed primarily in universities. As one critic claims, "The simple truth is that professional educators have not constituted a canon of essential knowledge or skills analogous to that which exists in law or medicine" (Hess, 2001, as quoted in Zeichner, 2003, p. 503). Although significant research argues otherwise (e.g., Zeichner, 2003), this criticism is the fuel that drives the supply-oriented recruitment solutions described above.

The more serious concern for professionalism as a policy response to the retention crisis is the risk that its structures and regulations will become bureaucratized and cement long-standing hierarchical norms of power and authority – norms that will continue to constrain teachers and limit their status. The history of American public schools is fraught with examples of well intentioned yet misguided reforms aimed at improving teachers and their practice (Oakes, Quartz, Ryan and Lipton, 2000). Rarely have these reforms relied on the professional judgment and reflective inquiry of teachers. Instead, "professional development" has typically meant passively listening to purported experts and implementing their recommendations – reminiscent of Frederick Taylor's quest to take the "brainwork" off the shop floor (Braverman, 1975, p. 113). Facing this history is an important step in dismantling the low status of teachers and ensuring their professional judgment is authentic and focused on learning.

The other major challenge faced by those who view the professionalization of teaching as a policy solution to the retention crisis is the extent to which it can be tailored to alleviate the problem in high-poverty schools. It is to this challenge that we now turn.

Creating Professional Learning Communities in High-Poverty Schools: Three Policy Arenas

Setting in motion conditions that enable qualified teachers to "collaborate with their colleagues in developing strong learning communities that will sustain them as they become more accomplished teachers" (NCTAF, 2003) is an extraordinary challenge within educational systems such as those in the United States. Core to this challenge is addressing deep inequities within the American system of mass public schooling – in this case the fact that qualified teachers are unevenly distributed in ways that leave the most impacted, high-poverty schools with a largely underqualified workforce. Although teacher education programs graduate enough certified teachers each year to meet the demand, few choose to teach in such challenging schools (Lankford, Loeb, & Wyckoff, 2002; Prince, 2003). By some accounts, high-poverty students are 12 times more likely to have teachers lacking full credentials than students in non-urban low-poverty schools (Harris, 2002) and recent data indicate that uncertified teachers leave at much higher rates than their certified peers, further increasing the staffing disparities (Henke et al., 2000). While the challenge to retain highly competent teachers affects all schools, the crisis is critical in high-poverty school districts, which historically suffer from a severe shortage of qualified teachers and typically fill vacancies with unlicensed teachers or full-time substitutes (Ingersoll, 1995, 1999; Darling-Hammond, 1999).

As reviewed above, recruitment and prescriptions such as scripted curricula, increased workloads, and out-of-subject teaching assignments are the most common strategies used to alleviate and manage the shortage of qualified teachers in high-poverty schools. Although it's fairly clear that these strategies perpetuate the cycle of dysfunction and high attrition, the dire need and immediacy of the problem faced by high-poverty schools and districts present a tough balancing act between short and longer-term solutions such as professionalization. Imagine helping a new teacher, perhaps one of 50, find a professional foothold – a mentor teacher, a teaching team, space for reflection – in an overcrowded, underfunded school. Imagine the task of preparing this new teacher for the challenges he or she will face in this school. And imagine the dim prospects for career development and advancement this teacher will face after a few years locked within a system with few qualified teaching colleagues, out-of-subject teaching assignments, and enormous workloads. It is to these challenges that the professionalism movement must speak in order to break the vicious cycle of attrition in high-poverty schools.

Three main policy arenas currently structure the long-term process of professionalization: specialized teacher preparation; induction and mentoring; and career advancement. These three policy arenas are the focus in many parts of the world. The following section briefly describes predominantly U.S. efforts underway in each arena to address the issue of retaining teachers in high-poverty schools.

Specialized Teacher Preparation

Increasingly, teacher educators worldwide are recognizing the importance of tailoring the learning of novice teachers to reflect the realities of high-poverty communities and their unique set of challenges. Yet a major gap in teacher preparation research, according to Wilson, Floden and Ferrini-Mundy (2001), is our lack of knowledge about how to prepare teachers for high-poverty schools. Over the past decade in the United States, there has been a call for multicultural teacher education programs that "challenge the ideological underpinnings of traditional programs, place knowledge about culture and racism front and center in the teacher education curriculum, include teaching for social justice as a major outcome, and value the cultural knowledge of local communities" (Cochran-Smith, 2003). Some teacher education programs have combined research-based, culturally responsive curricula with focused efforts at recruiting teachers of color in an attempt to prepare teachers who are knowledgeable of and committed to high-poverty students.

One example is UCLA's Center X Teacher Education Program (TEP), which takes a specialized approach to urban teacher preparation that is sensitive to the context of high-poverty communities within Los Angeles. An intensive two-year program leading to state certification and a master's degree, UCLA's core elements and principles are representative of the larger move towards multi-cultural teacher education:

– An explicit commitment to social justice, made real by continual struggle about what it means and how it is enacted in urban schools;
– Engaging a diverse group of faculty and teacher candidates in small, long-term learning communities (teams and cohorts);
– Viewing learning as social and dialogical inquiry within communities of practice;
– Constant grounding of practice in theory and of theory in practice, both in university courses and in K-12 fieldwork;
– Integrating the technical dimensions of teaching with the moral, cultural and political;
– Emphasizing the importance of knowing communities as well as knowing schools and classrooms;
– Extending formal preparation into the first year of teaching;
– Maintaining connections and support beyond the first year.

Center X teacher educators introduce students to a variety of theories with the intention of problematizing commonly accepted beliefs and practices surrounding ability, race, class, gender, language, difference, and so on. Following the growing body of sociocultural research on learning, the program maintains that its students learn as much – perhaps more – through enculturation into a critical, theory-rich learning environment as they do through explicit instruction in specific teaching skills and techniques (Putnam & Borko, 2000). As novices take on the skills, dispositions and beliefs of social justice educators, they deepen their understanding of self in the surrounding political economy – how their "everyday actions challenge or support various oppressions and injustices related to social class, race, gender, sexual preference, religion, and numerous other factors" (Zeichner, 1996).

Preliminary evidence – based on research of Center X graduates – suggests that teachers specially prepared to address the challenges of high-poverty school environments in the U.S. are retained at higher levels than their peers from traditional teacher preparation programs (Quartz et al., 2003). Since the founding of Center X in 1995, 913 students have been attracted to its specialized urban teacher education program. Most are female (79%), yet there is an extraordinary diversity in their ethnic and racial backgrounds: 35% are white; 25% are Hispanic; 6% are African-American; and 32% are Asian. As a research sample, the Center X graduates represent the population of highly qualified, diverse, and committed urban educators reformers clamor for. To date, Center X graduates are staying in teaching at higher rates than the national average and we are engaged in a significant longitudinal effort to understand the myriad of factors that contribute to these higher rates, including the characteristics of teachers attracted to UCLA's specialized program, features of the program itself and factors related to schools, communities and the teaching profession.

Induction and Mentoring

Early career teachers enter the classroom with a vast range of skills, abilities and dispositions, yet all need support during their first few crucial years if they are to beat the attrition odds. The National Center for Education Statistics identified "inadequate support from administrators" as the most frequently cited reason teachers gave for leaving their workplace or the profession (Bobbitt et al., 1994). Administrative and collegial support are particularly important for new teachers and are especially crucial for teachers in low-performing, high-poverty schools (Shann, 1998). Similarly, Center X graduates, who now teach in over 140 schools across and beyond Los Angeles, struggle to find like-minded colleagues and support structures in their schools. In most places, their specialized training is the exception, not the norm. In response, Center X created an Urban Educator Network to provide graduates with on-going professional development – tailored to address challenges found in high-poverty contexts – as they continue their learning within schools. For instance, urban teachers meet in inquiry groups to collectively reflect on the challenges they face in urban classrooms. Center X graduates also participate in summer seminars where they learn and apply critical research skills to pressing issues facing urban communities. These seminars engage teachers in creating an urban studies curriculum they can take back to their classrooms. Although these specialized efforts engage only a very small percentage of Los Angeles' teachers, they are proving effective at deepening the commitment and skills of urban teachers.

At the state level, policymakers have responded to the retention crisis by mandating induction support for new teachers. For example, California's Beginning Teacher Support and Assessment program (BTSA) aims to provide "formative assessment and individualized support based on assessment information for beginning teachers" (BTSA, 2003), ensuring that newly credentialed teachers receive structured mentoring and support during the years they are most likely to leave. Since 1992, BTSA has provided nearly 30,000 beginning teachers with a supportive professional network. Participation in these induction programs has been positively linked to higher rates of retention. A recent evaluation of California's BTSA program revealed that the retention rate for participating first- and second- year teachers was approximately 93 percent (Tushnet et al., 2003).

Nationwide, teachers who do not participate in induction programs are more than 73 percent more likely to leave the profession than those who receive induction support (Henke et al., 2000). Through induction programs, experienced teachers are entrusted with mentoring novices while simultaneously engaging in their own professional development, thus heightening perceptions of their own effectiveness, perceptions that have been linked to increased job satisfaction. For the novices, collaborating with an experienced mentor provides professional support as they begin facing the challenges of the job. Odell and Ferraro (1992) argue that it is the emotional support mentors provide to novices that contributes to their retention. Yee (1990) asserts that teachers value interactions with col-leagues more than any other form of professional stimulation. Unfortunately, teachers often report "that their opportunities for peer exchange are inadequate" (Yee, 1990, p. 113). Induction programs can provide a structured forum for such interaction.

While formal induction programs are indeed a promising policy response to the retention crisis, they often neglect a substantial proportion of teachers in high-poverty schools – the swelling ranks of under-prepared teachers. As Rogers (2003) reports, "uncredentialed teachers represent more than one third of the faculty at hundreds of schools in low income communities across Los Angeles County. In many schools ... the percentage of uncredentialed teachers rises above 50%." BTSA's stated intention is to support "fully-prepared first and second year teachers," discouraging districts from funding induction for the more than 32,000 state teachers holding emergency permits. Those with the least experience and weakest pedagogical foundations are thus those most often left to fend for themselves. As the chapter by Chin and Asera in this volume reports, states like California are redefining what counts as a "qualified" teacher in response to this under-prepared workforce and the national call for teacher quality, in effect lowering the bar far below the standard set by Center X and other specialized teacher education programs. Unfortunately, this will only serve to heighten the teacher retention crisis in high-poverty schools.

Career Development

Specialized preparation combined with early career induction and mentoring will increase the odds that teachers make it through their first few years in challenging high-poverty school workplaces. After that, the professional terrain shifts and teachers evaluate the long-term prospects of teaching as a career. Half of all turnover in schools is due to teacher migration (Ingersoll, 2001). As

Johnson and Birkeland (2003a) document, many teachers move around voluntarily in search of "schools that make good teaching possible" (p. 21). This is often a search for supportive principals and colleagues, reasonable teaching assignments and workloads, and sufficient resources. Given the scarcity of these conditions in high-poverty schools, teacher migration patterns typically flow from less to more affluent school contexts. As Johnson and Birkeland (2003b) report, "one of the most striking features of the data is that all of the Movers transferred to schools serving populations wealthier than in their original schools" (p. 599).

A less documented and potentially more positive form of migration is movement between full-time classroom teaching and other educational roles that may help ensure retention in the profession by providing educators with meaningful professional opportunities for learning and growth. We asked our sample of Center X graduates to identify not just their primary roles in education, but also additional or secondary roles. What emerged from extensive survey data was a portrait of active, professionally engaged urban educators. Across the board, Center X graduates reported that they take on a number of commitments beyond their classrooms. In this highly qualified teacher sample, more than half take university courses and participate in observational visits to other schools. Eighty percent are involved in regularly scheduled collaboration with other teachers on issues of instruction, and 95% attend workshops, conferences or trainings. Additionally, 44% of the educators report involvement with individual or collaborative research, 25% are part of a mentoring program, 20% participate in activist organizations, and 17% participate in a network of teachers outside of their schools. In addition to these professional development roles, a smaller percentage of graduates also take on leadership roles. These include department/grade-level chair (8%), mentoring other teachers (11%), administrators (2%), staff developers (13%), coaches (7%), activists (7%), coordinators (13%) or some other leadership role (22%). Overall, graduates report an average of five professional development and leadership roles in addition to their primary job responsibilities.

Whether or not these roles help educators develop strong learning communities that will sustain them as they become more accomplished professionals and enable their schools to improve over time is an important policy question to explore. Within our own data, educators with more roles were more likely to report that they stay in education because they find teaching to be a fulfilling and challenging career and they have good relationships with colleagues. They were also more satisfied with their opportunities for professional advancement and reported a higher degree of perceived respect from society (Goode, Quartz, Lyons, & Thomas, in press). But embedded in this issue is the very definition of an education professional. Is the push to take on more and more professional roles and responsibilities outside the classroom a positive one – one that will ultimately benefit students, improve schools, and curb attrition or one that will cement traditional hierarchies and structures? The repercussions of framing classroom teaching as a stepping stone to something larger, more important, and more respected are clearly problematic and significant efforts are underway to frame teaching as a profession rooted in the classroom.

As Johnson (2001) suggests, the National Board for Professional Teaching Standards (NBPTS) could lead to teaching as a staged career with multiple levels of accomplishment depending upon individual interest, energy, and ambition, all while retaining teachers within the classroom. Harman (2001), NBPTS's Director of Research, envisions creating new leadership roles such as teaching university classes and mentoring preservice teachers, designing and presenting professional development programs, and creating flexible administrative structures that allow teachers to take on new roles without leaving the classroom such as pairing two teachers to teach a single class, thereby providing time for each to pursue professional activities. Darling-Hammond (1997) echoes this recommendation:

> A new vision of the teaching career is needed that rewards the knowledge and expertise of those who work closest to children as highly as the skills of those who work furthest away and that makes those skills more widely available, thus enabling teachers to take on complementary hyphenated roles as school and program leaders, curriculum developers, mentors, staff developers, teacher educators, and researchers while they remain teachers (p. 327).

These efforts to professionalize teaching will, however, have to address the unique conditions of high-poverty schools – the challenge of finding like-minded competent colleagues, supportive leadership, and sufficient resources – to make this vision a reality.

Conclusion

As promising as these three policy responses to the teacher retention crisis are, they are clearly insufficient to address all the challenges associated with working in high-poverty communities. Such responses mask the limits of educational reform and policymaking – an enterprise fueled by a reform mill that churns out discrete programs to solve problems that are never discrete. Promoting a continuum of teacher learning within supportive school communities is a vision we can strive to approach through teacher preparation and induction programs as well as complementary professional roles, yet this hopeful vision should not deflect attention away from the political and economic conditions that fuel poverty. In a study of the teacher shortage in Tanzania, Towse et al. (2001, p. 649) describe the conditions of the nation's poor rural school, noting that "many Tanzanian primary schools lack such proper basic facilities as water, electricity, or a proper chalkboard." Similarly, high-poverty urban schools in the United States suffer from crumbling infrastructures and decrepit buildings that all too harshly contrast with the nation's more affluent public schools. Prioritizing teacher retention efforts is an important, if insufficient, step in addressing these inequities to ensure that all children have a qualified teacher.

Note

1. Support for the research reported in this chapter was generously provided through a grant from the Stuart Foundation. We wish to acknowledge the contributions of our colleagues Lauren Anderson, Joanna Goode, Eileen Lai Horng, Katherine Masyn, and Brad Olsen in the preparation of this chapter.

References

Adams, G. J., & Dial, M. (1994). The effects of education on teacher retention. *Education Policy Analysis Archives, 114*(3), 358–363.

Beginning Teacher Support and Assessment (2003). Retreived March 9, 2003 from the World Wide Web: http://www.btsa.ca.gov/BTSA_basics.html

Bobbitt, S. A., Leich, M. C., Whitener, S. D., & Lynch, H. F. (1994). *Characteristics of stayers, movers, and leavers: Results from the teacher follow-up survey: 1991–1992* (NCES 94–337). Washington, D.C.: National Center for Education Statistics.

Boe, E. E., Bobbitt, S. A., Cook, L. H., Whitener, S. D., & Weber, A. L. (1997). Why didst thou go? Predictors of retention, transfer, and attrition of special and general education teachers from a national perspective. *The Journal of Special Education, 30*(4), 390–411.

Braverman, H. (1975). *Labor and monopoly capital: The degradation of work in the Twentieth Century.* New York: Monthly Review Press.

Carroll, S., Reichardt, R., Guarino, C., & Mejia, A. (2000). *The Distribution of Teachers Among California's School Districts and Schools* (MR-1298.0-JIF). Santa Monica, CA: RAND Choy, S., Henke, R., Alt, M., Medrich, E., & Bobbitt, S. (1993). *Schools and Staffing in the U.S.: A statistical profile* (NCES 93–146). Washington, D.C.: National Center for Education Statistics.

Cochran-Smith, M. (2003). The multiple meanings of multicultural teacher education: A conceptual framework. *Teacher Education Quarterly, 30*(2), 7–26.

Coolahan, J. (2003). *Attracting, developing and retaining effective teachers: Country background report for Ireland.* Retrieved February 2, 2004 from http://www.oecd.org/dataoecd/62/22/19196740.pdf

CREDO (2001, August). *Teach for America: An evaluation of teacher differences and student outcomes in Houston, Texas.* Retrieved November 16, 2001 from http://credo.stanford.edu/TFA.report.final.pdf

Darling-Hammond, L (1999). *Teacher quality and student achievement: A review of state policy evidence* (Document No. R-99-1). Seattle, WA: Center for the Study of Teaching and Learning.

Darling-Hammond, L. (2000). Reforming teacher preparation and licensing: Debating the evidence. *Teachers College Record, 102*(1), 28–56.

Darling-Hammond, L., & Sclan, E. M. (1996). Who teaches and why: Dilemmas of building a profession for twenty-first century schools. In J. Sikula (Ed.), *Handbook of research on teacher education* (2nd Edition) (pp. 67–101). New York: Simon & Schuster.

Dianda, M. R., & Quartz, K. H. (1995). Promising new teacher support strategies and their costs. *Teacher Educational Quarterly, 22*(4), 45–62.

Dworkin, A. G. (1980). The changing demography of public school teachers: Some implications for faculty turnover in urban areas. *Sociology of Education, 53*, 65–73.

Education Week (2000). *Quality Counts 2000: Who should teach?* Bethesda, MD: Author.

General Teaching Council for England (2001). *Issues in the recruitment and retention of teachers.* London, England. Retreived June 6, 2003 from the World Wide Web: http://www.gtce.org.uk/gtcinfo/mori.asp

Goode, J., Quartz, K., Lyons, K., & Thomas, A. (in press). Supporting urban educational leaders: An analysis of the multiple roles of social justice educators. *Journal of Teacher Education and Practice.*

Grissmer, D. W., & Kirby, S. N. (1987). *Teacher attrition: The uphill climb to staff the Nation's schools.* Santa Monica, CA: The Rand Corporation.

Hanushek, E. A, Kain, J. F., & Rivkin, S. G. (2001). *Why public schools lose teachers.* Cambridge, MA: National Bureau of Economic Research.

Harris, L. (2002). *A survey of the status of equality of public education in California: A survey of a cross-section of public school teachers.* Public Advocates, Inc. Retrieved November, 1, 2002 from the World Wide Web: http://www.publicadvocates.org/equality_article-latest3.pdf.

Henke, R., Chen, X., & Geis, S. (2000). *Progress through the teacher pipeline: 1992–1993 college graduates and elementary/secondary school teaching as of 1997* (NCES 2000–152). Washington, DC: National Center for Education Statistics.

Henke, R., Choy, S., Chen, X., Geis, S., & Alt, M. (1997). *America's teachers: Profile of a profession, 1993–1994.* (NCES 97–460). Washington, DC: National Center for Education Statistics.

Ingersoll, R. (1995). Which types of schools have the highest teacher turnover? (Issue Brief No. IB-5-95). Washington, DC: National Center for Education Statistics.

Ingersoll, R. (2001). *Teacher turnover, teacher shortages, and the organization of schools.* Seattle, WA: Center for the Study of Teaching and Policy, January.

Ingersoll, R. (2002). The teacher shortage: A case of wrong diagnosis and wrong prescription. *Bulletin, 86*(631). Retrieved on January 5, 2003 http://www.principals.org/news/bltn_teachshort0602.html

Ingersoll, R. (2003a). *Who controls teachers' work: Power and accountability in America's schools.* Cambridge, MA: Harvard University Press.

Ingersoll, R. (2003b). *Is there really a teacher shortage?* Seattle, WA: Center for the Study of Teaching and Policy, September.

Ingersoll, R. M., & Alsalam, N. (1997). *Teacher professionalization and teacher commitment: A multilevel analysis.* Washington, DC: National Center for Education Statistics.

Johnson, S. M., (2001). Can professional certification for teachers reshape teaching as a career? *Phi Delta Kappan, 82*(5), 393–399.

Johnson, S. M., & Birkeland, S. E. (2003a). The schools that teachers choose. *Educational Leadership, 60*(8), 20–24.

Johnson, S. M., & Birkeland, S. E. (2003b). Pursuing a "sense of success": New teachers explain their career decisions. *American Educational Research Journal, 40*(3), 581–617.

Kim, E., & Han, Y. (2002). *Attracting, developing, and retaining effective teachers: Background report for Korea* (OECD No. OR 2002-8).

Kushman, J. W. (1992). The organizational dynamics of teacher workplace commitment: A study of urban elementary and middle schools. *Educational Administration Quarterly, 28*, 5–42.

Lankford, H. Loeb, S. Wyckoff, J. (2002). Teacher sorting and the plight of urban schools: A descriptive analysis. *Educational Evaluation and Policy Analysis, 24*(1), 37–62.

Lippman, L., Burns, S., McArthur, E., Burton, R., Smith, T., & Kaufman, P. (1996). Urban Schools: The Challenge of Location and Poverty. Retrieved December, 5, 2002 from the World Wide Web: http://nces.ed.gov/pubs/96184.html

Lortie, D. C. (1975). *Schoolteacher: A sociological study.* Chicago: University of Chicago Press.

Louis, K. S., Marks, H., & Kruse, S. (1996). Teachers' professional community in restructuring schools. *American Educational Research Journal, 33*(4), 757–798.

Macdonald, D. (1999). Teacher attrition: A review of literature. *Teaching and Teacher Education, 15*, 835–848.

Murnane, R. J. (1991). *Who will teach? Policies that matter.* Cambridge, MA: Harvard University Press.

Murnane, R. J., & Olsen, R. J. (1989). The effects of salaries and opportunity costs on duration in teaching: Evidence form Michigan. *Review of Economics and Statistics, 71*(2), 347–352.

National Commission on Teaching and America's Future (2003). *No dream denied: A pledge to America's children.* Washington: DC.

Nieto, S. (2003). *What keeps teachers going?* New York: Teachers College Press.

Oakes, J., Quartz, K. H., Ryan, S., & Lipton, M. (2000). *Becoming good American schools: The struggle for civic virtue in education reform.* San Francisco: Jossey-Bass.

Odell, S., & Ferraro, D. (1992). Teacher mentoring and teacher retention. *Journal of Teacher Education, 43*, 200–204.

Organization for Economic Cooperation and Development (2002). *Teacher Demand and Supply: Improving Teaching Quality and Addressing Teacher Shortages.* Working Paper No. 1 www.oecd.org/els/education/teacherpolicy

Prince, C. D. (2003). *Higher pay in hard-to-staff schools: The case for financial incentives.* Lanham, MD: The Scarecrow Press.

Popkewitz, T. S. (1994). Professionalization in teaching and teacher education: Some notes on its history, ideology, and potential. *Teaching and Teacher Education, 10*(1), 1–14.

Putnam, R. T., & Borko, H. (2000). What do new views of knowledge and thinking have to say about research on teacher learning? *Educational Researcher, 29*(1), 4–15.

Quartz, K., & The TEP Research Group (2003). "Too angry to leave": Supporting new teachers' commitment to transform urban schools. *Journal of Teacher Education, 54*(2), 99–111.

Rogers, J. (2003). The struggle continues: Quality teachers for all. *Teaching to Change LA, 3*(4). Retrieved June, 15, 2003 from the World Wide Web: http://tcla.gseis.ucla.edu/reportcard/archive/issue4.html

Rosenholtz, S. J. (1985). Effective schools: Interpreting the evidence. *American Journal of Education, 93,* 352–388.

Rosenholtz, S. J. (1989). *Teachers workplace: The social organization of schools.* New York: Longman.

Schlecty, P., & Vance, V. (1983). Recruitment, selection, and retention: The shape of the teaching force. *Elementary School Journal, 83,* 469–487.

Sclan, E. M. (1993). The effect of perceived workplace conditions on beginning teachers' work commitment, career choice commitment, and planned retention. *Dissertation Abstracts International, 54,* 08A (University Microfilms No. 9400594).

Shann, M. H. (1998). Professional commitment and satisfaction among teachers in urban middle schools. *The Journal of Educational Research, 92*(2), 67–74.

Skilbeck, M. and Connell, H. (2003). Attracting, developing, and retaining effective teachers: Australian country background report. Report prepared for the OECD. http://www.oecd.org/searchResult/0,2665,en_2649_201185_1_1_1_1_1,00.html

Spencer, D. A. (2000). Teachers' work: Yesterday, today, and tomorrow. In T. L. Good (Ed.), *American Education: Yesterday, Today, Tomorrow.* Chicago: University of Chicago Press.

Stinebrickner, T. R. (1999). Estimation of a duration model in the presence of missing data. *The Review of Economics and Statistics, 81,* 529–549.

Texas State Board for Educator Certification (2000). *The cost of teacher turnover.* Retrieved on November 4, 2003 from www.sbec.state.tx.us.txbess/turnover.pdf

Theobald, N. D. (1990). An examination of the influence of personal, professional, and school district characteristics on public school teacher retention. *Economics of Education Review, 9*(3), 241–50.

Towse, P., Kent, D., Osaki, F., & Kirua, N. (2001). Non-graduate teacher recruitment and retention: Some factors affecting teacher effectiveness in Tanzania. *Teaching and Teacher Education, 18,* 637–652.

Tushnet, N., Briggs, D., Elliot, J., Esch, C., Haviland, D., Humphrey, D., Rayyes, N., Riehl, L., & Young, V. (2002). *Final report of the independent evaluation of the Beginning Teacher Support and Assessment program* Retrieved on March 19, 2003 from http://www.ctc.ca.gov/reports/BTSA-Eval-2003-ExecSummary.pdf

Tyack, D. B. (1974). *The one best system: A history of American urban education.* Cambridge, MA: Harvard University Press.

Weiner, L. (2000). Research in the 90s: Implications for urban teacher preparation. *Review of Educational Research, 70*(3), 369–406.

Weiss, E. M. (1999). Perceived workplace conditions and first-year teachers' morale, career choice commitment, and planned retention: A secondary analysis. *Teaching and Teacher Education, 15,* 861–879.

Wilson, S. M., Floden, R. E., & Ferrini-Mundy, J. (2001). *Teacher preparation research: current knowledge, gaps, and recommendations.* Seattle, WA: Center for the Study of Teaching and Policy.

Yee, S. M. (1990). *Careers in the classroom: When teaching is more than a job.* New York: Teachers College Press.

Zeichner, K. M. (1996). Educating teachers for cultural diversity. In K. Zeichner, S. Melnick & M. L. Gomez (Eds.), *Currents of Reform in Preservice Teacher Education* (pp. 133–175). New York: Teachers College Press.

25

THE CULTURAL CONTEXT OF TEACHERS' WORK: POLICY, PRACTICE AND PERFORMANCE

Marilyn Osborn and Elizabeth McNess
University of Bristol, UK

The last decade of the 20th Century was a time of major policy change for schools and schooling. Teachers have found themselves at the centre of a generalised drive to increase the quality of education and improve outcomes for pupils in order to create a more skilled and educated workforce. Levin (1998) has referred to 'a policy epidemic' which is carried by agents such as the World Bank and the OECD to both developed and developing economies alike. As a result, a continuing de-regulation of commercial interests creating a global market for goods, services and labour has combined with increased technological solutions to the production and communication of knowledge, foregrounding education as the key ingredient in national economic development strategies.

In Western industrialised nations in particular, shifts in social attitudes and common structural problems such as changing work patterns, ageing populations, youth unemployment, poverty, exclusion and the assimilation of economic migrants have caused national governments to focus on the quality of their compulsory schooling systems (Green et al., 1999). Within Europe, for the first time, the 1991 Maastricht Treaty has placed education under the authority of the European Union (EU). Despite the principle of subsidiarity (which means that EU law must be framed in relation to existing national priorities and practice), national education systems are coming under pressure to engage in some form of restructuring and realignment (Karlsen, 2002). Both in Europe and beyond, a powerful discourse has ensured that the *market, managerialism* and *performativity* have combined to create what Ball (2003) has referred to as three interrelated 'policy technologies' which have been employed to control the work of teachers and the performance of schools.

These changes in the regulation of education systems have prompted commentators to speculate on the impact which such changes are having on the broad sweep of teachers' work and the extent to which they can retain their autonomy as professionals (Apple, 1986; Ball, 1994; Hargreaves, 1994; Robertson, 1996; Helsby, 1999; Smyth, Dow, Hattam, Reid, & Shacklock, 2000). Unfortunately,

International Handbook of Educational Policy, 507–525
Nina Bascia, Alister Cumming, Amanda Datnow, Kenneth Leithwood and David Livingstone (Eds.)
© 2005 *Springer. Printed in Great Britain.*

a tendency for some policy research to focus on either the meta-narrative of major shifts in the control and governance of education systems, or the evaluation of individual initiatives can reinforce a managerial perspective of the policy process. Generation and implementation have been constructed as distinct and separate 'moments', with generation followed by implementation in a direct, linear way. This can give rise to a structural-functionalist approach to policy analysis which looks for evidence of 'inputs' and 'outputs' and assumes a closed system of decision-making (Bowe & Ball, 1992). Policy becomes *what government does*, assuming a rational, 'top-down' and mechanistic process in which implementation is straightforward and unproblematic. Such a view takes little interest in what happens in the 'black box' of implementation, and puts less emphasis on the role of the involved actors or 'street level bureaucrats' (Lipsky, 1980) who can influence, or even subvert, policy in the process of implementation.

In contrast, the research reported in this chapter suggests that both the formulation and implementation of policy are complex and variable, and open to influence from many sources which need to be fully contextualised (Ozga, 2000). Rather than something which *gets done* to people, it is a continual process understood at the intersection of biography and history, as well as identity and structure (Ball, 1990; Whitty, 2002). Policy production does not happen in isolation but is influenced by the socio-historical context in which it arises and it, in turn, is altered through implementation. Policy, therefore, is a process as well as a product and, as such, has been considered in relation to an action-oriented perspective which sees those interpreting policy, in this case teachers, as also informing and amending policy by acting as 'policy makers in practice' (Croll, Abbott, Broadfoot, Osborn, & Pollard, 1994). Policy changes in the very process of implementation and can, therefore, be considered more a 'pattern of actions over a period of time' than a specific document.

This chapter argues that while similar educational policies are being enacted in many countries in response to global pressures, the impact of these policies on the actors involved may vary considerably as a result of the particular cultural context within which they are situated. Thus, a policy which may be global in origin may be mediated by national educational cultures, as well as cultures at school and teacher level, resulting in very different interpretations and responses. Both structure and agency interact to produce new interpretations of teachers' work in different cultural settings and it is particularly important not to underplay the role played by teachers' beliefs and values in interpreting, accommodating or resisting state policy. In making this case, the chapter reviews comparative findings on teachers' work, drawing particularly upon a programme of explicitly comparative research which has examined the impact of national policy change on teachers' work and professional identity in several European countries.

A Comparative Perspective

Since the beginning of modern forms of education, comparative educationists such as Sadler (1900), Kandel (1933) and Hans (1949), as well as sociologists such as Weber (1947) and Durkheim (1961) have sought to compare and contrast specific institutional arrangements for educational provision of particular times and places. Their goal was to understand the way in which prevailing economic and social imperatives were mediated by the ideological and cultural traditions of any particular society to produce the idiosyncratic characteristics of any one national education system.

More recently, data from international studies of pupil performance have fuelled the desire of national governments to seek accountability from their education systems in the race for economic competitiveness and led to an increase in research which seeks to compare the performance of different national systems. Such research centres on the search for 'best practice' and the isolation of specific characteristics which create 'effective' schools (Sammons, Hillman, & Mortimore, 1995; MacBeath & Mortimore, 2001). Again, like many policy studies, these tend to focus on macro agendas, concerned with variations in structural provision and the inputs and outputs of education provision rather than values, beliefs, and aspirations of the individual actors involved.

In contrast, other researchers have begun to seek understanding of the nuances of contextually specific experience by focusing on the individual actors at the school level. With their unique capacity to compare one context with another in a systematic way, such studies have a very significant role to play in generating insights into the more universal features of what it means to be a teacher as well as the more culturally and context specific variations. Thus, comparative studies are able to uncover conflicting priorities and illuminate the way in which teachers reconcile new policy demands with existing institutional practices (Gewirtz, Ball, & Bowe, 1995). Comparative studies show, for example, the extent to which the ability to mediate national educational policy in particular ways is a feature of teaching as a profession which transcends national and cross-cultural differences. When confronted with change, and in particular with reform imposed from above, a proportion of teachers in many countries, even those working in highly prescriptive, centrally controlled systems, will respond by subverting, mediating, reinventing, or developing a creative response (Menlo & Poppleton, 1999). Darmanin (1990), for example, demonstrates how Maltese teachers subverted some aspects of educational change. There is evidence of some teachers in Greece ignoring a rigid, over-prescriptive curriculum in selective ways (Krespi, 1995), while Hargreaves's study of Canadian primary teachers and the introduction of "preparation time" suggested that, although there was evidence for the intensification of teachers' work, this could not account for the whole range and complexity of teachers' responses (Hargreaves, 1994). Webb, Vulliamy et al.'s (1997) study of curriculum change in Finland and England shows how effectively some teachers could avoid or subvert change. Troman (1996), in a case study of English primary schools, writes of both the "new professionals" who were able to work with change, albeit in instrumental ways, and the "old professionals" who stuck to what they felt worked, regardless of policy directives. Many researchers have made the point that events and experiences in the personal lives of teachers are intimately linked with the performance of their professional role and their ability to mediate change (Goodson & Hargreaves, 1996). Thus many aspects of their personal and professional career trajectories, gender, age, life cycle and career stage (Huberman, 1993; Acker, 1999; Bascia & Young, 2001) are vital to understanding teacher cultures and response to change. As Hargreaves (1994) comments:

> *Teachers don't just have jobs. They have professional and personal lives as well. ... Understanding the teacher means understanding the person the teacher is* (p. viii).

Thus, to understand the complexities of teachers' response to policy change, it is vital not to ignore personal biographies and identities, teachers' values, emotions, and morale as well as efficacy. Comparative studies suggest that both structures and values vary across different national and local contexts, shaping teachers' social and professional values and leading to different expectations for teachers' work and professional identity (Broadfoot & Osborn, 1992; Metz, 1990; Louis, 1998) as the studies which follow demonstrate.

Changing Discourses of Professional Practice – The Empirical Evidence

The evidence presented in this chapter draws upon a series of linked research projects which sought to understand, in a cumulative way, the perceptions and priorities of teachers in three European contexts as their views of what it was to be a teacher were challenged by significant and wide-reaching policy change. The studies were comparative, collaborative and cumulative in nature, such that as a whole they present an account of the experiences of teachers and the impact of change on their work, identity and professional responsibilities. In reviewing the findings of this research, some conclusions have been drawn about the current thrust of policy-making with respect to the priorities identified for teachers and the impact this has had on the development of their professional practice. Attention is also drawn to the possible long-term effects that such a focus could have on the quality of teaching and learning and the ability of pupils to engage with the necessary skills for lifelong learning.

The Bristol-Aix Study

The *Brisrol-Aix (Bristaix) Study* was carried out by a collaborative team of researchers in England and France in the late 1980s. It involved primary teachers in both national contexts *before* the impact of the most recent wave of major educational reforms, and sought to understand the impact of history and culture on teachers' conceptions of professional responsibility and teacher identity (Broadfoot, Osborn, Gilly, & Bucher, 1993). At the time of the study, the two education systems provided a clear contrast. The French system was highly centralised with common programmes of study and attainment targets for all children identified centrally. In contrast, the system in England, at that time, was decentralised and locally determined with, apparently, much greater autonomy for teachers especially in matters of curriculum, pedagogy and assessment. The researchers wanted to explore the extent to which these historically and culturally different systems would influence teachers' views of their work and what it 'meant' to be a teacher (Nias, 1989). Given the many commonalities in schools and a common European heritage, would their teaching priorities be similar? Or, would the underlying aims and aspirations of the two systems impact on teachers' perceptions of the teaching and learning process, and the role of compulsory schooling in society?

The findings of the research suggested that teachers' conceptions of their professional responsibility in the two countries were characterised by two very different models of accountability. Teachers in France had a narrower, more restricted and more classroom focused conception of their role which centred on what they saw as their responsibility mainly for children's academic progress. Teachers in England, by contrast, saw themselves as having a more wide-ranging and diffuse set of responsibilities which encompassed widely dispersed goals relating to responsibilities outside, as well as inside, the classroom. These included extra-curricular and sometimes even community activities, all aspects of school relationships, accountability to parents, colleagues and the headteacher. They also had a strong consciousness of the need to justify their actions to others.

At their most extreme, then, a French teacher's perception of her role centred on "*meeting one's contractual responsibility*" and an English teacher's on "*striving after perfection*". Thus, based on what teachers said about their professional responsibility, four distinct dimensions of difference in the national context were identified. These were the *range* of professional activities undertaken, the relative *ambiguity* of the teacher's task, the *style* of pedagogy, and the relative importance to teachers of the *process*, as distinct from the *products*, of learning.

However, these findings were based on teachers' professed beliefs about their teaching. In the latter part of the study the team attempted to explore the relationship between teachers' expressed beliefs and their classroom practice using a more ethnographic and multi modal approach to the research. Members of the team shadowed 16 teachers and classrooms in each country using qualitative fieldnotes and interviews, teacher diaries and a systematic observation schedule. Striking differences in pedagogy, in classroom organisation and in teacher-pupil relations emerged which were far greater between the two countries than any of the differences observed within one country (for example in schools located in different socio-economic catchment areas) (Osborn & Broadfoot, 1992).

The sources of the very different styles of teaching identified were varied, stemming not only from shared experiences in schools in the two countries, but also from historical legacies and features of initial teacher training. However, it was clear from the way in which teachers in the two countries defined their *professional responsibility* that their beliefs about teaching were dramatically different and that the national policy context of the two educational systems played an important part. French teachers believed strongly in the need for a national curriculum as the basis for equality and unity in society. More immediately, however, they felt an overwhelming pressure to meet the attainment targets laid down for children by the end of the year. That strong sense of obligation to equip children with the skills and knowledge expected from a particular year grade so they would not be forced to "*redouble*" (repeat the year) was the source of much of the apparent conformity, the emphasis on rote learning, the didactic teaching methods, and the emphasis on bringing all children to a common standard, rather than on the differentiated teaching which was common in England. Thus the overwhelming pressure for a primary teacher in France was to:

> ... *make sure that my pupils acquire the knowledge and skills appropriate to the level of the class and to ensure their passage to the next class. Not to do so would be a professional and personal failure. One is always responsible for a child's failure, whatever the extenuating circumstances.* (French teacher of 10–11 year olds)

This contrasted sharply with the strongly held beliefs of teachers in England with regard to professional autonomy and a differentiated approach to curriculum and pedagogy which emphasised development of the individual child's intelligence and personality and included more diffuse goals such as:

> *Creating an atmosphere whereby children will learn through experience – moral and social norms, physical skills and aspects of health and hygiene, develop enquiring minds and creativity and generally to develop, progress and fulfil their potential.* (English teacher of 10–11 year olds)

The findings, therefore, underlined the power of specific contexts to shape the priorities of classroom teachers and drew policymakers' attention to the need to take this into account when implementing change. Major changes which were in opposition to teachers' often tacit understanding of their roles and responsibilities would be less likely to succeed.

These ideas were followed up in the next two linked studies in which the research teams were involved. Using the findings from the *Bristaix* study to identify teachers' priorities and practices before major policy reforms in both countries, a base-line of data was created which could be built on for the later *PACE (Primary, Assessment, Curriculum and Experience)* and *STEP (Systems, Teachers and Policy Change)* studies which sought to establish how far new reforms within the English and French systems had been successful in influencing primary teachers' practice. The aim was also to draw some conclusions concerning the management of change within an educational system and how it might be effectively accomplished.

The PACE and STEP Studies

In both England and France, major policy reforms in the late 1980s and early 1990s challenged teachers' fundamental professional perspectives. In England, the 1988 *Education Reform Act* established a quite different emphasis embodied in the imposition of a National Curriculum, national testing at Key Stages (7, 11 and 14 years) and explicit targets and expectations of achievement. Soon after, in France, the Jospin reforms (*Loi d'Orientation sur l'Education*) introduced pressure towards a more collaborative way of working and a more individualized pedagogy. In some ways the two systems, in policy terms, were moving closer to each other and, in each case, the reforms constituted a requirement on teachers to change not only their practice but also long-held beliefs concerning what and how to teach.

The findings of the *PACE* study (Pollard, Broadfoot, Croll, Osborn, & Abbott, 1994; Croll, 1996; Pollard & Triggs, 2000; Osborn, McNess, & Broadfoot, 2000) suggested that, in England over the course of the 1990s, there had been changes within the broader context of both schools and society which had influenced policy and practice. A growing concern with accountability within the public services had led to policy initiatives which, for some, had caused a disjunction between managerialist policy requirements and an older, more affectively-based professional identity. Some teachers in the study expressed a feeling of fragmented identity, torn between an official discourse which emphasized technical and managerial skills and a strongly held personal view which emphasized the importance of an emotional dimension to teaching:

> *Well, I don't know the children anymore. Well, I know them but there's no time to chat really. You feel that you are under this obligation to get work done and as a consequence ... no, I don't know the children ... This notion that we've got a certain amount to get through is just pressurizing – for the teacher and for the children. It's difficult to include the education of the whole child because of it.* (Teacher of 10 yr-olds, England)

And again:

> *I think it's (the new National Curriculum) awful. I think it's one of the most destructive things I've ever had the misfortune to deal with. I actually feel that my teaching's a lot worse now than it's ever been because it takes out the spontaneity that you can have. I have a timetable that I now have to work to. I have so many hours a week that I have to fulfil certain things. There is no flexibility and it doesn't allow for either the child who's distressed or they've got a problem. And I now feel that I pressurize my children into finishing their work.* (Teacher of 9 yr-olds, England)

These negative experiences were not the case for all teachers in the study. Evidence also supported the view that a new professionalism was emerging, especially amongst newer teachers who were more likely to find satisfaction within a more constrained and instrumental role:

> *I'm more focused when I plan an activity and because of the National Curriculum – this is a positive thing – I definitely do specify now what I'm*

intending the children to learn, whereas I think before, I planned an activity and was open to see what the children learned. Now, of course, you still do have exciting situations where children do learn all sorts of things that you didn't expect them to and they show all sorts of things that you didn't expect them to and they show all sorts of knowledge, skills, etc. that you didn't know they had, which is good, and honestly I'm still looking for this. But I think that I'm far more able now to explain to somebody else in more concrete terms what I'm doing, which I think is a good thing. (Teacher of 10 yr-olds, England)

So, while some teachers felt deskilled and restricted in their professional autonomy, there were others who had seized the potential for a margin of manoeuvre between the imposed centralized policies and their implementation. In a summative book on the PACE project findings, Osborn, McNess, and Broadfoot (2000) have argued that, while teachers' response to change varied from compliance to retreatism or resistance, some teachers' response to the reforms had been that of 'creative mediation', taking active control of the changes and gaining a new professional discourse (Woods & Jeffrey, 1997), including new professional practices in the process. As this teacher of 9 and 10 yr-olds explained:

If I am honest, I haven't let the changes affect my work. They have made me focus on different things, but I still feel I am prepared to follow the needs of the children at certain times, and to take risks. But part of me believes in the National Curriculum anyway. We have got to plan and think as a group with other teachers about the needs of the children.

The professional confidence to do this depended upon many variables at both institutional and individual levels which influenced teachers' stance towards change. These included school climate and culture, the socio-economic context, and teachers' personal biographies and career trajectories, including the teacher's gender, age and years of teaching experience. Perhaps most significant of all was the presence of a supportive and collaborative school climate and culture.

The findings supported the view that primary teachers in England during the 1990s had increased feelings of priorities being imposed from outside which had led to some loss of personal fulfilment and autonomy. External accountability had increased, especially through the establishment of the Ofsted (Office for Standards in Education, established in 1992) inspection service, and although personal and moral responsibility was still seen as important, there was some evidence of a shift in climate bringing teachers in England closer to their French colleagues. A covenant based on societal trust in the professionalism of teachers was being replaced with a contract based on the delivery of education to meet external requirements and national economic goals. The pressure of time and a demand to plan, assess and reach ever increasing, externally-defined targets had resulted in an environment in which, for pupils as well as their teachers, the affective or social and personal domain had been reduced in preference to the academic. In England, teachers' strong sense of professional responsibility had led to a high degree of apparent compliance with these changes which, in turn, resulted in a substantially increased workload and the undertaking of new professional tasks such as formal assessment. However, the coercive character of the reforms provoked an initially intense demoralization and sense of loss.

How did these findings compare with the experiences of teachers in France? The situation which the researchers found there was quite different from England. Although there appeared to have been identifiable shifts in both practice and underlying perspectives on the part of at least some teachers in France, there was a significant number who did not feel they had changed or would change. In this study, in seeking to understand the process of policy implementation, evidence of lack of change is arguably as significant as evidence of change itself. Equally, it is important to elucidate to what extent any such change is indeed a result of policy directives rather than of the teacher's own professional response to, for example, the perceived need of pupils or to particular characteristics of the working environment.

For many teachers in France, the notion of reform evoked a profound cynicism apparently born out of the large number of such initiatives in recent decades. As one teacher put it:

> *Les ministres passent, les enseignements restent et evoluent a leur rythme.*
> (Ministers come and go: teachers stay and change in their own time).

Another argued:

> *Les ministres passent et pensent tout changer*
> (Ministers come and go and think they can change everything)

To the world-weariness of many experienced teachers must be added a cynicism born of experience concerning how much life in the classroom is likely to respond to any such policy reform:

> *Il y a les belles idees; et il y a ce qui se passe en classe.*
> (There are beautiful ideas; and there are is what happens in class).

French teachers themselves identified a number of practical barriers to change, such as large classes, lack of suitable resources and even buildings. Lack of training and guidance left a significant number genuinely unclear how to implement a more individualized pedagogy. To such practical hurdles must be added the profound barriers of teachers' ideology and perceived constraint. Teachers in France described the expectations of pupils in the classroom and of their parents for particular activities to be taking place, the fear of disadvantaging pupils going into collège (secondary school) – in short the conservatism rooted in the familiar pattern of French education (Bourdieu & Passeron, 1990) – as inhibiting them from changing. More significantly, perhaps, the lack of sanctions which could be mobilised to enforce reform (only the occasional visit from an inspector) and the professional convictions of what it means to be a teacher rooted in more than a hundred years of tradition, make it relatively easy to understand why change in France was rather limited. In a teaching body traditionally subject to few external controls, there was less concern to conform to the reform's directives.

The ENCOMPASS Study

An interest in the potential of both European Union and global pressures to influence the education policies of individual nation states led to the next phase of the research programme which included the experiences of teachers within secondary education. Like England and France, Denmark was also experiencing change within its schooling system as a result of the 1992 *Act of the Folkeskole*. This had been driven, mainly, by the apparent underachievement of Danish pupils in international tests and concerns with the education of a growing immigrant population (Winther-Jensen, 2002). For this reason Denmark was included in the study to offer alternative perspectives on the work of teachers and the impact of policy. It offered a third dimension by representing a distinctive Nordic approach to the organisation of schooling which differed considerably from both the English and French approaches. The Danish system had grown out of a communitarian ideology which, while including regulation within a national framework, placed much emphasis on the retention of local power and the maintenance of a democratic system responsive to the views of teachers, pupils and the local community (Lauglo, 1990).

The teachers interviewed for the ENCOMPASS project taught in the lower secondary phase of compulsory education and were chosen to investigate the impact of policy on three different and culturally specific approaches to the role of the teacher (McNess, 2001; Osborn, Broadfoot, McNess, Planel, Ravin, & Triggs, 2003). In England, teachers were 'subject specialists' teaching classes of children across the age range from 11 to 16–18 years, and concentrating on one specific area of the curriculum. or most teachers, this was combined with an additional role as 'group tutor', which aimed to provide more affective support for the personal and social lives of a particular group of pupils. As one teacher explained, this could lead to a certain tension and separation between the two aspects of their work:

> *I view my role as a tutor fairly separately from my role as a teacher. In my role as a tutor I certainly am a lot gentler than my role as a teacher, so that the door is always open and they don't view me as being so disciplinarian that they can't feel that they can approach me any time on any basis.* (teacher of humanities, England)

There was some evidence that, in an effort to raise standards, there had been a re-focusing of the group tutor role to include more academic support and personal planning. Tutors were being required to monitor the progress of pupils using computer data in order to set targets, which would then be discussed with individual pupils. To some extent, teachers saw this as compromising the social and emotional aspects of the role and restricting still further the time and space available to engage with this aspect of their work.

Secondary teachers in France, like their primary colleagues, were expected to concentrate on the intellectual and academic domains of learning through their particular subject specialism. The social and emotional needs of individual pupils were met by a separate group of non-teaching colleagues led by the *conseiller principal d'éducation*. As one teacher in France explained:

> *(It is important) that the pupils know something ... his or her socialisation is not my priority, all that matters is my subject.* (teacher of mathematics, France)

[this and the following quote don't seem to quite match with each other] However, there was also some evidence that an increasing and more diverse school population, resulting from government policy aimed at increasing standards and extending the length of compulsory schooling (*massification*), had brought new pressures:

> *In France, education means mass participation. Okay, it's the same education for everyone, so social and personal development isn't something that concerns us ... although there are ministerial directives about looking for better strategies with pupils. But we don't have the means to do that sort of thing ... we neither have the time nor the locations to deal with pupils in that way ... to have more personal discussions with them, it just has not been provided for.* (teacher of history and geography, France)

Finally, teachers in Denmark perhaps uniquely at secondary level, usually combined elements of both subject specialist and group tutor within a single role: that of the 'class teacher' (*klasselærer*). The Danish class teacher was responsible for both the academic and the affective needs of a particular group of children, often for the whole of their compulsory schooling. Typically, they worked with a group of three to six other teachers who between them taught the whole of the curriculum to a single class group. As well as the academic, social and emotional needs of their class, the class teacher was also responsible for the maintenance of a close and regular contact with the parents of their pupils. The attributes needed for such a role were expressed in the following way by one teacher:

> *The class teacher should be engaging, able to understand their pupils' concerns and problems and live and grow together with their pupils ... the better children get along with each other the more power and energy they are able to use on learning. Learning will be hampered if you feel socially insecure.* (class teacher, Denmark)

This underlines a common concern with the integrative nature of the affective, or personal and social dimension in relation to the cognitive and academic aspects of learning.

Despite these clear structural differences, teachers within all three systems spoke in similar terms when asked about their aims and priorities. All were concerned that pupils should achieve academically, that they should grow and develop as individuals, and that they should acquire the skills and abilities which would enable them to take their place as future citizens and workers. These aims, while similar in their outcomes, were often expressed in terms which underlined the differing ideological influences from which they sprang:

> *I think the main political aim is to raise academic standards ... but personally I would say (the aim is) the development of the whole child, which includes fulfilling their academic potential, but also their development as a sound human being and their personal development – (to ensure that) they're not scarred in any way by their school experiences, or undermined, or they don't come out with an overriding sense of injustice, or failure, or loss of confidence.* (teacher of humanities, England)

> *I'm a maths teacher so my aim is to structure their thoughts, not only in maths. At secondary level, maths is a means of getting them to learn how to reason but it is a skill that will also help them in their future lives as citizens. I would say that my main aim as a maths teacher is to help pupils to develop into citizens who know how to reason and how to think.* (teacher of mathematics, France)

>> *It's important that the children like being here, otherwise they won't learn anything. But it is also important that they learn something and have a positive experience of being together. I think it's important that they treat each other in a proper fashion.* (class teacher, Denmark)

These quotes illustrate the importance of the development of the 'whole child' and the individualist nature of the educational process for teachers in England, the emphasis on intellectual and academic development for teachers in France, and the importance of collaborative working and democratic development for teachers in Denmark. For the English sample, however, there was an added dimension to their comments which highlighted a tension between the demands of policy and the teachers' own professional commitments, mirroring the findings of the earlier *PACE* study. Teachers in England were experiencing an increasing pressure to enable pupils to reach pre-set targets, as a measure of effective teaching and learning, and they considered that this could be at the expense of their generally more affective aims:

> *I think the main political aims are to raise standards, to raise academic standards, whatever the cost ... So I feel as though our backs are being thrashed in terms of assessments ... and, therefore, the values I might talk about as having myself in terms of pupil interaction, respect for pupils, if I'm feeling undermined by that (the pressure of assessment) will begin to slide ... I would say the development of the whole child is the name of the game ... that includes that their academic potential is fulfilled, of course it does, but it*

also includes their development as a sound human being. (teacher of humanities, England)

Global Pressures and a Re-ordering of Educational Priorities

What do these studies tell us about the impact of policy on the specific national contexts within which teachers work? Though the effects of globalisation are debated, this research provides some evidence that common pressures to compete in a global economy have focused attention on the achievement of pupils and the work of teachers. A common concern with efficiency and value for money, together with the need to produce a highly-skilled workforce for advanced economies have created similar trends in the enacting of education policy.

Despite this, there is also much evidence to suggest that the different national structures have given rise to different policy priorities which, in turn, have impacted differentially on approaches to teaching and learning. Thus, although there had been some relaxation of the system, the French teachers continued to work within a centrally-controlled framework which specified texts, timing and pedagogical approaches to teaching and tended to conform to a model of the teacher which emphasized the academic and intellectual. There was also some evidence that pressures from *massification* and the increasing variation within their student population were causing teachers in France to reassess the role of the affective and pastoral within teaching and learning. Meanwhile, in Denmark, a concern with low levels of pupil attainment in international tests and the need to accommodate an increasing number of immigrant children had brought pressure for a more differentiated approach to pupil learning and a reassessment of the role of the class teacher. Evidence suggested though that recent policy change had, in fact, supported and endorsed the role of the class teacher, enabling them to continue with an holistic approach to teaching and learning which included the personal and social development of pupils. Schooling in Denmark continued to rely very little on external control and gave teachers and pupils a great deal of pedagogic freedom. For teachers in England, the situation was very different. The imposition of new neo-liberalist policies had brought with them an increasing tension between the affective and academic areas of their work. Teachers at both primary and secondary levels were struggling to hold on to their commitment to the affective and pastoral, while at the same time being set ever increasing targets for the achievement of individual pupils in national testing.

The findings support the view that policy change within the three national contexts was presenting teachers with dilemmas. Where should they focus their attention? Should they be concerned with their pupils as learners or as emerging adults? Should they focus on increasing pupils' subject knowledge or help them with their personal and social development? Should teaching rely on discrete subjects or recognise the interrelated nature of knowledge by using cross-curricular work linked to pupil experience outside school? Should teachers encourage individual achievement at the expense of group co-operation? Should they encourage common goals or differentiate their teaching for individual children?

These studies have helped to emphasize how teachers approach their work in culturally specific ways. Within different systems, with different histories and different sets of professional values, some policy directives will be more difficult than others to accommodate. Global pressures to compete and conform will see the 'epidemic' (Levin, 1998) of policy initiatives spread widely but the way these common ideas are codified and implemented will depend upon the cultural values which underpin national systems. In general, French *collège* teachers continued to perceive their pupils as 'students' and promote a common core of learning for all pupils through a subject-orientated curriculum interpreted by autonomous professionals. Their colleagues in Denmark, on the other hand, generally worked collaboratively, recognising the importance of an affective component to learning. They engaged with the 'emerging adult' through a more holistic and democratic approach to knowledge which included both personal and social development and was more concerned with co-operation than individual achievement. For teachers in the English study, the picture was more ambiguous. A professional proclivity to engage more fully with the affective component of their work was at odds with a managerially-driven policy model which sought to be effective in terms of a narrowly defined measure of pupil attainment more in keeping with the academically-focused demands of policy. An emphasis on accountability had added to the administrative demands of their work, while a concern with target-setting, for themselves and their pupils, had also reduced the time and space for a more personally satisfying approach to pedagogy. A crowded and sometimes contradictory policy agenda continued to create competing demands which presented teachers with daily dilemmas in respect of their professional practice.

However, within these general national differences, there was also some evidence of commonalities across the three countries which could be developed through further research. Younger or more recently trained teachers tended to be more positive towards recent policy changes, they accepted the need to work more closely with colleagues and create a curriculum that would equip pupils for the changing work environment. They were also generally more satisfied with their roles and more accepting of the new challenges being placed upon them. Teachers in areas of social and economic deprivation were also, generally, more ready to fit their teaching around the lived experiences of their pupils. The different subject specialisms, in England and France, also had an impact on the ability of teachers to adapt their teaching to the needs of their pupils, with teachers of modern languages and the humanities especially proactive in this respect.

As other research shows, there is as yet little empirically based knowledge of the ways in which teachers' effectiveness in the classroom, or their willingness and ability to respond to policy change, grows and/or diminishes over the course of a career and in different contexts. Internationally there have been a number of studies of teacher career development – in the USA (Lightfoot, 1983; Fessler & Christensen, 1992); England (Ball & Goodson, 1985; Nias, 1989); Australia (Ingvarson & Greenway, 1984); Canada (Butt, 1984) and Switzerland

(Huberman, 1993). Huberman's study, the only significant longitudinal research carried out over a ten-year period with Swiss secondary school teachers, is particularly cited for its development of a non-linear, empirically-based schematic model of a five phase teaching career cycle. Fessler and Christensen's (1992) research also emphasises the non-linear nature of teacher development and conceptualises teacher development as consisting of a dynamic interplay between career cycle, personal environment, organisational environment and the growth of expertise. While some researchers have found that a teacher's commitment tends to progressively decrease over the course of their career (Fraser, Draper, & Taylor, 1998; Huberman, 1993) in response to factors such as pupil behaviour, parental demands and changes in education policies (Day, 2000; Louis, 1998; Tsui & Cheng 1999), others have found that, in some circumstances, level of commitment to teaching increases with teaching experience (Boylan & McSwan, 1998). Troman and Woods (2001) found that some teachers coped with the intensified work resulting from policy change by adjusting their careers. Some retired early or downshifted, relinquishing posts of responsibility, a step to "disengagement", or redefined their roles. Others "re-routed", finding new opportunities outside teaching or re-located to another school. However, for some teachers involved in our studies, in England particularly, there seemed to be a shift from a vocational to a more instrumental commitment to teaching and a progressive disinvestment of the self in teaching (Troman & Woods, 2001). All the studies discussed here point to the need for further comparative empirical research into the ways in which teacher career theory applies to different cultural contexts and to how teachers adapt to uncertainty and change over the lifetime of a teaching career.

Conclusion

So how do these findings help us understand the extent to which recent policy change has shaped what it means to be a teacher at the beginning of the twenty-first century? Evidence suggests that there is a potential for a disjunction between policy and practice. Teachers, especially in England, have become subject to a growing 'performance' model of practice, which seeks to govern not only the inputs and processes but also the outputs of education (McNess, Broadfoot, & Osbourn, 2003). Elliot (1996, p. 16) argues that this new emphasis on 'performativity' as a policy device is not simply or even mainly about raising standards, but rather plays a central role in *changing the rules which shape educational thought and practice ... part of a language game which serves the interests of power and legitimates those interests in terms of the performativity criterion.* The 'policy epidemic' which Levin (1998) speaks of suggests that such pressures will continue to spread to other national systems and there is already some evidence, especially within Denmark, that issues of effectiveness and performance are becoming more prominent (Klette, 2000; Rasmussen, 2000).

The findings also suggest that the implementation of policy is complex and filtered through the historical and cultural roots of national education systems.

The programme of comparative studies described here demonstrates the influence of both structure and agency as important influences on professional priorities and practice. The teachers studied were not the passive victims of imposed educational reform but had the potential to actively, and creatively, mediate policy change and in some cases to adapt, change or subvert it. In all three countries studied there is evidence of teachers seizing the potential for a margin of manoeuvrability between centralized policy change and its implementation. Both these and other studies suggest that teachers' response to change is multi-faceted and complex. They indicate the extent to which differences in teacher values and expectations of their work, sometimes referred to as 'cultures of teaching', are reinforced by policy and practice and "embedded" in particular policy contexts (McLaughlin & Talbert, 1993). Thus externally imposed require-ments are mediated by the perceptions, understandings, motivation and capacity of both individual and groups of teachers in different contexts to produce particular practices and actions. It follows that policy change is unlikely to be achieved by the imposition of centrally derived directives alone and that genuine reform needs to engage and challenge teachers' own values so that they become part of the reform process.

Endnotes

The Bristaix Study was funded by ESRC from 1984 to 1987 and was carried out by Patricia Broadfoot and Marilyn Osborn with Michel Gilly and Arlette Brucher.
The PACE Study was funded by the ESRC in three stages from 1989–1996 and included the following collaborators, Andrew Pollard, Patricia Broadfoot, Paul Croll, Marilyn Osborn, Dorothy Abbot, Edie Black, Elizabeth McNess and Pat Triggs.
The STEP Study was funded by ESRC from 1990 to 1991and included the following team members: Patricia Broadfoot, Marilyn Osborn, Claire Planel.
The ENCOMPASS Study was funded by the ESRC from 1998–2000 with a contribution from the Danish Research Council and included the following collaborators, Marilyn Osborn, Patricia Broadfoot, Elizabeth McNess, Claire Planel, Pat Triggs (*University of Bristol*), Birte Ravn and Thyge Winther-Jensen (*The Danish University of Education*), and Olivier Cousin (*University of Bordeaux 11*).

References

Acker, S. (1999). *The Realities of Teachers' Work: Never a Dull Moment*. London: Cassell.
Apple, M. W. (1986). *Teachers and Texts: A Political Economy of Class and Gender Relations in Education*. London: Routledge.
Ball, S. (1990). *Politics and Policy Making in Education: Explorations in Policy Sociology*. London: Routledge.
Ball, S. (1994). *Education Reform: A Critical and Post-Structural Approach*. Buckingham: Open University Press.
Ball, S. (2003). The teacher's soul and the terrors of performativity. *Journal of Education Policy, 18* (2), 215–228.
Ball, S., & Goodson, I. F. (1985). *Teachers' Lives and Careers*. London: Falmer Press.

Bascia, N., & Young, B. (2001). Women's careers beyond the classroom: Changing roles in a changing world. *Curriculum Inquiry, 31*(3), 271–302.

Bourdieu, P., & Passeron, W. (1990). *Reproduction in Education, society and culture* (2nd ed.). London: Sage.

Bowe, R., & Ball, S. J. (with Gold, A.) (1992). *Reforming Education and Changing Schools*. London: Routledge.

Boylan, C., & McSwan, D. (1998). Long-staying rural teachers: who are they? *Australian Journal of Education, 42*(1), 49–65.

Broadfoot, P., & Osborn, M. (1992). French lessons: Comparative perspectives on what it means to be a teacher. *Oxford Studies in Comparative Education, 1*, 69–88.

Broadfoot, P., Osborn, M., Gilly, M., & Bûcher, A. (1993). *Perceptions of teaching: Primary school teachers in England and France*. London: Cassell.

Butt, R. (1984). Arguments for using biography in understanding teacher thinking. In R. Halkes & J. K. Olson (Eds.), *Teacher thinking: A new perspective on persisting problems in education*. Lisse, Swets and Seitlinger B.V.

Croll, P., Abbott, D., Broadfoot, P., Osborn, M., & Pollard, A. (1994). Teachers and educational policy: Roles and models. *British Journal of Educational Studies, 42*(2), 333–47.

Croll, P. (Ed.) (1996). *Teachers, pupils and primary schooling: Continuity and change*. London: Cassell.

Darmanin, M. (1990). Maltese primary school teachers' experience of centralised policies. *British Journal of Sociology of Education, 11*(3), 275–308.

Day, C. (2000). Teachers in the Twenty-first Century: Time to renew the vision. *Teachers and Teaching: Theory and Practice, 6*(1), 101–115.

Durkheim, E. (1961). *Moral education: A study in the theory and application of the sociology of education* (E. K. Wilson and H. Schnurer, Trans.). New York: The Free Press.

Elliot, J. (1996). Quality assurance, the educational standards debate, and the commodification of educational research. *Curriculum Journal, 8*(6), 63–83.

Fessler, R., & Christensen, J. (1992). *The teacher career cycle: Understanding and guiding the professional development of teachers*. Boston: Allyn and Bacon.

Fraser, H., Draper, J., & Taylor, W. (1998). The quality of teachers' professional lives: Teachers and job satisfaction. *Evaluation and Research in Education, 12*(2), 61–71.

Gewirtz, S., Ball, S. J., & Bowe, R. (1995). *Markets, choice and equity*. Buckingham: Open University Press.

Goodson, I. F., & Hargreaves, A. (Eds.) (1996). *Teachers' professional lives*. London: Falmer Press.

Green, A., Wolf, A., & Leney, T. (1999). *Convergence and Divergence in European education and training systems*. London: University of London.

Hans, N. (1949). *Comparative education*. London: Routledge & Kegan Paul.

Hargreaves, A. (1994). *Changing teachers, changing times: Teachers' work and culture in the postmodern age*. London: Cassell.

Helsby, G. (1999). *Changing teachers' work*. Buckingham: Open University Press.

Huberman, M. (1993). *The Lives of Teachers*. London: Cassell.

Ingvarson, L., & Greenway, P. A. (1984). Portrayals of teacher development. *Australian Journal of Education, 28*(1), 45–65.

Kandel, I. L. (1933). *Comparative education*. Boston: Houghton Mifflin.

Karlsen, G. E. (2002). Education policy and education programmes in the European Union. In J. A. Ibanez-Martin & G. Jover (Eds.), *Education in Europe: Policies and politics*. Dordrecht, The Netherlands: Kluwer Academic Publishers.

Klette, K. (2002). Reform policy and teacher professionalism in four Nordic countries. *Journal of Educational Change, 3*, 265–282.

Krepsi, A. (1995). Greek primary teachers and the National Curriculum. Unpublished poster presentation British Educational Research Association Conference: University of Bath.

Lauglo, J. (1990). Factors behind decentralization in education systems: a comparative perspective with special reference to Norway. *Compare, 20*(1), 21–39.

Levin, B. (1998). An epidemic of education policy: what can we learn from each other? *Comparative Education, 34*(2), 131–142.

Lightfoot, S. L. (1983). The lives of teachers. In L. S. Shulman & G. Sykes (Eds.), *Handbook of teaching and policy*. New York: Longman.

Lipsky, M. (1980). *Street-level bureaucracy: Dilemmas of the individual in public services*. Russell Sage Foundation.

Louis, K. S. (1998). Effects of teacher quality of work life in secondary schools on commitment and sense of efficacy. *School Effectiveness and School Improvement, 9*(1), 1–27.

MacBeath, J., & Mortimore, P (2001). School effectiveness and improvement: The story so far. In J. MacBeat & P. Mortimore (Eds.), *Improving school effectiveness*. Buckingham: Open University Press.

McLaughlin, M., & Talbert, J. (1993). How the world of students and teachers challenges policy coherence. In S. Fuhrman (Ed.), *Designing coherent education policy: Improving the system*. San Francisco, CA: Jossey-Bass.

McNess, E. (2001). The school teacher: a universal construct? In C. Day & D. van Veen (Eds.), *Educational research in Europe Yearbook 2001*. Leuven: Garant Publishers.

McNess, E., Broadfoot, P., & Osborn, M. (2003). Is the effective compromising the affective? *British Educational Research Journal, 29*(2), 243–257.

Menlo, A., & Poppleton, P. (Eds.) (1999). *The meanings of teaching: an international study of secondary teachers' work lives*. London: Bergin and Garvey.

Metz, M. H. (1990). How social class differences shape the context of teachers' work. In M. W. McLauglin, J. E. Talbert & N. Bascia (Eds.), *The contexts of teaching in secondary schools: Teachers' realities*. New York: Teachers College Press.

Nias, J. (1989). *Primary teachers talking: A study of teaching as work*. London: Routledge.

Osborn, M., & Broadfoot, P. (1992). A lesson in progress? Primary classrooms observed in England and France, *Oxford Review of Education, 18*(1), 1992.

Osborn, M., McNess, E., & Broadfoot, P. (with Pollard, A., & Triggs, P.) (2000). *What teachers do: Changing policy and practice in primary education*. London: Continuum.

Osborn, M., Broadfoot, P., McNess, E., Planel, C., Ravn, B., & Triggs, P. (2003). *A world of difference: Comparing learners across Europe?* Buckingham: Open University Press.

Ozga, J. (2000). *Doing research in educational settings: Contested terrain*. Buckingham: Open University Press.

Pollard, A., Broadfoot, P., Croll, P., Osborn, M., & Abbott, D. (1994). *Changing English primary schools? The Impact of the Education Reform Act at Key Stage One*. London: Cassell.

Pollard, A., & Triggs, P. (with Broadfoot, P., McNess, E. and Osborn, M.) (2000). *What pupils say: Changing policy and practice in primary education*. London: Continuum.

Rasmussen, J. (2000). Construction of the Danish teacher on the basis of policy documents. In K. Klette, I. Carlgren, J. Rasmussen, H. Simola & M. Sundkvist (Eds.), *Restructuring Nordic Teachers: An analysis of policy texts from Finland, Denmark, Sweden and Norway* (pp. 38–108). Report No. 10/2000. University of Oslo, Institute for Educational Research.

Robertson, S. (1996). Markets and teacher professionalism: A political economy analysis, *Melbourne Studies in Education, 37*(2), 23–39.

Sadler, M. (1900). How can we learn anything of practical value from the study of foreign systems of education? In J. H. Higginson (Ed.) (1979). *Selections from Michael Sadler* Liverpool: Dejall and Meyorre.

Sammons, P, Hillman, J., & Mortimore, P (1995). *Key characteristics of effective schools*. London: Ofsted/Institute of Education, University of London.

Smyth, J., Dow. A., Hattam, R., Reid, A., & Shacklock, G. (2000). *Teachers' work in a globalising economy*. London: Falmer Press.

Troman, G. (1996). The rise of the new professionals? The restructuring of primary teachers' work and professionalism. *British Journal of Sociology of Education, 17*(4), 473–487.

Troman, G., & Woods, P. (2001). *Primary teachers' stress*. London: Routledge Falmer.

Tsui, K. T., & Cheng, Y. C. (1999). School organizational health and teacher commitment: A contingency study with multi-level analysis. *Educational Research and Evaluation, 5*(3), 249–268.

Webb, R., Vulliamy, G. (with Hakkinen, K., Hamalainen, S., Kimonen, E., Nevalainen, R., &

Nikki, M.) (1997). *A comparative analysis of curriculum change in primary schools in England and Finland*, York: University of York Department of Education.

Weber, M. (1947). *The theory of social and economic organisation* (A. M. Henderson & T. Parsons, trans.). New York: The Free Press.

Whitty, G. (2002). *Making sense of education policy*. London: Paul Chapman Publishing.

Winther-Jensen, T. (2002). Tradition and Transition in Danish Education. In R. Griffin (Ed.), *Education in transition: International perspectives on the politics and processes of change*. London: Symposium Books.

Woods, P., & Jeffrey, B. (1997). Creative teaching in the primary National Curriculum. In G. Helsby & G. McCulloch (Eds.), *Teachers and the National Curriculum*. London: Cassell.

26

SCHOOL IMPROVEMENT WITHIN A KNOWLEDGE ECONOMY: FOSTERING PROFESSIONAL LEARNING FROM A MULTIDIMENSIONAL PERSPECTIVE

Peter Sleegers, Sanneke Bolhuis and Femke Geijsel
University of Nijmegen, The Netherlands

Modern societies are gradually moving towards a knowledge economy in which knowledge productivity will be the dominant factor. The radical increase of information technology has already transformed modes of doing business, the nature of services and products, the meaning of time in work, and the processes of learning. These forces have contributed to a belief that knowledge production and continuous innovation are key to survival (Fenwick, 2001). Knowledge production, in fact, is crucial for the improvement of work processes, products and services, being demanded by our rapidly moving society. This situation stresses the importance of a competent workforce. As work in the new economy increasingly focuses on knowledge production, rethinking traditional ways of organizing work and creating powerful learning environments in organizations is crucial (Kessels, 2001).

By now, school organizations have encountered many of the same conditions and challenges experienced by their private-sector counterparts. Due to this transformation into a knowledge economy and confronted with the complex and insecure nature of recent educational innovations, schools have to deal with questions about how to manage knowledge and foster conditions for continuous professional learning (Leithwood & Louis, 1998; Toole & Louis, 2002). Although the imperative for professional learning appears to be indisputable, change processes are often unpredictable, evolutionary, and difficult to manage. So schools are faced with a rather complex situation.

In this chapter, we explore some of those complexities by focusing on the relation between knowledge production in schools and school improvement. Knowledge production can be understood from a psychological view as the signaling, absorbing and processing of relevant information, generating and disseminating new knowledge, and applying this knowledge to the improvement and innovation of schools (Bolhuis & Simons, 1999; Kessels, 2001). In this

International Handbook of Educational Policy, 527–541
Nina Bascia, Alister Cumming, Amanda Datnow, Kenneth Leithwood and David Livingstone (Eds.)
© 2005 *Springer. Printed in Great Britain.*

chapter, we also view knowledge production within its social context. Social-constructivist theory is used to understand the social context of the learning process and the social characteristics of knowledge. This brings us to view professional learning as a social process and knowledge as a social construction. In line with this, knowledge creation and learning may be conceived of as participating in the social construction of reality (cf. Berger & Luckmann, 1967) and learning to learn as learning how to participate in the social construction and reconstruction of reality.

Applying this line of reasoning to schools implies that the process of knowledge creation and production in schools requires the professional learning of individual teachers and administrators, as well as the development of collective professional learning processes within professional communities (Leithwood & Louis, 1998; Leithwood, 2000). The focus in school improvement within a knowledge economy is, therefore, on how teachers and administrators in schools collectively participate in the (re)construction of reality and learn to use innovations to change their practices, solve problems, and enhance teaching, learning, and caring (cf. Louis, Toole, & Hargreaves, 1999).

In this chapter, we first elaborate on the meaning of professional learning in schools within the context of a knowledge economy and the pressure for school improvement. This elaboration will result in a focus on professional learning as a multidimensional construct. Then we ask how professional learning can be fostered within the school organization. We examine research about the conditions fostering professional learning and schools as professional learning communities, as well as the theoretical bases of these topics. The chapter ends with a discussion of these issues from a more critical point of view and the question will be asked about the meaning of learning and education when we talk about change, and changing contexts. We point to some implications for educational policy, as well.

Professional Learning

The concept "professional" can be interpreted in the normative way as the standard that needs to be fulfilled by workers in a field like education. On the other hand "professional" may be understood as an adjective that simply refers to whatever belongs to the job in a field. Consequently, this first meaning of professional learning may be understood as a type of learning that is required of workers and characterized by certain qualities. But professional learning also refers to learning that comes from working in a professional field and may or may not contribute to quality. While professional education and training focus on the first meaning, it is often overlooked that professional learning, in the second sense, also occurs whether intended or not. This presents a major problem, since new learning always builds on previous learning of both types. In addition, this previous "learning in the workplace" is not understood very well within the mental models of learning that prevail in education. The dominant model focuses on the individual and puts cognitive understanding before action. We will argue that to understand and deal with continuous professional learning that is the heart of school improvement, different theoretical approaches are needed, cognitive and behavioral as well as social, historical, cultural and critical theory approaches.

School improvement is often pursued by means of providing teachers (administrators, and others) with new knowledge and skills. However, many teacher training and staff development programs do not predict very well what teachers and others will do next in their school. Many obstacles may hinder the "desired" behavior. Which obstacles? In the first place we may ask "whose desire was concerned?" What emotional and motivational value did teachers attach to these new knowledge and skills? Do the proposed knowledge and skills respond to any of the problems teachers experience or the goals they try to achieve? Do such programs appeal to teachers' convictions about what school is all about, and to their sense of professional identity? Or is consensus implicitly assumed, rather than actually co-constructed?

Secondly, the facilitation of teachers' learning may be impeded by the strong conviction that learning needs to precede behavior. This perception is rooted in the fact that our society has organized a huge educational system in order to learn before entering real life to "apply" knowledge in practice, and has for a long time been strengthened by cognitive learning theory. However, much "knowing about" does not lead to either knowing or to actual behavior. On the other hand, behavior may be reinforced and repeated, perhaps adapted and elaborated in the course of time, according to different circumstances and effects. One could say that, in order to adopt some new practice, behaving is at least an indispensable part of the learning process. The "expert" literature does pay attention to experience as an important contribution to expertise. Interestingly, this literature also recognizes that expertise is, in part, tacit. An expert teacher deals with students and problems that arise in an immediate, seemingly intuitive way, based on a long experience with similar situations, without having to think consciously and systematically about the nature of the problem and consequences of alternative ways to deal with the situation before acting. However, while the kind of behavior that results from experience is to a large extent tacit, experience does not automatically result in expertise, in expert behavior and desirable ways to handle problems in the profession. Teachers' professional learning in the workplace results in habitual ways of doing the job that may or may not represent quality work.

Thirdly, and most important, habitual behavior and thinking are not easily changed, as we know from our everyday experience. The conceptual change research in cognitive psychology, for example, studies problems of students' learning when they are asked to replace their everyday understanding of a phenomenon with a scientific understanding. The research demonstrates that the learner is likely to distort scientific understanding to make the new information fit to his/her prior knowledge, or else, and very often, to forget about the new information. Conceptual change research has identified several conditions that are important in facilitating such learning (Strike & Posner, 1985). These include 1) a feeling of dissatisfaction with prior knowledge, e.g., because of contradictory experiences or unsolved problems, 2) the new conception must at least make some sense to the learner, since completely incomprehensible information will be immediately rejected, 3) the new conception must appear plausible enough to invite further consideration, and 4) the new conception must be fruitful, that is solve problems in a better way than the prior conceptions did. For conceptual change to occur, search for preconceptions, compare and contrast preconceptions with new information, construct new conceptions, and evaluate new conceptions (Ali, 1990; Biemans, 1997). However, new understanding appears to vanish when it is not integrated in daily practice (Kikas, 1998). Conceptual change theory and research has focussed on acquiring scientific conceptions to replace prior understanding. But evidence from this research is applicable to professional learning when such learning requires the replacement of prior conceptions and/or behavior. To understand what is involved in changing daily practice, we need to turn to theory about more than cognition, located "in the head"; that is, theory about learning from cultural and historical perspectives, locating learning processes and results in social interaction. Culture may be defined as

> *"the pattern of basic assumptions that a given group has invented, discovered, or developed in learning to cope with its problems of external adaptation and internal integration, and that have worked well enough to be considered valid, and, therefore, to be taught to new members as the correct way to perceive, think, and feel as related to those problems"* (Schein, 1985, p. 3).

Since solutions to problems may have been invented long ago, even generations back, the correct ways to perceive, think, feel, and behave have become rather self-evident. They have turned into habits and are not discussed any longer. Discussions may emerge around elements of the solutions, or about new problems arising from the original solutions, without returning to the original problem however. It has become very hard to conceive of other solutions, and if anyone tries to do so, the resulting ideas are most often interpreted as "radical", "unrealistic", or worse. Teachers' behavior and learning are rooted in the cultural and historical phenomenon of our educational system, in school experiences from an early age. On numerous occasions everybody, including those without teacher training or teaching experience, has learnt what "school", "teaching", "learning", etc. mean. This implies that basic assumptions about why and how education is organized as it is in our society are not easily made explicit or criticized. When the well-known solutions that have been regarded valid as long as one can remember seem not to work as well anymore, it is very difficult to change; this is the case at the individual level of the teacher, at the group level within school, at the school level, at the level of the community involved (parents, policy makers, etc.). Old solutions are deeply engrained in the perception, thought and feelings of individuals. They are also strengthened through social interaction in diverse settings, and embedded in the organizational solutions, language, tools, and instruments.

From this perspective, the conditions of change prove to need some elaboration to include not only conceptual but also behavioral, not only individual but also culturally shared change. In general, the individual level will need completion with the sociocultural level, which may involve the school team as well as the local or larger community. Also, the steps of learning may turn out not to be linear, since the process of professional learning involves much more complicated patterns of thought and action than only conceptual change. Since teachers, and all others involved, are usually habituated to the accepted solutions of teaching, an explicit effort in raising awareness of the unsatisfactory quality of these solutions seems a necessary condition to reach the kind of dissatisfaction that frees the way to the consideration of alternatives. In fact, many beliefs are already in place to explain the contradictory experiences and unsolved problems. Raising awareness of uncritically accepted, implicit solutions needs discussion with others even when there is only a problem to be solved at the individual level, let alone when school development is involved. Strong counter-evidence of new solutions is necessary to provoke consideration of alternatives. New conceptions need not only to make some sense; they need to be attractive.

Solutions to problems better than the old solutions are attractive. But another part of attractiveness is that solutions are considered feasible. Becoming aware of the shortcomings of existing solutions and considering the possibility of alternatives appears to be strongly connected to a continuous and critical dialogue on what is aimed for in the school. A shared reframing of the problems schools are expected to solve is an essential part of school improvement.

Besides the difficulty of becoming aware of the sheer possibility of alternatives, changes may also threaten positions of power. Critical theory underlines the necessity of becoming aware of one's own habits and assumptions, but also focussing on the important role of dominance in the sociocultural context (Simons & Bolhuis, 2003). Teaching and learning play a part in the exertion and distribution of power in society. This happens, to a large extent, implicitly through socialization and self-evident cultural meanings. Power is expressed in the cultural meanings and imposition of these meanings as if they hold the only possible truth. So school improvement goals or changes will only be realized when a sufficiently powerful part of the school community is involved in constructing the new solutions and begins to consider these as valid ways to solve problems.

There is more to critical theory, however, that bears importance to issues of the knowledge economy and teachers' professional learning. Critical theory and critical pedagogy seek to raise consciousness and critical appraisal of the "truths" that are embodied and presented by schools and society. The rapid growth of knowledge also indicates the tentativeness of actual knowledge. And a multicultural world highlights the conflicts between "truths". Critical pedagogy challenges schools to recognize the oppressive effects of learning and to help students to reflect on what seems self-evident, to think of alternatives and possibly realize these. When schools are to prepare their students for lifelong learning in this world, they need to help students (and teachers) to deal with the uncertainties and provisional character of our understanding of the world, and to deal with the power dimensions of knowledge (Bolhuis, 2003). Teachers as well as students need to become aware of the part they play in the construction and reconstruction of reality (Berger & Luckmann, 1967).

Increasingly, we are coming to understand just how central dealing with uncertainty is to learning. While learning used to be – and is still often presented as – a way to reach certainty about the world, increasingly we are acknowledging the restricted, temporary and provisional state of what we learn in and outside school. The most important reason for schools to focus on learning how to learn is the simple fact that we live in a rapidly changing world. Learning requires unlearning, conceptual and behavioral change, at the individual as well as the social level. However, people as well as cultures differ in their tolerance of uncertainty (Hofstede, 1991; Huber & Sorrentino, 1996). People with a strong certainty orientation (a low tolerance of uncertainty) tend to stick to what they (believe to) know and do not like to investigate what is unknown to them. They are unwilling to risk discovering the need for change. Uncertainty-oriented people, on the other hand, tend to feel challenged by uncertain situations, and relish examining new information that contradicts their prior conceptions. The traditional school culture often reduces uncertainty in students', as well as in teachers', learning as much as possible. School organization and curriculum usually afford a kind of certainty (about what to do and what is true) seldom encountered in life outside school. Differences in certainty orientation among teachers, as well as students, within a school need to be taken into account in school improvement activities. While uncertainty-oriented teachers and students may enjoy changes, discussions, and collaborative work, certainty-oriented teachers may need support in a more gradual participation (Huber & Roth, 1999).

In short, to facilitate – and participate in – continuous professional learning, we need to adopt a multidimensional perspective on learning, combining the cognitive with the emotional and motivational as well as the behavioral aspects of learning, taking into account the implicit processes and results of learning as well as the explicit, relating the individual level of learning with several sociocultural levels, and being fully aware of the struggle for power and values involved in learning, and the responsibility professionals in schools should take.

School Organization and Professional Learning

If professional learning is as complex as we have portrayed it here, what can school organizations do to foster such learning for school improvement? This is a question that has been under discussion in the research literature since the late 1980s. And like professional learning, it has been viewed from multidimensional perspectives; the role of school leaders and school organization in fostering professional learning has been modeled using a variety of organizational and management approaches and strategies.

At the start of the 1980s, most studies in the field of school improvement and educational change reflected the so-called control-oriented approach (Rowan, 1990). This approach draws upon bureaucratic ideology and is grounded in organizational theories of control, economic rationality, and contingency (cf. Monk, 1989; Perrow, 1972). The idea is that student achievement can be improved by routinization of the schools' core technology through strengthening the schools' bureaucratic controls. People are viewed as rationally functioning creatures who can be steered towards desired behaviors by organizational structures and management. Thus, the role of the principal, for example, is conceived as essentially managerial in nature (cf. Bacharach & Mundell, 1995).

A control-oriented approach entails the school organization's bureaucracy to support professional learning only insofar as professional learning concerns the creation of new knowledge needed to realize small procedural changes (like using a newer version of subject method), not requiring fundamental new attitudes towards the profession of teaching. More significant changes in professional learning require different approaches.

During the 1980s, educational researchers began to reconsider the role of teachers from being objects or targets in the design of school organization into meaningful agents of change and active decision-makers. This reconsideration originated in the human relations model of organizations that stressed the importance of individuals' well being in an organization, as well as the importance of consensus and collegial relationships (Mintzberg, 1979). This revised view of teachers, in combination with increased demands on teachers to change, led to the call for alternative, more organic forms of school organization (Rowan, 1990). Rosenholtz's (1987, 1991) study of the school as a social workplace illustrates this reconsideration focusing more on the professional expertise and commitment of teachers rather than on control and coordination as mechanisms for improving the functioning of schools.

As Rowan (1990) argued, a more commitment-oriented approach emerged in the literature as a strategy for the organizational design of schools during the 1980s. As he argued, "collaborative and participative management practices will unleash the energy and expertise of committed teachers and thereby lead to improved student learning" (Rowan 1990, p. 354). A commitment-oriented approach draws upon human capital theory to support the importance of teachers' professional development (cf. Smylie & Hart, 1999), and motivational theories (e.g., Bandura, 1986; Ford, 1992) to conceptualize teachers' commitment to change. In this approach, people are viewed as subject to influence by others through motivational processes rather than through organizational rules and regulations. Central to the commitment strategy is the idea that teacher commitment can be built on the basis of personal identification with the goals and purposes of the school. This is fostered by the development of working arrangements, which increase teacher collegiality, participation in school-wide decision-making, and commitment to the profession (Hannay, 2003). The role of the principal is viewed as essentially inspirational and facilitative in nature (cf. Bacharach & Mundell, 1995; Leithwood, 2000).

Within a commitment strategy, interactive and experimental learning by members of the school organization is considered essential because most of the knowledge and expertise needed for school improvement can only be acquired on the job. Through interaction and commitment, moreover, the learning and professional development of individual teachers accumulates into the learning and improvement of the school as a whole (D. H. Hargreaves, 1994; Leithwood, 2000). As such, this strategy adopts a broader view of professional learning than the control strategy. Accordingly, the belief that professional learning can be managed and controlled is extended by the belief that professional learning can be stimulated by certain organizational conditions.

Inspired by the research of Rosenholtz (1990) and reflecting the commitment strategy, a wide range of studies has been executed into conditions that foster (or hinder) staff development (Smylie, 1988), organizational learning (Leithwood, Leonard, & Sharrat, 1998; Marks, Louis, & Printy, 2000), teacher commitment to change (Geijsel, Sleegers, Leithwood, & Jantzi, 2003; Leithwood, Steinbach, & Jantzi, 2002), school improvement (Hopkins, Ainscow, & West, 1994), and educational innovation (Geijsel, 2001). All of these issues are related to the professional learning of teachers, one way or the other. A review of these studies brings teacher participation in decision making, collaborative culture among teachers, collaborative planning, and a transformational style of school leadership to the front as the most important condition that potentially foster the professional learning of teachers (Sleegers, Geijsel, & van den Berg, 2002).

In addition to studies of conditions fostering professional learning, a second line of research emerged on the bases of commitment thinking and Rosenholtz's model of school as a social workplace. This research focused on the conception of the school as a professional community that gained attention during the 1990s (e.g., Bryk, Camburn, & Louis, 1999; Louis, Marks, & Kruse, 1996). Toole and Louis (2002) claim this body of research is grounded in the assumption that what teachers do together outside of the classroom can be as important as what they do inside in affecting school restructuring, teachers' professional development, and student learning (see also Louis & Kruse, 1995). Professional communities are viewed as a form of school culture that can provide a critical context for school improvement. And indeed, the conditions identified in the several studies referred to earlier, all appear to have their place in creating for the kind of collaborative cultures conceptualized as professional community (cf. Toole & Louis, 2002). Shared purpose, a collective focus on student learning, trust and respect, and reflective dialogue indicate the existence of professional community in schools. Together these conditions shape a way of thinking, interacting, organizing and leading that encapsulates the school as a professional community (see Toole & Louis, 2002, Figure 1, p. 255).

In all of the studies we have referred to so far, conditions are viewed as the main levers of either a school's capacity to change or the school as professional community. This mode of thinking is in line with system theory that takes the school as the unit of analysis. From a systems perspective, these conditions foster change at the teacher and community level as a prerequisite for improved student learning. Manipulating these conditions are a complex matter, however, because they concern both the school level (leadership, participation in decision making) and the teacher level (professional development, teacher motivation). Moreover, change as an outcome is conceptualized at the level of the organization (such as organizational learning and the building of a professional community), at the level of teachers (changed teaching practices), and the level of students (increased student engagement and learning).

Advanced analytic methods such as multilevel analyses and structural equation modeling are used to determine the effects of these conditions. Some such analyses of survey data support the chain of influence suggested to this point (e.g., Leithwood & Jantzi, 2000). This body of research has resulted in a knowledge base regarding conditions and their contextual antecedents and their impact which augments the conception of schools as communities in which students, teachers, school leaders and others involved, work, live and learn together. It also leads to the conclusion that improvement is always about the learning of those involved.

This knowledge base has not, however, resulted in an understanding of how learning processes of the various significant actors within the school take place and how these learning processes can contribute to educational improvements. These questions ask not so much for knowing which conditions matter under what circumstances, but for understanding how teachers, school leaders, team, and schools as a whole learn.

As mentioned in the previous section, professional learning is rooted in the situation that the professional is in and consists of the social construction of new knowledge. This is a situated, sociocultural, or social-cognitive perspectives on learning that defines knowing and learning processes of human participation in particular communities of practice (cf. Fenwick, 2001; see also: Spillane, Reiser, & Reimer, 2002). According to Billet (2001, p. 64), these perspectives stress the "need to understand more fully how workplaces afford opportunities that lead to the development of robust vocational knowledge. ... These reciprocal bases of participation and engagement in thinking, acting, and learning are referred to as co-participation at work." From such a perspective, we need to understand how schools as workplaces play a role in the social construction of knowledge and improvement.

It is exactly this issue that has recently gained attention in educational science literature and is referred to as "professional learning community". A central assumption of viewing schools as professional learning communities is that there is a great deal of untapped (implicit) knowledge already existing in schools and that this knowledge can become more explicit when teachers interact intensively in a way that Little (1990) described as "joint work". Toole and Louis (2002, p. 273) claim that "professional learning communities are most likely to capture the attention of educational leaders and policymakers as the key element in a changing world".

This learning community approach to studying organizational phenomena in education is rather new (cf. Imants, 2002; Bakkenes, De Brabander, & Imants,

1999; Imants, Sleegers, Witziers, 2001), suggesting that the school organization should be regarded as a meaningful construction of work content and work relationships by teachers, principals, students, and other participants. The key to learning, from this perspective, is not adaptation but creation and the free choice of individuals to participate in a social reality called organization and thereby to learn. The starting point for leading and steering individuals and the cooperative agreements, which they engage in organizations, is recognizing that individuals can make (intelligent) choices about behaviors and values that may have the potential to satisfy both individual and organizational needs. Discourse, dialogue, collaborative inquiry, informed debate about these choices is needed to foster human growth and development and, thus, to enable the creation of new knowledge. This is how the functioning of members of an organization, from an interpretive and sociocultural point of view, participate in professional learning communities described by Toole and Louis (2002).

Within this new approach, learning is conceptualized as a dynamic and cyclical process. The strict distinction between conditions and effects disappears (cf. Imants, 2002). As a result, the links between conditions for learning, learning communities, and school improvement are described as recursive relationships. Collaboration, participation, and transformational leadership, reflective dialogue and the like can be an input, throughput, or outcome of learning processes. They become *productive* when it concerns social constructions that make sense to those involved, for instance to teachers during their work with students and during their sharing with colleagues.

In this view of schools as professional learning communities, learning and change is about engaged participation in the shared practices of research, reflection, dialogue, and the co-construction of meaning and skill. So, not the individual nor internal cognitive processes are the unit of analysis, but instead the group, social interactions, and the community of users. For the analysis of social interactions within learning communities, the coordination principles, patterns of action, and participation in socially organized activity systems (Engeström, 1995, 1999) are relevant.

In sum, this section introduced a variety of organization and management theories to reflect on the question of what a school as an organization can do to foster professional learning as a way to realize school improvement. To effectively organize schools as workplaces where knowledge creation and professional learning occur in the interests of school improvement, we need to develop a multidimensional approach on the role of school leaders and school organization. In such a multidimensional approach, frameworks that enable interpretation of the functioning of schools as levers for school improvement will need to be combined with emerging conceptualizations of schools in terms of professional learning communities.

Towards Professional Learning from a Multidimensional Perspective

Current trends in school improvement often entail a shift to process-oriented instruction, which fosters self-directed learning in students. This is a quite demanding change and often requires new knowledge, skills, and attitudes from teachers. In a knowledge economy, we are expected to be able to create the new knowledge that is needed. This puts the professional learning of teachers in the center of school improvement. This chapter has described how we might understand and conceptualize this. We argued that a commitment-oriented approach to change provided the conditions needed for schools to act as professional communities. We also argued, however, for the need to further understand how professional learning actually takes place within such communities; how they *become* professional learning communities. Our answer was to view teacher's learning process as context-bound and embedded in the community of practice of the school. The social construction of reality in schools, however, can as easily reinforce traditional teaching as change teaching practice. Changing practice and thinking which has been functional for many years is not easy. A lot of experience has contributed to the practical knowledge of teachers. Prior knowledge is resistant to change. Experiential learning and critical thinking (reflection) therefore need to be intertwined to foster further learning and change. Emotional aspects are crucial in this process, because the teacher's identity is involved (van Veen & Sleegers, in press). So, critical reflection on assumptions, goals and values in the institutional context should be an essential part of teachers' collaborative learning and the school's culture (Zeichner & Liston, 1996) as well as critical reflection of teachers' emotions (cf. Hargreaves, 1998; Meijers & Wardekker, 2002; van den Berg, 2002). Initiation and facilitation of critical reflection in this broad sense, as well as the stimulation of enactment coming from such reflection might therefore be the essential mechanisms for professional growth and school development taking place simultaneously (cf. Clarke & Hollingsworth, 2002).

Conclusions

The view of professional learning developed in this chapter acknowledges that school improvement involves not only something happening outside that we have to keep up with and adapt to, but it involves also a process in which every teacher and school leader (or actually every member of society) is part of and should feel responsible for. This critical view defines professional learning as taking responsibility for the school-reality co-created by those who constitute it. This means that for teachers to learn, they need to engage actively in a constructive, goal-oriented process in which they monitor and decide on further action, participate in collaborative action and reflect in a school culture that is supportive of critical inquiry and action. For school leaders and others who are focusing on improving the functioning of schools as a whole, this means that they have to ensure that critical professional dialogue is going on. As Billet (2001) suggests, they must foster engagement in everyday work tasks, direct guidance (for example, coaching and modeling by experienced coworkers) and indirect guidance (for example, from observations of the workplaces and partially completed jobs). Following these three bases, according to Billet (p. 65), workplaces can afford learning through the quality of access to workplace activities and guidance.

Now is the time to expand school improvement research from modeling the impact of change capacity to better understanding the processes of social construction of knowledge as a means to increase our understanding of how to build and sustain capacity within schools. Sociocultural and social-cognitive perspectives, the modeling of professional learning communities as activity systems, and Billet's ideas on access to workplace activities and guidance offer promising directions for such research. Building on these directions, more systemic research needs to be done on change processes in schools as they happen "naturalistically" and locally, focusing on the learning of individuals, groups, and the school as a whole. We need to study the interaction and enactment of school leaders and teachers and use the conditions framework and concept of professional learning community to interpret what happens.

If we take this view of professional learning, what does it mean for the design of, and support for, such learning on the part of districts if not governments? In our view, educational reform efforts and educational change strategies need to pay more attention to the "naturalistic" and local change processes in schools. Most educational reforms are insufficiently differentiated to the social context of the school and policy makers often lack a systemic perspective on how to create responsive local structures for working with schools (Hopkins, 2001). As we have come to understand over the years, successful policy initiatives reflect a good fit between the aspirations and goals of the policy being implemented and the values and practices of the school. With regard to systemic change, policy therefore has to be concerned with enabling policy-makers, stakeholders, parents, schools and teachers to make connections and to synergize activities around common priorities (Fullan, 2000). What is needed is a local responsive and challenging infrastructure or what Fullan (2000) refers to as "cross-over structures": a variety of networks, agencies, offices and institutions that play a vital role in supporting the improvement work of schools.

In this respect, networks can be regarded as effective means for supporting innovation and school improvement. As identified by the OECD (1999), networks promote the dissemination of good practice, enhance the professional development of teachers, support capacity building in schools, and to a certain extent even challenge traditional hierarchical system structures and assist the process of re-structuring and re-culturing educational organizations and systems. In the context of system wide efforts for innovation, effective networking requires an evolving integrated typology of networks at different levels (groups of students, teachers, schools, parents, stakeholders, and policymakers). The challenge for those involved at all of these levels is to create supportive conditions and local infrastructures for both the implementation of the reform agenda and the innovation of the educational system. In doing so, networks can be a promising means for the stimulation of different forms of collaboration, multi-functional partnerships, engaged participation, knowledge creation, and professional learning.

References

Ali, K. S. (1990). *Instructiestrategieën voor het activeren van preconcepties. [Instructional strategies to activate preconceptions]*. Doctoral dissertation. University Brabant. Helmond: Wibro.

Bacharach, S. B., & Mundell, B. (1995). *Images of schools. Structures and roles in organizational behavior*. Thousand Oaks, CA: Corwin Press.

Bakkenes, I., de Brabander, C., & Imants, J. (1999). Teacher isolation and communication network analysis in primary schools. *Educational Administration Quarterly, 35*(2), 166–202.

Bandura, A. (1986). *Social foundations of thought and action: A social cognitive theory*. Englewood Cliffs, NJ: Prentice-Hall.

Berger, P. L., & Luckmann, T. (1967). *The social construction of reality*. Harmondsworth: Penguin Books.

Biemans, H. J. A. (1997). *Fostering activation of prior knowledge and conceptual change*. Doctoral dissertation. University of Nijmegen. Arnhem: Biemans.

Billett, S. (2001). Co-participation: Affordance and engagement at work. In T. Fenwick (Ed.), *Sociocultural perspectives on learning through work* (pp. 63–72). San Francisco, CA: Jossey-Bass.

Bolhuis, S. (2003). Towards process-oriented teaching for self-directed lifelong learning: A multidimensional perspective. *Learning and Instruction, 13*(3), 327–347.

Bolhuis, S., & Simons, R.-J. (2003). Naar een breder begrip van leren [Towards a broader understanding of learning]. In J. W. M. Kessels & R. F. Poell (Eds.), *Human resource development: Organiseren van het leren* [Human resource development: Organizing learning] (pp. 37–52). Groningen, The Netherlands: Samsom.

Bryk, A., Camburn, E., & Louis, K. S. (1999). Professional community in Chicago elementary schools: Facilitating factors and organizational consequences. *Educational Administration Quarterly, 35*, 751–781.

Clarke, D., & Hollingsworth, H. (2002). Elaborating a model of teacher professional growth. *Teaching and Teacher Education, 18*, 947–967.

Engeström, Y. (1999). Activitity theory and individualmand social transformation. In Y. Engeström, R. Miettinen & R. L. Punamäki (Eds.), *Perspectives on activity theory* (pp. 19–39). Cambridge: Cambridge University Press.

Engeström, Y., Engeström, R., & Kärkkäinen, M. (1995). Polycontextuality and boundary crossing in expert cognition: Learning and problem solving in complex work activities. *Learning and Instruction, 5*, 319–336.

Fenwick, T. (2001). Tides of change: New themes and questions in workplace learning. In T. Fenwick (Ed.), *Sociocultural perspectives on learning through work* (pp. 3–18). San Francisco, CA: Jossey-Bass.

Ford, M. E. (1992). *Motivating humans: Goals, emotions, and personal agency beliefs*. Newbury Park, CA: Sage.

Fullan, M. (2000). The return of large-scale reforms. *Journal of Educational Change, 2*(1), 5–28.

Geijsel, F. (2001). *Schools and innovations: Conditions fostering the implementation of educational innovations* (Dissertation). Nijmegen, The Netherlands: Nijmegen University Press.

Geijsel, F., Sleegers, P., Leithwood, K., & Jantzi, D. (2003). Transformational leadership effects on teachers' commitment and effort toward school reform. *Journal of Educational Administration, 41*(3), 228–256.

Hannay, L. (2003, April). *Orchestrating professional learning: The role of the school district*. Chicago: Paper presented at the annual meeting of the American Educational Research Association.

Hargreaves, A. (1998). The emotions of teaching and educational change. In A. Hargreaves, A. Lieberman, M. Fullan & D. Hopkins (Eds.), *International handbook of educational change* (pp. 558–575). Dordrecht, The Netherlands: Kluwer.

Hargreaves, D. H. (1994). The new professionalism: the synthesis of professional and institutional development. *Teaching and Teacher Education, 10*(4), 423–438.

Hofstede, G. (1991). *Cultures and organizations, software of the mind*. London: McGraw-Hill.

Hopkins, D., Ainscow, M., & West, M. (1994). *School improvement in an era of change*. London: Cassell.

Hopkins, D. (2001). *School Improvement for Real*. London/New York: Routledge/Falmer.

Huber, G. L., & Roth, J. H. W. (1999). *Finden oder suchen? Lehren und Lernen in Zeiten der Ungewiss-heit*. [To find or to look for? Teaching and learning in times of uncertainty]. Schwangau: Ingeborg Huber.

Huber, G. L., & Sorrentino, R. M. (1996). Uncertainty in interpersonal and intergroup relations: An individual differences perspective. In R. M. Sorrentino & E. T. Higgins (Eds.), *Handbook of motivation and cognition: The interpersonal context* (Vol. 3, pp. 591–619). New York: Guilford.

Imants, J. (2002). Relationships in the study of learning communities (book review). *School Effectiveness and School Improvement, 13*(4), 453–462.

Imants, J., Sleegers, P., & Witziers, B. (2001). The tension between organisational sub-structures in secondary schools and educational reform. *School Leadership & Management, 21*(3), 289–308.

Kessels, J.W.M. (2001). *Verleiden tot kennisproductiviteit* [Tempting for knowledge productivity]. Enschede, The Netherlands: Twente University Press.

Kikas, E. (1998). The impact of teaching on students' definitions and explanations of astronomical phenomena. *Learning and Instruction, 8*(5), 439–454.

Little, J. W. (1990). The persistence of privacy: Autonomy and initiative in teachers' professional relations. *Teachers College Record, 91*(4), 509–536.

Leithwood, K. (Ed.) (2000). *Understanding schools as intelligent systems*. Advances in research and theories of school management and educational policy: Vol. 4. Stamford: Jai Press.

Leithwood, K., & Jantzi, D. (2000). The effects of transformational leadership on organizational conditions and student engagement with school. *Journal of Educational Administration, 38*(2), 112–26.

Leithwood, K., Leonard, L., & Sharrat, L. (1998). Conditions fostering organizational learning in schools. *Educational Administration Quarterly, 34*(2), 243–276.

Leithwood, K., & Louis, K. S. (Eds.) (1998). *Organizational learning in schools*. Lisse: Swets & Zeitlinger.

Leithwood, K., Steinbach, R., & Jantzi, D. (2002). School leadership and teachers' motivation to implement accountability policies. *Educational Administration Quarterly, 38*(1), 94–119.

Louis, K. S., & Kruse, S. (Eds.) (1995). *Professionalism and community: Perspectives on reforming urban schools*. California: Corwin Press.

Louis, K. S., Marks, H. M., & Kruse, S. (1996). Teachers' professional community in restructuring schools. *American Educational Research Journal, 33*(4), 757–798.

Louis, K. S., Toole, J., & Hargreaves, A. (1999). Rethinking school improvement. In J. Murphy & K. Louis (Eds.), *Handbook of research on educational administration* (2nd ed.) (pp. 251–276). San Francisco: Jossey-Bass.

Marks, H. M., Louis, K. S., & Printy, S. M. (2000). The capacity for organizational learning: Implications for pedagogical quality and student achievement. In K. Leithwood (Ed.), *Understanding schools as intelligent systems (Advances in Research and Theories of School Management and Educational Policy* (Vol. 4, pp. 239–267). Stamford, CO: JAI Press.

Meijers, F., & Wardekker, W. (2002). Career learning in a changing world: the role of emotions. *Journal for the Advancement of Counseling, 24*(3), 149–167.

Mintzberg, H. (1979). *The structuring of organizations*. Englewood Cliffs, NJ: Prentice-Hall.

Monk, D. H. (1989). The education production function: Its evolving role in policy analysis. *Educational Evaluation and Policy Analysis, 11*(1), 31–45.

OECD (1999). *Innovating Schools*. Paris: OECD.

Perrow, Ch. (1972). *Complex organizations: a critical essay*. Glenview, Ill: Scott, Foresman & Co.

Rosenholtz, S. J. (1987). Educational reform strategies: Will they increase teacher commitment? *American Journal of Education, 95*, 534–562.

Rosenholtz, S. J. (1991). *Teachers' workplace. The social organization of schools*. New York: Teachers College Press.

Rowan, B. (1990). Commitment and control: Alternative strategies for the organizational design of schools. In C. Cadzen (Ed.), *Review of Research in Education, 16*, 353–389.

Sleegers, P., Geijsel, F., & van den Berg, R. (2002). Conditions fostering educational change. In

K. Leithwood & Ph. Hallinger (Eds.), *Second international handbook of educational leadership and administration* (pp. 75–102). Dordrecht, The Netherlands: Kluwer.

Smylie, M. A. (1988). The enhancement function of staff development: Organizational and psychological antecedents to individual teacher change. *American Educational Research Journal, 25*(1), 1–30.

Smylie, M. A., & Hart, A. W. (1999). School leadership for teacher learning and change: A human and social capital development perspective. In J. Murphy & K. S. Louis (Eds.), *Handbook of research on educational administration* (2nd ed.) (pp. 297–322). San Francisco: Jossey-Bass.

Schein, E. H. (1985). *Organizational culture and leadership.* San Francisco, CA: Jossey-Bass.

Simons, R-J., & Bolhuis, S. (2003). Constructivist learning theories and complex learning environments. To be published in R. H. Mulder & P. F. E. Sloane (Eds.), Preparation for the worksite in Europe; the construction of learning-teaching arrangements in vocational education and training. Oxford: *Oxford Studies in Comparative Education.*

Spillane, J. P., Reiser, B. J., & Reimer, T. (2002). Policy implementation and cognition: Reframing and refocusing implementation research. *Review of Educational Research, 72*(3), 387–432.

Strike, K. A., & Posner, G. J. (1985). A conceptual change view of learning and understanding. In L. H. T. West & A. L. Pines (Eds.), *Cognitive structure and conceptual change* (pp. 211–231). Orlando: Academic Press.

Toole, J. C., & Louis, K. S. (2002). The role of professional learning communities in international education. In K. Leithwood & Ph. Hallinger (Eds.), *Second International Handbook of Educational Leadership and Administration* (pp. 245–280). Dordrecht, The Netherlands: Kluwer.

van den Berg, R. (2002). Teachers' meanings regarding educational practice. *Review of Educational Research, 72*(4), 577–626.

van Veen, K., & Sleegers, P. (in press). How does it feel? Teachers' emotions in a context change. *Journal of Curriculum Studies.*

Zeichner, K. M., & Liston, D. P. (1996). *Reflective teaching: An introduction.* Mahwah, NJ: Lawrence Erlbaum Associates.

27

TEACHER INFORMAL LEARNING AND TEACHER KNOWLEDGE: THEORY, PRACTICE AND POLICY

Harry Smaller
York University, UK[1]

This chapter draws heavily on an empirical study which examined the ways in which elementary and secondary school teachers across Canada see and engage themselves, and each other, as informal learners. While "informal learning" has been explored for some time now in a number of social contexts, unfortunately there has been very little research undertaken in relation to teachers themselves, and therefore little literature in this area to draw on for comparative analysis. Other relevant studies are examined, particularly in relation to informal learning more generally and to comparisons between formal and informal learning undertaken by teachers and those in other occupational groups. While there are strong similarities between teachers working in Canadian public schools and their counterparts in classrooms in other "western" nations – at least in regard to formal and informal learning – hopefully the rather detailed descriptions provided in this study will allow readers to judge for themselves on this matter.

The research, spread over three years (1998–2001), involved a succession of activities: a national survey, a collection of teachers' weekly diaries, and a small number of in-depth interviews. In addition to data about formal and informal learning beliefs and activities, information about workload and general workplace conditions was also collected. Further, the initial survey was undertaken in parallel with a similar study involving the general Canadian population, which allowed for comparisons of the two groups in a number of important areas. In many ways the findings of this study seem to stand in significant difference to both received wisdom and official policy/practice in the areas of teacher learning, and teachers' professional development, and it is the purpose of this chapter to explore these differences. The chapter ends with a discussion of possibilities for the development of new/alternative policies and practices which might more appropriately align the present-day realities of teachers and teaching, with improvement of schools to better meet the needs and interests of an increasingly diverse student populations, living in increasingly complex socio-economic times.

Before engaging in a more detailed description of the procedures, findings and

International Handbook of Educational Policy, 543–568
Nina Bascia, Alister Cumming, Amanda Datnow, Kenneth Leithwood and David Livingstone (Eds.)
© 2005 Springer. *Printed in Great Britain.*

analysis of the research, it is important to explore some of the underlying themes which informed the development of the overall project.

First, this study is grounded in a critical understanding of a juncture between the discourses and realities of the schooling "reform" and "restructuring" movement rampant across most nations, north and south, and the shifting roles for teachers within this context. Discourses of "teacher change" and "teacher development" underpin both the rhetoric and reality of this domain of schooling "renewal" – in fact, it might be understandable why one might conclude that "need for change" in schools and schooling translated directly, and solely, to "need for change" in teachers and teaching.

Criticism and critique of state schooling systems, and the teachers within them, is not a new phenomenon. As revisionist historians have long since shown, centralized, compulsory schooling itself arose through a carefully calculated regime of condemnation of earlier, more community-based forms of education in many nations (Curtis, 1988; Gardner, 1984; Katz, 2001). Given this etymology, and the concomitant argument that the main purpose of these state schools was (and to a large extent, continues) to inscribe a particular, dominant culture of gender, race, class, ethnicity, religion, sexuality, and ability, it is not surprising that these systems and settings have been under critique almost since their inception. However, there is an argument that the schooling "reform" movement of the past two decades has been qualitatively different that previous eras, in at least two significant ways.

First, schooling reform is now more closely linked to transformations in the larger political economy of states, provinces and nations – a move to more globalizing, neo-liberal economies, including tighter control over, but less funding for, public sector social institutions (Ball, 1993; Economic Council of Canada, 1992; OECD, 1992).

Secondly, while the recent reforms in education continue to range across the many aspects of schooling – funding, governance, curriculum, resources, facilities, etc. – a strong argument can be made that the ways in which teachers have been singled out for special attention is quite unlike anything that has occurred before. Formerly, teachers were often addressed as a collective entity, and improvements to education were often associated with the need to improve material and intellectual conditions for teachers – resources, libraries, class sizes, salaries, benefits, pensions and job security. Even where and when teachers were seen to be in need of further education themselves, governments at various levels often moved to expand and improve teacher education programs, and/or to offer incentives for teachers to engage in further study, whether pre-service or in-service (see, for example, Althouse, 1967; Fleming, 1972; Tyack, 1976).

Today, however, teachers seem bathed in a different, and much more individualized, light. Individual teachers themselves, it is widely claimed, constitute the main "problem" in education, and need to be more carefully selected, trained, directed, evaluated, tested and controlled (Holmes Group, 1990; Labaree, 1992; Darling-Hammond, 1998; Darling-Hammond & Ball, 1998; OECD, 1998, Ontario Government, 2000). Often, these initiatives are being promoted through a rhetoric of a "need" for increased professionalism, and in at least two Canadian jurisdictions (British Columbia and Ontario), government-initiated and controlled "colleges of teachers" have been established, with a mandate to control the training, certification and practice of teachers (Ontario Government, 1995; Popkewitz, 1994). In many jurisdictions in Canada, the USA and Great Britain (among others), salaries, promotion, and even basic job tenure for individual teachers are increasingly being determined by teacher testing regimes, increased external evaluation of teacher practice, "success rate" of students on standardized examinations, league tables, etc. (OSSTF (Ontario Secondary School Teachers' Federation), 1999).

Underlying this thrust for new controls over teachers' classroom practice has been the insistence of the need for "improvement" of teachers skills and knowledge, the increasing calls for the introduction or expansion of compulsory in-service "professional development" programs for teachers, and the closely-related phenomenon of regular, and compulsory, teacher re-certification programs. In Ontario, for example, a compulsory re-certification program has been introduced, requiring engagement in arbitrarily-defined courses and programs, based partly on an official regime of "Standards of Practice" (Ontario Government 1999). Much less discussed, however, are the underlying foundations and parameters of such endeavors. Who, for example, controls the content and process of these plans? What are the assumptions about necessary or important knowledge? Are they based, and build upon, existing teacher knowledge, or otherwise?

The phenomenon of "teacher knowledge" itself has sparked increased interest among educational researchers in the past decade, and research in the area has taken a number of directions, including explorations about what it is, what it should be, how it is acquired and/or enhanced, and the nature of its relation to student and school success (Briscoe, 1994; Donmoyer, 1995; Gibson & Olberg, 1998; Klein, 1996; Ontario College of Teachers, 1999). To date, however, there has been much less attention paid to how teachers themselves see these matters personally – what they think is important to know and to learn, how they would like to engage in this learning process, and what they are already doing in this regard. These precise questions have born directly on the purpose and methodology of this study.

Directly linked to issues of control over teacher knowledge and teacher education are issues of professionalism. While there are many (differentiated, often oppositional) theoretical perspectives of this phenomenon, social stratification theorists such as Larson (1980) and Derber, Schwartz, and Magrass (1990) suggest that professionalization has been, and remains, an ongoing historic process, both concrete and ideological, whereby the status and authority of particular middle-class occupational groups have been enhanced through state intervention, in exchange for their social regulatory work in society overall (not to mention their own self-regulation). Teachers have historically not been part of the "inner circle" of the most-favoured occupational groups. To be sure, the official rhetoric surrounding their work has often been based on their purported "status" in, and importance to, society. Ironically however, precisely because of their importance as "proper" role models for future citizens, in most western nations the control over their selection, training, certification and practice has generally remained very much in the hands of government and/or its closely monitored agencies (see, for example, Atkins & Lury, 1999; Duman, 1979; Gorelick, 1982; Labaree, 1992; Lawn, 1996).

The contradictory nature of professionalism has been demonstrated in the recent context of neo-liberal schooling reform initiatives promoted and undertaken in many western jurisdictions. While the rhetoric of professionalism is often used in these contexts, the general import is usually that of the "need" for the "upgrading" or "retraining" of teachers. Given these strong ideological messages, it is not surprising that a recent Ontario survey found a significant percentage of parents (75%) in favour of requiring teachers to submit accounts of their learning activities to their principals (rather than being allowed to use their own professional judgements about their own in-service learning), and an even higher percentage (83%) in favour of principals being required to use provincial guidelines and methods to evaluate their teachers (Livingstone, Hart, & Davie, 2001, p. 32). To be sure, very few teachers, and certainly none of their unions, are opposed to on-going opportunities for further education and training. Many, however, are very concerned about the control over teacher learning being taken entirely out of the hands of teachers – leaving others with the power to determine unilaterally what shall be learned, how much, when, and in what manner. Among other aspects of this debate is the issue of "informal learning," and whether it will also be recognized in the mix.

Informal Learning

Few would argue that informal learning is not an important aspect of knowledge and skill acquisition, particularly at the workplace. For example, we often hear the expression "a steep learning curve on the job" – learning which seemingly occurs quite independent from any particular formal workshop or course. But what is it more precisely? When does or doesn't it happen? How is it recognized? Can and should it be measured? If so, how?

David Livingstone suggests that informal learning is

> any activity involving the pursuit of understanding, knowledge or skill which occurs outside the curricula of institutions providing educational programs, courses or workshops. ... Explicit informal learning is distinguished from everyday perceptions, general socialization and more tacit informal learning by peoples' own conscious identification of the activity as significant learning. The important criteria that distinguish explicitly informal learning are the retrospective recognition of both a new significant form of knowledge, understanding or skill acquired on your own initiative and also recognition of the process of acquisition (1999, pp. 3–4).

Similarly, Watkins and Marsick suggest that

informal and incidental learning is learning from experience that takes place outside formally structured, institutionally sponsored, class-room based activities. Informal learning is a broad term that includes any such learning; incidental learning is a subset that is defined as a by-product of some other activity. Informal learning can be planned or unplanned, but is usually involves some degree of conscious awareness that learning is taking place. Incidental learning, on the other hand, is largely unintentional, unexamined, and embedded in people's closely held belief systems (1992, p. 288).

In both cases, these definitions suggest that informal learning occurs apart from formal courses or institutions, but at the same time they carefully designate "explicitly" informal learning as that learning which is intentioned and/or iden-tified by the learner, as compared to "incidental" learning which is unintended (Watkins & Marsick) and/or unidentified (Livingstone) by the learner. As written, these two statements summarize concisely much of the discussion and debate, at least concerning definitions of the term informal learning. At the same time, however, implicit in concise definitional statements like these are a multitude of nuances and complexities. Given the relative informality of these forms of learn-ing, one can appreciate the difficulties in attempting to research the ways and extents to which they take place. However, the past three decades have seen a growing number of studies in this area (see Livingstone, 1999; also Boje, 1994; Garrick, 1996; Knowles, 1970; Penland; 1977; Tough, 1978). The research project described in this chapter is one attempt in this regard – both to document such learning among Canadian teachers, and to explore ways in which informal learning can be taken up more seriously in the context of schooling reform initiatives.

Canadian Teacher Learning Research Project – The Survey

The Canadian Teacher Learning Research Project was planned and undertaken in order to explore a number of interrelated issues: first the ways in which Canadian teachers see and engage themselves, and each other, as learners; secondly, the material and social conditions in which they undertake these learning activities; thirdly, the ways in which government policies and programs have served to influence these formal and informal learning activities.

For the first phase of this study, an eight-page survey questionnaire was mailed out in 1998 to nearly 2000 elementary and secondary school teachers across Canada. These teachers were randomly and proportionately sampled from the membership lists of the statutory teachers' associations in all ten provinces. (Given the mandatory membership legislation in place in all but one province, virtually every teacher working in a publicly-funded elementary and secondary school in Canada is included in these data-bases). The questionnaire surveyed respondents' activities and opinions about a range of their own learning activities: their engagement in formal workshops and continuing education courses, and their engagement in their own informal learning in their workplace, home, and community. In addition, there were the normal respondent background demographic questions, as well as questions relating to their engagement in the workplace, and their own computer/internet use. Many of the questions were developed in tandem with a parallel national public survey on formal and informal learning, undertaken by the New Approaches to Life-Long Learning (NALL) research collective in order to allow data comparisons (Livingstone, 1999). From the response rate of approximately 40%, a number of intriguing aspects were found worthy of analysis (see Smaller, Clark, Hart, Livingstone, & Noormohammed, 2000; Smaller, Clark, Hart, & Livingstone, 2001).

Teachers' formal learning pursuits. 86% of respondents stated that they had participated in one or more courses, workshops or other formalized learning activities in the past year. Of this group, 38% had taken one or two, 35% had taken three or four, and the remaining 27% had participated in anywhere from five to twenty such organized activities. It is interesting to note, by comparison, that in the general NALL Project survey of Canadian adult residents who are not in school, only 44% of respondents, and only 49% of those in the labour force, reported that they had engaged in similar pursuits in the past year.

Seniority and Learning Pursuits. Contrary to a general stereotype that teachers are less engaged in their own development as they get older, participation rates suggest that teachers overwhelmingly continue to engage in their own further formal education, regardless of their years of teaching experience. While there is a slight reduction in educational pursuits among those with more than twenty years of teaching seniority, well over eighty percent of these senior teachers said they were still participating in formal courses and workshops to enhance their own learning (and, as will be noted in the following sub-section, these senior teachers said they actually spent on average more hours per week in these educational pursuits). This pattern is in marked contrast to Canadian adults and the labour force in general where older, more experienced people are very unlikely to take further education courses (Livingstone, 1999)

Areas of Formal Learning. While the content of the courses and workshops taken by teachers varied significantly, a high percentage related directly to their work. Over three-fifths (61%) of all respondents reported engagement in "work-related" courses (curriculum, assessment, classroom management, etc.). In addition, over a third (37%) indicated they had taken computer related courses, 27% had taken academic courses, and 21% had taken recreation-related courses. In addition, 5% had taken language courses, and 7% indicated other kinds of courses.

Time spent on formal learning activities. On average, full-time classroom teachers (N = 506) reported spending 32 hours in actual attendance at courses and workshops over the past year. However, when work on course assignments, preparation and studying time was included in the overall amount of time taken up by these courses, teachers reported that they spent much more time on such formal, organized learning activities. Understandably, this time varied considerably among respondents, depending upon how much engagement they had had in the past year with such activities. However, overall teachers spent an average of over eight hours per week on formal learning activity.

Intragroup Variations. Within the overall respondent group, there were some significant variations in their engagement with these pursuits – depending upon gender, years of teaching experience, work location, elementary/secondary school, family status, and region of the country. In brief, teachers who taught secondary (as compared to elementary) school, those who had children at home, those who lived in the Atlantic provinces, those who had responsibilities outside of the classroom, and those with more than twenty years of teaching experience, were, on average, more likely to be engaged each week in their own further education activities. In addition, women teachers were more engaged in these activities than their male counterparts, and women with children at home were the most engaged of all sub-groups of teachers. However, there were no significant differences based upon rural-urban location of teachers.

Reasons for taking courses and workshops. Motivations varied for engaging in these formal courses and workshops. 19% of those respondents taking courses stated that one or more of the courses they had taken were part of a degree, diploma or certificate program at a university, community college, technical or business school, while 20% stated that one or more of their courses qualified them for additional certification related to their teaching credentials. Almost half (47%) of those taking courses reported that one or more of the courses and workshops were required or recommended by an employer (e.g., school board, principal), while 27% noted that one or more of these engagements had been required or recommended by some "other work-related organization (e.g., professional association, federation)."

Related to the matter of motivation, 54% of all those taking courses reported that they themselves had paid the fees for one or more of these activities. By comparison, 44% stated that fees had been paid at least once by their employer, 14% reported that courses had been paid by their union or professional association, and approximately the same number (13%) participated in courses which were paid jointly by their employer and union/professional association. 17% of respondents taking courses and workshops reported that one or more of these activities had no fees attached to them.

Future Plans. While 86% of responding teachers reported that they had taken one or more formal courses or workshops in the past twelve months, an even larger percentage (88%) stated that they would definitely (61%) or possibly (27%) take one or more courses in the future. Again, these numbers compare favourably with the general Canadian labour force, where only 70% indicated they would or might be so engaged (Livingstone, 1999). Those who were undecided, or stated that they would definitely not take further courses in the next few years, cited one or more reasons for this reluctance: too expensive (31%), courses held at inconvenient times and/or places (19%), family responsibilities (18%), no relevant courses available (17%), lack of employer support (14%), and health reasons (3%).

Teachers' Informal Learning

In addition to questions about teachers' engagement in formal courses and workshops, the survey questionnaire also asked respondents to think about the various ways they had engaged in informal learning, and the kinds of knowledges and skills they had acquired in this manner. For the purposes of facilitating responses in this area, respondents were asked to consider, in turn, learning which had taken place in four distinct locations: in their workplace, in their home, in their community, and elsewhere.

Informal learning in the workplace. Teachers were asked to identify any ways in which they had informally acquired new skills and/or knowledge over the past twelve months (that is, other than through organized courses or workshops) – things that would have assisted them in their present job, and/or would assist them in assuming new job responsibilities. Virtually all respondents (98%) stated that they were "learning on the job." 89% had informally gained new knowledge and skills about computers, while over 60% of all respondents indicated that informal learning had occurred in each of a number of other work-related areas – team-work/communication skills, teaching a particular grade/subject, class-room management, student problems, and keeping up with new teaching-related knowledge. (Among other themes, learning about extra-curricular student activities, and supervisory/management skills, were selected by 49% and 34% of respondents respectively.)

In a separate question, teachers were asked whether, in the course of their work in the past twelve months, they had informally engaged in learning in any of six specific work-related themes which were listed in the questionnaire. From this list, "Curriculum policy/development" was selected by well over two-thirds of all respondents (70%), while about one-half indicated they had acquired knowledge in each of "employee rights and benefits" and "teacher education/development" (54% and 47%). In addition, many respondents also indicated they had acquired knowledge and/or skills in the areas of "occupational health and safety" (35%), "environmental issues related to your work" (29%) and "equity/gender issues" (21%).

When asked what single most important knowledge, skill or understanding they had acquired informally, related to current or future paid employment, over one-quarter (27%) identified computers, approximately one fifth (19%) stated teacher education/development, 17% selected areas relating to curriculum policy/development/implementation. The remaining 37% of respondents to this question selected among 21 other themes (including student issues, team work/problem solving, employee rights, personal development, etc.).

When asked how this informal learning took place, 82% indicated that significant amounts took place collaboratively with colleagues. In addition, 63% also stated they engaged in informal workplace learning on their own. Other modes of informal learning included: interactions with students (24% of all respondents), with principals or school board administrators (27%) and with parents (14%).

Respondents were also asked to estimate the number of hours per week they were engaged in new informal learning activity in the course of their work. Overall, the average amount of time spent on informal learning on the job was almost four hours (3.9) per week. As compared to rates of formal learning activity, there were no gender differences indicated. However, elementary teachers were somewhat more active in this area than their secondary school counterparts.

Informal learning in the community. Among other questions, teachers were asked whether they were involved in volunteer community organizations, and if so, how frequently. Over three-fifths (61%) indicated they were involved, and of this group almost three-quarters (73%) stated that these activities had also provided them with an average of two hours per week of informal learning opportunity. When asked the most important knowledge, skill or understanding acquired as a result of this volunteer engagement, responding teachers cited 28 different themes, with "interpersonal skills," "community knowledge" and organizational/leadership skills" among the forefront (35%, 13% and 10% respectively). Interestingly, when asked if any of this informal, community-based learning could be applied to their paid employment, 90% expressed concurrence – with most stating that this learning was directly related to school-based education and teaching practices.

Other informal learning opportunities. Finally, teachers were asked if, in the past year, they had engaged in any recreational activities, either alone or with others, which might have occasioned informal learning of things they couldn't do, or didn't know, a year previous. A number of possibilities were listed for their consideration. 95% of all respondents indicated they had engaged in learning in this way. Again, computers rated high, with three-fifths of respondents, while four other themes were each selected by 40 to 45% of respondents – leisure/hobbies, sports/recreation, health issues, and finance/investing. On average, respondents reported that they had engaged in learning in this manner, for four hours in a typical week.

Related to these matters, it is certainly interesting to note that 86% of all respondents stated that they used computers at home, for an average 2 hours per week of computing time. In addition, over half of all respondents (53%) also reported using Internet as well, for an extra two hours per week. By comparison, data from the NALL national survey suggest that computer use at home among the general adult population is 56%, and by the general labour force, 64%.

Formal vs. informal learning preferences. When asked about preferences for modes of learning (course-based, or more informal), only 12% clearly favoured formal course-based learning, while a quarter preferred learning informally (whether on their own or with others). By comparison over 22% indicated that they favoured both modes equally, while almost half of all respondents (49%) stated that the decision depended in each instance upon what is to be learned. However, when to asked to choose outright between "formal courses" and "outside formal courses" (i.e., informal learning) as the more preferred mode for further learning, 58% selected informal modes, as compared to only 20% favouring formal approaches (14% wrote in "both" and 8% did not answer the question).

Future learning interests. Finally, teachers were asked what they were most interested in learning about in the next 12 months, both through formal and informal means. Over 80% (81%) of all respondents indicated that they had a definite interest in engaging in further formal learning activity, and over 80% of those expressed interest in further teacher development, either broadly or more specifically defined (e.g., teacher education, curriculum development/ implementation, further academic pursuits, student issues, ESL, computers, etc.). The remaining 18% of respondents selected from among 30 other areas of interest, ranging across the fields of work, further academic pursuits, and general interest areas.

While almost the same number of respondents (79%) also indicated they were interested in engaging in informal learning over the next 12 months, their selections of topics were somewhat more widely distributed. While 14% selected computers, and a further 11% expressed interest in pursuing further teaching and academic-related learning in informal ways, the remaining three-quarters of respondents selected from among the 27 other areas of informal learning interests.

Two further phases of the research project were undertaken, in order to generate more in-depth, qualitative data to provide further substance for overall analysis.

Second Phase – Teacher Diaries

The second phase of the research project involved the use of teachers' diaries to collect and analyze data on their daily activities. This is a method which has been used successfully in a number of jurisdictions, with a range of respondent types (teachers, housewives, other workers, etc.), for a variety of research purposes, and the work of a number of researchers was drawn upon to conceptualize and plan this project (see especially Peters and Raaijmakers 1998; Michelson, 1998; Harvey, 1984).

Respondents were selected from those who had participated in the first phase of the study, and who had agreed to identify themselves for this purpose. From this group, all 28 identified secondary school teachers working full-time in the province of Ontario were sent letters explaining the second phase of the research; 19 initially agreed to participate, and 13 eventually completed the tasks required. (This particular cohort was selected, partly because of its manageable size, partly because the project was based in Ontario, and partly because the Ontario

Secondary School Teachers' Federation was willing to fund this phase of the project.) Respondents were asked to record, for seven consecutive days, every activity in which they engaged over the 24 hours of each day of that time period. In particular, the informal learning aspects were emphasized, with the request to note, wherever possible, "when you believe that you have gained any new knowledge, understandings and/or skills, as a result of your activity during any specific activity," including "what you believe you have learned during that interval." Participants were also informed that an honourarium of $75.00 would be paid to those returning complete diary logs. 13 teachers submitted completed logs after a week's collection in November of 1999. In February of 2000, ten of these 13 respondents completed and submitted an additional week's diary. An analysis of these 23 weekly diaries proved very informative.

Given that these diary log forms required specific details for each activity undertaken during each 24 hour period, it was relatively straightforward to develop quite detailed reports and calculations on the kinds and amounts of activities undertaken each day by respondents. In total, these 13 respondents spent an average of 48.4 hours per week on duties directly related to their paid employment (with a range from 36.6 to 61.1 hours for those weeks reported). Of this total work week, the two most significant aspects were direct student instruction (19.8 hours) and course preparation/marking (17.6 hours). Other aspects, including student and parent counselling, student supervision, student extra-curricular activities, and administration/professional development activities, totalled a further 11.0 hours per week.

Informal learning. The entries in these diaries suggest that the life of a teacher – both at work, at home and elsewhere – is constituted as a never-ending series of informal-learning activities. For virtually every respondent, interactions with colleagues and students constituted the major engagement – in most cases, many times each working day The content of these discussions ranged widely – from specific school matters, to more general educational themes, to a wide variety of non-schooling-related issues. However, there was no question that much of this daily informal and often spontaneous interaction related directly or indirectly to the acquisition of new information and knowledge about the job at hand. In the words of one teacher, explaining a spontaneous late after-school discussion about upcoming report cards and parent interviews, "Our lunch and after school times are tantamount to [department] meetings."

On the one hand, these discussions often involved the specific issues of the moment. Typical and numerous were reports on information sharing about the interests and needs of students in their charge, such as Alice's "Lunch with colleagues – talked about some students at risk," and Dan, who "talked informally with V[ice] P[rincipal] – picked up from him a few bits of information about students who are having difficulty in my 10g [grade 10, general level] class." Equally numerous were discussions about course and program matters, such as John's report of having "Discussed law program with [student] counsellor," and Jim's "discuss[ion of program] problems and how they can be minimized re. failures." In this context, there were also a number of examples of respondents assisting colleagues directly with new learning. Jim, for example, was soon to leave the school, and spent much time one afternoon in a collaborative informal learning activity, "instructing teacher who will take my place upon retirement. This will be an ongoing procedure 3–4 times a week during this instructional time." Similarly, Eric reported on being in the school's "autoshop helping a colleague use a computer analyser to trouble shoot engine of Dodge van."

Also very numerous were reports on discussions relating to schooling issues more broadly. Understandably, given significant changes imposed by the provincial government during this time, many of the comments concerned these changes, and how they might affect existing courses and programs, teachers' workload, and the overall welfare of the students. Some reports, such as Eric's "Lunch with colleagues – primarily G[rade] 9 curriculum and its implementation in g[rade] 9 tech[nical subjects]" were noted in a fairly neutral manner. Other notations included explicitly stated concerns arising from their new understandings: "Lunch with tech teachers – discussion of effects on tech programs because of G10 new compulsory "civics" course – decimated G10 tech courses," and Jane's "discuss with colleagues Gr 9 material and cuts to Education – discussing how cuts to education will affect our work situation."

Finally, many other "informal learning" reports with colleagues involved themes and issues of more general interest and knowledge, such as Robert, who reported spending "15 minutes in staff room," during which time they discussed the "Nature of Things" program on prosthetics to be shown tonight," and Jeanne, who had a "Lunch/Sharing with colleagues – Learned about a couple of Internet sites." In addition to interactions with colleagues, many of the respondents also reported upon informal school learning which occurred for them in the context of their engagement with students, and in some cases, in phone conversations and meetings with their parents. As one respondent put it, these parent interactions provided opportunity for developing "listening skills and experience – not everything in counselling is as it first appears."

In addition to informal learning which took place at the school site, many of the respondents also reported on collegial interactions and related learning away from school and outside regular school hours. Sharing rides to and from school was a common venue for such activity. Eric reported that, "On route to work [we] discussed curriculum ... kids on my course, parent interviews, etc.," while Jane noted that in "travelling home with colleague – discussed Gr9 poetry and OAC Novel Study." Eric also reported on one evening at home, punctuated by "phone call from two colleagues – one off long term illness – other to advise me he will not be at work tomorrow – Thursday – not feeling good. Asks me to help organize lesson plan." Even evening and weekend social events seemed to involve discussion and sharing of knowledge and opinions relating to schooling and work. Jane reported on an evening "social; spent time at friends – discussed T[oronto] D[istrict] S[chool] Board budget," while Jeanne's "Staff Xmas Curling Tournament and Dinner" included "Informal learning, with colleagues on Time/Stress Management."

Other home activities were also often the source of new learning for our respondents. Computers constituted a major venue for such self-learning – both in relation to the acquisition of new skills and knowledge about the equipment and programs themselves ("help my spouse with computer – learned to format labels"), as well as using computers and the web to seek out new information on an infinite range of topics ("did my regular search for programming ideas – how to draw a transparent bitmap"; "check e-mails and info on school board network"). So-called "recreational" activities also served as learning opportunities for a number of respondents – particularly hobbies for respondents such as Jim who, on one occasion, was "preparing photo exhibit for May 2000 – learning framing technique so I can frame all work," while on another, was "read[ing]" – learning woodworking projects." Overall then, it is not difficult to conclude that home and community both served as important sites for informal learning for our 13 diarists.

The four most dominant "recreational" pursuits of these respondents were, in order, TV/video viewing, computer/internet use, reading books and magazines, and reading newpapers. TV/videos averaged 9.8 hours per week, and were fairly evenly balanced between programs which could be considered "entertainment," and programs such as news, documentaries and films, including films which were being previewed at home for school classroom use. Nine of the respondents reported on using computers at home, on average for 4.7 hours per week. In most cases, computers were used for "school work" – preparing course and lesson materials and tests, writing administrative reports, entering and processing student marks, and e-mailing colleagues and school administrators. Similarly, Internet use was highly related to searching for course material, books, etc. In addition, one respondent reported using e-mail for corresponding with family members, and another reported significant use of computer and Internet for writing, downloading and exchanging computer programs. In virtually every case, annotations were replete with many comments about the extent to which self-learning was taking place in the context of this computer use – "learned new computer skill" (Jeanne), "found new reference sites on Internet" (Jeanne), "learned how to program P.C. to use voice recognition software. This will take some time" (Barry), and so on. (These data certainly reflected findings of a recent national survey of the general Canadian public which indicated that teachers had the highest rate of access to computers and the Internet of any occupational groups in the country (Livingstone, 1999).

Books and magazines were read on an average of 2.7 hours each week, while newspapers were read 2.3 hours. In addition to general knowledge acquisition, several respondents punctuated their reports with comments about how this reading assisted them directly in their teaching work – articles on recent government, financial, scientific, and other events, fiction and non-fiction reading material for students in language courses, and so on.

In addition to their informal learning pursuits, nine of the 13 respondents indicated that they had participated in one to three "formal learning" events (e.g., workshops, presentations, meetings) over the course of the one or two weeks of diary reporting.

These diaries portrayed teachers who were all on-going, formal and informal learners, in both their paid workplaces and in many of the other sites in which they lived their lives. While these diaries provided a distinct picture of both the types of learning, and amount of engagement in each case, the third phase of the project, in-depth interviews, provided a very significant analysis of how respondents saw themselves as active learners in their workplace and elsewhere.

Phase Three – In-Depth Phone Interviews

For the purposes of further exploration of the data provided in the first two phases of the project, four of the 13 diarists from phase two of the study were sampled by categories of gender, age and geography; when contacted by telephone, all agreed to participate in individual telephone interviews. These interviews, conducted during 2000, ran between 45 and 60 minutes. All were taped and subsequently transcribed.

In order to provide a framework for exploring issues of learning with these four teachers, the interview questions focused on the provincial government's enactment of sweeping changes to the province's school system during the previous three years. Among many changes affecting secondary schools, teachers and students, specific province-wide initiatives were referenced: a) the complete revision of all syllabi and all courses for secondary schools in the province; b) introduction of a compulsory, standardized student assessment process, including revised standardized report cards; c) mandatory teacher involvement in student extra-curricular activities; d) a provincial statutory body to control teacher selection, training, examining, certification, registration, standards of practice, professional development and discipline (the Ontario College of Teachers); and e) an earlier, and short-lived, provincial government initiative to de-stream grade nine programs in the high school system. These government reforms served as a useful medium for exploring issues of teacher learning because they were universally applied across the province, and certainly well-known to all teachers.

Interviewees were asked to identify provincial government reform measures which they felt were particularly notable (if none came spontaneously to mind, then the initiatives described above were mentioned and the respondent asked to select one). They were asked to explain their understanding of these reforms and then to reflect on the ways in which they had come to learn about these undertakings. They were also asked to explore how it might have been that their colleagues in their respective schools came to be knowledgeable about and engaged in these initiatives. During this part of the interview there was considerable prompting to elicit reflections on ways in which learning may have taken place – "formal" opportunities such as workshops, meetings, presentations, circulars, and school announcements, as well as the more informal discussions among teachers, administrators, students and parents.

In spite of the enormity of these curricular, assessment and reporting changes, all four teacher interviews suggest that there was very limited, if any, formal opportunity to learn about the changes and what was required to implement them. Only two of the four respondents, for example, could recall any in-school staff meetings organized specifically to deal with curriculum and reform – one such event for each. In Jeanne's case, "the only formal session I've had was given by one of our teachers at school last year about evaluation and the new curriculum, but that's the only formal training I've received." John reported that his only formal meeting "was one on teacher advisory groups – [they] shortened the teaching day and extended the period of [workshop] time so we could learn how to do teacher advisory groups." Otherwise, reference to these reforms at formal staff gatherings seemed to consist only of announcements, such as Jeanne's summary that "it was all just documents received. Like our [team] leader said, they are now available in the office and the consultant, and he's there if I have questions." In short, as Barry noted, the entire curriculum assessment process for teachers in his school "just kind of fell in their laps." John's school seemed to be very similar to that of the other three schools being reported on – in his case, only one school-wide meeting on the subject of schooling reforms. As he frustratingly noted, the official approach to these reforms seemed to be, "Here's the change. Do it! And there's really little in-service ... you'll get memos stating that there's all this in-service available but the in-service never comes."

Given the dearth of access to structured professional development possibilities, and the immensity and significance of changes imposed on Ontario schools, it is not surprising that these interviews indicated that an immense amount of informal learning had taken place – not only with these four respondents, but also, to the extent that their observations are valid, with many or all of their colleagues as well. This informal learning about the reforms occurred in a number of ways, individually and collectively, and involved print materials, television and video, computers and the Internet, and discussions with others. While virtually all of these learning activities were intentioned by those involved, they occurred in a number of circumstances – from a long-planned-for evening of reading documents, to both planned-for and spontaneous meetings with one or two colleagues between classes, at lunch time, and before and after regular timetabled work hours.

All four respondents reported their own and colleagues' significant involvement in the reading of print materials related to the province's schooling reforms. Official reports, syllabi, guidelines, course profiles, booklets, memos, etc. turned out to be the main, if not sole, source of direct information. Jeanne, for example, talked about spending a month of her summer holidays reading all of the relevant guidelines and profiles she could obtain, and of the other respondents similarly reported on such activity. More than one respondent commented on how this individualized approach to learning about, and working on, the new mandated curriculum and assessment programs constituted a dramatic shift from an earlier mode of more engaged, collective activity. Barry remarked on this new phenomenon in the context of having to develop a new course of study for his guidance program. Similarly, John noted that these recent schooling

reforms meant a distinct change from earlier times when professional development, in-service training and curriculum development involved a more formal,
organized, collective way of learning. Now,

> primarily you're on your own, if you need to figure stuff out you ... and
> again, I don't have a lot of problems with that, as long as the resources are
> available, the materials, I don't mind doing the self-teaching thing. ... It's a
> gradual process trying to get your head around that because you're so
> accustomed to doing it the other way.

Informal interactions with their colleagues appeared by far the most significant
source of learning for all of the respondents interviewed. For example, although
Jeanne had devoted a significant part of her holidays to reading government
publications, she noted that "the document doesn't tell me a lot of details, doesn't
give me a lot of information, and I do have to go to someone else to find out."
One of several examples she gave occurred when she was attempting to understand the new requirements for assessing students in her program.

> Right now also I feel I'm learning a lot informally regarding the new
> curriculum – just by sharing with my colleagues. When I was making the
> new rubric ... I went to my colleague from the English department who has
> basically the same kind of program, a language program, and so I asked
> her advice on what she does ... and we discussed it and I was able to come
> to a better understanding. So that's the way we do it, just by discussing in
> the staff room.

All four respondents also reported on their use of computers and the Internet
to access information and programs related to the schooling reforms being
introduced. In some cases, this use involved downloading text materials which
were not otherwise easily available, for subsequent reading. In many other cases,
however, the computer was used more significantly to engage in learning about
specific programs. For John, this new approach of self-learning involved a
number of approaches, including

> a lot of work just on the Internet basically. I mean, that's helpful. I much
> rather learn, sort of, when I have the time and the more stuff that's posted
> on the Internet, the better. And I'm finding some stuff, like, on the
> Educational Network of Ontario. I mean, just having the course profiles
> on-line is very helpful too.

Jeanne as well reported on significant computer use, even though she was also
frank about the challenges which she herself faced in dealing with this medium.

> Myself I find I'm doing a lot of informal learning on the computer, tons of
> it ... for instance [there] is a program that's offered that has the four areas,
> and so on, and I downloaded it on my computer, well with my husband's
> help because also all that stuff is informal learning – the husband even helps

– and I realized how complex the program was. I couldn't make it work by myself.

The data collected in the three phases of this research project suggest that a vast majority of elementary and secondary school teachers are highly engaged in their own, on-going learning – through formal as well as intentioned and sponta- neous informal activity, both alone and collaboratively with colleagues. On the basis of comparisons with the parallel general population study undertaken concurrent with this project, the amount of time spent in these learning activities significantly exceeded those of virtually all other groups in the Canadian labour force, including those with similar educational backgrounds (Livingstone, 2000).

Teacher Knowledge and Informal Learning, Professionalism and Schooling Reform: What are the Connections?

In what ways can the understandings gleaned from this study be used to enhance schooling reform initiatives to ensure that schools can better represent the interests and needs of both an increasingly diverse student population, as well as our evolving communities? The data collected from this study already provides us with some important clues to this dilemma, to the ways in which teacher learning can be enhanced – or diminished – by the larger contexts of the workplace. Two will be explored briefly here, both in the context of their effects on teaching learning – first, teacher workload, and secondly, professionalism and relations of power.

Teacher Workload

Full-time respondents (n = 637) to the original questionnaire survey reported an overall workload of 47 hours per week, comprised of timetabled and non- timetabled work. On average, they were assigned 28 hours per week for working directly with students as well as such additional tasks as school administration, library coordination, administration, hall supervision, preparation and marking, and so on. Teachers reported that, on average they spent a further 19 hours per week on school related tasks – approximately 10 hours at school, and 9 hours at home and elsewhere. Such work included preparing courses and lessons, marking student work and extra-curricular activities; to communicating with students and parents; and participating in subject, school, board and federation meetings. This 47-hour average work-week is not unusual for teachers, as these findings are similar to those of studies of teachers in other jurisdictions – consistently, work weeks range from 45 to 53 hours for teachers across Canada, the USA, and Great Britain (Saskatchewan Teachers' Federation 1995; School Teachers' Review Body 2000; see also Drago, Caplan, Costanza, & Brubaker, 1999; Michelson & Harvey, 1999). In fact, the diaries of the second phase of the research revealed that virtually every one of the 13 respondents had been engaged in significantly more teaching-related work that they had self-reported on their survey questionnaires – in two cases, both women with children at home, by 75% and 35% respectively! This suggests that a number of recent studies in a number of jurisdictions that assess teacher workload on the basis of similar generalized estimations may also significantly under-represent actual work loads for teachers (see, for example, Alberta Teachers' Association, 2000; Harvey & Spinney, 2000; National Centre for Education Statistics (USA), 1997; National Union of Teachers, 2001; Raykov, 2001; Statistics Canada, 1994).

The diaries indicated clearly that a "normal" 8–5 work day, with time off for lunch, was certainly the exception rather than the rule. Lunches, if they happened at all, were often punctuated with ad hoc calls on teachers' time. Brian's comment exemplifies this situation: "12:10–12:30 – Eating lunch – dealing with students re. co-op application sheets – and with staff – seldom do you ever get to sit down for a sandwich." These diaries also revealed that much of the course preparation, and student marking and evaluation work undertaken by these teachers was performed in the evenings and on weekends. All respondents found it necessary to undertake such additional work, and on average, five days of each week were burdened with these extra hours. In total, a weekly average of 10.7 hours of work was undertaken outside of the regular 9 to 5 work day, with a range of 5 to 21 hours. In addition to working at home, during the two reporting weeks several teachers had noted that they had stayed at, or returned to their schools for evening events, including parents' nights and supervising at student dances and sport events.

The effects of this workload were certainly evident in relation to possibilities for organizing in-service activities related to the reform initiatives – all four interviewees commented, in one way or another, on the inability of school administrations, or teachers themselves, to develop successful collaborative learning opportunities. Barry, for example, expressed particular frustration of the attempts made in his school in this regard.

> The first time we went through that, in Guidance, we took it upon ourselves to do a lot of in-servicing with students and the staff. But, it came down to a timing issue. There's not enough time going around for anybody – It was essentially, 'here's the dates [for implementation], here's how to do it. ... We tried to do it through ... a concerted effort in some ways to free up the students on various themes and that would then free up the staff so we might have forty minutes here or there, and it worked for a while but then it just sort of disintegrated because it just became overwhelming ... it came out a logistics nightmare ... I don't think we really got a handle on it. and I would guess that we're probably just an average kind of example of what's going on out there.

To be sure, this is not a new issue for anyone involved with schooling. Too often, however, analyses of past professional development "failures" seem to venture no further than simply blaming teachers for poor planning or inappropriate prioritizing. If the findings of this study can be generalized in any way, it would appear teachers spend a lot of time in their own formal and informal learning related both to general professional development and the more immediate perceived needs related to changes in their classrooms and schools. What is lacking, perhaps, is any systematic, department or school-wide approach to organization for at least some of these learning activities. Could the workplace be organized (somewhat) differently, to take more advantage of teachers' learning interests? (Sleeger's chapter in this section considers this issue.) Traditional school structures are enduring entities, but is this an impossible challenge?

Professionalism and Relations of Power

Another intriguing theme arising out of this study was the way in which respondents talked about their learning in the context of their social relations with employers, government, students, parents and the "public," and the ways in which their own identities were continually being shaped and reshaped by their experiences with these reform measures. None of the interviewees had experienced any opportunity to participate in the conceptualization and planning of these initiatives, and judging from their comments, it was clear to them that their own knowledges and understandings were of little value or interest to those in charge of the change. What they had "learned" in this context was that the traditional ideology of professional engagement – certainly one in which they believed – was absent. John's observation that "we are being totally de-professionalized" equated, in this regard, with Norma's lament that teachers, "who have intelligent minds," were being totally ignored in this arena.

Jeanne was particularly explicit in her beliefs about this issue, and used the term "professional" more than once to explain her obligations in this regard. When initially asked in the interview about her understanding of the new schooling initiatives, she responded that "The government has a new reform, so it's my responsibility as a professional to make myself knowledgeable of what the reform is all about." She had engaged in considerable "professional reading ... [in order to] make sure that I'm abreast to these changes.". However, this sense of occupational responsibility in the context of these schooling reforms seemed to turn out to be very much a two-edged sword for Jeanne. As she explained,

> the feeling is also that it [the reform] was done very quickly, and that there were some big mistakes made on the part of the government ... and we had reaction from parents and students. They don't like it ... and then we end up with having to defend the mistake, and saying 'yeah we would prefer to say [that as well]' ... and so there was a lot of dissatisfaction there among the parents, and so we took a bit of the slack for that, and a lot of teachers don't like that of course, 'don't shoot the messenger' – that idea.

As she noted, this series of events had significantly affected her understandings of professionalism and identity. Even more problematic, perhaps, in the context of teacher development, were the direct references to power relations and the unilateral imposition of reform measures which teachers believed were fundamentally wrong for their students and for schooling generally. In fact, more than one respondent alluded to the clear statements made by the government in this regard. John noted, for example, that as compared to previous government reforms, where teachers felt they had some space to shape changes in ways they thought best,

> this time there's more attitude, just by the nature of the government, and when it says it's going to do, there are more people complying, and a lot of it, some of it's out of fear. It's a lot more, "cover yourself." ... [Teachers are finding] a whole lot more pressure on them. They're really under the microscope as far as they perform.

Given these findings relating to the complexities of teacher learning and teacher knowledge in our era of pervasive schooling reform, the recent work of Gitlin and Margonis (1995) in the USA is particularly informative. Intrigued by the ways in which teachers often came to be blamed for the failures in schooling reform initiatives over the years – often being portrayed as covertly resistant or openly opposed to change, either because of harbouring traditional (and therefore outmoded) views of education, or simply because of laziness and/or obstinacy – they began exploring other possible reasons for these reforms not being successful.

In spite of the purported differences in the literature between "first wave" and "second wave" schooling reformers, Gitlin and Margonis suggest both groups seem to concur with the general belief, as exemplified by studies such as Lortie's (1975), that most teachers are basically conservative, presentist, individualistic and "oversensitive to criticism." Not surprisingly, then, the ways in which both groups of schooling reformers prescribe change reflect these beliefs, albeit expressed in different ways. While the former group advocate "mak[ing] strong demands on the users" through "benevolently authoritarian forms of management" that create the need for teachers "to swim in new waters," develop commitment for the reform, and "accept it and even like it" (p. 383), the latter group tends to stress "engagement" with teachers through so-called "collaboration" – developing "collaborative school cultures" which, they claim, will help overcome the purported "isolation and alienation of teachers, making teachers more receptive to and engaged with educational reform" (p. 380). School collaboration, for this latter group, is seen as "a guiding approach for education reform" (p. 383).

Based on their close reading of this literature, however, Gitlin and Moralis suggest there are fundamental similarities. In both cases, changes are initiated and instituted from the outside, from the top down, and are designed to be implemented and monitored through the existing authority structures of the institution. For both "waves," teacher resistance and opposition is to be "overcome" one way or the other and the change process is to move ahead.

What is not present, argue Gitlin and Margonis, is any deep understanding or recognition of "teachers' knowledge" – teachers' deep understanding of schooling cultures and authority relations, the material conditions of work in their schools, and the nature, effects and outcomes of earlier attempts at change in their schools. Concerns raised by teachers about proposed changes are often viewed as representing an "habitual and emotional" attachment to traditional schooling routines, rather than ones engendered by reasoned analysis based upon their intimate knowledge of schooling. Overall there is a lack of any real understanding on the part of school reformers about the ways in which reform initiatives are taken up and analysed by teachers, and thus these reformers harbour considerable misunderstanding about reasons why teachers might seem unmotivated by specific externally-initiated calls for change, and may even challenge or resist such changes (see Bailey, 2000; Bascia, 1994, Blackmore & Kenway, 1995).

As further theoretical support for this position, Gitlin and Margonis draw on theories of resistance developed by Paul Willis (1977) and others to suggest that resistance, whether practiced by teachers or students, "is a political act that reflects an understanding of the hidden implications of schooling." This knowledge and understanding cannot always "be fully articulated by the actors," and as Gitlin and Margonis note, in relation to teachers' responses to top-down imposition of reforms,

> [T]he meaning of resistant acts ... is likely to remain ambiguous. On the one hand, resistance may be nothing more than laziness or an excuse of some kind; on the other hand, it can reflect important political insights. [However,] this ambiguity is used by school change researchers to discount resistance (p. 392).

Schooling reform initiatives often fail because educational reformers and school administrators fail to understand and incorporate the "good sense" of classroom teachers into their reform projects. In addition, in most if not all cases, important issues relating to existing authority relations in the school are definitively not part of the reform agenda – or even taken into consideration as a potential factor in determining the success of the proposed project.

> The pragmatic acceptance of school hierarchies in the school change literature reinforces the prevalent tendency to define teachers' resistant acts as unreasonable and obstructionist. It is ironic that overlooking these potential insights leads to a re-enactment of the push-pull cycle school change researchers hope to overcome. Thus, while resistant acts are likely to be ambiguous, they should not be immediately disregarded. They can direct our attention beyond the limits of the school change discourse to the fundamental institutional relations and school structures that help define relationships, roles, and the nature of teachers' work. Resistance can signify a political form of good sense (p. 393).

Gitlin and Margonis' empirical work for this study involved two aspects. First, they undertook a detailed examination of attempted changes in structures and accountability which had occurred in a particular school district over several years, and found (among other things) that these events had increased both bureaucratic relations, and workloads, for teachers. Secondly, they engaged in an ambitious program of interviews and ethnographic observations with teachers and administrators in one particular school in this same district, during the time when a new specific change initiative was being implemented. In many cases they found active opposition and resistance from teachers to what was being proposed and implemented. Based on these observations and follow-up interviews they concluded that teachers had, in fact, largely responded to this reform initiative on the basis of their knowledge of the existent material, social and authority relations in the school and district, and of the effects of earlier attempts by the district to induce top-down changes and reforms. Like Willis, they also found that among teachers interviewed there were those who could not always "fully articulate" these understandings. However, they concluded from this study that the earlier learning processes undergone by the teachers had certainly been both extensive and deep, and that their position on the current reform initiative was developed rationally through an intensive learning process. Certainly, the data from our national survey of teachers clearly substantiates these findings (see also, Bascia, 1994; Blackmore & Kenway, 1995).

Concluding Remarks

How can policy be informed by the kinds of findings apparent from this national survey of teachers' learning, and from similar studies? Can the theory and practice of teachers' informal learning be incorporated into – conjoined with – policies and programs designed to promote good teacher education and good schooling reform? Clearly, the data suggested in this study present a stark contrast to conventional notions of policy-driven, top-down teachers' professional development. Does the concept "policy" apply at all to something as intricate and complex as the ways in which teachers daily – both intentionally and spontaneously – go about learning new knowledges and skills related directly and indirectly to their work? Is this question itself an empirical one? Is it possible, for example, for a set of policies and programs for teachers' professional development to be developed which could successfully incorporate – build upon – existing teacher knowledge, teachers' perceived interests and needs, teachers' professional identities, and pragmatic workload issues?

   If this question applies to professional development programs intended to be general in nature – that is, to enhance teachers' learning and knowledge/skills more holistically – the answer is perhaps more straightforward and positive. As just one example, a province-wide program has recently been initiated in Nova Scotia, developed collaboratively and carefully by representatives of the ministry of education, the boards of education, the faculties of education and the teachers union in the province (a unique accomplishment in itself, given a traditional history – like that in many other jurisdictions – of suspicion, tension and even conflict – see Bascia's and Sachs' chapters in this section). Under this plan, each teacher in the province is required to file an annual report – to their local board and to the union – on their professional development activities for the previous year, listing their engagements in both formal and intentioned informal learning in a number of content and process categories. While a minimum number of 100 hours are required for continued certification each year, the first two years of reporting suggest three highly beneficial outcomes: first, a vast majority of teachers are now (or were already) far exceeding this level of expectation; secondly the existence of this teacher-centred approach to learning has encouraged even more self-engagement in this regard; and thirdly, that it has resulted in a more systematic and sustained self-learning regime for many teachers (Nova Scotia Teachers' Union).

If, however, the question applies to "desired" or "required" teacher learning in relation to a specific schooling reform initiative, the possibilities for success are much more complex. As suggested by the findings and analysis of the Canadian Teacher Learning research project and a number of similar explorations, chances of success might be highly predicated on a number of factors underlying the initiative – what is being "desired," and by whom; the extent to which teachers are involved with the conceptualization and development of the overall project (assuming they concur at all with its means and ends), including its "teacher-learning" components; and most importantly, the ways in which their workplaces might necessarily be altered to accommodate the concomitant formal and informal learning deemed necessary for the task at hand.

To be sure, such seemingly stringent requirements may well seem to be out of the realm of practicality or even possibility, especially in relation to schooling reform projects involving entire regions of a country. However, the sordid history of schooling reform in many jurisdictions, in both the recent and distant past, suggests that a qualitatively different approach is required. The studies explored in this chapter suggest that new initiatives must include a much more sophisticated understanding of the complexities of teacher formal and informal learning, teacher knowledge and teacher professional self-identity.

Notes

1. The author wishes to acknowledge the contribution of Rosemary Clark, Doug Hart, David Livingstone and Zahra Noormohammed to the two studies that are the basis of this chapter.

References

Alberta Teachers' Association (2000). *Teacher Workload Study*. Edmonton: Alberta Teachers Association.

Atkins, L., & Lury, C. (1999). The Labour of identity: Performing identities, performing economies. *Economy and Society, 28*(4), 598–614.

Althouse, J. G. (1967). *The Ontario teacher: A historical account of progress, 1800–1910*. Toronto: Ontario Teachers' Federation.

Bailey, B. (2000). The impact of mandated change on teachers. In N. Bascia & A. Hargreaves (Eds.), *The sharp edge of educational change: Teaching, leading and the realities of reform* (pp. 112–128) London: The Falmer Press.

Ball, S. (1993). Education, markets, choice and social class: The market as a class strategy in the UK and the US. *British Journal of Sociology, 14*(1), 3–20.

Bascia, N. (1994). Evaluation Report: "Creating a Culture of Change" Initiative. Report prepared for Ontario Ministry of Education and Training and the Ontario Teachers' Federation, June.

Boje, D. M. (1994). Organizational storytelling: The struggles of pre-modern, modern and postmodern organizational learning discourses. *Management Learning, 25*(3).

Blackmore, J., & Kenway, J. (1995). Changing schools, teachers and curriculum: But what about the girls? In D. Corson (Ed.), *Discourse and Power in Educational Organizations* (pp. 233–256). Toronto: OISE Press.

Briscoe, C. (1994). Cognitive frameworks and teacher practices: A case study of teacher learning and change. *The Journal of Educational Thought, 28*(3), 289–313.

Curtis, B. (1988). *Building the Educational State: Canada West, 1836–1871.* London: Althouse Press.

Darling-Hammond, L. (1998). Teachers and teaching: Testing policy hypotheses from a National Commission report. *Educational Researcher, 27*(1), 5–15.

Darling-Hammond, L., & Ball, D. (1998). Teaching for high standards: What policymakers need to know and be able to do. Pittsburgh, PA: Center for Policy Research in Education (CPRE) Policy Brief JRE-04.

Derber, C., Schwartz, W., & Magrass, Y. (1990). *Power in the highest degree: Professionals and the rise of a new mandarin order.* New York/Oxford: Oxford University Press.

Drago, R., Caplan, R., Costanza, D., & Brubaker, T. (1999). New estimates of working time for elementary school teachers. *Monthly Labor Review, 122*(4), April, 31–40.

Donmoyer, R. (1995). *The Very Idea of a Knowledge Base.* Paper presented at the Annual Meeting of the American Educational Research Association, San Francisco, April.

Duman, D. (1979). The creation and diffusion of a professional ideology in Nineteenth Century England. *Sociological Review, 27*(1), 113–138.

Economic Council of Canada (1992). *A lot to learn: Education and training in Canada.* Ottawa: Minister of Supply and Services.

Fleming, W. G. (1972). *Ontario's Educative Society, Volume 7, Educational Contributions of Associations.* Toronto: University of Toronto Press.

Gardner, P. (1984). The lost elementary schools of Victorian England. London: Croom Helm.

Garrick, J. (1996). Informal learning: Some underlying philosophies. *Canadian Journal for Study of Adult Education, 10*(1), 21–46.

Gibson, S., & Olberg, D. (1998). Learning to use the internet: A study of teacher learning through collaborative research partnerships. *The Alberta Journal of Educational Research, 44*(2), 239–241.

Gitlin, A., & Margonis, F. (1995). The political aspect of reform: Teacher resistance as good sense. *American Journal of Education, 103*(4), 377–404.

Gorelick, S. (1982). Class relations and the development of the teaching profession. In D. Johnson (Ed.), *Class and social development: A new theory of the middle class.* Beverly Hills: Sage.

Harvey, A (1984). *Time budget research.* Frankfurt/New York: Campus Verlag.

Harvey, A., & Spinney, J. (2000). *Life on and off the job: A time-use study of Nova Scotia teachers.* Halifax: St. Mary's University.

Holmes Group (1990). *Tomorrow's schools: Principles for the design of professional development schools.* East Lansing, Michigan: Author.

Katz, M. (2001). *The irony of early school reform: Educational innovation in mid-nineteenth century Massachusetts.* New York: Teachers College Press.

Klein, P. (1996). Preservice teachers' beliefs about learning and knowledge. *The Alberta Journal of Educational Research, 42*(4), 361–377.

Knowles, M. S. (1970). *The modern practice of adult education: Andragogy versus Pedagogy.* New York: Association Press.

Labaree, D. (1992). Power, knowledge, and the rationalization of teaching: A genealogy of the movement to professionalize teaching. *Harvard Educational Review, 62*(2), 123–154.

Larson, M. S. (1980). Proletarianization and educated labour. *Theory and Society, 9*(1), 131–154.

Lawn, M. (1996). *Modern times? Work, professionalism and citizenship in teaching.* London: Falmer Press.

Livingstone, D. W. (1999). Exploring the icebergs of adult learning: Findings of the first Canadian survey of informal learning practices. *The Canadian Journal for the Study of Adult Education, 13*(2), 49–72.

Livingstone, D. W. (2000). Reproducing Educational Inequalities in a Learning Society: Conceptual Gaps and Recent Canadian Research on Barriers to Adult Education. Revised version of paper originally presented at the International Symposium, "And the Walls Come Tumbling Down – Non-traditional Learners in Higher Education," University of British Columbia, Vancouver, August 1999.

Livingstone, D. W., Hart, D., & Davie, L. E. (2001). *Public Attitudes Towards Education in Ontario 2000.* Toronto: OISE Press.

Lortie, D. (1975). *Schoolteacher: A sociological study.* Chicago: University of Chicago Press.

Michelson, W. (1998). Time pressure and human agency in home-based employment. *Society and Leisure, 21*(2).

Michelson, W., & Harvey, A. (1999). Is teachers' work never done?: Time-use and subjective outcomes. Paper presented at the American Sociological Association, Chicago, August 8.

National Centre for Education Statistics (1997). Time spent teaching core academic subjects in elementary schools. Washington: U.S. Department of Education.

National Union of Teachers (2001). Teacher workload study: Extracts from the PriceWaterhouse-Coopers Interim Report Retreived March 6th, 2004 from http://www.teachers.org.uk/resources/pdf/exec_summary.pdf

Nova Scotia Scotia Teachers Union. Retrieved February 16th, 2004 from www.nstu.ca.

OECD (1992). *Schools and business: A new partnership.* Paris: OECD.

OECD (1998). *Teachers for tomorrow's schools.* Paris: Centre for Educational Research and Innovation.

Ontario College of Teachers (1999). *Professional learning survey results: Executive summary.* Toronto: Ontario College of Teachers.

Ontario Government (1995). Province to Proceed with Ontario College of Teachers. *Ministry of Education News Release Communique, November* 21.

Ontario Government (2000). *Ontario Teacher Testing Program.* Toronto: Ontario Ministry of Education.

OSSTF (Ontario Secondary School Teachers' Federation) (1999). *A Report on Teacher Testing.* Toronto: OSSTF.

Penland, P. (1977). *Self-planned learning in America.* Pittsburgh: University of Pittsburgh.

Peters, P., & Raaijmakers, S. (1998). Time crunch and the perception of control over time from a gendered perspective: The Dutch case. *Society and Leisure, 21*(2), 417–434.

Popkewitz, T. (1994). Professionalization in teaching and teacher education: Some notes on its history, ideology, and potential. *Teaching and Teacher Education, 10*(1), 1–14.

Raykov, M. (2001). Teachers hours of work and working conditions. Unpublished paper; OISE/UofT NALL Project.

Teacher Workload Study (1995). Regina: Saskatchewan Teachers' Federation.

School Teachers' Review Body (2000). *Survey of Teacher Workloads for 2000.* London: Department of Education and Employment.

Smaller, H., Clark, R., Hart, D., Livingstone, D., & Noormohammed, Z. (2000). *Teacher learning, informal and formal: Results of a Canadian Teachers' Federation Survey.* Toronto: OISE/UT NALL Working Paper Number 14.

Smaller, H., Clark, R., Hart, D., & Livingstone, D. (2001). *Informal/formal learning and workload among Ontario Secondary School Teachers.* NALL Working Paper #39–2001.

Statistics Canada (1994). Teacher workload in elementary and secondary schools. *Education Quarterly Review, 1*(3), 11–16.

Tough, A. M. (1978). *The Adult's Learning Projects: A fresh approach to theory and practice in adult learning*; Second Edition. Toronto: Ontario Institute for Studies in Education.

Tyack, D. (1976). Pilgrim's progress: Toward a social history of the superintendency. *History of Education Quarterly, 32*(4), 257–300.

Watkins, K. E., & Marsick, V. J. (1992). Towards a theory of informal and incidental learning in organisations. *International Journal of Lifelong Learning, 11*(4), 287–300.

Willis, P. (1977). *Learning to labour*. Farnborough: Saxon House.

28

NO TEACHER LEFT UNTESTED: HISTORICAL PERSPECTIVES ON TEACHER REGULATION

Cecilia Reynolds
University of Saskatchewan, Canada

The idea of testing teachers to ensure that they will help students achieve high standards is not something new, but it has long been a contentious area of policy development and implementation. In this chapter, I consider recent controversial shifts in Ontario government policies on teacher education programs, an entry to the profession test, teacher re-certification and professional learning requirements. In each of these policy areas, I describe the historic context and give international comparisons. I also discuss elements of debates surrounding implementation. These debates shed light on past and present struggles for control over teachers and teacher's work.

An important backdrop to this discussion is a consideration of teaching as a profession and the paradoxical nature of teacher's professional autonomy. Writing on this topic, Harry Smaller and I observed that "teachers have always been under structural controls" (Reynolds & Smaller, 1997, p. 15), even though those structures have changed over time, that "professionalism has worked to foster the development of state controls (however subtle) over teachers and their work" (p. 16), although we have been careful to point out that "There has been a rich history of ways and means through which teachers (and other groups) have accommodated and resisted these state incursions into schooling and teaching" (p. 16).

The sociological literature on professionalism was dominated from the 1930s to the 1960s by structural functionalist views. This approach drew heavily on lists of characteristics to define occupations as professions. Within this approach, teaching was declared a "semi-profession," and while the functionalist paradigm of professions within which the semi-professions thesis is located has been largely displaced, the semi-professions thesis remains the one which many people still imagine when they consider teachers. The neo-Marxist view, however, proposes that the state (influenced by elites) mediates professional work and uses efficiency as a yardstick. The post-modern perspective suggests that professionals enter into "contractual reciprocity" and agree to be governed, while simultaneously striving to govern themselves (Reynolds & Smaller, 1997). These perspectives

International Handbook of Educational Policy, 569–577
Nina Bascia, Alister Cumming, Amanda Datnow, Kenneth Leithwood and David Livingstone (Eds.)
© 2005 *Springer. Printed in Great Britain.*

help us understand government rationales and public reactions in Ontario and elsewhere to new policies regarding teachers and teaching.

The Ontario Historical Backdrop

As early as 1846 in Ontario, the Common School Act "removed in principle most of the educational autonomy enjoyed by local educational consumers and put in place a set of administrative structures in which respectable members of local elites would be charged with much of educational management" (Curtis, 1988, pp. 114–115). Over the next 150 years, numerous policies were designed and implemented to control who might become a teacher and how they would need to be prepared for their important role. Most of those policies mirrored similar ones taken up in the United States, England, France and several other European nations. They were part of an overall vision of a school system that was highly organized, routinized and centralized. This was the vision held by Egerton Ryerson, who held the role of Superintendent of Education for thirty-two years in the mid 1800s in what was to become Ontario.

In 1847, Ryerson established what were called "normal" schools for the training of new teachers. These schools attempted to "normalize" the preparation of teachers for a common curriculum to be taught in all schools across the province. Using a rhetoric of professionalism, Ryerson and other promoters of publicly funded schools argued for the need for teachers who had academic aptitude and achievement. But the normal schools also became sites to ensure that teachers had a high degree of "moral self-regulation". Records of these schools show notes by staff of a number of infractions that could lead to expulsion, including if male students attempted to talk to female students (Reynolds & Smaller, 1997, p. 29). These records also show a system of examination or teacher testing.

In the early years of Ontario's publicly funded school system, teaching certificates were issued by district Superintendents. Renewal required an annual trip to the district seat and an examination before the educational official. Inconsistency in the actual implementation of this examination process is well documented. While one applicant stated that his test consisted of having to spell the word "summons," others reported having to wrestle with a two hour rigorous test of their ability in Reading, Grammar, Arithmetic and Geography (Reynolds & Smaller, 1997, p. 33). Records suggest that certification in these times depended largely on the subjective assessment of local elites as to not only the ability of teachers but also the "propriety" of individuals who wanted to teach (Reynolds & Smaller, 1997, p. 34). By the 1870s, teachers in Ontario needed to pass examinations each year and these were sent to the Department of Education in Toronto for marking.

Gradually, such state run examinations were phased out, teacher unions developed, and teacher education programs became the responsibility of the universities. All of this, however, remained controversial, and there were a number of Royal Commissions over the years that investigated how teachers should be selected, educated and monitored. One of the most recent of these

Royal Commissions in 1995 led to the establishment of a College of Teachers in 1998, designed as a "self-regulatory" body for the teaching profession in the interest of the general public of the province.

Against the historic backdrop just described, the Ontario Ministry of Education announced in June 2001 that it would initiate a new "teacher testing program" in order to achieve excellence in teaching. The plan for this program grew out of an election promise in 1999 by the provincial Premier, Mike Harris, who was seeking re-election. His Conservative Party claimed that they would deliver "quality" education. The overall initiative included new and more rigorous curriculum from kindergarten to Grade 12, a standardized testing program for students, new School Council regulations, and a Code of Conduct to help create safe environments in Ontario's schools (Ontario Ministry of Education News Release, June 7, 2001). For teachers, it meant a new Regulation that would allow the Ontario College of Teachers to accredit teacher education programs and additional qualifications courses. It also meant the establishment of an Ontario Teacher Qualifying Test for new teachers, an induction program for first year teachers, and a new performance appraisal scheme. The most contentious issue, however, was the plan for re-certification for practicing teachers.

The Global Context

Initiatives for teachers similar to those undertaken by the Harris government in Ontario were underway in this time period in other parts of Canada, in the United States, the United Kingdom, Australia and New Zealand, as well as many other nations. For a critical discussion by a group of international education scholars of these and other school reforms, see *Equity and Globalization in Education* (Reynolds & Griffith, 2002).

In the neighboring province of Quebec, a 1993 report, *The Challenge of Teaching Today and Tomorrow*, called for a renewal of the teaching profession through more stringent admission requirements into teacher training, better training programs, and support for new teachers. The Quebec plan also called for active participation by all educational partners and a new look at professional development activities by teachers aimed at improving teaching practices (Ontario College of Teachers, 2000, p. 49).

In Alberta, one of Canada's Western provinces, the 1998 *Teacher Growth, Supervision and Evaluation Policy* set the Teaching Quality Standard. The TQS mapped out a system whereby new teachers would be granted an Interim Professional Certificate which would become a permanent Professional Certificate only after two years of successful teaching and the completion of an annual professional growth plan prepared by each "individual teacher in the context of the employment setting" (Ontario College of Teachers, 2000, p. 51).

In the United States in 1998, *Key State Policies on K-12 Education: Standards, Graduation, Assessment, Teacher Licensure, Time and Attendance – A 50 State Report* provided a "state by state profile for work on state standards for teacher licensing, teacher assessment instruments for use in licensing of new teachers and professional development requirements for licensing renewal" (Ontario College of Teachers, 2000, p. 35). In 1996, the National Commission on Teaching and America's Future had issued a report that proposed "far reaching changes in the way the nation prepares, licences and recruits teachers." Critics of this report, such as Ballou and Podgursky (2001), argued that it effectively "would transfer considerable regulatory control out of the public domain to private education organizations" (p. 1). These same critics felt that the evidence base for such a move was weak and that the Commission had not made good use of available research.

Despite criticisms, and many difficulties in terms of implementation, a number of states attempted to "test" teachers during this time period. Flippo (2002) has outlined how the Educational Testing Service, a for-profit private company, has contracts with up to thirty-five states. Flippo explains that these tests were set into motion to deal with perceived deficiencies in teacher education programs, a decline in participation of minority persons in the teaching profession, shortages of teachers in particular fields, and a poor public image of teachers. But none of these issues were adequately addressed through testing initiatives. Indeed, lawsuits in places such as Georgia and California questioned the legality and validity of tests being used by companies such as ETS. An initial testing program in Texas in 1986 proved to be such a failure that it was discontinued in favor of developing standards and a new test, as well as a parallel re-designed teacher appraisal system which included a required professional growth plan (Ontario College of Teachers, 2000, p. 38).

Re-certification plans in the United States also ran into difficulties over this same time period. In Illinois in 1997, a government mandate required teachers to re-certify "every five years on the basis of a professional development program" (Reynolds & Hart, 2001, p. 8). Critics of this plan point out that it is highly individualized and since it is not tied to practice, it does not address actual competency or performance in any direct way. Connecticut, New York, and New Jersey have re-certification plans based on set numbers of hours and critics of such plans (primarily teacher unions) have argued that they are punitive. Equally contentious are re-certification plans in states such as Massachusetts, Wisconsin, and Ohio. Lawsuits have been brought against the governments in these states and there are fears about local administrators using such schemes as part of teacher evaluation. More successful was a plan in Idaho where a State Board provides credit for activities which must be directly tied to the filed School District Professional Development Plan. Also successful was a scheme in Hawaii where there was no required re-certification, but credits could gain salary improvements for teachers (Reynolds & Hart, 2001).

In 1998 in Australia, the Senate Employment, Education and Training References Committee gathered evidence throughout Australia and published *A Class Act: Inquiry into the Status of the Teaching Profession*. The approach here has been to develop sets of Professional Standards that will guide professional growth for teachers (Ontario College of Teachers, 2000, p. 38). In New Zealand, the national Teacher Registration Board took responsibility for re-certifying teachers. This body grants a three-year "practicing certificate" to individuals who have been successful teachers and who have participated in professional development activities over the three year period (Reynolds & Hart, 2001, p. 5).

In England, Wales and Scotland, the emphasis has been on standards and improved initial teacher training. The British Teacher Training Agency (TTA) has outlined national Standards and the Scottish Office Education Department released a list of teacher competencies in 1993 (Ontario College of Teachers, 2000, p. 47).

In France, there are "seven different examinations for the teaching profession" (Ontario College of Teachers, 2000, p. 48). The Instituts Universitaires de Formation des Maitres (IUFM) is responsible for both pre-service and in-service professional development. After passing an initial examination, aspiring teachers must consult a reference list of the skills they need to acquire. On-going professional learning is seen as a natural part of the process of working as a teacher.

Ontario Policies as a Case in Point

In Ontario, standards for teachers developed in the 1990s can be seen as a regulation mechanism. The Standards of Practice for the Teaching Profession came out of the College of Teachers. The College brochure outlining these standards declared that they are part of the self-regulation function of the College and "provide the foundation for pre-service and in-service programs accredited by the Ontario College of Teachers (Ontario College of Teachers, 1999, p. 1). In effect, the standards provided a means to hand over to the state an increased control over teacher education programs. An Accreditation Regulation (Ontario Gazette, 2002), passed after considerable controversy with the universities and the teacher unions, gave the College of Teachers the right and the responsibility for accrediting all teacher education programs in the province, including programs for on-going professional development for teachers. These programs must demonstrate that they match the Standards of Practice.

Since the 1970s, Ontario pre-service teacher education programs have been conducted in universities. While each university followed regular internal reviews, the new accreditation process, which began in the late 1990s, called for extensive documentation every five years by the universities and a visit by a panel selected by the College of Teachers. During the three-year pilot process for accreditation, controversies arose over the College's infringement of university autonomy. In British Columbia, the other Canadian province with a College of Teachers, this "infringement" had gone as far as dictating which texts might be used. Following court battles, the BC government stepped in and reworked the purview of the College. In Ontario, court battles also ensued. Eventually a compromise position was reached and the powers of the College were mitigated by strong statements in the new Accreditation Regulation outlining the rights of the universities, including a valid appeal route concerning the accreditation decision by the College (Ontario College of Teachers, 2003, p. 22).

Despite the fact that all teacher education pre-service programs would now undergo external evaluation, the Harris government pushed forward with their promise to "test" teachers. There was much criticism of this new plan. The government claimed there was a crisis in public confidence in schools and teachers. Surveys such as the one conducted by Livingstone, Hart and Davie (2003) showed that while satisfaction levels regarding public schools had plummeted between 1989–1993, levels had improved following that period (p. 10). In 2002, for example, 71% of parents surveyed said they were satisfied with the job teachers were doing (p. 8). Despite this, and against several recommendations by the College of Teachers in their report, *Maintaining, Ensuring and Demonstrating Competency in the Teaching Profession* (2001), the government of the day pushed forward to make good on their promise of a teacher testing program. This move angered teachers, and the implementation of new policies to bring about this program has been fraught with difficulties.

The plan for a written test originally was meant for all practicing teachers in the province but, when provincial teacher unions strongly opposed this move, an Ontario Teacher Qualifying Test (OTQT) for all graduates of pre-service programs became the compromise. The OTQT was implemented for the first time in the Spring of 2001. The implementation process was so flawed, however, that the government had to "back down" at the final moment and declared that new teachers needed to write the test but that the scores for 2001 would not "count" as that year would be considered a pilot. This decision came after almost everything that could go wrong with a test of this type did go wrong.

The government had hired the Educational Testing Service (ETS) to design and deliver the test. Immediately there was an outcry about an American private agency being able to adequately work within a bilingual Canadian setting. The general public slowly became aware of the fact that only Ontario graduates of pre-service programs needed to take the test in order to be allowed to teach in the province following the completion of their teacher education program. New teachers who had taken programs in the United States, Australia, or in other places were free to teach immediately and were to be provided with several years to "learn the Ontario system" before being required to take the OTQT. This angered the Ontario universities who already felt that they were in sharp competition with "off-shore" (out of Canada) programs in teacher education. Students in Ontario teacher education programs marched in protest of the test and one candidate actually arrived in a clown suit on the test date to show derision for the whole process. The students' anger was based on a faulty communication network that provided them with inadequate details about where and when the test would be. People at ETS clearly did not understand how big Ontario was, as one operator suggested that a student take the subway from Toronto to North Bay to take the test. Nor did the ETS personnel speak French.

Promising to improve these glitches, ETS proceeded to set up an improved mechanism for the following year. But a firm decision to have only one test date in April backfired when an unexpected and severe snowstorm on that date played havoc with students' ability to get to test sites, particularly in northern parts of the province. There was an additional test date a few days following, but the same test was administered and cries of unfairness rang out since many who sat for the second test date had the benefit of having seen the test on the internet. Serious critiques of the validity of the test were mounted by educational researchers (Portelli, Solomon, Majawamariya, Dibos, Gathayenya, Manoukian, & Price, 2003) and promises for future legal action were made by teacher union officials. Researchers claimed that "the overwhelming majority of participants [in our study] felt that the Ontario Ministry of Education launched the teacher-qualifying test for purely political reasons rather than for educational concerns" (Portelli, et al., 2003, p. 3).

Delivering on the teacher testing promise, the Ontario government also ran into serious blocks regarding their policies for teacher re-certification and a Professional Learning Plan (PLP). The re-certification plan has been opposed by both the College of Teachers and the teacher unions, but the government has moved forward under the claim that such a process is necessary "to ensure that teachers keep their skills and knowledge up to date" (Ontario College of Teachers, 2001, p. 21). Teachers said that they feel insulted by the mandatory nature of the scheme since, contrary to government claims, studies have shown that Ontario teachers are actively promoting their own professional growth (Browne, 1999; Smaller, Clarke, Hart, & Livingstone, 2001). The new "learning plan" requires that all teachers "complete a minimum of 14 professional learning courses every five years to maintain their license to teach" (Ontario College of Teachers, 2001, p. 17). To oversee this plan, the government has set up a Professional Learning Committee. Most members of this committee are selected from the College of Teachers, but the Minister of Education reserved the right to appoint up to five members to the committee. This decision and the extensive infrastructure needed at the College to handle all the necessary data entry brought the wrath of teachers, many of whom have threatened to boycott the scheme. Indeed, one of the teacher unions systematically boycotted universities giving courses that could be credited to the plan by refusing to supervise preservice teachers' practicum experiences in schools where its members worked.

The dilemmas in Ontario, as in other sites where re-certification has been initiated recently, are about how to tackle the "nettle of competency" (Reynolds & Hart, 2001, p. 21) for teachers. How can performance evaluation be clearly separated from professional learning? What is the link between personal judgements by teachers about their learning needs and local, district or state-wide priorities? To what sorts of bodies do we delegate the professional development plan for teachers, and should this be locally monitored or done through a state-wide system? Who picks up the costs, not only monetary but in terms of staff time? In this time period in Ontario, the Harris government, like bodies elsewhere, seems to have stepped forward with policy statements that were not sufficiently supported by well designed implementation processes. The result was anger, frustration, confusion, and resistance. Working relationships among educational stakeholders were severely damaged.

Summary

Educational policy, such as the Ontario teacher testing regulations, must be considered in light of historic backdrops and conditions in the broader context. In the Ontario case described in this chapter, it is helpful to clarify how earlier debates about teacher professionalization intertwine with debates concerning self-regulation and autonomy. A central question remains: Who should control teachers and teachers' work? Should it be local elites as in days gone by? Should it be teacher unions? What is the role of bodies such as a College of Teachers? Is it appropriate to pass control along to private companies, such as a testing agency like ETS in the United States, or for-profit boards or agencies such as Britain's Teacher Training Agency (TTA) or the National Council for the Accreditation of Teacher Education (NCATE) in the United States?

Another crucial question regarding educational policy, such as the one described in this chapter, is: "What is the role of educational research and researchers in terms of policy formation and implementation?" In numerous venues around the world, educational researchers have been asking this question. As competition to obtain funding for educational research heats up, sources of that funding have increasingly become tied to government and/or particular private interests. How can researchers maintain their autonomy? Who controls educational researchers and educational research? How does the paradox of professionalism play out for those in teacher education and/or in research about teachers and teachers' work?

The answers to the questions I have just posed will vary, but raising such questions and having a debate based upon multiple views is critical if we are to enhance our understanding of the longstanding and continuing struggle to regulate teachers and their work in our schools.

References

Ballou, D., & Podgursky, M. (2001). Reforming teacher preparation and licensing: What is the evidence? *TCRecord.org* Retrieved December 19th, 2001 from http://www.tcrecord.org/Content.asp?ContentID = 10524

Browne, L. (1999). Teachers pursue professional learning. *Professionally Speaking*, Ontario College of Teachers, December.

Curtis, B. (1988). *Building the educational state: Canada West, 1836–1871*. London: Falmer Press.

Flippo, R. (2002). Repeating history: Teacher licensure testing in Massachusetts. *Journal of Personnel Evaluation in Education, 16*(3), 211–229.

Livingstone, D. W., Hart, D., & Davie, L. E. (2004). *Public attitudes towards education in Ontario: The 14th OISE/UT Survey*. The Ontario Institute for the Study of Education of the University of Toronto.

Ontario Ministry of Education (2001). News release: Government takes next steps to support student achievement through teacher excellence. Retrieved June 8th, 2001 from http://www.edu.gov.on.ca/eng/document/nr/01.06/nr0607.html

Ontario College of Teachers (2003). Pilot process was an important lead up to accreditation regulation. *Professionally Speaking*, March.

Ontario College of Teachers (2001). Teacher testing: Government pushing ahead. *Professionally Speaking*, June.

Ontario College of Teachers (2000). *Maintaining, ensuring and demonstrating competency in the teaching profession.* Toronto: Ontario College of Teachers, April.

Ontario College of Teachers (1999). Standards of practice for the teaching profession. Toronto: Ontario College of Teachers.

Ontario Gazette (2002). *Accreditation of Teacher Education Programs Ontario Regulation*, 347/02 1581.

Portelli, J., Solomon, P., Mujawamariya, D., Dibos, A., Gathenya, W., Manoukian, R., & Price, J. (2003). *A critical analysis of the Ontario Teacher Qualifying Test: Teacher candidates' perspectives.* Preliminary research report released in February.

Reynolds, C., & Griffiths, A. (Eds.) (2002). *Equity and globalization in education.* Calgary: Detselig.

Reynolds, C., & Hart, D. (2001). *Approaches to re-certification: A selected survey of current practices.* A Report to the Ontario Ministry of Education, April.

Reynolds, C., & Smaller, H. (1997). *Professionalism as paradox: Past and present struggles for control over teachers' work in Canada.* Paper presented at the Eighth International Conference of the International Study Association on Teacher Thinking, October, Kiel, Germany.

Smaller, H., Clarke, R., Hart, D., & Livingstone, D. (2001). *Informal and formal learning among Ontario secondary school teachers.* Report as part of the New Approaches to Lifelong Learning (NALL) project at OISEUT.

29

TEACHER PROFESSIONAL STANDARDS: A POLICY STRATEGY TO CONTROL, REGULATE OR ENHANCE THE TEACHING PROFESSION?

Judyth Sachs
University of Sydney, Australia

The idea of standards for the teaching profession has been circulating in education policy discourses and public debates in Australia, the UK, the USA since the mid 1990s. The rise of education policies in support of professional teaching standards needs to be seen in the light of broader public sector reforms which have sought to contribute to increased efficiency and effectiveness of bureaucracies through systems of performance management of staff, increased demands for public accountability, and increased regulation by central government. Such policy processes need to be seen in the light of government priorities which, as Mahony and Hextall observe, have been preoccupied with debates about standards which have centred on, "how these terms are defined, second, by whom, and third, on how improvement of effectiveness is to be achieved" (2000, p. 8). This chapter is organized around three questions: i. what discourses inform the standards debate and the development of teacher professional standards? ii. What are some emerging issues relating to teacher professional standards? and iii. What alternative strategies could the teaching profession itself use to seize the agenda towards a profession led strategy?

The political nature of the content and oversight of teacher professional standards is often underplayed by taking as unproblematic the meanings and objectives of standards policies. This may be an intentional strategy used by policy makers to promote a neutral and natural view of standards as good sense or common sense. As Andrew observes, "in this era of standards, writers use the term in many different ways, seldom bothering to unpack the differences in meaning; standards become the answer to all questions. They are thought to provide the magic ingredient to restructuring all education" (1997, p. 168). The very term has become a site of struggle between various interest groups – bureaucracies, teachers' unions and teachers themselves.

Ball (1990) argues that policies are intended to bring about idealized solutions

International Handbook of Educational Policy, 579–592
Nina Bascia, Alister Cumming, Amanda Datnow, Kenneth Leithwood and David Livingstone (Eds.)
© 2005 *Springer. Printed in Great Britain.*

to diagnosed problems. They embody claims to speak with authority, they legitimate and initiate practices in the world, and they privilege certain visions and interests. They set the limits for what can be thought and done in educational practice both inside and outside of classrooms. Policies and practices as they are developing in the UK and Australia relating to teacher professional standards can be seen in this way. The analysis of policy texts is useful here since such texts represent the legal obligations of teachers, the types of activities that are mandated by the state and how those activities are to be implemented and monitored.

Inherent in any policy document are a set of discourses that set the framework for what is to be represented and how it is to be enacted. Gee, Hull, and Lankshear (1996) capture the complexity of discourse which they describe as a set of related practices.

> A discourse is composed of ways of talking, listening, reading, writing, acting, interacting, believing, valuing and using tools and objects, in particular settings at particular times, so as to display or to recognise a particular social identity. ... The Discourse creates social positions (or perspectives) from which people are 'invited' (summoned) to speak, listen, act, read and write, think, feel, believe and value in certain characteristic, historically recongnisable ways, in combination with their own individual style and creativity. (p. 10)

I have argued elsewhere (Sachs, 2003a) that managerial discourses shape the form and content of policies relating to teacher professional standards. These managerial discourses are concerned with ensuring public accountability, both through the language that is used but also by engendering a sense of 'trust' insofar as the application of 'standards frameworks' will improve the quality and provision of education. Within the current political climate managerialism presents a strong and authoritative discourse (Clarke, Cochrane, & McLaughlin, 1995). This is part and parcel of the transformation of the public sector worldwide over the past decade through new management reforms. A second, and closely linked phenomenon, is the current practice of policy borrowing – bureaucrats look to the policies of other systems both for reference and for comparability. These reforms with their emphasis on accountability, efficiency, effectiveness and economy have ensured a 'sameness' across many policy documents.

The policy texts and discourses around the issue of teacher professional standards compliment and are informed by the logic of public sector reform, in particular the need for education bureaucracies in general and teachers in particular to become more accountable not only in terms of what they teach but also how they teach. Accordingly as Strathern (2000) observes, managerial rationality is centred on the notion that institutional behaviour can be shaped if the right kind of reinforcement is combined with the right kind of information.

In this chapter I examine some of the rhetorics embodied in policies and debates concerning teacher professional standards in three national contexts and suggest that these initiatives are an attempt by the state to control the teaching profession. I conclude the chapter with the proposal for a role for the teaching profession in the oversight and monitoring of professional standards, through what I refer to as an activist teaching profession (Sachs, 2003a). An activist teaching profession anticipates that teachers and others interested in education will be able to defend and understand themselves better. It is founded on the basis of transformative professionalism which serves the best interests and aspirations of not only the teaching profession itself but all of those interested and participating in schooling and education. The characteristics of transformative professionalism include: inclusive membership, collaborative and collegial social and professional relationships. It is flexible and progressive and is accordingly responsive to change, it is policy active and self regulating.

Professional Standards As A Technology Of Control?

Standards regimes need to be examined within the context of broader public sector reforms – especially the imperatives for government and its instrumentalities to be more accountable and to have in place a system to monitor activities and outcomes. Seen within this light professional standards represent a dimension of the audit society (Power, 1999) and an aspect of audit cultures which currently characterise public institutions (Strathern, 2000). Under the strictures of an audit society, surveillance and inspection go hand in hand. Regulation, enforcement and sanctions are required to ensure its compliance. Of its professionals it requires self-ordering, based not on individual or moral judgment, but rather upon meeting externally applied edicts and commands. It requires 'regulatory mechanisms acting as 'political technologies' which seek to bring persons, organisations and objectives into alignment (Shore & Wright, 2000, p. 61).

The development of standards has been part of a two pronged initiative by governments and bureaucracies in the United Kingdom, Australia, and the USA to improve the educational performance and outcomes of education systems and the practices of teachers in classrooms. Debates and initiatives regarding teacher professional standards have been concerned with two orientations: the use of standards to improve performance and the use of standards as a basis for reforming the teaching profession. In some settings these standards have been imposed and used by governments as regulatory frameworks and bureaucratic controls over teachers, particularly as they relate to licensing and certification procedures. In other instances they are used as an initiative for teachers to gain professional control over what constitutes professional work. Darling Hammond, writing from a US perspective, argues, "Recently developed professional standards for teaching hold promise for mobilising reforms of the teaching career and helping to structure the learning opportunities that reflect the complex, reciprocal nature of teaching work" (1999, p. 39). Two sets of tensions are present. First, where has the initiative to develop the standards come from and how the standards are monitored? Whether standards are developed and imposed by state mandated regulatory bodies or by the profession itself, the issue of standards is neither straightforward nor unproblematic to the teaching profession. Mahony and Hextall demonstrate the complexity of the task.

> In examining standards it is important to examine them for their clarity, consistency and coherence, as well as the values, principles and assumptions that underpin them. They also need to be examined in terms of fitness of purpose – are they capable of doing the work they are intended to do? And is this consistent with the broader purposes of their institutional setting? Procedurally, standards can be investigated in terms of their establishment and formation, with all the questions of accountability and transparency that this entails. They can also be questioned in terms of the manner in which they are translated into practice and the consequences, both manifest and latent, which follow. More broadly, there is a set of issues to consider in relation to the culture and ideology of standards as a widespread phenomenon operating across both the private and public sectors in England and elsewhere. (2000, p. 30)

Governments have been attracted to a commonsense approach to the use of professional standards. Standards are viewed as instruments for identifying minimum levels of achievement in various aspects of practice, to define what teachers should be able to do and what they should know that is they embody a "technical" conception of teaching (Bascia & Hargreaves, 2000; Darling-Hammond, 1999). Implicit in this commonsense view of teacher professional standards are three goals: first, to present an uncritical view of professional standards, to accept that the teaching profession will benefit from the external application of professional standards, and paradoxically, through the rhetoric of a professionalising agenda, use the standards as a strategy to control teachers and the teaching profession. The application of bureaucratic forces such as rules, mandates and requirements as the means to provide direct supervision, standardized work processes or standardized outcomes to control or regulate teaching (Sergiovanni, 1998). Indeed what might be seen to be commonsense here has significant implications for teacher autonomy and teacher professionalism.

Apple claims that

> ... a set of national or state standards, national or state curricular, and national or state tests would provide the conditions for thick morality. After all, such regulatory reforms are supposedly based on shared values and common sentiments that also create social spaces in which common issues of concern can be debated and made subject to moral interrogation. Yet what counts as "common" and how and by whom it is actually determined, is rather more thin than thick. (2001, p. 84)

Clearly, then, common sense versions of standards are problematic. While sometimes there is an element of good sense in them, more often than not complex issues are simplified and reduced to meaningless cant.

A second but no less important tension within commonsense definitions is a tendency to focus on standardisation of practice rather than the development of standards that can have wide applicability across various contexts and settings or even of improving the level of standards achieved. Much of the content of standards frameworks are acontextual – there is little acknowledgement of how a teacher's experience, workplace environment and history can significantly shape a teacher's performance as codified within the standards framework.

The Politics of Standards Setting

Three empirical cases are used to demonstrate the origin and political processes, and the discourse/rhetoric of standards setting. These cases indicate how standards' agendas have been used differently by governments and teacher professional associations to improve the standing and practices of teachers. Furthermore, they clarify the 'political' differences between regulatory and developmental approaches to standards setting (Mahony & Hextall, 2000). Regulatory approaches can be used as a managerialist tool for measuring the efficiency and effectiveness of systems, institutions and individuals. Developmental approaches on the other hand provide opportunities for teachers' further professional learning, and are often aimed at improving the quality of their teaching throughout their careers.

The following similarities characterise a developmental approach to teacher professional standards in UK, Australia and the US:

- A student centred approach to teaching and learning
- Systematic forms of monitoring for the purposes of accountability
- A view that teachers should be life long learners
- A commitment to teachers improving their professional knowledge and practice.

While regulatory approaches across the three examples are characterised by:

- A focus on accountability
- A technical approach to teaching
- Monitoring teacher performance
- External imposition of the standards by a government instrumentality

That there are commonalities and similarities in approaches to standards should not be surprising. The practice of policy borrowing referred to earlier and the use of 'international experts' leads to a homogenisation of practice. While the local politics and priorities may differ, there is a common desire both to improve the provision of education to students and to make teachers more accountable for their practice.

In the UK, Australia and US both of these approaches to standards are evident, but there is an emerging drift from developmental to regulatory approaches to standards. In the UK for example, the development of the National

Professional Standards (NPS) can be seen both as providing a centralised specification of 'effective teaching' and as the codification of relations between managers and managed (Mahony & Hextall, 2000, p. 32).

In the UK between 1994 and 1998 the Teacher Training Agency (TTA) developed a framework of National Standards for Teaching, which, in their words, would 'define expertise in key roles' (TTA, 1998, p. 1). Furlong et al. (2000) claim that policies in the late 1990s sought to exploit the new control system by specifying the content of professional education in detail. They claim that "two strategies were involved: first, the transformation of competencies into more elaborate 'standards'; second, the development of a national curriculum for initial teacher education in English, mathematics, science and information and communication technology" (pp. 149–150).

In the UK, the move to standards emerged from the competencies debates. This move was to define the content of teacher training in much more explicit detail than before. As the circular stated, 'the standards have been written to be specific, explicit and assessable and are designed to provide a clear basis for the reliable and consistent award of Qualified Teachers Status (QTS)' (DfEE, 1997, p. 6). Millett (1997) suggests that the standards for the award of Qualified Teachers Status set out in more detail than ever before the core knowledge, understandings and skills on which effective teaching rests. These standards replace more "general 'competencies' which had been in force previously and apply to all those assessed for QTS no matter what initial training course or route to teaching they may be on" (quoted in Furlong et al., 2000, p. 150).

Attempts in Australian states to develop and implement teacher professional standards illustrate the political nature of standards setting. Louden (2000) has identified two evolutionary phases in the development of professional teaching standards in Australia. The first wave of standards, prior to 1999, was domi-nated by:

> the large State government school systems, and influenced by competency based conceptions of standards ... There standards are characterised by long lists of duties, opaque language generic skills, decontextualised perfor-mances, and expanded range of duties, and weak assessments (Louden, 2000, p. 118).

Ownership by the teaching profession itself has been a key characteristic of some recent initiatives in Australia. Accordingly, an emerging second wave of standards developments is being largely led by professional associations. For example The Australian College of Educators, the largest national professional association in the country, has been trying to establish a structure and set of processes to achieve a commonly agreed upon set of teacher professional standards. To date while there have been several public forums and much associated debate there are few tangible outcomes, in particular a set of accepted standards have not been put in place across the country. Other curriculum associations such as the English Teachers Association and the Science Teachers Association are develop-ing standards along the lines of the American National Board for Professional

Teaching Standards. Both of these subject associations have been concerned with writing standards for 'highly accomplished teachers' or 'excellence in teaching'. While the professional associations have accepted the standards, they have not as yet been implemented systemtically by education systems.

More recently Gregor Ramsay (2000) was commissioned by the NSW government to review teacher education and the teaching profession.His final report recommended that the New South Wales Government establish an Institute of Teachers whose primary purpose is to enhance the level of professionalism of teachers and teaching. The Institute would be responsible for:

- The establishment and promulgation of performance standards at designated stages of development as a teacher, together with standards of ethical practice for teachers;
- The accreditation and disaccreditation of teachers against such ethical standards, determining related requirements for maintaining and extending or removing such accreditation, and maintaining records of teachers so accredited;
- Endorsing and disendorsing courses and programs of teacher education, both initial and continuing;
- Advising the Government and the community on issues relating to teacher quality and professional standards, and on qualifications, profile and experiences of teachers employed throughout the state. ... (Ramsay, 2000, p. 147)

To date the Institute has been established, and a set of Draft Standards are in the processes of validation. The draft standards will ensure that teachers:

- Know their subject content and how to teach that to students;
- Know their students and how they learn;
- Plan, assess and report for effective learning;
- Communicate effectively with their students;
- Create and maintain safe and challenging learning environments through classroom management;
- Continually improve their professional knowledge and practice; and
- Are actively engaged members of their profession and the wider community.

The standards were developed through a process of consultation with international and national experts, focus groups across the State and professional associations. Interestingly while their intention can be seen to be towards a developmental rather than a regulative form of standards a focus on performance at various stages of a teacher's career gives the standards a somewhat regulatory flavour.

In Australia it is clear that the issue of teacher professional standards is not so much whether a system of professional standards should be established but rather how. To do this will require political will, resources and the ' buy in' by the teaching profession itself. Indeed at the time of writing this chapter the

Australian government Department of Education, Science and Training published *a National Statement on Teacher Standards, quality and professionalism* (Department of Education, Science and Training, 2003) which was compiled by a cross-section of stakeholders within the profession. In this document the position is that "Professional standards for teaching should be the responsibility of and owned by, the teaching profession in collaboration with other key stakeholders" (p. 5) There is still conceptual fuzziness in the document as the following statement reveals. "Standards should recognize the value of both generic and subject specific standards (p. 3). How this will be translated in practice either at a policy level or a structural level is yet to be revealed.

The United States provides a third example of the development of a strong teacher professional standards initiative. Like Australia, the provision of education is a state responsibility. Nevertheless, there have been central government initiatives to support the development of professional standards.

The National Board for Professional Teaching Standards (NBPTS) was established in 1987 in response to significant criticism of education and the standard of education performance and provision in the US as presented in the report *A Nation at Risk*. The NBPTS is a non profit, non partisan and non governmental agency governed by a 63 member board of directors, the majority of which are teachers. The NBPTS's mandate was to establish rigorous standards regarding the practice of accomplished teachers. The standards are organised around a set of five propositions about effective teaching and accomplished teachers:

- Commitment to students and their learning;
- Knowledge of the subjects they teach and how to teach those subjects to students;
- Responsibility for managing and monitoring student learning;
- Systematic reflection on their practice and learning from experience
- Membership of learning communities

NBPTS (1996 introduction)

The NBPTS's standards provide descriptors setting expectations of accomplished professionals. They are subject and age specific rather than generic. When complete there will be twenty six statements on standards, such as those for Early childhood/Generalist (ages 3–8) Early Adolescence/Science (ages 11–15) and Adolescence through young Adulthood/English Arts (ages 14–18+). To date only 16 of the twenty three standards have been completed.

While there is considerable support by state legislatures (40 state legislatures support it to date), members of the teaching profession and professional bodies such as The Council of Chief State School Officers, the National Association of State Boards of Education and the National Education Association, the NBPTS has had its critics. Tom (2000), for example, notes that "all is not going well with the National Board process":

Three problems with National Board certification – the slow development of certificate areas, the small number of certified teachers, the high cost of assessment process to teachers – are all problems which grew out of the National Board processes, or might reasonably have been anticipated to follow from that process. A fourth problem, however, is something that Darling Hammond and other supporters could not have foreseen in the mid-1980s: the accountability movement. (pp. 19–20)

Interestingly, while the standards have been developed at a national level, the Federal government does not have jurisdiction over state education matters. Nevertheless, it is interesting to note that 40 states have taken up the National Board's standards. At issue here is a mismatch between the use of standards at the national level to contribute to the professionalization of teaching, while at the state level the agenda was increasingly that of accountability and improving student learning outcomes by improving the quality of teaching. As Tom claims, "the states agenda is firmly focused on teaching quality measured in terms of a teacher's ability to produce student results on state mandated K-12 assessment" (2000, p. 20).

Clearly, then, standards are being used by different organizational players for different political and ideological ends. Such tensions contribute to confusing the purpose and potential of standards for the teaching profession and make them a battle ground for competing interests and expectations. Time and energy is thus spent on the politics and the potential, and the practices around standards are often left to languish.

Professionalism and Teaching Standards?

An uncritical gaze would suggest that, like motherhood, standards are in the best interests of teachers, students and the teaching profession, and indeed this may well be the case. The need to be cautious about the limitations of standards is expressed by Darling Hammond (1999, p. 39):

Teaching standards are not a magic bullet. By themselves, they cannot solve the problems of dysfunctional school organizations, outmoded curricula, inequitable allocation of resources, or lack of social supports for children and youth. Standards, like all reforms, hold their own dangers. Standard setting in all professions must be vigilant against the possibilities that practice could become constrained by the codification of knowledge that does not significantly acknowledge legitimate diversity of approaches or advances in the field; that access to practice could become overly restricted on grounds not directly related to competence; or that adequate learning opportunities for candidates to meet standards may not emerge on an equitable basis.

The issue of standards then has both political and professional dimensions. In the UK the change of language from 'competencies' to 'standards' represented these two dimensions. Rather than the notion of a minimum ability as implied in the word 'competency', the idea of 'standards' of professional training crossed easily into government concerns to raise educational standards more generally. As such the change in term had political advantages, making enforcement even more difficult to resist. Who after all could be opposed to raising standards? (Furlong et al., 2000, p. 151).

While in the eyes of its advocates, teacher professional standards may well enhance the status of teachers and contribute to their on-going professional learning, nevertheless, there are likely to be costs which will have some influence on teachers' classroom performance, their professional engagement and their receptiveness to change. David Hargreaves (1994) describes the ways in which work intensification occurs in teaching. He argues that intensification leads to a lack of time to retool one's skills and keep up with one's field. It creates chronic and persistent overload (as compared with the temporary overload that is sometimes experienced in meeting deadlines), which reduces areas of personal discretion, inhibits involvement in and control over longer term planning, and fosters dependency on externally produced materials and expertise.

A tension emerges through the implementation of teacher professional standards. There is strong evidence to suggest that the work of teachers is being intensified (Apple, 2000; Smyth, Dow, Hattam, Reid, & Shacklock, 2000) that is, teachers are being required to be more accountable by employing authorities and communities are placing greater expectations and demands on extra curricula and pastoral activities. It follows then that a mandatory application of teacher professional standards on top of teachers' already heavy workload will make the task of teaching even more demanding. The danger with teachers accepting the challenge of using a standards framework as a source of professional learning is that they become complicit in their own exploitation and the intensification of their work. Acceptance of a standards-based framework for teacher on-going learning becomes an ideological tool for teachers to do more under the rhetoric of increasing their professionalism and status. Hence professionalism under the guise of standards becomes a tool for employers demanding more of teachers. The implementation of a standards framework puts teachers in a double bind. If they do not have a set of publicly documented standards like other 'professions' then they are seen not to have the same professional status as those professions who do have these codified frameworks. At the same time, by undertaking professional development activities as outlined by Ingvarson (1998), they contribute to the intensification of their work. For standards to contribute to the on-going professional learning of teachers, participation in standards based professional development must be seen as an integral part of teachers' work and time must be allocated for this to occur.

Given this situation, a profession led initiative would be seen to be far more attractive to teachers. The challenge for those developing standards frameworks is twofold. First is how to accommodate the ambiguities and uncertainties of a changing and fluid education policy agenda while at the same time providing teachers and the community with clear guidelines as to what constitutes good practice. Second is how issues of teacher professionalism are debated and developed in order to enhance the quality and status of teaching in order to facilitate and improve student learning. How these are achieved takes the development of teacher professional standards into new and likely highly politically charged territory. Dealing with these challenges will require resolve, courage and political and professional care. Indeed it means that we think about professional teaching standards differently. Being profession driven puts the locus of control on the teaching profession. For its success it means that teachers will have to be mobilised to speak collectively and to develop strategies to work towards the common interests of the whole profession rather than focussing on sectional interests and agendas of small sub-groups. This type of collective action (Sachs, 2003b) acts as a strategy to take stock of what is happening in communities, schools and classrooms. People working collectively in such ways are able to motive and sustain each other, test ideas, debate strategies and negotiate shared meaning about how best to improve the status and practice of teachers. This type of work has previously been undertaken by subject or professional associations. However, to be more effective a broader constituency needs to be mobilized. It would be one in which teachers, community members and other interested parties debate and negotiate what are the purposes of standards and questioning how can they be used to develop and improve teachers' practice and students' learning.

An Alternative Approach to Teacher Professional Standards

Given my obvious preference for developmental rather than regulatory standards, what would these look like? The following assumptions could underpin profession-wide strategy for teacher professional standards.

- The purpose of teacher professional standards should be developmental rather than regulatory
- Engaging in on-going learning in order to keep up to date with subject area knowledge and pedagogical skills should be mandatory. In most other professions, especially law and medicine, practitioners are expected to engage in a minimum amount of professional learning.
- In line with the above, the focus for standards should be context specific for teachers' particular needs. At different stages of their careers teachers have different needs and similarly, the context in which teachers work shape their professional learning needs.
- Representatives of various teachers' groups should have responsibility for the development and oversight of professional teaching standards. These should come from as broad a constituency as possible representing the various schooling sectors (government and non-government schools), different levels (pre-school, primary and secondary) subject area specializations, as well as principal professional bodies (primary and secondary), teacher unions, teacher educators, education employers as well as parent

and citizen groups. The development of coalitions and alliances among various constituencies is power building to achieve social and political ends (Sachs, 2003b).
• The content of teacher professional standards should encompass professional, practical and personal skills and attributes.

The set of assumptions provided above complement the tenets of an activist teaching profession (Sachs, 2003a). The development of standards for teaching is a collective enterprise of all of those who are interested in improving the quality of teaching and student learning outcomes. We have to resist any attempts by those who define teaching too narrowly and work against those who advocate a 'teach to the test' syndrome of a narrow set of teaching attributes. We need to acknowledge that conceptions of good teaching are changing, and that the knowledge and research base of teaching and learning are expanding. This is all occurring at a time when there are significant cultural and social changes, which impinge on how competent teaching is defined and judged.

Professional standards for teachers which make the distinction between self interest and self control have significant potential to provide the necessary provocation for teachers to think about their work, classroom activities and professional identity in quite fundamentally different and generative ways. They also have the potential for teachers to develop a framework to think and talk about their work. Clearly both developmental and regulatory approaches have their strengths and weaknesses. However, my preference would be more towards the developmental approach than the regulatory one. The expectations and demands of external accountability need to be balanced with the developmental requirements of teachers to improve their practice and improve student learning outcomes. To achieve this, opportunities are required for teachers to identify, debate and negotiate the form and content of teacher professional standards. This should be done both collectively and individually. Teaching standards then could be seen as a centre piece for a profession that is mature and confident about its place in society. Standards are developed collegially and overseen and monitored in a collective and professional way. Thus teachers are active in their creation and become activist professionals in their implementation.

Conclusion

In this chapter I have suggested the need for a more developmental and profession driven form of professional teacher standards. Indeed professional learning should be a strong professional value but also a commitment by teachers and systems to enhance teacher and student performance.

In a perfect world, any set of professional standards for teaching needs to be owned and overseen by the profession itself. It is politically important that these standards are not primarily self-interested, but rather are concerned with a broader professional project. These standards should not be seen as a government imposed regulatory framework, which promotes one particular view of teaching and what it means to be a teacher. Furthermore, the establishment of professional control, rather than a reactive stance of self-interest will take time to develop. The development and implementation of professional standards which have currency among teachers as well as the broader society is no simple task. Indeed, while there are attempts to align the teaching profession with other professions such as engineers, architects and the like in terms of certification and registration, the uniqueness of the teaching profession must be acknowledged, as well as the various contexts in which teaching occurs. While any attempt to develop a 'one size fits all' version of standards may be attractive to governments, it may not be in the best interests of teachers teaching in remote areas, in difficult schools, or in multi-age settings where their competence will be judged on the basis of some idealized notion of what competent, or excellent teaching might be. There needs to be some flexibility regarding the form of the standards to recognize the fact that context plays an important role in influencing how teachers teach, what they teach and the learning outcomes of their students (Sachs, 2003b).

Teachers need not be captured by or held captive to a standards policy agenda. Rather they need to grasp the opportunity for professional and intellectual leadership to ensure that developmental rather than regulatory standards inform the development and application of policy. This is a political project and it requires teachers to think and act differently – especially about their role in society. Moreover, at its core it requires that the wider community think differently about teacher professional standards and how such thinking can be used as a provocation to rethink practice rather than constrain it.

I end the chapter supporting the idea of professional teacher standards, but on the proviso that they do not lead to standardization of practice or of the teaching profession being controlled by the State. A strong, competent and autonomous teaching profession is in the best interests of all of those working in the field of education. Furthermore, it is something that everyone who has a commitment to education must be willing to invest time and energy in achieving.

References

Andrew, M. (1997). What matters most to teacher educators. *Journal of Teacher Education, 48*(3) 167–176.

Apple, M. (2001). *Official knowledge: Democratic education in a conservative age* (2nd edition). New York: Teachers College Press.

Ball, S. (1990). *Politics and Policy Making in Education*. London: Routledge.

Bascia, N., & Hargreaves, A. (Eds.) (2000). *The sharp edge of change:Teaching leadership and the realities of reform*. London: Falmer.

Clarke, J., Cochrane, A., & McLaughlin (Eds.) (1995). *Managing social policy*, London: Sage.

Darling-Hammond, L. (1999). *Reshaping teaching policy, preparation and practice: Influences on the National Board for Teaching Professional Standards*. Washington: AACTE Publications.

Department for Education and Employment (DfEE) (1997). *Teaching: High status, high standards* (Circular4/98). London: DfEE.

Department of Education, Science and Training (2003). Report of a National Forum on Standards, Quality and Teacher Professionalism, Commonwealth of Australia.

Furlong, J., Barton, L., Miles, S., Whiting, C., & Whitty, G. (2000). *Teacher education in transition*, Buckingham: Open University.

Gee, J., Hull, G., & Lankshear, C. (1996). *The new work order: Behind the language of capitalism*. Sydney: Allen and Unwin.

Hargreaves, D. (1994). The new professionalism: The synthesis of professional and institutional development. *Teaching and Teacher Education, 10*(4), 423–438.

Ingvarson, L. (1998). Teaching standards: Foundations for professional development reform. In A. Hargreaves, A. Lieberman, M. Fullan & D. Hopkins (Eds.), *International handbook of educational change*. Netherlands: Kluwer.

Louden, W. (2000). Standards for standards: The development of Australian professional standards for teaching, *Australian Journal of Education, 44*(2), 118–134.

Mahony, P., & Hextall, I. (2000). Reconstructing teaching: Standards, performance and accountability. London: Routledge/Falmer.

Millett, A. (1997). Letter to Providers, 26 June London: TTA.

National Board for Professional Teaching Standards (1996). About the National board: what teachers should know and be able to do: Introduction. Retrieved December 5th, 2003 from http://www.nbpts.org/standards/intro.html

Power, M. (1999). *The audit society: Rituals of verification*. Oxford: Oxford University Press.

Ramsay, G. (2000). *Quality matters: Revitalising teaching: Critical times, critical choices*. Report of the Review of Teacher Education, New South Wales.

Sachs, J. (2003a). *The activist teaching profession*. Buckingham: Open University Press.

Sachs, J. (2003b). *Teacher activism: Mobilising the profession*. Plenary Address presented to British Education Research Association conference, Herriot Watt University, Edinburgh. September 11–13.

Sergiovani, T. (1998). Markets and community strategy for change: What works best for deep changes in schools. In A. Hargreaves, A. Lieberman, M. Fullan & D. Hopkins (Eds.), *International handbook of educational change*. Netherlands: Kluwer.

Shore, C., & Wright, S. (2000). Coercive accountability. In M. Strathern (Ed.), *Audit cultures*. London: Routledge.

Smyth, J., Dow, A, Hattam, R. Reid, A., & Shacklock, G. (2000). *Teachers' work in a globalizing economy*. London and New York: Falmer.

Strathern, M. (Ed.). (2000). *Audit cultures*. London: Routledge.

Teacher Training Agency (TTA) (1998). *Initial teacher training: Performance profiles*. London, TTA.

Tom, A. (2000). *Teacher education reform in the United States: Thrusts, assumptions and implications*. Paper presented to Symposium 'Repositioning Teacher Education', The University of Sydney, Australia.

30

TRIAGE OR TAPESTRY? TEACHER UNIONS' WORK IN AN ERA OF SYSTEMIC REFORM[1]

Nina Bascia
Ontario Institute for Studies in Education of the University of Toronto, Canada

Teacher unions – also known as federations, associations, and teachers' professional organizations – are part of the educational landscape of many countries. The extent to which they have made substantive contributions to educational policy-making corresponds to the authority teachers have had, historically, to shape the terms of their own practice. Recently, as public educational governance has been radically altered in many jurisdictions, teachers' organizations – and teachers themselves – have been further sidelined from influencing educational policy directions (Bascia, 1999; MacLellan, 2002). In Britain and New Zealand, for example, teachers' organizations were essentially outlawed when the sweeping reforms of the past decade and a half significantly changed the locus of educational decision-making. Though they have returned, their influence and roles are not the same as they had been. Several Canadian provinces have recently reduced teacher association purview and membership rights. In the U.S., public relations between policy makers and teachers' organizations seems to have recently fallen to an all-time low as the federal Secretary of Education called one of the two national teachers' unions a "terrorist organization." Beyond this, currently prevalent policy directions – centrally-driven large-scale reforms that emphasize standards for teaching and learning and accompanying accountability mechanisms – de facto challenge organized teachers' participation in shaping policy and practice by enshrining what had previously been negotiable in central legislation.

While much of this section of the Handbook focuses on the substantive domains of current teaching policy, this chapter emphasizes the politics-in-practice of reform, describing emerging trends in the roles teacher unions play in Canadian and U.S. efforts to improve the quality of teaching. While teachers' organizations are typically absent from teacher policy analyses (except when they are viewed as obstructive to improvement), this chapter focuses in particular on the organizational strengths that teacher unions possess, their unique contributions to teaching policy, and the challenges they face. It does so by presenting and contrasting two broad conceptions of systemic reform in support of improving teacher quality, one of which can be characterized as "triage" and

International Handbook of Educational Policy, 593–609
Nina Bascia, Alister Cumming, Amanda Datnow, Kenneth Leithwood and David Livingstone (Eds.)
© 2005 *Springer. Printed in Great Britain.*

the other as "tapestry." When held up to a standard of reform as triage, teacher unions appear to provide little that is relevant. Considered in relation to a notion of systemic reform as a tapestry of efforts, on the other hand, teacher unions appear to provide several unique and important functions within the larger educational policy system.

Most educational policy research has viewed unions as not quite legitimate decision makers, at best benign or irrelevant but frequently obstructive, rarely visionary, and tending to promote mediocrity. There is not much empirical research on unions' roles relative to educational quality, and much of the reform research has ignored unions or attempted to make do with scant evidence. The few policy documents that have noted unions' productive reform efforts (e.g., National Commission on Teaching & America's Future, 1996) are encouraged by a handful of cases of innovation rather than being able to report on more widespread trends. Research that has focused specifically on teacher union activities and priorities has presented a somewhat different picture of these organizations, as potentially productive contributors to policy and practice whose efforts are constrained by a range of factors. In particular, researchers have noted that unions are limited by the bureaucratic tendencies of the educational system itself (Johnson, 1983, 1984), by the legal parameters of collective bargaining (Carlson, 1992; Larson, 1977), and by the difficulty of fairly representing a membership with diverse priorities and occupational needs (Bacharach & Mitchell, 1981; Bascia, 1994, 1998, 2000; McDonnell & Pascal, 1988). Even when unions attempt to overcome these limitations, they encounter difficulties in maintaining effective, proactive positions within policy systems where they have little formal authority and where policy directions change with some frequency (Bascia, 1994; Bascia, Stiegelbauer, Watson, Jacka, & Fullan, 1997; Johnson, 1987; Kerchner & Koppich, 1993; Kerchner & Mitchell, 1988).

This chapter draws upon over a decade of research on teacher unions' roles in educational reform (Bascia, 1994, 1998a, 1998b, 2000, 2003, in press; Bascia et al., 1997; Lieberman & Bascia, 1990), focusing on recent attempts by organizations in the U.S. and Canada to improve teacher quality within the context of current reform directions. Some of this research (e.g., Bascia et al., 1997; Lieberman & Bascia, 1990) was commissioned on behalf of union organizations concerned about their ability to improve the quality of educational practice. Other studies (e.g., Bascia, 1994, 2000, 2003) were part of larger research projects that explored the relative impact of a variety of influences on teaching quality. (The stronger tradition of policy and program evaluation in the U.S. extends to teacher organizations themselves; most of the Canadian studies were initiated by researchers rather than organizations and funded by competitive research grants.) Rather than providing a "snapshot" of union activities in relation to particular reform initiatives at a particular time, as most union reform research has done, the chapter is a longer term assessment of unions' efforts by comparing contemporary activities with those reported across several decades. The unions described in this chapter reflect a broader range in terms of their reputations for reform; the degree to which they have initiated, supported and/or resisted reform; their size, organizational complexity, and resource bases; their ability to convincingly articulate comprehensive reform strategies; and the depth, range, and coherence of their reform efforts. Each, however, has demonstrated an increased commitment to improving the quality of teaching in recent years (some are leaders in this regard); and each has been constrained in its reform efforts by common features of current reform preferences.

In the past two decades, the notion of "systemic" large-scale, centrally-driven reform has driven educational policy making not only across the U.S. but also internationally (Ball, 1998; Earl, Bascia, Hargreaves, Watson, & Jacka, 1998; Whitty, Powers, & Halpin, 1998), but it is neither a timeless nor a static concept. Emerging from some U.S. policy analysts' dissatisfaction with piecemeal, incremental reform efforts of the 1970s, 80s and early 90s, "fragmented authority and multiple short-term and often conflicting goals and policies" (Smith & O'Day, 1990, p. 238; see also Timar, 1989) that failed to significantly improve educational practice, the concept of systemic reform identified policy levers that might ensure "successful school workplaces for teachers and students" (Smith & O'Day, 1990, p. 236). Smith and O'Day argued that, in the U.S., states were the most critical policy actors in turning around poor teacher quality and unsuccessful schools because states have constitutional responsibility for educational funding. The equitable distribution of resources and "alignment among key elements of the system" (Knapp, 1997, p. 230) were seen as both necessary and requiring centralized control. Specifically, many (though not all) of the domains identified by policy analysts as crucial to improving teaching quality – teaching standards, licensure requirements, and curriculum and student assessment mechanisms – are more readily addressed by centralized efforts. Such thinking can become tautological: Knapp (1997), for example, noted that systemic reform efforts tend to focus on assumptions about which "aspects of teaching ... are most reachable by policy action" (p. 232). This, in effect, is a "triage" approach to reform.

Where Smith and O'Day argued that centrally-driven, large-scale policy was the most effective way to ensure teacher quality, *What Matters Most: Teaching for America's Future* (National Commission on Teaching and America's Future, 1996), another highly influential U.S. document, focused on naming specific policy domains – for establishing professional standards for teaching, improving teacher education and ongoing professional development, teacher recruitment and retention, establishing a career continuum in teaching, and reorganizing schools in ways that focus resources more directly on teaching activities. *What Matters Most* cautioned that such strategies are mutually reinforcing and must be undertaken simultaneously: "The first step is to recognize that these ideas must be pursued together – as an entire tapestry that is tightly interwoven. Pulling on a single thread will create a tangle rather than tangible process" (p. vii).

The "tapestry" metaphor invoked in *What Matters Most* does more than assert that multiple aspects of educational improvement be addressed all at once. It builds upon notions, which emerged in the U.S., Canada, Australia and other countries in the mid to late 1980s, that a range of institutional players had both the right and the responsibility to shape and support educational reform (Bascia, 1996; Ogawa, 1994; see also Sachs' chapter in this volume), that experimentation is useful and that building capacity – of individual educators, school organizations and staffs, and school systems – is a necessary prerequisite to bringing about and sustaining educational improvement.

As many other chapters in this handbook illustrate, systemic reform increasingly has emphasized the primacy of standards and accountability measures; mandates rather than capacity building have been the policy instruments of choice (see McDonnell & Elmore, 1987); and the role of the state and the authority of formal administrative positions rather than networks of support. "Alignment of key elements of the system" and "those aspects of teaching [which] are most reachable by policy action" (Knapp, 1997, p. 232) have become the primary focus of policies intended to improve teacher quality. Early advocates for systemic reform argued for the development of locally appropriate responses to state policy, for a harnessing of local, experimental, diverse reform strategies, "the energy and professional involvement of the second wave reforms [combined] with a new and challenging state structure to generalize the reforms to all schools" (Smith & O'Day, 1990, p. 234). But both reduced public spending for education and the loss, over the past several years, of both teaching and system competence as a generation of seasoned educators has retired, have contributed to the streamlining of policy systems we have come to equate with systemic reform. The convergence of tighter educational budgets and the centralizing tendencies of systemic reform have resulted in fewer resources, less diversity and experimentation, an emphasis on traditional roles and activities for educators (teachers teach, administrators evaluate), reporting systems that emphasize accountability rather than bi-directional or lateral informing, a policy system that emphasizes standardization rather than allowing for contextual diversity, and an infrastructure that is lean on support for teaching. This "triage" model of reform sums up pertinent features of the current policy context that are significant in terms of how teacher unions must operate. Like most models, it creates both possibilities and constraints.

Holding Teacher Unions up to a Standard

Two fundamentally divergent tendencies, consistent with the "triage" and "tapestry" metaphors, have shaped the histories of Canadian and U.S. educational systems: their centralizing, hierarchical natures, on the one hand, and on the other hand their capacity to respond to and include an expanded range of participants through democratic governance structures. Teacher unions have both contributed to and been affected by the recurring tensions between these two tendencies. Educational historians have described how the establishment of large urban educational systems about a century ago created a new bureaucratic order organized hierarchically and governed by administrative "experts" who claimed the authority to tell teachers, for the first time, what and how to teach (Darling-Hammond, 1997; Prentice & Theobald, 1991). One enduring result of the educational systems' architectural plan has been that this power structure has been hard-wired in, so to speak: the dominant status of administrators has been maintained, while the involvement of teachers in educational policy making has been more tenuous and less pervasive (Carlson, 1992). At the same time, these bureaucratic structures have frequently been contested by teachers and others; teacher unions first emerged in response to the establishment of school system apparati of the 19th and early 20th centuries (Gitlin, 1996; Larson, 1977; Murphy, 1990; Smaller, 1991; Urban, 1982).

The most common standard to which teacher unions have been held, since their inception, is the degree to which their priorities are congruent with prevailing policy directions and administrative preferences. Teachers' organizations became established members of the establishment in Canada through provincial Education Acts between the 1930s and 1940s. In the U.S., their involvement did not become significant until the 1960s and 70s, as state after state passed legislation enabling collective bargaining; the literature emerging during this period first raised concerns about the challenges unions might pose to district- and school-level administrative discretion (Englert, 1979; Johnson, 1983, 1984; Kerchner & Mitchell, 1986; Russo, 1979; Simpkins, McCutcheon, & Alec, 1979; Williams, 1979).

In a comprehensive assessment of U.S. teacher union activity with respect to educational reform in the 1980s, McDonnell and Pascal suggested that unions could take three possible stances toward reform: they could oppose or resist policies "that challenged their traditional interests, adapt to this new set of circumstances and accommodate various reform options espoused by others, or play an active role in shaping new approaches to teacher policy" (1988, p. 16). The news media and most policy researchers are highly critical of teacher unions because they essentially assume that compliance or alignment should be the standard by which these organizations' actions are judged. While they are not a common topic of policy research, when they do attract attention, they are often viewed as focused on irrelevant issues, such as increasing teacher salary even in tight fiscal contexts, and with promoting bureaucratic solutions rather than promoting quality teaching and learning. Unions are portrayed as lacking legitimate authority and out of touch with what really matters – which in turn makes it difficult for union staff and officials to establish credibility and work proactively within the educational policy system. A recent review of teacher union research in the U.S. publication *Education Week* concluded that "[r]egardless of where they stand, one thing unites the few researchers who actually study unions and the many commentators who have an opinion on them: everyone wants them to change" (Bradley, 1996).

A body of evidence emerging over the past decade and a half suggests that the tapestry metaphor might provide a useful way of assessing teacher unions' efforts with respect to educational reform than triage. That is, in a model of reform requires the leadership and involvement of multiple players within the larger educational system, teacher unions could be assessed according to their unique advantages and constraints relative to other organizations and the extent to which they contribute to educational systems' capacity to support quality teaching and learning. As *What Matters Most* (1996) noted, while teacher unions contribute to some of the counterproductive aspects of educational practice, they are not solely responsible for them; further, it suggested that unions had also been responsible for many gains in teacher quality:

> [Traditional bargaining agreements] have sometimes established or continued conditions that are inimical to change. As contracts have evolved within school bureaucracies and have mirrored the systems in which they are embedded, many have come to include rules that are restrictive during a time of reform. The same is true of many federal, state and local regulations, whose roots in old systems and procedures can be frustrating when changes are sought. ... Although it doesn't make nightly news, teacher groups have often been at the forefront of the movement to improve schools and enact greater quality assurances in teaching. (1996, p. 56)

Teacher Unions and the Current Reform Context: New Ways of Working

To a great extent, teacher unions' effectiveness is shaped by formal educational policy system parameters. States and provinces have and execute their authority to define and redefine the purview and authority of teacher unions. Legal frameworks determine whether collective bargaining is permitted and by what terms it will be carried out. In schools, at the district level, and with respect to the policy-making processes of the state, the substantive involvement of union members (teachers), staff and elected officials in decision making is conditional, subject to the willingness of administrators and elected officials to consider their "advice." While labour laws can be modified and the productivity of working relationships between union staff and decision makers certainly vary, the basic terms of union involvement restrict them from participating as equal or even consistently effective partners in educational decision making (Bascia, 1998b; Carlson, 1992; Humphries, 2001; Larson, 1977). Frequent changes in administrative and state/provincial leadership tend to divert at least some of unions' organizational energy away from sustained attention to reform as personnel work to establish their credibility with new decision makers (whose views of unions often follow commonplace assumptions about their illegitimacy and irrelevance) (see Bascia, 2003; Bascia et al., 1997).

With states and provinces claiming their right to set teaching and learning standards, to hold educators accountable and to control educational spending, it would appear that there would be little space for the less formal influence of teacher unions at state or district levels. Coupled with reduced interest in program innovation, where unions have been particularly active with respect to new forms of support for teaching, there would seem to be fewer available opportunities for teacher leadership. Such trends ultimately may be borne out: a stronger administrative structure with reduced purview for local decision making as well as state-level innovation could result in less proactive reform activity on the part of teacher unions. Indeed, some union organizations have become more reactive and/or defensive in their approaches (Bascia, in press). But many other teacher organizations attempt to deliberately compensate for the formalization of the educational system: they reject simplistic, reactive and idealistic positions in favor of more nuanced and generous responses. While McDonnell and Pascal's (1988) typology of union actions as resistant, accommodating or initiating with respect to reform is conceptually useful, many unions incorporate elements of all three positions as they attempt to mitigate against, influence, enrich and/or change the larger educational policy system. They do this by not only challenging but also working around and compensating for some of the prevailing features of the current reform movement: by investing in partnerships and relationships and thereby reducing their own marginalization vis-a-vis the formal administrative structure; by providing intellectual and resource capacity to the educational system to challenge the prevailing "triage" approach to reform; and by attempting to balance increased centralization and the primacy of the formal authority structure by working across levels and locales.

Investing in Partnerships and Relationships

Teacher unions increasingly work strategically with others in the educational system to not only initiate but also to sustain coherent and comprehensive reform. In the U.S., at the local level, the establishment of (or at least the attempt to establish) substantive labor-management is increasingly common. For example, in a study of several U.S. unions conducted between 1999 and 2002, the Washington Education Association supported local affiliates with training in collaborative rather than adversarial bargaining, and when local officials request assistance resolving a school- or district-level conflict, state association staff focused their efforts on identifying the substantive root of the problem rather than laying blame. In New York City, the United Federation of Teachers (UFT) staff worked with school, community school district and Board of Education staff to tailor professional learning programs and targeted intervention initiatives (for instance, in schools having difficulty complying with federal and state special education regulations, and for schools on state probationary review which must make serious efforts to improve their educational programs or face the prospect of being shut down). The UFT and the Alberta Teachers' Association (ATA) in Canada also exemplify trends by some teachers' organizations in both countries of working with parents, both at the organizational level through joint lobbying and collaborative initiatives and by providing a range of ways for parents to become more knowledgeable and more actively involved in their children's education. A number of teachers' organizations in both countries have been strengthening and reestablishing relationships with university schools of education to foster joint responsibility for ongoing teacher development (see Bascia, in press).

Some teacher unions reach out to schools' communities by helping support the formation of school-community partnerships. The UFT had a dedicated staff person developing sustained relationships with school-parents – through a range of learning opportunities so parents can support their children through greater understanding and involvement in their homework; through involvement with teachers and other educators through school-based Teacher Centers; and by attempting to develop a strategic alliance between the UFT and organized parent groups such as the PTA. An idea promoted by the National Education Association in the U.S. and adopted by teachers' organizations in both countries involves communications units in focused public awareness campaigns in support of public education.

Contributing to the Educational Infrastructure

As organizational players in their respective educational contexts, many teacher unions actually have provided system capacity by providing fiscal and human resources for new initiatives (or to keep existing practices from being decimated). An increasingly common example of this trend lies in the area of professional development for teachers and others (see Bascia, 1998a, 2000, 2003, 2004). Where educational funding has been reduced and local jurisdictions have been unable to provide adequate workshops, courses, induction support, school-based professional learning strategies to help teachers improve their classroom performance – to address new curriculum and teaching standards and to improve the academic success of low-performing students – teachers' organizations have attempted to make up the difference. And where educational policy has focused professional development resources exclusively on improving teachers' classroom performance, unions have expanded their array of professional development offerings to help teachers, principals, parents and other educational partners understand and interact more effectively in the broader educational milieu – in school, district and community settings – that they understand as providing crucial support for classroom teaching.

In the U.S., the WEA is a good example of union contribution to educational infrastructure (see Bascia, 2003). Its staff, many of whom had worked for other state educational agencies in the past and could call upon longstanding relationships and working knowledge, had several strategies for continuing their work within the state policymaking infrastructure: for example, its lobbyist met weekly with lobbyists from other state agencies; it sponsored collaborative projects, such as legislation with other agencies such as Washington State's Office for State Public Instruction, and then provided training and support for new teacher assistance, peer assistance and review programs; it conducted research for other state and district organizations; and it staffed and provided funding for a statewide network of regional professional education advisory boards that will develop and deliver locally appropriate professional development for educators. The WEA conducted research not only for its members, and not only with respect to collective bargaining; it actually established a database to track variations across districts and over time on local factors that otherwise would not be kept, since the state does not do so. The WEA also ensured the human resources necessary to ensure the development of regional professional learning agencies – plans which involved not only WEA staff and members but staff from the state department of education.

In Canada, the ATA exemplifies trends evident in both countries for not only assuming aspects of support for educational delivery that otherwise would not be available, but also asserting its own preferences for reform (see Bascia, in press). While other teachers' organizations in both countries have argued that it is the formal system's responsibility to support teachers' work, the ATA has perceived such gaps as opportunities to challenge provincial government primacy. For example, supporting the province's interest in site-based decision-making but finding neither models nor technical assistance forthcoming from the ministry of education, the ATA developed informational packets and training for school staffs. When the government mandated a new teacher evaluation scheme, it was the ATA that became the official source of information, essentially endorsed by the government, by seeking and winning the contract for training, essentially defining their purpose and content. Similarly, when the government legislated school councils in the mid-1990s, the ATA chose to support the plan and, with the assistance of other stakeholders including the Alberta Home and School Council Association, it developed the official resource manual and training for school council participants, essentially managing to determine the shape of this reform.

Beyond their capacity for immediate response and support for daily practice, teacher organizations appear to serve as test-beds for certain kinds of innovations that might take years of planning and strategic work to come to fruition (see also Bascia, 1998a). Professional development options, and in particular support for beginning teachers (through induction, mentor teacher and peer review programs), are obvious examples of initiatives that originated in union organizations, at the instigation of members, officials or staff, and have come to be seen as necessary supports for teaching. Many other, less obvious and less visible examples exist: curriculum initiatives, and peer mediation and other anti-violence programs, represent district-specific efforts to improve classroom and school practices (Bascia, 1998a, 2000, 2004). At the policy level, working ideas into and through the legislative process may take many years. Such long-term efforts are only visible by looking within union organizations and examining the work educators have done, sometimes over many years, to keep particular goals or programs alive even and especially when there is little interest or support elsewhere in the formal educational system.

A final way that teacher unions provide infrastructural support is by creating opportunities for educators to develop skills and relationships and learn the workings of the larger educational system. Because unions work and enable work in so many locations and levels, and because at least to some extent educators can work through union organizations on initiatives of their own

design, these informal learning opportunities (see Bascia, 2000) extend possibilities for leadership development beyond what is available within the formal
administrative hierarchy. This learning and growing sense of possibility for the
work of individual teachers as well as groups of educators can enrich the
educational system.

In all of these ways, teacher unions participate in shaping educational policy
and practice by both helping define the content of reform and providing educators and other involved groups with skills training and information to help them
increase their competence within the larger educational system.

Dealing with Increased Centralized Control

As formal educational authority has become more centralized over the past
decade, with states and provinces asserting legislative control over educational
practice through funding formulas, curriculum standards, accountability mech-
nanisms, and licensure requirements, it would seem reasonable to expect that
teacher union activity would also concentrate at the state level, particularly in
terms of attempts to influence the content of legislation. Influence and access to
central decision making bodies is increasingly crucial to teacher unions, and
local teachers' organizations that can afford it will tend to hire their own
lobbyists rather than working exclusively through the state teachers' organization. But rather than only mirroring the recent centralizing tendencies of the
formal system, at least some teacher organizations have continued developing,
refining and expanding their range of relationships and strategies in ways that
contrast with and in some ways compensate for these trends in the larger policy
environment.

Unions have attempted to enhance their roles as conduits between their own
members and formal educational systems and, simultaneously, as vehicles for
teachers, administrators, parents and others to expand their skills, information,
and ability for understanding and acting effectively in the current educational
system. These efforts can be seen in the expansion of their communications units
and publications efforts, the growing array of their research initiatives, and in
their attempts to reach out to and work with other organizations and staff on
an ever-increasing range of offerings.

Some teacher unions also try to compensate for the hierarchical, centralized
nature of authority in the educational system through the working patterns and
portfolio assignments of staff. In traditional union organizations, staff associated
with professional development, collective bargaining and other organizational
priorities interact with distinctly different groups and constituents (government
officials, administrators, "teacher leaders," teachers in trouble) and maintain
distinctly different views of the world. Similar to teachers in secondary schools
or other complex organizations, differences in the world views of staff in different
units of teacher unions can result in a rich program of organizational "products,"
but they can also result in inadequately informed decision making and costly
internal turf wars (see Bascia, 2000). Some union organizations deliberately

attempt to compensate for these balkanizing tendencies: staff who interact with legislators and state and district agencies may also spend part of their time in the field, working with teachers in classrooms and other work settings. They may travel around their states or districts to learn what is occurring in multiple educational contexts, to ensure that they are visible and that their programs work and are appealing in a wide variety of settings (see also Bascia, in press). Perhaps even more significantly, staff may take care to distribute information about problems and innovations from the field across the organization through a range of deliberate organizational processes, including complex portfolios for individual staff members, cross-unit job-sharing, frequent and routine debriefing sessions, and efforts to build equitable and mutually informing relationships between short-term elected officials (who come from the field) and long-term dedicated staff.

Another strategy favored by some teachers' organizations is to provide a variety of non-mandatory offerings from which local organizations (district-level unions, schools) and individual teachers can choose and fashion to suit their local contexts and needs. Even while state policies have become more standardized and compulsory in their intent, some teacher unions seem to have taken to heart the lessons of program evaluation research: just as with reforms promoted through the formal educational system, no single union reform initiative is attractive, meaningful, and effective across a group of teachers of any diversity. This represents a change from unions' tendency, in recent decades, like many state and district agencies, to identify a single reform and place unreasonable hopes in its potential for educational improvement (see Bascia, 1994, 1996, 1998a, 2000; Bascia et al., 1997). The strategy of providing a "menu" of diverse and flexible options (see Hargreaves, 1994) may be the result of union staffs' awareness of the growing bimodal distribution of teachers (veterans and brand new teachers) as well as of differences in student populations and teaching conditions across urban, suburban and rural areas. A typical example of this menu approach is a wide range of professional development options for teachers (including not only topic but also timing, location, pedagogical structure, and unit to be addressed – individual teacher vs. whole school staff).

These deliberate strategies by some of the teacher unions challenge and contrast with the hierarchical, standardizing, triage model of reform and support delivery in effect across the country. Interviews with union officials and staff suggest that they represent conscious attempts to compensate for the reduction of system capacity of in recent years.

Teacher Unions' Substantive Contributions to the Tapestry of Reform

While prevailing opinion views teacher unions as uncommitted to educational improvement, research that has focused directly on their efforts suggests a somewhat different picture – of organizations concerned about educational quality as it is manifested in and through teachers' work. This concern may be evident even when the directions unions choose appear to contradict prevailing policy preferences. While there has been much of a speculative nature written about the negative impact of union presence on educational practice, most actual empirical research has revealed a more nuanced picture, with union officials attempting to establish productive working relationships with district and school administrators and to compensate for the limitations of the educational bureau- cracy (Kerchner & Mitchell, 1986; Johnson, 1983, 1984, 1987). Starting in the second half of the 1980s, Charles Kerchner and colleagues Douglas Mitchell and then Julia Koppich first articulated and then supported unions in adopting a stance of "joint stewardship" for educational reform (Kerchner & Mitchell, 1988; Kerchner & Koppich, 1993) by trading adversarial for cooperative practices and working with decision makers to support local school reform (Bascia, 1994; also Lieberman & Bascia, 1990; Rosow & Zager, 1989). These ideas became influential in both the U.S. and Canada among teacher unionists. Empirical studies that followed described both changes in local governance to involve union leaders and members in substantive decision making and various reforms in support of increased teacher quality, such as school- and district-level support, innovation in initial teacher education, teacher recruitment and retention, and a wide range of professional development strategies (Bascia, 1988a; Bascia et al., 1997; Johnson, 1988; Murray & Grant, 1998; Martin Macke, 1998).

Kerchner and Mitchell's assertion, in the late 1980s, that teacher unions were entering a new phase of their evolution, moving beyond organizing, contract maintenance and adversarial relationships to cooperation and reform-minded- ness may have been a bit overly confident – evaluation research (e.g., Bascia et al., 1997; Lieberman & Bascia, 1990) has revealed the fragility of these new arrangements and the enduring, intractable nature of major union concerns. But there is also some evidence to support Kerchner and Mitchell's claims that these organizations are evolving, or are at least different from the ways most of the literature has portrayed them. Within many organizations are individuals who have read the research critical of teacher unions and are concerned about their organizations' capacities to respond effectively to a changing reform climate. As an organizational type, teacher unions are becoming more interested in and able to initiate and support innovation.

Teacher organizations' major activities are actually consistent with many of the recommendations identified by the National Commission on Teaching and America's Future report (1996) especially with respect to teacher recruitment and retention; reinventing teacher preparation and professional development; and ensuring that school workplaces support teaching and learning (Bascia, in press). Union efforts in these domains suggest that these organizations may be more than the recalcitrant "dinosaurs" as they are viewed in much of the policy research. The work that has been done in these areas, particularly with respect to attraction and retention and professional development, in some cases are in the forefront of reform development. Some teacher unions appear to be contribut- ing substantively, at various levels and locations of the educational system, on a range of initiatives, large and small, to influence policy, provide technical support, and to assume responsibility for various aspects of the larger educational enterprise that they view as inadequate or unaddressed.

This is, of course, an aggregate assessment. No single organization possesses either the intellectual or resource capacity to cover all the bases. While such reform-mindedness is a general trend, each does this work in a particular way, to a greater or lesser degree, with varying degrees of success. While unions have been viewed as platforms for "enlightened" or "short-sighted" union leaders, it is important to consider the organizations' roles as political players in the larger policy making environment of districts and states or provinces (Bacharach & Mitchell, 1981). Such analyses help explain the extent of teacher unions' effectiveness in promoting teacher quality.

Teacher unions do not function in a vacuum; they work within the larger educational milieu. Not only do social, legal and fiscal realities shape unions' work; even more fundamentally, they must contend with what might be called the operative discursive or conceptual framework that underlies current educational policy goals. Two sets of related notions seem especially germane to how deeply and effectively unions can contribute to educational reform. The first pertains to prevailing thinking about teaching and teachers; the second focuses more specifically on assumptions about teacher unions themselves.

As noted earlier, the prevailing model of systemic reform emphasizes centralized state control and a strengthened administrative structure, standards, and policies that emphasize compliance, and reduced funding for education and a significant turnover within the teaching force. This model and these conditions have emerged from but also have reinforced a conception of teaching as technical work and teachers as technicians (see Bascia & Hargreaves, 2000; Darling-Hammond, 1997). This conception of teaching stands in sharp contrast with the prevailing assumptions embedded in the reforms of the later 1980s, which viewed teaching as intellectual work. Expectations that good teaching is a matter of obedience and compliance, and that poor teaching is the result of resistance, deny the possibility of both informed judgement by teachers and the importance of the quality of teachers' working conditions – fiscal and human resources, professional relationships, opportunities to learn, and so on.

When a technical conception of teaching prevails, teachers' concerns as expressed through their unions are viewed as insubordination or irrelevance. Further, when a technical conception of teaching prevails, unions must necessarily focus on attempting to improve basic conditions. Related to prevailing conceptions of teachers are assumptions about the actual and potential roles of their organizations. The limits of teacher unions' legal purview contribute to a view of these organizations as labor- rather than professionally-oriented (see Carlson, 1992; Larson, 1977; Mitchell & Kerchner, 1983). In Canada, where provinces have comparable authority to US states over educational policy and where "triage" reform is also the current model, teachers' organizations have recently lost significant ground with respect to the terms and purview of bargaining and their roles in helping shape provincial education policy (Bascia, 1998c; 2002, in press). Some have actually managed to claim high moral ground and to take advantage of emerging gaps in service delivery to shape the nature of school programs (developing curriculum, providing professional development and even defining the terms of school based management frameworks). But others have responded in increasingly reactive ways, urging teachers to refuse to comply with government mandates, offering fewer supports for teaching, and engendering increased tensions with the public as well as with their members. The tensions experienced by such organizations suggest that possessing sufficient internal capacity to "take the high road" with respect to educational reform is necessary, but it is not sufficient in policy settings where teacher unions are extremely disadvantaged relative to the power of the formal administrative hierarchy.

Summing up: Teacher Unions' Contributions to Educational Policy and Practice

Recent research on teacher organizations in Canada and the U.S. reveals that these organizations are more deeply and broadly involved in educational reform, and in improving teacher quality in particular, than previous studies have suggested. To a greater or lesser extent, these diverse organizations – large and small, with reputations for reform and with reputations for resistance to reform – demonstrate a commitment to involvement in improving the quality of teaching and learning by investing in relationships with administrators, policy makers and others, and by supporting and initiating a range of reform projects. Their ambiguous insider-outsider roles encourages them to both attempt to influence the formal educational system and to compensate for it through a variety of informal mechanisms.

Their capacity to conceptualize and work to implement programs and practices to improve teacher quality by challenging, supporting, and initiating reform strategies – taking stock of current conditions and filling in or compensating for inadequacies in support for teaching quality – suggests that it is useful to think about unions' value as contributing to a "tapestry" of reform. It suggests that the "triage" model of reform which currently drives educational policy making and practice may not be appropriate or adequate for judging unions' contributions to reform. Further, it suggests that the familiar dichotomy between union support for traditional "bread and butter" or "professional" concerns is not necessarily the best way to assess whether unions are on the right track. A more productive standard might be the extent to which teacher unions can persuasively articulate the positive relationship between teaching and learning quality such that policy makers and administrators in the greater educational system are persuaded to work with them rather than against or in spite of them.

Teacher unions that accomplish this work do so through a series of deliberate organizational strategies that involve staff with diverse skills in ongoing relationships with other players in the educational environment. Such unions invest organizational effort into ensuring their ability to continue to be responsive to changing conditions in the realms of practice and policy making. Their intellectual and resource capacities as organizations make important differences in their ability to carry out this work. Changing notions about teaching, teachers and teacher unions prevailing in the larger educational environment also have strong effects on their success. Over at least the last couple of decades teacher unions have contributed substantively to the capacity of the educational system at classroom, school, district, state and national levels, in ways that are particularly salient during an era of reduced funding and infrastructure support for education. Their ability to do this is somewhat tenuous where and when teachers experience inadequate support from the system as a whole.

Teacher unions are not uniform in their goals, abilities, or successes; indeed, their strength lies in their ability to respond to changing conditions, to recognize gaps and to invent new solutions, and in their two-way relationships with their teacher-members and policy makers. It might be useful, however, to spell out the unique contributions they make and could make: they are sites for creativity and innovation, for professional learning, and for developing and fostering educational leadership for individuals and for educational systems. They also serve a corrective function, a reality check when policy and practice lead to reduced support for teacher quality. The multiple functions teacher unions provide are critical to educational improvement.

Note

1. This chapter is drawn from a longer report of the same name produced for the Center for the Study of Teaching and Policy at the University of Washington (Document R-03-1), June 2003, and funded by the Office of Educational Research and Improvement (OERI) of the U.S. Department of Education. Additional research was supported by the National Education Association in the U.S., the Connaught Fund of the University of Toronto, and the Social Sciences and Humanities Research Council (SSHRC) of Canada. The author wishes to thank Ann Lieberman and Julia Koppich for their thoughtful comments on the longer report.

References

Bacharach, S. B., & Mitchell, S. M. (1981). Interest group politics in school districts: The case of local teachers' unions. In Samuel B. Bacharach (Ed.), *Organizational Behavior in Schools and School Districts* (pp. 495–526). New York: Praeger.

Ball, S. (1998). Big policies, small world: An introduction to international perspectives in Educational policy. *Comparative Education, 34*(2), 119–136.

Bascia, N. (1994). *Unions in teachers' professional lives: Social, intellectual and practical concerns.* New York: Teachers College Press.

Bascia, N. (1996). Caught in the crossfire: Restructuring, collaboration, and the "problem" school. *Urban Education, 31*(2), 177–198.

Bascia, N. (1998a). Teacher unions and educational reform. In A. Hargreaves, M. Lieberman, Fullan & D. Hopkins (Eds.), *International Handbook of Educational Change.* The Netherlands: Kluwer.

Bascia, N. (1998b). Teacher unions and teacher professionalism: Rethinking a familiar dichotomy. In B. Biddle, T. Good & I. Goodson (Eds.), *International handbook of teachers and teaching.* The Netherlands: Kluwer.

Bascia, N. (1998c). Collective bargaining under fire. *Orbit*. Toronto: OISE/University of Toronto, 19–21.

Bascia, N. (2000). The other side of the equation: Teachers' professional development and the organizational capacity of teacher unions. *Educational Policy, 14*(3), 385–404.

Bascia, N. (2001). Do teacher unions have demonstrated potential to promote positive forms of pedagogical, curricular and organizational change that benefit student learning? *Journal of Educational Change, 2*(2), 65–70.

Bascia, N. (2003). Triage or tapestry: Teacher unions' contributions to systemic educational reform. Report prepared for the Center for Teacher Policy, University of Washington, and the Office of Educational Research & Improvement, US Department of Education, Washington, DC.

Bascia, N. (2004). Teacher unions and the teaching workforce: Mismatch or vital contribution? In M. Smylie & D. Maretsky (Eds.), NSSE Yearbook chapter.

Bascia, N. (in press). Learning through struggle: How the Alberta Teachers' Association maintains an even keel. In K. Church, N. Bascia & E. Shragge (Eds.), *Informal learning: Making sense of lived experience in turbulent times*. Waterloo, Ontario: Wilfred Laurier Press.

Bascia, N., & Hargreaves, A. (2000). The sharp edge of change. In N. Bascia & A. Hargreaves (Eds.), *The sharp edge of educational change: Teaching, leading and the realities of reform* (pp. 3–27). London: The Falmer Press.

Bascia, N., Stiegelbauer, S., Watson, N., Jacka, N., & Fullan, M. (1997). *Teacher associations and school reform: Building stronger connections*. External review of the NCI Learning Laboratories Initiative. Prepared for the National Education Association, Washington, DC Toronto: Ontario Institute for Studies in Education of the University of Toronto.

Bradley, A. (1996). Education's "dark continent." *Education Week*, December 4.

Carlson, D. (1992). *Teachers and crisis. Urban school reform and teachers' work culture*. New York: Routledge Chapman & Hall.

Darling-Hammond, L. (1997). *The right to learn: A blueprint for creating schools that work*. San Francisco: Jossey-Bass.

Earl, L., Bascia, N., Hargreaves, A., & Jacka, N. (1998). *Teachers and teaching in changing times: A glimpse of Canadian teachers in 1998*. Report prepared for the Canadian Teachers' Federation. Toronto: International Centre for Educational Change, Ontario Institute for Studies in Education of the University of Toronto.

Englert, R. (1979). Collective bargaining in public education: Conflict and its context. *Education and Urban Society, 11*(2), 255–269.

Gitlin, A. (1996). Gender and professionalization: An institutional analysis of teacher education and unionism at the turn of the Twentieth Century. *Teachers College Record, 97*(4), 588–624.

Hargreaves, A. (1994). *Changing teachers, changing times*. London: Cassell.

Humphries, S. (2001). Types of relations between states and organized teachers as exemplified in education reform. Unpublished doctoral thesis, Universite de Montreal.

Johnson, S. (1983). Teacher unions in schools: Authority and accommodation. *Harvard Educational Review, 53*(3), 309–326.

Johnson, S. (1984). *Teacher unions in schools*. Philadelphia: Temple University Press.

Johnson, S. (1987). Can schools be reformed at the bargaining table? *Teachers College Record, 89*(2), 269–280.

Johnson, S. (1988). Pursuing professional reform in Cincinnati. *Phi Delta Kappan, 69*(10), 746–751.

Kerchner, C. T., & Koppich, J. E. (1993). *A union of professionals: Labor relations and educational reform*. New York: Teachers College Press.

Kerchner, C., & Mitchell, D. (1986). Teaching reform and union reform. *Elementary School Journal, 86*(4), 449–470.

Kerchner, C., & Mitchell, D. (1988). *The changing idea of a teacher's union*. Philadelphia: Falmer Press.

Knapp, M. S. (1997). Between systemic reforms and the mathematics and science classroom: The dynamics of innovation, implementation and professional learning. *Review of Educational Research, 67*(2), 227–266.

Larson, M. S. (1977). *The rise of professionalism: A sociological analysis*. Berkeley: University of California Press.

Lieberman, A., & Bascia, N. (1990). *The trust agreement: A cooperative labor compact.* Report for the Stuart Foundations. Berkeley: Policy Analysis for California Education (PACE).

MacLellan, D. (2002). Two teachers' associations and the Ontario College of Teachers: A study of teacher and State relations. Unpublished doctoral thesis, University of Toronto.

Martin Macke, S. (1998). Teacher unionism: Back to the future. *Contemporary Education, 69*(4), 180–181.

McDonnell, L. M., & Pascal, A. (1988). *Teacher unions and educational reform.* Washington, DC: RAND.

McDonnell, L. M., & Elmore, R. (1987). Getting the job done: Alternative policy instruments. *Educational Evaluation and Policy Analysis, 9*(2), 133–152.

Murray, C., & Grant, G. (1998). Teacher peer review: Possibility of pipedream? *Contemporary Education, 69*(4), 202–204.

Murphy, M. (1990). Blackboard unions: The AFT & the NEA 1900–1980. Ithaca, NY: Cornell University Press.

National Commission on Teaching & America's Future (1996). *What matters most: Teaching for America's future.* New York: National Commission on Teaching & America's Future.

Ogawa, R. (1994). The institutional sources of educational reform: The case of school-based management. *American Educational Research Journal, 31*(3), 519–548.

Prentice, A., & Theobald, M. (Eds.) (1991). *Women who taught: Perspectives on the history of women and teaching.* Toronto: University of Toronto Press.

Rosow, J., & Zager, R. (1989). *Allies in education reform.* San Francisco: Jossey-Bass.

Russo, J. (1979). Changes in bargaining structures: The implications of the Serrano decision. *Education and Urban Society, 11*(2), 208–218.

Simpkins, E., McCutcheon, A., & Alec, R. (1979). Arbitration and policy issues in school contracts. *Education and Urban Society, 11*(2), 241–254.

Smaller, H. (1991). A room of one's own: The early years of the Toronto Women Teachers' Association. In R. Heap & A. Prentice (Eds.), *Gender and education in Ontario* (pp. 103–124). Toronto: Canadian Scholar's Press.

Smith, M., & O'Day, J. (1990). Systemic school reform. In S. Fuhrman & B. Malen (Eds.), *The politics of curriculum and testing* (pp. 223–268). Bristol, PA: The Falmer Press.

Timar, T. (1989). The politics of school restructuring. *Phi Delta Kappan, 71*(4), 264–275.

Tyack, D., & E. Hansot (1982). *Managers of Virtue: Public School Leadership in America, 1820–1980.* New York: Basic Books.

Urban, W. J. (1982). *Why teachers organized.* Detroit: Wayne State University Press.

Whitty, G., Powers, S., & Halpin, D. (1998). *Devolution and choice in education: the state, the school and the market.* Buckingham: Open University Press.

Williams, R. (1979). The impact of collective bargaining on the principal: What do we know? *Education and Urban Society, 11*(2), 168–180.

SECTION 4

Literacies

Section Editor: Alister Cumming

31

IMPROVING RESEARCH-POLICY RELATIONSHIPS: THE CASE OF LITERACY

Ben Levin
Government of Ontario and Ontario Institute for Studies in Education of the University of Toronto, Canada

Why and How Research Affects Policy[1]

Problems in the relationship between research and policy are often bemoaned, perhaps especially so in education. Researchers complain that the knowledge they generate is not read, understood or used by policy-makers, a problem that tends to be attributed to the malign influence of politics. Policy-makers, on the other hand (in which category I include politicians as well as senior officials) complain that research does not speak to the important problems they face, or is too qualified, inconsistent or unrealistic to be a useful basis for their work.

The argument is an old one, but it has taken on renewed importance in recent years as research has come to occupy a more prominent role in public discourse around policy in many areas.

The growing interest in research is supported by several developments in contemporary societies. More educated populations are more likely to be interested in what research might have to say. Programs in the media give increasing mention to research in various fields, even if the reporting of research may not always be as careful as might be wished. The phenomenal growth of the Internet and its increasing use by a wide range of people as a way to get current information on many different topics is another illustration of this interest. Governments are more likely than used to be the case to try to make the claim that their policies are supported by evidence. Research conjures up images of science and of objectivity, and thus has a particular kind of appeal to the public imagination.

In part the interest in research can be linked to a growing awareness of the complexity of the main problems that confront humanity (Homer-Dixon, 2000). Over the last few decades we have learned that issues of long-term significance are what Rittel and Webber (1973) called 'wicked problems' – they cannot be avoided and yet have no obvious solution. Under these circumstances we need

International Handbook of Educational Policy, 613–628
Nina Bascia, Alister Cumming, Amanda Datnow, Kenneth Leithwood and David Livingstone (Eds.)
© 2005 *Springer. Printed in Great Britain.*

to learn more if we are to be able to address these issues with any chance of success.

These trends apply to education, but education also has some particular characteristics that affect the role that research can play. Education is a value-laden activity, inextricably connected to our broadest aspirations for society. It embodies a wide range of purposes that are not always mutually consistent. People agree on educational goals only at the most general level, with many conflicts not only about goals but about desirable means of carrying them out.

Education also has less history of basing policy and practice on research than do some other fields, although it seems likely that each policy area thinks that other areas are doing better in this regard (personal communication with John Lavis, Canada Research Chair in health knowledge transfer, McMaster University). Many factors contribute to the particular status of research in education, including the relatively low status of teaching as an occupation, the relatively recent arrival of education as a field of study in the university, and the many different disciplines that contribute to the field (Lagemann, 2000). Because everyone has gone to school, professional knowledge about education is not seen to be as esoteric or specialized as knowledge in fields such as health or law or engineering.

In recent years there have been pointed criticisms of education research in several countries including Britain (Hargreaves, 1996; Hillage, Pearson, Anderson, & Tamkin, 1998), France (Prost, 2001), Australia (McGaw, Boud, Poole, Warry, & McKenzie, 1992), and the United States (Coalition for Evidence-Based Policy, 2002). To give a rather extreme example, a website closely linked to the U.S. Education Department (www.w-w-c.org/about.html) notes: "Our nation's failure to improve its schools is due in part to insufficient and flawed education research. Even when rigorous research exists, solid evidence rarely makes it into the hands of practitioners, policy-makers and others who need it to guide their decisions." While Canada has not had the same level of public debate about education research, discussions among education ministers and senior officials in which I have participated evidenced much unhappiness with the contribution of research, or at the least a strong sense that the contribution should be stronger than it is.

Despite the relatively poor reputation of education research one can point to many instances where research has played an important role in shaping policy and practice. Some examples include:

- Understanding the importance of children's early years in shaping their later success and the possibilities for interventions;
- Realizing the importance of parental and family interaction to children's development and education;
- Supporting the moving of children with disabilities from segregated settings into regular schools and programs;
- Learning about the number of students dropping out of school and the reasons for their doing so;

- Understanding the importance of assisting adults with low levels of literacy;
- Realizing both the importance of and difficulties in providing high quality professional development for teachers;
- Recognizing that much short-term training for the workplace has very weak payoffs;
- Revealing ways in which second language learners can best be helped to integrate into a new language and society; and
- Appreciating the link between good nutrition and ability to concentrate and learn.

Research in Australia (DETYA, 2000) and in the U.S. (Biddle & Saha, 2002) has found that very large majorities of school principals and policy-makers believe that their work is actively informed by research, though in a variety of largely indirect ways.

Efforts to improve links between research and practice are not new. The ERIC system and the network of regional educational labs in the U.S. have had a longstanding focus on issues of research impact, with considerable success in many areas. However partly as a result of the current criticisms, new interest in the role of research in education has developed (Davies, 1999; Levačić & Glatter, 2001), and various initiatives in this direction have been undertaken in recent years in education. The National Education Research Forum in England (www.nerf-uk.org) and the various initiatives under that umbrella are an excellent recent example of a thoughtful effort to improve the role of research. In Canada, important efforts have been made by the Social Sciences and Humanities Research Council of Canada (SSHRC) through programs such as the Community-University Research Alliances or the Initiative on The New Economy, through joint ventures with other agencies including the Council of Ministers of Education, and through changes in the regular research grants programs to give greater weight to what SSHRC calls 'knowledge mobilization'.

If research in education has in fact had substantial impact, why is there so much criticism of it? Part of the concern grows from the frequent assumption that there should be a direct line between research and subsequent policy and practice such that research findings point unambiguously to what governments, educators, or learners should do. There are many important questions of education policy and practice where research does not yet provide much guidance. Most of education is concerned with producing significant and lasting change in how people think or behave, yet on the whole we do not know very much about how to do this, either in schools or in other settings. Policy-makers are often faced with difficult alternative choices around how to use resources; again, research often has little to say about what choices are best. There are good reasons, conceptual and practical, for these limitations in research – to mention two, the issues are often very complex and the total education research effort is comparatively small – but the lack of clear direction is understandably frustrating for users.

At the same time, researchers have their own set of complaints about governments. Research in education is not well funded anywhere in the world, and certainly not in Canada (OECD, 2002), which makes it hard to produce substantive, reliable and timely results. Researchers may also feel that their work is disregarded if it does not fit the predispositions of decision-makers, or that it gets distorted to meet other political or bureaucratic needs. Like the criticisms of research by policy-makers, these a   have some truth to them.

Understanding the problems in relationship of research to policy is easier if one recognizes that researchers and policy-makers inhabit very different worlds, with different sets of incentives, constraints and pressures that shape their work. Although these two worlds do connect with each other in a variety of ways, they are also linked by another sector consisting of various people and organizations that are interested in using research to shape policy and practice. A model of research use, then, might usefully start with the idea of three different contexts – the context of research production, the context of research use, and the various mechanisms that act as links between these two settings. This conceptualisation is illustrated in Figure 1.

An important implication of this conceptualization is that the gaps and misunderstandings between researchers and users do not arise from people's faults, but from the realities of their contexts. Of course improvements can and should be made, but these efforts should start from a realistic understanding of why people act as they do and what kinds of changes might be possible.

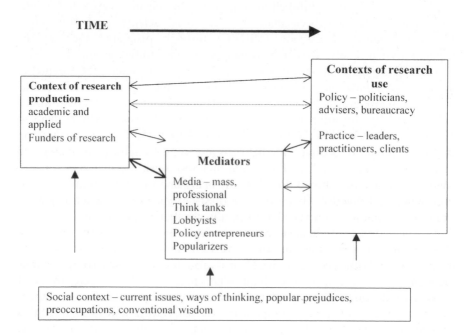

Figure 1.   Elements of Research Impact.

It is also important to recognize that the terminology around research impact is quite inadequate. The wording of 'producers' and 'users' is itself problematic in that it implies a one-way flow of information and a passive role on the part of 'users'. In reality people move back and forth among these three contexts, the relationships run in multiple directions, and so-called 'users' are not just passive recipients of the work of researchers but active constructors of knowledge and action in their own setting.

I will not in this paper talk about the context of research production, which is shaped largely by the mores, rewards and habits of the academic world. I want to focus instead on the world of government policy, which is where, in Canada, most of the important decisions about education policy are made.[2] To speak effectively and meaningfully to policy-makers, researchers must understand something of that world. The next section of this paper gives some description of the world of policy, followed by some suggestions on how the links between research and policy could be strengthened.

The Dynamics of Government[3]

A fundamental starting point is that the use of research – indeed, knowledge use in general – in government can only be understood as part of the overall process of government and especially the influence of politics. In my experience politics is an intensely rational activity. Politicians are no more self-serving or indifferent to knowledge than are researchers or civil servants. However the premises behind political rationality are not necessarily the same as those governing education or research. Understanding the use of research in government requires an understanding of the factors that affect elected governments. Although these descriptions arise largely from my own experience, they are also supported by a substantial literature on the dynamics of government (referenced more fully in Levin, 2005a).

Governments have Limited Control over the Policy Agenda

Although every government comes to office with a set of policy ideals or commitments, the reality is that much of what governments attend to is not of their own design or preference; governments have to be in whatever businesses people see as important. Government agendas are certainly shaped in part by political commitments, party platforms, and the views of key political leaders. Governments do try to keep a focus on meeting the commitments they made when elected. However they are also influenced, often to a much greater extent, by external political pressures, changing circumstances, unexpected events and crises.

As soon as a government is elected, various groups try to influence its agenda in accord with their own. This is in many ways the essence of the political process. It means that politicians are constantly bombarded with requests or demands to do things, stop doing things, increase funding, decrease funding, pass legislation, repeal other legislation, and so on. As people have become better educated and better organized, the number and intensity of the pressures on politicians has risen. Nor are people necessarily reasonable or consistent in their demands.

Unanticipated developments can also affect political agendas. When the unexpected happens, whether an economic downturn, a natural disaster, or some other new development, governments must respond in some way, even if that means taking attention and resources away from other activities that were high on the priority list. As Dror put it, there is "at any given moment a high probability of low probability events occurring. In other words, surprise dominates" (1986, p. 186). September 11, 2001 remains a perfect example of how many plans are rendered null by something unusual and unpredictable.

While some of the pressures on government relate to very important, long-term issues, others may concern small short-term details. However one cannot assume that the former will always be more important than the latter. Sometimes very small items can turn into huge political events. For example, a single instance of a problem can undermine an entire system that may actually be working reasonably well, as those working in health care or child welfare or immigration or corrections know only too well.

Governments are particularly susceptible to issues that take on public salience through the media (Levin, 2005b). As most people get their information about public events from the mass media, an issue that is played up in the media often becomes something that a government must respond to, even if the issue was no part of the government's policy or plan. Media coverage is itself motivated by a number of considerations, but long-term importance to public welfare is not necessarily one of them (Edelman, 1988). Indeed, novelty is an important requisite for the media in order to sustain reader or viewer interest, so that governments are likely to be faced with an ever-changing array of issues supposedly requiring immediate attention.

Insofar as research becomes an issue on the public agenda, it will necessarily be of concern to governments. The results of research, whether on a new health treatment or results of education tests or new data on crime rates can often become part of the public policy agenda, sometimes to the surprise of many including the researchers.

There is Never Enough Time

Governments are in some sense responsible for everything. Government leaders have to make decisions about a vast array of issues – from highways to the environment, from financial policy to education, from health to justice systems. And, as just noted, they are likely to face an unending set of pressures on their energy and attention. A cabinet member not only has responsibility for her or his own area of jurisdiction – which can itself be enormously complicated and fraught with difficulties – but is also supposed to participate in collective decision-making on a wide variety of other matters facing the government. Each issue has to be considered not only in terms of its substance, but from the standpoint of public attitudes and political implications. The nature of political life is such that there is no respite from these demands. A politician may leave her or his office, but almost every social encounter will also lead to new pressures or requests.

There is, consequently, never enough time to think about issues in sufficient depth. Some sense of this pace is captured in the TV program *The West Wing*, except that the real situation is generally more messy even than this portrayal, with more simultaneous demands and pressures being handled. Senior government leaders, both politicians and civil servants, work under tremendous time pressures, in which they are expected to make knowledgeable decisions about all the issues facing them within very short timelines and without major errors. This is impossible but it is nonetheless what we expect from our leaders.

The result is that important decisions are often made very quickly, with quite limited information and discussion. This is not because politicians necessarily like making hurried or uniformed decisions, but because this is what the office requires. The stress of multiple issues is one of the reasons that policy implementation tends to get short shrift. As soon as one decision has been made there is enormous pressure to get on to the next issue. Even with the best intentions, it is hard to get back to something from months ago to see how it is progressing, since so many other issues have meanwhile arrived on the doorstep demanding immediate attention.

Politics and Policies are Both Important

Everything in government occurs in the shadow of elections. Every government is thinking all the time about how to improve its prospects for being re-elected. Some people find this cynical, but it is hard to see what else politicians could do. After all, concern for re-election is at least partly about doing what most people want, and presumably we elect governments for precisely that purpose. A government that does not satisfy people will be tossed out most of the time. The British cabinet minister in the TV series *Yes Minister* understandably reacted with dismay when his chief advisor, Sir Humphrey, called for taking a courageous stand, since this meant doing something unpopular. We vilify our politicians for ignoring our wishes, so we can hardly be surprised if they go to great lengths to try not to offend.

At the same time, governments are often genuinely concerned about the results of their actions and policies. They do want to fulfill their commitments to voters, and programs and policies are the means of doing so. Moreover, a mistaken policy can create very large political costs.

There is, to be sure, a cynical side to the concern with public perception in that governments sometimes do attempt to manipulate public opinion, give the perception of action even when they are not doing much, and focus on image rather than substance. Rhetoric is a vital part of politics (Levin & Young, 2000), and government statements of intention cannot necessarily be taken at face value. Governments can and do use research as one of the vehicles to support their rhetoric, something that may become more common as the prominence of research increases.

People and Systems Both Matter

Much of what a government does is shaped by the individuals who happen to occupy critical positions, regardless of their political stripe. Any political party is likely to contain a wide range of views and positions; to put it in statistical terms, the within-group variance in ideas in a party is likely to be quite a bit larger than the variance between one party and another. So the individuals who come to hold certain positions are important. Some ministers carry quite a bit of weight in Cabinet and can get their way on important issues, while others have difficulty getting their colleagues to support any major policy thrust. Some politicians are intensely pragmatic and willing to reshape policy in light of changing pressures or public preferences, while others are deeply committed to particular values and work hard to promote and implement a course of action over years even in the face of substantial opposition. Some Cabinet ministers or key political operatives may be ignorant or even dismissive of research while others understand and use it well.

The nature of government systems also matters. The roles of various departments and central agencies, the relative power of individual ministers vis a vis central government, the way in which issues come to Cabinet and the kind of information that accompanies them, are all important in shaping the way policies are constructed and delivered. Some governments or agencies have given a prominent role to research units. For example, in Canada Statistics Canada and the (recently disbanded) Applied Research Branch of Human Resources Development Canada have both played important evidence-based policy roles. Where such functions are institutionalized there is more potential for research to be available when needed and in an appropriate form. Insofar as research has public credibility it will also tend to have more cachet with politicians.

A Full-time Opposition Changes Everything

Imagine how your work might change if there were people whose full-time job it was to make you look bad. Imagine also that they could use less than scrupulous means of doing so and that there was a tendency for people to believe their criticisms ahead of your explanations. Might that not change the way you went about your work?

Yet that is precisely the situation facing every elected government. Oppositions are there to oppose. They will work hard to show how government actions are wrong, venal, or destructive. In doing so they will not always be particularly concerned with balance or fairness in their accounts. Research is also used by the opposition to support its political stance, which is one reason governments are not always anxious to do or publish empirical work. As a minister once said to me in refusing to release research reports done by my unit, "You don't ask a dog to fetch the stick you use to beat it."

While many people decry negativity in politics, politicians use this strategy not necessarily because they like it, but because they think it works. If conflict is what attracts public attention, then conflict is what politicians will create, since public attention is what they must have. A politician friend once told me that he got far more publicity and recognition from a certain public relations gesture that he knew was rather narrow than from any number of thoughtfully articulated policy papers, so the public relations gesture would continue. The problem is that over time an emphasis on the negative can certainly increase voter cynicism and thus worsen our politics.

Beliefs are More Important than Facts

Researchers are often convinced that policy ought to be driven by research findings and other empirical evidence. From a political perspective, however, evidence is only one factor that shapes decisions, and it will often be one of the less important factors. I have had politicians tell me on various occasions that while the evidence I was presenting for a particular policy might be correct, the policy was not what people believed, wanted or would accept. As Bernard Shapiro, whose extensive experience includes a stint as Ontario Deputy Minister of Education, put it, "All policy decisions are made by leaping over the data." (Remarks at the Conference on Policy Studies, University of Calgary, May 10, 1991).

For politicians, what people believe to be true is much more important than what may actually be true. Beliefs drive political action and voting intentions much more than do facts. Witness the strength and depth of public support for various measures that clearly fly in the face of strong evidence. Many people continue to believe in capital punishment as a deterrent for crime, or that welfare cheating is a bigger problem than income tax evasion. Others are convinced that amalgamating units of government saves money, or that free tuition would substantially increase accessibility to post-secondary education for the poor, or that retaining students in grade will improve achievement even though in all these cases a strong body of evidence indicates otherwise. Where beliefs are very strongly held political leaders challenge them at their peril. As Marcel Proust put it,

> The facts of life do not penetrate to the sphere in which our beliefs are cherished ... they can aim at them continual blows of contradiction and disproof without weakening them; and an avalanche of miseries and maladies coming, one after another, without interruption into the bosom of a family, will not make it lose faith in either the clemency of its God or the capacity of its physician. (*Swann's Way*)

Just as problematic is that people do not have to be consistent in their attitudes, either across issues or over time. As Arrow pointed out long ago, public preferences do not necessarily line up in rank order (1970). The same people who demand more services from governments may also demand lower taxes. Those who in one year argued vehemently in favor of reduced government spending might the following year be just as impassioned when pointing out the negative consequences of the reductions. People can and do hold inconsistent beliefs, but political leaders must do their best to accommodate these inconsistencies in some way.

Not everything in government is subject to all these constraints. The reality is that given the number of issues any government must handle at any time, only a few will be high enough on the political or public agenda to get significant time and attention from ministers and political staff. Many activities of government are not of much public interest unless something dramatic happens. Few people pay attention to the management of water quality until someone gets sick or dies. The scope for research to influence policy may be as great or greater for issues that are not high on the political radar screen (Levin & Wiens, 2003). However as soon as an issue gets onto the public agenda, it will be of interest to politicians and all the problems noted will apply. On most other issues civil servants will play an important or even decisive role in shaping what a government does. Politicians and civil servants live in quite different environments (Levin, 1986). As a result, although they sometimes work closely and well together, at other times there can be substantial distrust with each party feeling that the other is ignorant and wrong-headed.

Knowledge Use and Agenda Setting

Despite all these constraints, governments do set agendas and take actions. Kingdon (1994) described political agendas as being created from the intersection of political events, defined problems and possible solutions. When the right mix of the three comes together, political action follows.

Political events might include such elements as timing in the electoral cycle, changes in individuals in key roles, or unusual events that create a political requirement to respond. Defined problems can come from many sources. Many groups, including a whole range of lobby and service organizations, work actively to create the perception that a particular issue requires political action. The media can play a critical role in noting, or even advocating, some condition as constituting a problem. One can easily list such diverse examples as spousal abuse, taxation levels, global warming or international trade as issues where active campaigns were undertaken to convince voters and politicians that some action was needed.

Definition of a problem also requires the generation of solutions. People are much more disposed to act on problems when they see the possibility of doing something that is feasible and will make a difference. Solutions are advanced by the same set of actors who try to define problems. In fact, much of the promotion of problems is done in order to generate support for a policy solution (Stone, 1997). At the same time, people who may share the view that something is a problem can also differ enormously in regard to the best solution. Everyone would agree that establishing good literacy skills is a vital goal, but the strategies people advocate for achieving that goal differ considerably, from stressing particular reading problems to focusing on family literacy and early childhood, to believing that more testing is the answer.

Research plays a part in defining both problems and solutions. However its role in both cases is largely mediated through third parties. Research comes to policy-makers indirectly, through the civil service, through the media, or through the work of people and organizations who make it their business to try to influence policy by using research. These latter are sometimes known as knowledge brokers or policy entrepreneurs (Mintrom, 2000).

Third parties recognize what many researchers do not – that the impact of an idea depends on its public salience more than on its empirical validity. That is why the main route for research to have impact is through its entry into the ongoing public debate on ideas and policies. If we look back at the list of areas where research has had a positive impact, it is clear in every case that the impact occurred over many years, and that research mattered not because a minister read a study and acted on it, but because ideas that were once seen as outlandish gradually came to be seen as desirable or even as conventional wisdom – and vice versa.

That process does not happen by accident. It is almost always the result of sustained effort by many people who realize that to affect public policy you have to enter into the political process in some way. Usually this work is not done by researchers but by policy advocates. Sometimes researchers themselves take on the role of advocate but more often they either rely on others or they simply provide the work – even unknowingly – that is adopted and used by others, with or without their approval.

Doing policy relevant research, or trying to link research to policy has its dangers.

In French the same word – 'politique' – is used for policy and for politics, a useful reminder that policy is part of the political world. As a struggle for power, politics is often a particularly ruthless business. Naïve researchers – or even those who are not so naïve – can get badly burned when they find their work being used to support a political position or argument that they find inappropriate or even disreputable.

Implications for Literacy Policy

The ideas developed in this paper suggest some general implications for the relationship between research and policy, and some particular slants for literacy policy.

The description above suggests several lines of action to improve the links between research and policy. One line is to improve the research production side so that research findings are communicated more clearly and effectively in a variety of ways, and so that policy-makers are more aware of what research is being done and what conclusions are being drawn. Some indication of steps in this direction has been given earlier, but much more could be done – a subject for another paper. A second line involves building stronger links between researchers and policy-makers through a whole variety of means, including face to face and other forms. It is also important to ask who the key users of research would be, and what are the barriers that prevent stronger connections?

We tend to focus on what researchers should do differently, but even if Canada produced the best research in the world, many of our key user organizations, including governments, have very limited capacity to find, understand and apply the research. For example very few school boards have any research use capacity and many of the umbrella provincial and national organizations, such as those of school boards or school administrators, also run shoestring operations. Finally, there is inadequate appreciation of the role of third parties in the research impact process. Those interested in better links between research and practice need to recognize that working with third parties is a critical part of the effort.

Literacy issues present some particular challenges and opportunities in linking research to policy. Literacy remains a very high profile policy concern in Canada, and one that is by no means limited to education. There is strong continuing interest in learning more about how to improve literacy levels. However this will not happen simply by researchers telling policy-makers what we have learned.

Although researchers are gradually achieving a degree of consensus on many aspects of literacy education, we should not expect the public or our political leadership to be aware of or understand this consensus any time soon. As already mentioned, it can take years for research results to become widely known and accepted even under relatively good conditions. These conditions include active champions and proponents on the issue who are well connected or effective in the public and political arena as well as synergies between the ideas being proposed and existing or emerging conventional wisdom. The further from current thinking a new idea is, the harder it is to get purchase in the public mind and therefore to have an impact on policy.

In the case of literacy, the situation is difficult for at least three reasons. First, twenty years of the 'reading wars', with heated debate over issues such as phonics vs whole language, have left many parents as well as policy-makers feeling confused about what might be true. Since much of the confusion was stirred up, or at least exacerbated, by vigorous if not vicious arguments among researchers, there is less willingness to believe researchers when they now claim to have reached agreement on some of the main points of contention. The heated debate in the United States over the recent National Reading Panel report (e.g., Coles, 2003) shows that these issues are by no means resolved.

Second, because early literacy involves important questions about the future of children, it is also a subject that will rouse strong emotions. People will be reluctant to take a gamble with something new even if it is widely recognized that current practice is not satisfactory, because the cost of mistakes is so high.

New research findings will take time and careful dissemination before they will be credible. Governments are likely to move very cautiously on this front until and unless they sense broad public support for a particular course of action. Moving public opinion in this area will also not be easy and will require sustained effort by a range of actors. Much of the discussion of these new results will have to occur through third parties such as parent groups and organizations of educators.

Third, research on literacy comes from a variety of disciplines and perspectives, ranging from neurology to psychology to pedagogy to architecture. The Canadian Learning and Literacy Research Network (www.cllrnet.ca), a very important vehicle for Canadian research in this area, brings together more than 100 researchers in a wide variety of fields who do not necessarily agree even on the important questions let alone on the answers to them. All these disciplines can make important contributions to our knowledge, but the multiplicity of perspectives is confusing to lay audiences.

Research impact is also affected by the degree of structure that already exists in a given area of policy or practice. The better established current practices are, and the larger the network of groups and organizations tied into those practices, the harder it will be to change them and, generally, the more reluctant policy makers will be to try. Elementary school teaching of reading, for instance, is a longstanding practice that is difficult to change even when a substantial effort is made (Earl, Watson, Levin, Leithwood, Fullan, & Torrance, 2003). Literacy advocates will need to think about the areas where interest is likely to be high and resistance relatively low.

Two areas connected to literacy development seem to be promising candidates for policy action. One of these is early childhood. We have an increasing understanding of the powerful impact of early childhood experience on literacy (developed more fully in Levin, 2003b). Aspects of children's experience such as their nutrition, health and housing are important to eventual literacy but currently substantially disconnected in policy terms from efforts to improve literacy. Early childhood also offers institutional and political possibilities for change that are in many ways more promising than those related to schools. Because the sector is less developed, there is much less institutional inertia and resistance to experimenting or to changing policies and practices in this area. Public acceptance of the importance of equity in early childhood care is also likely to be stronger than in some other areas of education. The broad interest in work done by the OECD (OECD, 2001) shows the growing importance of early childhood in national policy, an importance that is due in no small measure to effective promotion of the findings of research (e.g., McCain & Mustard, 1999).

Another area that seems highly attractive is family literacy efforts, which seem to be both important and not very controversial (e.g., Logan, Peyton, Read, McMaster, & Botkins, 2002). The efforts that have been made in this direction are still quite small in scale despite quite a bit of suggestion that this is an area where the return on investment could be quite high (Earl et al., 2003). Nor are there yet well established organizations and patterns of provision that might inhibit a bolder approach.

There are undoubtedly other areas related to literacy in which there is strong potential for research to shape policy. The key thing is for researchers to think strategically about where the chances are greatest to influence policy, and to focus on those areas.

Conclusion

One should not be unrealistic about what is possible in the relationship between research and policy. Research will never replace politics, nor should it. Although research findings are important, we also know that they are not immutable, and that in some cases yesterday's certain knowledge has turned out to be today's reprehensible practice. Research will never be more than one part of what political decision-makers need to take into account in making decisions, and given a conflict between what researchers say and what the population believes, the latter will almost always be the winner.

At the same time, I remain an optimist about the potential contribution that research can make to policy and practice in education in the near future. We are only beginning to think about how this might be done and to try various strategies. Doubtless some of these strategies will turn out to be unproductive, but over time we are certain to learn more about what works under what conditions. With sustained effort research can help improve policy and therefore outcomes for children and families. Research may never be the complete guide to policy and practice in literacy or any other area, but there is no doubt that it can play a more important role than it currently does.

Endnotes

1. Much of the work on which this paper was based was done as a Visiting Scholar for the Social Sciences and Humanities Research Council of Canada in 2002–03. I thank Marc Renaud, President of SSHRC, for the opportunity to undertake this work, and many other colleagues at SSHRC and elsewhere who helped me think about these issues. I also thank many colleagues in the Government of Manitoba and other governments during my time as Deputy Minister, who helped deepen my understanding of the realities of that world. However all ideas, interpretations and errors are solely mine and nothing in this paper should be taken as representing the policy or opinion of SSHRC or any other organization. The ideas in the first section of this chapter are developed more fully in Levin (2003a).
2. School boards are another important site for education policy making. The political dynamics around school boards are different from those I will outline here in some important respects, which is why I do not focus very much on them.
3. This section provide a brief discussion of issues about government and its relationship with education that are developed more fully in my book, *Governing education* (Levin, 2005a).

References

Arrow, K. (1970). *Social choice and individual values* (2nd edition). New Haven, CT: Yale University Press.

Biddle, B., & Saha, L. (2002). *The untested accusation: Principals, research knowledge, and policy making in schools.* Westport, CT: Ablex.

Coalition for Evidence-Based Policy (2002). Bringing evidence-driven progress to/ education. Report to the US Department of Education, November, 2002. www.excelgov.org.

Coles, G. (2003). *Reading the naked truth: Literacy, legislation and lies.* Portsmouth, NH: Heinemann.

Davies, P. (1999). What is evidence-based education? *British Journal of Educational Studies, 47*(2), 108–121.

Department of Education, Training and Youth Affairs (DETYA) (2000). *The impact of educational research.* Canberra: DETYA.

Dror, Y. (1986). *Policy-making under adversity.* New Brunswick, NJ: Transaction Books.

Earl, L., Watson, N., Levin, B., Leithwood, K., Fullan, M., & Torrance, N. (2003). *Watching and learning 3: Final report of the OISE/UT evaluation of the implementation of the National Literacy and Numeracy Strategies.* Prepared for the Department for Education and Skills, England. http://www.standards.dfes.gov.uk/literacy/publications.

Edelman, M. (1988). *Constructing the political spectacle.* Chicago: University of Chicago Press.

Hargeaves, D. (1996). Teaching as a research-based profession: possibilities and prospects. Teacher Training Agency Annual Lecture. London: TTA.

Hargreaves, D. (1999). Revitalising educational research. *Cambridge Journal of Education, 29*(2), 239–250.

Hillage, J., Pearson, R., Anderson, A., & Tamkin, P. (1998). *Excellence in research in schools.* London: Department for Education and Employment/Institute of Employment Studies.

Homer-Dixon, T. (2000). *The ingenuity gap.* New York: Knopf.

Kingdon, J. (1994). *Agendas, alternatives and public policies* (2nd edn). New York: HarperCollins.

Lagemann, E. (2000). *An elusive science: The troubling history of education research.* Chicago: University of Chicago Press.

Levačić, R., & Glatter, R. (2001). 'Really good ideas?': Developing evidence-informed policy and practice in educational leadership and management. *Educational Management and Administration, 29*(1), 5–25.

Levin, B. (2003a). Connecting research to policy and practice. Paper presented to the Canadian Society for the Study of Education, Halifax. Available at http://home.cc.umanitoba.ca/~levin/what %27s_new.htm.

Levin, B. (2003b) Approaches to equity in policy for lifelong learning. Paper prepared for the OECD. Available at http://home.cc.umanitoba.ca/~levin/what %27s_new.htm.

Levin, B. (2005a). *Governing education.* Toronto: University of Toronto Press.

Levin, B. (2005b). Government and the media in education. *Journal of Education Policy, 19*(3), 271–284.

Levin, B. (1986). Uneasy bedfellows: Politics and programs in the operation of government. *Optimum, 17*(1), 34–44.

Levin, B., & Young, J. (2000) The rhetoric of educational reform. *International Journal of Comparative Policy Analysis, 2*(2), 189–209.

Levin, B., & Wiens, J. (2003). There is another way. *Phi Delta Kappan, 84*(9), 658–664.

Logan, B., Peyton, T., Read, C., McMaster, J., & Botkins, R. (2002). Family literacy: A strategy for educational improvement. Washington: National Governors Association. www.nga.org/center/divisions

McCain, M., & Mustard, J. F. (1999). Early years study. Toronto: Publications Ontario.

McGaw, B., Boud, D., Poole, M., Warry, R., & McKenzie, P. (1992). Educational research in Australia: Report of the review panel of research in education. Canberra: Australian Government Publishing Service.

Mintrom, M. (2000). *Policy entrepreneurs and school choice.* Washington: Georgetown University Press.

OECD (2001). *Starting strong: Early childhood education and care.* Paris: OECD.

OECD (2002). Educational research and development in England: Examiners' report. Paris: OECD. CERI/CD(2002)10.

Prost, A. (2001). *Pour un programme stratégique de recherche en éducation. Report to the ministers de l'Éducation nationale et de la Recherche.* Report of the working group named by M Prost. Paris: Ministère de l'Éducation nationale.

Rittel, H., & Webber, M. (1973). Dilemmas in a general theory of planning. *Policy Sciences 4*, 155–159.

Stone, D. (1997). *Policy paradox.* New York: Norton.

32

LITERACIES IN EARLY CHILDHOOD: THE INTERFACE OF POLICY, RESEARCH, AND PRACTICE

Dorothy S. Strickland
Rutgers, the State University of New Jersey, USA

In Early Education, Social Policy is Educational Policy

Interest in early education as a key determinant to school readiness has steadily increased in recent years. There is good reason for this. Research demonstrates that early learning experiences are linked with later school achievement, emotional and social well-being, fewer grade retentions, and reduced incidences of juvenile delinquency and that these outcomes are all factors associated with later adult productivity (Barnett, 1995; Yoshikawa, 1995).

> Long before children knock on the kindergarten door, during the crucial period from birth to age five, when humans learn more than during any other five-year period, forces have already been put in place that encourage some children to shine and fulfill their potential in school and life while other forces stunt the growth and development of children who have just as much potential. (Hodgkinson, 2003, p. 1)

While Hodgkinson was speaking of children in the United States, the same could be said of young children no matter where they live.

It is impossible to talk about young children without discussing social policies that effect their families. For example, high mobility among children is frequently cited as a factor contributing to poor academic achievement. According to Lee and Burkam (2002), of the 281 million people who live in the U.S., 43 million move each year, the highest known migration level of any nation. Low-income young children move more often than their middle-income peers. Hodgkinson (2003) gave an example of two states within the United States, Pennsylvania and Florida, that serve vastly different clientele in terms of transience. The high level of transience in one of these states makes it extremely difficult to provide services for a rapidly changing clientele:

International Handbook of Educational Policy, 629–644
Nina Bascia, Alister Cumming, Amanda Datnow, Kenneth Leithwood and David Livingstone (Eds.)
© 2005 *Springer. Printed in Great Britain.*

Eighty percent of the people who live in Pennsylvania were born there, making education and health care easier to provide since the client group is very stable. But in Florida, only 30% of the residents were born in the state. Large number of teachers may start and end the year with 24 students, but 22 of those 24 are different from the students they welcomed the first day of school. The same could be true for daycare centers. A daycare center in Pennsylvania will be a more stable place in terms of child and staff turnover than a similar center in Florida. Transience is a reality we cannot afford to ignore. (Hodgkinson 2003, p. 4)

In many countries early childhood education and care exists within "the deeply embedded tradition of using public policy to promote the healthy development of children" (Knitzer, 2001, p. 81). This is true in many European countries, such as Sweden, Finland, Norway, France, and Italy. On the other hand, the United States and the United Kingdom share many similarities in their approach to early care and education. Americans have conflicting views about the role of the federal government in both providing – and paying for the early care and education of children (Cohen, 2001; Knitzer, 2001). In the United Kingdom, child care – particularly for children aged three and under – is the financial responsibility of parents, and takes place in private nurseries or family daycare provider settings. The U.K. government does fund state-maintained primary schools, but these settings only provide full-time education to four and five-year olds in Scotland, England, and Wales, because these ages mark the beginning of compulsory schooling for young children in the U.K. (Aubrey, David, Godfrey, & Thompson, 2000). In both countries, there is increased awareness of the need to address both educational and social policies in order to effect useful change (as reported by Ackerman & Martinez, 2002).

A review of early childhood education and care policy across twelve post-industrial, "information-age" countries suggests that the term "early childhood education and care" (ECEC) includes all arrangements providing care and education for children under compulsory school age, regardless of setting, funding, open hours, or programme content (Organization for Economic Co-operation and Development, 2001). This framework reflects the growing consensus in the participating countries (Australia, Belgium [Flemish and French communities], the Czech Republic, Denmark, Finland, Italy, the Netherlands, Norway, Portugal, Sweden, the United Kingdom, and the United States) that "care" and "education" are inseparable concepts and that quality services for children necessarily provide both (p. 14).

In the United States, the increased focus on early education has largely centered on young children's literacy development and its relationship to success in beginning reading. The Committee on the Prevention of Reading Difficulties in Young Children (Snow, Burns, & Griffin, 1998) recommended that "all children, especially those at risk for reading difficulties should have access to early childhood environments that promote language and literacy growth and that address a variety of skills that have been identified as predictors of later reading achievement" (p. 8).

The contribution of *early care and education* (ECE) to the cognitive develop-ment and school success of children who are economically and socially disadvan-taged has become a vital public issue (Barnett, 1998). Concern about lagging academic achievement among poor children has led policy makers and educators to increase their efforts to foster early literacy development. Strong early literacy programs are viewed as a means to bridge the gap in educational achievement between those who are succeeding and those who are not. For poor children, access to early literacy is often tied to opportunities for early care and education. For all children, but particularly for poor children, it is impossible to talk about policies associated with early literacies without talking about the social context in which children live. Regardless of where children live, social policies and educational policies are highly interdependent. Childcare policies are often related to other social and family policies, and public involvement in childcare is linked to more comprehensive policy goals (Cochran, 1993).

Early Literacies: Attention and Contention

Increased emphasis on preschool literacy education has brought attention to the content and the processes by which young children are educated in early child-hood settings. Historically, early childhood education has centered on children's physical and social development. Oral language and reading aloud to children were central to most curricula, but there was a virtual aversion to anything that might be construed as "pushing" children before they were "ready." Getting children ready to read was left to the end of kindergarten or during the beginning of first grade. During this period, children were engaged in a variety of explicit "reading readiness" activities including letter identification, letter-sound relation-ships, and a variety of visual-perceptual tasks (Galda, Cullinan, & Strickland, 1993).

During the latter part of the twentieth century, a convergence of early literacy research caused many researchers and educators to rethink their ideas about how young children learn and develop literacy. Research by Clay (1975, 1982, 1991), Dyson (1982), Holdaway (1979), and Teale and Sulzby (1985), among others, helped to spawn an emergent literacy perspective on young children's literacy learning that emphasized the young child's ongoing development of skill in reading and writing from infancy. An *emergent literacy perspective* offers several important understandings about the nature of children's literacy learning and the educational environment needed to support it. These include:

(1) *Literacy learning begins early in life and is ongoing.* It does not wait for kindergarten or first grade. Starting from infancy, the informal and playful things that adults do to promote children's language and literacy really count.
(2) *Learning to read and write is a developmental process.* Although language and literacy is ongoing from infancy, the activities in which children engage differ according to their age and maturity.

(3) *Literacy develops concurrently with oral language.* What children learn about listening and talking contributes to their ability to read and write. Language and literacy work together.

(4) *Learning to read and write are social and cognitive endeavors.* Young children need to talk, move about, sing, and generally interact with others as they learn.

(5) *Children are active participants in the processes of learning language and literacy.* Literacy activities for young children need to be meaningful and purposeful to them and appropriate to their age and development.

(6) *Storybook reading, particularly family storybook reading, has a special role in young children's literacy development.* Shared book experiences and the verbal interactions they promote help to broaden children's knowledge of print and their background knowledge.

(7) *Learning to read and write is nurtured by responsive adults.* Adults provide the social and educational contexts that support learning. They act intentionally as they plan opportunities for age appropriate literacy activities.

(8) *Literacy learning is deeply rooted in a child's cultural milieu and family communications patterns.* What children have already learned at home can be used to build literacy experiences (Galda, Cullinan, & Strickland, 1993, pp. 75–76).

Research associated with the term "emergent literacy" has been expanded by a growing body of investigations into the development of early literacy skills in children ages zero to five. The work of Yopp (1992), Dickinson and Tabors (2001), Goswami (2001), Richgels (2001), and Torgesen, Morgan and Davis (1992), among others, took a closer look at some of the skills and abilities possessed by young children that might predict later reading outcomes. Specific abilities in oral language, phonological awareness, letter recognition, and concepts about print began to emerge as key areas of attention for research on literacy development and the "early literacy predictors" to reading success. In the United States, a National Early Literacy Panel (NELP) was formed to conduct a synthesis of the scientific research regarding the development of early literary skills in children, ages zero to five, including parental and home effects on that development (National Center for Family Literacy, 2003). The stated purpose of that review is to "contribute to education policy and practice decisions that affect early literacy development and the role of teachers and families in supporting children's language and literacy development" (p. 1).

The growing body of understandings about young children's literacy development is consistent with new findings from brain research. The 1990s brought an unprecedented number of studies on the brain, causing it to be termed the "decade of the brain" (Wolfe & Brandt, 1998, p. 8). Perhaps one of the most important findings is that "our environment, including the classroom environment, is not a neutral place. We educators are either growing dendrites or letting them wither and die. The trick is to determine what constitutes an enriched environment" (p. 11).

New findings about early brain development that provide insights into early literacy development include: (1) how a brain develops hinges on a complex interplay between the genes a person is born with and the experiences the person has; (2) early experiences have a decisive impact on the architecture of the brain and on the nature and extent of adult capacities; (3) early interactions do not just create a context; they directly affect the way the brain is "wired"; (4) brain development is non-linear. There are prime times for acquiring different kinds of knowledge and skills; (5) by the time children reach age three, their brains are twice as active as those of adults. Activity levels drop during adolescence (Families & Work Institute, 1997, p. 18).

Ramey and Ramey (1998, 2000) proposed a conceptual framework for understanding human development, which they call *biosocial developmental contextualism*. They interpret children's development as occurring within a complex and dynamic system in which the environments in which children are reared play a major role in their development. Biology and experience are not pitted against each other but rather are conceptualized as reciprocal and interdependent processes that influence development. They contend that deeply held beliefs that success in life is largely determined by genetic predispositions and individual factors may adversely influence society's investment in children.

Conceptual frameworks such as *emergent literacy, biosocial developmental contextualism*, and the growing body of research detailing *early literacy predictors to reading success and school readiness* provide the research base for thinking about early literacy curriculum and instruction. Together, with the existing research on overall child development, these constructs offer much needed guidance to educators and policy makers as they seek to shape early childhood education policy for young children.

Early Literacies and the Curriculum

The new understandings, described above, about young children's early literacy development have been widely embraced by the research community and by early literacy teacher educators, but they have been slow to find their way into the curricula of the early childhood classroom. Well trained in child development but less so in early literacy, many early childhood educators have expressed concern about emphasizing reading and writing too early with young children. Often, the notion of early literacies is construed to mean direct instruction of the alphabet, tracing letters, and heavy duty phonics instruction, rather than an intentional focus on children's meaningful encounters with print and in guiding them in talk about print encounters both in and outside of school in their daily lives.

In the midst of this ambivalence, several key policy reports and literacy initiatives in the United States (e.g., Snow, Burns, & Griffin, 1998; No Child Left Behind, 2001) have criticized current early childhood curricula as being inadequate in terms of cognitive development and support for language and literacy. Head Start has been the recipient of much of the concern (Bowman, Donovan, & Burns, 2000). Early childhood programs, particularly those serving the poor, are generally viewed as inadequate in producing school-ready children capable of succeeding academically. The call for strengthening the academic curriculum has been met with both applause and dismay. Some embrace the idea of rethinking the curriculum to better integrate language and literacy throughout the day. Others express grave concerns about curriculum imbalance. Head Start advocates remind us that its original mission stressed the physical, social, and emotional welfare of children and their families. And, they add, Head Start has had success in this area (Bowman, Donovan, & Burns, 2000). Advocates of balanced, developmentally appropriate practice, also remind us that cognitive development is only one part of the equation (Strickland & Barnett, in press; see chapters by Pressley and by Willows, this volume).

The need to better articulate what it means to provide an early childhood curriculum that fosters a print-rich environment, oral language development, phonological and phonemic awareness, concepts about print, knowledge of the alphabet, and writing related behaviors, using approaches that are appropriate to the age and maturational development of children is at the heart of the controversy surrounding curriculum. Indeed, the controversy and discontent surrounding curriculum issues may lie more with the means than the goals. Brief descriptions of each curriculum component follows:

A print-rich environment is one in which print is displayed in ways that are meaningful and purposeful where children are actively involved in its use.

Oral language curriculum goals include the development of children's listening and speaking vocabulary and their ability to engage in conversations that extend beyond the here and now. Children are helped to build capacity to initiate and respond appropriately in conversation and discussions with peers and adults.

Phonological awareness is a broad term that includes *phonemic awareness*, the ability to hear, identify, and manipulate the individual sounds – phonemes – in spoken words. Phonological awareness also refers to oral work involving rhymes, words, and syllables.

Concepts about print include the notion that print involves meaning, the concept of letters, words, and directionality.

Alphabet knowledge involves the identification of the letters of the alphabet.

Writing-related activities involve children in observing adults write for specific purposes and participating in that process to the extent that they are capable. Children are given opportunities to use writing for various purposes in their play activities and to experiment with writing instruments.

Even as these ideas begin to take hold within the early childhood community, issues surrounding new technologies add yet another dimension to the many curriculum decisions to be faced. As Smith (2002) reported in her research describing a toddler's experiences with CD-ROM story books with his mother, "the play associated with computer use involved the use of language and the development of new understandings about the technological concepts related to this new medium of storybook" (p. 10). Smith linked the child's responses to hypertext to Sulzby and Teale's (1991) notion of the development of independent functioning with storybooks. According to their theory, children's exploration of storybooks with an adult participant follow a routine pattern, with the emergent reading typical of two-year-olds consisting of labeling and commenting on items in pictures. From this initial form of reading, children move toward a more conventional reading of storybooks.

The inclusion of various *new* technologies in early childhood settings is inevitable. Technologies are included among the many literacies to which young children are exposed and in which they want to be involved. The United Kingdom's Grid for Learning is useful example: "The broad aim of the Grid is to help raise education standards by providing teachers, students and education institutions with access to information and communications technologies (ICT)" (Lankshear & Knobel, 2002). Early education is included among the target areas for this initiative. Concern for the Grid's early efforts aimed at young children prompted Lankshear and Knobel to state, "the Grid may have headed down an unfortunate and counter-productive road so far as young learners are concerned. If our assessment is correct, it will take a considerable change in direction and mindset to put it on a course that will enable the Grid to be a productive force for early literacy development" (p. 180). Concerns include: inciting boredom with online literacy practices; fostering the mislearning of new forms of literacy; dumbing down new forms of literacy acquisition; impeding development of responsibility for on-line actions (referring to policing and surveillance procedures) (p. 180).

It is clear that policy makers and educators need to keep current understandings about early literacy development in mind as they make decisions about the inclusion and use of technology in early childhood settings. Whether the technologies are old or new, they need to be used in ways that are consistent with what is known about how children learn.

Early Literacies and Teacher Quality

Dramatic changes in the educational expectations for young children, and for the early literacy curriculum to which they are exposed, strongly suggest the need to improve the overall quality of the workforce engaged in early childhood education. This must be done through recruitment, improved professional development, and better pay and working conditions. Once again, these issues point to a mixture of social and educational policy. There is widespread agreement about the need for teacher preparation to meet new curricular demands (Snow, Burns, & Griffin, 1998; Strickland & Snow, 2002). The quality of staff working with children in ECEC programs have a major impact on children's early development and learning. Research shows the links between strong training and support of staff – including appropriate pay and conditions – and the quality of ECEC services (Bowman, Donovan, & Burns, 2000; Whitebrook, Howes, & Phillips, 1998). Not the least among the challenges related to upgrading the quality of early childhood literacy programs is the need for a well trained workforce and the infusion of a program of ongoing professional development.

Requirements for teacher education in early childhood settings varies from country to country. Finland, France, Norway, Japan, and the United Kingdom have relatively high national teaching standards for early childhood educators (Pritchard, 1996). In the past, the U.S. has had minimal educational requirements for preschool staff. However, proposed legislation, the School Readiness Act of 2003 (Head Start Reauthorization) provides for the improvement of teacher quality in Head Start: "The bill would ensure that a greater number of Head Start teachers are adequately trained and educated in early childhood develop-ment, particularly in teaching the fundamental skills of language, pre-reading and pre-mathematics" (Bill Summary, House Education and the Workforce Committee, May 22, 2003.) This legislation would require all new Head Start teachers to have at least an associates degree (i.e., two years of higher education) in early childhood education or a related field within three years and 50 percent of Head Start teachers nationwide to have at least a bachelors degree by 2008. This will put a heavy burden on center administrators to find well-trained professionals to work in their centers, which traditionally have paid low wages. Issues related to maintaining a work force that, at least in part, reflects the local community must also be addressed. In addition to issues related to recruitment and teacher education, are issues related to the content of the teacher education curriculum.

It is clear that standards are increasing for both children and teachers. The demands regarding what early childhood teachers need to know and do have changed dramatically. Described in broad terms, teachers of young children need to know the importance of oral language competencies, early literacy experiences and family literacy in children's learning to read. They need to be able to foster a wide range of literacy related dispositions and competencies, including a love of literacy and the development of vocabulary, phonological awareness, and print-related knowledge. They must be able to use a variety of instructional methods that are age and developmentally appropriate and have the ability to adjust those methods to the specific needs of individuals.

The growing trend to generate standards for early childhood education may be the best indication of a felt need to specify curriculum content and child outcomes for early education programs. Figure 1 shows one small section of a broad set of standards for early childhood education (CTB/McGraw Hill, 2003). Trends toward greater accountability at the early childhood level will, no doubt, require early childhood agencies to produce and adhere to a set of standards such as these if they wish to gain access to certain funding streams.

Policy and Accountability

Policies that influence government funding of early childhood care and education have rendered a new emphasis on accountability. This trend had already

Figure 1.   Domain 2: Basic Symbol Systems of Each Child's Culture

Guideline IV: Literacy and Language Learning

Goal 1 – Listening

Building on their prior listening experiences children can develop the abilities to identify sounds in their environment and distinguish between and among them. Children listen actively, attending to what they hear with purpose and gain meaning and understanding. Children learn that listening to others, to stories, poetry, and songs brings them joy and pleasure.

Guideline IV, Goal 1, Objective 1	Children Will Discriminate Between Sounds In Their Environment
Children Will Need to Experience:	Benchmarks
. Listening to sounds in their environment.	Children Should Be Able To:
. Creating sounds.	. Identify sounds in their environment such as animal sounds, traffic noises, music, human speech.
. Singing and listening to music.	
	. Create sounds by singing and making music.

Vignette

A group of crows landed in some trees surrounding the playyard. Excited over something or other the crows cawed and cawed. It was quite a cacophony. Taking advantage of the cawing, the teacher sat on a bench next to three-year old Joshua. She said, "Listen to those crows! What a racket!"

Joshua looked up at the crows and replied, "They fighting, they fighting." "The crows are fighting?" responded his teacher. "Yep," Brian said as the crows continued their cawing, "They fighting – they using fighting voices,," Joshua said demonstrating his ability to identify sounds, and discriminate between environmental sounds.

Continued

appeared with initiatives focused on beginning reading in the United States and the United Kingdom. In the U.S., such initiatives as No Child Left Behind (2001) requires states to establish "adequate yearly progress" goals and timetables that ensure all students meet or exceed particular levels of proficiency. In the U.K. the National Literacy Strategy also has a strong accountability component. Critics are quick to express their concern about the high stakes associated with these kinds of assessments relative to promotion and for the possibility of narrowing the curriculum to the content of the test.

In reflecting on the first four years of the National Literacy Strategy in England, Shiel (2003) stated, "it is apparent that it has been successful to a point. We know that scores of 11 year-olds have risen dramatically. However, it is unclear to what extent higher test scores reflect real gains in literacy" (p. 694). Critics generally laud the goals of these national initiatives. At the same time, they express concern about the relatively narrow conceptualization of literacy

Fig. 1.   *Continued*

Standard I, Goal 1, Objective 2	Children Will Listen Attentively
Children Will Need to Experience:	**Benchmarks**
. An environment in which free expression of ideas, feelings and emotions is fostered and children are encouraged to talk, listen, discuss and even argue with each other.	**Children Should Be Able To:** . Listen with attention and without distraction or interruption.
. Listening to a variety of stories, poetry, songs, chants.	. Respond to the ideas, feelings and thoughts expressed orally by others, such as running to help a child who has fallen and telling a crying
. Arrangements are made for family members to read, sign, recite the same stories, poetry, songs, and chants.	child "It's OK, don't cry". . Recognize the purpose of listening, noting details by using new ideas and information in their play. . Make judgments about what they hear, telling parts of stories they liked, or that frightened them.

Vignette

"Ms. Johnson, Ms. Johnson, come look at our city," pleaded four-year old Juanita, who was finishing building a city of blocks. After Ms. Johnson agreed that Juanita and her friends had indeed built a marvelous block city, Ronald asked, "Now where are the lights, Ms. Johnson, now we need lights." "Why do you need lights?" asked Ms. Johnson. "Because we're building the city that goes to bed hanging lights all around it's head. We need lights." Ms. Johnson, who often read Langston Hughes' poem The City in which the "city goes to bed hanging lights around its head," realized that these children were listening attentively and incorporating details of their listening into their play, building a city of blocks.

Continued

represented by large scale standardized assessments, the substantial challenge to educators in terms of reasonable expectations for students, and the danger of defining literacy solely in terms of test performance (Linn, Baker, & Betebenner, 2002; Shiel, 2003).

Nevertheless, as policy makers move toward systemic education reform from pre-kindergarten through grade 12 and the attendant promulgation of standards for the performance for children, teachers, and programs, it is not surprising that these will be increasingly tied (implicitly or explicitly) to government legislation along with requirements for accountability and curriculum improvement. A growing number of educators and policy makers are advocating universal access to preschool for all children regardless of income (Zigler, 2002). This can only come about through large-scale funding with accompanying policies and regulations set by national bodies often far from the actual delivery of service.

The impending call for accountability in the form of performance measures for children has prompted early childhood educators to find means to assess young children's growth in all areas of the curriculum in ways that are consistent with their age and developmental needs. Shepard, Kagan, and Wirtz (1998) suggested four major purposes for early childhood assessment: (1) to support learning; (2) for identification of special needs; (3) for program evaluation and

Fig. 1. *Continued*

Guideline IV, Goal 1, Objective 3	Children Will Listen For Pleasure And Enjoyment
Children Will Need to Experience:	**Benchmarks**
. Listening as others read and tell a variety of stories, poems, songs and chants.	**Children Should Be Able To:**
. Entering into dialogues with others about stories, poems and chants.	. Request specific stories, poems, songs and other music.
. Listening to a variety of types of music including songs, chants and instrumental music.	. Repeat parts of stories and poems.
. Families who share their cultures' chants, songs, music, poems and stories.	. Show pleasure and enjoyment during listening activities, smiling, laughing and responding in appropriate ways.
	. Enter into dialogues while listening to others, stories, poems and chants.
	. Increase their listening attention span from a moment or two to listening to an entire story, poem, or chant.

Vignette

Three-year old Shaval running outside to play was heard singing "Trip, trap, trip trap, tripety trap, trap, trip-traptey, trip," illustrating that she could was familiar with the folk tale Three Billy Goats Gruff and could repeat parts of story with enjoyment and pleasure.

Guideline IV, Goal I, Objective 5	Children Will Be Able To Identify Letter-Sound Relationships
Children Will Need to Experience:	**Benchmarks**
. Listening to alphabet books.	**Children Should Be Able To:**
. Explicit teaching of letter names and sounds in a meaningful context.	. Identify the letter that begins their name and its sound.
. Hear and recall numerous rhymes, poems, chants and alliteration.	. Pick out other words that begin with the same letter/sound as their names.
	. Begin to identify a few consonant letter/sound correspondence in words in familiar rhymes, poems, and chants, including those with alliteration.

Vignette

"Look," said Carl's teacher as four-year old Carl was hanging his coat in his cubby shortly after he had joined the preschool group. Your name begins with a c just like coat and cubby." "Oh," said four-year old Carl, "I know that C C C, Carl, cubby, cup. But what I want to know is when are the cubbies coming to stay in the cubbies?" This vignette illustrates that young children can learn letter names and sounds through first-hand experiences. Nevertheless, their preoperational thinking, the idea that some type of cub would come to live in their cubbies, dominates their thinking.

monitoring trends; and (4) for high-stakes accountability (p. 7). They also offered a set of principles for early childhood assessment that can serve to guide policy makers and practitioners:

> Assessment should bring benefits for children; be tailored to a specific purpose and be reliable, valid and fair for that purpose; policies should be designed recognizing that reliability and validity of assessments increase with children's age; be age-appropriate on both content and the method of data collection; linguistically appropriate, recognizing that to some extent all assessments are measures of language; and parents should be a valued source of assessment information and an audience for the assessment results (pp. 5–6).

Early Literacies and Parent Involvement

Through the last three decades there has been an emerging consensus that the quality of relations between schools and families plays an integral role in student success. Parents' involvement in children's education has been emphasized as a particularly important aspect of the school-family relationship, with significant implications for children's education (Mattingly, Prislin, McKenzie, Rodriguez, & Kayzar, 2002). Indeed numerous studies have shown that parent involvement is correlated with higher student academic achievement, better student attendance, and more positive student and parent attitudes toward education (Eccles & Harold, 1996). Nevertheless, studies of family literacy programs have shown mixed results and raised important questions about their effectiveness. Researchers attribute this, not so much to the value of encouraging parents to be involved in their children's education, but to the need for more rigorous research to determine what kinds of programs work best (Barnett, 2002; Hayes, 2002).

In their review of early childhood programs, Strickland and Barnett (in press) discuss the lack of overall consistency of program success among the home-based early childhood programs. Many factors may contribute to this. Families participating in home-based programs may be among the most needy. Family instability and the lack of daily attention that can be provided in center-based programs may also influence results. However, even center-based programs often lack consistency and sustained quality regarding parent involvement. Researchers and evaluators attempting to study these programs find it difficult to control for parental participation and follow-up. Despite these problems, parent education and involvement remain extremely important part of the policy considerations for early literacy programs. Much more needs to be done, however, to determine the best mix of home-school links to support children's education.

Some Policy Recommendations

Educators customarily think in terms of the links between research and practice. However, there is a growing awareness that policy is an equally significant component of our professional pursuits. Educational policies help to convey to us, as educators, what to do, how to do it, and for what purposes (Stevens, 2003, p. 662). This may be even more salient in the area of early literacies, where issues related to working mothers, social welfare, and childcare may be linked to early education policies. Ball (1990) defined policy as the captured essence of values. This crystallization can occur in print but can also be conveyed through speeches and images, as values and shared understandings of those values are complex aspects of policy, mediated by words images, and actions (Lingard, Henry, Rivzi, & Taylor, 1997).

In their *Thematic Review of Early Childhood Education and Care Policy*, the Organization of Economic Co-operation and Development (OECD, 2001) identified eight key elements of policy likely to promote equitable access to quality early childhood care and education. Based on a study involving a diverse set of countries, contexts, circumstances, values, and beliefs, these policy elements are intended to be broad and inclusive. The policy recommendations relate well to the content I have already offered in this chapter. They speak to the dynamic interface of social and educational policies that influence the quality of literacy programs in early childhood settings. Eight key elements required for a systematic and integrated approach to policy development and implementation:

- A clear vision for children from birth to 8 years that is coordinated at centralized and decentralized levels;
- A strong and equal partnership with the "regular" education system;
- A universal approach to access, with particular attention to children in need of special support;
- Substantial public investment in services and the infrastructure;
- A participatory approach to quality improvement and assurance;
- Appropriate training and working conditions for staff in all forms of provision;
- Systematic attention to monitoring and data collection; and
- A stable framework and long-term agenda for research and evaluation (p. 11).

The importance of early education is generally agreed upon. Many countries are taking a second look at the educational needs of the very young with a special focus on those who are economically and socially disadvantaged. There is a growing awareness that early literacies play a special role in supporting overall school success and in producing a better educated and productive citizenry. As governments rethink early childhood education and care, it becomes clear that social and educational policies are interdependent. Indeed, they are dynamic, interactive, and increasingly influenced by research. Rigorous and credible research in the social welfare and educational sectors is critical if policy makers and educators are to make informed decisions for children and families. Early literacies will no doubt be central to the research and to the decision making.

References

Ackerman, D., & Martinez, M. C. (2002). Who pays, who attends, and who teaches? A comparative study of early care and education in the international community. Unpublished paper. New Brunswick, NJ: Rutgers University.

Aubrey, C., David, T., Godfrey, R., & Thompson, L. (2000). *Early childhood educational research: Issues in methodology and ethics.* London: Routledge Falmer Press.

Ball, S. (1990). *Politics and policy making in education.* New York: Routledge.

Barnett, W. S. (2002). Preschool education for economically disadvantaged children: Effects on reading achievement and related outcomes. In S. Neuman & D. K. Dickinson (Eds.), *Handbook of early literacy* (pp. 421–443). New York: Guilford Press.

Barnett, W. S. (1998). Long-term effects on cognitive development and school success. In W. S. Barnett & S. S. Boocock (Eds.), *Early care and education for children in poverty* (pp. 11–44). Albany, NY: State University of New York Press.

Barnett, W. S. (1995). Long-term effects of early childhood programs on cognitive and school outcomes. *The Future of Children, 5*(3), 25–50.

Bowman, B., Donovan, M. S., & Burns, M. S. (Eds.). (2000). *Eager to learn: Educating our preschoolers.* Washington, DC: National Academy Press.

Children's Defense Fund. *The state of children in America's union: A 2002 action guide to leave no child behind.* Washington, DC: Author.

Clay, M. (1975). *What did I write?* Auckland, New Zealand: Heinemann.

Clay, M. (1982). *Observing young readers.* Exeter, NH: Heinemann.

Clay, M. (1991). *Becoming literate: The construction of inner control.* Auckland, New Zealand: Heinemann.

Cochran, M. (Ed.) (1993). *International handbook of childcare policies and programs.* Westport, CT: Greenwood Press.

Cohen, S. S. (2001). *Championing child care.* New York: Columbia University Press.

CTB/McGraw-Hill LLC. (2003). *Pre-Kindergarten standards: Guidelines for teaching and learning.* Monterey, CA: McGraw-Hill. Retrieved June 9, 2003 from http://www.ctb.com

Dickinson, D. K., & Tabors, P. O. (2001). *Beginning literacy with language.* Baltimore, MD: Brookes Publishing.

Dyson, A. H. (1982). The emergence of visible language: Interrelationships between drawing and early writing. *Visible Language, 16,* 360–381.

Eccles, J. S., & Harold, R. D. (1996). Family Involvement in children's and adolescents' schooling. In A. Booth & J. F. Dunn (Eds.), *Family-school links: How do they affect educational outcomes?* (pp. 3–34). Mahwah, NJ: Lawrence Erlbaum Associates.

Families and Work Institute (1997). *Rethinking the brain: New insights into early development.* New York: Author.

Galda, L., Cullinan, B., & Strickland, D. S. (1993). *Language, literacy, and the child.* Orlando, FL: Harcourt.

Goswami, U. (2001). Early phonological development and the acquisition of literacy. In S. Neuman & D. K. Dickinson (Eds.), *Handbook of early literacy* (pp. 111–125). New York: Guilford Press.

Hayes, A. (April, 2002). High-quality family literacy programs: Child outcomes and impacts. *Connecting, 1*(4), 1–2.

Hodgkinson, H. (2003). *Leaving too many children behind: A demographer's view of the neglect of America's youngest children.* Washington, DC: Institute for Educational Leadership.

Holdaway, D. (1979). *The foundations of literacy.* Sidney, Australia: Ashton Scholastic.

Knitzer, J. (2001). Federal and state efforts to improve care for infants and toddlers. *Future of Children, 11*(1), 79–97. Retrieved May 21, 2003 from http://www.futureofchildren.org/usr_doc/volllno1ART6%2Epdf

Lankshear, C., & Knobel, M. (2002). Children, literacy and the U.K. National Grid for Learning. *Journal of Early Childhood Literacy,* 167–194.

Lee, V., & Burkam, D. (2002). *Inequality at the starting gate.* Washington, DC: Economic Policy Institute.

Lingard, B., Henry, M., Rivzi, F., & Taylor, S. (1997). *Educational policy and the politics of change.* London: Routledge.

Linn, R. L., Baker, E. L., & Betebenner, D. W. (2002). Accountability systems: Implications of requirements of the No Child Left Behind Act of 2001. *Educational Researcher, 31*(6), 3–16.

Luke, A. (December, 2002). Making literacy policy differently: Globalisation, diversity, and semiotic economics. Presentation at the 52nd Annual Meeting, National Reading Conference, Miami FL, USA.

Mattingly, D. J., Prislin, R., McKenzie, T. L., Rodriguez, J. L., & Kayzar, B. (2002). Evaluating evaluations: The case of parent involvement programs. *Review of Educational Research, 72,* 549–576.

National Center for Family Literacy (March, 2003). Synthesis of Scientific research on development of early literacy in young children. Occasional paper.

No Child Left Behind Act of 2001, Pub. L. No. 107–110, 115 Stat. 1425 (2002).

Organisation for Economic Co-operation and Development (OECD). (2001). *Starting strong: Early childhood education and care.* Paris: Authors.

Pritchard, E. (1996). Training and professional development: International approaches. In S. L. Kagan & N. E. Cohen (Eds.), *Reinventing early care and education* (pp. 126–134). San Francisco: Jossey-Bass.

Ramey, L., & Ramey, C. (1998). Early intervention and early experience, *American Psychologist, 53*(2), 109–20.

Ramey, L., & Ramey, C. (2000). Early childhood experiences and developmental competence. In S. Danziger & J. Waldfogel (Eds.), *Securing the future: Investing in children from birth to college* (pp. 122–150). New York: Russell Sage.

Richgels, D. (2001). Invented spelling, phonemic awareness, and reading and writing instruction. In S. Neuman & D. Dickinson (Eds.), *Handbook of early literacy research* (pp. 142–158). New York: Guildford Press.

Shepard, L., Kagan, S. L., & Wirtz, E. (1998). *Principles and recommendations for early childhood assessments.* Washington, DC: National Education Goals Panel.

Shiel, G. (2003). Raising standards in reading and writing: Insights from England's National Literacy Strategy. *The Reading Teacher, 56*(7), 692–695.

Smith, C. R. (2002). Click on me! An example of how a toddler used technology in play. *Journal of Early Childhood Literacy, 2,* 5–20.

Snow, C. E., Burns, M. S., & Griffin, P. (Eds.) (1998). *Preventing reading difficulties in young children.* Washington, DC: National Academy Press. Stevens, L. P. (2003). Reading first: A critical policy analysis. *The Reading Teacher, 56*(7), 662–668.

Strickland, D. S., & Barnett, W. S. (2003). Literacy interventions for preschool children considered at risk: Implications for curriculum, professional development, and parent involvement. In C. M. Fairbanks, J. Worthy, B. Maloch, J. Hoffman & D. Schallert (Eds.), *National Reading Conference Yearbook* (pp. 104–116). Oak Creek, WI. National Reading Conference.

Strickland, D. S., & Snow, C. (2002). *Preparing our teachers: Opportunities for better reading instruction.* Washington, DC: National Academy Press.

Sulzby, E., & Teale W. (1991). Emergent literacy. In R. Barr, M. Kamil, P. Mosenthal & P. D. Pearson (Eds.), *Handbook of reading research* (Vol. 2, pp. 727–757). New York: Longman.

Teale, W., & Sulzby, E. (1985). Emergent literacy: New Perspectives on young children's reading and writing. In D. S. Strickland & L. M. Morrow (Eds.), *Emerging literacy: Young children learn to read and write* (pp. 1–15), Newark, DE: International Reading Association.

Torgeson, J. K., Morgan, S., & Davis, C. (1992). Effects of two types of phonological awareness training on word learning in kindergarten children. *Journal of Educational Psychology, 84,* 364–370.

Whitebrook, M., Howes, C., & Phillips, D. (1998). *Worthy work, unlivable wages: The national childcare staffing study, 1988–1997.* Washington, DC: Center for the Child Care Workforce.

Wolfe, P., & Brandt, R. (1998). What do we know from brain research? *Educational Leadership,* 8–13.

Yopp, H. K. (1992). Developing phonemic awareness in young children. *The Reading Teacher, 45,* 696–703.

Yoshikawa, H. (1995). Long-term effects of early childhood programs on social outcomes and delinquency. *The Future of Children, 5*(3), 51–75.

Zigler, E. (2002). Reflections – Where do we go from here? In B. Bowman (Ed.), *Love to read* (pp. 83–93). Washington, DC: National Black Child Development Institute.

33

BALANCED ELEMENTARY LITERACY INSTRUCTION IN THE UNITED STATES: A PERSONAL PERSPECTIVE

Michael Pressley
Michigan State University, USA

As I write this chapter in late 2003, I reflect that I cannot count the number of invitations I have received in the past few years to talk about balanced reading instruction, particularly in the elementary grades. Even more uncountable are the number of references I have seen in print in the past few years to "balanced instruction." Plugging "balanced instruction," "balanced teaching," and "balanced literacy instruction," into the data bases of the electronic booksellers, I come up with more than 20 titles on the topic. Balanced literacy instruction seems very much to be "in." Perhaps I should feel good about that, since I wrote the first book on the topic (Pressley, 1998) and then, as I broadened my perspective on it, revised that book (Pressley, 2002), anticipating I will do so again (Pressley, 2006?). The fact of the matter is that I do not feel so good about all of the activities claiming to be about balanced instruction. There are many who are using the variations of the term, "balanced instruction," in ways that are very different that I intended and in ways that do not inspire confidence in me that children's literacy will be much advanced by their efforts.

What is "balanced literacy instruction" from my perspective? It involves explicit, systematic, and completely thorough teaching of the skills required to read and write in a classroom environment where there is much reading of authentic literature – including information books, and much composing by students. Balanced literacy instruction is demanding in every way that literacy instruction can be demanding. Students are expected to learn the skills and learn them well enough to be able to transfer them to reading and writing of texts. Yes, this is done in a strongly supportive environment, with the teacher providing a great deal of direct teaching, explanations and re-explanations, and hinting to students about the appropriateness of applying skills they have learned previously to new texts and tasks. As children learn the skills and use them, the demands in balanced classrooms increase, with the goal of the balanced literacy teacher being to move students ahead, so that every day there is new learning;

International Handbook of Educational Policy, 645–660
Nina Bascia, Alister Cumming, Amanda Datnow, Kenneth Leithwood and David Livingstone (Eds.)
© 2005 *Springer. Printed in Great Britain.*

every day students are working at the edge of their competencies and growing as readers and writers.

I emphasize in introducing my perspective on balance that this is not a position I invented, but rather one I stole! The concept reflects how excellent primary-grades language arts teachers do what they do. It reflects the teaching of primary-grades teachers who produce high engagement and achievement in their students. My only contribution was to come and document their teaching and find that there was strong resemblance in pedagogy across such classrooms. I'll relate more about how I discovered this perspective on balance.

For now, note that this view of balanced literacy instruction contrasts with other perspectives on beginning literacy instruction that are sometimes referred to as balanced by their supporters. Balanced literacy instruction (i.e., the instruction in the most engaging and effective of primary-grades classrooms) is not teaching of skills if and when a student demonstrates a need to learn a skill, which seems to me to be the surviving form of whole language instruction (Weaver, 1994). Nor is balanced literacy instruction delaying of holistic reading and writing in favor of learning phonemic awareness and phonics skills. It isn't greatly foregrounding skills instruction over reading of books and student composing. That is, balanced literacy instruction as presented here is not consistent with what some skills advocates are calling balanced literacy instruction, viewing skills learning (especially phonics skills) as gates that children must pass through before they can read and write (Moats, 1999).

Lest you think that I am offering "straw men" extremes as comparisons, on the left hand side of my desk this morning is the supposedly balanced curriculum guide of a city in Michigan, a guide that includes no systematic teaching of basic reading and writing skills, and on the right hand side of my desk is a curriculum that forefronts the reading of decodable books in first grade to the exclusion of other texts and no real student composition. I have paged through many similar manuals in the past few years as I have talked my way around America, hosted by states, intermediate school districts, and individual schools supposedly interested in balanced literacy instruction. Whole language and skills instruction extremes that are referred to as balanced by their proponents are common in American literacy instruction. They are not the instruction I favor, and they are not like the instruction in the most engaging and effective classrooms, settings where beginning readers and writers are reading and writing with enthusing and growing in literacy as they do so.

How Did I Develop My Position on Balanced Literacy Instruction?

In the early 1990s the whole language versus phonics (or skills instruction) debate was bubbling over. From about the fourth week of August to the second week of September, the popular media in the U.S. always focus on education. In the early 1990s, a very hot, start-of-school issue for the media was whole language versus phonics, featured in articles in popular magazines and segments on the network television magazines. In those days, I was not really part of the debate, but somehow, the media thought I was. There were interviews by several popular magazines and even a TV segment on camera in Rockefeller Center discussing the difference between whole language and other approaches. Lots of adults who had learned to read with Dick and Jane or through explicit phonics instruction wanted to know how children could learn to read without the skills instructions, work books, or basal readers with systematically increasingly difficult text. How could they learn to read from listening to the teacher read a half dozen story books a day, complemented by choral reading of big books, topped off by writing in response to literature, with the resulting writing sometimes having no capitalization, correctly spelled words, or punctuation?

That was, in part, because, in the early 1990s, whole language was driving the school day in many elementary classrooms around the United States. The movement was fueled by a few events. The largest curriculum decision-making entity in the U.S. is the state of California. In the late 1980s, California decided that their elementary reading instruction would be literature-driven. They decided in favor of whole language, a perspective that enjoyed the support of a number of vocal curriculum theorists, including Frank Smith (1971, 1975, 1979) and Kenneth Goodman (1986). Many California educators had been persuaded by whole language advocates that reading was about meaning making and best accomplished by children being immersed in real reading and writing, with skills instruction played down. Skills could be taught when children needed them. Skills instruction was definitely much less prominent in whole language classrooms than in the elementary classrooms of the 1960s and 1970s, which had been driven largely by published basal reading series.

Other states followed California, including some of the biggest players in the textbook market: Texas and Florida. Publishers had to change their ways in a hurry. Some offered literature sets to schools, rather than anything resembling the traditional basal reader. Others offered anthologies that physically resembled basal readers, but which were filled with real children's literature rather than stories about Dick and Jane. New teachers' editions made little mention of the skills instruction that was so prominent in the reading programs of the past. What was emphasized was literature experience and responding to literature through writing. So, the Bay Area Writing Project (Kamp, 1983) held sway in California, while the National Writing Project (Gray & Sterling, 2000) swept the nation, and elementary classrooms everywhere had daily writer's workshops!

Although research analyses concluded that whole language was either no better than the basal approach or slightly worse in the case of weaker readers (Stahl & Miller, 1989), whole language was very popular in professional education associations that counted many teachers as members, including the International Reading Association and the National Council of Teachers of English. The teachers pointed to their own experience as evidence, making strident assertions for the superiority of whole language, which they perceived as putting decision making in the hands of teachers, over other approaches, which they perceived as putting decision making in the hands of publishers, researchers, and others far removed from the classroom experience. For a sampling of just how forcefully opinionated whole language leaders could be, see Edelsky (1990). Whole language was an educator-led, populist movement that prevailed in elementary reading in the United States in the early 1990s.

Three events in autumn 1993, however, did more than anything to impress me that I should become more interested in primary-level language arts instruction. One was that my son, Timothy, began grade 1. He began grade 1 in the classroom of a committed whole language teacher, who was among the leaders in the school district with respect to curriculum decision making. Tim heard lots of stories at school, did much choral reading, and struggled to do some writing. He wrote many stories about soccer because he liked soccer, and because soccer was a word he knew how to spell. Tim was more than a little miffed that his teacher would never tell him how to spell words that he wanted to use in his writing, since he knew that his invented spellings were wrong, and Tim did not like being wrong!

Frankly, it did not take long for both my wife, Donna, whose doctorate was in developmental psychology specializing in the area of reading development, and me to feel that Tim was not learning to read at the rate or near the level that we expected in first grade. Our response was to teach Tim, with Donna, in particular, spending a great deal of time reading with him, making certain he knew the letter-sound associations and could decode words. Our home had always been filled with age-appropriate books during Tim's preschool years. The collection expanded by hundreds of books during the first grade year.

As Tim thrived in reading with Donna as tutor, I became aware that other children in the class were not thriving. We lived in a very small village in upstate New York in those days. When I picked up Tim at school or went to the post office or filled up my tank or attended a sporting event, I encountered other parents from Tim's class, and there were frequent conversations that included expressions of concern about how reading was being taught in Tim's school, and, in particular, in the first grade classroom that Tim attended. That is, in fall 1993, continuing into spring 1994, I lived in a village that was reflecting on the value of whole language versus more traditional reading instruction. A question I heard repeatedly as I roamed that village that year was, "What can I do to get my child reading?" I knew from first hand experience in autumn 1993 that there was grass roots parental dissatisfaction with whole language, with many parents anxious about the slow progress their children were making in reading and writing. In the decade since then, I have been in many conversations that detailed similar parental reactions in cities, towns, and villages across the United States, as primary-grades students experienced whole language in the early 1990s.

The second event of autumn 1993 that jolted my interest in whole language occurred at the National Reading Conference's annual meeting. There was a debate between whole language and skills advocates. Because I was at another session when the debate occurred, I did not attend it. I did hear about it for the remainder of the meeting, however, and, shortly after the debate occurred, I would be drawn into it. A decision was made to publish the debate with commentary (Smith, 1994). Although I still do not know why – for I really was not doing research that touched on the whole language versus phonics (skills instruction) debate at the time, I was tapped to be a commentator. Although my remarks conceded that the skills instruction group probably had more scientific evidence in their corner, I found that I was very uncomfortable siding with either the whole language or skills instruction advocates. That feeling was accentuated by a third event in the autumn of 1993.

In autumn 1993, I entered a series of discussions with Ruth Wharton-McDonald that would change my professional life profoundly. I was teaching at the University of Albany, where Ruth was a graduate student. Ruth had studied at Harvard with Jeanne Chall, the most famous commentator in *The Great Debate* (Chall, 1967) about beginning reading instruction. Wharton-McDonald came to Albany wanting to do work on beginning reading instruction. In the school year 1993–94, she and I reflected on potential research that she might do; the whole language versus skills instruction debate was prominent in our thinking.

As I worked on the published commentary about the National Reading Conference debate (Pressley, 1994), Ruth and I came to an insight. Both she and I had spent a great deal of time in primary-grade classrooms. We realized that the instruction described by the great debaters on both sides did not sound much like the instruction we had seen in very many first grades, including some that seemed to be producing high achievement in reading and writing.

As Ruth and I read the work of the great debaters additionally, we came to another insight. Although the researchers in these debates had spent time in instructional settings that featured instruction they favored, that was pretty much the limit of their direct experience of primary-grades classrooms (except, of course, that much earlier in life, they had attended primary school). None of the great debaters had sought out classrooms where literacy achievement was clearly very high, with the goal of determining how effective primary-grades teachers, in fact, produce high achievement. Ruth and I decided to do just that, joined in the venture by another graduate student, Jennifer Hampston, who was also interested in beginning reading achievement.

Wharton-McDonald, Pressley, and Hampston (1998)

Designing a study that would illuminate what goes on in effective grade-1 classrooms was the first challenge, since there was no precedent literature with respect to that problem. At that time, I had recently completed a series of ethnographic studies of comprehension instruction (see Pressley et al., 1992), work that revealed the methods used by teachers who were very effective in teaching comprehension strategies. The applause for that research was great, so that my confidence in ethnographic approaches was high. That accounts, in part, for why Ruth and I decided to do an ethnography of grade-1 reading instruction, in particular, very effective grade-1 teaching. We conducted observations across the school year, complemented by interviews of the observed teachers, resulting in grounded theories about how each classroom operated (Strauss & Corbin, 1998). Through cross-case analyses, we constructed a theory of how effective grade-1 classrooms differ from less effective ones, that is, how grade-1 classrooms producing high achievement differ from those that are not so successful in developing children as readers and writers.

Then came the challenge of identifying effective grade-1 teachers. Although now in 2003, it might seem obvious to look for classrooms where there was great value attributed to standardized achievement test scores (Sanders & Horn, 1994), there were no achievement tests being given to grade 1 students in New York in those days. Our decision was to contact area school administrators and request that they nominate very effective grade-1 teachers, teachers they would be willing to show to parents or other visitors to their schools. We were emphatic that we did not want any weak teachers nominated. We received 10 such nominations of teachers who were willing to be observed, with 9 of them continuing to work in the schools for the entire 1994–95 school year, when the observations were made.

From the very first observations, Ruth, Jennifer, and I recognized a difference that distinguished some of the teachers we were observing from others. In some of the classrooms – three, to be exact – the students were intensely engaged in literacy learning.

They were always reading and writing, always learning something. When one task was completed (e.g., rereading a story with a partner), they turned their attention to another task (e.g., composing a response to the story that was just reread). Moreover, it did not matter when we visited such classes because almost all of the students were productively on task most of the time.

In contrast, there were three classes in the sample that were just the opposite. Intense engagement in reading and writing – in fact, any sustained academic attention to reading or writing – was rare in these classes. Two of these three teachers were emphatically identified with whole language philosophy. These teachers were determined that skills instruction would be downplayed. They succeeded to the point that we hardly ever observed any skills instruction! In fact, one of the most uncomfortable moments in the study came when one of these teachers caught a student attempting to sound out a word. When the student explained that his mother suggested he sound out words, the teacher remarked, "I don't care what your mother says. Look at the picture for clues."

Then, there were three classrooms where student engagement was more variable. Some of the time, these three teachers came up with activities that elicited student attention, but often they failed to do so. At a typical moment, some of the students would be reading and writing productively, and some would be doing nothing or something not likely to advance their literacy skills (e.g., paging through a picture book without seeming to process what was on the pages, playing a board game without obvious academic connection).

As the study continued, we noticed that there were important associations between the engagement status of the classrooms and student achievement. First, with respect to reading, there was clear evidence that the students in the most engaging classrooms were reading at a more advanced level than the students in the other classrooms. For example, all of the grade-1 classrooms had leveled books in them. By the end of the year, the students in the three engaged classrooms were reading books at higher levels than the students in the other classrooms. The most striking contrast was with students in the three least engaged classrooms, with some students in those classrooms still reading books that had been read in the middle fall by many students in the three most engaged classrooms. There was definitely a difference in reading achievement.

There was also a difference in writing achievement. By the end of the year in the most engaged classrooms, compositions were much longer (i.e., two or more pages in length), more coherent, and more impressive with respect to usage, mechanics, and spelling than in the other six classrooms in the study. In the three highly engaged classrooms, sentences were capitalized and punctuated appropriately. High frequency words were spelled correctly and lower frequency words were invented spellings that reflected the sequence of sounds in the words. The printing was neat and the spacing appropriate. In contrast, in the weakest classrooms, two or three sentences was the norm, with these sentences often not capitalized or punctuated appropriately. A much higher proportion of words were spelled inventively, with the inventions often not well mapped to the sound sequences in the words. Writing achievement definitely varied as a function of student engagement.

Did the teaching differ in these classrooms? Absolutely and unambiguously! There were three striking dimensions of difference with respect to the teaching:

(1) The most effective teachers were teaching all the time, using a variety of whole group, small group, and one-on-one instructional tactics to teach, which was an integration of literacy and content (i.e., students often read and wrote about social studies and science topics). The teaching was also an obvious balancing of skills instruction and holistic literacy experiences. Often, as many as 20 skills an hour would be covered, some planned and others in response to students' needs.

(2) The most engaging teachers were constantly teaching to motivate students, employing a wide range of tactics to do so (Pintrich & Schunk, 1996). Thus, they praised specific accomplishments of students (e.g., "This is an exciting story you are writing, with it making a lot of sense from beginning to end"). They encouraged students to recognize their successes as due to appropriate effort and their failures as reflecting lack of effort. The most engaging teachers also chose stories and classroom activities that were interesting for students.

(3) The classroom management was so good in the most engaging classrooms that it was difficult to know what the disciplinary policies were. In two of the three classrooms, the observers did not see a single disciplinary event during the year of observations.

In contrast, the teaching in the least engaging classrooms was much less intense, with the teacher teaching less and relying on seat work more. When students in the least engaged classes were at their desks, their teachers did not monitor their progress and their needs for support nearly as closely as the teachers in the most engaging classrooms. There were few mini-lessons in response to specific student needs. The disciplinary policy was easy to discern in these classrooms; the teachers often cited students for misbehavior, especially talking and general inattention, the hallmarks of low academic engagement. These teachers did not positively motivate much. In fact, they often acted in ways to undermine motivation (e.g., telling students that tasks were difficult, perhaps too difficult for them; presenting tasks that were, in fact, very boring; giving tasks that either were very easy or impossibly difficult).

In short, Wharton-McDonald et al. (1998) found that engaging classrooms were classrooms where achievement was high. These were also the classrooms in the study with the most intense teaching, best management, and extensive efforts to motivate students. What we discovered was that excellent beginning reading instruction was not consistent with either of the extremes that are in the beginning reading curriculum and instruction marketplace. Rather than being skills instruction or whole language, engaging and effective beginning literacy instruction is an intense balancing of skills instruction and holistic literacy experiences, in a well-managed, motivating classroom setting.

A National Followup

As part of the federally funded National Center for English Learning and Achievement, Ruth Wharton-McDonald and I, along with a number of other colleagues around the U.S., would follow up on the Wharton-McDonald et al. (1998) study, essentially doing the same investigation in New York, New Jersey, Texas, Wisconsin, and California, observing a total of 29 teachers (Pressley, Wharton-McDonald et al., 2001; Pressley, Allington et al., 2001). The results of this study can be summarized succinctly. We found what Wharton-McDonald et al. (1998) found. A bonus, however, was that we administered a standardized reading test, with the data from that making clear that the real winners in classrooms served by exceptionally balanced teachers were the weakest readers, those most at risk for reading failure.

Initial Presentation of the Results

The results of these studies were first presented at conferences in 1995, 1996, and 1997. It was clear from the first such presentations that we had a set of results that were compelling to many. These sessions especially attracted individuals who had vast experience in primary-grades classrooms. Many such attendees were emphatic that they had observed teachers like our best ones as well as many more that were like the more typical and weak teachers we had documented. They made clear to us that they felt we had gotten it right: Teachers who intensively balance diverse forms of instruction – including systematic skills instruction, reading of real literature, and composing – manage their classrooms well; they do much to motivate their students, and they are the teachers who produce the highest achievement.

We also came to realize, however, that our work was threatening to some. You might have guessed that it would be the whole language advocates, since the movement was so predominant across the nation. In fact, that turned out not to be the case.

Reactions from a Member of the Federal Government

In December 1997, Dick Allington and I were invited to participate in a news conference hosted by the Education Writers of America. It was a long session, beginning at 4:00, with a short dinner break in the middle, continuing to about 7:00. When I arrived at the meeting room, I was somewhat surprised that a large number of reprints were stacked in the back of the room, delivered courtesy of the National Institute of Child Health and Development (NICHD). The articles summarized NICHD-sponsored efforts to understand reading disabilities. Just before 4:00, the head of the branch of NICHD that funded research on reading disabilities, G. Reid Lyon, arrived, along with Louisa Moats, and offered every reporter a complete set of the NICHD preprints and reprints that were on the back tables.

More surprising was that, during the news conference, Dr. Lyon insisted on providing answers to reporters' questions and challenging the answers given by Allington and me, despite the fact that he had not been invited to participate in the news conference. I left the session well aware that Dr. Lyon was not convinced that balanced instruction was the answer to beginning reading problems. He firmly believed that beginning reading difficulties are caused by phonological deficits, ones that often can be cured with explicit phonics instruction (e.g., Lyon, 1997). He also knew that the nation would soon be barraged with that opinion. His remarks in Baltimore in December 1997 were a prelude of what was to come.

1998-Present: The National Reading Panel, No Child Left Behind, and the Reading First Perspective on Balance

During the year before the Education Writer's event, I learned that a report commissioned by the National Research Council (Snow, Burns, & Griffin, 1998), *Preventing Reading Difficulties in Young Children*, was circulating in draft form. In a number of informal conversations with reading research colleagues, Dr. Lyon was portrayed as very concerned about its content, specifically, that it did not focus sufficiently on NICHD-sponsored research and did not go far enough in supporting phonological skills instruction as the principal means of preventing beginning reading instruction. Supposedly, Lyon and his NICHD colleagues felt that another report was needed. In 1997, the U.S. Congress authorized the NICHD to form a National Reading Panel (2000; henceforth, NRP), charged to summarize the scientific evidence related to reading instruction.

The National Reading Panel

The decision as to what would be reviewed by the NRP seemed determined before the NRP ever met, at least in the eyes of one member of the Panel (Yatvin, 2002). Ultimately, what was covered was grouped into research on phonemic awareness, phonics, fluency, vocabulary instruction, comprehension, teacher education, and computer technology in reading instruction. The NRP also decided from the outset to limit itself to experimental and quasi-experimental research, which meant that qualitative studies, such as the ones conducted by Wharton-McDonald, me, and our colleagues, would not even be considered.

Two years later, the NRP released its results. Rather than entitling their report so that it was clear they had selectively sampled the literature, the NRP chose a title that suggested much more. Their report was entitled, *Report of the National Reading Panel: Teaching Children to Read: An Evidence-Based Assessment of the Scientific Research Literature on Reading and Its Implications for Reading Instruction.* One major finding of the report was that teaching phonemic awareness, phonics, vocabulary, and comprehension strategies to children improved reading instruction. The NRP also concluded that reading fluency can be encouraged through repeated reading with teacher guidance. The report included evidence to support professional development of reading instruction, with such professional development changing how teachers teach and impacting student achievement.

There was much ado about the NRP in spring 2000 and beyond. Several members of the NRP traveled the country to explain the findings. An executive summary was published, although the government provided complementary copies of the entire 450 page report, with it freely available on the web as well. One American reader proved to be more important than other readers, however. George W. Bush pledged during his presidential campaign in 2000 that no child would be left behind, if he were to become president, and part of his vision for assuring children's academic development was based on the NRP.

No Child Left Behind and Reading First

The new Bush administration would reauthorize the elementary and secondary school act, entitled *The No Child Left Behind Act of 2001* (107th Congress; see http://www.ed.gov/ legislation /ESEA02/107–110.pdf). This law enabled a program known as *Reading First*, which is intended to provide federal funds to transform reading education in kindergarten through grade 3. The charge is that primary literacy education be transformed into scientifically-based reading instruction, with the work of the NRP the reference for the type of reading instruction mandated by the law. Schools receiving Reading First dollars must put into place reading programs that include: (1) phonemic awareness instruction, (2) teaching of phonics, (3) instruction aimed at increasing reading fluency, (4) teaching of vocabulary, and (5) comprehension strategies instruction. These schools receive professional development emphasizing the five Reading First factors as well as funds to purchase materials that support teaching of phonemic awareness, phonics, fluency, vocabulary, and comprehension strategies.

What has been striking to me since I first encountered this five-factor answer, which is offered as scientifically-based reading instruction, is that there is no evidence – experimental, correlational, or qualitative – that establishes this package as a package as effective in improving reading achievement. In fact, in the decade of looking for and at effective primary-grades classrooms, my colleagues and I have not encountered an effective classroom – or an ineffective one for that matter – that forefronts these five factors. This mixture was not advanced by scientists, as is suggested by the phrase "scientifically-based reading instruction," but rather reflects policymakers' interpretations of science. That is, they believe because there is evidence that each of the five Reading First factors promotes reading achievement, all five together is all that is needed to assure that students will make progress. Such a translation is just one more version of skills instruction disguised as balanced literacy instruction (Moats, 1999).

In the past, policy shifts in literacy education resulted in rapid changes in published curricular products. That was also true in the case of Reading First. Some of the most up-to-date, published reading programs include the Reading First components prominently. Even so, these published programs are much fuller because state frameworks call for more than the components emphasized in Reading First, including reading of and responding to excellent literature, composition, and building important cultural knowledge. Thus, not surprisingly, many of the publishers' products purchased with Reading First funds include much more than the five Reading First factors. As the co-author of one of them, I am aware of efforts to do all that is possible to encourage broadly balanced reading instruction, which encourages everything from letter-sound processes to word recognition to reading and responding to literature that is part of conceptually-driven units. Such published materials also include much demand for student writing in response to reading, as well as demands for students to do library and internet research. The programs that compete with the one I co-authored are all doing what they can to encourage such balance as well.

In summary, there is now a national policy, Reading First, that is pushing for balancing of skills, with the policy stimulating the development of published programs that include those skills. Because states demand holistic reading and writing, the result is curricular products that encourage a reasonable balance of reading and writing competencies. I suspect that there is going to be even more pressure for balance, however, because states are changing their standards and expectations, with those changes being in the direction of more balanced literacy instruction.

More Balanced State Frameworks and Standards

As I write this chapter, I am serving as the chair of a committee in my home state of Michigan that is charged with getting the state K-8 language arts expectations to the point that they are acceptable by an organization, Achieve,

Inc. (see <achieve.org>), that vets the adequacy of the state's education standards. As we prepared the Michigan standards, Achieve, Inc. recommended that
we look at the standards for several states that they felt were doing it well,
for example, California (see <http://www.csun.edu/~hcbio027/k12standards/
standards/ela.html>) and Massachusetts (see <http://www.doe.mass.edu/
frameworks/ela/0601.pdf>).

Only very balanced teaching could produce the results demanded by these
standards. The expectation in 2003 in these states is that students acquire the
full range of reading skills across their years of schooling, from phonemic
awareness, knowing the alphabet, and letter-sound association to being able to
read many different types of texts with understanding. Elementary students are
expected to acquire worthwhile cultural knowledge through their reading, knowledge that will empower them to understand and react to documents in secondary
school and later adult life. With respect to writing, the expectations are that
students will learn the many writing skills (e.g., usage, mechanics, spelling) well
and, as they do so, they will learn how to plan, draft, revise, and complete a
variety of types of compositions, from letters sent in the mail to persuasive essays
to poems and plays. Students will also learn how to listen and respond appropriately in discussions about literature. They are expected to learn how to give oral
presentations, ones that are planned, drafted, and revised to the point that the
student can deliver the message at an appropriate pace and with appropriate
tone and expression, and respond to questions about the comments the student
delivered.

My reading of these standards documents is that the states are now moving
far ahead of the five factor expectations of Reading First. I could not miss that
most of the recommendations in the state documents I just reviewed could be
defended on the basis of scientific evidence, including my own work on effective
primary-grades instruction. State officials, who work closely with well-informed
educators as they craft frameworks and standards for the state, are evidence-
demanding and balanced in their thinking these days, encouraged to do so by
external vetting, such as is being done by Achieve, Inc.. The result is states'
standards consistent with my vision of balanced literacy instruction (Pressley,
2002), with teaching expected to produce skillful students who can read well
and widely, write well and persuasively, and communicate intelligently with the
many types of individuals and for the many purposes the contemporary world
contains.

Beyond Reading First to Balanced Evidence-Based Instruction

There are converging reasons to be optimistic that elementary language arts
instruction in the United States is going to be more balanced in the future. One,
we now have a better vision of what excellent elementary language arts looks
like, at least at the primary grades. My own work is complemented by that of
others who have observed that the most certain achievement in language arts
occurs in classrooms where skills and holistic literacy experiences are balanced,

classroom management is strong, and the teaching is massively motivating (Gipps, McCallum, & Hargreaves, 2000; Perry & VandeKamp, 2000; Perry, VandeKamp, Mercer, & Nordby, 2002). Two, although the policies of No Child Left Behind emphasize skills instruction, the implementations are being carried out in ways that support balancing of skills instruction and holistic reading and writing. Most emphatically, many school districts are complying with Reading First by purchasing comprehensive programs that include much skills instruction but also much real reading and writing. Three, agencies evaluating state standards (i.e., Achieve, Inc) are providing high praise for states that have standards that require years of balanced teaching if they are to be met.

That said, the challenges ahead are enormous. First of all, there are many, many players that do not get it with respect to balance. The *de facto* whole language and *de facto* skills-emphasis programs that portray themselves as balanced reflect many people's substantial lack of understanding of the concept of balanced literacy instruction, from district-level educators to publishers.

Second, although the governmental pressures towards balance are there, the balance is entirely with respect to language arts elements. There is little to no attention in No Child Left Behind, Reading First, and state standards documents to classroom management and motivation of students, which are two huge components in effective and engaging classrooms. In fact, recently, my colleagues and I have conducted several studies examining in greater depth how excellent primary-grade teachers motivate their students. The answer is that they are doing something motivating every minute of every school day, using every motivational mechanism ever studied, while simultaneously, doing nothing to undermine student motivation (Bogner, Raphael, & Pressley, 2002; Dolezal, Welsh, Pressley, & Vincent, 2003; Pressley et al., 2003). I think that both federal and state efforts to improve language arts instruction must pay greater attention to the motivational aspects of instruction if their reform efforts are to be maximally successful.

Third, there is no reason to believe that teachers can be transformed quickly into teachers that resemble the most effective teachers that my colleagues and I have studied. In fact, Alysia Roehrig and I have worked on an intensive, year-long mentoring approach for the past several years; only some of the participating teachers have made progress, and even those teachers who make progress do so slowly. Pressley and El-Dinary (1997) studied elementary teachers who were trying to learn how to teach comprehension strategies. A minority made great progress over the course of a year. That really effective, balanced primary-grades teachers invariably have been teachers for a while (5 or more years, typically) probably indicates that engaging, balanced, achievement-producing teachers are not born but rather become better over time. In short, my research-based experiences with professional development make clear to me that there will be no quick transformation of teachers.

That said, I think every elementary teacher should try to become more like the most engaging and most effective elementary teachers. In short, they should commit to all of the following:

- Aim for a strong balancing of skills instruction and holistic literacy experiences in elementary language arts. Teach the skills as explicitly and systematically as students require them to be taught. Make certain that students use their skills as they read and write, encouraging them to be reading texts at the edge of their competence and for writing to improve day by day, week by week, and month by month. Teachers must demand that students' writing improves both from the bottom up (i.e., excellent mechanics, spelling, and usage must be encouraged) and the top down (i.e., students must learn to plan, draft, and revise as they write).
- Connect reading, writing, and content learning, so that literacy instruction and content instruction are occurring all day.
- Teach a lot. Effective, engaging teachers are always teaching, either the entire class, or a part of the class, or individualized lessons directed at particular student needs. In the most engaging classrooms, instruction begins before the morning bell rings (i.e., as soon as the students enter the room) and concludes after the final bell. Students are so enthused about what they are doing that often they will stay in during recess to continue reading or writing or working on a project.
- Scaffold students. That is, monitor students as they read aloud and write, and provide mini-lessons that move them along. All of the engaging teachers we have studied are more like athletic coaches than anything else, watching their students carefully to provide just the instruction they need.
- Do all that is possible to motivate students, especially encouraging them to be self-regulated. Such self-regulation is possible when tasks and goals are well matched to a student's competence, requiring effort to accomplish but well within reach with such effort. Let your students know that you have high expectations about them, that you are certain that they can learn a great deal, that they can become good readers and writers.
- Have a management plan, although management is much less of an issue with effective instruction, when everyone is busy and motivated.

As I make these recommendations, I know what the reaction of many will be, "Isn't he forgetting that there are now skills-loaded tests that hold teachers accountable? How will students in such classrooms do on such tests?" Well, when my colleagues and I looked at this issue formally, the students did just fine (see Pressley, Allington et al., 2001, Chapter 3). I'll close, however, with a true story about one of the most engaging classrooms my colleagues and I have studied.

In spring 1999, the state of Indiana was developing a new first grade test and piloting it, including in the classroom of Nancy Masters (see Pressley, 2002; Pressley, Dolezal et al., 2003 for extensive descriptions of Nancy's teaching), an engaging grade-1 teacher, who worked in an inner city school. I had witnessed another pilot classroom earlier in the week, one overseen by a more typical teacher, and the students in that class were struggling with the test. Not only did Nancy's students not struggle, every student answered every question correctly. Nancy's balanced teaching prepared her students well for the test! It is time to find ways to assure that more students experience the type of primary education that occurs in the classrooms of Nancy Masters and teachers like her.

References

Bogner, K., Raphael, L. M., & Pressley, M. (2002). How grade-1 teachers motivate literate activity by their students. *Scientific Studies of Reading, 6*, 135–165.

Chall, J. S. (1967). *Learning to read: The great debate.* New York: McGraw-Hill.

Dolezal, S. E., Welsh, L. M., Pressley, M., & Vincent, M. (2003). How do grade-3 teachers motivate their students? *Elementary School Journal, 103*, 239–267.

Edelsky, C. (1990). Whose agenda is this anyway? A response to McKenna, Robinson, and Miller. *Educational Researcher, 19*(8), 7–11.

Gipps, C., McCallum, B., & Hargreaves, E. (2001). *What makes a good primary school teacher?: Expert classroom strategies.* London: Routledge Falmer.

Goodman, K. S. (1986). *What's whole in whole language?* Richmond Hill, Ontario: Scholastic.

Gray, J., & Sterling, R. (2000). *Teachers at the center: A memoir of the early years of the National Writing Project.* San Francisco: Berkeley CA: National Writing Project.

Kamp, G. (1983). *Teaching writing: Essays from the Bay Area Writing Project.* Portsmouth NH: Boynton/Cook.

Lyon, R. (July 10, 1997). *Report on learning disabilities research. Testimony before the Committee on Education and the Workforce.* Washington, DC: U.S. House of Representatives.

Moats, L. C. (1999). *Teaching reading is rocket science: What expert teachers of reading should know and be able to do.* Washington, DC: American Federation of Teachers.

National Reading Panel. (2000). *Report of the national reading panel: Teaching children to read: An evidence-based assessment of the scientific research literature on reading and its implications for reading instruction: Reports of the subgroups.* Washington, DC: National Institute of Child Health & Human Development, National Institutes of Health.

107th Congress (2001). *The no child left behind act of 2001.* Washington, DC: United States Congress.

Perry, N. E., & VandeKamp, K. O. (2000). Creating classroom contexts that support young children's development of self-regulated learning. *International Journal of Educational Research, 33*, 821–843.

Perry, N. E., VandeKamp, K. O., Mercer, L. K., & Nordby, C. J. (2002). Investigating teacher-student interactions that foster self-regulated learning. *Educational Psychologist, 37*, 5–15.

Pintrich, P. R., & Schunk, D. H. (1996). *Motivation in education: Theory, research, and applications.* Englewood Cliffs NJ: Prentice-Hall.

Pressley, M. (1998). *Reading instruction that works: The case for balanced teaching.* New York: Guilford.

Pressley, M. (2002). *Reading instruction that works: The case for balanced teaching* (2nd ed.). New York: Guilford.

Pressley, M., Allington, R., Wharton-McDonald, R., Block, C. C., & Morrow, L. M. (2001). *Learning to read: Lessons from exemplary first grades.* New York: Guilford.

Pressley, M., Dolezal, S. E., Raphael, L. M., Welsh, L. M., Bogner, K., & Roehrig, A. D. (2003). *Motivating primary-grade students.* New York: Guilford.

Pressley, M., & El-Dinary, P. B. (1997). What we know about translating comprehension strategies instruction research into practice. *Journal of Learning Disabilities, 30*, 486–488.

Pressley, M., El-Dinary, P. B., Gaskins, I., Schuder, T., Bergman, J. L., Almasi, J., & Brown, R. (1992). Beyond direct explanation: Transactional instruction of reading comprehension strategies. *Elementary School Journal, 92*, 511–554.

Pressley, M., Wharton-McDonald, R., Allington, R., Block, C. C., Morrow, L., Tracey, D., Baker, K., Brooks, G., Cronin, J., Nelson, E., & Woo, D. (2001). A study of effective grade-1 literacy instruction. *Scientific Studies of Reading, 5*, 35–58.

Sanders, W. L., & Horn, S. (1994). The Tennessee Value-Added Assessment System (TVAAS): Mixed-model methodology in educational assessment. *Journal of Personnel Evaluation in Education*, *8*, 299–311.

Smith, C. B. (Moderator) (1994). *Whole language: The debate* (pp. 155–178). Bloomington IN: ERIC/REC.

Smith, F. (1971). *Understanding reading – A psycholinguistic analysis of reading and learning to read.* New York: Holt, Rinehart, & Winston.

Smith, F. (1975). *Comprehension and learning: A conceptual framework for teachers.*

Katonah, NY: Owen. Smith, F. (1979). *Reading without nonsense.* New York: Teachers College Press.

Snow, C. E., Burns, M. S., & Griffin, P. (1998). *Preventing reading difficulties in young children.* Washington DC: National Academy Press.

Stahl, S. A., & Miller, P. D. (1989). Whole language and language experience approaches for beginning reading: A quantitative research synthesis. *Review of Educational Research, 59*, 87–116.

Strauss, A., & Corbin, J. (1998). *Basics of qualitative research: Grounded theory procedures and techniques* (2nd ed.). Newbury Park CA: Sage.

Weaver, C. (1994). *Understanding whole language: From principles to practice* (2nd ed.). Portsmouth, NH: Heinemann.

Wharton-McDonald, R., Pressley, M., & Hampston, J. M. (1998). Outstanding literacy instruction in first grade: Teacher practices and student achievement. *Elementary School Journal, 99*, 101–128.

Yatvin, J. (2002). Babes in the woods: The wanderings of the National Reading Panel. In R. L. Allington (Ed.), *Big brother and the national reading curriculum: How ideology trumped evidence* (pp. 125–136). Portsmouth NH: Heinemann.

34

EVIDENCE-BASED STATE LITERACY POLICY: A CRITICAL ALTERNATIVE

Allan Luke

National Institute of Education, Nanyang Technological University, Singapore

My research in literacy education in the 1980s and 1990s pivoted on three related educational questions. How do the selective traditions of curriculum, instruction and evaluation in schools lead to the stratified production of textual and discourse practices? What are the material consequences of school-acquired practices for students as they enter work, leisure and civic life? How might approaches to "critical literacy" and "multiliteracies" alter inequitable results and consequences of literacy education?

Beginning from a sociology of school knowledge, I and others looked at how literacy was constructed textually across a range of sites. These included ideological and linguistic accounts of educational policies; media reports; curriculum and textbooks; face-to-face classroom discourse; and, tests and examinations. With many colleagues in Queensland, we developed prototypes of critical literacy, media literacy and mulitliteracies that had been widely implemented across Australia. I also worked in teacher education with regular in-service in schools and districts for over two decades. But like most curriculum researchers and teacher educators, I had no direct involvement in the making of state educational policy.

In 1998, I was well into my term as Dean of Education at the University of Queensland. I was invited by the Queensland state ministry (Education Queensland) to take up the position of Deputy Director General of Education for the state for a fixed term (1999–2000). I subsequently was Chief Educational Advisor to the Minister until 2003. Like Canadian counterparts in Manitoba and British Columbia, and UK counterparts under the Blair government, I was crossing over from academy to government, from the social fields and orthodoxies of research to those of civil service.

As Deputy Director General of Education, my charge was to initiate reforms that would prototype for Queensland's 1200 state schools and 750,000 students new approaches to curriculum, pedagogy and assessment. These aimed to address the challenges of new community cultures, new knowledges and technologies,

International Handbook of Educational Policy, 661–675
Nina Bascia, Alister Cumming, Amanda Datnow, Kenneth Leithwood and David Livingstone (Eds.)
© 2005 *Springer. Printed in Great Britain.*

and globalised economies. The results were three major initiatives, all ongoing to some degree four years later:

- *New Basics*: 'futures-oriented' curriculum and pedagogical reform that included new curriculum categories, integrated project work in lieu of standardised testing, and a systematic focus on 'productive pedagogies' as the core of school renewal;
- *Productive Pedagogies*: a system-wide focus on pedagogy (and not testing or curriculum reform) as the core work of teachers, and the implementation of a new critical metalanguage for talking about teaching and learning;
- *Literate Futures*: a state strategy for literacy that aimed to improve literacy achievement through the development and implementation of 'whole school' plans based on community and staff audits.[1]

This chapter is a narrative account of policy making, an auto-ethnography that describes both arbitrariness and motivated 'play' of discourse in the sites of local policy development. I use this to make a case for evidence-based educational policy. But I argue that such an approach should be based on a rich, multi-perspectival, hermeneutic social science, rather than the narrow positivist approaches advocated in the US and UK. I then describe *Literate Futures* (2000), the Queensland state literacy strategy developed with Peter Freebody and Ray Land. The chapter concludes with a discussion of the strategy four years on. Drawing on sociological models of capital (Albright & Luke, in press; Bourdieu, 1992), I make the case for literacy-in-education policy as a subset of sustainable, broader educational, social and economic policy.

A Policy Auto-ethnography

After I had moved into the state bureaucracy, I continued to attend evening seminars with graduate students on the state and policy discourses. Our studies included Nikolas Rose's *Powers of Freedom* (1999), where Rose's model of governmentality draws from Foucault but also from the genealogical studies of mathematics and statistics by the Canadian philosopher Ian Hacking (1996). Rose documents the emergence of a modernist state premised on the calculability of the human subject, where 'countability' prefigures neoliberal moves towards government based on institutional performance and measurement. At the same time, I was reading recent work by Habermas (1998), where he argues that legal, juridical discourse is a bridge between "facts and norms".

Drawn as they are from the two distinctive strands of contemporary Western philosophy, these works offer differing but complementary accounts of how evidence-based social policy might work. In Rose's case, an avalanche of numbers overrides and drives the discourses of ethical decision-making, enabling technocratic rationality to take on a life of its own in the constitution of governance and governmentality. In Habermas' view, it is only a dialogic, hermeneutic social science that stands to mediate facticity, in all of its various forms, and social norms. This is the work of the formation of law, achieved through the ethical conditions and very possibility for dialogue, discourse and consensus. While they offer strikingly different critiques of the state and, epistemologically accounts of social facts and realities, both nonetheless view policy, law and social regulation as shaped and achieved through constituent discourses towards identifiably ethical and moral ends. Whatever their epistemological departure points, their actual applications to the analysis of contemporary educational and social policy turn on a key point of discourse: what will count as science?

Moving from these discussions each week back into the corporate board room of senior government bureaucracy was, simply, an out-of-body experience. For a while my life had become the kind of boundary crossing 'halfie' narrative described recently by Foley, Levinson and Hurtig (2001) – a lived political/personal dialectic of emic/etic, insider/outsider relations. Though committed in formal policy and ideology to a broad liberal and neo-socialist agenda of social justice and equality, the state government I was working with, like virtually all of its counterparts in postindustrial nations, was characterised externally as moving inexorably towards a neoliberal political economy that was 'beyond left and right' (Giddens, 1996).

What follows is a composite narrative of my first 'high stakes' senior policy meetings. The topic on the boardroom table was school size. We were discussing the opening of new schools and the politically sensitive issue of school closures. I waited for Rose's avalanche of numbers. I waited for technocratic economic rationalism. I waited for the ideal speech situation (not really). None arrived. After the fact, I made a list of the speech acts used, in the Habermasian tradition treating them as a taxonomy of dialogic 'truth claims'. The claims were:

- Precedent: "We always have done it this way".
- Political: "The unions would never let us do it." "That constituency would never wear it". "We'd never get that through cabinet".
- Fiscal: "We can't afford it". "Where is the money coming from?".
- Evidence: "Look at the data". "Look at the test scores".
- Philosophy: "We believe in ..."

Curiously, the latter two categories were invoked least frequently, a pattern which developed across many such meetings. Further, the exchanges shifted fluidly, sometimes wildly between the different categories, and, as is typical in face-to-face discussions, there was little explicit, self-conscious marking of such shifts.

As researchers and theorists – there are many language games we can play in trying to analyse and objectify the operations of power in such situations. We could undertake critical discourse analyses of such claims, or break them down as Aristotelian forms of knowledge, view them as taxonomic shifts in logical grounds, or, as Habermas might, take them as speech acts with particular locutionary, illocutionary and perlocutionary characteristics. But I experienced them as something more akin to the ebbs and flows of what Blackmore and

Sachs (1998) have referred to as an "emotional economy" of educational admin-istration. To a newcomer, they were more like unpredictable musical riffs, pre-sented with affective force, their effects greatly dependent on the gendered and hierarchical authority of the speaker and her/his individual agency, and affiliated knowledge and power relations. As an aside, it is indeed curious that we generally treat classroom interaction and school leadership in such terms but fail to apply such analytic constructs to policy analysis – treating it as a relatively simple instance of dominant ideology, as static interpellating text, rather than something which is historically produced through discourse generative zones, everyday exchanges of capital and face-to-face dynamics. Perhaps this is simply because such exchanges have historically been barred from researcher or public scrutiny – though current journalistic accounts over the decision-making processes and dynamics of the Bush "war cabinet" are narrative ethnographies of the workings of power (e.g., Clarke, 2004).

For now, let me make the point that policy formation appeared to entail far more of an arbitrary play of discourse and truth, power and knowledge than I had anticipated, notwithstanding how it is justified in press releases, Hansard, or Green Papers, or how it is critiqued in our own critical theory. More pertinent to this handbook, the use of evidence – whether psychometric, sociometric, factor-analytic, multilevel, case-based, ethnographic, or qualitative – appeared far less systematic, far less 'calculating' than Rose's account, and far less indicative of a dominant ideology than many of our own critical policy analyses since Apple (1982) have led us to believe.

My experience convinced me that we could only move systematically towards a redressive educational agenda and project of social justice if, indeed, we reworked and reappropriated an evidence-based approach to policy development away from narrow, neoliberal educational orientations to accountability. Without a broad array of evidence and data, targeting and moving specific redressive strategies was difficult, arbitrary and piecemeal, more likely to entail add-on activities and token distribution of funds. But the grounds and shape of policy required are of a very different order than the test-driven approaches so influential in most North American and UK contexts at present.

Economy and School in Transition

In most Australian states, the major policy settings for 'reform' have been in place for some years now. These consist of: (1) standardized achievement testing in literacy and numeracy at key junctures in schooling; (2) the ongoing updating and implementation of curriculum documents. Under these broad auspices, "outcomes-based education" brings together Tylerian models of curriculum with the aforementioned neoliberal policy approaches to the appraisal of student performance. At the same time, the defacto national agenda has been to move towards (3) school-based management, where principals can make semi-autono-mous decisions about school programming, structures and procedures, ostensibly to ensure the improvement of (1) above and the better implementation of (2) above. The effects of this approach are compounded and, perhaps, confounded by the emergence of powerful market forces, with the Catholic and Independent sectors differentially funded but less explicitly regulated in terms of testing performativity and curriculum. Though on different timelines in various states, this general suite of reforms has evolved for two decades. But what remains unclear is how these reforms logically extend to the matter of literacy education.

This is, indeed, a contradictory matter. For on the one hand, the approach to 'evidence-based' policy that draws upon aspects of 'steering from a distance' and surveillance is exemplified in *No Child Left Behind*[2] and the UK *National Literacy Program*,[3] where the basic strategy consists of the specification of target outcomes, the standardisation of teaching via centrally-mandated textbooks and programs, and centralised control via the monitoring of outcomes on standardised, norm-referenced, pencil-and-paper reading tests. As this chapter goes to press in 2004, Australia is engaged in its own latest round of 'phonics wars' – phenomena that, as in North America, have tended to come and go cyclically in postwar periods of major social, economic and cultural upheaval (Green, Hodgens & Luke, 1994).

But what if we were to build literacy strategies from, inter alia, the 'other' putative principles of neoliberal reform – local school autonomy and community responsiveness and accountability – and augment them with a model which draws directly from the lessons of over a decade of work in the broader field of literacy studies (e.g., Barton, Hamilton, & Ivanic, 2000)? What if we were to build an approach to literacy education based on the findings of critical social science – qualitative and quantitative – and not the narrow bands of 'experimental science' that the *National Reading Panel* (National Institute of Child Health and Human Development, 2000) operated from?

Such an approach might stress local, school-level analyses of community-literacy needs, audits and local mobilisation of available teacher professional expertise and discourses, the study of community linguistic and cultural profiles, and an assaying of the developmental and sociopractical needs of specific communities of learners. These, rather than the large scale mandating of a single approach or textbook/curriculum package would form the basis for school-specific literacy education plans, that would include justified choices of materials, approaches and assessment strategies to be taken up by schools. Literacy-in-education policy making, then, could be about the coordinated mobilisation and alignment of resources and capital – human and discursive, pedagogical/professional and economic/infrastructural – rather than the identification and implementation of teaching method per se (Luke, Land, Kolatsis, Christie & Noblett, 2002).

Understandably, many systems administrators, senior civil servants and, indeed, literacy educators would see this as a tall order, as 'too hard', given available levels of teacher expertise, and the actual levels and kinds of technical and theoretical knowledge that would be necessary. This is a very real problem given teacher deskilling through the over-proliferation of basal reading-type series and highly variable teacher training in language arts, literacy, second-language teaching and reading education within larger educational systems. But indeed this is the direction we proposed for Queensland.

In 2000, Peter Freebody, Ray Land and I were commissioned to review literacy education in Queensland and to develop a five-year literacy strategy for the 1300 state-run primary, secondary and middle schools, 30,000 teachers and three quarters of a million students in the state of Queensland, Australia's third most populous state, known for its Barrier Reef, large tropical fruit, a problematic racial and political history and, most recently, its eclectic intellectual and practical project of critical literacy. As noted above, the review was the third piece in a series of major policy developments undertaken by the state government – beginning with *Education 2010* (Education Queensland, 1999), the *School Restructuring Longitudinal Study* (Lingard et al., 2002) and the New Basics curriculum reform (Luke et al., 1999). The latter reform document had implemented a version of the New London Group's (1996) "multiliteracies" in 36 trial schools.

The brief from the government for the literacy strategy was twofold. First, we were charged with identifying strengths and weaknesses in current practice with an eye to the improvement of student literacy outcomes. Second, unlike UK and US policies, we moved to develop a durable literacy strategy that considered and addressed the impacts of economic globalisation on Queensland children and youth: the profound social effects of the unequal spread of capital and declining social infrastructure, the new skill and job demands generated by digital technologies, the shift to service and semiotic, information and symbol-based economies, and the new forms of textual practice and identity in play on the internet and other communications technologies.

These are not abstractions, but changed material and sociodemographic conditions for Queensland communities – with attendant changes in the 'narratives' and grammars of people's life pathways:

- *Spatialised poverty*: with 20% of families living below the official poverty line, particularly in rural primary economy areas, indigenous areas but also in low wage mortgage belts, fringe cities where a white underclass has developed, a gradual movement towards more of a binary divide in the distribution of wealth; youth unemployment in these same areas was often in the range of 60–80% and many teachers and social workers were reporting second and third generation structurally unemployed;
- *Changing job markets*: with the cumulative effects of two decades of economic restructuring, the casualisation, outsourcing and subcontracting of the workforce was accompanied by a proliferation of service and information work, with a concomitant shift from traditional male-dominated jobs requiring physical dexterity to semiotic, data and social interactional skills.

The net result was a "delinearisation" of life pathways from school to work and further education, employment, underemployment and unemployment (Luke &

Luke, 2001) that to date had not been empirically documented or described on any scale within government. These are recursive, non-linear and somewhat less predictable life trajectories that indicate both the volatility of employment conditions. Although all Australian state governments undertook what were termed "pathway" studies in the late 1990s, we were unable to account for where drop outs and graduates go, from what 'streams' into what social fields and institutions, when, how they might return to education, with what capital and consequences. One of the additional responses to these structural economic conditions was an increased intrastate and interstate mobility of the school-aged population, particularly as younger families moved in search of work and affordable housing. At the same time, general retention rates in Queensland and across Australia are in decline, with 74% of the year 8 cohort completing year 12 and the percentage of students leaving schools for the (state-subsidised) independent and religious schools at about 30%. This overall picture – as much sociodemographic as psychometric – provided a working context for situating and localising literacy problems and proposed interventions.

Our four-month work program in 2000 involved a reanalysis of student achievement data from Queensland schools, a review of various other state, national and regional approaches to literacy policy, and a state-wide public and professional consultation that involved stakeholder consultation with relevant professional organizations, teacher educators, and parents in public meetings and school visits. As much as this could be taken as a scientific survey of literacy standards, then, it was equally an exercise in public policy discourse formation among the state's key educational constituencies. From the consultation, we collected and coded over 2000 statements and slightly over 250 written positions for a discourse analysis of key words and themes. *Literate Futures* (Luke, Freebody & Land, 2000) was endorsed by the state government in October 2000 and is currently under implementation.

Our findings on literacy instruction were assisted by several larger-scale studies that we had been involved in – both of which involved extensive systematic classroom observation, something missing from many attempts at state policy. These were a federally-funded study of early literacy home/school transitions and social class (Freebody et al., 1996) and a state-funded study that involved the analysis and description of pedagogy in 1200 classroom lessons over a three year period (Lingard et al., 2003). Our overall findings were:

- *Writing Instruction:* that the overall focus of the 'text in context' and 'genre' approaches to writing over a decade was effective, though there was still some way to go in teacher knowledge of functional grammar;
- *Reading Instruction:* that, while about a third of all children were picked up by a face-to-face reading diagnostic as struggling in year 2, according to existing testing systems, roughly 80% of children were leaving Year 3 with basic functional decoding skills. There was fifth grade 'slump' evidence, with residualisation of skills for almost 10% of students by year 5. The majority of schools lacked a systematic focus on reading, often with eclectic

approaches from a range of training backgrounds, often deployed irrespective of student need or data on achievement and background;

- *Inclusive Instruction*: that, despite an increase in numbers of students from non-English speaking backgrounds to about 15%, and the mainstreaming of students with learning disabilities and a range of special education needs, teachers were struggling to provide these students with appropriate or effective intervention;

- *Secondary Literacy Programs*: that secondary schools did not have in place diagnostic systems to identify and help non-readers, programs for increasing comprehension or literacy across the curriculum, or sufficient reading specialists or staff expertise;

- *Multiliteracies*: that despite expanded hardware infrastructure, schools were slow to adapt to new digital literacies, with most teachers sticking to traditional print models and the "IT" expertise principally concentrated in maths and science education.

While factors such as gender, ethnic/linguistic background were predictors of early reading achievement, the schools most 'at risk' were those from the aforementioned communities hit the hardest by new patterns of spatialised poverty. It was clear to us that some of the strategies we would have to enlist could be 'generic' and 'across-the-board'. Our principal assumption was that schools and the system had to have highly localised responses. Without these, there was a danger of misdirection of fiscal and human resources – and mismatch of instructional approach to student background and need.

Several schools that we had visited had an over-reactive emphasis on 'basic skills'. This had led to some extremely unbalanced programs. We visited one such program that declared itself with full parental support a "basics" school featuring an exclusive emphasis for the initial years of schooling on phonics, word study and quota spelling. Not surprisingly, their reading comprehension scores at year 6 were low and there were real problems in the students' writing. This is the kind of program 'skew' that leads on from an over reliance on test scores and commodified single method approaches. It also corroborated the findings of the Queensland School Restructuring Longitudinal Study (Lingard et al., 2003). Replicating previous research designs by Newmann et al. (1996), the Queensland study provided case and systems-wide data that indicated that overall levels of "intellectual quality" and depth were low. Several teachers and principals interviewed in that study stated that the narrowing of the curriculum for purposes of basic skills instruction had already begun among middle and lower achievement schools.

At the same time, the strategy of choice in responding to the new poverty was the proliferation of "pull out" programs, that is, augmenting, specially funded programs for diagnosis and remediation of the bottom quartile of students. These included: learning support programs, Aboriginal and Torres Strait Islander programs, ESL support, Reading Recovery, speech pathology and school psychology. In many schools, there was no coherent coordination between these programs and we had very little state-wide data about their efficacy. At the school level, performance gains achieved through pull-out programs often were difficult to sustain where there was little focus on changing mainstream pedagogical practices.

Literate Futures, then, sent out a mixed message. While there was hardly evidence of a literacy crisis, it was clear to us as literacy researchers that schools could improve their overall strategies and approaches to literacy, particularly for those children from lower socio-economic backgrounds (cf. LoBianco & Freebody, 1997). However, the complexity and diversity of the problem required something other than a 'one size fits all' approach. Quite the contrary, in the vast majority of schools, a 'back to the basics' or strongly coordinated reemphasis of code and alphabetic knowledge might have been counterproductive. If indeed the more general claims of Newmann et al. (1996) and Lingard et al.'s (2003) Queensland work held, in fact, the challenge was how to provide intellectual quality, depth, higher order thinking and connectedness to the world, as readily as it might be to ensure that necessary basic skills were achieved.

An Alternative Policy

Part of the achievement of *Literate Futures* was that it captured the complexity of literacy and education in transition. Certainly two decades of literacy research since the pivotal publication of *Ways with Words* (Heath, 1983), *Literacy in Theory and Practice* (Street, 1984), and *The Psychology of Literacy* (Scribner & Cole, 1981) taught us some very simple lessons worth heeding: that literacy is constructed, contested and put to work by individuals not as a universally portable, transferable and applicable set of skills. Rather the "functions and uses of literacy", their affiliated social meetings and capital value, depend upon and occur in the context of a range of social "contexts of use" and "contexts of acquisition" (Heath, 1986). Therefore to change and reshape literacy, its practices and uses in sustainable ways, our efforts must engage the full breadth and depth of social institutions where families and individuals live their everyday lives.

If we move beyond the view of literacy education as simple pedagogic machinery for the transmission of basic skills, a literacy-in-education policy *in situ* can only be based on a rich, triangulated, and multiperspectival social science. To our colleagues in the legislatures and civil service, we can argue that this is just simply a matter of the construction of better, more sustainable and potentially more efficacious social policy – with less risk of short term effects (however electorally attractive these might appear), collateral and unintended effects, and fiscal waste.

This isn't to say that improved test scores and the systematic teaching of coding skills are not a key part of the picture. But they are indeed part of a picture that needs shaping, moulding and structuring, as social and educational policy sets out to do, in relation to a range of other factors. Simply, knowing the complexity of literacy, its communities and learners, and indeed, the complexity of schools as industrial organisations engaged with change – we took a harder and more ecologically valid road: one that focused on changing schools as professional and pedagogic cultures where literacy teaching could be done, wilfully but differently; and one that focused on how those changes might connect with and enlist other kinds of capital and knowledge, cultural and linguistic resources in the community.

Furthermore, where we re-analysed the test score data in terms of location, social class, and ethnic/linguistic diversity – it became apparent that the problem was not a generic early reading problem that could be solved by a singular pedagogic intervention. That is, to follow Heath (1986) again, we wanted to change the "contexts of acquisition" – classroom teaching and learning – in relation to changes in the "contexts of use", communities, new workplaces and new pathways. No basal could do this.

Literate Futures mandated the following policy strategies:

1. *Whole School Planning*: Each school was tasked with the 18–24 month development of a school literacy strategy. That strategy had to be based on data that included diagnostic net and test scores but also local audits of community linguistic and cultural resources (Moll, 1989), audits of existing teacher expertise. On this basis, instructional modes and curricula would be set out. These would involve the setting of "distance-travelled" performance targets benchmarked against "like-schools" of similar community demographic and socio-economic backgrounds.
2. *Balanced Programs*: Each school had to adopt a "balanced approach" to the teaching of reading based on the "four resources" model (Freebody & Luke, 1990; Luke & Freebody, 1996). This requires that teachers make principled decisions based on analyses of their analysis of student performance data and student linguistic and community resources. These decisions would tilt the program balances between "coding", "semantic", "pragmatic" and "critical" practices of literacy. While it acknowledges the need for a coherent common vocabulary on reading instruction, the report does not assume that there is a universally effective or valid 'method' or curricular commodity that will be relevant or worthwhile for all student communities.
3. *Multiliteracies*: Each school was encouraged to engage with "multiliteracies", the blending of information technologies and traditional print literacies. The focus here was meant to push literacy paradigms in schools towards on-line communications, mass media and digital cultures.
4. *Professional Development*: There was a recognition that the state system and schools needed to rebuild and refocus their professional development resources and networks to achieve 1, 2 and 3 above. The problem was particularly acute given the age-bifurcation of the workforce, with a significant 'generation gap' arising in staffrooms. Our observation was that much of the expertise needed to systematically improve literacy and solve many of the problems was in the schools, but that it was dispersed and not

sufficiently recognised. Hence, the proposed audits of staff expertise in 1 above.

Literate Futures thus set out a different educational approach from that underway in many systems: in its refusal to get 'sucked into' the reading wars debate, in its focus on school/community analyses and linkages, and in its focus on the capitalization on and development of teacher expertise. Our focus in the strategy is as much to reframe the professional development capacity of educational systems as teachers' "social capital". The strategy contrasts sharply with a compliance approach that targets short and medium term improvement of test scores via the standardization, surveillance and control of teacher classroom behaviour and methods. It is based on the premise that teacher learning and professionalisation, rather than deskilling and centralized control, have the potential for more flexible and sustainable approaches to these problems.

Finally, its futures orientation is based on the assumption that an overly zealous focus on short-term surface performance gains may fail to engage with the educational challenges facing schools and systems, governments and economies: new textual and semiotic economies, blends of oral, print and technologically-mediated language and multiliteracies, and the large-scale generational shift in teacher population, expertise and technological competence as schools approach 2010.

Aftermath: Sustainable Policy and the Alignment of Capital

In the midst of all of this, one seasoned bureaucrat turned to me and said: in one electoral cycle, if you can achieve one substantive reform or change, you've done very well. To be honest, there were times after *Literate Futures* when our decision to challenge teachers' professionalism, to engage and build professional development and training opportunities that brought teacher educators, researchers and curriculum consultants into closer 'problem-solving' relationships with schools seemed too hard. For the mobilisation of different, appropriate and powerful methods and approaches, curriculum and instruction, funding and staffing at the local level – while maintaining some degree of control and accountability over the whole process by tracking centrally whole school plans, progress towards targets, and professional development activities – is far more complex than mandating a textbook series and expanding testing. In such cases, it is not wholly a matter of whether the teachers or principals or students are up to the task. It is at least in part whether your bureaucracy is kitted up to drive dynamic, diverse patterns of local institutional development and change – a task requiring systematic approaches to formative evaluation, coordination of qualitative and quantitative data collection, and a critical interpretive capacity in central office.

In the four years since *Literate Futures* several trends have become apparent. While we can't attribute such short and medium term results to policies in implementation variable,[4] the primary reading scores have trended upward. In the 2002 test results, almost 90% of children met the year 3 state standard for reading. However, there is a persistent 'fifth grade' slump, with 20% of all children failing to meet state standards. Further, secondary schools have been far slower to develop and implement their comprehensive school plans. At the same time, the suite of reforms beginning in 2000 led to major and ongoing pedagogic dialogue amongst teachers and among teacher-educators across the state.

In several Aboriginal schools and lower socio-economic community schools, whole school planning, *New Basics* curriculum reform and other interventions were affiliated with major performance gains. But it would be presumptuous of us as policy-makers to take credit for these. For they typically occurred in relation to dynamic community and professional mobilisations of social and economic capital to support educational efforts of the school – nothing short of local 'campaigns' to make a difference. One of the indirect lessons of our strategy to date is that face-to-face pedagogic change can make a difference when and where it is tied to the wholescale development of schools as professional learning cultures (Newmann et al., 1996; Lingard et al., 2003).

But similarly, whether and how school based literacy achievement can be translated into improved educational consequences and life pathways depends as much on the availability of other forms of capital in communities: from economic capital via gainful and meaningful work, to non-discriminatory and enabling social networks and institutional relations, to community environments that recognise and encourage school-acquired knowledge as 'counting', as having symbolic and real power in communities. In this regard, we can only really assess the impacts of literacy-in-education planning as a subset of broader educational policy that includes school reform and professional renewal. And even then its success in changing lives is as contingent on coordinated, localised social and economic policies of the kinds that governments and corporations struggle to deliver across the silos of welfare, health, education, and employment policies (Luke, 2003). A key function of government, then, is to make available the requisite kinds and combinations of capital, and to try to establish and enable the social, economic and linguistic fields where these forms of capital can be deployed.

In *Academic Distinctions* (1996) James Ladwig argued that for a critical realist approach to educational research that enlists both qualitative and quantitative, hermeneutic and positivist paradigms in a constructive dialogue about the reform of educational systems and their social consequences. We now need evidence-based social policies derived, inter alia, from a critical, hermeneutic social science that draws from a range of disciplinary discourses and fields. Such an approach, I would argue, would provide a more complex, theory-driven analysis using and triangulating a range of social statistical, demographic, economic, sociological, ethnographic as well as psychometric data sources.

It would move away from a reductionist focus on outcomes qua standardised norm-referenced achievement test scores towards a broader analysis of how educationally acquired capital has material consequences in individuals' and communities' pathways through and via emergent economies and institutions. It would bring to bear the kinds of multilevel statistical analysis (e.g., structural equation modelling) that have come into their own, enabling the theoretical and empirical documentation of complex networks of mediating social and educational effects – including and focusing on the possibilities of pedagogical practice – in lieu of causal, hypodermic models of psychological effects. We would begin to use statistical and value adding analyses to begin to account for how forms of difference (multiple aspects of subjectivity) work together to constitute enabling and disenabling forms of capital, and how such forms of difference can be differentially remediated through curriculum and instruction. We would use ethnographic, case study and discourse analytic work to test hypotheses, to build models, and to instantiate the trends and clusters that emerge from such an analysis.

At the same time, we would push to prototype and expand a range of models of "authentic assessment" (Newmann et al., 1996) in ways that would normatively redirect schools and systems away from, rather than towards, a teleology of basic skills towards models that stress critical, higher order and advanced engagements with intellectual fields and discourses that count. Finally, we would engage in longitudinal tracking of life pathways in ways that would enable us to understand the consequences of education beyond simple heightened test scores and retention rates. This is the kind of work we began in Queensland in the late 1990s, and it forms the core of work currently underway in Singapore.[5]

All of the components of a multidisciplinary, interpretive social science are at hand to engage in powerful and cohesive approaches to evidence-based policy – in literacy, in education, and in affiliated social and economic policy. The current gratuitous attacks on educational research, and the deliberately naïve polarisation of qualitative/quantitative, experimental/interpretive are but smokescreens. We need and could enlist all of them to make critical, informed and sustainable literacy-in-education policy.

The question is only in part about whether and how teachers and schools can change. The prior question is whether governments, bureaucracies and education systems themselves have the intellectual resources, the research infrastructure and capacity, and, indeed, the psychological maturity and electoral patience to understand, articulate and promote complex and multidimensional strategies needed by unprecedented educational, social and economic contexts. And even then, they must stay the course.

Acknowledgement

Thanks to Peter Freebody and Ray Land for *Literate Futures* and other projects; Kim Bannikoff for mentoring; Alister Cumming and Siti Masturah Bte Ismail for editorial assistance; Terry Moran for envisioning and enabling these and many other reforms in Australian education.

Notes

1. For documentation see the Education Queensland website:
    http://education.qld.gov.au/corporate/newbasics/;
    http://education.qld.gov.au/curriculum/learning/literate-futures;
    http://education.qld.gov.au/public_media/reprots/curriculum-framework/productive-
    pedagogies/
2. See http://www.ed.gov/nclb/landing.jhtml
3. See http://www.standards.dfes.gov.uk/literacy/
4. This is part of the problem, of course, for while one can't technically assume responsibility for gain scores, the press and parliamentary opposition will undoubtedly hold you responsible for any losses.
5. See http://www.crpp. nie.edu.sg

References

Albright, J., & Luke, A. (Eds.) (in press). *Bourdieu and literacy education*. Mahwah, NJ: Lawrence Erlbaum.

Apple, M. W. (1982). *Education and power*. London: Routledge.

Barton, D., Hamilton, M., & Ivanic, R. (Eds.) (2000). *Situated literacies*. London: Routledge.

Blackmore, J., & Sachs, J. (1998, July). Performativity, passion and academic work: The making of self and self-management. Paper presented at Winds of Change: Women and the Culture of Universities Conference, Sydney, Australia.

Bourdieu, P. (1992). *Language and symbolic power*. J. B. Thompson (Ed.). Palo Alto, CA: Stanford University Press.

Clarke, R. (2004) *Against all enemies*. New York: The Free Press.

Education Queensland (1999). *Education 2010*. Brisbane: Education Queensland.

Foley, D. A., Levinson, B. A., & Hurtig, J. (2001). Anthropology goes inside: The new educational ethnography of ethnicity and gender. *Review of Research in Education, 28*, 37–98.

Freebody, P., Ludwig, C., Gunn, S., Dwyer, S., Freiberg, J., Forrest, T., Gary, S., Hellsten, M., Herschell, P., Luke, H., Rose, J., & Wheeler, J. (1995). *Everyday literacy practices in and out of schools in low socioecononmic urban communities*. Canberra: Department of Employment, Education and Training.

Freebody, P., & Luke, A. (1990). Literacies' programs: Debates and demands in cultural contexts. *Prospect: A Journal of Australian TESOL, 11*, 7–16.

Giddens, A. (1996). *Beyond left and right*. Palo Alto, CA: Stanford University Press.

Green, W., Hodgens, J., & Luke, A. (1991). *Debating literacy: A documentary history of literacy crises in Australia, 1946–1990*. Sydney: Australian Literacy Federation.

Habermas, J. (1998). *Between facts and norms*. Boston: MIT Press.

Hacking, I. (1996). *The taming of chance*. Cambridge: Cambridge University Press.

Heath, S. B. (1983). *Ways with words*. Cambridge: Cambridge University Press.

Heath, S. B. (1986). Critical factors in literacy development. In S. DeCastell, A. Luke & K. Egan (Eds.), *Literacy, society and schooling* (pp. 196–209). Cambridge: Cambridge University Press.

Ladwig, J. (1996) *Academic distinctions*. New York: Routledge.

Lingard, R., Ladwig, J., Mills, M., Hayes, D., Gore, J., & Luke, A. (2001). *Queensland school reform longitudinal study: Final report*. Brisbane: Education Queensland.

LoBianco, J., & Freebody, P. (1997). *Australian literacies: Informing national policies on literacy education*. Melbourne: Language Australia.

Luke, A. (2003). Literacy and the other: A sociological approach to literacy research and policy in multilingual societies. *Reading Research Quarterly, 38*(1), 132–141.

Luke, A., & Freebody, P. (1996) The social practices of reading. In S. Muspratt, A. Luke & P. Freebody (Eds.), *Constructing critical literacies* (pp. 227–242). Creskill, NJ: Hampton Press.

Luke, A., Freebody, P., & Land, R. (2000). *Literate futures*. Brisbane: Education Queensland.

Luke, A., Land, R., Kolatsis, A., Christie, P., & Noblett, G. (2002) *Standard Australian English and language for Queensland Aboriginal and Torres Strait Islander students*. Brisbane: Queensland Indigenous Education Consultative Body.

Luke, A., Land, R., Matters, G., Herschell, P., & Barrett, R. (1999) *New basics technical papers*. Brisbane: Education Queensland.

Luke, A., & Luke, C. (2001) Adolescence lost/childhood regained: On early intervention and the emergence of the techno-subject. *Journal of Early Childhood Literacy, 1*, 145–180.

National Institute of Child Health and Human Development (2000). *Report of the national reading panel*. (NIH Publication No. 00-4769). Washington, DC: US Government Printing Office.

New London Group (1996). A pedagogy of multiliteracies: Designing social futures. *Harvard Educational Review, 66*, 60–92.

Newmann, F. et al. (1996). *Authentic assessment*. San Francisco: Josey Bass.

Rose, N. (1999). *The powers of freedom*. Cambridge: Cambridge University Press.

Scribner, S., & Cole, M. (1981) *The psychology of literacy*. Cambridge, MA: Harvard University Press.

Street, B. (1984). *Literacy in theory and practice*. Cambridge: Cambridge University Press.

35

LITERACIES IN ADOLESCENCE: AN ANALYSIS OF POLICIES FROM THE UNITED STATES AND QUEENSLAND, AUSTRALIA

Katherine Schultz* and Bob Fecho[†]

*University of Pennsylvania, USA; [†]University of Georgia, USA

Look outside of the school walls in nearly every community and you will find examples of adolescents deeply engaged in literacy practices. In Australia, a young man composes a flyer for a lawn-mowing service (Knobel, 1999). Teenagers in Nepal exchange love letters mixing home and school languages (Ahearn, 2001). In the U.S. suburbs, youth race home to read and respond to each other's web logs (or blogs), public journals that are proliferating among adolescents (Nussbaum, 2004). Shivering in his car, waiting to make a drug deal, a young man writes poetry to express his critique of the societal and institutional structures that constrain his life choices. Across town, his high school classmate composes a play in an afterschool club in order to make sense of her cousin's untimely death (Schultz, 2003). In a range of settings, responding to a multitude of purposes and audiences, youth gather to document their lives through film, music, photographs, poetry, and political posters posted on the Internet, played out in public performances and written in private spaces they alone occupy. They offer critique and celebration, despair and optimism, unity and diversity.

If we look and listen closely enough at the right moments and in the right places, we will notice that literacy practices initiated and sustained by youth are flourishing. Outside of classrooms, literacies often traverse multiple modalities combining music, pictures and words in new and often groundbreaking ways (Hull, 2003; Hull & Zacher, in press; Schultz & Vasudevan, in preparation). In some instances these same practices find their way into classrooms. Teachers ask students about their poetry. On-line writing including zines, blogs and other new forms of media are incorporated into classroom reading lists. Teachers work with students to pursue their interests and write about what matters to them, whether it is graphic hip hop verse, analyses of cultural epochs, or letters to campus newspapers (Fecho with Green, 2004). In numerous classrooms, students and teachers uncover opportunities for in-school and out-of-school literacies to transact in complex and often surprising ways.

However, even as students and educators are expanding our understandings

International Handbook of Educational Policy, 677–694
Nina Bascia, Alister Cumming, Amanda Datnow, Kenneth Leithwood and David Livingstone (Eds.)
© 2005 *Springer. Printed in Great Britain.*

of the audiences, purposes and forms of literacy, policy initiated at the federal, state and district levels often continues to define literacy in ever more parochial terms. Extending their sphere of influence, yet masking their fiscal responsibility, policymakers have codified literacy in increasingly narrow ways through regulations and curricular mandates. Although many educators might understand adolescents to be engaged in literacy practices across the borders of school and community when they write messages to one another in a variety of electronic and traditional media, literacy policies enacted at distance from classrooms too often direct teachers and curriculum towards discrete tasks that are keyed to a narrow range of assessment measures and prescriptive teaching.

The opening description of the varied ways in which some youth are engaged in literacy learning on their own in and out of school is not meant to hide the very real pictures of disengagement among adolescents, particularly in urban schools. In the U.S., there are persistently high dropout rates, particularly in urban and rural areas and for Latino and African American students (e.g., Greene & Winters, 2002; NCES, 2000), and there is abundant evidence of students failing to graduate and schools failing to meet the needs of or to engage their students (e.g., Anyon, 1997; Fine & Weis, 2003; Lipman, 1998; Schultz, 2002). While the national focus in the U.S. and countries around the world is on early literacy, dropout rates in the U.S. have persisted at high rates particularly for students of color, suggesting the urgency to maintain a focus on literacy learning and retaining students in their adolescent years. Greene (2001) reported that in 1998 the national graduation rate was 71%. For white students the rate was 78%, while it was 56% for African-American students and 54% for Latino students. The social and economic consequences of dropping out of school, and not attaining the necessary literacy knowledge, skills and practices are steep (e.g., Greene, 2001) although not necessarily clear-cut. While on one hand we can paint a picture of abundance and activity, there is always the contrasting portrait of struggle and failure in our discussion of adolescent literacy.

In each of these descriptions, a multitude of tensions are at play. The conclusion that youth are deeply engaged in literacy practices outside of school while failing school subjects is far too facile, as are the valorization of literacies in the community and the characterization of literacies at school as stagnant (Hull & Schultz, 2002; Schultz, 2003). Key to our discussion is the ways these examples point to how socially constructed policies, institutions, and media both reflect and ignore the needs of individuals served by these institutions. To illustrate this point, we turn to a small rural community in the U.S. for an extended example.

The Test and Nothing But the Test

Kate, a secondary teacher in a rural school, called our attention to Virgil, one of her students. It seems that Virgil was confronted with passing a high school exit exam, a high stakes standardized test established by his state as a requirement for graduation. As Kate described him, Virgil was not "the type of student who takes the test lightly, belligerently scribbling slack answers" and generally shrugging off the test. Instead, he had followed many of the unwritten rules required of a good student about to re-take a complicated exam: He attended and participated in school regularly, sought help, practiced, got rest the night before, ate well the day of the test, and gathered support and confidence from people who cared about him.

Nor is Kate the kind of teacher who disregards such tests. She may not agree with their intention, but she understands the role they play in the lives of her students. In fact, all of her students except Virgil had passed the exam. But she wasn't about to rest on this success and, in the months prior to Virgil's re-taking the exam, she worked closely with him, "not just teaching him how to read and write and think, but teaching him how to pass the test." Moreover, Virgil's foster parents – the couple who had adopted this Native American child and rejoiced when, finally, in fourth grade he emerged as a reader – had helped him study and practice at home. Yet, given all this support and effort, Virgil, for the third time, was in danger of not passing the exam.

Kate believed Virgil to be a victim of policy. As she wrote:

> So, legislators who decided that a single test would somehow fit every student in our great state ... what about Virgil? ... What about a young man whose foster parents, friends, and teachers continue to encourage him while you, a government body unfamiliar with the real-life, blood-and-guts, day-to-day reality of education, require that he pass a test that he really and truly *cannot pass* (emphasis in the original) if he wants to earn a diploma? What are you saying to him? What are you trying to prove? What is your point, your purpose? Whose life, whose hide, are you trying to save here?

Furthermore, Kate herself was becoming a victim of policy. In her effort to help her student, she read through his completed exam and, following her instincts as a conscientious and careful teacher, analyzed the data at hand for insight into how best to continue her efforts. She made no attempt to correct Virgil's work; she simply wanted to know how best to support his learning in the moment, rather than waiting for months when the reported scores would be all but useless. When administrators from her state department of testing heard she had done this, they issued a reprimand that she had "violated test security" and restricted her from discussing the particulars of this story we render here using pseudonyms and vague references. As Kate wrote, "Virgil, I want to shout from the rooftops for you," but "part of test security is not sharing the details of the injustice done to you today."

As it turns out, Kate was wrong in her projections. Virgil did pass the test. Barely. Testing proponents would see this as a victory. Their argument would be that Virgil had been challenged by the test and, through hard work and perseverance, had met that challenge. From our perspective, however, this vignette is less about whether or not Virgil succeeded, although we applaud both Virgil and his support community for their successful efforts. We are more concerned about the *why* of this policy. What, we wonder, is the intent of this policy? Whose voices get heard and whose are silenced in the creation of policies such as these? Whose needs are being served, what are those needs, and what is the cost in time and effort as well as funding?

There is a tension in Virgil's story between the collective efforts of the school community and the distance that separates that community from the policymakers. What are the needs of individual students and local districts, who gets to define them, and are those needs being served well by policy being made in state and national capitals? This line of questioning leads us to wonder whose voices get heard when policy gets made and who, for that matter, gets to make policy? We wonder about the intent of policy, whether it is enacted with the intent to limit and constrict – to be the lone voice of authority – or is there an intention built into policy that tries to embrace and include, that seeks dialogue as opposed to smothering it? Finally, Virgil and Kate's story reminds us that policy is more than words on paper, that it is a set of actions meant to be carried forward and those actions transact daily with millions of lives. As is the case with Virgil and Kate, lives get changed daily by policy in ways, we suspect, that those who write these policies are often unaware.

Further, we can guess that there are narrow definitions of literacy embedded in these tests that fail to account for the myriad ways Virgil and his peers may engage in literacy practices in their daily lives. Current theoretical perspectives on literacy, especially those described by the New Literacy Studies (e.g., Gee, 1996; Street, 1993) and characterized as multiliteracies (Cope & Kalantzis, 2000; New London Group, 1996) suggest that importance of revealing, understanding and addressing power relations embedded in literacy practices. Tests present a standardized and distant conception of literacy, while the local practices enacted by individuals are situated in social interactions across multiple contexts. In short, literacy practices are often messy, idiosyncratic and rarely captured by single measures. Recognition of these tensions leads us to a conceptual framework that captures these complexities.

Framing Policy with Bakhtinian Theory

We enter this discussion of literacy policies through an exploration of one of Mikhail Bakhtin's theories of language. A Russian linguist and literary theorist writing in the early part of the 20th century, Bakhtin (1981) offered a view of language that characterized it as inherently social and always undergoing transformation. Our language becomes our own only after we have appropriated it from others. Central to Bakhtin's description of language use is the concept of dialogue. In particular, Bakhtin argued that language continuously experiences centripetal or unifying tensions at the same time that it experiences centrifugal or disunifying tensions. Furthermore, he argued that this is a healthy state for language. The centripetal forces enable ease of communication across a wider audience while the centrifugal forces allow individuals to see themselves and their needs in the language. This variation keeps language from becoming static and lifeless.

Hermans and Kempen (1993), two social psychologists, have suggested that if we accept Bakhtin's concept of language as existing in a continual state of tension between unification and disunification, then identity creation, the way we construct ourselves through language, undergoes similar tensions. They argue that our identities are complex structures continually under construction and that we present identities of self that are at once unified and in dialogue or conflict with the range of roles and voices we use to represent ourselves, hour-to-hour and even minute-to-minute. Like language, the play of these unifying and disunifying forces makes for a healthy presentation of self. Drawing on these theoretical perspectives, Pintaone-Hernandez (2002) claimed that communities operate under the same tensions when they engage in a healthy and sustaining process that acknowledges the dialogue between forces that unite and forces that keep them in flux. Too much of either force is problematic for the life of the community.

If we accept that policy is an attempt to use language to mediate the ways individuals transact within a community through institutional practices, then – similar to language (Bakhtin, 1981), identity (Hermans & Kempen, 1993), and community (Pintaone-Hernandez, 2002) – policy is subject to centripetal and centrifugal tensions. Following that line of argument, healthy policy is predicated upon a relative balance of those tensions. As policymakers try to standardize and unify policy at any level of government, a myriad of local constituencies pull and tug at that policy causing its simultaneous disunification. These tensions serve to keep policy both stable and fluid. We wonder, then, what it means to see the making of policy through this Bakhtinian lens, to regard policy as a framework for the sphere it purports to influence, yet fluid enough to respond to a range of needs within that sphere.

Working from this theoretical stance, in this chapter we examine governmental adolescent literacy policies in two locations – at the federal level in the U.S. and at the state level in Queensland, Australia – in order to raise questions about their assumptions and purposes. In doing so, we wonder about a number of concerns that cast a spotlight upon the play of centrifugal and centripetal tensions inherent in policy. First, what counts as literacy, literacy pedagogy, and literacy practice as construed by the policy? Secondly, whose voices are represented in and whose needs are being served by the policy. Next, how rigid or fluid is the policy? Finally, in what directions does this policy seem to be pointing the field of adolescent literacy and what guidance does it offer practitioners?

Our purpose for this chapter is to suggest some guidelines for conceptualizing and enacting literacy policy that addresses the complex lives and goals of adolescents at the beginning of the 21st century. It is not our intent to weigh in on the effectiveness of particular policies. Instead we use a lens offered by Bakhtinian theory to focus on two exemplars in order to understand and raise questions about the competing tensions and silences of policies that guide literacy teaching and learning for adolescents.

A Comparison of Two Educational Policies in the U.S. and Queensland, Australia

In this chapter we present two exemplars that reflect two points along a complex and multidimensional continuum, rather than a historical or contemporary review of literacy policies in countries around the world. These exemplars are not meant to represent "good" and "bad" policy or two extremes, but rather to present two illustrative approaches to literacy policy for adolescents. The No Child Left Behind legislation of the U.S. is an example of federal policy that has had a deep impact on state and district policies and practices, shifting the balance in the national, state, and local control of education in the United States (U.S. Department of Education, 2001). This legislation has had the effect of overriding state and local reform measures, replacing existing programs with systematic and federally mandated testing schedules. The literacy practices for adolescents promoted by this legislation are unspecified, leaving them open to interpretation by local schools and districts that nonetheless are required to test this age group. The research behind the literacy policies is derived from large-scale experimental studies on early reading. In contrast, Literate Futures, the policies from Queensland, Australia were developed in conjunction with leading literacy researchers working across university and governmental settings and who articulated conceptions of multiliteracies (e.g., New London Group, 1996; see chapter by Luke, this volume) that are responsive to the changing times and current literacy theory. This policy was written to be shaped by local constituencies. In the following sections, we briefly examine the literacy policies in the two countries to raise questions about adolescent literacy policies and practices.

Adolescent Literacy Policy at the National Level in the U.S.

Overview. In the U.S., the major emphases of federal policy in education have been on standardized testing and the implementation of national curriculum standards. In the early part of the 21st century, under the leadership of President George W. Bush, the focus has shifted from standards to standardized testing and the standardization of curriculum. Hailed by politicians and the media as the most sweeping national educational legislation in the United States since the Sputnik-motivated reforms of the 1960s, U.S. President Bush's *No Child Left Behind Act of 2001* has had a profound impact on schools. The legislation ties federal funding to achievement levels as measured by standardized tests. As a result, in many school districts across the country, teaching has been reduced to the preparation for these tests. Similar legislation, with an emphasis on basic skills, has become increasingly common in many countries around the world.

A close examination of the No Child Left Behind (NCLB) legislation reveals that adolescent literacy is rarely mentioned in its 1100 pages. On the first page of the U.S. legislation, the authors state:

Children who enter school with language skills and pre-reading skills (e.g., understanding that print reads from left to right and top to bottom) are more likely to learn to read well in the early grades and succeed in later years. In fact, research shows that most reading problems faced by adolescents and adults are the result of problems that could have been prevented through good instruction in their early childhood years. (U.S. Department of Education, 2001, p. 1)

This typifies the stance of the legislation toward adolescent literacy. Most of the money connected with the NCLB legislation is targeted for young children through programs such as Head Start, Even Start, and a newly funded program called Reading First. Thus adolescent literacy policy is largely absent at this moment in the United States. Although states are expected to set up accountability systems and display adequate yearly progress at all grade levels, the funding for these mandates, while minimal at the elementary level, is practically absent for older students.

Definitions of literacy. Definitions of adolescent literacy or frameworks for teaching older students are missing from the current NCLB legislation. Its focus on early literacy implies either that those definitions and understandings should be extrapolated to guide the teaching of older children or a belief that an infusion of money and attention on early literacy will trickle up to adolescents. In effect, the current policy advocates "inoculation" for young children to prevent the "disease" of illiteracy or failure for adolescents and adults. In the absence of specified policy for older students, testing becomes the default policy that guides curriculum decisions. Definitions of literacy contained within the testing materials form the backbone of literacy curricula designed to prepare students to pass tests. Money is spent on testing materials and test prep courses, leaving teachers without materials that will either engage students deeply in learning or prepare them for their futures beyond passing the tests.

In a speech during his presidential campaign in 1999, U.S. President George W. Bush stated that he planned to make testing the cornerstone of his reform. He made his stance on testing clear when he stated:

Without testing, reform is a journey without a compass. Without testing, teachers and administrators cannot adjust their methods to meet high goals. Without testing, standards are little more than scraps of paper. Without testing, true competition is impossible. Without testing, parents are left in the dark. (Bush, 1999, quoted in Hillocks, 2002, p. 9)

Central to the NCLB legislation is the emphasis on testing every year, administering the NAEP test in fourth and eighth grades, and the establishment of a system that operates on the basis of rewards and sanctions for increasing test scores or adequate yearly progress.

Missing from this federal literacy policy and the surrounding rhetoric is a discussion of broader definitions of literacy suggested by current theory and, perhaps more importantly, descriptions of actual pedagogy and practice that should accompany the focus on raising scores. In place of frameworks to guide practice there is a mandate to use research-based programs based on scientific research methodology. In particular, with its emphasis on teaching reading in the early grades, there is little focus on practices for teaching adolescents. The single focus on high stakes testing tends to restrict curriculum to the kinds of knowledge tested (e.g., Hillocks, 2002). For instance, high school English teachers in Philadelphia have been instructed to replace novels with books produced by Kaplan, a company that tutors students to raise scores on standardized tests. Test prep is the new order of the day.

In addition, the focus on basic skills in the NCLB legislation belies the shifting emphasis toward technology and new forms of literacy in the globalized workplace. As Luke (2002, p. 189) explained:

[we are in] a historical moment where there appears to be an apparent delinkage between skill and knowledge production by schools and educational institutions and the emergent appetites for human capital of the new economies. From this perspective, we could ask how the current policy orientations towards basic skills fit into education systems where there are highly inexact correspondences between what schools produce and what elite and non-elite sectors of the new economy demand.

Definitions of reading in current legislation and the reports – such as the Report of the National Reading Panel (National Institute of Child Health and Human Development, 2000) – that are the basis for the legislation are narrow. Reading is defined as decoding, word recognition, fluency, vocabulary development and comprehension of literal meaning rather than a set of sociocultural practices situated in local contexts. Further, these definitions are based on the notion that research on early literacy can be extended to literacy learning during adolescence. The definitions of literacy or reading in current legislation are tied to school-based practices with no recognition of the learning that occurs outside of the school walls (e.g., Hull & Schultz, 2001, 2002).

Whose voices are represented in the policy? The No Child Left Behind legislation is written in terms of rewards and sanctions. As such it is positioned to define the federal role in K-12 education and to act as a mechanism to promote parent and child choice in terms of schools and teachers. Specifically, the four major areas of the legislation include: (1) increased accountability through an emphasis on performance goals, mandated testing schedules and sanctions for schools failing to meet specified benchmarks or adequate yearly progress goals, (2) greater choices for parents and children if schools fail to meet accountability goals or teacher quality measures, (3) greater flexibility for the use of federal funds, and (4) an emphasis on research-based programs including a focus on early (K-3) reading through Reading First grants.

As described above, the legislation does not account for a broader definition of literacy that might reflect adolescents' literacy practices in a changing world, nor does it take into account the pedagogies already enacted in classrooms that might engage students in their learning. Voices of parents and students are included only in that they are given opportunities to transfer out of "failing" schools, an option that has not proved viable in the first year of the law's implementation (Orfield, 2004.) Teachers are assumed to be technicians whose responsibility is to implement programs written and approved by outsiders who are likely unfamiliar with their local contexts. As the supporting materials for NCLB (www.ed.gov) state:

> *No Child Left Behind* puts special emphasis on determining what educational programs and practices have been proven effective through rigorous scientific research. Federal funding is targeted to support these programs and teaching methods that work to improve student learning and achievement.
>
> Reading programs are an example. *No Child Left Behind* supports scientifically based reading instruction programs in the early grades under the new Reading First program and in preschool under the new Early Reading First program. Funds are available to help teachers strengthen current skills and gain new ones in effective reading instructional techniques.

There is no provision for teachers, building administrators, or local professional development teams to determine which programs or even which instructional techniques are most likely to work in local contexts with particular groups of students. Further, adolescent literacy practices fall outside of the discussion of programs and practices, but not outside of the testing mandates. Schedules for testing in grade levels from 6th to 12th grades are carefully outlined in the legislation. Represented in the legislation are the voices of individuals at each level of the education system who monitor compliance and test scores, linking both to funding.

Flexibility of the policy. The absence of a specified policy presents school personnel who work with adolescents with both constraints and opportunities. Freed by the absence of direct mandates from the federal government for literacy programs and pedagogical practices, state and local school districts can develop their own guidelines. Yet this freedom is constrained by both the ambitious performance goals tied to high stakes testing as well as the paucity of resources tied to these benchmarks that are unattainable to many school districts. The absence of language around adolescent literacy provides an opportunity for educators to develop local policies and practices that are responsive to the youth and also the current time period. At the same time, the definitions of literacy are adapted from reports such as those from the National Reading Panel (NICHD, 2000) that focus on young children, thus narrowing the possibilities for adolescent classrooms and high schools.

Literacy policy in the U.S. has been built on a research base that does not take into account current literacy theory, such as the New Literacy Studies mentioned above, or research on adolescent literacy practices in the current times.

Future directions. This legislation is clearly pointing to greater federal control of literacy policies and practices through an increased focus on standardized test and accountability based on test score gains. Across the U.S., state and local reform plans have been replaced by new priorities to increase test scores in reading and math in grades 3 to 8. This new legislation mandates goals that are higher than any that have been achieved in high poverty districts in this country (Orfield, 2004). Equity is defined by this legislation, as equal expectations while there is little provision for the equalizing of funding that would support all children to achieve the same test scores. Specifically, in terms of adolescent literacy, this legislation imposes an early literacy model and focus that is increasingly narrow and tied to standardized tests and adapted neither to this specific age group nor the current times. The reliance on increased test scores as a measure of success imposes a static conception of literacy moving forward into the future and one that is imposed from the outside rather than a situated understanding of literacy practices. In the section that follows, we provide a glimpse into the legislation that arose from a different set of assumptions about both literacy and policymaking.

Adolescent Literacy Policy at the State Level in Queensland, Australia

Overview. Literate Futures is the literacy initiative implemented by Education Queensland (EQ) the state department of education. This set of policies was written in response to a study describing the state of literacy and literacy teaching in the region at the end of the 20th century and predicting what it might look like in the year 2010. This study – which EQ commissioned two prominent literacy researchers, Allan Luke and Peter Freebody, to conduct (Education Queensland, 2000a) – is comprehensive and detailed in its findings and strategy suggestions. As characterized by EQ, the work attempts to (1) respond more effectively to the challenges raised by diverse student and school communities as well as the diversity of adolescent experience; (2) focus on whole school change and community partnerships; (3) engage educators in a dialogue in search of a range of productive pedagogies; and (4) consider and address the implications of new technologies, multiliteracies, and new work practices. As Roger Slee, Deputy Director General of Education for the State of Queensland, writes in his forward to the position paper for Literate Futures, "What is advocated here is not a single new approach, a defined method of teaching, or a prescribed set of materials," but instead "is an opportunity for all teachers to identify what students need to learn, know, and experience to be effective readers now, and in the future, in the wider range of life worlds in which they operate." (Education Queensland, 2002a, iv).

Rather than taking a prescriptive and punitive approach to reforming literacy instruction, the policies gathered under Literate Futures provide a framework and a baseline of what schools are required to enact, while allowing schools some flexibility in how they respond to those requirements. For example, all schools p-12, are expected to generate and implement "a strategy for action to improve students' literacy learning" (Education Queensland, 2002b) and have a timeline for doing so. To support these dialogues within and across schools, EQ has provided a book, a video, and a CD that have been designed by educators working with the State Department of Education and are meant to be used interactively and as needed by schools as they develop their plans. Furthermore, the government acknowledges both the hard work already done by teachers in addressing these issues as well as the complexity of the task at hand. Therefore, the language of the Literate Future publications both acknowledges and addresses the tensions educators and administrators might face in the implementation of these plans in individual classrooms.

Definitions of literacy. Literacy, as configured by EQ in their Literate Futures documents is a complex social construct that is constantly undergoing change as new technologies, changes in the workplace, and shifting populations transact with the ways we teach and learn language. In fact, care is taken in this literature to illustrate how literacy has changed since the 1950s and why educators need to consider those changes as they construct pedagogy. As the Literate Futures report notes, " being a child, being an adolescent, and, indeed, becoming literate, have changed in some fundamental ways. The tool kit of basic skills that served many of us well in the 1950s is inadequate today" (Education Queensland, 2000a, p. 7). The Teacher Summary Version (2000b) of that report constructs literacy through a matrix of four roles of the literacy learner – code breaker, meaning maker, text user, and text analyst – and three communication media – oral, print, and multimedia. It argues that a strong literacy program helps students to become proficient in all four literate roles as well as across a range of media. Although care is taken to note the need for students to become proficient in breaking codes as language learners, equal care is taken to impel teachers to consider that a mark of literacy is the ability to read critically.

Defined as "the flexible and sustainable mastery of a repertoire of practices with the texts of traditional and new communications technologies via spoken language, print, and multimedia" (Educational Queensland, 2000b, p. 3), literacy is broadly configured and intimately tied to the world outside school walls. According to this policy, issues of changing social structures, cultural diversity, globalization, the continuing advent of rapidly growing information and communication technologies, and shifting views of work, the workplace, and the workforce all need to be considered when constructing society's needs for future literacies and the teaching that will support such literacy practices. An implication of this policy is that it is not enough for schools to catch up with these changes, but there is a need to anticipate the future and try to keep one step ahead. The result is that the definition of literacy is in flux. The conception of literacy at the start of this program probably won't be the same conception five or ten years into the future.

Whose voices are represented in the policy? As the teacher summary to the Literate Future report (Education Queensland, 2000b, p. 3) begins:

> The task for the educational community – teachers and administrators, parents and community stakeholders, researchers and teacher educators – is to begin a rigorous and ongoing debate over which repertoires of literacy practices students will need in the economies, cultures, communities, and

institutions of the new Queensland. To begin that debate requires that we define literacy in broader, more future-oriented terms than previously.

Although the voices of students seem to be missing from this discussion, nonetheless this policy casts a fairly wide net in terms of audience and responsibility. That this paragraph is taken from a teacher summary is also significant in that the governmental authors of the report saw it as necessary to speak directly to teachers and to enlist their support of the policy. This is in contrast to the U.S. NCLB legislation, which provides extensive materials for parents and few materials for teachers and students.

It is core and basic to this policy that schools are situated in communities and that communities differ in terms of their needs, resources, and modes of approaching and addressing issues. Given this diversity, schools p-12 are required to enter into dialogue not only among themselves and their communities, but also with useful research and theory-based frameworks (Education Queensland, 2000b). Educators working for the state have developed support materials for the initiative and these materials advocate inquiry into issues rather than prescribing canned or standardized curriculum. On the other hand, student test outcomes are not ignored by this policy. In looking at such data, the report cautions, care should be taken to note that although the current data does not indicate a widespread crisis in literacy, certain groups – e.g. boys, non-native English speakers, rurally-isolated students – struggle more with school and literacy. In addressing the needs of these struggling groups, however, care should be taken to understand the situated nature of literacy and learning. The assumption should not be made that promising practices in one community will necessarily translate into another community, no matter how similar it may seem. The overriding message being sent by the EQ policy is that the government has a baseline set of requirements that local schools need to adhere to, but this set of requirements is open to dialogue with local and global stakeholders.

Flexibility of the policy. Literate Futures strikes a balance between providing enough structure for individual school communities to use in the development of their literacy strategies while leaving enough play in the structure to allow those communities to develop strategies that speak more directly to their own needs. This balance is evident in the various policy documents. First, the policy argues that a "reanalysis of studies of literacy in the United States show that there is no magic method or single approach that produces improved literacy outcomes for all" (Education Queensland, 2000b, p. 11). On the other hand, the policy argues against a kind of educational relativism where anything is acceptable. Instead, Literate Futures clearly states that the best literacy programs create an "informed and theorized balance" (Education Queensland, 2000b, p. 12) of a range of ideas that fit into an agreed upon philosophic stance developed through dialogue and across time within a single community.

Further evidence of this dialogue can be found at the Literate Futures website where whole school literacy planning is supported through a five-step process: (1) reflect on current literacy practice; (2) investigate who is struggling with literacy in the community and why; (3) consider the ways social, cultural, economic, and technological changes are transacting with the community; (4) learn more about literacy and what current research might suggest; and (5) organize ways to sustain and grow programs (Education Queensland, 2002c). In the same vein, a Literate Futures position document argues that it is not a step-by-step guide on how to use the initiative's support materials, but instead endeavors to situate those materials in the planning process and help stakeholders consider key issues. Throughout the many documents that either delineate or support the policy, the tone of the texts of Literate Futures policy is one of an invitation to explore within a judicious, but necessarily bounded frame.

Future directions. As has been indicated in a number of places above, EQ set out to separate itself from what was labeled the "basic literacy tool kit of the 1950s" (2000a, p. 3) and instead imagine literacy in a world where "new communication technologies, globalised economies, and world cultures are altering – and will continue to alter – the way we live and work" (Anstey, 2002, p. 3). All supporting documents are marked by discussions of the importance of situated literacies and multiliteracies, and the very name of the policy – Literate Futures – determines the stance this work will take. As the document *New Times, New Literacies* (Anstey, 2002, p. 1) states in its opening paragraph,

> There is a need to think about literacy for lifelong learners in new ways. We need to equip students with the ability to combine and recombine existing and new literacy skills in different ways, for new purposes and with new technologies.

By encouraging dialogue and exploration into the needs and issues of the local community, the policy of Literate Futures imagines literacy as deeply embedded in sociocultural, sociohistorical, and sociopolitical issues. Furthermore, there is no disjuncture between early years and adolescent literacy; learners are seen as literate individuals who need support in their literacy practices as they and their surroundings grow and change.

Discussion and Implications

To this point, we have looked at federal literacy policy in the U.S. and state literacy policy in Queensland, Australia, particularly as they relate to the acquisition of literacy practices by adolescents. In this final section, we want to consider the two literacy policies from our initial theoretical framework to eke out some understandings about the way these policies either seek a balance of centrifugal and centripetal tensions or skew one way or the other. Ultimately, we're interested in what such an analysis might imply for policymakers considering issues of adolescent literacy.

When we explore No Child Left Behind through this lens of centrifugal and centripetal tensions, we find the policy to be unbalanced toward creating unification through standardization. It is policy intended to narrow definitions, limit critique and interpretation, and constrain the range of resources. The language is one of authority that seeks to monitor content and pedagogy in literacy classrooms through pervasive testing and restriction of resources. Although it purports to give more flexibility to local districts, in fact, that flexibility is dependent on raising test scores to often unattainable levels given the diversity of students and their needs. For example, the provision that allows parents to remove their children from poorly performing schools and to place them into schools that have higher performance indicators is both under funded and without legal support. The better performing schools are under no obligation to accept students from the struggling schools and often refuse to do so (Snyder, 2003; Sunderman & Kim, 2004). Constructed primarily by governmental policy-makers working within a narrow literacy paradigm, NCLB has a voice and tone that denies the sociocultural complexities of the lives of those who are poor and disenfranchised, even as it claims to speak in their interest.

We are beginning to see the price of such single-mindedness and lack of deference to a range of constituencies and voices. Calling NCLB "the most sweeping intrusions into state and local control of education in the history of the United States," the Republican controlled Virginia House of Representatives voted 98 to 1 to ignore NCLB policy, even at the cost of loss of revenues (Becker & Helderman, 2004, p. A.01, see also Paulson, 2004). This lawmaking body felt NCLB negated or obstructed their own statewide efforts to advance literacy education. Additionally, organizations like the National Council of La Raza (NCLR) and the National Association for the Advancement of Colored People (NAACP), groups representing parents whose children have frequently been left behind in the past, have raised concerns about the effectiveness of NCLB regarding their constituencies and the lack of funding to support the work (NAACP, 2003; NCLR, 2002). Simultaneously, professional teaching organizations like the National Council of Teachers of English and the International Reading Association, whose rich and broad body of research has largely been ignored by federal policymakers, have raised questions about the narrowness of NCLB (IRA, 2001; NCTE, 2002).

In addition, there is an ever-growing body of research that indicates that educational reform, in order to succeed, must take local stakeholders into account (Allington, 2002). For example, a policy brief by a non-profit research organization describes a study they conducted of recent and tumultuous reform in the Philadelphia School District (Research for Action, 2002). That report cites five lessons learned from that experience, and of those five lessons, four specifically speak to the problems caused when policymakers are unwilling to include a means for dialogue with local stakeholders when making policy (Christman & Rhodes, 2002). In particular, the researchers argue that school reform needs to be forged in the spirit of collaboration, particularly with the intent for reform leaders to value the input of principals, teachers and parents. Without such invited dialogue, these local stakeholders have little substantive access through which to shape the policy.

Where NCLB tends to eschew dialogue and skew toward a monophonic stance, the Literate Futures policy of Queensland opens itself to polyphony. In contrast, the Queensland policy attempts to incorporate dialogue through offering blueprint for schools to develop pedagogies and strategies for students in this particular historical moment. At the same time, this policy encourages educators to draw on multiple resources to look forward to what tools students will need to meet the challenges and opportunities in the future. This ambitious policy attempts to address the push and pull or the centripetal and centrifugal forces we described in the opening of this chapter. Rather than a complete reliance on local practices that would pull out from the center, or an imposition of uniform mandates that might pull everything into the center, the policy strikes a balance. The notion of frameworks with baseline expectations allows for literacy policy to be fluid, yet contained, flexible, yet held to external controls.

Current U.S. federal policies were written and supported by a bipartisan group of politicians aimed at holding schools accountable for high standards in literacy and mathematics. The legislation seems to speak to district offices, local districts, building administrators and teachers in strict, punitive tones holding out a system of sanctions and rewards, while inviting parents, or local constituents to exercise choice. In Queensland, Australia, the primary voices behind the policies were academic researchers who sought ways to implement literacy policies that were responsive to current knowledge about literacy and learning. Although respectful to students and teachers, the voices of these two stakeholders only seemed to come into play once the policy framework was enacted. We are left to wonder, what would policy look like that incorporated the voices and perspectives of a range of students and teachers, especially early on as policy is created? Is such a conception of policy possible on the national level? Can policy begin with understandings of local contexts and build upwards, rather than beginning at a broader level and generalizing to the individuals?

Our analysis of these two policies leads us to several broad guidelines for constructing literacy policies for adolescents. First, we believe that dialogue is critical to policy creation, and it is exactly that dialogue which is rarely represented in policies at any level. Local, state, and national discussions of educational policy that seek inclusion of the greatest number of diverse voices can, from our stance, produce the kind of substantive dialogue that enables the enactment of reflective policy that, even as it is being generated, opens itself to future reconsideration. Second, policies must be forward looking. They should be responsive to the moment and contain provisions to address the educational needs of the future. Third, adolescent literacy policies must begin with a careful consideration of the developmental and learning trajectories of this age group. In addition, to knowledge of adolescents as an age group or adolescence as a developmental stage, policies must reflect youth's literacy practices in and out of school. Policy should both reflect and prompt youth's interest in new forms of literacy across multiple modalities and in a range of new media. Current literacy theory provides a critical knowledge base for conceptualizing the practices and content of this policy. Finally, policy should reflect local contexts as much as possible. As a rule of thumb, we think that the further the authority is from the constituency it serves and the greater that constituency is in number, the more general and open-ended the educational policy needs to be. Therefore, policy written in Washington, DC to serve schools as diverse as those in Patagonia, AZ and Philadelphia, PA needs to serve as touchstones and discussion points from which local policy can be evolved rather than mandates that all must follow to the letter.

We want to conclude by bringing this discussion of adolescent literacy policy back into the classrooms occupied by teachers and students like Kate and Virgil. Ultimately, classrooms are where all educational policy discussions end. It is our sense that neither Kate nor Virgil expects school to be a place where anything goes, where students aren't expected to strive toward learning goals and high standards and where teachers are only accountable to themselves. We and they understand the need for policy that provides stability and shape to education across a range of schools and districts. But what we particularly heard in the frustration expressed by Kate and Virgil is their need for dialogue and an opportunity to engage in local interpretation of policy written far away and, in some instances, long ago. We don't think it is Kate's desire to be *the* voice; she just wants to be *a* voice along with Virgil and others with different expertise and perspectives.

However, we think two simple beliefs needs to be acknowledged. Teachers like Kate – strong, creative intelligent teachers who are professionally active and see their classrooms as places of reflection and negotiation – have, do, and will engage in dialogue with and locally interpret national policy, no matter what the intention of the policymakers. Furthermore, adolescents like Virgil will continue to see their teenage years as a time of hope and struggle. Policy and practices that address the literacy and learning of this age group and the classroom-generated practices of their teachers should embody and be responsive to the needs of both, as well as other local stakeholders. It is incumbent on legislators sitting in offices at a distance from middle and high schools to reach out to the teachers and students in them, embracing their complexities and incorporating their needs and desires into policy.

References

Ahearn, L. M. (2001). *Invitations to love: Literacy, love letters, and social change in Nepal.* Ann Arbor: University of Michigan Press.

Allington, R. L. (2002). *Big brother and the national reading curriculum.* Portsmouth, NH: Heinemann.

Anyon, J. (1997). *Ghetto schooling: A political economy of urban educational reform.* New York: Teachers College Press.

Anstey. M. (2002). *New times, new literacies.* Brisbane, Australia: Education Queensland.

Bakhtin, M. (1981). *The dialogic imagination* (C. Emerson & M. Holquist, Trans.). Austin, TX: The University of Texas Press.

Becker, J., & Helderman, R. (2004, January 24). Va. seeks to leave Bush law behind: Republicans fight school mandates. *The Washington Post*, p. A.01.

Cope, B., & Kalantzis, M. (Eds.) (2000). *Multiliteracies: Literacy learning and the design of social futures.* London: Routledge.

Christman, J. B., & Rhodes, A. (2002). *Civic engagement and urban school improvement: Hard-to-learn lessons from Philadelphia.* Philadelphia, PA: Research for Action.

Education Queensland. (2000a). *Literate futures: Report.* Brisbane, Australia: Author.

Education Queensland (2000b). *Literate futures: The teacher summary version.* Brisbane, Australia: Author.

Education Queensland (2002a). *Introducing literate futures: Reading.* Brisbane: Australia, Author.

Education Queensland (2002b) *Projects.* Retrieved February 13th, 2004 from http://education.qld.au/curriculum/learning/literate-futures/projects.html

Education Queensland (2002c) *Whole school literacy planning.* Retrieved February 13th, 2004 from http://education.qld.au/curriculum/learning/literate-futures/wsl-planning.html

Fecho, B. (with A. Green), (2004). Learning as Aaron. In B. Fecho (Ed.), *"Is this English?" Race, language, and culture in the classroom.* New York: Teachers College Press.

Fine, M., & Weis, L. (2003). *Silenced voices and extraordinary conversations: Re-imagining schools.* New York: Teachers College Press.

Gee, J. P. (1996). *Social linguistics and literacies: Ideology in discourses* (2nd ed.). London: The Falmer Press.

Greene, J. P. (2001). *High school graduation rates in the United States.* New York: Center for Civic Innovation at the Manhattan Institute.

Greene, J. P., & Winters, M. A. (2002). *Public school graduation rates in the United States* (Civic Report #21), New York: Center for Civic Innovation at the Manhattan Institute.

Hermans, H., & Kempen, H. (1993). *The dialogical self: Meaning as movement.* San Diego, CA: Academic Press.

Hillocks, G. (2002). *The testing trap: How state writing assessments control learning.* New York: Teachers College Press.

Hull, G. (2003). Youth culture and digital media: New literacies for new times, *Research in the Teaching of English, 38*(2), 229–233.

Hull, G., & Schultz, K. (2001). Literacy and learning out of school: A review of theory and research, *Review of Educational Research, 71*(4), 575–611.

Hull, G., & Schultz, K. (Eds.) (2002). *School's Out!: Bridging out-of-school literacy with classroom practices:* New York: Teachers College Press.

Hull, G., & Zacher, J. (in press). What is after-school worth? Developing literacies and identities out-of-school, *Voices in urban education.* Annenberg Institute for School Reform. Brown University, Providence, Rhode Island.

International Reading Association. (2001). On US government policy on the teaching of reading. Retrieved March 24th, 2004 from http://www.reading.org/positions/reading_policy.html

Knobel, M. (1999). *Everyday literacies: Students, discourse, and social practice.* New York: Peter Lang.

Lipman, P. (1998). *Race, class, and power in school restructuring.* Albany: State University of New York Press.

Luke, A. (2002). What happens to literacies old and new when they're turned into policy. In D. E. Alvermann (Ed.), *Adolescents and literacies in a digital world.* New York: Peter Lang.

National Association for the Advancement of Colored People. (2003, September). NAACP opposition to school vouchers. Retrieved on March 23rd, 2004 from http://www.naacp.org/work/washington_bureau/schoolVouchers093003.shtml

National Center for Education Statistics (2000). *Dropout rates in the United States: 2000,* Washington, DC: U.S. Department of Education.

National Council of La Raza (2002). The No Child Left Behind Act: Implications for local educators and advocates for Latino students, families, and communities. Retrieved February 13th, 2004 from http://www.nclr.org/policy/briefs/IB8NoChildLeft.pdf

National Council of Teachers of English (2002, November). NCTE resolution on the Reading First initiative. Retrieved February 13th, 2004 from http://www.ncte.org/about/press/rel/107601.html.

National Institute of Child Health and Human Development (2000). *Report of the National Reading Panel. Teaching children to read: An evidence-based assessment of the scientific research literature on reading and its implications for reading instruction* (NIH Publication No. 00-4769). Washington, DC: U.S. Government Printing Office.

New London Group (1996). A pedagogy of multiliteracies: Designing social futures. *Harvard Educational Review, 66*(1), 60–92.

Nussbaum, E. (2004, January 11). My so-called blog. *New York Times* (Section 6, p. 33).

Orfield, G. (2004). Introduction. In G. L. Sunderland & J. Kim (Eds.), *Inspiring vision, disappointing results: Four studies on implementing the No Child Left Behind Act*. Retrieved February 15th, 2004 from http://www.civilrightsproject.harvard.edu/

Paulson, A. (2004, February 11). An education rebellion stirring. *Christian Science Monitor*. Retrieved February 15th, 2004 from http://www.csmonitor.com/

Pintaone-Hernandez, A. (2002). *Literacy narratives toward identity and community in a first-grade classroom*. Unpublished master's thesis, University of Georgia, Athens, Georgia, U.S.

Research for Action. (2002). *Lessons from Philadelphia about building civic capacity for school reform*. Philadelphia, PA: Author.

Schultz, K. (2002). Looking across space and time: Reconceptualizing literacy learning in and out of school. *Research in the Teaching of English, 36*(3), 356–390.

Schultz, K. (2003). *Listening: A framework for teaching across differences*. New York: Teachers College Press.

Schultz, K., & Vasudevan, L. (in preparation). Multi-media storytelling as method: Insights from documenting the literacy practices of youth in and out of school.

Snyder, S. (2003, October 12). "No Child Left Behind:" law bumps into hard reality. *The Philadelphia Inquirer*, p. A01.

Street, B. V. (1993). (Ed.), *Cross-cultural approaches to literacy*. NY: Cambridge University Press.

36

ASSESSING LITERACIES

Caroline V. Gipps* and J. Joy Cumming†
*Kingston University, UK; †Griffith University, Australia

Assessment is not an uncontested term. Assessment can include a range of activities – formal examinations, orals/vivas and practicals, multiple-choice tests, and open-ended assessment tasks–to elicit performance. The evaluation or judgement of that performance can be made by peers, teachers or external agencies. These different types of assessment do not simply embody a range of choice of activity; they are based on different underlying conceptions of knowledge and of learning. We can describe assessment as being on a continuum that has psychometric and measurement models of *testing* at one end and interpretivist/ constructivist models of *assessment* at the other, with a new variant of the latter, *assessment for learning*, in which assessment is an integral part of the learning process (Gipps & Stobart, 2003).

In the psychometric model there is an assumption of the primacy of technical issues, notably standardisation and reliability. Because of the norm-reference base individuals are compared with one another, so we need to be certain that the test was carried out in the same way for all individuals, that it was scored in the same way, and that the scores were interpreted in the same way. Within this model, standardisation is vital to support the technical reliability of the test. However, these requirements can have a negative effect on the construct validity and curricular impact of the test because only some material and certain tasks are amenable to this type of testing. The psychometric model was based essentially on a 'scientific' model of certainty and objectivity: the assumption that certain things (e.g., skills or abilities) exist 'out there' and need only to be captured in test content to be measured accurately or objectively.

Newer developments in assessment – performance assessment, "authentic" assessment, portfolio assessment, and so forth – are part of a move to design assessment that supports learning and provides more detailed information about students (Wolf, Bixby, Glenn, & Gardner, 1991). Furthermore, in the postmodern world, assessment is seen to be value laden and socially constructed. To see assessment as a scientific, objective activity is misconceived (Broadfoot, 1994; Wolf et al., 1991). The modernist view is that it is possible to be a disinterested observer, while the postmodernist view is that such detachment is not possible.

International Handbook of Educational Policy, 695–713
Nina Bascia, Alister Cumming, Amanda Datnow, Kenneth Leithwood and David Livingstone (Eds.)
© 2005 *Springer. Printed in Great Britain.*

We are social beings who construe the world according to our values and perceptions; thus, our biographies are central to what we see and how we interpret it. Similarly in assessment, performance is not "objective"; rather, it is construed according to perspectives and values of the assessor, whether the assessor is the one who designs the assessment and its "objective" marking scheme or the one who grades open-ended performances.

In the traditional model of teaching and learning, the curriculum is seen as a distinct body of information, specified in detail that can be transmitted to the learner. Assessment here consists of checking whether the information has been received and absorbed. Standardised achievement tests evaluate students' abilities to recall the facts learned and to apply them in a routine manner. Even items which are designed to assess higher-level activities often require no more than the ability to recall the appropriate formula and to make substitutions to get the correct answer. This conception is built on models of learning that see learning as a process in which new information is transmitted to the learner and is learnt (as given) in a linear hierarchical way (Gipps, 1994).

In contrast, constructivist models see learning as requiring personal knowledge construction and meaning making, and as involving complex and diverse processes; such models therefore require assessment to be diverse, in an attempt to characterise in depth the structure and quality of students' learning and understanding. More intense, even interactive methods, such as essays, performance assessments, and small group tasks and projects, are needed to assess understanding. The implications of sociocultural approaches to learning for assessment practise are significant too: The requirement in this frame is to assess process as well as product, the conception must by dynamic rather than static, and attention must be paid to the social and cultural context of both learning and assessment (Gipps, 2002).

We are not arguing that one approach is *good* and another *bad*: the key issue is around *fitness for purpose*. The more open approach to assessment is possible only for certain purposes. For external assessment at the system level and for high stakes purposes, forms of standardisation that lead to high reliability are of key importance. For assessment used in the classroom and for diagnostic or formative purposes, such attention to reliability is less relevant, and the main focus is on validity and use of results at the classroom or school level. It is important to consider the most appropriate balance between reliability and validity in assessments for different purposes as well as the level of detail of the information provided. For these reasons there inevitably is a tension between good classroom practice in assessment and the design of tests used in national and international surveys. Much of the assessment described in the rest of this chapter is part of national, even international, assessment programmes, and these purposes have determined the models of assessment adopted.

Models of Literacy and Literacy Assessment

Just as assessment is not an uncontested term, models of literacy are also diverse and contested. At the simplest level, developments in models of literacy follow a similar continuum to models of assessment, from a generic functional literacy model compatible with a psychometric model of assessment to constructivist models of literacy as social practice, compatible with constructivist models of assessment (Street, 1995).

Even within a functional literacy model, diverse definitions exist. Literacy can be defined as reading and writing only (i.e., dealing with written text) or can include oral/aural skills, viewing of symbolic representations, and critical thinking. A major distinction in functional literacy definitions is the context or purpose: literacy for school success or functional literacy for life skills, for example, "reading to learn or reading to do" (Mikulecky et al., 1987). Functional literacy curricula can incorporate cultural components (Scribner & Cole, 1981). National and international literature such as Shakespeare or the Koran may be incorporated for deeper study or as texts in assessment. More standardised and controlled approaches to assessment generally restrict the degree to which the meanings of such texts can be challenged. Other important issues in designing assessment of functional literacy include accommodation of language backgrounds other than the language of instruction and assessment, and special needs (e.g., whether the text and questions for a standardised reading comprehension can be read aloud to students, and the degree of emphasis on standard English).

Technology such as computers and the Internet is emerging as a significant issue for literacy curriculum and assessment. Research is only beginning on the role and impact of technology on the simplest components of a functional literate definition of reading and writing. Communication is changing forms of literacy as students in developed nations use technology to access information and create reports in multimedia forms. Gender differences in functional literacy outcomes may be reversed if technologically-based literacy is the focus (Cumming, Wyatt-Smith, Ryan, & Doig, 1998).

Thus, even an apparently simple model of literacy as a generic functional skill may require diverse assessment practices. While functional literacy assessments are often undertaken using psychometric approaches, constructivist models of assessment are equally compatible.

Constructivist models of literacy that focus on the embeddedness or situatedness of literacy practice within cultural and other contexts are similarly diverse. Focuses vary from multiliteracies (Cope & Kalantzis, 1999) including multimedia literacies (Lemke, 2001), literacies in and out of school including curriculum literacies (Cumming & Wyatt-Smith, 2001), to the role of discourse (including pedagogic discourse) in structuring identity (e.g., Bernstein, 1996). Both learning in school and behaving may be culturally-defined through literate behaviours (Gee, 1992). At the extreme of the social-constructivist continuum, then, literacy and social identity are intertwined. Literacy educators at this end of the spectrum argue that a major purpose of literacy development of the individual should be for the development of students' capacity to critically assess, rather than the moulding of students towards, a socially-defined norm.

Constructivist models of literacy need constructivist models of assessment and create additional challenges for large-scale, comparative or high stakes assessments. Assessments using portfolios or performance assessments that match assessment tasks to communities of practice and individual context address constructivist model issues but are limited for the extremes of literacy interpretations. The more situated the perception of appropriate literacy practice for an individual, the more the construction of comparable assessments, or even the 'rightness' of responses, becomes difficult.

Constructivist models of literacy and assessment embed issues such as diversity based on cultural, language-background and special needs. However, the technological interface must still be considered. Indeed, access to technology interacts as a further cultural issue for literacy assessment outcomes.

Various other models of literacy lie along the literacy continuum, or perhaps on intersecting dimensions. These include models related to the nature of language structures and development, such as systemic functional linguistics (Halliday, 1994) and genre (e.g., Christie & Martin, 1997), semiotics (Kress, 2001), and so on. We do not attempt to summarise all models of language and literacy nor models of learning skills such as decoding and meaning-making – whether within functional or constructivist models of literacy (Freebody & Luke, 1989) – or developing of learning processes such as metacognitive and strategy skills. To the extent that these models are incorporated in literacy policies, they will impact upon assessment needs.

In summary, literacy assessment that is *fit for purpose* depends on the literacy policy that is implemented through curriculum and assessment, the models of literacy or literacies that the policies implicitly or explicitly endorse, and the reason for the assessment. The following section discusses various literacy assessment policies and practices for England, Australia, Canada, and the United States, as well as a number of international comparative studies.

National Level

England and Wales

Assessment in England and Wales is very much centrally directed with a National Curriculum assessment programme and school-leaving examinations that contain a broad range of approaches from formal written examinations and standardised tests, to standard assessment tasks and externally assessed coursework.

The National Curriculum consists of programmes of study (defining what is to be taught) and attainment targets which are the basis for assessment. The National Curriculum for English consists of three attainment targets: speaking and listening, reading, and writing. The programmes of study for reading detail both the knowledge, skills and understanding to be taught, and the breadth of study (a range of literary and non-literary texts). The reading attainment target covers the age range from 5 to 14, with eight levels of attainment, each defined by a level description; these are in turn further defined by 'question focuses'. In reading, progression is characterised by:

- ability to read increasingly demanding texts, using a repertoire of reading strategies;
- development in response to texts, including analysing and evaluating; and
- reading for information.

The following principles structure the design of the national assessments for Reading:

- The tests must reflect the knowledge, understanding and skills, and the breadth of study, set out in the programmes of study and the attainment target. But any one year's test cannot cover the whole range. Each year's test must include a range of reading skills and text types. Over the years, the tests must include as wide a variety as possible of skills and text types.
- The programmes of study for reading also have an attitudinal component. The general requirements include 'interest and pleasure' and 'enthusiastically', in addition to the ability to read independently. In test development, this translates into a principle that texts should be well written and interesting or entertain the children as readers. This requirement for an authentic engagement with texts leads to a practice of using full-length texts or extended extracts.
- A further underlying principle is that children's responses to texts will draw on their own experiences and understandings, and will therefore differ somewhat from child to child. Because of this, most questions in any text are required to be open, allowing the child to give his or her own view, explanation or opinion in response to the text.
- Although most questions are open, closed questions are also used (multiple choice, matching, numbering, true/false, etc.). One purpose of these is to support the inexperienced reader in establishing a basic understanding of the main points of the text. A further use of closed questions is to articulate an abstract understanding that children would be unlikely to be able to express clearly themselves.

(Rémond & Sainsbury, 2002)

The tests focus not only on literal understanding but also, increasingly with age and level, inference from the text and evaluation.

Within the national assessment programme, at age 7 and 11 a real effort has been made to provide reading and writing tasks and tests that are contextualised, use "real" material as a stimulus, and require pupils to do tasks that are similar to classroom tasks, to enhance validity. The national curriculum itself separates out reading, writing, speaking and listening, and in the national assessment programme reading, writing, spelling (and handwriting at age 11) are evaluated separately – although they are usually elicited within the same test/task.

At age 7 there is a "read aloud" test also: A running record is made of reading in order to judge use of reading strategies (phonic, graphic, syntactic, contextual) and ability to express understanding orally. This detailed information is of use to the class teacher, but it is also reported externally in relation to the level reached. This is an example of the design tension we referred to in our introduction: Good quality assessment tasks provide detailed information for the teacher, but this is aggregated to a global level for reporting to parents and at a national level with questions around adequate reliability for the latter purpose.

At the primary school level, as well as national assessment, a range of more open-ended, performance-based assessments of reading are used at the choice of schools/teachers. Informal reading inventories have been developed that help teachers to assess the skills that students have mastered. These inventories can include checklists to assess attitudes to reading, checklists of examples to assess phonic skills (e.g., knowledge of initial and final letters), lists of books read by the student, activities to assess comprehension, and "miscue" techniques for analysing reading aloud. To assess comprehension, teachers will often ask questions after the student has read aloud about the content of the story, or about what may happen next, while the "running record" (Clay, 1985) uses a notation system to record miscues during reading. Miscue analysis is essentially a formalised structure for assessment while hearing children read. When miscue analysis is used, reading aloud develops from a practice activity to a more diagnostic one. The teacher has a list of the most common errors children make, along with a set of probable causes. By noticing and recording in a systematic way the child's errors and analysing the possible causes, teachers can correct misunderstandings, help the child develop appropriate strategies, and reinforce skills. In other words miscue analysis is essentially an informal diagnostic assessment and teaching tool.

At age 14 (end of Key Stage 3) the national curriculum assessment for reading involves a separate reading booklet containing three texts and 15 questions of various formats as well as a Shakespeare reading task which focuses on extracts from two scenes of a Shakespeare play studied in class, with detailed written responses to the extracts. There are also two writing tasks, and pupils are given separate levels for reading and writing (as well as English overall) as they are at ages 7 and 11.

In the (school-leaving) examinations at 16 there was a stage when all "English" assessment was done via coursework (i.e., projects and extended essays) assessed both internally and externally, rather than through examinations. However, this was deemed to be politically unacceptable and now there is a maximum limit (50%) which may be assessed by coursework. The rest is by formal written examination. This is an example of external factors driving an assessment structure which is less acceptable to most English teachers.

Australia

Each of the states and territories in Australia develops a curriculum framework for English (literacy) and has a system of external standardised literacy assessment at varying year levels. Curriculum frameworks are outcome-based, with various stages of development. Stages are not synonymous with grade level; hence a student's achievement is recorded against standards within the stages, not grade level.

In 1999, the Ministerial Council on Education, Employment, Training and Youth Affairs (MCEETYA) endorsed national standards and reporting in the Adelaide Declaration on National Goals for Schooling in the twenty-first Century. The goals included the attainment of "skills of numeracy and English literacy; such that, every student should be numerate, able to read, write, spell and communicate at an appropriate level". This statement underpins the National Literacy Benchmarks for Reading, Writing, and Spelling, developed through a consensus process over some years, for Years 3, 5 and 7. The benchmarks state minimum standards of reading, writing and spelling for success in schooling. The initial consultations identified a number of literacy strategies as important benchmarks for student progress in early literacy. However, the final National Literacy Benchmark descriptors reflected aspects of literacy that could be assessed in simple standardised forms.

States and territories report performance against the benchmarks by extracting data from their own assessment system. However, the state system-level data are designed to assess a range of literacy performance. In general, assessment policies for all states and territories endorse principles of standards-based, criterion-referenced, teacher-based assessment. Statewide assessments can include teacher-based assessment as part or all of the assessment undertaken. Literacy policy statements for school-level assessments include cross-curricular literacy, reading, writing, listening, speaking, viewing, and critical thinking. Critical literacy is endorsed by most syllabuses, although functional literacy definitions focusing on school literacy are most prevalent. The genre approach to writing is most common. Assessment policies encourage formative and summative assessment, continuous assessment, and selection of assessment tasks that suit community needs. This flexibility can address issues of authenticity and contextuality, as well as student engagement and interest.

Victoria's policy, AIM (Achievement Improvement Monitor), incorporates five components: Classroom Assessment, Homework Guidelines, Comprehensive Reporting, Learning Improvement, and Statewide Testing. Assessments are based within Victoria's standards framework. The policy notes the role of classroom observation and other teacher-based assessment strategies. AIM incorporates standardised teacher-assessed writing tasks for Years 3 and 5, evaluated on three criteria, texts and contextual understanding, linguistic structures and features, and strategies (VCAA, 2002). Computers may be used for students with special learning needs. Other standard resources such as dictionaries are available. Drafting is expected. Work can be spread over two or three days but must be undertaken at school. Teachers are expected to lead discussion on the writing topic, observe and record strategies each student demonstrates in drafting and revising. Discussion with other students can occur during drafting. Final drafts must be written alone. Detailed marking rubrics and examples are provided for teachers.

Centrally-assessed tasks in English reading and writing conventions, spelling, and writing are also undertaken. The reading and writing conventions involve multiple choice and short answer questions. Spelling involves an editing task and dictation. The writing outcome is seen as a single finished draft. In addition to the statewide assessment in English in Years 3, 5, and 7, "teachers working in the early years of primary school undertake baseline assessments of students on entry and assessments of reading progress at the end of Prep, Year 1 and Year 2" (VCAA, 2001, p. 7). Overall for Preschool to Year 10, assessment is against 6 stages.

In New South Wales, the Basic Skills Tests for Years 3 and 5 incorporate reading, language use, and identification of correct punctuation and spelling. Accommodations are made for students with special needs. In addition to the Basic Skills Tests of Years 3, 5 and 7, English Language and Literacy Assessment (ELLA) occurs for students in Years 7 and 8. All students are assessed early in Year 7 and schools can opt to assess again in Year 8 to gauge progress (NSWDET, n.d.). Assessment involves writing (two tasks, reading (comprehension of a range of texts) and language (structure). Outcomes for all English stages include talking and listening, reading and writing, with each component having a number of aspects. Statements of expected learning enable teachers to make direct comparisons from classroom assessment activities. For example, for Writing for the subcomponent Handwriting and Computer Technology, a Stage 1 outcome standard is "WS1.12 Produces texts using letters of consistent size and slope in NSW Foundation Style and using computer technology".

The 2003 Queensland English syllabus (Preschool to Year 10) defines literacy through three strands: cultural, operational and critical with three sub-strands of speaking and listening, reading and viewing, and writing and shaping. Key learning outcomes for all elementary level subjects include oral and written communication, as do subjects in the final years of secondary schooling. Queensland has had a Year 2 Diagnostic "Net" since 1995, aimed at identifying students in the early years in need of assistance in literacy and numeracy. A kit provides teachers with a range of tasks to be administered individually with students in order to make a comprehensive diagnosis of their reading and writing strengths and weaknesses. The tasks are similar to the standard reading and writing diagnostic tools used in the language profiles in England.

In addition to assessing other areas, Western Australia undertakes statewide assessment of expository and narrative speaking skills of students in a small group at the system level. A sample level descriptor is:

Level 6

Students explore ideas in discussions by comparing their ideas with those of their peers and building on others' ideas to advance the discussion. They generate a comprehensive and detailed response to the topic.

(Forster, 2001, p. 12)

The Australian Capital Territory also assesses listening, speaking and viewing as components of the Years 3 and 5 literacy assessments.

Canada

Like Australia and the U.S., Canada is a confederation of provinces, each with its own program of literacy curriculum and assessment. Canada has an additional complexity of bilingual education and an issue for assessment is the "harmonization" of English and French assessments.

At the national level, the Council of Ministers of Education, Canada, initiated the *School Achievement Indicators Program* (SAIP) in 1989 to provide a national assessment of language skills, for a nationally random sample of 13- and 16-year olds (CME, 1999). Areas are assessed on a four-yearly cycle with Reading and Writing last assessed in 2002. Individual achievement is not identified. The framework for assessment was developed using a nationwide consensus approach. The national policy addresses contextuality and authenticity issues of large-scale assessments by seeking to reflect as much as possible classroom curricula and methods. Reading assessments use booklets of readings from recognized literature, essays, and newspaper articles of varying lengths (up to four pages), genres, and difficulty. For reading, students 'read selections and responded to questions individually' (CME, 1999, p. 2). Questions are a combination of multiple-choice and constructed responses. The constructed responses require students to:

- express opinions about the texts,
- explain something in the texts,
- make judgements about textual information,
- extract ideas from the texts, or
- relate concepts in the texts to their personal experiences.

(CME, 1999, p. 5)

As for England, the assumptions for the reading assessment are that student responses reflect:

- the personal experience the student brings to the reading task,
- the student's language base (vocabulary and language strategies),
- the complexity of the textual information, and
- the difficulty of the task.

(CME, 1999, p. 5)

The national writing assessment for Canada extends standardised practices of most nations in the quest for authenticity. The assessment follows purpose and genre theories in writing, allowing the initial discussion, writing of first drafts and revision using normally available reference books such as dictionaries and thesauruses. In the recent assessment "students had two and a half hours to complete the assessments. The writing assessment permitted them to discuss the theme in a group, prior to the date of testing, and with a partner, for the first 10 minutes of the testing time" (CME, 1999, p. 2). Students were permitted to use computers if they "normally used them for composition work" while "students who had accommodations made for them in the classroom were allowed those accommodations". Extra time was at the discretion of the teacher.

For writing, the assumptions are that 'A student's writing fluency depends on:

- the personal experience that the student has with written language,
- the degree to which the student's language base (background and environment) allows expression of ideas, and
- the complexity of the writing task.

(CME, 1999, p. 6)

Criteria and standards rubrics were developed for assessment. Development of both English and French forms of assessment and rubrics were undertaken in parallel. Assessment is against five levels of competence using criteria that "explain the increasing sophistication of the responses" and by exemplars of student work for each level (CME, 1999, p. 5). A student's work has to reflect a level description consistently. The data are used to compare performance in different jurisdictions as well as to chart performance over time by the use of common passages.

Within Canada, we can consider the literacy curriculum and assessment program of British Columbia (B.C.) as one example of a provincial system, given that each province in Canada has unique jurisdictional authority for education. B.C. has 12% of students enrolled in ESL instruction, predominantly students with Asian backgrounds. All students undertake a common English language assessment (or French if this is their first language) at 13 years old while 16 year olds are assessed in common English, communications and technical and professional communication tasks in grade 11 or 12. Assessments are developed to match learning outcomes statements that reflect content standards developed for the province as a whole.

Expectations are made at Grade level. The curriculum emphasises "practical application of communication skills by focussing on reading, writing, oral communication, and media literacy. The new curricula emphasize the literary, informational, and mass media applications of language as well as critical and creative thinking" (CME, 1999, p. 40). External assessments are regarded as snapshots of student achievement to be interpreted in conjunction with other assessment data. All students are also assessed at the provincial level annually in reading and 'first-draft' writing in Grades 4, 7 and 10.

The Reading Comprehension Specifications use narrative and poetry literature texts and "information" texts, including illustrations and graphic materials (<bccanreading_specs.pdf>). The three major assessment criteria are "Identify and interpret key concepts and main ideas", "locate, interpret and organize details" and "critical analysis". The Writing Specifications require students to undertake two tasks, short responses and a longer task (<bccanreading_specs.pdf>). Students are offered choices in topic or through prompts. "Purpose, audience and form" are to be made clear. The genre is changed for different grades and years. Standards for the national assessments are criteria-based, using the B.C. Performance Standards for Writing (www.bced.gov.bc.ca/classroom_assessment/perf_stands/writing.htm).

The British Columbia Performance Standards focus 'exclusively on *performance assessment* (original emphasis)' (BCME, 2002, p. 1), that is, that students "are asked to apply the concepts they have learned to complete complex, realistic tasks" in a criterion-referenced assessment environment. However, as standards are expressed in grade-level expectations, students are reported as Not Yet Within Expectations, Meets Expectations (Minimal level), Fully Meets Expectations (grade level), Exceeds Expectations. Hence there is a normative component to reporting.

The standards provide teachers with a guide or benchmark for their classroom-based observations and assessments. They allow teachers to provide assistance where a student has difficulty with a task. Thus the standards can serve both formative and summative purposes. The standards for reading include Reading literature and Reading for information, including strategies of reading.

United States of America

The states of the U.S.A. have independent systems of literacy assessment and reporting at state and community levels. The recent No Child Left Behind legislation requires states to report students' performance and progress each year against literacy standards. It is too early to evaluate the impact of this legislation on state assessment policy and practice.

At the national level, the National Assessment of Educational Progress (NAEP) was established as national policy to assess "what America's students know and can do" and "to measure achievement at the national level and to measure trends in academic progress" (Hombo, 2003, p. 59). It is congressionally-mandated. Areas of schooling are assessed each year on a rotational basis, for representative samples of students from each state. Recent legislation provides a new role for NAEP in benchmarking annual state measures.

The NAEP Writing Assessment has been modified over time to reflect recent research on writing instruction and assessment. The original framework was developed nationally through a consensus process. The current policy endorses a "process writing approach", that is, that good writing is the result of drafting, editing and revision, and a genre approach:

> The fundamental aim of writing is to communicate. However, its purpose, audience, form, and subject matter vary according to the specific writing situation. Good writers can communicate well in a range of situations. They can perform a variety of writing tasks – from business letters to stories, reports, and essays.

> (NAGB)

The NAEP documents note that NAEP outcomes reflect students' capacity to write in large-scale testing situations as opposed to authentic, and drafting, writing contexts. The current assessment includes:

- Assessment of narrative, informative, and persuasive writing.
- A set of writing topics that incorporate a variety of stimulus materials, audiences, and forms of writing.
- Expanded assessment time: 25 minutes per topic for grades 4, 8, and 12, with some 8th- and 12th-graders receiving a 50-minute task.
- A special page accompanying each topic for students to plan and organize their writing.
- A 6-point scoring criteria (with recommendations that rubrics should be adjusted to suit the task).

To address contextuality and student motivation, materials are chosen to provide a variety of stimulus including "varying the presentation of the test, providing manipulative materials, and providing visual presentations of the prompt" (NAGB, 2003). Writing performance is assessed against three levels, Basic, Proficient and Advanced. Language mechanics (spelling, punctuation, capitalization, grammar) are one component of the overall rubric (NAGB, 2003, p. 41).

The NAEP Reading framework reflects a view of reading as a 'dynamic, interactive process.' 'Reading includes the ability to understand and use written texts for enjoyment and to learn, participate in society, and achieve one's goals' (NAGB, 2003, p. 1). The contexts for NAEP reading include "reading for literary experience", "reading for information" and "reading to perform a task" as well as four ways the reader may respond to a text: "forming a general understanding", "developing interpretation", "making reader/text connections", and "examining content and structure". Students are given booklets of reading materials, half the questions are multiple-choice, half are constructed -response questions. Task materials are selected to be authentic. Texts "generally available" to students including stories, magazines and informational books. Accommodations are made for students with disabilities, as well as for English-language learners including extra testing time, individual or small-group administrations and multiple testing sessions (NAGB, 2003, p. 25).

The NAEP Reading is seen to provide "a broad picture of what our nation's students should be able to read and understand at specific grade levels. Students use various skills and strategies in the reading assessment. However, NAEP does not report on strategies such as finding a detail or summarizing a plot. This is in keeping with NAEP's role as an assessment of overall achievement rather than a diagnostic test for individual students" (NAGB, 2003, p. 5). All questions are designed to emphasise critical thinking and reasoning. Scoring rubrics are developed for each open-ended question, for example:

Evidence of Partial or Surface Comprehension

These responses provide an opinion about the author. These opinions go beyond simply "yes" or "no" by demonstrating some understanding of the information in the article. They fail to provide appropriate evidence from the article to support their opinion concerning the author's abilities. (NAGB, 2003, p. 45)

Oral reading has also been assessed in a subsample of students in 2002. Second-grade students were taped reading a passage aloud. Readings was rated by fluency and accuracy, the latter including omissions, corrections and insertions. Meaning-change and self-correction were noted to reflect reading theory concerns with strategic use of contextual clues to assist skills reading. The results for this study are forthcoming.

International Level

There are three major sets of international assessments. Two are at school level: the IEA (the International Association for the Evaluation of Educational Achievement) and PISA (Programme for International Student Assessment). One is at the adult level, the IALS (International Adult Literacy Survey). All have a focus on assessing literacy.

The IEA survey, named PIRLS (Progress in International Reading Literacy Study) of students in grade 4, around nine years of age, took place in 2001 in 36 countries and its results were due to be reported in spring 2003. Its aim was to assess reading literacy across a range of countries and to relate students' achievements to a wide range of background factors (Rémond & Sainsbury, 2002). Its definition of reading literacy is: the ability to understand and use those written language forms required by society and/or valued by the individual. Young readers can construct meaning from a variety of texts. They read to learn, to participate in communities of readers, and for enjoyment.

Readers are regarded as actively constructing meaning, using reading strategies effectively and knowing how to reflect upon what they have read. The texts and items are organised along two dimensions: purposes for reading and processes of comprehension. Two broad purposes for reading are recognised in the PIRLS framework:

- reading for literary experience and
- reading to acquire and use information.

These correspond to the main uses of literacy amongst children of this age, suggested by the definition above.

There are four processes of comprehension represented by the items in the PIRLS tests:

- focus on and retrieve explicitly stated information
- make straightforward inferences
- interpret and integrate ideas and information
- examine and evaluate content, language and textual elements

Question types are split roughly equally between multiple choice and open ended, with lengthy scoring guides for the latter.

The first PISA study in 2000 assessed literacy in reading, mathematics and science but with a major emphasis on reading literacy (Harlen, 2001, p. 3):

> The notion of being literate has for some time been extended beyond the ability to read and write. The term now generally carries the connotation of being able to engage effectively with different aspects of modern life. Hence it is common to refer to being technologically literate, scientifically literate, even politically and socially literate. Being literate in these various respects indicates having the knowledge and skills that are needed by everyone, not just those who will be specialists in, or make a career using knowledge in, one of these areas. The emphasis is not on mastering a body of knowledge but on having and being able to use a general understanding of the main or key ideas in making informed decisions and participating in society.

What is unusual about the PISA studies is that they assess young people's capacity to use their knowledge and skills in order to meet real life challenges, rather than merely looking at how well they have mastered a specific school curriculum. Students have to understand key concepts, to master certain processes and to apply knowledge and skills in different situations.

The target sample is 15 year olds, and in 2000 about 265,000 students from 32 countries took part (28 of which are OECD members). Students were assessed on:

- retrieving information
- interpreting text
- reflecting on and evaluating a text

The scales were divided into levels, so, for example, a student deemed to be at Level 5 in their ability to reflect on and evaluate a text was able to "critically evaluate or hypothesise, drawing on specialised knowledge. Deal with concepts that are contrary to expectations and draw on deep understanding on long or complex texts." At the other end of the scale, at Level 1 in this area, a student was able to "Make a simple connection between information in the text and common, everyday knowledge."

In PISA reading literacy is defined as: "the ability to understand, use and reflect on written texts in order to achieve one's goals, to develop one's knowledge and potential, and to participate effectively in society." Reading literacy is thus seen as a dynamic process with many dimensions.

PISA uses a mixture of continuous prose passages that are narrative, expository or argumentative, and non-continuous texts that present information in other ways, such as lists, forms, graphs and diagrams. Texts are chosen from those which have been constructed for reading for: public purposes, private purposes, learning and education, and specific work-related purposes (Turner, Bakker, & van Lent, 2002).

To analyse and describe reading proficiency, three scales were developed, based on the type of reading task. These scales describe students' skills in retrieving information, in interpreting text, and in reflection and evaluation. For each of the scales, five levels of proficiency have been described. The three scales were also used to develop an aggregated composite of overall reading proficiency. That scale locates reading performance along a single line with a mean of 500, and a standard deviation of 100.

On publication of the main report (OECD, 2001) most attention focused on country differences in the overall proficiency scale. Within education systems, however, analysis of performance on the three reading scales would be more valuable. Critiques of the design of the studies (Bonnet, 2002) and the production of a single scale (Goldstein & Wood, 1989) have been made.

The *International Adult Literacy Study* of 1990 (OECD, 1997) collected data from a random sample of adults aged 15 to 65+ in many countries. Each adult was individually interviewed. Results are likely to underestimate adult literacy difficulties as in general adults in institutions, or in countries such as Australia in isolated areas, were excluded. The study assessed three aspects of literacy: prose literacy, document literacy, and quantitative literacy. Each aspect was defined as unidimensional and generic in nature, determined by the form of the material and task to be performed, not by the context or culture of the "reader". The focus was on life skills literacy. Texts included images, tables and graphs and questions elicited meaning-making and higher-order skills of extracting, interpreting and inferring meaning. Questions were multiple-choice. No writing was involved. Results from the study have been widely published with national governments paying some heed to the outcomes. Ongoing analyses raise issues of cultural comparability of definitions of, and forms of, functional literacy assessment (Blum, Goldstein & Guerin-Pace, 2001; Cumming, 1996).

Conclusion

Our discussion of literacy assessment policy and practice across a number of nations reveals a breadth of literacy models and assessment practices. The policies show that careful consideration is being given to more constructivist models of literacy and assessment. Many system-level assessment practices incorporate innovations that extend assessment beyond written text, paper-and-pencil tests and multiple-choice items. However, for reporting purposes detailed information is "collapsed" into a scale or level score. The contextuality of literacy learning and performance is recognised as important, and systems try to address equity issues of special needs and cultural diversity. British Columbia incorporates technological elements in literacy assessment if that is the usual practice of students. This is still the area where we expect most innovation, both in curriculum frameworks and assessment practices in literacy, will occur in the twenty-first century.

The concepts emerging from this discussion form a schema that countries can use to undertake a critical examination of their literacy framework and assessment policy.

Sector

Is the literacy assessment policy seamless across sectors, that is, elementary, middle, secondary school or do different policies and practices exist?

If different policies exist, consider the following issues for each as well as the impact of the differences on student performance and learning.

Syllabuses

Is the literacy assessment policy clearly indicated in core areas such as English and reading? Is literacy a focus of other curriculum areas?

Definition

What aspects are the focus of literacy assessment (reading, writing, spelling, listening, speaking and so on)? What definition of literacy is provided (functional, genre, critical and so on) or implicit? To what degree does the definition identify cultural context and/or situatedness of task as aspects of literacy development and performance?

Technology Interface

How is technology incorporated in literacy policy and literacy assessment policy? What information is available about student access to and use of technology to support literacy development?

Equity

Do the literacy assessment policies accommodate cultural diversity, special needs?

Has opportunity to learn been considered?

Assessment Model

What models of assessment (psychometric, constructivist, assessment for learning) are indicated by the literacy assessment policies? What guidelines are given to practitioners for effective classroom assessment of literacy? How well do the assessment policies in practice match the different literacy policies in place? How are issues of contextuality, authenticity and student engagement addressed? What evidence is available about the impact of the literacy assessment policies on students' literacy performance? Will the use of assessment results affect teaching and learning practice?

The most overriding issue, though, is how well do the assessment practices *fit the purpose*?

In sum, views of literacy are rapidly changing. As our conceptions of literacy change and expand, so a wider range of assessment practice is needed to do justice to these broad definitions. Conceptions of assessment are also going on apace (see Gipps & Stobart, 2003) with development of assessment tasks, ways of evaluating knowledge, skills and performance, and an opening up of the assessment relationship between assessor and learner. A number of researchers in the field are trying to bring these two strands together (Wyatt-Smith & Cumming, 2003; Johnson & Kress, 2003). However, the political climate is one of meeting targets and achieving standards which in turn demands a particular form of testing which prioritises consistency and technical reliability and uses a single score or level as the result (so it can be used in tables of performance or for easy comparison). This not only militates against providing broad assessment data, but where such assessment regimes are high stakes it also tends to deaden pedagogical creativity in classrooms. Our *fitness for purpose* theme suggests a range of literacy assessment programmes for the school, national, and international levels, each designed (in terms of sample, assessment tasks, locus of reference, structure of results) to fit its particular purpose.

References

Bernstein, B. (1996). *Pedagogy, symbolic control and identity. Theory, research, critique.* London: Taylor and Francis.

Blum, A., Goldstein, H., & Guerin-Pace, F. (2001). International Adult Literacy Survey (IALS): An analysis of international comparisons of adult literacy. *Assessment in Education: Principles, Policy and Practice, 8*(2), 225–246.

Bonnet, G. (2002). Reflections in a critical eye: On the pitfalls of international assessment. *Assessment in Education: Principles, Policy and Practice, 9*(3), 387–399.

Broadfoot, P. (1994). Approaches to quality assurance and control in six countries. In W. Harlen (Ed.), *Enhancing quality in assessment* (pp. 26–52). London: Chapman.

British Columbia Ministry of Education (BCME) (2002). *B.C. performance standards: Reading.* British Columbia: B.C. Ministry of Education, Student Assessment and Program Evaluation Branch.

Christie, F., & Martin, J. R. (Eds.) (1997). *Genres and institutions: Social processes in the workplace and school.* London: Cassell.

Clay, M. M. (1985) *The early detection of reading difficulties* (3rd ed.). Auckland, New Zealand: Heinemann.

Cope, B., & Kalantzis, M. (Eds.) (1999). *Multiliteracies: Literacy learning and the design of social future.* New York: Routledge.

Council of Ministers of Education, Canada (CME) (1999). *School Achievement Indicators Program.* Toronto: Council of Ministers of Education, Canada.

Cumming, J. J. (1996). The IEA studies of reading and writing literacy: A 1996 perspective. *Assessment in Education: Principles, Policy and Practice, 3*(2), 161–178.

Cumming, J. J., Wyatt-Smith, C. M., Ryan, J., & Doig, S. (1998). The literacy-curriculum interface. The literacy demands of the curriculum in post-compulsory curriculum. Brisbane: DEETYA/ Griffith University.

Cumming, J. J., & Wyatt-Smith, C. M. (Eds.) (2001) Examining the literacy-curriculum connection. Special issue of *Linguistics in Education, 11*(4), 295–312.

Forster, M. (2001). *A policy-maker's guide to systemic assessment programs.* Melbourne: ACER.

Freebody, P., & Luke, A. (1989) On becoming a fluent reader. *Prospect, 5*(7), 7–16.

Gee, J. P. (1992). What is literacy? In Shannon, P. (Ed.), *Becoming political: Readings and writings in the politics of literacy education* (pp. 21–29). Portsmouth, NH: Heinemann.

Gipps, C. (1994). Beyond testing: Towards a theory of educational assessment. London: Falmer.

Gipps, C. (2002). Sociocultural perspectives on assessment. In G. Wells & G. Claxton (Eds.), *Learning for life in the 21st century* (pp. 73–83). Oxford: Blackwell Publishers.

Gipps, C., & Stobart, G. (2003). Alternative assessment. In T. Kellaghan & D. Stufflebeam (Eds.), *International handbook of educational evaluation* (pp. 549–575). Dordrecht, The Netherlands: Kluwer.

Goldstein, H., & Wood, R. (1989). Five decades of item response modelling. *British Journal of Mathematical and Statistical Psychology, 32,* 139–168.

Halliday, M. A. K. (1994). *An introduction to functional grammar* (2nd ed.). London: Edward Arnold.

Harlen, W. (2001). The assessment of scientific literacy in the OECD/PISA project. *Studies in Science Education, 36,* 121–146.

Hombo, C. M. (2003). NAEP and No Child Left Behind: Technical challenges and practical solutions. *Theory into Practice, 42,* 59–65.

Johnson, D., & Kress, G. (2003). Globalisation, literacy and society: redesigning pedagogy and assessment. *Assessment in Education: Principles, Policy and Practice, 10,* 5–14.

Kress, G. (2001). 'You've just got to learn how to see': Curriculum subjects, young people and schooled engagement with the world. In J. Cumming & C. Wyatt- Smith (Eds.), *Literacy and the curriculum: Success in senior secondary schooling* (pp. 12–20). Melbourne: ACER Press.

Lemke, J. (2001). Multimedia literacy demands of the scientific curriculum. In J. Cumming & C. Wyatt-Smith (Eds.), *Literacy and the curriculum: Success in senior secondary schooling* (pp. 170–181). Melbourne: ACER Press.

Mikulecky, L. et al. (1987). *Training for job literacy demands: What research applies to practice.* University Park: Institute for the Study of Adult Literacy, Pennsylvania State University. (ERIC Document Reproduction Service No. ED 284 968).

National Assessment Governing Board (NAGB). *Writing framework and specifications for the 1998 National Assessment of Educational Progress.* Washington, DC: U.S. Department of Education.

National Assessment Governing Board (2003). *Reading framework for the 2003 National Assessment of Education Progress.* Washington, DC: U.S. Department of Education.

New South Wales Department of Education and Training (n.d.). *English language and literacy assessment (ELLA) for students in Years 7 and 8.* Authors.

OECD (1997). *Literacy skills for the knowledge society.* Paris: OECD.

OECD (2001). *Knowledge and skills for life: First results from PISA 2000.* Paris: OECD.

Rémand, M., & Sainsbury, M. (2002) *Reading literacy: Sharing understandings.* Unpublished Paper, National Foundation for Educational Research in England and Wales (NFER), Slough, UK.

Scribner, S., & Cole, M. (1981). *The Psychology of literacy.* Cambridge, MA: Harvard University Press.

Street, B. (1995). *Social literacies: Critical approaches to literacy in development, ethnography and education.* London: Longman.

Turner, R., Bakker, S., & van Lent, G. (September, 2002) *PISA from 2000 to 2003 – 'Profiles and proficiency'.* Paper presented at the Conference of the International Association for Educational Assessment (IAEA), Hong Kong. www.iaea2002.hkea.edu.hk

Victorian Curriculum and Assessment Authority (VCAA) (2001). *Consultation paper: Assessment and reporting in Victorian schools.* Melbourne: VCAA.

Victorian Curriculum and Assessment Authority (VCAA) (2002). *AIM years 3 And 5 testing 2002 guide for principals and teachers.* Melbourne: VCAA.

Wolf, D., Bixby, J., Glenn, J., & Gardner, H. (1991). To use their minds well: nvestigating new forms of student assessment. *Review of Research in Education, 17*, 31–74.

Wyatt-Smith, C. M., & Cumming, J. J. (2003). Curriculum literacies: Expanding domains of assessment. *Assessment in Education: Principles, Policy and Practice, 10*, 47–59.

37

LITERACIES IN FAMILIES AND COMMUNITIES

Kendall A. King* and Nancy H. Hornberger†
*Georgetown University, USA; †University of Pennsylvania, USA

Over the last three decades, research on family and community literacy practices has moved from the periphery to center stage in a quest to understand which policies best support the acquisition and development of literacy skills among diverse populations. Indeed, some of the most important theoretical insights concerning the nature and acquisition of literacy in the last twenty-five years have come from research focusing on contexts *outside* of traditional school domains, that is, in homes and communities (Hull & Schultz, 2002). Correspondingly, within policy circles, addressing family and community roles in literacy development is increasingly viewed as essential for "breaking the cycle of illiteracy" and for resolving many countries' "literacy crises" (Auerbach, 1989).

Defining what is meant by the terms *literate* or *literacy* has long been a source of controversy in policy and in the domains of theory and research. Policy-oriented definitions of literacy vary widely, including views of literacy as a basic skill, but also more sophisticated definitions that incorporate notions of functionality and critical thinking. The national census of India, as an example of the former, defines a literate person as one who is above seven years of age and can both read and write with understanding in any language (DPEP, 2003). In contrast, the widely used policy definition employed in Australia is that "effective literacy is intrinsically purposeful, flexible and dynamic, involves the integration of speaking, listening, and critical thinking, and reading and writing" (DEET, 1991, p. 5; in Hammond, 2001). A further complication is that literacy is often defined in the context of only one language. For instance, the U.S. National Literacy Act of 1991 defines literacy as "an individual's ability to read, write, and speak in English" (Sapin & Padak, 1998, p. 3; also see Kaplan & Baldauf, 1997).

Policy discourse on literacy has concomitantly tended to assume a strong human capital effect in relation to the labor market, stressing that the acquisition of literacy skills is critical for an individual's employment and for the nation's economic development (Auerbach, 1989; Lo Bianco, 2001). Indeed, literacy has been equated with a much wider set of attributes as well; as Baker (2003, p. 78) noted,

International Handbook of Educational Policy, 715–734
Nina Bascia, Alister Cumming, Amanda Datnow, Kenneth Leithwood and David Livingstone (Eds.)
© 2005 *Springer. Printed in Great Britain.*

literacy is variously said to cultivate values, norms of behavior and codes of conduct, to create benign citizens, develop powers of thinking and reasoning, enculturate, emancipate and empower, provide enjoyment and emotional development, develop critical awareness, foster religious devotion, community development and not the least to be central to academic success across the curriculum.

Scribner and Cole's groundbreaking (1981) work on literacy and cognitive skills among the Vai peoples of Liberia called into question many such assumptions concerning the transformative power of literacy while at the same time drawing attention to the importance of community literacy practices. Scribner and Cole were interested in whether literacy in and of itself or educational training more generally led to enhanced cognitive skills. The Vai presented an excellent research population for this question as they were trilingual (in Vai, English and Arabic) and made use of three scripts, each of which were learned in different community contexts. After extensive comparative cognitive testing, Scribner and Cole concluded that literacy in and of itself made little difference in cognitive performance. While specific types of literacy tended to promote particular types of cognitive skills, they found no evidence of the great cognitive divide between literates and illiterates suggested by previous research and policy.

In recent years, many researchers, especially those focused on family and community literacy issues, have critically examined the notion of literacy from a theoretical perspective. Much of this work has focused on understanding literacy as a social and cultural activity, rather than as an isolated cognitive skill. Brian Street (1984, 1993) described these two approaches to literacy as the *autonomous model*, which tends to conceptualize literacy as a discrete cognitive ability, and the *ideological model*, which views literacy as a varied and fluid cultural practice. Early ideological approaches can be traced back to Basso's (1974) argument that despite claims of a "crisis of illiteracy," there was little understanding of how best to conceptualize literacy, nor was there any knowledge of how reading and writing were used in social life. Basso (1974) called "for a study of the relationship between school and the world outside it and specified that the focus should be an inventory of one community's needs and resources" (Hull & Schultz, 2002, p. 14).

The ideological model is generally characterized by a rejection of the traditional categories of *literate* or *illiterate*, as well as the assumptions concerning the characteristics or outcomes traditionally associated with those categories (Baynham & Prinsloo, 2001). This approach to literacy is also shaped by the working assumptions that literacy consists of fluid, purposeful social practices which are embedded in broader social goals, cultural activities, power relationships and historical contexts (Barton & Hamilton, 2000). In recent years, the ideological approach to understanding literacy practices in homes, communities and schools is most prominently represented by what is known as the New Literacy Studies (NLS) (Gee, 1996; Street, 1993). A central area of research for the NLS has been non-dominant or non-mainstream literacy practices which have typically fallen outside the traditional constructions of literacy. For instance, Street (1984), in his study of an Iranian village, described the literacies that were part of everyday life of people who had been classified by the national literacy instructors as 'illiterate'. These included the literacies needed to engage in buying and selling market goods and religious Qur'anic literacy practices.

These contrasting perspectives on literacy form the backdrop of our discussion of community and family literacy policy. In what follows, we first outline two broad categories of policy approaches which have dominated the field of family and community literacies in the past three decades, along with the theoretical assumptions underlying those approaches, largely based on what has come to be known as the "home-school mismatch hypothesis." We then take up two of the new directions in empirical and theoretical work on family and community literacies, and their implications for policy: namely work on multilingualism and literacy, and on language planning and literacy policy.

Traditional Policy Approaches to Family and Community Literacies

Broadly speaking, traditional policy approaches to family and community literacy can be classified into two types: those which attempt to promote school-like literacy activities or literate practices in homes and families; and those which attempt to bring what has been learned about family and home practices into schools. The former policies and programs often attempt to reach adults, children, and entire families in non-traditional settings, that is, outside of formal, mainstream educational institutions. Examples include parenting classes which promote book-reading activities and 'effective parenting' skills; adult second language and literacy programs held in community settings; and activities designed to help parents assist with children's homework and understand how the school system functions. The latter approach includes many of those policies and programs promoted under the rubric of 'bilingual' or 'multicultural' education, but also more targeted classroom or school efforts, for instance, to incorporate a community's story-telling styles into class discussion activities or to involve students in community research projects which highlight the knowledge and expertise within the community and use that as the basis for literacy instruction and formal school learning.

While this distinction is not perfect or precise – indeed, one can envision programs which fall into neither or both of these categories – it provides a useful means of organizing the existing research and policy approaches. More importantly, it highlights the two divergent theoretical orientations which have shaped many policies. A central assumption of the first policy approach has been that families and communities are best served by the acquisition of formal, 'school-like' literacy practices, and that effective policies should help home and community practices more closely resemble what happens in schools. The second policy approach, in contrast, is guided by the belief that the most effective way to promote literacy acquisition is for schools and other formal educational institutions to more closely reflect the communities and families they serve. The underlying assumption is thus that formal educational institutions, not the families themselves, are in need of reform.

Both of these approaches, however, share an even more basic assumption – that family and community literacy practices often differ from those of the school and that these differences must be addressed in order for learners to most effectively and successfully acquire academic, schooled literacy (Cook-Gumperz, 1986). This assumption, often known as the home-school mismatch hypothesis, is in turn founded on a strong and convincing line of empirical research in the (linguistic) anthropology of education, which has developed over the last thirty years and more, beginning with the seminal book, *Functions of Language in the Classroom* (Cazden, John, & Hymes, 1972). In the sub-sections of this chapter which follow, we first introduce the home-school mismatch hypothesis and then expand on this policy distinction, providing examples and discussing policies and programs which characterize these two orientations towards family and community literacy.

Home-school Mismatch

As literacy practices in culturally and linguistically diverse communities have become better understood, so too has understanding of the relationship between a community's cultural practices surrounding language and literacy and students' school experiences. A major stimulus for the increased attention of policy-makers on family literacy practices has been the substantial evidence which has surfaced in recent decades that the home environment plays a critical role in fostering children's literacy abilities (Sulzby & Teale, 1996) and is a key determinant of educational success (Au & Jordan, 1981; Heath, 1982, 1983; Philips, 1972, 1983; Purcell-Gates, 2000).

Prior to entering formal schooling, children engage in interactional routines and are exposed to extended family discourse in the home. These early language socialization experiences play a formative role in children's emergent language and literacy abilities and provide them with essential skills for developing literacy and academic competence, such as narrative abilities and print concepts (Beals, De Temple, & Dickinson, 1994; Pellegrini & Galda, 1993; Reese, 1995; Schieffelin & Ochs, 1986; Snow, 1991). A community's cultural beliefs and values also influence the general patterns of communication in the home. These cultural differences are reflected, for instance, in comparative ethnographic language socialization research which consistently describes Latino homes as highly social environments in which family and non-family members engage in multiparty conversations (Delgado-Gaitán, 1994; Fant, 1990; cited in Ninio & Snow, 1996; Valdés, 1996). Leyendecker, Lamb, Schölmeric and Fracasso (1995), for example, found that in Central American homes, infants' interactions were mostly with multiple social partners, whereas European-American infants' interactions were mostly with one adult at a time. Furthermore, while European-American mothers tend to focus on cognitive skills and task-specific goals (e.g., organizing a narrative chronologically), mothers in Latino homes stress interpersonal skills and social conversational goals (e.g., including all those present in the conversation) (Eisenberg, 1986; Harwood, Miller, & Irizarry, 1995; Melzi, 2000).

Research strongly suggests that these types of communication differences influence children's language and literacy interactions in the classroom, as well as their general school performance. Heath's now classic work (1983), for example, clearly demonstrated how the distinct cultural patterns of communication in black and white communities in the southern U.S. differentially prepared children for language and literacy tasks at school. For instance, Heath found that some children were unable to respond to known-answer questions about the labels and characteristics of events; this skill was part of some children's everyday family and community experiences and an important component of classroom discourse. Children who were not able to engage in this type of discourse, in turn, often failed to participate successfully in school language and literacy routines.

Heath's explanation of school failure is part of a large body of work that has investigated how cultural and linguistic mismatch across home and school contexts influences children's engagement and participation in the classroom and teachers' assessment and treatment of students (see also Erickson & Mohatt, 1982; Michaels, 1991; Michaels & Collins, 1984; Philips, 1972, 1983; Shultz, Florio, & Erickson, 1982). These and other studies document innumerable instances where linguistic and cultural practices in the home conflict with expectations for the child and learning practices at school. However, as suggested below, in many instances, it is not difference itself which creates the problem, but rather the interpretation of this difference as a deficit rather than a resource (Ruiz, 1984).

School to Home: Bringing Official Literacy Practices into Communities and Families

Given the well documented differences between home and school language and literacy practices in many communities, one policy approach to improving school literacy for culturally and linguistically different populations has been to attempt to bring official literacy practices into communities and families. This approach overlaps with the most widespread conception of 'family literacy,' that is, "performing school-like literacy activities within the family setting" (Auerbach, 1989, p. 166). As Auerbach observed, from this vantage point, the successful development of literacy and language skills is closely linked to the culture of school and to mainstream literacy practices, and at the same time, cultural practices of the home, and life demands in general, "are seen as taking parents away from literacy development and as conflicting with the demands of schooling" (such as doing homework) (1989, p. 166). Traditional family literacy programs from this perspective, then, essentially attempt to instill more and better school-like practices into families' daily routines. This deficit-oriented view of family literacy is interwoven with the fact that in nearly all contexts, family literacy programs, either explicitly or implicitly, are targeted at 'at-risk', low income, and often minority families.

This orientation is evident in current U.S. family literacy policy, for instance, where family literacy is defined as the provision of voluntary services which are of sufficient intensity and duration "to make sustainable changes in a family (such as eliminating or reducing welfare dependency) and that integrate all of the following activities: (a) interactive literacy activities between parents and their children; (b) equipping parents to partner with their children in learning; (c) parent literacy training that leads to economic self-sufficiency; (d) appropriate instruction for children of parents receiving parent literacy services" (H.R. 1385, passed by the House in 1997; in Sapin & Padak, 1998, p. 3). The primary U.S. federal program which has been established to implement this policy is known as the "Even Start Family Literacy Program," first authorized in 1988, which aims to "break the cycle of poverty and illiteracy by improving the educational opportunities" of low income families by integrating early childhood education, adult basic education, and parent skills classes into one unified program (Even Start legislation, Part B, Title 1 of the Elementary and Secondary Education Act; in Sapin & Padak, 1998, p. 3).

These types of policies are founded on research suggesting that effective family literacy programs yield numerous benefits for participating parents and children. There is evidence, for instance, that successful family literacy programs improve both child and parent reading, writing, and language skills, as well as their attitudes towards reading, writing, teachers and school; other research indicates that family literacy programs help families to establish closer relationships, to value education, and to have fewer health problems (see Padak & Rasinksi [1994] for a review; Paratore, Melzi, & Krol-Sinclair [2003] for case studies). However, not all research findings are clear-cut. Parents who participate in family literacy programs, as an example, tend to show only modest gains in literacy skills (Sapin, 1996). Some of the mixed findings no doubt are due to the weak evaluation component of many family and community literacy programs (Sapin, 1996); however, other issues, such as the deficit premise of many programs, may also play a role (see Valdés [1996] for further discussion of deficit-oriented family literacy programs).

Of all family and community practices, the greatest amount of attention has been given to the importance of parent-to-child book reading. Since the late 1960s, research has provided evidence that supports the importance of parental book reading for children's own reading success. By 1985, the U.S. Commission on Reading, charged with reviewing the research concerning children's reading development, concluded that "the single most important activity for building the knowledge required for eventual success in reading is reading aloud to children" (Anderson, Hiebert, Scott & Wilkinson, 1985, cited in Paratore, Melzi, & Krol-Sinclair, 2003, pp. 101–102). These findings have directly influenced U.S. family literacy policies and programs; for instance, evaluations of Even Start Programs report that 94% provide support for reading, storytelling, and pre-reading activities in families (Tao, Khan, Gamse, St. Pierre, & Tarr, 1998).

As suggested above, the ideological underpinnings of many of these types of program merit scrutiny. Auerbach (1989) has argued that implicit in this "transmission of school practices" model are five core assumptions: (1) that literacy (and education in general) are not valued in these students' homes; (2) that family and community literacy involves a one-to-one transfer of skills from parent to child; (3) that successful acquisition of literacy skills is dependent upon parents' abilities to engage their child in school-like literacy events in the home; (4) that school practices are sufficient, while home practices are the critical factor in determining successful literacy acquisition; and (5) that parents' cultural, personal and economic inadequacies are an impediment to the development of their children's literacy skills. Clearly, a difference as deficit premise predominates here.

Home to School: Bringing Community and Family Practices into Schools

An alternative policy approach to improving schooled literacy acquisition for linguistically and culturally different populations has been to bridge the home-to-school gap by attempting to bring community and family practices into schools. This approach to literacy policy is linked to those definitions and interpretations of literacy which tend to view literacy as including "a range of activities and practices that are integrated into the fabric of daily life" (Auerbach, 1989, p. 166). From this perspective, "doing schoolwork and developing literacy are not necessarily synonymous ... The acquisition of literacy skills is seen in relation to its context and uses: literacy is meaningful to students to the extent that it relates to daily realities and helps them to act on them" (1989, p. 166).

An early example of a successful attempt to bring community literacy and language practices into the school was that of the Kamehameha Early Education Program (KEEP) initiated in the 1970s for native Hawaiian children. Based on ethnographic research in native Hawaiian communities, KEEP teachers set up collaborative 'peer-learning centers' in the classroom and incorporated a community speech event called 'talk story' into the literacy curriculum. Both innovations successfully integrated home and community discourse patterns into classroom learning activities, thus minimizing home-school cultural incongruence and maximizing literacy acquisition (see Au & Mason, 1983; Villegas, 1991; Watson-Gegeo & Boggs, 1977).

The Navajo maintenance bilingual education programs which were developed at Rough Rock and Rock Point schools beginning in the 1960s offer excellent examples of successful efforts to recognize and empower community experts and community expertise in the context of the school, thus enhancing children's literacy learning. Not only were Navajo young people recruited as teachers, but also Navajo elders have from the very beginning directed and guided the development of the curriculum and have provided hands-on, face-to-face instruction in Navajo traditional ways as well (see Holm & Holm, 1995; McCarty, 2002).

Significantly, in both of the above examples, difference is seen as a resource on which schools can draw, rather than a deficit to be overcome. However, these programs tend to be the exceptions rather than the norm. For instance, language and literacy practices of urban, immigrant populations have traditionally not been accorded attention in school literacy contexts, with generally negative consequences for their literacy acquisition. Skilton-Sylvester (2002), in her discussion of Nan, a Cambodian girl in Philadelphia who was an unsuccessful writer at school and prolific writer at home, suggested ways in which out-of-school literacy resources "can be a foundation for school literacy if we are able to read the word and the worlds that children bring with them to school and help them engage in new and related words and worlds as they use writing to do the social work of school" (p. 88). For instance, Nan's oral discourse, visual communication and drawing skills could have been capitalized upon in a classroom in which "oral and visual meaning-making exist alongside written communication, where both teachers and students are an authentic audience for the written work of others in the classroom, and where the purposes for writing are connected to multiple real reasons why class members would want to communicate with each other" (2002, p. 87). Clearly, we still have much headway to make for educational policymakers and practitioners to come to view linguistically and culturally different literacy practices as resources rather than deficits and for the home-school mismatch hypothesis to serve its full usefulness in improving literacy acquisition and development.

Beyond Mismatch: New Directions in Research and Policy on Family and Community Literacies

As suggested above, in recent years there has been a gradual shift away from the deficit model of family literacy and towards one that explicitly recognizes the fact that home literacy practices do in fact exist, though they vary from community to community and are different in important ways from school literacy activities (Sapin, 1996). Perhaps most significantly, researchers and policymakers have begun to conceptualize family literacy in much broader terms than heretofore, moving beyond school-based definitions and reflecting the ideological or cultural approach to literacy. For instance, the International Reading Association defines family literacy as the way parents, children, and extended family members use literacy at home and in their communities. This definition includes literacy activities which are purposefully initiated by a parent, as well as those which come about as families conduct the business of their daily lives (International Reading Association Family Literacy Commission, 1994; in Sapin & Padak, 1998, p. 5).

There is also evidence that the home-school mismatch hypothesis itself, with its emphasis on the role of cultural differences in academic failure, only captures one aspect of the relationship between home and school. This is in part because the mismatch hypothesis is by definition rather uninterested in describing and analyzing continuities between home and school. As an example of recent work which moves beyond the traditional mismatch paradigm, Volk and De Acosta (2001), in their ethnographic study of home, community, and school literacy practices among Puerto Ricans in the U.S., highlighted the ways in which home and school practice both diverge and overlap. They reported that Puerto Rican parents engaged in direct literacy instruction with their children at home, often using teacher-like language and practices, but that the nature of literacy practices, the purposes of literacy events, and what counts as literacy tended to differ from school to community. "What counted as literacy at home and in the community were primarily social interactions with familiar texts containing significant and useful knowledge," while in contrast, "what counted as literacy in school was a progression from social to individual interactions with print" (pp. 219–220). Thus, although the home-school mismatch literature has identified cultural differences that may exist in the nature and structure of parent-child conversations and shown how these differences often shape the nature of students' school experiences and the likelihood of their academic success, it also may overemphasize the discontinuities across the two contexts.

Moreover, the home-school mismatch explanation also fails to consider adequately the role of power and resistance and how these are negotiated in the home and classroom. For instance, young students' silence in the classroom (cf. Philips' [1972] work with Warm Springs Indians) has been interpreted as the result of cultural and communicative differences, but might also as be understood as resistance to mainstream school practices, norms and values (Heller & Martin-Jones, 2001). Among older Latino students in rural U.S. classrooms, in turn, academic silence has been interpreted as resistance to academic content decisions which exclude students' "identity, experiences, and vernacular word choices" (Lincoln, 2003, p. 155).

Two lines of work emerging in the last twenty years offer new perspectives on the above-mentioned shortcomings of the mismatch hypothesis, that is, the emphasis on discontinuities and the inadequate attention to power and resistance. Research on literacy attitudes and practices in multilingual communities has led to the formulation of a theoretical framework on biliteracy which emphasizes continuities (as well as discontinuities) across the development, media, content, and contexts of biliteracy in two or more languages. Simultaneously, work in the area of literacy policy as an aspect of language planning has highlighted the potential of indigenous or local literacy programs as vehicles for communities to empower themselves from the bottom up. Both of these new research directions hold direct policy implications.

Multilingual Literacies and the Continua of Biliteracy

As Martin-Jones and Jones pointed out in the introduction to their volume on *Multilingual Literacies* (2000), the term is laden with meaning. Literacies in the plural signals, from within the New Literacy Studies, an understanding of literacies as social practices (Street, 2000), while multilingual, rather than bilingual, signals, from within the sociolinguistic study of bilingualism, an awareness of the multiplicity and complexity of communicative repertoires in multilingual settings. Martin-Jones and Jones further explicated that: (1) the use of *multi* rather than *bi* signals that the communicative repertoires under study include not just two, but many, communicative means (i.e., media of biliteracy: languages, dialects, styles, registers, channels, modes of expression, etc.); (2) *multi* signals the multiplicity and complexity of communicative purposes associated with the repertoire of languages and literacies (in contexts of biliteracy); (3) the use of *multi* takes account of multiple paths of acquisition and varying degrees of expertise within individuals' and groups' communicative development (of biliteracy); and (4) that it focuses attention on the multiple ways people draw on and combine the codes in their communicative repertoires to make meaning as they negotiate and display cultural identities and social relationships (the content of biliteracy) (Hornberger, 2000, pp. 353–357).

Hornberger's Continua Model of Biliteracy (Hornberger, 1989, 2003; Hornberger & Skilton-Sylvester, 2000) provides a framework that incorporates and elucidates many of these complex issues. For Hornberger, biliteracy includes "any and all instances in which communication occurs in two (or more) languages in or around writing" (1990, p. 213). The Continua Model depicts the development of biliteracy along intersecting continua of first language-second language, receptive-productive, and oral-written language skills; through the medium of two (or more) languages and literacies whose linguistic structures vary from similar to dissimilar, whose scripts range from convergent to divergent, and to which the developing biliterate individual's exposure varies from simultaneous to successive; in contexts that encompass micro to macro levels and are characterized by varying mixes along the monolingual-bilingual and oral-literate continua; and with content that ranges from majority to minority perspectives and experiences, literary to vernacular styles and genres, and decontextualized to contextualized language texts (see Figure 1).

The notion of the continuum conveys that all points on a particular continuum are interrelated, and the intersecting and nested relationships among the continua convey that all points across the continua are also interrelated. In addition, the Continua Model also highlights the power relationships which surround literacy practices in general and biliteracy in particular; that is, there tends to be an implicit privileging of one end of the continua over another (e.g., literate contexts of biliteracy over oral ones; second language development over first language; majority content over minority; and successive exposure over simultaneous exposure). The Continua Model thus offers a framework in which to situate research, teaching, and policy, enabling us to focus on one or more dimensions while highlighting the fact that in order to fully understand any particular instance of biliteracy, we need to take account of all dimensions represented by the continua. (See Hornberger 2003 for fuller discussion of the Model and case studies which have made use of it.)

While abstract in nature, the Continua Model is grounded in the research literature on literacy, and has direct implications for family and community literacy policy. For instance, the Model can be used as a tool to assist in the development of effective (multi)literacy policies for particular regions or communities. One clear implication of the Continua is that the most successful literacy

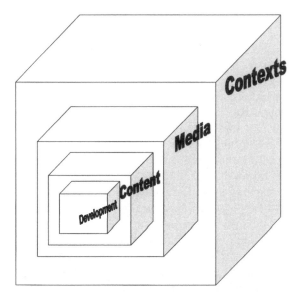

Nested relationship among the continua of biliteracy

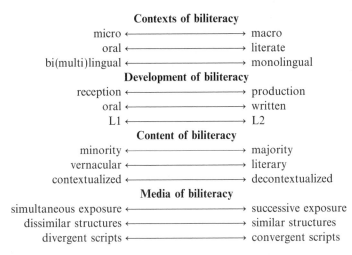

Figure 1. The Continua of Biliteracy (from Hornberger 2003, with kind permission from Multilingual Matters)

policies in terms of providing the greatest opportunities for full literacy development are those which allow and encourage individuals to draw from all points of the Continua. Focusing on the media of biliteracy, another important insight is the importance and value of "program structures and instructional approaches which make a strength rather than a weakness out of learners' criss-crossed, simultaneous acquisition of (exposure to) two languages and literacies, and the need for language planning that devolves agency and voice to those whose varieties and discourses are at stake" (Hornberger & Skilton-Sylvester, 2003, p. 62). Mercado (2003), for instance, in her comparative analysis of three middle-school Latino students in New York City public schools, showed how "spontaneous biliterate development" was often invisible or misinterpreted, revealing the "untapped potential for intellectual development in formal learning contexts such as schools that resides in bilingual/multidialectal communities" (pp. 167–168).

In addition, the Continua Model provides a powerful tool for the analysis, assessment and potential revision of existing policies. Two international research reports illustrate this well. Baker (2003), in his discussion of historical and present literacy practices in Wales, highlighted, among other themes, how the Continua Model allows for insightful analysis of Welsh language and literacy policy, and in particular the (risky and controversial) decision to promote Welsh usage in all high status domains, including text books and novels, television programming, internet sites, computer programs, and signage and packaging. Thus, the Welsh policy does not promote diglossia – a supposedly safe separation of Welsh and English into different domains of usage – but rather provides bilinguals with the opportunity to use Welsh in many different high status domains. Baker argued that in the case of the Welsh language and literacy policies, the aim has been to move along all twelve dimensions of the continua as far as possible towards the traditionally more powerful ends of these dimensions (i.e., towards literary content, successive exposure, and written development). Moving along these twelve dimensions and bringing what was traditionally a family and community language into public and school domains thus can be understood as a means for increasing the power of Welsh language literacy and also for "contesting the traditional power weighting of the continua by paying attention to and granting agency and voice to actors and practices that have traditionally been at the less powerful ends of the continua" (Hornberger & Skilton-Sylvester, 2000, p. 99; in Baker, 2003, p. 87).

In South African language and literacy policy, the Continua Model also has provided a framework for action and reflection (Bloch & Alexander, 2003). Since July of 1997, official language policy has promoted bilingual (and in some cases, multilingual) education for all South African students, emphasizing additive bilingualism, the maintenance of home languages, the promotion of biliteracy, and the official use of each of the country's eleven official languages. Through their analysis of literacy and language policy in a primarily Xhosa-speaking school, and in particular the attitudes associated with using languages other than English for formal literacy functions, Bloch and Alexander showed that "at the less powerful end of the continua, much can be done to initiate changes in people's perceptions about making use of the possibilities for their languages and literacies as well as in their capabilities to take control of such changes" (2003, p. 17). The Continua model thus provides a tool for analyzing many of the complex and interrelated factors which come into play in the development and use of literacy skills and practices, allowing us to take into account both the autonomous and ideological literacy issues outlined above as well as the connections across home, school, and community contexts.

Literacy Policy as Language Planning from the Bottom up

With the increased recognition of literacy as a social and cultural practice and the greater understanding of the role of home factors in promoting school success, family and community literacy policy has grown in significance as an area of language planning in recent decades (Kaplan & Baldauf, 1997; Street, 1994). While literacy is often conceptualized as an educational issue, as Barton (1994) rightly pointed out, literacy is at heart a language issue, meaning that "every literacy programme in the world, every literacy initiative, every government statement, every act by an aid agency has behind it a theory of language and also a theory of literacy" (p. 3).

Literacy policy is rooted, either explicitly or implicitly, in at least one of three types of language planning: status planning (concerning the allocation of functions of languages/literacies), corpus planning (about the form or structure of languages/literacies), and acquisition planning (concerning efforts to influence the allocation of users or the distributions of languages/literacies). At the same time, literacy planning potentially draws from either policy planning or cultivation planning approaches. Hornberger, building on Neustúpny's (1974) early distinction, noted that policy planning tends to focus on "matters of society and nation, at the macroscopic level, emphasizing the distribution of languages/ literacies, and [is] mainly concerned with standard language" (1994, p. 79). Cultivation planning, in contrast, is "seen as attending to matters of language, at the microscopic level, emphasizing ways of speaking/writing and their distribution, and [is] mainly concerned with literary usage" (1994, p. 79). (See Hornberger [1994] for an expanded discussion.)

These two language planning approaches (policy and cultivation) and three language planning types (status, acquisition, and corpus) are best understood within Hornberger's (1994) integrative framework of language planning goals. (See Table 1.) While the parameters of the framework are formed by the matrix of language planning types and approaches, it is the language planning goals which "identify the range of choices available within those parameters" (1994, p. 79). In other words, the language/literacy planning types and approaches do not in and of themselves set or determine policy; rather, it is the goals assigned to them that shape policy.

Among the various language planning goals listed in Table 1, we mention just two, both from the Andean context, to illustrate how these goals intersect with family and community literacy policy-making, as well as the bottom-up nature of many language policy decisions. As a first example, the status planning goal of *revival*, which refers to the restoration of a language with few or no speakers, or a literacy with few or no users, to use as a normal means of communication within a community, is evident in the case of the Quichua language in Saraguro, Ecuador. In this highland Andean indigenous community, residents – who are

Table 1.   Language planning goals: An integrative framework (Hornberger, 1994)

Approaches	Policy Planning (on form)	Cultivation Planning (on function)
Types	Goals	Goals
Status Planning (about uses of language)	Standardization status Officialization Nationalization Proscription	Revival Maintenance Interlingual communication International International Spread
Acquisition planning (about users of language)	Group Education/School Literature Religion Mass Media Work	Reacquisition Maintenance Foreign Language/ Second Language Shift
Corpus planning (about language)	Standardization Corpus Auxiliary code Graphization	Modernization Lexical Stylistic Renovation Purification Reform Stylistic simplification Terminological unification

increasingly Spanish-dominant – collectively decided to revitalize or revive their native or heritage language, Quichua (King, 2001). These efforts entailed teaching Quichua language and literacy in formal school domains, but also promoting Quichua language and literacy within homes and communities. Community signs, for instance, were reposted in Quichua, some visual-supplementary materials at community meetings were presented in Quichua, and parents were encouraged to support children's Quichua language/literacy development at home.

Intertwined with the status and cultivation planning goal of revival at the community level was the corpus and policy planning goal of *standardization* at the national level. Standardization, in the context of literacy planning, generally refers to the development of a literacy norm which supplants regional and social literacies (Ferguson, 1968; Hornberger, 1994). In the Ecuadorian context, the process of standardizing Quichua was formally initiated in 1981, when representatives of the different Ecuadorian varieties of Quichua agreed upon a unified variety. Quichua language planners, most of whom were themselves indigenous political and education leaders, made decisions in two areas: a unified writing system, consisting of twenty consonants and three vowels; and lexical modernization and purification, primarily through replacement of Spanish loan words with neologisms. These decisions were codified in subsequent dictionaries and grammars (CONAIE, 1990; MEC, 1982) and constituted a major step towards the standardization of Ecuadorian Quichua, which came to be known as *Quichua Unificado*. Standardization was intended to facilitate the development of Quichua literacy and educational materials and to contribute to the maintenance and revival of the language at the community level. Despite the new written standard, it was expected that the regional varieties would continue to exist in their spoken forms (CONAIE, 1990).

These two examples of bottom-up efforts to achieve literacy planning goals – one of revival, the other of standardization – illustrate the distinct nature of each type of goal, and concomitantly, how the goals relate and interconnect. These examples in particular and the framework in general also remind us that independent of the specific language or literacy planning goal, success is most likely if multiple goals are pursued along multiple dimensions simultaneously (Fishman, 1979). More broadly, the framework has proven powerful not only in explicating language and literacy policy types, approaches and goals, but also in underlining the importance of moving beyond traditional top-down approaches to language and literacy planning (also see Hornberger, 1996a, 1996b).

Implications for Policies

The theoretical shifts outlined above, including trends moving beyond the autonomous model of literacy and traditional home-school mismatch paradigm towards conceptualization of linguistic and cultural differences as resources rather than as deficits, and towards increased recognition of multilingual literacies and language planning as a grassroots community activity, are not unrelated. Rather, they are convergent and indeed together reflected in current work on family and community literacy policy. For instance, the most recent research-based recommendations concerning the best practices for family literacy programs serving adult English language learners suggest that four components are critical: (a) sufficient intensity and duration to allow for adequate instructional time; (b) a focus on middle- and high-school-age children as well as early childhood learning; (c) building on parents' existing language and literacy skills, including those in their first languages; and (d) respecting families' cultures and ways of knowing, and in particular recognizing the many strengths and resources that parents have, which may be different from the mainstream, but not deficient (National Center for ESL Literacy Education, 2002; see also Weinstein-Shr, 1992).

We further suggest that while these approaches have been shown to be effective for minority language parents in particular, they also constitute ideal practices for working with all families. Such 'best-practices recommendations' are supported by recent research which has underlined the many ways in which low-income and minority parents support their children's literacy development. For instance, Paratore, Melzi and Krol-Sinclair (2003), in their analysis of Latino parents participating in an intergenerational literacy project, found that even parents with diverse levels of education and English proficiency reported engaging in different types of literacy events at home, with no significant relationship between the parents' level of education and parent-child book reading.

These findings and recommendations reflect the field's growing recognition that family literacy consists of much more than promoting the achievement of children in school (Weinstein-Shr, 1992). Concomitantly, there is increasing consensus that successful "programs that aim to strengthen families and communities while promoting school achievement do not locate 'the problem' with parents, but see the task as a reciprocal one of enabling parents to understand schools while enabling school personnel to understand and take into account the realities of parents" (1992, p. 5). The best community literacy programs not only view parents as a resource, but also take steps to empower them and give them greater control over their education. Rivera (1999), for instance, described the critical pedagogy approach adapted by El Barrio Popular Education Program, a community-based, adult-education program in New York City which caters to Puerto Rican and Dominican women. The program, which is committed to participatory education and the development of bilingualism and biliteracy, successfully integrated the teaching of Spanish-language literacy and basic education with ESL, computer technology and popular research through research designed and conducted by the student participants. The program implemented pedagogy that recognized that "the community was not only a source of knowledge, but also knowledge itself" (1999, p. 498). Programs such as this one point to the essential future directions for community and family literacy policy and programs.

References

Anderson, R. C., Hiebert, E. H., Scott, J., & Wilkinson, I. (1985). *Becoming a nation of readers.* Washington, DC: U.S. Department of Education, National Institute of Education.

Au, K. H., & Jordan, C. (1981). Teaching reading to Hawaiian children: Finding a culturally appropriate solution. In H. T. Trueba, G. P. Guthrie & K. H. Au (Eds.), *Culture and the bilingual classroom: Studies in classroom ethnography* (pp. 139–152). Rowley, MA: Newbury House.

Au, K. H., & Mason, J. M. (1983). Cultural congruence in classroom participations structures: Achieving a balance of rights. *Discourse Processes, 6,* 145–167.

Auerbach, E. R. (1989). Toward a social-contextual approach to family literacy. *Harvard Educational Review, 59*(2), 165–181.

Baker, C. (2003). Biliteracy and transliteracy in Wales: Language planning and the Welsh national curriculum. In N. H. Hornberger (Ed.), *Continua of biliteracy: An ecological framework for educational policy, research, and practice in multilingual settings* (pp. 71–90). Clevedon, UK: Multilingual Matters.

Barton, D. (1994). Globalisation and diversification: Two opposing influences on local literacies. *Language and Education, 8*(1&2), 3–17.

Barton, D., & Hamilton, M. (2000). Literacy practices. In D. Barton, M. Hamilton & R. Ivanic (Eds.), *Situated literacies: Reading and writing in context* (pp. 7–15). London: Routledge.

Basso, K. (1974). The ethnography of writing. In R. Bauman & J. Sherzer (Eds.), *Explorations in the ethnography of speaking* (pp. 425–432). Cambridge, UK: Cambridge University Press.

Baynham, M., & Prinsloo, M. (2001). New directions in literacy research. *Language and Education*, *15*(2&3), 83–91.

Beals, D. E., De Temple, J. M., & Dickinson, D. K. (1994). Talking and listening that support early literacy development of children from low-income families. In D. K. Dickinson (Ed.), *Bridges to literacy: Children, families and schools* (pp. 19–42). Cambridge, MA: Basil Blackwell.

Bloch, C., & Alexander, N. (2003). *A luta continua!* The relevance of the continua of biliteracy to South African multilingual schools. In N. H. Hornberger (Ed.), *Continua of biliteracy: An ecological framework for educational policy, research, and practice in multilingual settings* (pp. 91–121). Clevedon, UK: Multilingual Matters.

Cazden, C., John, V., & Hymes, D. (Eds.) (1972). *Functions of language in the classroom*. NY: Teachers College.

CONAIE (Confederación de Nacionalidades Indígenas del Ecuador). (1990). *Ñucanchic shimi 1.* Quito: MEC/DINEIIB/CONAIE.

Cook-Gumperz, J. (1986). Literacy and schooling: an unchanging equation? In J. Cook-Gumperz (Ed.), *The social construction of literacy* (pp. 16–44). New York: Cambridge University Press.

DEET (Department of Employment, Education, and Training) (1991). *Australia's language: The Australian language and literacy policy*. Canberra, Australia: DEET.

Delgado-Gaitán, C. (1994). Consejos: The power of cultural narratives. *Anthropology and Education Quarterly, 25*, 298–316.

DPEP (District Primary Education Programme) (2003). Concepts and definitions in educational planning – educational attainment. Retrieved June 20, 2003 from http://www.dpepmis.org/webpages/concept %20for %20web/Main_O_index.htm.

Eisenberg, A. R. (1986). Teasing: Verbal play in two Mexicano homes. In B. B. Schieffelin & E. Ochs (Eds.), *Language socialization across cultures* (pp. 182–198). New York: Cambridge University Press.

Erickson, F., & Mohatt, G. (1982). Cultural organization of participation structures in two classrooms of Indian students. In G. Spindler (Ed.), *Doing the ethnography of schooling* (pp. 132–174). New York: Holt, Rinehart and Winston.

Fant, L. (1990). Turntaking in Swedish and Spanish group discussions. Paper presented at the International Pragmatics Conference, Barcelona, Spain.

Ferguson, C. A. (1968). Language development. In J. Fishman, C. A. Ferguson & J. Das Gupta (Eds.), *Language problems in developing nations* (pp. 27–35). New York: John Wiley and Sons.

Fishman, J. (1979). Bilingual education, language planning, and English. *English World-Wide, 1*(1), 11–24.

Gee, J. P. (1996). *Social linguistics and literacies: Ideology in discourses* (2nd edition). London: Falmer.

Hammond, J. (2001). Literacies in school education in Australia: Disjunctions between policy and research. *Language and Education, 15*(2&3), 162–177.

Harwood, R., Miller, J. G., & Irizarry, N. L. (1995). *Culture and attachment: Perceptions of the child in context.* New York: Guilford Press.

Heath, S. B. (1982). Questioning at home and at school. A comparative study. In G. Spindler (Ed.), *Doing the ethnography of schooling* (pp. 102–131). New York: Hold, Rinehart, and Wilson.

Heath, S. B. (1983). *Ways with words: Language, life and work in communities and classrooms.* Cambridge: Cambridge University Press.

Heller, M., & Martin-Jones, M. (2001). Introduction: Symbolic domination, education, and linguistic difference. In M. Heller & M. Martin-Jones (Eds.), *Voices of authority: Education and linguistic difference* (pp. 1–28). London: Ablex Publishing.

Holm, A., & Holm, W. (1995). Navajo language education: Retrospect and prospects. *The Bilingual Research Journal, 19*, 141–165.

Hornberger, N. H. (1989). Continua of biliteracy. *Review of Educational Research, 59*(3), 271–296.

Hornberger, N. H. (1990). Creating successful learning contexts for bilingual literacy. *Teachers College Record, 92*(2), 212–229.

Hornberger, N. H. (1994). Literacy and language planning. *Language and Education: An International Journal, 8*(1–2), 75–86.

Hornberger, N. H. (Ed.) (1996a). *Indigenous literacies in the Americas: Language planning from the bottom up.* Berlin: Mouton.

Hornberger, N. H. (1996b). Language planning from the bottom up. In N. H. Hornberger (Ed.), *Indigenous literacies in the Americas: Language planning from the bottom up* (pp. 357–366). Berlin: Mouton de Gruyter.

Hornberger, N. H. (2000). Multilingual literacies, literacy practices, and the continua of biliteracy. In M. Martin-Jones & K. Jones (Eds.), *Multilingual literacies: Reading and writing different worlds* (pp. 353–367). Philadelphia: John Benjamins.

Hornberger, N. H. (Ed.) (2003). *Continua of biliteracy: An ecological framework for educational policy, research, and practice in multilingual settings.* Clevedon, UK: Multilingual Matters.

Hornberger, N. H., & Skilton-Sylvester, E. (2000). Revisiting the continua of biliteracy: International and critical perspectives. *Language and Education: An International Journal, 14*(2), 96–122.

Hull, G., & Schultz, K. (2002). Connecting schools with out-of-school worlds: Insights from recent research on literacy in non-school settings. In G. Hull & K. Schultz (Eds.), *School's out! Bridging out-of-school literacies with classroom practice* (pp. 32–57). New York: Teachers College Press.

International Reading Association Family Literacy Commission (1994). *Family literacy new perspectives, new opportunities.* Newark, DE: International Reading Association.

Kaplan, R. B., & Baldauf, Jr., R. B. (1997). *Language planning: From practice to theory.* Clevedon, UK: Multilingual Matters.

King, K. A. (2001). *Language revitalization processes and prospects: Quichua in the Ecuadorian Andes.* Clevedon, UK: Multilingual Matters.

Leyendecker, B., Lamb, M., Schölmeric, A., & Fracasso, M. (1995). The social worlds of 8- and 12-month-old infants: Early experiences in two subcultural contexts. *Social Development, 4*(2), 194–208.

Lincoln, F. (2003). Language education planning and policy in middle America: Students' voices. In N. H. Hornberger (Ed.), *Continua of biliteracy: An ecological framework for educational policy, research, and practice in multilingual settings* (pp. 147–165). Clevedon, UK: Multilingual Matters.

Lo Bianco, J. (2001). Policy literacy. *Language and Education, 15*(2&3), 212–227.

Martin-Jones, M., & Jones, K. (2000). Introduction: Multilingual literacies. In M. Martin-Jones & K. Jones (Eds.), *Multilingual literacies: Reading and writing different worlds* (pp. 1–15). Philadelphia: John Benjamins.

McCarty, T. L. (2002). *A place to be Navajo: Rough Rock and the struggle for self-determination in indigenous schooling.* Mahwah, New Jersey: Lawrence Erlbaum Associates.

MEC (Ministerio de Educación y Cultura). (1982). *Caimi ñucanchic shimiyuc-panca.* Quito: MEC/ PUCE.

Melzi, G. (2000). Cultural variations in the construction of personal narratives: Central American and European-American mothers' elicitation discourse. *Discourse Processes, 30*(2), 153–177.

Mercado, C. (2003). Biliteracy development among Latino youth in New York City communities: An unexploited potential. In N. H. Hornberger (Ed.), *Continua of biliteracy: An ecological framework for educational policy, research, and practice in multilingual settings* (pp. 166–186). Clevedon, UK: Multilingual Matters.

Michaels, S. (1991). Dismantling of narrative. In A. McCabe & C. Peterson (Eds.), *Developing narrative voice* (pp. 305–351). Hillsdale, NJ: Lawrence Erlbaum.

Michaels, S., & Collins, J. (1984). Oral discourse styles: Classroom interaction and acquisition of literacy. In D. Tannen (Ed.), *Coherence in spoken and written discourse* (pp. 219–244). Norwood: NJ: Ablex.

National Center for ESL Literacy Education (2002). *NCLE Fact sheet: Family literacy and adult English language learners.* Washington, DC: NCLE.

Neustúpny, J. V. (1974). Basic types of treatment of language problems. In J. Fishman (Ed.), *Advances in language planning* (pp. 37–48). The Hague: Mouton.

Ninio, A., & Snow, C. E. (1996). *Pragmatic development.* Boulder, CO: Westview Press.

Padak, N., & Rasinski, T. (1994). Family literacy: Who benefits? (Occasional Paper No. 2). Kent, OH: Kent State University.

Paratore, J. R., Melzi, G., & Krol-Sinclair, B. (2003). Learning about the literate lives of Latino families. In D. M. Barone & L. M. Morrow (Eds.), *Literacy and young children: Research-based practices in early literacy* (pp. 101–118). New York: Guilford Press.

Pellegrini, A. D., & Galda, L. (1993). Ten years after: A reexamination of symbolic play and literacy research. *Reading Research Quarterly, 28*(2), 163–175.

Philips, S. (1972). Participant structure and communicative competence: Warm Springs children in community and classroom. In C. B. Cazden, V. John & D. Hymes (Eds.), *The cultural politics of English as an international language* (pp. 370–394). London: Longman.

Philips, S. (1983). *The invisible culture: Communication in classroom and community on the Warm Springs Indian reservation.* New York: Longman.

Purcell-Gates, V. (2000). Family literacy. In R. Barr, M. Kamil, P. Mosenthal & P. D. Pearson (Eds.), *Handbook of reading research* (Vol. III, pp. 260–276). Mahwah, NJ: Lawrence Erlbaum.

Reese, E. (1995). Predicting children's literacy from mother-child conversations. *Cognitive Development, 10,* 381–405.

Rivera, K. M. (1999). Popular research and social transformation: A community-based approach to critical pedagogy. *TESOL Quarterly, 33*(3), 485–500.

Ruiz, R. (1984). Orientations in language planning. *NABE Journal, 8*(2), 15–34.

Sapin, C. (1996). Book Review: *A Survey of family literacy in the United States* and *Family literacy: Connections in schools and communities.* (Publication No. 039-0600-0007). Kent, OH: The Ohio Literacy Resource Center, Kent State University.

Sapin, C., & Padak, N. D. (1998). *Family literacy resource notebook.* Kent, OH: The Ohio Literacy Resource Center, Kent State University.

Schieffelin, B., & Ochs, E. (1986). *Language socialization across cultures.* New York: Cambridge University Press.

Scribner, S., & Cole, M. (1981). *The psychology of literacy.* Cambridge, MA: Harvard University Press.

Shultz, J. J., Florio, S., & Erickson, F. (1982). Where's the floor? Aspects of the cultural organization of social relationships in communication at home and in school. In P. Gilmore & A. A. Glatthorn (Eds.), *Children in and out of school* (pp. 88–123). Washington, DC: Center for Applied Linguistics.

Skilton-Sylvester, E. (2002). Literate at home but not at school: A Cambodian girl's journey from playwright to struggling writer. In G. Hull & K. Schultz (Eds.), *School's out! Bridging out-of-school literacies with classroom practice* (pp. 61–90). New York: Teachers College Press.

Snow, C. E. (1991). The theoretical basis for the relationship between language and literacy in development. *Journal of Research in Childhood Education, 6*(1), 5–10.

Street, B. V. (1984). *Literacy in theory and practice.* New York: Cambridge University Press.

Street, B. V. (Ed.) (1993). *Cross-cultural approaches to literacy.* New York: Cambridge University Press.

Street, B. V. (1994). What is meant by local literacies? *Language and Education, 8*(1&2), 9–17.

Street, B. V. (2000). Literacy events and literacy practices: Theory and practice in the New Literacy Studies. In M. Martin-Jones & K. Jones (Eds.), *Multilingual literacies: Reading and writing different worlds* (pp. 17–29). Amsterdam: John Benjamins.

Sulzby, E., & Teale, W. (1996). Emergent literacy. In R. Barr, M. L. Kamil, P. B. Mosenthal & P. D. Pearson (Eds.), *Handbook of reading research* (Vol. II, pp. 727–757). Mahwah, NJ: Lawrence Erlbaum.

Tao, F., Khan, S., Gamse, B., St. Pierre, R., & Tarr, H. (1998). *National evaluation of the Even Start family literacy program* (1996 Interim Report ED 418 815). Bethesda, MD: Abt Associates.

Valdés, G. (1996). *Con respeto: Bridging the distances between culturally diverse families and schools.* New York: Teachers College Press.

Villegas, A. M. (1991). *Culturally responsive pedagogy for the 1990s and beyond.* Princeton, NY: Educational Testing Service.

Volk, D., & De Acosta, M. (2001). 'Many different ladders, many ways to climb ... ': Literacy events in the bilingual classroom, homes, and community of three Puerto Rican kindergartners. *Journal of Early Childhood Literacy, 1,* 193–224.

Watson-Gegeo, K. A., & Boggs, S. T. (1977). From verbal play to talk story: The role of routine in speech events among Hawaiian children. In S. Ervin-Tripp & C. Mitchel Kernan (Eds.), *Child discourse* (pp. 67–90). New York: Academic Press.

Weinstein-Shr, G. (1992). Family and intergenerational literacy in multilingual families. ERIC/NCLE Digests. National Center for ESL Education. Washington, DC: ERIC Document Reproduction Service.

38

LITERACIES AND MEDIA CULTURE

Ursula A. Kelly

Memorial University of Newfoundland, Canada

The 'mediatization' or 'digitalization' of culture through rapid technological advances in media communications has had and will continue to have a profound impact on what it means to live, to work, and to learn in a culture of accelerated change. Communication and meaning-making-modes of individual and collective expression, creativity, representation are at the heart of culture. When changes occur to technologies of meaning-making, social tensions and anxieties escalate around issues of ownership, influence and effect, infrastructure and content, and access and opportunity. Much of this tension and anxiety can be traced to commonly cited, strongly held (yet highly debatable) beliefs about the relationship of *literacy*, as its pertains to a specific medium or media, to a plethora of 'social goods' including democratic participation, morality, health, and economic well-being. Here, literacy is defined as both a knowledge relationship and a set of cultural practices which enables one to manipulate communications media for a variety of meaning-making purposes. In this sense, then, literacy is both relational and contextual. Literacy is a central project of education. In these times of unprecedented change, it is important to ask of education its place in addressing the numerous and profound implications for (changes in) literacy in the context of contemporary culture.

This chapter traces the place of education in relation to media culture through an examination of the shifts in discourses, meanings, and practices which have accompanied concerted, systematic attention to media culture and literacy practices in both governmental (often curricular) and cultural policies and community-based initiatives. With a backdrop of global, corporate and digital culture, its accompanying life/work changes and challenges, and the increasing educational success gap between the disadvantaged and advantaged, I focus on literacy, media culture and policy through a central question: What literacies now, for what purposes, and with what policy support? To address this question and its related issues, I consider four areas: an international snapshot of educational attention to media culture: an overview of competing discourses within media education and their attendant versions of the individual, the social, and the civic; an analysis of how media literacies are framed within existing policy,

International Handbook of Educational Policy, 735–747
Nina Bascia, Alister Cumming, Amanda Datnow, Kenneth Leithwood and David Livingstone (Eds.)
© 2005 *Springer. Printed in Great Britain.*

with what meanings and agendas; and, finally, a discussion of what kinds of policy initiatives might support a dynamic, progressive, and educationally potent engagement of media literacy practices.

Multimedia/Multiliteracies: An Educational Snapshot

International attention to media culture in education coincided with the advent of mass media communications. Since the 1950s, the United Nations Educational, Scientific, and Cultural Organization (UNESCO) has focussed its attention on education and media and, by the early 1960s, had made its first declarations regarding the need for education which encouraged a critical perspective on media culture. The interest of UNESCO in media education centred on the imbalance between countries where media were produced and owned and those where media content was received, and the threats to cultural autonomy such imbalance posed, in both developed and developing countries. In subsequent decades, various UNESCO initiatives – research, curriculum development, conferences – were undertaken while, simultaneously, in several countries, educational inroads were forged by teachers who argued, from a number of competing ideological perspectives, that media education was an essential component of contemporary citizenship. In 1999, at its Vienna Conference on "Educating for the Media and Digital Age", UNESCO expressed a renewed commitment that "media education is part of the basic entitlement of every citizen, in every country of the world, to freedom of expression and the right to information and is instrumental in building and sustaining democracy." By then, media education had found some formal place – albeit a sometimes contested one – in various levels of curricula in several developed countries (e.g., Canada, England, South Africa, Australia, and parts of Europe). Strong community – and organization-driven initiatives were established in others (e.g., U.S.A., India, and Israel).

Coincident with these initiatives was the development of a burgeoning and increasingly sophisticated scholarship which argued eloquently for the centrality of the study of media in education, at all levels, and within teacher education. Yet, despite nearly a half-century of development in media culture, educational attention remains uneven, sporadic, contradictory, and terribly out of step with many of the most compelling theoretical advances regarding media, education, and literacy. In an educational climate marked by public preoccupation with benchmarks, standardized testing, competencies, outcomes, and (inter)national ratings, media education can appear tangential. Despite concerns about literacy featuring heavily in this context, its meanings are usually so deeply constrained as to lose the central educational role of an expanded notion of literacy, one which neither surrenders to the strictures of the medium of print and an alphabetic literacy nor abandons their centrality.

A central point here is the relationship between the study of media and of literacy. In scholarship, pedagogy, and policy there is no easy or settled congruity between media *education* and media *literacy*, although the terms are often used interchangeably in all three areas. Yet, initial inroads into an expanded notion of literacy came from a focus, even sometimes only implicit, on literacy in media education through attention to such goals as critical viewing and writing media which were easily aligned with traditional literacy practices of reading and writing. Many media educators recoil at the use of the word literacy in relation to their work, in part due to a fear that it limits the scope of media study. However, such perceptions are based on a narrow conception of literacy as skills and competencies which ignore much of the insight accrued through what is often called the 'new' literacy studies. This recent literacy research, largely sociocultural in nature and concerned with expanded notions of literacy-literacies or multiliteracies (Cope & Kalantiz, 2000) – has solidified an inextricable and mutually beneficial connection which, when clarified in policy and practice, offer immense educational potential in these times.

The 'new' literacy educators, many of whom are school-based teachers of English Language Arts, provide some of the most compelling arguments for the place of media culture in literacy education. These arguments come from a grassroots perspective on the high toll accrued daily of restricted notions of literacy and from the unique view provided from a 'sandwiched' position between the often narrow rhetoric and policies of governments, couched almost entirely in economic terms, and the lived limits of institutionalized education-excessive, competing demands which exist in the face of compromised working conditions, scarcity of resources, limited teacher education, insufficient professional development, and stringent and narrow notions of accountability. These teachers know well what Gunther Kress (2000, p. 157) noted:

> The focus on language alone has meant a neglect, an overlooking, even a suppression of the potentials of all the representational and communicational modes in particular cultures; an often repressive and systematic neglect of human potentials in many of these areas; and, as a consequence, of the development of theoretical understandings of such modes. Semiotic modes have different potentials, so that they afford different kinds of possibilities of human expression and engagement with the world, and through this differential engagement with the world they facilitate differential possibilities of development: bodily, cognitively, affectively ... [T]he single, exclusive and intensive focus on written language has dampened the full development of all kinds of human potentials.

This point turns attention to the dominant notion of literacy as a practice of exclusion while it also draws a connecting line to the earliest concerns of media educators, the right to produce, to express, and to communicate on one's own individual and cultural terms: meaning-making as a creative practice of freedom. The contemporary world offers new challenges for both media and literacy education. The points of convergence are strong; the enormity of challenges would suggest a concerted alliance is more useful than any research or policy designed, intentionally or not, to create discrete turf.

Competing Discourses and Contested Visions

Central to the concerns of those who initially lobbied for media education was the potential colonizing impact of media on what were believed to be often unwitting populations. The United States led the world in communications technology; other, less powerful, countries saw its imperialist powers and consumer ideologies taken to new extremes with these enhanced forms of communications. Critical awareness was seen as a buffer, a means through which people could measure, judge and choose based on a working knowledge of the complexities of media production and distribution, form and meaning, and context and effect. In this sense, media education espoused, through this democratic urge, an explicit political agenda. Given this predominant early agenda, it is not surprising that media education in the United States is less extensive than in many other developed countries. As Keval Kumar (2000) noted, "[i]t appears that subject peoples and subject nations have been converted to the [media education] movement much earlier than those parts of the world that dominated the media" (p. 12).

Based on an international study of media education, Andrew Hart (1998) outlined three media education paradigms which emerge consistently across countries and which represent generational phases of development in a half-century of media education: inoculatory/protectionist; discriminatory/popular arts; and critical/representational/semiological. These paradigms represent discursive practices in relation to media education-meaningful ways of constructing media education which are systemic and partial, that is, political. Hart stressed that paradigmatic practices are not pure; they usually coexist and often share platforms, albeit, for varying political purposes. Douglas Kellner (1998) presented 'approaches' to media study, but his categories resonate with the paradigms of Hart and his researchers. For Kellner, there is the traditional protectionist approach, a media arts approach (akin to Hart's popular arts approach), a media literacy approach, concerned with decoding and analyzing media texts, and a critical media literacy, most closely aligned with the critical/representational paradigm of Hart. Critical media literacy:

> builds on these approaches, analyzing media culture as products of social production and struggle, and teaching students to be critical of media representations and discourses, but also stressing the importance of learning to use the media as modes of self-expression and social activism. (Kellner, 1998, p. 113)

As Kellner implied and Hart (1998) importantly noted, paradigmatic differences register both ideologically and pedagogically. For example, discourses of inoculation and protectionism can be often aligned with elitist ideologies and transmission pedagogy. The popular/media arts paradigm which focuses on the intricacies of individual media can be often aligned with liberal humanist and expressive ideologies and student-centred pedagogy. The representation paradigm is concerned with broader issues of cultural and institutional power and politics, is ideologically based in resistance politics, and uses a situated, participatory pedagogy of cultural analysis and critique (Hart, 1998, p. 18). The interrelated, corresponding historical trends in forms of literacy education-cultural literacy, progressive literacy, and critical literacy-are obvious (Ball, Kenny, & Gardner, 1990; Kelly, 1997). What is interesting about Kellner's categories, however, is the inclusion of media literacy as a separate approach. Many who practice media literacy education would argue that it is inherently critical and political. What Kellner's emphasis on a critical media literacy does is highlight the broad-based political critique and social activism which is an invaluable characteristic of the notion of 'critical' in any critical literacy.

Implicit in these different paradigms and approaches are competing notions of learners and learning, but also implicit are competing notions of the social and the civic. It is in these connections – among education, learning and the civic subject – that policy always implies and actively constitutes an ideal subject/citizen. For example, the 'idealized citizen' implied in cultural literacy differs from that of critical literacy. It can be argued that cultural literacy encourages intellectual passivity and critical thinking as a form of discriminatory practice based on prescribed and naturalized categories of stratification, thereby attempting to ensure the maintenance of a social status quo. Critical literacy, on the other hand, conceives of intellectual creativity as social engagement and critique, a political practice of deconstruction of preordained categories and accepted practices and reimagined alliances across social and cultural differences.

In a paper commissioned by the International Reading Conference, Donna Alverman (2001) addressed the issue of what literacy pedagogy might best match the contemporary circumstances of young people's lives. She (2001, p. 2) pointed out:

> [Youth] find their own reasons for becoming literate – reasons that go beyond reading to acquire school knowledge of academic texts. This is not to say that [such] academic literacy is unimportant; rather, it is to emphasize the need to address the implications of youth's multiple literacies for classroom instruction.

Alverman pointed to the long-established tension-a hallmark of education in cultural literacy – between school literacies and so-called popular literacies, those literacies commonly practiced by students in informal settings outside the institutional limits of schools. Kathleen Tyner (1998, p. 8) added further to the point:

> Since at least the 1960s, there has been a growing bifurcation between the literacy practices of compulsory schooling and those that occur outside the schoolhouse door. The literacy of schooling, based on a hierarchical access to print literacy, is increasingly at odds with the kinds of constructivist practices necessary to accommodate the more diverse, interactive, and less linear media forms made available by digital technologies.

Many literacy educators recognize how this divide described by Alverman and Tyner inhibits literacy success for a wide-range of students (Alverman & Heron, 2001: Comber, 2002; Lankshear, Gee, Knobel, & Seale, 1998; Knobel, 2001). To constrain notions of literacy is to encourage social inequity. This 'lesson' is part of what students may come to realize as part of a critical multiliteracies approach. Many popular, multiple literacies are developed and strengthened in out-of-school youth activities such as unprecedented community-building through online writing and communication, high levels of independent knowledge production and acquisition using online search engines and digital databases, varied and creative expressions of personal and collaborative mean-ing-making through digital media productions, and new, diversified transnational 'virtual' collectivities committed to social change worldwide. As Alverman (2001, p. 19) indicated, adolescents who appear most 'a risk' of failure in the academic literacy arena are sometimes the most adept at (and interested in) understanding how media texts work, and in particular, how meaning gets produced and consumed. These same adolescents are also often adept at constructing a critique of a social order that systematically disenfranchises many of them, both in and out of school.

The implications here of how policy frames literacy education – using what definitions, promoting what objectives, and for what broader purposes – are immense. The obvious need to expand how literacy is understood and 'measured' is one issue. What must also be carefully considered are the ideological directions in which multimedia literacy education might go. Adolescents attuned to and skilled in a multimedia environment, unsurprisingly, will resist educational mes-sages – of the sort associated with inoculatory, protectionist, cultural literacy paradigms – intended to 'inform' them of 'bad media'. No policy, however widespread, can ensure the success of literacy programs which are narrowly and ill-conceived, ignore learners' existing knowledge, are inattentive to the cultural contexts of their lives, and deflate their best inclinations to engage and to better their worlds – in other words, programs which do not have the characteristics which encourage and recognize wide-ranging success.

Policies and Politics: Exemplars

The countries which have made significant advances in media literacy education – Canada, Australia, South Africa, Israel, and England, for example – are those where its study has been institutionalized, largely through legislation into public school curricula, in particular, into English Language Arts. The impetus for such inclusion varies depending on context and political agenda. In South Africa, for example, media literacy education is part of the ongoing project to deconstruct and dismantle educational ideologies and cultural practices associated with apartheid. In Israel, on the other hand, media literacy education is part of the creation, protection and maintenance of the Jewish state and Jewish cultural integrity. In Australia, Canada, and Scotland, for example, the initial impetus was the increased threat of American and British cultural imperialism.

In Canada, where education is provincially mandated, Ontario has led the way in policy support, with media literacy being a component of study in the provincial curriculum since the late 1980s, and a required component since the mid 1990s. Propelled by the dedicated grassroots work of the provincial Association for Media Literacy and the Jesuit Communication Project, media literacy education in Ontario has become a reference point for initiatives in other parts of Canada and worldwide, demonstrating the potential power of community-based efforts. The Media-Awareness Network, a Canadian multi-corporate-sponsored educational organization whose massive website is utilized worldwide as a resource for media literacy education, draws heavily on the work of both these organizations. In the absence of professional development, such resources importantly support but also often define – and unfortunately limit – what media literacy education will be for teachers. By the mid-1990s, other Canadian provinces, for example the western provinces through the Western Canadian Protocol for Collaboration in Basic Education and the eastern provinces through the Atlantic Provinces Education Foundation, had developed curricula which also enshrined media study through an expanded notion of literacy. The convergence of media literacy and literacy education is evident in the Atlantic Provinces Education Foundation (1996, p. 1):

> This curriculum identifies the development of literacy as a priority. The curriculum anticipates that what it means to be literate will continue to change as visual and electronic media become more and more dominant as forms of expression and communication. As recently as one hundred years ago, literacy meant the ability to recall and recite from familiar texts and to write signatures. Even twenty years ago, definitions of literacy were linked almost exclusively to print materials. The vast spread of technology and media has broadened our concept of literacy ... [T]he curriculum at all levels extends beyond the traditional concept of literacy to encompass media and information literacies, offering students multiple pathways to learning through engagement with a wide range of verbal, visual, and technological media.

This expanded notion of literacy is text-based, albeit with an expanded concept of text, and the agenda for study is clearly economically driven: "To participate fully in today's society and function competently in the workplace, students need to read and use a range of texts" (p. 1). Such statements are typical of those describing a multimedia and multiliteracies focus in much new English Language Arts curricula in Canada, Australia, New Zealand, and the United Kingdom. While such statements suggest a more innocuous media literacy approach, as described by Kellner (1998), curricula in both Canada and Australia explicitly support opportunities for critical media literacy education. Despite these advances, research by the Canadian Race Relations Foundation (1999) into the status of multicultural, anti-racism and media education in all Canadian provinces and territories found that, while there exists broad support for these areas, progress is compromised by continued lack of resources, inadequate teacher professional development, and inadequate education of new teachers by faculties of education.

In Great Britain, where a National Curriculum dictates the program of study in schools, there are also interesting examples of 'policy convergence'. The Department for Culture, Media and Sport, through a general statement of policy, *Media Literacy Statement: 2001*, suggested the moral agenda of media literacy education. In concert with the Department for Education and Skills and the directives of the National Curriculum, this policy focuses on media literacy as an aspect of citizenship education whereby "critical awareness of the media and the literate and self-aware use of [Information and Communications Technology] ... will become increasingly necessary for the health and protection of citizens". To this end, what is envisioned is:

> a multi-tiered and flexible system of regulation, with an emphasis on co-and self-regulation that is designed to adapt itself to the changing environment it will oversee [of which] promoting greater media literacy and critical viewing skills must be one important response.

The explicit attention to the self-regulating state subject who, it is implied, will make 'appropriate' decisions regarding media culture is noteworthy and reminiscent of the earliest moral agenda of mass print literacy. However, as many literacy researchers continue to point out, there is no convincing evidence of such a social and moral effect of literacy (Graff, 1987; Tyner, 1998). While such strong but uninformed assumptions about the effects of literacy are prevalent as belief, ideal and myth-literacy as "the key to national unity, social order, good character, and economic progress" (Tyner, 1998, p. 33) – they are hardly the basis of informed public policy.

Yet, the conflation of mass literacy and moral righteousness persists. In the United States, where education is state-mandated, a series of initiatives in the 1990s led to the rapid expansion of media literacy education. As a result, there exist many examples of state and national organizations committed to the promotion of programs based on principles of creative production and critique. The work of the Media Education Foundation, founded by Sut Jhally, is but one of many. Nonetheless, protectionist-driven initiatives are still evident, as seen in the work of the Center for Media Education (Heins & Cho, 2002). Perhaps the most glaring example, however, is the highly prescriptive and influential policy statement on media education of the American Academy of Pediatrics. The statement calls for, among other things, a media education which alerts pediatricians to "the public health risks of media exposure" and it asks its members to encourage all levels of government "to explore mandating and funding universal media education programs" (pp. 2–3). Such stringently protectionist sentiments can often fuel and direct much school-based media literacy education, as well.

In its report, *Media Literacy: An Alternative to Censorship* (Heins & Sho, 2002), The Free Expression Policy Project traced the history and contemporary place of media literacy education in the United States, noting that, while media literacy education is coming of age, it is still marked by censor-oriented, inoculation approaches which have resulted in a plethora of protectionist policy statements from various levels of government and high-profile organizations. Arguing for policy based on intellectual freedom and the First Amendment, one in which "critical thinking [is recognized as] an essential skill for all citizens in a democracy" (p. 38) and as the goal of media literacy education, they call for "a clear statement of national purpose to promote media literacy as an essential part of basic education" (p. 39).

As the spread of media literacy education is gauged, some attention is also required to the 'repeat colonization' which is happening in terms of program adoption and adaptation. As Keval Kumar (2000) noted, those interested in promoting media education in India have modelled their work on programs in existence in developed countries. Noting the highly rigid structure of education in India and the barriers it presents for the inclusion of media literacy education in schools, he highlighted the need for indigenous programs which arise from the specificities of culture and context. Kumar (2000, p. 12) argued for a grassroots approach to media literacy education which "places the community at the centre of any efforts in media education" and the goals of which are "development and liberation of the community as a whole rather that the production of critically autonomous individuals or discriminating adults, or even the protection of individuals against manipulative media." Kumar's points shore up the ethnocentricity of dominant notions of media literacy education and are a reminder of another level of reflexivity required of media literacy education itself.

Policy differences and debates such as those outlined in this section are at the forefront of media literacy education and, as the examples suggest, they resonate internationally. The debate is framed not solely by whether to support media literacy education. More important and, perhaps, more contentious, are the debates about what versions of media literacy education to support. Other issues must also be addressed. For example, with the increasing involvement in and co-optation of media literacy education programs by the very corporations such programs need to critique, questions of efficacy are obvious. As well, the extent to which media literacy education has and will become an integral part of popular literacy education programs in developing countries continues to highlight the pressing issues of access and cultural autonomy first highlighted by UNESCO in the 1960s. These debates require greater and more diversified forms of public address.

Future Policy Considerations: Ongoing Challenges/Renewed Directions

In an analysis of contemporary educational reform proposals, Colin Lankshear (1998, p. 356) pointed out that "reform proposals are enactive texts that are connected to projects to change how we think and act (by changing our cultural models of things like learning, teaching, and schooling)." Lankshear argued that contemporary reform proposals are marked by a preoccupation with an economic imperative, what he called the *economization* of literacies (pp. 353, 369), which can be seen in the emergence of four different constructions of literacy, each of which is tied in specific ways to global economic needs. Lankshear contended that these constructions constitute a new word order – stratifications within literacies – as part of an emerging new work order – hierarchies of work in a global corporate culture.

The literacies to which Lankshear referred – lingering basics; new basics; elite literacies; and foreign language literacy (p. 357) – warrant further articulation for they reveal the stratifications within literacy and add crucial insights into current debates around it. In Lankshear's research, lingering basics is a construction of literacy preoccupied with the skills of encoding and decoding, a series of competencies and tools that form the basis of all other learning. The new basics add the importance of 'higher order' skills of critical thinking, problem solving and analysis to the baseline tools of encoding and decoding. Elite literacies involve "high level mastery of subject or discipline literacies" (p. 360) – for example, technological literacy and scientific literacy – which enable innovation and advancement. Foreign language literacy focuses on second and additional language proficiency.

Lankshear's analysis is a reminder that a mere expansion of literacies is by no means a guarantee of greater freedom or social equity. The history of literacy has demonstrated time and again that technologies of literacy are adopted unevenly and are uneven in their effects. Any technology can be used for the advancement or the containment of people. Literacy – its availability, meanings, and usage – is situated and relational, that is, tied to issues of power. The dangerous underside of new literacies is their (in ways, already realized) potential for commodification and use to advance and enhance already deep social divisions (Lankshear, 1997). Directions in literacy at all levels must encourage a critical estimation of and resistance to these divisions and the economic imperatives that solidify them.

The contemporary digital culture, with its condensed media order and convergent technologies, and the accompanying heightened tensions of cultural diversification and homogenization, press the envelope of policy development in literacy. In this sense, lobbying for media literacy education or technological literacy is not enough. These new educational times require greater vigilance and new, more creative and more carefully articulated alliances to strengthen demand and shore up support for more informed policy. Areas which share common concerns – arts, literacies, technologies, media – need to rethink the basis of their separateness. The *literacy* in visual literacy, technological literacy, and media literacy must be developed, just as the arts, technology and media of literacy must, as well. This project of educational advancement is a partnership which must resist 'turf protection' and work from points of common, carefully articulated purpose. Such alliances can be more effective in promoting and redefining school success.

Educationally, literacies attendant to multimodalities and multimedia require broad-based competencies and approaches. One of the weak links in the chain between progressive policy and effective media literacy education is teacher education. Despite expanded notions of literacy and curricular direction regarding media and multiliteracies, teacher education has not provided teachers the appropriate spaces to develop their thinking in these areas (Hart, 1998; Heins & Cho, 2002; Lankshear et al., 1997). Teacher education programs more frequently than not omit media literacy education as a requirement. And while few teacher educators would argue that new teachers need to be technologically savvy, too rarely this point translates into mere familiarity with and ability to use digital technology. But general familiarity and proficiency are relatively low order expectations and, while necessary, they cannot and should not displace critical awareness and pedagogical effectiveness. Teacher educators are implicated in this problem when enthusiasm for technology is allowed to occlude a self-reflexive stance, and education in 'critical' media literacy becomes little more than 'educational' exercises in expressions of corporate enthralment.

On the public front, the paucity of thought which marks much literacy debate itself suggests the need for a public literacy project. If it can be said that "schools regulate access to orders of discourse" (Cope & Kalantzis, 2000, p. 18), the success of this historically shameful project of confining literacy is widely evident in how ill-formed public debate is around the complexities of literacies and the intricacies of contemporary media culture and our engagement of it. For this reason, it is essential that discussion be discursively broadened. To facilitate this move, literacy education researchers need to produce, to compile, and to present publicly and with greater consistency the evidence that challenges the claims of outmoded notions of literacy and its effects and that which demonstrates the educational benefits of multiliteracies. This research dissemination project can be enhanced in many ways, some of the most effective being through alliances of researchers, teachers, and community cultural workers. Other ways include seizing a space in public discourse through the opportunities offered by media itself.

The public debates about literacy and literacy policy are monopolized by voices which espouse belief as fact and which recite a chorus of rhetorical ideals which ignore research-based insight. Policy that reiterates to people what they believe may well be politically expedient, but it will not improve public education. The protectionist paradigm may predominate in policy support for media literacy education because it is a comfortable partner with the kinds of economic and social conservatism which surrounds talk of literacy and so-called literacy crises and social decay. Literacy cannot afford support for any of its numerous sectors at such costs to vision, inclusion, and justice. Policy change which seriously supports a broad-based multiliteracies education requires massive funding, resource support, and public (re)education. In a testing-obsessed educational culture where standardized testing has become an educational industry – in Canada, for example, students complete various tests, to the yearly sum of millions of educational dollars (Sokoloff, 2002) as part of province wide, nationwide, and international assessments – ratings and scores designed to test marketplace competencies and desirable characteristics of a globally competitive workforce too often drive educational policy. As Michelle Knobel (2001, p. 1) pointed out, "government responses to New Times around the world have focused on constraining what students learn by means of national curricula, increased national and state testing, accountability checks for teachers, and mandated standardized tests." She called on educators to problematize such tests and to rethink what counts as literacy learning and literacy 'failure' according to such tests.

Such powerful, controlling trends can sometimes seem so entrenched as to feel irreversible. But alterative visions with which to forge a different direction are available. In 1994, a group of literacy educators from several countries gathered in New London, New Hampshire to consider the future of literacy teaching. The ground-breaking work produced by this 'New London Group', which builds on concerted efforts of many literacy educators worldwide, attempts to articulate a broad-ranging project for literacy education in a context of change. At the heart of this project is a notion of civic pluralism in which difference is seen as productive. Bill Cope and Mary Kalantzis (2000, p. 15), two members of the New London Group, put it this way:

Civic pluralism changes the nature of civic space, and with the changed meaning of civic spaces, everything changes; from the broad content of public rights and responsibilities to institutional and curricular details of literacy pedagogy. Instead of core culture and national standards, the realm of the civic is a space for the negotiation of a different sort of social order; an order where differences are actively recognized; where these differences are negotiated in such a way that they complement each other; and where people have the chance to expand their cultural and linguistic repertoires so that they can access a broader range of cultural and institutional resources.

Such a civic space would refuse corporate governance and practices of homogenization and stratification. It would, instead, enable creative citizenship, not in order to fuel an economic agenda but, rather, to enhance human potential, expressive capacities, and an awareness of connected living. To begin to even realize such a vision may well require that policy itself – the interests and practices it has traditionally enshrined – be radically rethought, as well.

References

Alverman, D. E. (2001). *Effective literacy instruction for adolescents*. Executive Summary and Paper Commissioned by the National Reading Conference. Chicago, IL: National Reading Conference.
Alverman, D. E., & Heron, A. H. (2001). Literacy identity work: Playing to learn with popular media. *Journal of Adolescent and Adult Literacy, 45*(2), 118–22.
American Academy of Pediatrics. (1999). Policy statement: Media education (RE9911) *Pediatrics, 104*(2), 341–343.
Ball, S., Kenny, A., & Gardiner, D. (1990). Literacy, politics, and the teaching of English. In I. Goodson & P. Medway (Eds.), *Bringing English to order* (pp. 47–86). London: Falmer Press.

Canadian Race Relations Foundation (1999). Curricula and special programs appropriate for the study of portrayal of diversity in the media. Retrieved February 27, 2003 from http://www.crr.ca/en/mediacentre/newsreleases/emedcen-newsreldivinmediareppg1.htm

Comber, B. (2002, July). *Critical literacy: Maximising children's investments in school learning.* Draft discussion paper presented at the Resource Teachers: Literacy Training Programme, Christchurch, NZ.

Cope, B., & Kalantzis, M. (Eds.) (2000). *Multiliteracies: Literacy learning and the design of social futures.* London: Routledge.

Department of Culture, Media and Sport. (2001). *Media literacy statement: 2001.* Retrieved February 27, 2003 from http://www.culture.gov.uk/pdf/mediallit2001.pdf

Foundation for the Atlantic Canada English Language Arts Curriculum (1996). Halifax: Department of Education and Culture, Government of Nova Scotia.

Graff, H. J. (1987). *The legacies of literacy.* Bloomington: Indiana University Press.

Hart, A. (Ed.) (1998). *Teaching the media: International perspectives.* Mahwah, NJ: Lawrence Erlbaum.

Heins, M., & Cho, C. (2002). *Media literacy: An alternative to censorship.* New York: Free Expression Policy Project.

Kellner, D. (1998). Multiple literacies and critical pedagogy in a multicultural society. *Educational Theory, 48*(1), 103–122.

Kelly, U. (1997). *Schooling desire: Literacy, cultural politics, and pedagogy.* New York: Routledge.

Knobel, M. (2001). I'm not a pencil man: How one student challenges our notions of literacy "failure" in school. *Journal of Adolescent and Adult Literacy, 44*(5), 404–414.

Kress, G. (2000). Design and transformation: New theories of meaning. In B. Cope & M. Kalantzis (Eds.), *Multiliteracies: Literacy learning and the design of social futures* (pp. 153–161). London: Routledge.

Kumar, K. J. (2000, October). *Media education in India: Strategies, trends, visions.* Paper presented at the Stockholm Media Education Conference, Stockholm.

Lankshear, C. (1998). Meanings of literacy in contemporary educational reform proposals. *Educational Theory, 48*(3), 351–372.

Lankshear, C., Gee, J. P., Knobel, M., & Seale, C. (1997). *Changing literacies.* Buckingham: Open University Press.

Sokoloff, H. (2002, October 2). Federal cuts threaten student tests: Provinces. *National Post,* A2.

Tyner, K. (1998). *Literacy in a digital world: Teaching and learning in the age of information.* Mahwah, NJ: Lawrence Erlbaum.

United Nations Educational Scientific and Cultural Organizations (UNESCO) (1999, April). *Media education – Renewing UNESCO's commitment.* Retrieved February 27, 2003 from http://www.culture.gov.uk/pdf/mediallit2001.pdf

United Nations Educational Scientific and Cultural Organizations (UNESCO) (1999, April). Recommendations adopted by the Vienna conference "Educating for the Media and Digital Age". Retrieved February 27, 2003 from http://193.170.81/cn/vs/media/impact/resolution.html

39

TECHNOLOGY AND LITERACIES: FROM PRINT LITERACY TO DIALOGIC LITERACY

Carl Bereiter and Marlene Scardamalia
Ontario Institute for Studies in Education of the University of Toronto, Canada

A web search on the phrase "technology and literacy" will locate thousands of documents, almost all of which deal with "technological literacy" or ways of integrating technology into literacy instruction. Except for vague and optimistic pronouncements, there is very little about what technology can contribute to literacy development and almost nothing about how technology should figure in an education system's literacy policy. The confusion between "technological literacy" and "technology for literacy" is especially unfortunate. The two are worlds apart and there is no reason to assume that people who speak learnedly about the first have knowledge relevant to the second. Educational policies need to be concerned with both, but the semantic overlap between the two is far from providing a reason to stretch one policy to cover them. What tends to get neglected in the confusion is "technology for literacy." This chapter endeavours to remedy that neglect.

First, however, we note a point made by many of the writers on technology and literacy: New technology has brought with it an expanded conception of literacy. The kinds of documents available on the web and circulated as e-mail attachments may include, in addition to written language, logos and typographical ornamentation, pictures, graphs, hypertext links, animations, video segments, sound bites, and Java applets. Each of these components has its technology, with which students must become proficient if they are to produce such documents themselves. Although this is a new expectation for schools to meet, its principal challenges are those of finances, scheduling, and professional development. Indeed, the common report is that if the technology is available and teachers are confident in letting students use it, the learning of new media skills takes care of itself.

Where research is relevant is in (1) harnessing technology to the solution of long-standing problems of literacy and (2) addressing the higher-level skills called for in a knowledge-based economy. On both of these counts, most of the technology currently in use in schools is disappointing. Although it makes limited contributions, it does not take advantage of available scientific knowledge,

International Handbook of Educational Policy, 749–761
Nina Bascia, Alister Cumming, Amanda Datnow, Kenneth Leithwood and David Livingstone (Eds.)
© 2005 *Springer. Printed in Great Britain.*

let alone push the envelope. This is unlikely to change unless educational decision-makers become more sophisticated in their demands.

The main contribution to policy-making that we hope to make in this article is to raise the expectations of decision makers in terms of what they could be demanding from technology providers. In the early days of information technology use in schools the emphasis was on comfort level, ease of integration into existing activities, and the "Wow!" factor. Vendors accommodated brilliantly to these demands, and continue to do so. But as teachers become more familiar with technology, they are more prepared to deal with software of some complexity, to experiment with new educational possibilities enabled by technology – and they are less easily "wowed." In short, they are ready for something more. Accordingly, we focus in the following sections on what "something more" could consist of as regards literacy development.

There are many paths that could be followed in exploring the potential of technology for literacy development. The path we follow here will seem familiar at the outset but will then shift to unfamiliar and uncharted territory. The path starts with reading and writing as commonly taught and practiced and moves from there toward what we will call "dialogic literacy." This is an ancient literacy, of which the Socratic dialogues have traditionally served as the model. Modern information technology not only provides a means by which such dialogues can overcome restrictions of time and space, it affords means by which dialogue can become more dynamic, democratic, and creative. Dialogue can be seen to underlie all the knowledge-creating disciplines and professions. Thus dialogic literacy, we shall argue, is the fundamental literacy for a "knowledge society," and educational policy needs to be shaped so as to make it a prime objective.

Technology and Print Literacy

Indicative of the changes wrought by technology in the landscape of literacy is the fact that we no longer have an entirely suitable term for literacy as traditionally conceived. We adopt the term "print literacy" here, while assuming that the term also embraces the diminishing species of handwritten documents and also documents that may be produced by dictation or use of speech-to-text technology. Although the means for encoding and decoding written text may change, there is little basis for the belief that print literacy, as broadly conceived, is becoming obsolete. If anything, the increasing complexity of knowledge in almost all fields is placing increasing demands on people's ability to compose and comprehend written text (OECD-OCDE, 2000).

Research makes it clear that reading and writing comprise a number of separable skills (Stanovich & Cunningham, 1991). Technology has demonstrated just how separable these skills are. There are separate pieces of software that can translate text into speech and speech into text, check and correct spelling, spot grammatical errors, evaluate style, and even produce summaries of documents. On the other hand, technology is not yet up to the level of integrated competence that enables a person to read a handwritten note on a refrigerator door and alter meal plans accordingly. Not surprisingly, therefore, learning technology has tended to focus on subskills rather than on a wholistic approach to print literacy. One of the more legitimate complaints against subskill approaches to literacy is that many of the identified subskills are tangential ones unrelated to the actual cognitive needs of learners. Traditional workbooks are full of exercises in sequencing and classification, word-picture matching, sound-picture matching, and questions about paragraph content that are not based on any theory or evidence but are closely aligned with the kinds of items that appear on reading achievement tests. Unfortunately, much learning technology simply transfers these dubious exercises to an electronic medium, with some enhancement of their entertainment value but no significant change in pedagogy.

Phonemic Awareness Training

Phonemic awareness is awareness of identifiable parts (for instance, a set of 40 or so speech sounds) that in various combinations make up the spoken words of a language. Its importance in learning to read an alphabetical language is now well established (Adams, 1990; Treiman, 2000). Available computer software can handle parts of the training that call on the learner to recognize speech sounds – for instance, by making same-different judgments or counting syllables – but the technology of speech recognition is not yet up to the level of accuracy required for software to handle the complementary part of the training that calls on the learner to produce the sounds – for instance, by producing a word that rhymes with a presented word or replacing one vowel sound with another in a spoken word. Because phonemic awareness is a personal acquisition, much influenced by prior language experience, software that could individualize training would do much to enhance early literacy teaching.

Decoding Instruction

Phonics instruction has two components, called "analytic" and "synthetic." The analytic component, commonly carried out through workbook exercises and word analysis, may be thought of as an extension of phonemic awareness training, extending it to the relations between word sounds and spellings. The synthetic component involves what is popularly called "sounding-out" as a means of decoding unfamiliar written words. In recent decades, beginning reading instruction in English-speaking countries – in both "traditional" and "whole language" classrooms – has been largely confined to the analytic component, whereas research strongly supports an emphasis on the synthetic (National Reading Panel, 2000). Computer-based instruction and exercises can easily handle the analytic component, and that is what most of the available software does. The synthetic component, however, requires speech recognition at a level beyond existing technology. Thus an unfortunate result of the introduction of computers into primary grade classrooms has been to encourage an increased emphasis on the analytic component, which already tends to be over-emphasized, and to encourage further neglect of the synthetic.

Assisted Oral Reading

The decoding of print, whether by "sounding out" or by visual recall, can impede reading comprehension if it is slow and laborious, as it tends to be in the early years and as it tends to remain with poor readers. A tested means of building up fluency is oral reading, with a teacher or aide helping out in the recognition of difficult words, so as to allow fluent reading to proceed. In practice, this has meant either round-robin oral reading or individual tutoring. Recently developed applications, however – specifically, Soliloquy's Reading Assistant (http://www.reading-assistant.com/) and Project LISTEN's Reading Tutor (Mostow, Aist, Burkhead, et al. (2003) – have proven capable of performing the helper role in oral reading, a boon to teachers who do not have aides capable of doing that work. This helper role requires speech recognition, but computer recognition of words-in-context is much more successful than recognition of isolated words or word sounds, which makes computer-assisted oral reading feasible even when computer-assisted synthetic phonics is not.

Comprehension Strategy Instruction

Much of what is called "teaching comprehension" consists merely of the teacher asking comprehension questions. This activity is easily carried out by computer, and there is an almost unlimited supply of software for this purpose; but its value, except as rehearsal for test-taking, is questionable. Reading research has demonstrated more potential gain from teaching students to be strategic in their approach to reading. Comprehension strategies are mental actions carried out during the course of reading for the purpose of solving comprehension problems, making connections, or otherwise getting more out of the reading than is gained by a more passive approach. There is ample evidence that such strategies distinguish good from poor readers, that younger readers make relatively little use of them, that they are teachable, and that teaching them yields gains in comprehension (National Reading Panel, 2000). However, it is also the case that few teachers teach them and that enabling students to incorporate comprehension strategies into their normal practice requires much more intensive teaching than is usually devoted to it. It is much easier to teach procedures that are carried out after reading or during interruptions of it than to teach processes that must go on covertly during reading. Again, the role of technology seems to be to increase the emphasis on what is easiest to implement. What makes the teaching of comprehension strategies inherently difficult is that it must intervene in an ongoing and typically over-learned process. It is within the realm of possibility that a computer could provide strategy coaching on an ask-for-help basis. This has proved successful in other contexts (e.g., Davis & Linn, 2000). The student who experiences a comprehension difficulty could hit a key and the computer, instead of supplying an explanation of the difficult text passage, could suggest an appropriate strategy for dealing with the difficulty. Much more challenging, but foreseeable as a possibility in artificial intelligence, is for the computer to detect comprehension difficulties by analyzing the oral reading speech stream, eye fixations, and other clues, and prompt strategy use even when the student is unaware of a difficulty. In summary, computer-assisted teaching of comprehension strategies lies in the future; it would be a mistake to assume that existing software claimed to "teach comprehension" actually does so.

Summarization

Straddling reading and writing is the production of summaries. Summarization during reading is a strategy used by good readers (Pressley & Afflerbach, 1995); summarization after reading is a well-recognized study skill. The accuracy of a summary is an indicator of level of comprehension. And the ability to produce a cogent summary is a useful composition skill. For both practical and ideological reasons, however, summarization has not played a large role in literacy teaching. New technology may change that. Latent Semantic Analysis is a technology that can both evaluate how closely a summary maps on to the content of a text and detect important missed or distorted points. Summary Street, an instructional tool based on this technology, enables students to test their own comprehension and to revise their summaries in pursuit of a higher score (Kintsch, Steinhart, Stahl, & LSA Research Group, 2000).

Vocabulary Instruction

Limited vocabulary is a serious handicap in both reading and writing. Various direct and indirect approaches to vocabulary development have been tested, with generally positive results. The consensus seems to be that vocabulary needs to be approached in a variety of ways – that students need to encounter and use a word often and in varied contexts in order for it to become part of their active vocabulary. An analysis of vocabulary development software by Wood (2001) indicates that there is considerable variety in the kinds of experience different software applications provide, suggesting that an assortment of such resources could contribute to overall growth of vocabulary.

Teaching Writing Mechanics and Conventions

Users of the leading word processor will already be familiar with the strengths and limitations of computer intervention in writing mechanics and style. From an educational standpoint an important issue is whether this kind of software supports the learning of spelling, grammar, and style conventions or whether it merely compensates for the lack of such learning. There appears to be marvellously little concern about this issue, compared to concerns about the parallel issue of pocket calculators and arithmetic. Instead, curriculum standards often treat word processor use (along with spell checkers and the like) as a composition skill in its own right. Reviewing research at the post-secondary level, Goldfine (2001) found that the effects of word processor use were largely negative, resulting in the development of more careless and mindless writing habits. Rather than advocating the avoidance of word processors, however, Goldfine suggested, for instance, turning off the spelling and grammar checkers until after students have done their own proofreading, then turning them on so that students could compare the errors they detected to the errors detected by the machine.

Teaching and Supporting Composing Strategies

Essentially the same story can be told here as with reading comprehension strategies. There are identifiable strategies that distinguish expert from less expert writers; these strategies are teachable; teaching them improves writing. But teaching them is difficult because, again, it means intervening in an ongoing process. However, if the student is composing on a computer the possibilities for context-sensitive intervention in the form of cues or suggestions are much greater than with reading. We are not aware of any software in which coaching is based on analysis of the actual text being produced by the student, but several applications interact with the student on the basis of the student's indicated goals and plans. Two that have produced positive results are the Writing Partner (Zellermayer, Salomon, Globerson, & Givon, 1991) and MAESTRO (Rowley & Meyer, 2003).

In summary, technology has so far made limited contributions to the teaching of print literacy, but these contributions are offset by a tendency to emphasize the aspects of literacy instruction that are easiest to implement on a computer. In this way, instructional software provides unbalanced instruction and reinforces a bias toward low-level cognitive processes (even when it is touted as teaching thinking skills). None of this is likely to change unless educational decision-makers become more sophisticated in their demands. The past quarter-century has seen an amazing growth in understanding of print literacy, and this under-standing is readily available to software developers; but until there is pressure from customers, they have no incentive to upgrade.

Contexts for Development of Print Literacy

A criticism that may be brought against all the approaches discussed in the preceding section is that the skills they teach are decontextualized. Computers have played an ambiguous role with regard to contexts for literate activity. On one hand, desktop publishing, web publishing, and e-mail have made it possible for students to write for real and extended audiences. According to numerous reports, this is a great motivator and encourages students to take greater care with their writing. (The most serious attention to style and mechanics we have seen occurred when third-graders were producing work that would be read by students in a higher grade.) On the other hand, instructional software, as discussed in the preceding section, has contributed to decontextualization rather than creation of a meaningful context.

The principal response to the problem of contextualization has been *project-based learning.* (Much of the activity is reflected in web sites that provide project descriptions and resources and ways to connecting with other projects. As of July, 2003, a web search on "project-based learning" locates more than 50,000 documents, and restricting the search to any particular country's domain name will reveal that project-based learning has truly taken hold world-wide). As promoted in countless workshops and professional development courses, project-based learning involves students working in small groups to gather information on a topic or issue of interest and use it to produce a report, usually a multimedia document or slide presentation. Projects can be carried out using standard Web browsers, word processors, and presentation tools, but software specifically designed to facilitate school projects is also available.

There are wide variations in what project-based learning actually amounts to. At one extreme, it is merely a dressed-up version of the traditional school "project" or research report. It is still essentially a cut-and-paste operation, except that the cutting and pasting are now done with software tools. Both the meaningfulness of the context and its relevance to literacy development are questionable. More highly developed and researched approaches to project-based learning, however, put the main emphasis on content rather than presentation (e.g., Bell, Davis, & Linn, 1995; Marx, Blumenfeld, Krajcik, & Soloway, 1997). Generally, considerable pains are taken to ensure that the projects are engaging ones that are relevant to important ideas or issues in a field of study. Accordingly, they are normally considered as approaches to science education or education in some other content field rather than as literacy education. In contrast, the traditional "projects" or "research reports" are often treated as a part of language arts education, with recipes for producing them appearing in language arts textbooks.

From a literacy perspective, the issue in considering project-based learning is what kind of environmental press it creates for literacy. To what extent do project activities create a need for more careful reading, deeper comprehension, clearer exposition, more convincing argumentation and the like? Evidence is lacking to answer this question, but it does seem fair to say that project activities are not usually designed with such objectives in mind.

Dialogic Literacy

In recent years a number of different strands of thought and research have produced a heightened recognition of the role that discourse plays in the advancement of scientific knowledge and understanding (Gross, 1990; Simons, 1990). This is a development that deserves equal attention in other subject fields, although its contrast to earlier views is not so easily apparent. Ever since the curriculum reforms of the 1950s, the received wisdom has been that hands-on experimentation is the heart of science. The new view does not deny the importance of experimentation, but it holds that knowledge advances by bringing experimental findings into a sustained discourse the purpose of which is to advance the state of knowledge and understanding. The same can be said about empirical research in history or any other field. This so-called "rhetorical turn" in the philosophy of knowledge clearly places a heightened emphasis on literacy. Moreover, it places emphasis on a level of literacy considerably higher than the levels that normally figure in curriculum guidelines, standards, and tests.

Functional literacy may be defined as the ability to comprehend and use communication media to serve the purposes of everyday life. We will define "dialogic literacy" as *the ability to engage productively in discourse whose purpose is to generate new knowledge and understanding.* This definition is not tied to any particular representational medium, so long as the medium is one through which people can interact in a knowledge-building way. In chemistry, for instance, dialogic literacy may require the ability to comprehend and express ideas using the conventions of chemical diagrams (Schank & Kozma, 2002).

The term "dialogic literacy" is not original with us but appears in some of the literature on college writing instruction (e.g., Coogan, 1999; Cooper, 1994). There, however, dialogic is contrasted to monologic literacy, mainly in political terms: Dialogue is seen as democratic, whereas monologue is seen as authoritarian. From this standpoint, dialogic literacy is treated as a practice to be instituted rather than as a competence to be acquired. The closest we have seen to treating dialogic literacy as an attainment is in some discussions of problems in sustaining high-quality discourse in e-mail or threaded discussions (e.g., Shamoon, 2001). In the present discussion we explicitly treat "dialogic literacy" as an attainable competence. To speak of dialogic literacy in this sense is to imply that people may possess it in varying degrees and that it is continuously improvable.

Dialogic literacy, like other literacies, involves many skills and attributes and is context-dependent. That is, the ability to contribute through conversation to knowledge creation in one context does not ensure that the same will suffice in another context. The defining skills of dialogic literacy are those without which one's ability to contribute to knowledge advancement will be limited in any conversational context. What might those indispensable skills be? Lists of dialogue skills that address this "necessary but not sufficient" criterion have a certain obviousness about them. They are the kinds of things anyone would think of when asked, "What do you need in order to be a good participant in a dialogue?" For instance: Dialogue is a conversational practice. Like sports, exercising, or other practices, you build skills as you work at it. Some important dialogue skills to practice are:

- Allowing others to finish their thoughts;
- Respecting others' thoughts, feelings, views, and realities, even when they differ from your own; or

- Listening deeply without needing to fix, counter, argue, or resist (Conway, 2001).

Research on conversation or dialogue skills is not very helpful in extending the skills list beyond the obvious. Most of this research deals with young children, second-language learners, pathological cases, or artificial intelligence programs. In all these cases mastering the obvious skills represents a sufficient challenge.

The Dialogue Project at MIT, founded by physicist David Bohm and carried forward through the influential work of Peter Senge (1990), has helped pin down the concept of dialogue by contrasting it with discussion: Discussion is aimed at settling differences, whereas dialogue is aimed at advancing beyond the participants' initial states of knowledge and belief. Dialogue is purposeful, but it does not have a fixed goal. The goal *evolves* or *emerges* as the dialogue proceeds. Ability to sustain this open-ended yet goal-directed character would seem to be a hallmark of dialogic literacy.

Technological Supports for Knowledge Building Dialogue

Related to the distinction between discussion and dialogue is a distinction we have proposed in the treatment of ideas between "belief mode" and "design mode" (Bereiter & Scardamalia, 2003). In belief mode, the concern is with truth, evidence, and coherence. Rational argument is the preferred form of discourse in belief mode. In design mode, the concern is with the usefulness and improvability of ideas. Collaborative, problem-solving dialogue is the preferred form of discourse. Design mode is clearly the most relevant to Knowledge Age occupations. It is central to the work of research groups, design teams, and innovators in knowledge-based organizations. Schooling, however, has traditionally been carried out almost exclusively in belief mode and accordingly has put the emphasis on argumentative as opposed to problem-solving or knowledge building discourse. This emphasis persists, even in areas like science education where one might suppose that problem-solving dialogue would prevail (e.g., Kuhn, 1993). Correspondingly, technology to support or teach dialogue skills has, with one notable exception, focused on argumentation.

It should be noted, however, that most of the software used in education is not conducive to either type of dialogue. We have in mind the ubiquitous chat rooms, bulletin boards, listserves, and discussion forums that accompany course management systems and other learning ware. All of these favor brief question-answer or opinion-reaction exchanges. Extended discussion that goes deeply into an issue or problem is a rarity (Guzdial, 1997; Hewitt & Teplovs, 1999). Although a dedicated instructor can sometimes guide discussion to deeper levels, the technology itself wars against this by the hierarchical structure of message threads, the inability to link across threads, the typically chronological ordering of contributions, and above all the lack of any means of introducing a higher-order organization of content – the synthesis or subsuming idea that is the emergent result of the most successful dialogues. Technology that overcomes these limitations is technically possible and is in fact available (Scardamalia, 2002; Scardamalia, 2003).

Whereas the communication software in common use represents technical variations on e-mail, technology designed to foster dialogue generally has some theoretical basis. For instance, several applications to support argumentation are based on Toulmin's (1958) model of argument. The elements of logical argument identified by Toulmin are used to structure and label dialogue contributions and are the basis of hints to the users (Cho & Jonassen, 2002). The principal software to support knowledge building discourse, Knowledge Forum®, is based on theoretical ideas of knowledge processes, such as the distinction between knowledge-telling and knowledge-transforming strategies in writing (Scardamalia & Bereiter, 1987), and a conception of expertise as progressive problem-solving (Bereiter & Scardamalia, 1993).

Knowledge Forum is characterized, not as a writing or discourse tool, but as a *collaborative knowledge building environment*. This implies that the knowledge work of the group is centrally carried out in Knowledge Forum. Other knowledge-related activities such as experimentation and model-building produce results that are brought into the environment, where they become additional objects of inquiry and discussion. Rather than being based on a message-passing model, like conventional online environments, Knowledge Forum is based on a knowledge evolution model. Instead of producing a string of messages, participants produce an evolving mutlimedia hypertext that objectifies the knowledge that is being built. Mentors, visiting experts, or classes in different schools are brought into the process, not through message exchanges, but through entering the environment and joining in the work going on there (Scardamalia, 2003).

Dialogue presupposes a shared goal that is valued by the participants. The mere airing of opinions (no matter how passionately held) or, alternatively, the holding of mock debates and the solving of artificial problems do not provide contexts conducive to the development of dialogic literacy – regardless of the technological supports that may be provided. Accordingly, it seems essential that fostering dialogic literacy be part of a more general movement toward engaging students with big ideas and deep principles. This implies that the main work of developing dialogic literacy should go on in subject-matter courses rather than in language arts or media courses. Most of the innovative work on dialogue is, in fact, being carried out in science education, history education, and other knowledge-rich fields, rather than being treated as an objective in itself.

Regardless of context, a further issue is the structuring of dialogue. Harking back to the distinction between dialogue and discussion, a fair generalization about classroom activity structures is that they support discussion rather than dialogue. When there is dialogue – a deliberate attempt to advance the state of knowledge – the teacher typically plays the leading role, as is specifically the case with Socratic dialogue (Collins & Stevens, 1982). The result, however, is that dialogue skills are mainly exercised by the teacher, leaving the students in a reactive role. A vital role for technology is to change that structure, so that students are taking the initiative for moving dialogue ahead toward its emergent goal. This requires that the technology be more than a discussion environment, that it have the properties of a knowledge-building environment (Scardamalia, 2003).

Policy Implications: Making Dialogic Literacy a Priority

The need to prepare students for work in knowledge-based organizations is widely recognized. Curriculum guidelines and standards already include, under headings such as "21st Century Skills," objectives thought to be in line with emerging post-industrial needs. As regards literacies, these objectives frequently take a technical, media-centered approach: Students are expected to become proficient in the use of word processors, computer-based image-processing and presentational software, to learn how to perform web searches, handle e-mail, participate in web forums, and so on. Although there is no denying that these are useful skills, it is important to recognize that they are the digital-age equiva-lents of learning to hold a pencil, use a card catalog, and format a business letter. In other words, they are low-level skills that are nowhere near sufficient to prepare students for "knowledge work."

Higher-order Knowledge Age skills are also recognized. These generally have to do with collaboration, initiative, communication, and creativity. The almost universally endorsed way of folding these, along with the technical skills, into a learning package is by means of collaborative "projects" (Moursund, 1999). It is here, however, that "knowledge work" tends to degenerate into traditional "school work." Projects are typically run off according to a formula that, except for a greater emphasis on collaboration and electronic media, has undergone no significant change in the past century: Choose a topic, narrow the topic, collect material, organize it, produce a draft, edit the draft. The criticisms that have been levelled for generations against this ritualized practice apply to many school projects: It is basically an exercise, the product has no authentic purpose, and it is not preparation for anything other than more school work of the same kind.

Conclusion

In this chapter we have argued for "dialogic literacy" as an over-arching objective. In every kind of knowledge-based, progressive organization, new knowledge and new directions are forged through dialogue. Post-industrial management style calls for broadening the base of those who participate in the dialogue. The dialogue in Knowledge Age organizations is not principally concerned with narrative, exposition, argument, and persuasion (the stand-bys of traditional rhetoric) but with solving problems and developing new ideas. So, to be effective participants, people have to be able to marshal their communication skills in the joint pursuit of problem solutions and conceptual advances.

Bringing Knowledge Age dialogue into the classroom will require a change much more profound than the adoption of new activity structures or a shift from an instructivist to a constructivist philosophy (Bereiter, 2002). It will require repurposing education so that innovation and the pushing forward of knowledge frontiers are authentic purposes. Only through such a systemic transformation can we reasonably expect that education will provide an environment for the cultivation of new Knowledge Age literacies.

References

Adams, M. J. (1990). *Beginning to read: Thinking and learning about print*. Cambridge, MA: MIT Press.

Bell, P., Davis, E. A., & Linn, M. C. (1995). The knowledge integration environment: Theory and design. In *Proceedings of the computer supported collaborative learning conference* (CSCL '95: Bloomington, IN) (pp. 14–21). Mahwah, NJ: Lawrence Erlbaum Associates.

Bereiter, C. (2002). *Education and mind in the knowledge age*. Mahwah, NJ: Lawrence Erlbaum Associates.

Bereiter, C., & Scardamalia, M. (2003). Learning to work creatively with knowledge. In E. De Corte, L. Verschaffel, N. Entwistle & J. van Merriënboer (Eds.), *Unravelling basic components and dimensions of powerful learning environments* (pp. 55–68). EARLI Advances in Learning and Instruction Series. North-Holland: Elsevier.

Bereiter, C., & Scardamalia, M. (1993). *Surpassing ourselves: An inquiry into the nature and implications of expertise*. La Salle, IL: Open Court.

Cho, K. L., & Jonassen, D. H. (2002). The effects of argumentation scaffolds on argumentation and problem solving. *Educational Technology: Research & Development, 50*(3), 5–22.

Collins, A., & Stevens, A. L. (1982). Goals and strategies of inquiry teachers. In R. Glaser (Eds.), *Advances in instructional psychology* (pp. 65–119). Hillsdale, NJ: Lawrence Erlbaum Associates.

Conway, F. (2001). *Effective communication*. Corvallis, OR: Oregon State University Extension & Station Communications.

Coogan, D. (1999). *Electronic writing centers: Computing in the field of composition*. Westport, Conn: Ablex.

Davis, E. A., & Linn, M. C. (2000). Scaffolding students' knowledge integration: Prompts for reflection in KIE. *International Journal of Science Education, 22*(8), 819–837.

Goldfine, R. (2001). *Making word processing more effective in the composition classroom*. Urbana, IL: National Council of Teachers of English.

Gross, A. G. (1990). *The rhetoric of science*. New Haven, CT: Yale University Press.

Guzdial, M. (1997). Information ecology of collaborations in educational settings: Influences of tool. *Proceedings of the computer support for collaborative learning conference, CSCL'97*, 83–90.

Hewitt, J., & Teplovs, C. (1999). An analysis of growth patterns in computer conferencing threads. *Proceedings of the computer supported collaborative learning conference, CSCL'99*, 232–241.

Kintsch, E., Steinhart, D., Stahl, G., & LSA Research Group. (2000). Developing summarization skills through the use of LSA-based feedback. *Interactive Learning Environments, 8*(2), 87–109.

Kuhn, D. (1993). Science as argument: Implications for teaching and learning scientific thinking. *Science Education, 77*, 319–337.

Marx, R. W., Blumenfeld, P. C., Krajcik, J. S., & Soloway, E. (1997). Enacting project-based science. *Elementary School Journal, 97*, 341–358.

Mostow, J., Aist, G., Burkhead, P., Corbett, A., Cuneo, A., Eitelman, S., Huang, C., Junker, B., Sklar, M. B., & Tobin, B. (2003). Evaluation of an automated reading tutor that listens: Comparison to human tutoring and classroom instruction. *Journal of Educational Computing Research, 29*(1), 61–117.

Moursund, D. (1999). *Project-based learning using information technology*. Eugene, OR: International Society for Technology in Education.

National Reading Panel (2000). *Teaching children to read: An evidence-based assessment of the scientific research literature on reading and its implications for reading instruction: Reports of the subgroups*. Washington DC: National Institute of Child Health and Development.

OECD-OCDE (2000). *Literacy in the information age: Final report on the international adult literacy survey*. Paris: OECD-OCDE; Ottawa, Canada: Statistics Canada.

Pressley, M., & Afflerbach, P. (1995). *Verbal protocols of reading*. Mahwah, NJ: Erlbaum.

Rowley, K., & Meyer, N. (2003). The effect of a computer tutor for writers on student writing achievement. *Journal of Educational Computing Research, 29*(2), 169–187.

Scardamalia, M. (2002). Collective cognitive responsibility for the advancement of knowledge. In B. Smith (Eds.), *Liberal education in a knowledge society* (pp. 76–98). Chicago: Open Court.

Scardamalia, M. (2003). Knowledge building environments: Extending the limits of the possible in education and knowledge work. In A. DiStefano, K. E. Rudestam, & R. Silverman (Eds.), *Encyclopaedia of distributed learning* (pp. 269–272). Thousand Oaks, CA: Sage Publications.

Scardamalia, M., & Bereiter, C. (1987). Knowledge telling and knowledge transforming in written composition. In S. Rosenberg (Eds.), *Advances in applied psycholinguistics: Vol. 2. Reading, writing, and language learning* (pp. 142–175). Cambridge: Cambridge University Press.

Schank, P., & Kozma, R. (2002). Learning chemistry through the use of a representation-based knowledge building environment. *Journal of Computers in Mathematics and Science Teaching, 21*(3), 253–279.

Senge, P. M. (1990). *The fifth discipline: The art and practice of the learning organization*. New York: Currency Doubleday.

Shamoon, L. (2001). *Intercollegiate e-democracy project guide for faculty*. Available, July, 2003, at http://www.trincoll.edu/prog/iedp/facultyguide.htm.

Simons, H. W. (Ed.) (1990). *The rhetorical turn: Invention and persuasion in the conduct of inquiry*. Chicago: University of Chicago Press.

Stanovich, K. E., & Cunningham, A. E. (1991). Reading as constrained reasoning. In R. J. Sternberg & P. A. Frensch (Eds.), *Complex problem solving: Principles and mechanisms* (pp. 3–60). Hillsdale, NJ: Lawrence Erlbaum Associates.

Toulmin, S. (1958). *The uses of argument*. Cambridge, MA: Cambridge University Press.

Treiman, R. (2000). The foundations of literacy. *Current Directions in Psychological Science, 9*(3), 89–92.

Wood, J. (2001). Can software support children's vocabulary development? *Language Learning and Technology, 5*(1), 166–201.

Zellermayer, M., Salomon, G., Globerson, T., & Givon, H. (1991). Enhancing writing-related metacognitions through a computerized writing partner. *American Educational Research Journal, 28*(2), pp. 373–391.

40

ADULT LITERACY POLICY: MIND THE GAP

Nancy S. Jackson
Ontario Institute for Studies in Education of the University of Toronto, Canada

In June 2003 the Canadian government released a Parliamentary Committee report calling for a first-ever "pan-Canadian accord on adult literacy and numeracy skills development." Such an accord would commit the federal, provincial and territorial governments to work together to "significantly increase the proportion of adults with higher-level literacy skills" (Longfield, 2003, p. 1). In taking this initiative, Canadian policy would fall in step with the proclamation of the UN Literacy Decade (2003–2012) and its goal of increasing literacy levels by 50% (UNESCO, 2003). It would also draw the Canadian policy discourse into alignment, rather belatedly, with other OECD countries where frameworks for comprehensive national provision have emerged throughout the decade of the 1990s.

The proposal for a national system across Canada has been pursued by literacy advocates with a blend of hope and caution. This is based in the knowledge that literacy campaigns and large scale policy initiatives elsewhere have come and gone in the past, but the hoped for targets remain elusive nearly everywhere around the globe. Comprehensive frameworks of provision have promised not only raised levels of literacy functioning, but also a "system" for doing so that is consistent, efficient, effective and accountable. But mounting evidence suggests that these systems are fraught with contradictions, and even advocates are "having doubts" about their reliability.

In this chapter I examine the murky terrain that lies between policy and practice in comprehensive literacy frameworks in the United Kingdom, the United States, Australia, and South Africa as well as in Canada. In preparing the manuscript, I kept a list of words from recent publications that serve as signposts to the kind of gaps or troubles I wanted to discuss. Informed literacy watchers seem to write increasingly about distortions, ruptures, contradictions, tug-of-war, tensions, distractions, reversals, and competing values. Policy and reporting frameworks (including assessment, performance monitoring, and quality assurance) are said to mislead, exclude, narrow, reduce and re-orient the needs and intentions of teachers and learners. In the face of such dilemmas, many resilient and bureaucratically savvy literacy practitioners are said to be

International Handbook of Educational Policy, 763–778
Nina Bascia, Alister Cumming, Amanda Datnow, Kenneth Leithwood and David Livingstone (Eds.)
© 2005 *Springer. Printed in Great Britain.*

"gaming the numbers" and "circumventing the rules" to "survive." Growing numbers of others are reported to be over-burdened, stressed, disillusioned, burned out, and leaving the field. This chorus of voices is remarkably similar across national, international, and intercontinental boundaries, fuelling a growing sense that literacy workers are becoming "enrolled as agents to a project" that is increasingly not their own (Hamilton, 2001, p. 191).

There is a growing and varied literature, in print and on-line, about these troubles. From my perspective, the most helpful and hopeful of these accounts connect such thorny reporting problems to underlying theoretical debates between functional versus social or practice-based conceptions of "what counts" as literacy itself. This chapter begins within the context of these debates, although the examples I will use here focus on routine administrative rather than pedagogical elements of reporting. In all cases, literacy practitioners ineluctably determine what counts or – what is made to count – through the routine daily work of record keeping and reporting to funders. As others have commented, such reporting work is itself a highly complex form of literacy practice that remains remarkably under-examined (Darville, 2002; Derrick, 2002a, 2002b; Hamilton, 2001). This terrain is also vast, and the picture presented here is necessarily selective and sketchy. But I hope the issues raised will be familiar to a wide range of readers and the analysis suggestive of useful ways to investigate the policy challenges currently being faced across national and international boundaries.

This focus on policy frameworks reflects a growing interest in the adult literacy field in improving our own "policy literacy." Experienced literacy advocates describe themselves as "well-practiced in the art of working in the cracks" but less effective at "engag[ing] with the central processes of policy formation and decision-making (Hamilton, 1997, p. 147). Even language theorists point out that the theories of language that have largely guided the literacy field in past are "not by themselves adequate to the task of guiding action in the "messy" policy arena of our times" (Wickert, 2001, pp. 86–87; Barton, 2001). Policy processes are coming to be recognised as a specialised form of textual practice and subject to examination as such. According to Barton, (2001, p. 100) "writing is not just speech written down ... [but] ... a distinct form of meaning-making" that is increasingly the object of theorising in language studies and elsewhere.

Sociologist Dorothy Smith described this phenomenon as "textually mediated social organization" (1990a, 1990b, 1999) that has become increasingly central to understanding institutional arrangements over the past century. In her view, texts have a unique capacity not only to "make meaning" but to actively to organize social action based on those meaning across a variety of settings by "transposing the actualities of people's lives and experience into the conceptual currency by which they can be governed" (Smith, 1990a, p. 14). Darville has taken up this analysis in the field of literacy (1998, 2001, 2002) pointing out that literacy reporting frameworks accomplish precisely this work of "organizing and coordinating" literacy teaching across settings. They do so in part by "holding the meaning of words constant" and thus creating "a stable object for discourse, for policy, and institutional action" (Darville, 1998, p. 1). This system of coordinating he calls the "literacy regime" (2001) emphasising the "complex institutional arrangements by which literacy is worked up ... as an issue for public attention ... and regulated as an arena of action" (2000, p. 1).

The tension between this "stable object of discourse" and the "messy" world of literacy practice is the focus of investigation in this chapter. I will attempt to show the relevance of such an analysis to the dilemmas facing literacy workers internationally. First, I draw briefly on international literature that associates the dilemmas noted above with the rise of comprehensive policy regimes. Then I turn to the question of how these concerns might be theorised and investigated empirically as textually mediated troubles. I give a brief example from policy documents and reporting practices in Ontario. Finally, I conclude with comments on how this perspective on policy analysis might contribute toward new strategies of engagement with policy formation.

The Rush to Systems – and Contradictions

Any reporting on policy developments across the range of jurisdictions I have identified is necessarily selective. I have focused on events of the past two decades that I believe will be familiar internationally. In each jurisdiction, I have drawn selectively on literature that has already synthesised local reports and thus offers an overview of the changes and the debates surrounding them. My concern here is not to establish the representativeness of any of the views reported here, but rather to investigate how it might happen that such curiously similar concerns could arise across such a broad reach of time and space. I begin below with the United States, where such debates have been rapidly escalating in recent months.

United States

For information about the United States I have drawn on the work of Juliet Merrifield (1998) who has usefully reviewed many of these issues. Merrifield identified the decade of the 1990s as the turning point in the U.S. between the "campaign" model of literacy work and the rise of a more comprehensive literacy policy framework. She outlined a history of interlinking state and national efforts to establish a coherent national delivery system and an integrated national accountability system with objective measurements and performance indicators. The lynchpin for these efforts came in March 1997 with the launching of the National Outcome Reporting System Project (Merrifield, 1998; Sticht, 2001).

According to many observers, "coherence" has not come smoothly in the U.S. Writing in 1998, Merrifield described the adult basic education system as still "a complex and incomplete system characterized by diverse and multiple funding sources, institutional arrangements, goals and objectives" but with the emphasis on accountability brought to "center stage." (p. 4) With accountability came what she called a "rush to measurement," despite lack of clear goals and objectives and limited capacities of local programs to collect valid data. Even the federal U.S. General Accounting Office reported in 1995: "the data the Department receives are of questionable value. ... Because state and local client data are missing or inaccurate, attempts to make the program accountable may be compromised" (GAO, 1995, p. 33, cited in Merrifield, 1998, p. 38).

So already by 1998, insiders were warning that the U.S. system was plagued not only by what "cannot (yet) be known" but also by the fact that "what we do know is problematic" (Merrifield, 1998, p. 38). Along with other "myriad difficulties" related to staffing and resources, Merrifield identified a problem she called "lack of understanding" of the purpose of data collection. She wrote, "When asked to report numbers, literacy programs will indeed report numbers – but when they see no purpose in the numbers ... do not use them themselves etc. ... there is little incentive to make the numbers accurate" (Merrifield, 1998, p. 40, 48). And when measurement for its own sake becomes important, she observed, programs learn quickly to "game the numbers."

Things seem not to be improving. In 2003, the first report from the new National Reporting System brought data suggesting not only that targets are not being met, but that many community programs are dropping out of federal funding schemes altogether. In addition, in a curious number of cases, the data showed little relationship, or indeed an inverse relationship, between hours of instruction and the rate of learner achievements when compared between states. According to well-known observers like Thomas Sticht, the report itself warns against using such data to make comparisons between states, because measures vary from state to state. But that calls into question the usefulness of a "national" database designed precisely to inform the U.S. congress about the "system" as a whole (2003, p. 5).

Merrifield has warned that such troubles are more than growing pains. Even with a growing technical capacity to measure, thorny questions remain about what to measure. "What is counted usually becomes 'what counts'" and "... measuring the wrong thing is a problem in many government endeavours." Indeed, as I will show below, such systemic troubles are not unique to the United States.

United Kingdom

Here I have drawn mainly on the work of Mary Hamilton and Jay Derrick, both well-known commentators on the U.K. scene. They identified the 1990s, as in the U.S., as a period of transition from "a patchwork of community programs relying on volunteers, diverse institutions, and varied funding streams" to a unified system of national provision (Hamilton & Merrifield, 2000, p. 245). This picture is based primarily on developments in England and Wales; but according to Hamilton, Macrae and Tett (2001), policies there have influenced events as well in Scotland and Northern Ireland over this period.

The Further and Higher Education Act of 1992 marks the beginnings of a unified system of National Vocational Qualifications (NVQs) tied to a set of national training targets and quality assurances, bringing adult basic education provision largely within the colleges of further education (Hamilton & Merrifield, 2000). This new comprehensive system was meant to offer equivalences and pathways through "the maze of different vocational qualifications" and "bridge the divide between academic and vocational qualifications" (2000, pp. 247–248).

But while these changes promised to expand and streamline the provision of services, according to critics it has also had the contradictory effect of throwing up new barriers to access for many adults (retired, on disability, etc) who are not job-seekers. It also brought Adult Basic Education (ABE) within a new management process involving "strong central pressures ... for national account-ability, documented performance and quality control, accreditation through a standardised national curriculum and tests" described "limited and limiting" (Hamilton & Merrifield, 2001, p. 244). Furthermore, both ABE learner and teacher credentials have been linked into the NVQ system (Hamilton et al., 2001, p. 36; Hamilton, 1997, p. 136).

Thus, according to its critics, along with a more formalised, recognised and secure system of provision has become "a redefinition of what counts as literacy, as well as its goals and means" (Hamilton, 1997, p. 131). The result is predomi-nantly "a strongly controlled and narrowly focused approach to literacy and numeracy" (Hamilton et al., 2001, p. 36) leading those committed to a broader, community-based literacy practice to lament that their "visions of literacy have moved farther into the distance" (Hamilton, 1997, p. 131).

According to Jay Derrick (2002a, 2002b) some of these problems are systemic. Performance measurement, per se, is not the problem, he argues, since govern-ment funders are "entitled to be satisfied that money is being spent effectively and efficiently" (2002a, p. 1). So the "big question is how to provide a regulatory framework that ensures support for learning ... without ... unduly circumscribing or distorting it" (2002a, p. 1). Furthermore he warns, given that performance measures are "proxies for the real quality they purport to measure", they raise the possibility of powerful distortions or "data and analysis which [are] all but meaningless." (2002b, p. 2) These are ideas that I will return to later in this chapter.

Australia

Australia has a recent history of very robust policy in language and literacy, accompanied by lively academic and practitioner debate. For an overview, I have drawn primarily on a collection of papers on "policy activism" edited by Joseph Lo Bianco and Rosie Wickert (2001). These writers report that interest in a national policy for adult literacy began in the late 1980s, and was given impetus across the states through the adoption in 1991 of The Australian Language and Literacy Policy. Between 1990 and 2000 there was a major influx of funds leading to rapid growth across a range of types of provision. But, as in the United Kingdom, all this took place in the context of the integration of language and literacy into the Vocational Education and Training sector and the Training Reform Agenda (Falk, 2001, p. 205). In this context, there was "an explosion of research and development activity" (Wickert, 2001, p. 80) leading to the development of a nationally consistent approach in the form of a competency-based curriculum and the introduction of a National Reporting Framework. So, according to Wickert (2001) "after "years of neglect and ignorance of this issue by state and territory governments" there was the sense amongst literacy advocates that "'our time had come' in policy terms" (p. 80).

But these developments also brought results that were unanticipated and seen by some literacy advocates to be contradictory to their values and intentions. Wickert (2001) wrote, "the experience of 'having a policy' seemed to trigger the dismantling of what they had known as adult literacy in Australia, as the newly visible adult literacy became subject to the dominant vocationalist discourses and the disciplining effects of the 'new public management'" (p. 83). According to Lo Bianco (1997), "Perversely to some extent because of these policies, adult ESL and adult literacy face a crisis" (p. 1).

> [Provision] although greater, is fragmented and insecure, the workforce has become increasingly casualised, ... infrastructure support has dematerialised, working conditions have worsened, curriculum has been "colonised" by competency-based approaches. In the eyes of many, adult literacy has come to be "sublimated" to a centralised, controlling, assessing, monitoring, information-demanding mechanism (Lo Bianco, 1997, cited in Wickert, 2001, p. 82).

Thus, by 2002, less than a decade after the achievement of a national policy, and despite the successes of a decade of expanding provision, literacy advocates in Australia were said to be "losing ground" (Castleton & McDonald, 2002) and the prevailing mood among practitioners was "pessimistic" (Lo Bianco, 1997, p. 1). Meanwhile, growing pessimism in Australia did nothing to dampen the enthusiasm of the new South African government for using the comprehensive Australian framework as the model for their own new policy initiative.

South Africa

Writing about a unique historical period in South Africa, with unprecedented changes following the election of the ANC government in 1994, Catherine Kell's reports of literacy policy dilemmas have a familiar ring. She wrote of "the noblest of intentions" producing contradictory outcomes, leading to a "serious rethinking of the overall approach to policy and provision" (2001a, p. 94). Prior to 1994, according to Kell (2001a), there was a wide range of modes and sites of practice with "no overall state regulation, no canon, no professional structure, and no agreed-upon measure of success." "Adult literacy work ... commanded tremendous moral authority, and the dominant discourse around literacy was deeply embedded in the narrative of the struggle against apartheid, with the concept of empowerment, learner centredness and relevance placed in the centre" (p. 95).

But since 1999, a new urgency has appeared in public discourse, with ABE portrayed as the technology of "African Renaissance" needed to bring South

Africa "from backwardness into modernity" (Kell, 2001a, p. 97). This new economic imperative has led to a broad restructuring of adult education provision involving an intensive and costly process of formalisation and standardisation (Kell, 2001a, p. 95). Key elements of the restructuring included the adoption of a National Qualifications Framework (NQF), the introduction of outcomes-based education, "unit standards" accompanied by curriculum packages ... all governed by a Sectoral Education and Training Authority and a national examination board.

According to Kell, results of this comprehensive new system have been complex and contradictory. In teaching, standards have taken the place of curriculum, and procedures have replaced content. Limited resources and inadequate teacher training have fuelled a booming market in "teacher-proof" instructional materials and the circulation of mock exams has promoted teaching to the test (Kell, 2001a, 2001b). Formerly active networks of NGOs have been largely excluded from field, along with the learner populations (both rural and urban) in greatest need of assistance. Kell (2001a, 2001b) described the new National Qualifications Framework as a "huge virtual jungle gym" hovering over the country with "supposedly vertical and horizontal learning pathways" becoming "new currencies of exchange." In this context, Kell argued that literacy is "desired" or even "yearned for" by many, but has been reduced to a sign, "an empty cipher ... a simulacrum" (2001b, p. 206).

Kell specifically proposed foregrounding and theorising these troubles around the notion of a gap, or gaps. Her own primary focus is on the ever-widening gap between literacies as "practiced in everyday life" and those "provided" in the adult education sector. But more broadly, she has pointed to the "gap" between the " standardisations and normalisations" of policy and "messy lived practices of those who are targets of policy" (2001b, p. 197). This way of formulating the issues is helpful and suggestive of the direction I take in the remainder of this chapter.

Textually Mediated Troubles

Taken together, these cautionary tales from around the globe suggest that such troubles with comprehensive literacy "regimes" are, as Merrifield has said, more than "growing pains." On the contrary, the troubles seem, perversely (Lo Bianco, 1997) to be as systemic as the policies with which they are associated.

The question I want to further explore here is how we might more systematically investigate and theorise such pervasive troubles. But I want to use "theorise" in a particular manner prescribed by institutional ethnography, that is, to develop something like a map (Campbell & Gregor, 2002; Smith, 1999) that can show us how and where to look in order to find these troubles being produced in the routine, everyday world of practice – both the practice of policy making and the practice of program delivery. This systematic understanding is key to finding an effective strategy for change.

There is now said to be a "wealth" of ethnographies that investigate literacy in various ways through the lens of everyday practice (Street, 2003). There is also growing consensus that such practice-based research needs to focus not only on learners and learning, but also on what literacy workers, administrators, and government officials do every day in the name of literacy (Derrick, 2002b; Hamilton, 2001, Lo Bianco, 2001). In Canada, Darville (1998, 2001, 2002) has long been an advocate of such a focus, using an approach to inquiry known as institutional ethnography (Campbell & Manicom, 1995; Smith, 1987). This approach explores the "insider knowledge" of workers – whether on the front lines or in the offices of government – in order to trace how literacy work is defined, organized, and coordinated in everyday activity.

A careful "trace" of everyday experience of "coordination" quickly reveals the significant place of texts in what literacy teachers and administrators "do" every day. As we have seen around the world, increasingly their work involves the use of "standardised and standardising documentary processes [such as] ... curricular frameworks, performance indicators, assessment tools, reporting frameworks" which allow a wide range of activities in delivery agencies to be made accountable in uniform terms (Darville, 1998, p. 4). A growing chorus of voices identifies these reporting arrangements as somehow central to the "malaise" in literacy work. They are said to "measure the wrong things" or embody the "wrong values" (Merrifield, 1998). But exactly how this happens, not just occasionally but systematically it seems, is rarely made the subject of investigation on its own terms (Darville, 2002; Smith, 1990). Institutional ethnography takes this question as its central focus of investigation, guided by the concept of "textual mediation."

The following example will briefly identify the kind of terrain that could be systematically "mapped" using institutional ethnography. I cannot properly illustrate institutional ethnography as a research method, per se, since I present no proper ethnographic data. But I can typify one aspect of the method by showing the importance of investigating "the problem" from more than one standpoint in everyday practice.

In this case, I identify two locations of everyday practice, indeed literacy practices in every sense of the word, that would need to be investigated: one is in the front line agencies where workers are required to routinely compile and submit program data to their governments; the other is in government offices where public servants carry out the daily routines of administering literacy policies. Since I have already set the stage in this paper by introducing broadly "the problem" of "gaps" as experienced by literacy workers around the world, I will turn here to describe how a piece of this same "gap" is seen from the vantage point of the government officials. Then I will return again to the story as experienced by front line literacy workers.

In this case, my source of data about the government point of view is not ethnographic, but textual. It is a public document in Ontario, the 2002 Annual Report of the Provincial Auditor, which identified a problem they called "misleading" results in the annual reporting on literacy programs in the province. Briefly stated, the contentious issue was the methods used for reporting the percentage of clients who achieved the target outcomes of "getting a job" or "going on to further education or training" after completing or leaving a literacy program. Staff in agencies delivering programs are required to collect this information through follow-up surveys three months following the exit of any student from their programs. These data are reported to the Ministry responsible for literacy, which in turn is required to report this information in their Annual Report to the provincial treasury. In Ontario, the Ministry apparently omitted this information from its 2000/2001 Annual Report, which led to some investigations by the Auditor's office.

The Auditor's report pointed to several layers of activity, but for the sake of brevity here, I will discuss only one. That is, according to the Auditor, agencies had not used "consistent practices" in implementing and reporting the required follow up survey. After reviewing the raw data, the auditor concluded that, on average, the community agencies had attempted to implement the follow-up survey with only about 60% of the total clients who had "left" or "completed" during the fiscal year, and were successful in getting survey results from only about 28% of those they had attempted to reach (Government of Ontario, 2002, p. 306–307). Nevertheless, internal documents concluded that "80% of participants got a job or went on to further education or training" (2002, p. 306). According to the Auditor, this figure "could lead one to assume" that 80% of total clients had a positive outcome (higher than the original performance target of 70%), which they said was "misleading."

The Auditor criticised the agency reports for "distort[ing] reported results" by excluding "lost contacts," making final outcome reports "unreliable". Here we seem to have an instance of agencies being charged with "gaming the numbers." But let's look more closely at what might be going on here, and for whom.

It is important to note (and then to investigate empirically) how the Auditor's understanding of "reliable" is mediated by institutional accountabilities. The Auditor's office also reports annually, in this case to the finance department, where they are required to show performance of programs against target outcomes that have been defined in advance in the business plans for the Ministry (in this case, getting a job or going on to further education/training). Thus for the Auditor, problems of "consistency" and "reliability" of data are defined explicitly in this relation to their own needs for and uses of information.

But keep in mind that all these levels of reporting take place in text, where the numbers and categories of the written report are taken to refer to, indeed to stand in for, the actualities of teaching and learning. But when we look again, and more closely, at these same reporting procedures from the standpoint of literacy workers and learners, the picture gets even more complex and interesting. There we discover that such required categories and calculations stand in a highly mediated relationship to the lived reality of the people – both practitioners and learners – they purport to represent. Exploring this disjuncture throws into question their fundamental "reliability" from the standpoint of the field, and serves to suggest that other aspects of standardised reporting may appear more "objective" in theory than they can ever be in practice.

I will discuss just one point – that is the apparently straightforward idea that learners actually "exit" community programs in a manner that permits them to be first counted as "leaving" and then surveyed three months later. On the surface, this idea seems like common sense. But it produced peels of laughter from the group of experienced community-based literacy workers in Toronto with whom I discussed this example. Of course, they assured me, some literacy students do formally "complete" and "exit" the program and/or make a successful transition to a job or another setting of education or training. But this expectation applies best to students taking higher levels of literacy instruction through a school board or community college (at least in urban centres where there are such options). But the reporting requirements do not recognise these distinctions.

In community-based programs, the actuality of learning usually presents quite a different picture. According to my informants, a typical student in a community program at the basic levels of instruction might come to the program for a while and seem to be making good initial progress, gaining confidence as a learner. But then the person may suddenly disappear, usually without notice. With luck, this student will reappear in a few weeks, explaining that his partner or her kids got sick and so s/he couldn't come to class for a while. That's nothing remarkable from the student's point of view; just a "reliable" fact of life as she knows it. When the student does return, s/he may continue for many weeks, until one day s/he suddenly disappears again. A literacy worker in a community agency is not paid to be a case worker who follows up when students fail to attend. She may call anyway, but in many cases she will never know what happened until she meets a neighbour one day in the local grocery story. There, between the cereal and soup cans, she learns that the missing student's husband/wife lost his/her job and suddenly the family moved "up north somewhere" where they could stay with relatives until they find new work. The literacy student in question did not come into the program, announce her "exit" and provide a forwarding address. As the experienced literacy workers point out, if the student had this kind of bureaucratic literacy "skills," she probably would not be in the literacy program in the first place. Nor would there be any way to report any new job s/he may have moved to.

So here we see that "what counts" as "reportable" using the "consistent and reliable" reporting practices may well not reflect the actual circumstances of learning for the student. When the lives of community literacy students are economically unpredictable, so will be their attendance in literacy programs. If the rules and procedures are followed consistently, such students will be "counted" – not once but several times – as failures for the programs that serve them. Through a process of textual-mediated reporting, they will be counted once as a "lost contact" (failure) when the agency is unable to contact them using their prescribed ("consistent") procedures for a follow-up survey. Then they will be counted again when the records show they "failed" to complete the program and "failed" again to reach the target of going on to work or further training.

Agency workers tell me that they have repeatedly advised the Ministry that the data, as requested, will give a poor and misleading picture of what is actually being achieved in literacy services. But this problem is not easily solved, since the Ministry is accountable through another layer of textual mediation involving categories that "normalise" and "standarise" literacy services in the terms of their business plan. Seen in this broader perspective, it is not surprising that there is an imperative, at all levels of the system, to "crunch the numbers ... to survive." Do these "troubles" originate with poorly trained (or dishonest) literacy workers? Or government officials? Or are we looking at the "social organization of "gaming" as a rational bureaucratic practice? We can speculate with some confidence that systematic ethnographic research would reveal similar pressures in reporting relationships across the national literacy systems discussed in this paper.

The routine production of texts that make literacy work appear to conform to the expectations of funders is an example of the production of a "virtual and virtuous reality" (Castleton, 2000). It is virtual because the orderly appearance is produced only on paper, not in the lives of learners or workers. And it is virtuous because it is a high normative version of what government officials need the lives of literacy learners to look like in order to make them more administerable.

Managing through Textual Visibility

The literacy reporting practices discussed here are an instance of what McCoy (1998) and other critical accounting theorists have called the production of "textual visibility." This involves "an analytic exercise" through which organizational activities, including the most routine work processes, can be recorded and displayed at a distance from the original activity (1998, p. 403). The choice and manner of selection, organization and display is carefully designed to facilitate the evaluation of these activities for purposes that most often differ from the intentions and priorities of the actors themselves. So while "good" literacy teachers may have their eyes on the needs of the learners, "good" government officials are more likely to have their eyes on program targets. These individuals may be equally good at their jobs. But they have different institutional needs and thus different views of what good program reporting would look like. The question is, "good" for whom and for what purposes?

According to McCoy, a routine purpose for management accounting is to produce "knowledge for others." Particularly in large scale managerial processes such as the ones we have been examining here, the most useful knowledge is "knowledge for which [individuals] can be held accountable" (1998, p. 407). According to McCoy, this use of knowledge is typical of contemporary management methods in general. But it is particularly common in relations of accountability between funders and funding recipients, "where grant recipients ... report on their activities through documents prepared using accounting categories and procedures imposed by the more powerful organization" (1998, p. 396).

This generic description of standard management accounting fits very well the type of reporting relationships that would typically be part of the literacy policy regimes discussed here. That is, funding agencies (governmental or otherwise) design reporting frameworks that "make textually visible" selected aspects of the daily activities of literacy learners, teachers and administrators. But importantly, what funders want to know for their purposes is a particular "slice" of the lived reality of literacy teaching and learning. As one experienced government official said to me in a research interview many years ago, "There's a lot of things we don't want to know, so we don't ask."

The partialness of such standardized reports is not an oversight or a mistake; it is central to their role as a technology of management. Paradoxically, such managerial measures are powerful in part because they are seen to be an "objective" picture of the activities described (McCoy, 1998). They do indeed give a picture that is "objective" in some senses of the word: coming from the outside rather than inside, attempting to be consistent on every occasion, and so forth. But this does not make them "neutral" or impartial. (McCoy, 1998). On the contrary, according to McCoy such accounts play "an active conceptual role in setting the terms in which organizational activities can be thought discussed and evaluated." They teach people "to compare what they do ... with established standards." In this way, management accounting serves as a form of control from a distance as "people learn to carry out their activities with reference to the accounting representations that will be made of them, and when they learn to understand [their work] in the terms provided by the accounting visibility" (McCoy, 1998, pp. 396–397).

As in the example above from Ontario, administrators and senior officials learn to "bring in" their programs within the desired targets, as represented in the reporting framework. Regardless of the values or intentions of individuals, or how they "prefer to view" their situation, individuals are "constrained to adopt the accounting categories and the schema that operates them" in order to meet their own accountabilities and thus to survive as a program (McCoy, 1998, p. 397). Thus reporting frameworks are about not just "recording" but also "shaping" what people do. According to McCoy (1998):

> Changing the visibility provided by accounting – what is identified, measured, compared; and what staff can be held accountable for – is one of the most powerful ways to refashion an organization from within [and to] articulate ... work processes ... to hitherto unconsidered relevances. This sort of change is an important dimension of public sector restructuring. (pp. 397–398)

Seen through this lens, the pervasive "gap" with which the literacy field is struggling around the globe comes into a fresh perspective. Here we have the beginning of a "map" that tells us where to look to trace the practical activity of coordination between "local" and "distant" (Street, 2003) moments and sites in the "extended division of labour" (Smith, 1990) of literacy policy and its implementation. We begin to see how "systems" that get it wrong (measure the "wrong things" or embody the "wrong values") are organized and sustained through routine textual practices – the "regulatory paraphernalia" (Derrick, 2002b) – designed to give governments "less complexity and more governability (Pusey, 1981 quoted in Moore, 1996, p. 38).

Conclusions: From Practice to Policy

I have made a broad and somewhat speculative case about the nature of "troubles" facing literacy workers across several continents. The argument is this: that the much reported "gaps" between policy and practice that are distressing literacy workers from country to country are not idiosyncratic, however distinct they may be in their particulars. Rather, they can be seen as a systematic feature of a textually mediated mode of governance that is increasingly in evidence in the adult literacy sector not only in Ontario, but also in Washington, London, Canberra, Ottawa, and Pretoria, as well as many other places beyond the scope of this paper. These "gaps" are a routine product of the way that literacy work is currently regulated through a virtual world of texts. The messy details of peoples' lives and learning are translated into standardised and objectified categories through which they can be counted and made administerable as the object of policy. Smith (1987, p. 3) described this as "the creation of a world in texts as a site of action." All of this is available to empirical investigation through careful ethnographic research.

The case made here also suggests that, just as the "gaps" are systemic, so is the growing practice of "gaming the numbers." Rather than a failure of honesty or training, this practice can be seen as a "rational" (not to say desirable) bureaucratic response to a systemic contest over what counts as "real" in literacy work. This contest is organised in taken for granted ways by competing and sometimes conflicting interests between funders and users of literacy services, with literacy workers often feeling caught in the middle. Indeed, in the policy environment of advanced capitalism, such differences are not only systemic, but likely inevitable, whether funders or providers are located in the private or public sector.

But the systemic character of these troubles is not cause for despair. On the contrary, the present analysis points to alternatives to despair and burnout by showing that the problems faced by literacy practitioners may not be entirely remote and inaccessible. That is, they arise in part through practical activities that literacy workers themselves implement every day, albeit according to designs that are mostly not of their own choosing. If practitioners have a hand in executing them, this may provide some leverage to negotiate their character. This strategy presumes "the field" can decide what a better "design" would look like for the governance of literacy provision. Figuring this out will take time, but meanwhile there may be more room than we think to choose, in small but significant ways, how they govern daily choices (see Lo Bianco, 2001; Sanguinetti, 2001).

Indeed there is an emerging view across continents about principles for a better design for policy and governance. This view centres on socio-cultural theory and the critical insights of the New Literacy Studies (see Edwards, 2001). To date, these principles have been mostly applied to issues of pedagogy. But as Derrick (2002a) and Merrifield (1998) have both argued, there is a "pressing need" to extend this thinking to issues of performance management and other aspects of governance. According to Derrick, there are already some hopeful steps in this direction, in the United States and Scotland, both using more of a "minimum specifications" approach to governance, which allows scope for practitioners to set their own paths toward agreed-upon goals. He describes such an approach as "an enabling framework, rather than a restrictive delimiting one" (Derrick, 2002a, p. 2), that could be applied to administrative as well as pedagogical accountability. Such a framework has the potential to nourish and sustain, rather than suppress and distort, the wealth of practice-based knowledge that already exists about forms of literacy provision that combine "mutual learning and dialogue [with] democratic management" (Hamilton, 1997, p. 146). In other words, it could even restore hope to a battered field of literacy practitioners.

Acknowledgements

For introducing me to very helpful literature, I want particularly to thank Mary Hamilton and Katrina Grieve. For inspiration and feedback on drafts, I want to thank Richard Darville and a handful of experienced literacy practitioners who remain anonymous.

References

Barton, D. (2001). Directions for literacy research: Analyzing language and social practices in a textually mediated world. *Language and Education, 15*(2/3), 92–104.
Campbell, M., & Gregor, F. (2002). *Mapping social relations.* Aurora, ON: Garamond Press.
Campbell, M., & Manicom, A. (1995). *Knowledge, experience and ruling relations: Studies in the social organization of knowledge.* Toronto: University of Toronto Press.
Castleton, G. (2000). Workplace literacy: Examining the virtual and virtuous realities in (e)merging discourses on work. *Discourse, 21*(1), 91–104.
Castleton, G., & McDonald, M. (2002). A decade of literacy: policy, programs and perspectives. (A paper prepared for the Adult Literacy and Numeracy Australian Research Consortium). Brisbane, Queensland Centre: Griffith University.
Darville, R. (1998). Nowadays I read myself to sleep: Media narratives in the adult literacy regime. Paper presented at the Pacific Sociological Association, San Francisco.
Darville, R. (2001). The literacy regime. Unpublished manuscript, Carleton University, Ottawa.
Darville, R. (2002). Policy, accountability and practice in adult literacy work. Paper presented at the Canadian Association for Studies in Adult Education (CASAE) Ontario Institute for Studies in Education, Toronto. Retrieved July 6th, 2003 from http:www.oise.utoronto.ca/.CASAE/cnf2002/2002_Papers/darville2002w.pdf
Derrick, J. (2002a). What could a socio-cultural approach to literacy, numeracy, and ESOL practice be, and how does this align to current practice? [Paper one for Economic and Social Research Council Seminar,18 October]. ESRC Adult Basic Education Seminar Series. Retrieved July 6th, 2003 from http://www.education.ed.ac.uk/hce/ABE-seminars/papers/ABE1-JayDerrick.pdf

Derrick, J. (2002b). A socio-cultural approach to literacy numeracy and ESOL practice: A practice perspective. [Paper two for Economic and Social Research Council Seminar, October 18]. ESRC Adult Basic Education Seminar Series. Retrieved July 7th, 2003 from http://www.education.ed. ac.uk/hce/ABE-seminars/papers/ABE1-JayDerrick2.pdf

Edwards, V. (Ed.) (2001). *New directions in literacy research: Policy, pedagogy, practice.* Special Issue of *Language and Education, 15*(2/3).

Falk, I. (2001). Sleight of hand: Job myths, literacy and social capital. In J. L. Bianco & R. Wickert (Eds.), *Australian policy activism in language and literacy* (pp. 203–220). Melbourne: Language Australia.

General Accounting Office (1995). Adult education: Measuring program results has been challenging. Report to Congressional requesters. Washington, DC: US General Accounting Office (GAO/ HEHS-95-153).

Hamilton, M. (1997). Keeping alive alternative visions. In J. P. Hautecoeur (Ed.), *Alpha97: Basic education and institutional environments* (pp. 131–150). Toronto: Culture Concepts Publishers.

Hamilton, M. (2001). Priviledged literacies: Policy, institutional process and the life of the international adult literacy survey. *Language and Education, 15*(2–3), 178–196.

Hamilton, M., Macrae, C., & Tett, L. (2001). Powerful literacies: The policy context. In J. Crowther, M. Hamilton & L. Tett (Eds.), *Powerful literacies* (pp. 23–42). Leicester: National Institute of Adult Continuing Education.

Hamilton, M., & Merrifield, J. (2000). Adult learning and literacy in the United Kingdom. In J. Comings, B. Garner & C. Smith (Eds.), *Annual Review of Adult Learning and Literacy* (Vol. 1, pp. 243–303). San Francisco: Jossey-Bass.

Kell, C. (2001a). Literacy, literacies and ABET in South Africa: on the knife-edge, new cutting edge, or thin end of the wedge? In J. Crowther, M. Hamilton & L. Tett (Eds.), *Powerful literacies* (pp. 94–107). Leicester: The National Institute of Adult Continuing Education.

Kell, C. (2001b). Ciphers and currencies: Literacy dilemmas and shifting knowledges. *Language and Education, 15*(2–3), 197–211.

Lo Bianco, J. (1997). Policy proliferation: Can literacy cope? *Fine Print: A Journal of Adult English Language and Literacy Education, 20*(1), 3–11.

Lo Bianco, J. (2001). From policy to anti-policy: How fear of language rights took policy-making out of community hands. In J. L. Bianco & R. Wickert (Eds.), *Australian policy activism in language and literacy* (pp. 13–44). Melbourne: Language Australia.

Lo Bianco, J., & Wickert R. (Eds.) (2001). *Australian policy activism in language and literacy* (pp. 13–44). Melbourne: Language Australia.

Longfield, J. (2003). *Raising adult literacy skills: The need for a pan-Canadian response* (Report of the Standing Commitee on Human Resources Development and the Status of Persons with Disabilities). Ottawa: House of Commons, Canada.

McCoy, L. (1998). Producing what the deans know: Cost accounting and the restructuring of postsecondary education. *Human Studies, 21*, 395–418.

Merrifield, J. (1998). Contested ground: Performance accountability in adult basic education. Report #1. National Center for the Study of Adult Learning and Literacy. Retrieved July 10th, 2003 from www.gse.harvard.edu/~ncsall/research/report1.pdf

Moore, H. (1996). Why has competency-based training become the 'solution'? *Prospect, 11*(2), 28–45.

Ontario, Government of (2002). Annual report of the provincial auditor of Ontario. Retrieved May 20th, 2003 from www.gov.on.ca/opa/english/ro2t.htm

Sanguinetti, J. (2001). Pedagogy, performativity, and power. Paper presented at the International Literacy Conference, Cape Town South Africa.

Smith, D. E. (1987). *The everyday world as problematic: A feminist sociology.* Toronto: University of Toronto Press.

Smith, D. E. (1990a). *The conceptual practices of power: A feminist sociology of knowledge.* Toronto: University of Toronto Press.

Smith, D. E. (1990b). *Texts, facts and femininity: Exploring the relations of ruling.* London: Routledge.

Smith, D. E. (1999). *Writing the social: Critique, theory and investigations.* Toronto: University of Toronto Press.

Sticht, T. (2001). Reforming adult literacy education: Transforming local programs into national systems. El Cajon, CA. Retreived June 6th, 2004 from www.nald.ca/fulltext/sticht

Sticht, T. (2003). Federal accountability system fuels the decline of the adult education and literacy system of the United States. National Literacy Advocacy List sponsored by American Association of Adult and Continuing Education. Retrieved August 25th, 2003 from aaace-nla@lists.literacytent.org

Street, B. (2003). What's "new" in New Literacy Studies? Critical approaches to literacy in theory and practice. *Current Issues in Comparative Education, 5*(2), 1–14.

UNESCO (2003). Message from the Director General of UNESCO to mark the launch of the United Nations Literacy Decade, 2003–2012. Retrieved March 14th, 2003 from http://portal.unesco.org/edu

Wickert, R. (2001). Politics, activism and processes of policy production: Adult literacy in Australia. In J. Lo Bianco & R. Wickert (Eds.), *Australian policy activism in language and literacy* (pp. 75–91). Melbourne: Language Australia.

41

SHAPING LITERACY POLICY: FROM ABSTRACT IDEALS TO ACCOUNTABLE PRACTICES

David R. Olson
Ontario Institute for Studies in Education of the University of Toronto, Canada

> The noblest acquisition of mankind is SPEECH, and the most useful art is WRITING. The first eminently distinguishes MAN from the brute creation, the second, from uncivilized savages. (Astle, 1784, p. 1)

> The focus of education [is] to raise the levels of literacies for all students. (Ontario Royal Commission on Learning, 1994, p. 35)

> We're recommending a new body, an office of learning Assessment and Accountability, consisting of a small number of experts in education and assessment, and reporting directly to the legislature ... to evaluate and report on the success of Ontario's education policy. (Ontario Royal Commission on Learning, 1994, p. 53)

Literacy is universally recognized as critical to the functioning of a modern society and, by the United Nations, as a human right. The sentiment behind such policy may be traced to Aristotle's discussion of the importance of writing in *Interpretation*, and literacy came to be seen as fundamental to human and social development in the 18th century Enlightenment. With the rise of nation states, literacy in the national language became an instrument of nation building, and state-sponsored bureaucratic school systems were set up to meet those responsibilities. In the past two decades, state concerns that the schools were not meeting their responsibilities led to new levels of accountability, including state-wide testing and mandated curricula. However, in drafting policies and goals for their school systems, legislators tend to offer extravagant "wish lists" of what they would like to see achieved, lists that are empirically implausible and that consequently result in failure. Worthwhile policies must match goals with human and material resources in order to be achievable. Accountability has meaning only in terms of these plausibly achievable goals.

The formation of educational policy is the responsibility of government not academics. Yet academics can usefully enter this discourse both by acquainting legislators with the literature, that is, with what is known about the successes

International Handbook of Educational Policy, 779–791
Nina Bascia, Alister Cumming, Amanda Datnow, Kenneth Leithwood and David Livingstone (Eds.)
© 2005 *Springer. Printed in Great Britain.*

and failures of previous attempts at reform and, more importantly, by making clear to policy makers the options available and their likely consequences. Previous reviews have shown that policy initiatives in the past are largely addressed to "remedying abuse" of earlier policies rather than addressing the second responsibility of academics, namely, to set out so far as possible the dimensions and choices amongst which policy makers are free to choose. Roughly, these are: (1) Are we to define literacy broadly or narrowly? (2) How do these definitions determine criteria to be used for judging success? (3) Who is to be given responsibility for the achievement of these criteria? (4) What entitlements does the meeting of these responsibilities earn?

Defining Literacy

Literacy is defined in the *Oxford English Dictionary* as "the ability to read and write," that is, as a basic personal competence. In order to turn the definition into a policy, one must address two more specific questions, first, "how well?" – that is, the question of standards, and second, "read what?" – that is the question of content. Neither of these questions is straightforward, and ignoring them has resulted in many of the failures of attempted educational reforms.

Consider first, the question of "how well?" It is a relatively simple matter to define competence in terms of "grade levels." Children are said to read at a 4th grade level or a 12th grade level if their performance is equivalent to the average or mean performance of children at that grade level. Traditional, norm-referenced tests readily allow such classifications. Yet it is well known that reading level is in fact poorly correlated with actual grade level in that the reading levels of children in a single 6th grade class typically range six years, some children reading at the 3rd grade level, and others at the 9th grade level. If graduation from one grade to the next were based on reading at one's grade level, one-half of the children would fail. That is just the logical implication of norm-referenced testing. For this reason many jurisdictions have attempted to spell out standards for "criterion-referenced" tests that would detail what one must know to pass, to graduate, or to earn a credential. Although enthusiasm for this tack continues to run high, it quickly runs into the more general constraint on all such initiatives pointed out by Satz and Ferejohn (1994, p. 72). They point out that only if one narrows the goals sufficiently can one design an efficient method for their achievement; the more broadly defined the less likely they are to be achieved. The British press recently reported that only some 40% of middle school graduates could spell the word "particularly." No doubt if the goal of literacy were narrowed to bringing that level to 100% a system could be developed to achieve that end. But no one knows how to design a system to get all children to spell all or most English words competently, yet that is a more defensible goal. Policy makers therefore have a choice. Either one can define precisely and narrowly goals of dubious value and assure that all children achieve them or they can define goals more broadly and validly with the unwanted consequence that some children will fail to meet them.

Some proposals have been made to translate the goal of a general literate competence into sets of specific skills and by assuring the achievement of each of the many specific ones ultimately achieve the more general. As appealing as this idea may be it runs against the fact that although complex skills do assume some subsidiary ones, no one has yet succeeded in listing and enumerating the items of knowledge or skill that add up to literate competence. Conversely, no one has yet succeeded in analyzing the complex competence we think of as literacy into a finite set of subsidiary skills. Although some analysis, however incomplete, is required for any pedagogy, the resulting sub-skills themselves remain largely unanalyzed. To illustrate, the mastery of punctuation is not a unitary sub-skill but rather is tied into literate competence more generally.

To turn the narrow conception of "the ability to read and write" into a worthwhile educational goal, this definition is amended to state "the ability of read and write well or skillfully" with the difficulties of assessment that I have discussed. And second it is amended to address the question of "read what?" Simple decoding or simple transcription ignores the form and content that makes up literate competence. The narrow answer to "read what?" would be "read English," that is, the ability to put what one says into written form and to read back what one had written. Indeed, this is a useful first stage of learning to read and write, and statistics about basic literacy should perhaps be confined to this ability. Assessments of adult literacy misleadingly assess more esoteric reading skills such as reading literature or a newspaper or one's telephone bill. Because such assessments ignore the actual reading requirements for particular adult roles they give a wildly inaccurate yet widely cited estimate of levels of adult literacy.

But this basic or narrow conception of literacy is quickly surpassed in that literacy in a literate society includes the ability to read so-called "authorless" or "autonomous" texts, that is, texts in which the document itself may be the only thing that the writer and the reader have in common (Olson, 1977; Harris, 1986). The context, purpose, social relation, and common ground cannot be assumed but rather have to be constructed around the document. Such authorless texts may be further classified into types or forms know as genres such as narratives, expository texts, instruction manuals, poetry and the like. Literary genres bear some similarity to their oral forms, a similarity that aids in their acquisition. Yet they are sufficiently different that learning to read and write in these genres is a major concern of the school. The literate competence required to read and understand a nursery rhyme differs radically from that required to read science or mathematics or, for that matter, Scripture.

To "read what" raises not only genre but also content. Reading and writing may be about animals or about atoms. Genre and content are interdependent but must be distinguished if literacy policy is to be distinguished from educational policy more generally. Animals may figure in a scientific explanation or in a fantasy story and literate competence requires that one know how to distinguish between those genres. However, reading either scientific explanations or stories about animals does assume some knowledge about animals, for example, that they share certain behavioral and internal properties. Because one cannot read and write without some such knowledge, some writers are tempted to define literacy in terms of that content, as for example, scientific literacy. This clouds the conception of literacy unnecessarily (Norris & Phillips, 2003). It would seem preferable to bracket the content by assuming some shared background knowledge of readers and writers within which literate competencies operates while acknowledging that this is a working assumption rather than an established principle.

Returning to "reading what", then, to be literate requires that one not only read and write what one would or could say but also that one be able to distinguish genre, that is, types of discourse such as poetry and prose or narrative and expository texts. But further it requires that one master the accompanying metalanguage, that is, the concepts and words for "talking about text" by referring to the genres, their properties and their normative interpretations. As Haas and Flower (1988) discovered, many able readers identify words, locate information, and recall content and yet provide a paraphrase when asked to analyze, summarize when asked to criticize, and simply retell when asked to interpret. The ability to summarize, paraphrase, compare, discuss, outline are more general than any specific content and therefore constitute an important part of the skills of literacy. Admittedly, it is difficult to summarize an account of the habits of animals if one knows little about animals other than that set out in a document, yet summarizing is an aspect of literate ability.

Other metalinguistic concepts that are essential for referring to, discussing, editing, and interpreting various types of documents are also essential aspects of literate competence. These include obvious concepts such as words, sentences, paragraphs as well as more subtle ones such as main point, topic sentence, assumptions, arguments, conclusions, evidence, theory, and still more subtle concepts such as literal and metaphorical and truth and validity. These metalinguistic concepts are frequently taken for granted rather than made into objects of instruction, an oversight with unfortunate consequences as these concepts tend to be well-known by children in highly literate families but not by those from less literate ones (Olson & Astington, 1990). To the extent that content-based forms of knowledge such as literature or science are document-based they may be viewed as an outgrowth of literacy without being central to literacy policy. That is, it is legitimate to examine a person's literate competence independently of their more specialized forms of knowledge. The relation of literate competence to other branches of knowledge is, nonetheless, important and is highlighted by programs that examine writing across the curriculum.

Further, it is now widely recognized that high levels of personal literacy are possible only in a literate society. A literate society is one in which literacy earns or entitles one to some social advantage such as credentials, jobs or other forms of access to the literate institutions – science, law, literature, religion, government, economy – of the larger society. Thus it is useful to distinguish the personal literacy skills of an individual, from "societal literacy," the literacy embodied in social institutional arrangements such as written law, disciplined knowledge, formal contracts, documentary practices and bureaucratic management systems (Elwart, 2001). This social definition is introduced to indicate the close relation between the literate competencies of an individual and the social practices of the larger society. Literacy both contributes to and is sustained by literate institutions, civil society, and the rule of law. Further, it is important in highlighting the responsibilities of governments and other agents in the creation of a literate society.

Both definitions have a place in the formulation of literacy policy as a set of achievable goals. Historically, both educational literacy programs have been seen as failing because the goals set out are more like "wish lists" than they are relevant and achievable. Achievable goals must be spelled out in the contexts of application. Both (a) standards in terms of earning access to more advanced programs and (b) standards in terms of plausibly achievable for particular students or groups of students must be spelled out. And achievable goals must be spelled out for various agents in the educational system.

The goal of universal literacy is that every member of the society develop sufficient competence to cope with the reading and writing demands of everyday life as well as the more specialized competence required for employment. Standards for acceptable competence have changed over the past century from an elementary school education to a high school diploma. Not everyone currently meets these standards and the various initiatives – intensifying efforts or assigning students to different programs – have yielded disappointing results. Defining standards that are both worthwhile and achievable remains a critical task but one that cannot be solved by social mandates but rather must be negotiated with various agents. This is especially true for adult learners who very much set their own goals and monitor their own achievements, dropping out when they are met.

Responsibilities and Entitlements for Literacy Development

The recent policy initiative emerging from the United States Department of Education bears the appealing title "No child left behind" (NCLB, 2002). Like its predecessors it fails the test of achievability, that is, it is set out in terms of arbitrarily high goals and assessments with little regard for the various agents responsible for meeting those goals, while ignoring entirely the responsibilities of the learners themselves. Consequently, such a policy statement betrays an unbecoming taste for control over various educational agents rather than a dedicated search for goals and methods that may be shared by the various agencies involved. Furthermore, whereas such mandates make clear the responsibilities and entitlements for achieving literacy goals for teachers and students (and penalties for not achieving them), they tend to hide the responsibilities and entitlements for other levels of the system, including government. For this reason, I have chosen to set out policy suggestions in terms of responsibilities, one of which is to negotiate achievable goals, rather than in terms of fixed goals and accountabilities for achieving them. Meeting these responsibilities is what earns the various agents their entitlements whether they be tax dollars, salaries, or credentials.

Literacy policy requires that the responsibilities of various levels of government and agencies be clearly distinguished. Although our concern is primarily with those of the public schools, other agencies clearly have a role. Childhood health, poverty, stable families and housing all have an impact on learning. Educational policy may be expanded to incorporate responsibility for all of these factors. My own view (Olson, 2003) and that of Ravitch (2000) is that schools tend to fail by taking on broad responsibilities that they cannot meet and that obscure their primary mission, namely, providing the resources and teaching needed to achieve their more specific academic goals. Even if we confine our attention to those of the public school, the responsibilities of those occupying different roles – for example, learner, teachers, parents, school, or funding agency – differ in important ways. This analysis would permit one to answer in a court of law: "Who is at fault in case of failure?" and "Who earned their entitlements in case of success?"

Learners

Ultimately it is the learner's responsibility to acquire various forms of literate competence as well as the knowledge required to participate and exploit the resources of a literate society. Learners take on this responsibility for acquiring literate competencies in lieu of a variety of rewards and entitlements such as personal interest and access to other goals. Literacy cannot be merely imposed, but providing the conditions necessary for acquiring literacy are the responsibility of parents, teachers, schools and Ministries of Education.

Parents

Under the law, parents are required to send their children to school or to provide equivalent instruction. But they can also be encouraged to prepare children for school by reading to them, for example, and by participating in the educational programs of the school.

Teachers

Teachers are responsible for mediating between the needs of the learners and the stated and assessable goals of the school. Teachers may be faulted for, that is, held accountable for, the failure to provide not only the needed information but also for providing it in an accessible form, that is, attuned to the needs of the learners. Training teachers so that they recognize and meet these responsibilities is a critical part of literacy policy. Part of that teacher education involves acquiring the specialized knowledge of how children learn to read and write and some optimal methods for helping children learn to read and write. The knowledge to be acquired is not simply that of applying the strategy "what works" but rather the knowledge that allows the teacher to make informed decisions about the needs and progress of individual children relative to the norms of the society (Olson, 2004).

Schools, Boards, and Administrators

School administration is responsible for providing the resources needed to make instruction possible and successful. These responsibilities include not only providing a workable environment, limiting the number and diversity of learners, for example, as well as a degree of surveillance and supervision to see that teachers have the competence and resources needed to meet their responsibilities.

Ministry of Education

Whether education is the legislated responsibility of a nation, province, or state varies by country. The literacy policy set by the relevant government jurisdiction not only spells out which conceptions of literacy it intends to address and the indices of competence that will be taken as indicating success or failure. It also has responsibility for conveying to both teachers and students these goals in terms of workable curricula, texts and materials and suitable forms of assessment (see below).

Federal Government

A federal government has primary responsibility for the development of a literate society with functioning institutions such as those of the economy, the law, and the sciences that are transparent, well documented, and that comply with "the rule of law". Yet, the federal government can also facilitate personal literacy through adult education, preschool education, as well as programs to combat poverty. It can also aid the provincial or local educational systems by providing quality published materials including standard assessment forms that may be used for guiding program development, instructional programs, and the like.

Governments have responsibility for helping citizens achieve their own goals to the extent that these goals are seen as in the public interest. These include the literate skills needed to participate in the public institutions of a civil society, including the political system, the economy, the justice system, and the arts and sciences of the society. These include literacy in the official language(s) of a country. Public support for "heritage languages" and for sectarian religious and cultural beliefs is questionable and would be justifiable only if such support could be shown to contribute to more general social goals.

The Educational Research Establishment

Educational researchers and theorists are part of an international network of scholars with responsibilities for participating in and making available advances in the understanding of each of these levels of activity. They have the task of conducting the research that provides the knowledge that allows each of the agents to make informed decisions about their practices. Researchers have special responsibility for advancing the "knowledge-base', the specialized knowledge that underlies the profession and for sharing the knowledge with practitioners through teacher-training and retraining programs. It is important to note that researchers provide information not control; they do not tell educators what to do but rather provide the theory and information that may be of use to those who do make policy and practice decisions.

On Creating a Literate Society: Literacy Curricula, Literacy Programs, and Literacy Standards

As I have pointed out, a policy for literacy specifies the kinds and levels of knowledge that make up literate competence in a particular society. It indicates the kinds or types of documents to be read and written, the metalinguistic concepts needed for thinking about them, and the levels of proficiency involved in dealing with them. Instructional units would be specified in such a way that teachers and students can recognize what the goals are and when the goals have been met. Further, goals would be specified in such a way that valid and objective assessments of their achievement can be designed. The closer the forms of assessment correspond to the specific goals of the program, the more likely they are to be achieved. Hence, it is vital that the goals and the programs designed to achieve them are in fact important and valid. Narrowing the goals to the point of triviality may make them more achievable and more easily assessed; broadening them to include a set of ideals such as "no child left behind" or "a universal high level of literacy" makes them unachievable. Balancing goals to the personal and material resources in the local context is crucial. Yet determining what exactly is entailed in being able to read, write, and interpret documents of various types is the first step in elaborating a literacy policy.

Standards or benchmarks to be achieved at various levels of education are problematic. While it is possible to align assessment with curriculum, it is more difficult to set and measure standards. Levels of literacy are always relative to the population tested. As we have seen, while it is not difficult to provide norms based on the average performance for grade eight children, it is difficult, some would say impossible, to specify what competence is in more absolute terms.[1] That is, one may detail curricular goals and assess their achievement, but performance on any test will still provide only norms relative to a population. Benchmarks designating the goals of a literacy program are more useful for designing programs than they are for the assessment of absolute standards.

Nor can standards be set independently of the learners. Learners will adopt a goal only if they have a reasonable prospect of attaining it. How to maintain acceptably high standards and yet keep all learners involved is a perennial problem traditionally addressed by program diversification but with questionable results (Ravitch, 2000).

Responsibility and Accountability

Accountability requires that assessments be made to determine if various agents have met their responsibilities, thereby earning their entitlements. School inspector reports, graduation rates, drop-out rates, program diversity, as well as student assessments have all traditionally played a role. Formal and informal tests are an important part of this process and serve a number of quite different functions, but it is a serious mistake to assume that one test can serve all of these functions.

Historically, tests have served two primary functions, one, to provide a basis for awarding credentials and, two, for adjusting instruction to learner's needs. More recently, they are seen as providing information as to the effectiveness of the educational system as a whole, of particular schools, and as a basis, often quite dubious, for allocating credit and blame.

Governments or states, school boards or districts, schools, teachers and students all require information on their success in meeting their obligations, and all may be held accountable for success and failure and all may earn entitlements through meeting their obligations, but, as mentioned, these obligations vary from agency to agency. We may summarize these in a preliminary way in terms of the judgements to be made as follows:

- What entitlements are to be earned (e.g., student promotion, school honors, tenure, salary increments, re-election to governing bodies)?
- What decisions are to be made? By whom?
- What kinds of evidence are relevant to such decisions?
- Are decisions based on single, "one-shot" evidence or on a variety of sources? How is evidence to be accumulated over time?

Consider how each of these considerations apply to each of the agents (student, teacher, school, board, state) involved in achieving an acceptable level of literacy:

- *Students* earn promotion and ultimately a credential (a diploma) by achieving a certain standard or level of competence. Tests may be used to determine if they meet that standard, along with other data, such as portfolios or assessment of a year's work. Objective tests help minimize variability of standards across classrooms and schools. Teachers' tests provide evidence to students as to whether or not they are earning those credentials.
- *Teachers* use tests (and assignments) to hold students responsible for their work to see that it meets the norms and standards that lead to the earning of credentials. Teachers can also use tests (and assignments) to detect gaps in learning and understanding and to see if the curriculum is lining up with the criteria to be assessed.
- *Schools* may make use of student achievement scores as one factor among many to revise programs, reassign teachers, and adapt to the special needs and interests of the local community.
- *School boards or districts* may use a variety of forms of data, including test

scores of students, to judge strengths and weaknesses of schools, the curriculum, faculty, distribution of resources, and the fit of the school program to the needs of the local community. No one bit of information is ever decisive; professional experience and judgment is required.

- *States* are concerned that students actually earn the credentials they are awarded and that teachers and schools earn their salaries on the basis of their success in helping students achieve those credentials.

Implementation

Tests and other indications of achievement serve several purposes. One, they provide the system with evidence that students have earned an academic credential, that is, that students have taken responsibility (an obligation) and earned a credit (an entitlement). Second, tests can help to articulate the criteria that students and teachers can use in taking on an obligation, say, in deciding to earn a credit in English, Science, or Mathematics.

What is involved in earning a credit is largely determined by the course of study, the subject, the resources including textbooks, and topics that make up the curriculum. In many jurisdictions, teachers (and schools) have some latitude in decisions whether to pass or fail students. Objective, province- or nation-wide tests may help to standardize these decisions and to make students and teachers more clearly responsible for success and failure. There is now a widespread initiative in the U.S., the U.K., and Canada of subjecting every student to nation- or province-wide tests either every year, every three years, or prior to graduation. A second possibility has not been tried, that of developing an objective test that could be used to evaluate the validity and reliability of the more locally adjusted assessments and tests. That is, if local schools adjust their programs to local needs, and assess student progress in those terms, there is still a need to determine that the levels achieved are appropriate for the awarding of credentials. A national, standardized test could be used to assure that local tests are valid and reliable by giving the standardized tests to a small sub-sample of the tested group and calibrating standards accordingly. Informal observations suggest that local teacher-made tests have fallen out of favor. If systematic local testing were part of every school program, states would feel less compelled to devise and enforce state-wide testing.

Many governments believe that objective test data should be added to other criteria of school performance such as drop-out rates and college admissions to hold educational systems accountable for the resources they are granted. Just as students have to reach some standard to earn a credential, so too, schools and teachers may have to meet some standard if they are to be judged a success. What to do with "failing schools," "failing teachers," and "failing students" is always somewhat problematic. Addressing this issue in terms of rewards (incentives) or punishments clouds the more basic problem of linking entitlements and obligations. Teachers and students work hard or harder if the effort entitles them to the goals they seek. For students, these are clearly to earn a credit and to some extent to be the best in the class. For teachers, the entitlement to tenure, salary, and the regard of one's peers comes from meeting the obligation of helping students and the school as a whole reach their goals. Incentives come from helping one's students achieve or surpass a previously established norm. Whether financial incentives based on competition with one's peers adds to the more basic incentive to meet one's obligations remains both uncertain and unpromising (Tyack, 1995).

Routine assessment is a central part of teaching. Teachers and students both need to know that students are on-line to achieve a credit, such as passing a course. Tests made by commercial publishers and teachers are widely available but not widely used, and there is seldom any policy directing their use. Sorting out the available tests and locating the lacuna may be an important first step to an assessment policy.

Further Considerations on a Literacy Policy

Literacy is both an ideal and a series of practical, achievable goals. "A nation of readers" and a society ordered by "the rule of law" are worthy aspirations that guide literacy policy, but they are far from feasible, assessable goals. Plausibly achievable goals vary with individuals and with institutions. Societies allocate funds to foster goals in the public interest, such as those that lead to employability or good citizenship. But the society may define these goals either too broadly or too narrowly. Adults pursue literacy for a variety of personal purposes including the study of religious texts and reading to their children as well as to enhance their employability. Yet it is also true that literate adults are more likely to raise literate children, hence, encouraging literacy for even private purposes may be in the public interest. Economic advancement is only one goal among many for pursuing literacy. Schools are not responsible for all forms and degrees of literacy. Defining the goals in such a way that schools can realistically accept responsibility for achieving them is the purpose of a literacy policy.

Conceptions of Basic Skills

Schools are given the responsibility for creating both literate persons and a literate society. Yet to meet the standards of accountability, they necessarily narrow their goals. The risk in narrowing the goals to the "basic skills" of reading, writing and mathematics is that of losing the more general purposes of literacy and schooling. Literate competence is broader than basic skills but narrower than the disciplines served by documentary practices such as science, literature or government. While literacy is not correctly seen as content neutral, there is a justifiable distinction between literate competence and the specialized knowledge of the disciplines. On the other hand one cannot define literate competence independently of the types of written discourse important to the society. Therefore, reducing reading to word identification at the expense of comprehension, analysis, and interpretation is a serious oversimplification. On the other hand, adopting too broad a goal for literacy, such as the enjoyment of literature, may lead to an underestimate of the importance of the mechanics of language and literacy. Ministry guidelines and assessments must allow professionals the latitude they need to achieve an appropriate balance.

Assessment of Literacy

There is a tradeoff between objective assessments and the breadth of literacy goals. Simple skills are readily assessed objectively sometimes by a single item; understanding documents is difficult to assess objectively and requires professional judgment. Which skills are taken to be basic and universal is not obvious and is subject to research and analysis.

While relative judgments are straightforward, absolute judgments are not. Norm-referenced tests necessarily put 50% of the people who take them below the mean. So-called "criterion-referenced" tests or "benchmarks" are no less relativistic than others. To be useful, test items must discriminate, and therefore yield a distribution of scores with an average score. So half of the responses will fall below that average score. Such tests serve useful functions, but student assessment and the awarding of credentials cannot be based exclusively on such tests.

"High stakes" tests that bear the major burden for a decision, must be valid and reliable. Establishing that requires considerable research. In general, the more important a decision, the more important it is to use multiple sources of information – tests, projects, interviews, and so forth.

Literacy policy is the attempt to turn a widely shared belief in the importance of literacy for personal and social development into specific goals for which particular agencies – including the state and federal governments as well as teachers and students – may undertake some responsibility in order to earn their entitlements. Assessment may be addressed in terms of entitlements and obligations. If one is to earn an entitlement, say to pass to the next grade, one must meet the obligations or responsibilities associated with that entitlement. These entitlements and obligations differ for different agents – states, school boards, schools, teachers and students. Assessment is essential to determine that each agency meets its obligations. It is tempting to believe that a single test can serve several purposes simultaneously. This assumption is in question. Once the functions of various agents in the educational system are specified it becomes clear that several forms of assessment are called for. Many lines of evidence are relevant; tests are only one, and if relied on too heavily may narrow educational goals. Yet tests aid in clarifying the goals of literacy programs and in providing a reliable base for the granting of entitlements including credentials. It is misleading to think of entitlements as "incentives"; they are not inducements to extra effort but rather criteria for meeting one's obligations. Only by sorting through them can one design a literacy policy for a society or its schools.

Notes

1. When absolute standards are set and tested for the results tend to be lower than on traditional norm-referenced tests yet the correlations remain relatively high (e.g., $r = 0.65$). For example, about 75% of those who scored either high or low on the standards-based assessment test also scored high or low on the norm-referenced test (Schoenfeld, 2002). Consequently, the higher failure rates on the former simply demonstrate that the "absolute" standards are arbitrarily high.

References

Astle, T. (1784). *The origin and progress of writing*. London.

Elwert, G. (2001). Societal literacy: Writing culture and development. In D. R. Olson & N. G. Torrance (Eds.), *The making of literate societies* (pp. 54–67). Oxford: Blackwell.

Haas, C., & Flower, L. (1988). Rhetorical reading strategies and the recovery of meaning. *College Composition and Communication, 39*, 30–47.

Harris, R. (1989). How does writing restructure thought? *Language and Communication, 9*, 99–106.

No child left behind (2002). Washington, DC: United States Department of Education.

Norris, S., & Phillips, L. (2003). How literacy in its fundamental sense is central to scientific literacy. *Science Education, 87*, 224–240.

Olson, D. R. (1977). From utterance to text: The bias of language in speech and writing. *Harvard Educational Review, 47*, 257–281.

Olson, D. R., & Astington, J. A. (1990). Talking about text: How literacy contributes to thought. *Journal of Pragmatics, 14*, 705–721.

Olson, D. R. (2003). *Psychological theory and educational reform: How school remakes mind and society*. Cambridge: Cambridge University Press.

Olson, D. R. (2004). The triumph of hope over experience: A response to Slavin. *Educational Researcher, 33*, 24–26.

Ravitch, D. (2000). *Left back: A century of failed educational reforms*. New York: Simon & Schuster.

Ontario Royal Commission on Learning (1994). *For the love of learning*. Toronto: Publications Ontario.

Satz, D., & Ferejohn, J. (1994). Rational choice and social theory. *Journal of Philosophy, 91*(2), 71–87.

Schoenfeld, A. (2002). Making mathematics work for all children: Issues of standards, testing, and equity. *Educational Researcher, 31*(1), 13–25.

Tyack, D. (1985). Reinventing schooling. In D. Ravitch & M. Vinovskies (Eds.), *Learning from the past: What history teaches us about school reform* (pp. 191–216). Baltimore: Johns Hopkins University Press.

42

LITERACY IN DEVELOPED AND DEVELOPING COUNTRIES

Armin Triebel

Free University of Berlin, Germany

Ideas about literacy have featured prominently on the policy agenda for decades, with few sharp differences between developed and underdeveloped societies. But research on literacy policies has reached a turning point today. The first testimony of this trend is the wish of many scholars to evaluate what the outcomes of the past 50 years of literacy research and innumerous literacy programs have been. Second, literacy has become an interdisciplinary field (Barton, 1994), and anthropology has made considerable contributions to it. Third, literacy has come to be seen as an element within a web of practical activities and community commitments (Etzioni, 1993; Selznick, 1992). Literacy work has been full of both enthusiasm and disappointment. The antagonisms of literacy and the discontinuities of history are the subject of the present chapter.

Recent research has shown that there is a close link between the role of the individual in a community and that person's literacy practices. But discussion of the role of literacy in society has been hampered, to this day, first by the belief that literacy generates social change, and second by the belief that a script changes a person's cognitive abilities. For a long time the etic approach dominated policy debates (cf. Pike, 1967; Pike had contrasted the etic, outsider perspective, with the emic, or insider, approach which he favored). An etic perspective was evident in the aggressive wording of the literacy campaigns of the 1970s (*eradication* or *elimination* of illiteracy, *attack, front line workers*), which contrasted with their peace-orientated ideology. Today, two notions are crucial. The first is embedding. There is ample evidence that literacy is embedded in a system of social functions and cultural processes. Being a component of the social system, literacy is connected with agency. Hence, policies in the broad sense of collective action are the second context of literacy.

The Meanings of Literacy in the 20th Century

A Variety of Definitions

While emphasizing the individual communication act, most definitions of literacy have been rather unsophisticated with regard to explaining literacy in terms of

International Handbook of Educational Policy, 793–812
Nina Bascia, Alister Cumming, Amanda Datnow, Kenneth Leithwood and David Livingstone (Eds.)
© 2005 *Springer. Printed in Great Britain.*

an individual quality. Instead, particular qualifications such as the ability to decipher and interpret a bus schedule or topics related to "What Every American Needs To Know" have been enumerated in a rather arbitrary way (Hirsch, Kett, & Trefil, 1988; cf. Curtis, 1990, p. 10). The ways in which an institution or society defines literacy implies a definition of the culture's "collective identity" more generally. Literacy is an expression of cultural and political aims, and it is used to designate social roles in a society. In this respect literacy is always an essentially normative notion and an instrument of politics, and it varies with time and place (with each definition having different political consequences, as Street, 1990, has demonstrated). This is true also with respect to classifications of literacy levels. They, too, are subject to renewed political evaluation. Thus, for example, from a definition that declares literacy being the ability to perform reading and writing tasks needed in everyday life, "a vision emerges of a citizen who should not aspire beyond the modest rounds of getting a job, going to work, and coming home in the evening to read the newspaper" (Winterowd, 1989, p. 4f.).

A committee of experts on the standardization of educational statistics, convened by UNESCO in November 1951, recommended the following definitions (*50 Years of Education*, p. 123), which are still used today in UNESCO's "Human Development Reports":

> A person is considered literate who can both *read* with understanding and write a short, simple statement on his everyday life. A person is considered *semi-literate*, who can read with understanding, but not write, a short simple statement on his everyday life.

This definition is "a minimal, functional criterion, couched in terms of an individual's circumstances" (Selden, 1981, p. 34). Research studies and education programs in the USA since the late 1970s have paid tribute to the fact that cultural values and tradition highly correlate with literacy performance. The U.S. National Institute of Education extended research into the meaning of literacy for specific cultural groups and the society at large. In 1956 a definition of functionality was promulgated under the auspices of UNESCO in terms that were slightly more responsive to emic (i.e., insider like, culture-specific) perspectives (Gray, 1956, p. 24):

> a person is functionally literate when he has acquired the knowledge and skills in reading and writing which enable him to engage effectively in all those activities in which literacy is normally assumed in his culture or group.

The Persepolis Declaration clearly contained a political will, but was not as clear in discriminating between literacy, basic education, and societal participation (UNESCO, 1975, pp. 2–3). It "considered literacy to be not just the process of learning the skills of reading, writing and arithmetic, but a contribution to the liberation of man." It proclaimed: "Literacy is not an end in itself. It is a fundamental human right." It said "literacy creates the conditions for the acquisition of a critical consciousness of the contradictions of society in which man lives", declared "Literacy work [...] would constitute the first stage of basic education," and concluded that "true education" must be "open to a fertile dialogue with other civilizations." But on balance, UNESCO, while still acknowledging certain group contexts, threw overboard any impulse for social change and political progress and returned to a narrow skills approach, which remained within the boundaries of functional literacy For administrators or teachers implementing literacy standards the concept of functional literacy has, since early on, betrayed a pedagogically top-down orientation. In consequence and in the long run, more influence accrues to the state.

With the Experimental World Literacy Program (UNESCO, & UNDP 1976) the strategy of big literacy campaigns was abandoned, and the policy of selected functional literacy projects was launched (UNESCO, 1997, p. 120). Functional literacy came to the fore in the Education-For-All program, adopted by the Conference at Jomtien in 1990. The rhetoric of the conference put basic education on a continuum that connected subsistence economies and elaborate abilities. Basic learning needs should:

comprise both essential learning tools (such as literacy, oral expression, numeracy, and problem solving) and the basic learning content (such as knowledge, skills, values, and attitudes) required by human beings to be able to survive, to develop their full capacities, to live and work in dignity, to participate fully in development, to improve the quality of their lives, to make informed decisions, and to continue learning.

The OECD employed, in the Adult Literacy Survey 1994–98, a shortened version of a definition of functional literacy (Literacy in the Information Age, 2000, p. x):

the ability to understand and employ printed information in daily acitivities, at home, at work, and in the community to achieve one's goals, and to develop one's knowledge and potential.

The strategy of "strengthening livelihoods with literacy" (Oxenham, Diallo, Katahore, Petkowa-Mwangi, & Sall, 2001) does without any political claims whatsoever.

Recent definitions include the political and economic determinants of literacy and, secondly, take an emic perspective, as in Kenneth Levine's (cited in Hunter, 1987, p. 25) statement:

Literacy in general becomes the *exercised* capacity to *acquire* and *exchange* information via the written word. Functional literacy is taken to be the possession of, or access to, the competencies and information required to accomplish those transactions entailing reading and writing in which an individual wishes or is compelled to engage. [italics in original]

Up-to-date approaches no longer rest on the contrast of orality and literacy nor discuss the trajectory from one to the other, but assume the cohabitation of both in society (Hautecoeur, 1994, p. 15; Wagner, 1993) and allow for a variety of forms of literacy:

> Literacy may be considered as the semiotic process of playing with the codes to deconstruct and reconstruct meanings and strategies of communication.

There is also a tendency to detach literacy from individual performance and define it in terms of community development (as in Hubik, 1994, p. 197):

> By (cultural) literacy, I mean the ability of a regionally and structurally delimited community to create relationships, processes and institutions aimed at a multi-faceted social, spiritual and mental cultivation of that community, based on its own indigenous resources.

The Crisis of Literacy

The sense that research on literacy is now at a turning point arises from the apparent failure of more than 40 years of struggle for alphabetization (i.e., basic literacy education). Experts have deplored, after decades of investment and countless literacy campaigns and programs, the persistence of high drop-out rates and seeming relapse into illiteracy in many so-called developing countries (Comings & Kahler, 1984, p. 3; Elwert, 1997; Harman, 1976; Lockheed & Verspoor, 1990; Mueller, 1996, pp. 2, 10; Nascimento, 1990; Ouane, 1996; Rogers, 1993; Triebel, 2001; Wagner, 1995, pp. 344, 354). Basing efforts at literacy education on the colonial culture and language have had marginal or undesired effects, for example, in countries such as Senegal (Lüsebrink, 1990).

Moreover, statistical evidence on literacy is felt to be lacking. Such was, for example, the complaint by the World Bank after 30 years of lending funds to improve literacy (Oxenham et al., 2001, p. 18). UNESCO (1990, p. 5; cf. Triebel, 1998) estimated that adult illiteracy for all countries as of 1970 was at 890 million (840 million in low- and middle-income countries, International, 1995), i.e. roughly 38% of all persons aged 15 years and older. As of 1990 the figure was 948 million or 26%. In the developing countries only the figure was at 842 and 917 million (or 55% and 35%) in 1970 and 1990 respectively.

The Jomtien Conference agreed on the figure of 960 million with regard to the 1980s (Inter-Agency Commission, 1990, Preamble). The World Bank (International Bank for Reconstruction and Development, 1995, p. 41) estimated with regard to 1995 that there were 900 million illiterate adults in low- and middle-income countries. For the year 2000 the estimates ranged from some 870 million "to a probably more realistic 1 billion plus" (Wagner, 2000, p. 13). The numbers of people classified as illiterate extracted from the Human Development Reports published by the UNDP corroborate these numbers, as shown in Table 1.

In many cases the numbers of illiterates increased while illiteracy rates dropped (e.g., in the Sub-Saharan and Southern Asian countries or the average of all developing countries), or illiteracy rates and numbers increased (e.g., in Mali).

Table 1. Aggregate illiteracy 1970–2001, Selected Regions

Human Development Report [category]	Year	Adult literacy rate Total [%]	Adult literacy rate Male age 15+ [%]	Adult literacy rate Female Age 15+ [%]	Illiterate adults (15+) [mill.]	Illiterate females (15 +) [mill.]
All developing countries	1970	43 46 48	53	33	842*	
	1985	63 60	71	50	870	
	1990	65 67	75	55	920	600
	1991	69 68			900 860	600 550
	1992	70	79	62	860	540
	1995	74		66		
	2000	75		67		
	2001					
Least developed countries	1970	25 29 30	33	16		
	1985	39 37	47	27	150	150
	1990	45	56	33	170	
	1995	49	59	39		
	2000	53		43		
	2001	53		44		
Arab states	1970	31 30			50*	
	1985	46			59*	
	1990	51	63	39	60	50
	1995	57 56	67	44		
	2000	62		50		
	2001	61		49		
South Asia	1970	31 32 33	44	19	302*	
	1985	44 41	54	28	374*	
	1990	48 42	55	29	380 397*	
	1995	51	63	37		
	2000	56		44		
	2001	56		45		
Sub-Saharan Africa	1970	26 27 28	34	17	115*	
	1985	44 48	59	38	134*	
	1990	50 47	58	36	140 139*	80
	1995	57	66	48		
	2000	62		54		
	2001	62		55		
Medium human development countries	1970	53 57 60	67	48		
	1985	69 71	81	61	370	
	1990	76 72	84	67		
	1992	79 80 78	89	70	320	230
	1995	80 81	90	77	300	200
	2000	79		72		
	2001	78		72		

continued

Table 1. *Continued*

Human Development Report [category]	Year	Adult literacy rate Total [%]	Adult literacy rate Male age 15+ [%]	Adult literacy rate Female Age 15+ [%]	Illiterate adults (15+) [mill.]	Illiterate females (15 +) [mill.]
Low human	1970	29 31	40	17		
development	1985	35 41	54	29	500	
countries	1990	49 43	63	39		
	1992	49 48	62	35	500	300
	1995	51	63	38	530	330
	2000	50		39		
	2001	55		45		

Sources: Human Development Reports 1990 up to 2003. If more than one figure is given, the figures vary according to the source. If no entry, data are not available.
*Wagner, 1995, p. 342.

The overall figures hide considerable differentials. Linguistic minorities, who are often also poor, tend to be concealed by national language statistics. Limited literacy often is connected with marginality and with membership in a minority group, as is the case in many developing countries (Donzelot, 1991; Rosanvallon, 1995). Another common feature is the relative ineffectiveness of literacy campaigns for the female part of the populations. In the face of this situation, the consultant for non-formal education in the German Education, Science, and Documentation Centre simply concluded that illiteracy was unlikely to be overcome by formal education (Müller, 1991, p. 48; see the reports in *Norrag News 19*, 1996, which are, for the most part, in a pessimistic tone).

Illiteracy takes on different forms in economically advanced countries with strong education systems, although in the U.S.A. in the mid-1980s at least 5% of 21- to 25-year-olds were evaluated as simply not being able to read or write (Kaestle, Campbell, Finn, Johnson, & Mikulecky, 2001: cf. Smith, 1998; U.S. Young Adult Literacy Survey, 1985: cf. Kirsch & Jungeblut, 1986; Kirsch, Jungeblut, Jenkins, & Kolstad, 1993; Kozol, 1985). Moreover, almost 25% had problems reading texts that required inferences and understanding *across* sentences. The recent proclamations of a crisis in literacy, as measured by the distribution of reading, writing and numeracy skills among the populations of Western countries, has been a shock to the wider public (Baumert, Schmitz, Clausen, Hosenfeld, & Köller 1997; Baumert, Klieme, Neubrand, Prenzel, Schiefele, & Schneider, 2001; Nascimento, 1990; OECD, 2001; Pompougnac, 1996). In 1990, the German UNESCO-Commission presumed that 3 million citizens, i.e. 5% of the population in the Federal Republic of Germany, could be labeled as "habitual illiterates" (Deutsche UNESCO, 1991, pp. 9–209). Fresh evidence has been furnished through the International Adult Literary Survey (IALS) which was conducted in 1994 to 1998 and covered 20 countries, mostly with highly developed

Table 2. Comparative Distribution of (Lowest and Highest) Literacy Levels in 2 of 3 Literacy Domains, 1994 to 1998: Countries with Highest and Lowest Proficiency According to Percentage of Population Aged 16 to 65

Country	Prose Literacy		Numeracy	
	level 1	level 4/5	level 1	Level 4/5
Sweden	7.5%	32%	7%	36%
U.S.A.	21%	21%	21%	22.5%
Germany	14%	13%	7%	23.5%
United Kingdom	22%	17%	23%	19%
Chile	50%	2%	56%	3%

Source: IALS (Literacy in the Information Age, 2000, pp. 136–137).

economies (Gläss, 1990; Husfeldt, 2001; Literacy in the Information Age, 2000). With regard to the understanding of texts, between 7.5% and 50% of the national populations only reached the lowest performance level, and between 1.6% and just over 30% the highest level.

Certain findings in these surveys are relevant to theories and policy. In many cases, the level of competence in literacy and the education level did not necessarily correspond. Although basic education proved to be, with marked differences across countries, the most important route to literacy, there were other powerful predictors such as labour force participation, parent's education, and social demand for the use of literacy.

Literacy versus Orality?

For years the debate about the "great divide" between oral and literate cultures diverted attention from the varied individual and institutional functions of literacy in every society (Triebel, 1997). The great-divide-model (which Street, 1993, called "the autonomous model of literacy") was interested in the difference between the type of society without any writing system and a society with, at least, some literate competence. It missed the mark insofar as neither oral communication nor the epistemic difference between orality and literacy is a crucial issue in the politics of development. There are, even in highly literate cultures, areas of symbolic use that cannot be put down in writing. Modern Europe is not the only region in which oral traditions and literate elements have coexisted in one and the same culture (Raible, 1998, p. 23). The restriction of literacy to a small proportion of the total population's access to the legal system is another instance of the coexistence of orality and literacy. The introduction of Islam in west African societies from the thirteenth century resulted in the formation of *proto-literate* societies (Goody, 1986). Historians have raised the objection that many societies have had many levels of competence in both reading and writing at the same time (Clanchy, 1979; Goody, 1968, pp. 4–20;

Goody & Watt, 1968, p. 36; Stock, 1983). The idea of two cultures, one literate and the other oral, however, worked itself into public consciousness. It was fed by two lines of thinking, one concerning the philosophy of literacy and the other concerning the technology of literacy.

The Philosophy of Literacy Approach

A long-established tradition has tied written literacy to democracy, rationality, and modernity (e.g., Eisenstein, 1979; Goody, 1968, 1986; Lefevre & Martin, 1976; Lilley, 1966; Lüsebrink, 1990; Oxenham, 1980). According to this view the conclusion, in the eyes of the European educated classes, was irresistible, that only a writing system like the Greek twenty-four-letter-alphabet would set free the "savage" mind and produce progress. Additional support came from the experiments of Luria (1982, pp. 199–209), which proposed a theory of the cognitive development of the human species. Since Goody and Watt's epochal essay (1968) there was no doubt that orality was contrary to progress (Olson, 1977, 1991; Ong, 1982; Saenger, 1982). The oral culture was said to have been empathetic, close to the human lifeworld, and agonistically toned. Pre-literate cultures were declared prelogical as well as prehistoric, a view that amounted to the claim that history only begins with writing (e.g., Illich & Sanders, 1988, p. 7). Vilém Flusser was one of the last scholars who elaborated the idea that linear thinking, allegedly made possible by the Greek alphabet, was the logical form of modern societies (Flusser, 1992, pp. 139–140). The distinction between pre-literate and literate cultures according to this line of thinking had practical consequences on developmental policies (as cited in Scribner & Cole, 1981, p. 14 from UNESCO working group papers):

> The illiterate man's thought [...] is, in fact, a series of images, juxtaposed or in sequence, and hence it rarely proceeds by induction or deduction. The result is that knowledge acquired in a given situation is hardly ever transferred to a different situation to which it could be applied.

The policy of developmental agencies of promoting literacy education that involved the learning of European languages, which proved to be over the years a failure, was derived from this erroneous premise.

The Technology of Literacy

The philosophy of literacy approach and the technology of literacy approach are closely related even though they differ diametrically in their evaluation of the oral. This approach, which became famous for introducing mass communication and which is connected with the names of two Canadian scientists from Toronto, Harold Innis and Marshall McLuhan, was, in the beginning, a reading of the history of mankind and an interpretation of the great civilisations, their role, and their characteristics in history. Innis' view was back to good old orality (Innis, 1951, p. 190). And McLuhan did not set much hope in the critical intellect to overcome manipulation and mystification; formal education, so his conviction was, would not help anyway. Another classical scholar, Eric A. Havelock, in his pioneering work, *Preface to Plato* (1963), spelled out the idea that the world of oral culture was Paradise lost. All of the keywords that later played a role in the comparison of literate and oral societies had already been brought up in Innis' works in the 1940s (Innis, 1951, p. 95ff.). An economist with strong historical interests from the start, he was occupied with the *imagery of cultures*; he termed these their *technology*. He did not shy away from daring generalizations when drawing, from the democratic reforms under Solon and Cleisthenes, a straight line to Protestantism, the printing press, and to industrial culture.

Though making general assertions about the whole of a society, the communication approach was directed, principally, at the individual and to the effects a text for reasons of its make-up produces in a person. Or, to paraphrase, McLuhan's (1962) famous maxim, the text *is* the message. Goody spoke of the "*individualizing* tendency of a literate technology" which, as he saw it, linked up with the division of labour and the greater emphasis literate religions placed on individual paths of righteousness. If writing becomes understood as a technique rather than a social practice it is apt to acquire a dynamic or "logic" of its own: Literacy shapes the human mind, as Havelock put it, and the "technologizing of the word" was said to *restructure* thought (Havelock, 1963; Ong, 1982).[1]

Literacy Policies

Three ideas have had a determining influence on practical action for literacy in the last four decades: democracy, modernization, and the paradigm of enlightenment. Resultant policies have drawn, to varying degrees, on the aforementioned assumptions about history and the nature of society.

The Politics of Education

After the Second World War and fascism there grew a sense of mission to bring democracy to the world, and its vehicle was to be the written word. The comparative politics approach connected "urbanization" and "widespread literacy" to economy, mass communication, and societal participation. This approach, invigorated by James Coleman (e.g., Almond & Coleman, 1960, p. 532), was substantiated by Daniel Lerner's comparative study of modernization processes (Lerner, 1958, p. 55). Compulsory education and "the proportion able to read in one language" functioned as two primary indicators of the transition process from tradition to modernity among others. This process took society, so was the simple assumption, from oral communication systems to the printing press. Literacy was an important step on the way to the integration of a society and to nation-building.

A political commitment of a less liberal sort appeared in the 1970s when the pedagogy of political empowerment sought to bring emancipation to the underprivileged. Illiteracy was seen to be injustice *per se* (Freire & Macedo, 1987,

p. vii; Freire, 1970), and attacking it meant, at the same time, campaigning for solidarity and self-confidence among the oppressed against the alienating forces of the capitalist system (Curtis, 1990, p. 6). Much of the attraction which Freire's "conscientisation policy" exerted on the leftist public was due to these ideas. What distinguished the literacy-for-social-change approach, however, was the notion of agency being linked with literacy. The normative content of literacy was once more being activated in the politics executed by developmental agencies. In this context, literacy was seen to serve as a means of overcoming traditionalism and promoting modernization (e.g., Bhola, 1984, Bhola, H., & Bhola, J., 1984; Delors, 1996; Haggis, 1992; Lockheed & Verspoor, 1990; Schwöbel, 1982; UNESCO, 1976). The repeated catchphrase was "to make the world a better place to live in."

The Economics of Modernization

In the years of economic take-off following the end of the Second World War the belief that the acquisition of reading and writing skills is causally linked to economic growth seemed so convincing as not to be questioned in any essential way (Anderson, 1966; Galbraith, 1964). It was backed up by a misinterpretation of European history which easily served in those years as a global model for development. The "economic rationale" of literacy still influences the politics of international development agencies like the World Bank and the OECD to this day. The very title of the OECD survey of adult literacy, *Literacy, Economy and Society* (OECD, 1995) said it all. At the core of that argument were human capital theory and rational choice theory. Investment in education should lead to improvements in the quality of the labor force, which would result in reducing poverty, improving living standards, creating self-sustaining economic growth, and ensuring political stability (International Bank for Reconstruction and Development, 1995). The dependency of economic performance on the literacy of a society has been called into question, though (Fischer, 1970; Graff, 1996; Wagner, 1995, pp. 343, 345). Observation of everyday life shows that this economic rationale does not apply necessarily to the lives of individuals. Decisions, on the individual level, for investment in education remain dependent on social and cultural preconditions. Even Western countries have been experiencing, in recent years, a serious set-back in the returns on higher education. Beliefs in the symbiotic connection between modernization and economy (insofar as economy was understood in terms of economic welfare) were dashed during the 1970s on the global level. The politics of modernization often ended in mass poverty. Economic growth, if it appeared, did not lead to a proportional increase in employment. The results of literacy achievements turned out to be disappointing.

The Strategy of Schooling

By 1946 UNESCO had made basic education its special policy for the "eradication" of illiteracy. This was to be realized by large-scale literacy campaigns. On the occasion of the International Literacy Year in 1990, the UN, UNICEF, UNDP, and the World Bank adopted these policies (cf. United Nations General Assembly, 2002). The World Conference on Education For All (EFA) at Jomtien made basic literacy a world-wide campaign. Jacques Delors, the then chairman of the International Commission on Education for the 21st Century, articulated the shift from political development theory to educational policy making when he said: "policy-makers [...] cannot leave it to market forces or to some kind of self-regulation to put things right when they go wrong" (Delors, 1996, p. 29). From these premises, literacy policies since 1990 have been reduced to consider education the path to participation and tolerance, to social and economic development, with alphabetical skills being one integral element in education (Inter-Agency Commission, World Declaration 1990, article 1). The profession of teachers has taken on the commitment to shape human minds by teaching them literacy skills in the hope that literacy would be thus "a means by which millions of individuals can transform themselves and their societies" (Fordham, 1983, p. 11). On the occasion of the World Education Forum in Dakar in 2000, which was to evaluate the achievements since Jomtien, one had to realize that none of the goals of the previous 10 years had been attained. Drop-out rates and disparities within and between countries remained high. Awareness of this phenomenon seems to have given rise, in recent years, to reconsider literacy policies. The need was felt to establish more and better evaluation techniques in order to understand the forces that come into play in education and literacy.

Societal Literacy

The 1990s not only brought a revival of schooling strategies but also fresh concepts of literacy (e.g., Street, 1993). The new literacy studies profited from various new perspectives established in the 1980s. Discourse analysis, in the wake of the "linguistic turn," took as the object of study larger units of language than the word or the sentence (cf. Stubbs, 1980). The ethnography of communication (Hymes, 1974) blended with anthropology, which was to become in the 1990s a sort of leading discipline within the social sciences (Elwert & Giesecke, 1987). The concept of "literacy event" coupled any piece of writing with its associated interactive situations (Heath, 1983). Grillo (1989) drew attention to the social activities through which communication is produced. Instead of literacy skills, "literate behaviour" became the word of the day. The emic perspective was compelling for research. A consensus slowly emerged that changing the societal environment and thus creating the demand for literacy was a precondition for sustained literacy (Elwert, 2001).

Historical research provides an abundance of proof of the social and institutional embedding of the processes of literacy. The theory of insular centers of literacy applies both to developed and developing countries (Triebel, 2001; cf. "spheres of activity" in Scribner & Cole, 1981, p. 236 and "kulturelle Systeme" in Giesecke, 1992, p. 75).

Historical Findings

The concept that script had its own potential to change society needs to be revised in the light of historical experience. Rather, a reliance on script must be seen as the result of specific social processes of change. Social change in Europe, including processes of economic change, created nuclei of modernization around which other centers of literacy could develop. It took a long time for these insular centers of literacy to grow so much and branch out so extensively that one could speak of literacy having taken hold of all society. This was the case in Europe only by the nineteenth century, that is, 400 years after the invention of the printing press. The first accounts that simple folk could read turned up during the industrial age (i.e., marked by the invention of the steam engine in 1769 in England). The call for mass education rang out only when, in the nineteenth century, industrial society was in need of a skilled workforce and emerging national armies were short of adequately trained recruits (Triebel, 1997). Literacy did not permeate whole populations at one time but commenced in scattered places (e.g., religious areas, seats of government, or academies). It found its way through texts, for which society produced a demand (Schenda, 1970). Certain occupational groups, social classes, or bearers of special functions were forerunners of literacy (e.g., scribes, administrators, civil servants and employees, landed gentry and propertied urban entrepreneurial classes) (Haarmann, 1996; Messerli & Chartier, 2000; Nissen, Damerow, & Englund, 1993; Rix, 1992).

Favourable to the emergence of literate behaviour were the related factors of identity formation (Assmann, 1998–2001), urbanization, and the integration of local urban commercial centers into distant markets, mercantile development, and a well-developed traffic system (Lévi-Strauss, 1974, p. 299; but for obstructive factors, see Cipolla, 1969; François, 1989). Factors which touched the emergence of a public sphere were the praise of the "common good," the call for "good governance," and development of the polity (Giesecke & Elwert, 1983; Wagner, 1995, p. 347). Stimuli for the demand for literacy and its dissemination among the public were, as many authors have emphasized, the experience of discontinuity, theological dispute, or interruptions in the life-course (McKitterick, 1990).

Table 3.   Estimated percentages of the population of Central Europe (over 6 years of age) who might have been able to read*

1770	25%
1830	40%
1870	75%
1900	90%

*Compiled from Schenda (1970, p. 444f). The figures are not to be interpreted as a time-series sequence.

The Social Context

The historical experience with literacy reconsidered from a sociological perspective leads to further insights into the potential of literacy. The common denominator of historical and sociological research is the concept of social embedding. Literacy is tied to institutional arrangements (and concepts such as "institution", "life world", societal subsystem, or domain of knowledge; "textual community" in Olson, 1994, p. 273). The process of becoming literate takes place, firstly, within a "domain". Literacy is combined, secondly, with a certain way of conceptualizing the world. To be literate a person must be familiar with a network of conventional arrangements. A person has to be subjected to a socialization process which provides answers to questions such as the following: What is an argument? What is "legitimate" knowledge? What are the legitimate ways of learning something?

There are institutional arrangements of outstanding influence. An institutional arrangement whose heritage has not yet been overcome is colonialism. Market capitalism gave vigor to literacy. Throughout history the social context where literacy flourished was the small capitalism of the marketplace and the workshop (Braudel, 1985). A special institution that has been repeatedly referred to in research on literacy is law. Legal texts, statute books, and contracts spear-headed written culture. Law is the trustee of another institution that is less conspicuous, namely the regularity of procedure (Elwert, 2001). In the nexus of law and economy, property rights are central to inspiring confidence and have, historically, operated in the take-off point for literate culture and modern economies in Europe (North & Thomas, 1973). Another institution that creates and employs literacy is political power. So the nation-state is a prominent social context of literacy. The example of nationalism shows that literacy is closely connected with the emergence of collective identity (Street, 1994). Collective identity defines an imagined community which constitutes a public, and a public and literacy have always been concomitant.

The Future of Literacy

In the course of the last decade researchers and many practitioners have shifted from the monolithic concept of literacy to the reality of literacies which exist in the same place at the same time, connected with various identities hosted in the same person. The concurrence of a variety of vernaculars, each tied to its specific institutional arrangement, is an example (e.g., in regards African states, Reh, 1981; in regards India, Daswani, 2001). In the past, the process of becoming literate was a slow one that never took hold of the whole of society at once because it was dependent on social change. One problem of literacy policy in development projects today is that many, from pedagogical or ideological grounds, have had the idea that literacy competences might be implemented in a society top down without the necessary structural changes being set in motion, through, for example important structural conditions as the emergence of nuclei of civil society, private economy, and impartial law. It was for a long time a serious misjudgement by many educators that literacy itself would lead to egalitarianism and democracy. They overlooked historical experience which showed that state-run literacy programs were a matter of concern, for example, to Fascist Italy (Glück 1987, p. 155) and Stalinist regimes in East Europe (i.e., "logocracy" in Anghel, 1994).

"Best Practice"?

What is needed in the near future is an appraisal of literacy policies in light of the issues I have discussed above. Harping on quantities for the purposes of assessment continues to be popular with national literacy programs, which tend to measure success as numbers of enrollments. Very often programs suffer from the non-existence of a particular need on the part of the would-be learner (see chapter by Jackson, this volume). Although loads of books and reports on literacy programs, and attempts to evaluate them, have been published, comparative appraisals of best practices are rare (but see examples from Africa, India, South America, and the Philippines in Olson & Torrance, 2001, pp. 121–316). With the telephone and television the problem of creating literate environments has merged with the question of the role of new media that are not linked to the written word. With the Internet a media has arrived which is based on writing as well as on pictograms.

Literacy, Distance Learning, and New Media

Since Marshall McLuhan predicted, over a quarter century ago, the fall of the book-age and the rise of the pictoral era, the decline of literate culture in developed countries has increasingly been a source of dread. Flusser projected the idea that a culture of images could not bring about the ability to draw conclusions, produce abstract ideas, and develop concepts on the modern world. In his view, the post-histoire was the age of the picture, when binary logic would prevail and enlightenment come to an end. This argument assumes that the electronic world of images is a world of emotions and irrationality and a culture of images cannot convey the ability to draw conclusions, think in abstract terms, or develop concepts (cf. Lüsebrink, 1990, p. 2).

Today we have arrived, in the developed countries, at a society which is shaped profoundly by pictures and orality. But the question of whether the Internet and television will ruin literate culture remains open (Bonfadelli & Bucher, 2002, especially the chapter by Ulrich Saxer). The Internet demands such a highly-developed infrastructure, both with regard to technologies and mental orientation, that its contribution to the development of literacy will be limited. If the take-off into self-sustained literacy gains impetus, however, it may be a powerful incentive. The Internet internationalizes the mass media, creating a powerful communication channel to overcome state-created restraints on public debate (e.g., as has been seen recently in Iran or China). If community building and identity formation are the crucial variables at the basis of literacy, distance-learning, for this very reason, will be of limited value. The telephone, medium-range broadcasting stations, and the press are more likely to be triggering influences. Hubik (1994) described how television in the Czech Republic before and after 1990 gave multi-faceted literacy a platform and thus supported community development. The village-based approach in Brasil (i.e., the Solidarity in Literacy Program, Contribution to the Hamburg Congress on "The Making of Literate Societies", Brasilia 2001), in the ABET Programme in South Africa, or in Senegal (Olson & Torrance, 2001) are examples. In these cases, the basis for the introduction of written culture into a community are (a) the recognition that semi-literate people are able to cope in some way with everyday life and (b) respect for their indigenous modes of oral communication. Steps in these directions involve, for example, taking up traditional ceremonies like coronation days; introducing written communication through signs, posters, mural papers, or the drawing of maps; establishing reading rooms that also function as community centers and meeting places; and publishing books for local markets. Problems can arise, however, from national governments being suspicious about too much independent activity, and of elites, who may be rival to the government, uprising. The concerns of Article 1 of the Jomtien Declaration – quality of life, empowerment, tolerance, morale, community sense, and humanistic values – will have to be made "profitable" for both the individual and the polity. By acknowledging this, politics will return – not, however, with the idealist emphasis of former days but with a more pragmatic look at the real interests of people and the "habits of their hearts".

Note

1. Even Elwert and Giesecke (1987) did not abandon the comparison of standard languages and high-tech systems for their self-dynamics (p. 433). The influence of the philosophical approach manifested itself in their insisting that literacy is the condition for mathematical reasoning and other forms of meaningful behavior while their basic argument was that a standard national language is dependent on social structure and social practices.

References

Almond, G. A., & Coleman, J. S. (Eds.) (1960). *The Politics of developing areas.* Princeton, NJ: Princeton University Press.

Anderson, C. A. (1966). Literacy and schooling at the development threshold. In C. A. Anderson & Bowman, M. (Eds.), *Education and economic development* (pp. 159–183). London: Frank Cass.

Anghel, F. (1994). Functional literacy in Romania – Between myth and reality. In J.-P. Hautecoeur (Ed.), *Alpha 94: Literacy and cultural development strategies in rural areas.* Toronto: Culture Concepts.

Assmann, A. (Ed.) (1998–2001). *Erinnerung, Geschichte, Identität* [Memories and identity: Remembering history] (4 vols.). Frankfurt: Suhrkamp.

Barton, D. (1994). *Literacy: An introduction to the ecology of written language.* Oxford: Blackwell.

Baumert, J., Schmitz, B., Clausen, M., Hosenfeld, I., & Köller, O. (1997). *TIMSS: Mathematisch-Naturwissenschaftlicher Unterricht im internationalen Vergleich. Deskriptive Befunde* [Third

International Study of Mathematics and Sciences: An international comparison of teaching math and natural sciences]. Berlin: Max-Planck-Institut für Bildungsforschung.

Baumert, J., Klieme, E., Neubrand, M., Prenzel, M., Schiefele, U., & Schneider, W. (Eds.) (2001). *PISA 2000: Basiskompetenzen von Schülerinnen und Schülern im internationalen Vergleich* [Basic competence in children: An international comparison]. Opladen: Leske + Budrich.

Bhola, H. S. (1984). *Campaigning for literacy*. Paris: UNESCO.

Bhola, H. S., & Bhola, J. K. (1984). *Planning and organization of literacy campaigns, programs and projects*. Bonn: Deutsche Stiftung für internationale Entwicklung (DOK 1240 C/a).

Bonfadelli, H., & Bucher, P. (Eds.) (2002). *Lesen in der Mediengesellschaft. Stand und Perspektiven der Forschung* [Reading in the literate society: The state of the art and the perspectives of the future]. Zürich: Pestalozzianum.

Braudel, F. (1985). *Sozialgeschichte des 15.–18. Jahrhunderts. Der Alltag* [Social history from the 15th to 18th centuries: The history of everyday life]. München: Kindler.

Cipolla, C. (1969). *Literacy and development in the west*. Harmondsworth, UK: Pelican.

Clanchy, M. T. (1979). *From memory to written record: England. 1066–1307*. Cambridge, MA/London: Harvard University Press & Edwin Arnold.

Comings, J., & Kahler, D. (1984). *Peace Corps literacy handbook*. Washington. Retrieved June 6, 2003 from http://www.peacecorps.gov.

Curtis, L. R. (1990). *Literacy for social change*. Syracuse, NY: New Readers Press.

Daswani, Ch. J. (Ed.) (2001). *Language education in multilingual India*. New Delhi: UNESCO.

Delors, J. (1996). Education: the necessary utopia. In UNESCO (Ed.), *Learning: The treasure within* (pp. 11–33). Paris: UNESCO.

Deutsche UNESCO-Kommission (Ed.) (1991). *Die Alphabetisierung geht weiter – Pressestimmen am Ende des Internationalen Alphabetisierungsjahres 1990* [Alphabetization continues: A press report at the end of the International Year of Literacy]. Bonn: UNESCO-Pressespiegel.

Donzelot, J. (Ed.) (1991). *Face à l'exclusion: le modèle français.* [Resist exclusion: The French model]. Paris: Esprit.

Eisenstein, E. L. (1979). *The printing press as an agent of change. Communications and cultural transformations in early-modern Europe*. Cambridge: Cambridge University Press.

Elwert, G. (1987). Die gesellschaftliche Einbettung von Schriftgebrauch [The social embedding of writing]. In D. Baecker, & et al. (Eds.), *Theorie als Passion* (pp. 238–268). Frankfurt: Suhrkamp.

Elwert, G. (1997). Pas de développement sans culture écrite. Réflexions sur la persistance de la pauvreté dans les pays moins avancés d'Afrique. [No development without literate culture: Reflections on the persistence of poverty in the lesser developed countries of Africa]. *D + C – Développement et Coopération*.

Elwert, G. (2001). Societal literacy: Writing culture and development. In D. R. Olson & N. Torrance (Eds.), *The Making of literate societies* (pp. 54–67). Malden, MA: Blackwell.

Elwert, G., & Giesecke, M. (1987). Technologische Entwicklung, Schriftkultur und Schriftsprache als technologisches System [Written language and literacy as technologies: The role of technological change]. In B. Lutz (Ed.), *Technik und sozialer Wandel* (pp. 418–438). Frankfurt: Campus.

Etzioni, A. (1993). *The Spirit of community: Rights, responsibilities, and the communitarian agenda*. New York: Crown Publishers.

Fischer, J. (Ed.) (1970). *The Social sciences and the comparative study of educational systems*. Scranton, NJ: International Textbook Company.

Flusser, V. (1992). *Die Schrift. Hat Schreiben Zukunft?* [Script: Does writing have a future?] Frankfurt: Fischer.

Fordham, P. (Ed.) (1983). *Co-operating for literacy: Report of an international seminar held in Berlin, October 1983*. Toronto & Bonn: International Council for Adult Education & German Foundation for International Development.

François, E. (1989). Alphabetisierung und Lesefähigkeit in Frankreich und Deutschland um 1800 [Literacy in France and Germany from 1800]. In H. Berding & E. François, & H.-P. Ullmann (Eds.), *Deutschland und Frankreich im Zeitalter der Französischen Revolution* (pp. 407–425). Frankfurt: Suhrkamp.

Freire, P. (1970). *Pedagogy of the oppressed*. New York: Herder and Herder.

Freire, P., & Macedo, D. (1987). *Literacy: Reading the word and the world.* South Hadley: Bergin and Garvey.

Galbraith, J. K. (1964). *Economic development.* Cambridge, MA: Harvard University Press.

Giesecke, M. (1992). *Sinnenwandel, Sprachwandel, Kulturwandel: Studien zur Vorgeschichte der Informationsgesellschaft* [Desires change, languages change, and cultures change: Studies in the prehistory of the information society]. Frankfurt: Suhrkamp.

Giesecke, M., & Elwert, G. (1983). Literacy and emancipation: Conditions of the literacy process and cultural revolutionary movements (16th century Germany and 20th century Bénin). *Development and Change, 2,* 255–276.

Gläss, B. (Ed.) (1990). *Alphabetisierung in Industriestaaten? Europäische Probleme beim Umgang mit den Kulturtechniken Lesen und Schreiben* [Problems of literacy in the industrial countries of Europe] (2nd ed.). Bonn: Deutsche UNESCO-Kommission.

Glück, H. (1987). *Schrift und Schriftlichkeit. Eine sprach- und kulturwissenschaftliche Studie* [Script and literacy: A study in linguistics and the humanities]. Stuttgart: Metzler.

Goody, J. (1968). Introduction. In J. Goody (Ed.), *Literacy in traditional societies* (pp. 1–26). Cambridge: Cambridge University Press.

Goody, J. (1986). *The Logic of writing and the organization of society.* Cambridge: Cambridge University Press.

Goody, J., & Watt, I. (1968). The Consequences of literacy. In J. Goody (Ed.), *Literacy in traditional societies* (pp. 27–68). Cambridge: Cambridge University Press.

Graff, H. J. (1996). The persisting power and costs of the literacy myth. *Literacy Across the Curriculum 12*(2), 4–5.

Gray, W. S. (1956). *The teaching of reading and writing.* Chicago: UNESCO/Scott Foresman.

Grillo, R. (1989). Anthropology, language, politics. In R. Grillo (Ed.), *Social anthropology and the politics of language* (pp. 1–24). London: Routledge.

Haarmann, H. (1996). *Early civilization and literacy in Europe: An inquiry into cultural continuity in the Mediterranean world.* Berlin: Mouton.

Haggis, S. (1992). *Education for all: Purpose and context.* Paris: UNESCO.

Harman, D. (1976). Nonformal education and development. In D. Harman (Ed.), *Expanding recurrent and nonformal education.* San Francisco: Jossey-Bass.

Hautecoeur, J.-P. (1994). Opening reflections: Literacy in rural areas; orientations for action research. In J.-P. Hautecoeur (Ed.), *Alpha 94: Literacy and cultural development strategies in rural areas* (pp. 7–24). Toronto: Culture Concepts.

Havelock, E. (1963). *Preface to Plato.* Cambridge, MA: Harvard University Press.

Heath, S. B. (Ed.) (1983). *Ways with words: Language, life and work in communities and classrooms.* Cambridge: Cambridge University Press.

Hirsch, E. D., Kett, J. F., & Trefil, J. S. (1988). *The Dictionary of cultural literacy: What every American needs to know.* Boston: Houghton Mifflin.

Hubik, S. (1994). Television and literacy: Development in the Czech Republic. In J.-P. Hautecoeur (Ed.), *Alpha 94: Literacy and cultural development strategies in rural areas* (pp. 197–209). Toronto: Culture Concepts.

Hüfner, K., Naumann, J., & Meyer, J. (1984). *Comparative education policy research: A world society perspective.* Berlin: Free University.

Hunter, C. (1987). Literacy: What do the definitions tell us? *Convergence (Literacy in the industrialized countries: A Focus on practice), 20*(3–4), 23–26.

Husfeldt, V. (2001). *Literalität, Bildung und Beschäftigung* [Literacy, cultivation of the mind, and employment]. Berlin: Waxmann.

Hymes, D. (1974). *Foundations in sociolinguistics: An ethnographic approach.* Philadelphia: University of Pennsylvania Press.

Illich, I., & Sanders, B. (1988). *ABC: The alphabetization of the popular mind.* San Francisco: North Point Press.

Innis, H. (1951). *The bias of communication.* Toronto: University of Toronto Press.

Inter-Agency Commission (UNDP, UNESCO, UNICEF, WORLD BANK) (Eds.) (1990). *World declaration on education for all and framework for action to meet basic learning needs, adopted by the World Conference on Education for All, Jomtien*. New York: UNICEF House.

International Bank for Reconstruction and Development (Ed.) (1995). *Priorities and strategies in education: a World Bank review*. Washington, DC: The World Bank.

Kaestle, C. F., Campbell, A., Finn, J. D., Johnson, S. T., & Mikulecky, L. J. (2001). *Adult literacy and education in America*. Washington, DC: US Department, Office of Educational Research.

Kirsch, I., & Jungeblut, A. (1986). *Literacy: Profiles of America's young adults. Final report of the National Assessment of Educational Progress*. Princeton, NJ: Educational Testing Service.

Kirsch, I., Jungeblut, A., Jenkins, L., & Kolstad, A. (1993). *Adult literacy in America*. Washington, DC: U.S. Department, Office of Educational Research.

Kozol, J. (1985). *Illiterate America*. Garden City, NJ: Anchor Press, & Doubleday.

Lefevre, L., & Martin, H.-J. (1976). *The Coming of the book*. London: NLB.

Lerner, D. (1958). *The Passing of traditional society: Modernizing the Middle East*. Glencoe: The Free Press.

Lévi-Strauss, C. (1974). *Tristes tropiques* [Unhapppy in the tropics] (J., & D. Weightman, trans.). New York: Atheneum.

Lilley, S. (1966). *Men, machines and history*. New York: International Publishers.

Literacy in the Information Age (2000). *Final report of the International Adult Literacy Survey*. Toronto: OECD.

Lockheed, M. E., & Verspoor, A. M. (1990, March). *Improving primary education in developing countries: A review of policy options*. Paper presented at the World Conference on Education for All, Bangkok, Thailand.

Luria, A. R. (1982). *Language and cognition*. Washington, DC: Winston Wiley.

Lüsebrink, H.-J. (1990). *Schrift, Buch und Lektüre in der französischsprachigen Literatur Afrikas: Zur Wahrnehmung und Funktion von Schriftlichkeit und Buchlektüre in einem kulturellen Epochenumbruch der Neuzeit* [Reading and literacy in francophone Africa]. Tübingen: Niemeyer.

McKitterick, R. (1990). Introduction. In R. McKitterick (Ed.), *The uses of literacy in early mediaeval Europe* (pp. 1–10). Cambridge: Cambridge University Press.

McLuhan, M. (1962). *The Gutenberg galaxy. The making of typographic man*. Toronto: University of Toronto Press.

Messerli, A., & Chartier, R. (Eds.) (2000). *Lesen und Schreiben in Europa, 1500 – 1900. Vergleichende Perspektiven – Perspectives comparées* [Reading and writing in Europe: Comparative history, 1500–1900]. Basel: Schwabe.

Mueller, J. (1996). *Literacy and non-formal (basic) education: Still a donor priority?* Education For Development Occasional Papers, I, 3. London: Education For Development.

Müller, J. (1991). Alphabetisierung im Rahmen des integrierten Grundbildungsansatzes der UNESCO. In I. Neu-Altenheimer & B. Sandhaas (Eds.), *Grundbildung. UNESCO-Schwerpunkt der neunziger Jahre* [Literacy on the basis of UNESCO's approach to integrated basic education] (pp. 38–51). Bonn: Deutsche UNESCO-Kommission.

Nascimento, G. (1990). *Illiteracy in figures*. Geneva: UNESCO, IBE.

Nissen, H. J., & Damerow, P., & Englund, R. K. (1993). *Archaic bookkeeping: Early writing and techniques of economic administration in the ancient Near East*. Chicago: Chicago University Press.

North, D. C., & Thomas, R. P. (1973). *The Rise of the western world: A new economic history*. Cambridge: Cambridge University Press.

Olson, D. R. (1977). From utterance to text: The bias of language in speech and writing. *Harvard Educational Review*, 47(3), 257–281.

Olson, D. R. (1991). Literacy and objectivity: the rise of modern science. In D. R. Olson & N. Torrance (Eds.), *Literacy and orality* (pp. 149–164). Cambridge: Cambridge University Press.

Olson, D. R. (1994). *The world on paper: The conceptual and cognitive implications of writing and reading*. Cambridge: Cambridge University Press.

Olson, D. R., & Torrance, N. (2001) (Eds.), *The Making of literate societies*. Malden, MA: Blackwell.

Ong, W. J. (1982). *Orality and literacy: The technologizing of the word*. London: Methuen.

Organisation for Economic Co-operation and Development (OECD). (2001). *Knowledge and skills for life: First results from the OECD programme for international student assessment (PISA).* Paris: OECD.

Organisation for Economic Co-operation and Development (OECD) (Ed.) (1995). *Literacy, economy and society: Results of the first International Adult Literacy Survey.* Paris: OECD.

Ouane, A. (1996). *Literacy for the twenty-first century: The future of literacy and literacy of the future.* Paper prepared for UNESCO seminar. Hamburg: UIE.

Oxenham, J. (1980). *Literacy: Writing, reading and social organization.* London: Routledge and Kegan Paul.

Oxenham, J., Diallo, A. H., Katahore, A. R., Petkowa-Mwangi, A., & Sall, O. (2001). *Strengthening livelihoods with literacy: Report of a study of programmes of adult education and training that have attempted to incorporate either training for livelihood skills into mainly literacy instruction, or literacy instruction into mainly strengthening livelihood skills (Draft).* Bonn: Institute for International Cooperation of the Geman Adult Education Association.

Pike, K. (1967). *Language in relation to a unified theory of the structure of human behavior* (2nd ed.). Paris: Mouton.

Pompougnac, J.-C. (1996). *Illetrisme: Tourner la page?* [Illiteracy: Turn the page?] Paris: Hachette.

Raible, W. (Ed.) (1998). *Medienwechsel. Erträge aus 12 Jahren Forschung zum Thema "Mündlichkeit und Schriftlichkeit"* [Twelve years of research on orality and literacy]. Tübingen: Narr.

Reh, M. (1981). Sprache und Gesellschaft [Language and society]. In B. Heine et al. (Eds.), *Die Sprachen Afrikas* (pp. 513–557). Hamburg: Buske.

Rix, H. (1992). Thesen zum Ursprung der Runen [Where the runes originated]. In L. Aigner-Foresti (Ed.), *Etrusker nördlich von Etrurien, Akten des Symposions von Wien – Schloß Neuwaldegg, 2.–5. Oktober 1989* (pp. 411–441). Vienna: Verlag der Österreichischen Akademie der Wissenschaften.

Rogers, A. (1993). The world crisis in adult education. A case study from literacy. *Compare, 23,* 159–175.

Rosanvallon, P. (1995). *La nouvelle question sociale.* [The new social question]. Paris: Seuil.

Saenger, P. (1982). Silent reading: Its impact on late medieval script and society. *Viator, 13,* 367–414.

Schenda, R. (1970). *Volk ohne Buch. Studien zur Sozialgeschichte der populären Lesestoffe 1170–1910* [People without books: Studies in the social history of popular reading: 1170–1910]. Frankfurt: Klostermann.

Schwöbel, H. (1982). *Erziehung zur Überwindung von Unterentwicklung. Curriculumentwicklung emanzipatorischer Alphabetisierung und Grunderziehung zwischen Tradition und Moderne. Das Beispiel Somalia* [Education to overcome underdevelopment: Creating a curriculum for literacy towards emancipation. Basic education between tradition and modernity, the case of Somalia]. Frankfurt: dipa.

Scribner, S., & Cole, M. (1981). *The Psychology of literacy.* Cambridge, MA: Harvard University Press.

Selden, R. (1981). Literacy: Current problems and current research. In *Fifth Report of the National Council on Educational Research: Fiscal years 1978–1979* (pp. 30–40). Washington, DC: U.S. Government Printing Office.

Selznick, P. (1992). *The moral commonwealth: Social theory and the promise of community.* Berkeley, CA: University of California Press.

Smith, M. C. (Ed.) (1998). *Literacy for the 21st century.* Westpoint, CT: Praeger.

Stock, B. (1983). *The Implications of literacy: Written language and models of interpretation in the eleventh and twelfth centuries.* Princeton, NJ: Princeton University Press.

Street, B. (1993). Introduction: The new literacy studies. In B. Street (Ed.), *Cross-cultural approaches to literacy* (pp. 1–21). Cambridge: Cambridge University Press.

Street, B. (1994). Cross-cultural perspectives on literacy. In J. Maybin (Ed.), *Language and literacy in social practice* (pp. 139–150). Avon, UK: The Open University.

Street, B. V. (1990). *Cultural meanings of literacy.* Geneva: UNESCO, IBE.

Stubbs, M. (1980). *Language and literacy.* London: Routledge & Kegan Paul.

Triebel, A. (1997). *Cognitive and societal development and literacy: A report on the state-of-the-art of research on literacy.* Bonn: German Foundation for International Development.

Triebel, A. (1998). Il est temps de réévaluer notre politique des langues. *D + C – Développement et Coopération* [Development and cooperation].

Triebel, A. (2001). The Roles of literacy practices in the activities and institutions of developed and developing countries. In D. R. Olson & N. Torrance (Eds.), *The Making of literate societies* (pp. 19–53). Malden, MA: Blackwell.

United Nations General Assembly (Ed.) (2002). *United Nations literacy decade: Education for all. International plan of action, implementation of General Assembly resolution 56/116 (Report of the Secretary-General)*. Washington, DC: United Nations (A/57/218).

UNESCO, & UNDP (Eds.) (1976). *The Experimental world literacy programme. A critical assessment.* Paris: UNESCO.

UNESCO International Co-ordination Secretariat for Literacy (Ed.) (1975). *Declaration of Persepolis. International Symposium for Literacy, Persepolis, 3–8 September 1975*. Paris: UNESCO.

UNESCO (Ed.) (1990). *Compendium of statistics on illiteracy*. UNESCO Statistical Reports and Studies, 31. Paris: UNESCO Office of Statistics.

UNESCO (1997). 50 Years of education. http://www.unesco.org/education/educprog/ 50y/ brochure/ 1.htm.

Wagner, D. (2000). Adult literacy: A Herculean task. *UNESCO Sources, 122*, 13–14.

Wagner, D. A. (1993). *Literacy, culture, and development: Becoming literate in Morocco*. Cambridge: Cambridge University Press.

Wagner, D. A. (1995). Literacy and development: Rationales, myths, innovations, and future directions. *International Journal of Educational Development, 15*(4), 341–362.

Winterowd, W. R. (1989). *The Culture and politics of literacy*. Oxford: Oxford University Press.

World Conference on Education For All. (1990). *Final report*. New York: UNICEF.

SECTION 5

Workplace Learning

Section Editor: David Livingstone

43

THE CHANGING NATURE OF EMPLOYMENT AND ADULT LEARNING POLICIES: UNLOCKING CREATIVE FORCES

Paul Bélanger
UQAM/CIRDEP, Canada

The driving social forces operating in the emergence of work related adult learning policies could not be fully understood without referring to the ambiguous changes taking place in the nature of employment and at workplace. In late modernity, the work context has been gradually but profoundly transformed by strong underlying trends, almost fleeting micro-changes, operating over decades. This has led to an increase and a transformation of adults' aspirations and social demand for learning throughout their life.

After describing, in the first section, how the transition toward reflexive production is fuelling advances in adult learning participation and policies, we will re-examine, in different and broader terms, the requirement of productivity, often referred as the main economic factors behind the rise in demand for learning. This reassessment will help us, in a third section, to state some key issues in current work-related adult learning policies and underline the meaning of these changes for unlocking creative forces in all sectors of activity.[1]

The Economic Changes Behind the Rise in Learning Demand

Demand for adult learning tends, in public discourses, to be recognised mainly in relation to the requirements of economic productivity and changes in ways to produce, which call for an ongoing development of skills and capacities of adult populations (Bélanger & Federighi, 2000). The last decade has seen an upsurge in governmental discourses on competition and ways to curb unemployment, tied to the need to raise skills levels and adopt adult learning policies, a trend strongly supported by OECD (1996, 1999; OECD-CERI, 1992, 1995). Over this period, we have seen, in "post-industrial" countries, a proliferation of national and international reports and conferences on adult learning and the continuing development of human resources.[2] By the end of the century, politicians and business leaders alike had integrated the "learning solution" into their

International Handbook of Educational Policy, 815–827
Nina Bascia, Alister Cumming, Amanda Datnow, Kenneth Leithwood and David Livingstone (Eds.)
© 2005 *Springer. Printed in Great Britain.*

analysis of the work crisis. It is now standard, in any discussion of economic globalisation and of new technologies integration towards productivity increase to include continuous skill development scheme. In Great Britain, this was the subject of a series of reports and policy statements by the Manpower Services Commission and later by the Department for Education and Skills.[3] Their argument is a refusal to invest in lifelong learning can hold back economic growth. This same plea can be found in 1994 in Australia[4] where the then Prime Minister stated publicly that, to compete and prosper, his country needed to harness all its resources and most importantly the talent and energy of the adult population.

In the United States, the reports *A Nation at Risk* (National Commission on Excellence in Education, 1983) and *Work Force 2000* (Hudson Institute, 1987), have established similar link between development of human resources and international competition. In *The Work of Nations*, Robert Reich (1991), the former US Secretary of Labour, stated that the main strengths of his country on the eve of the 21st century were the abilities and skills of its people, and that this strategic resource must become a top priority.[5] We could also mention reports from Canada,[6] Finland[7] and Norway,[8] as well as, in 2002, the new *Québec Government Policy on Adult Education and Continuing Education and Training* (Québec, 2002). All of these reports emphasise that it is impossible to meet the challenge of regional economic integration without developing continuing education and adopting active policy towards the labour market.

Similarly in 1993, the Commission of the European Communities published a white paper[9] stating that, for growth and competitiveness, education and particularly work-related adult learning are so central that they should be deemed a "catalyst for changing society". Since that date, this Commission has held five conferences on adult education[10] emphasising each time "the need to give all adults the opportunity to improve their skills throughout life". The same argument articulated around the concept of *learning society* was recalled and publicized by the European Commission (EC, 2001), through its famous *Memorandum on lifelong learning*.

A spotlight has then been thrown in many countries and in intergovernmental networks (see also OECD-CERI 1995) on the need for an intra-generational rise in skills and capacities. Indeed, schooling for young people, alone, will not be able to develop the capabilities of "working" populations quickly enough, since most of those who will be adults in the next two decades have already completed their initial education. I argue that important changes in mode of production, spurred by economic globalisation, are acting as a catalyst of such trends: competition in expanded markets is exerting additional pressure that accelerates changes in the mode of production, creating, in many sectors, a general demand a higher level of skills and more comprehensive basic competencies (Bélanger & Valvidielso, 1997; Statistics Canada, 2002).

The current transformation of adult learning policies is a much more complex and ambiguous process than a repeated linear adjustment to recurrent technical changes in production. The shift in the articulation between mode of production and competency requirement carries many contradictions. First, rise in skills requirements is not a widespread tendency, but rather a trend already dominant in certain leading sectors and indicative of future developments in others. Second, this observation does not negate the existence of opposite situations where the introduction of new technology tends to lower skills levels (Braverman, 1974; Aronowitz & DiFazzio, 1994). Third, job enrichment tends to remain proportional to position in occupational hierarchy. Fourth, this rise in learning demand is definitely linked to the jobs crisis and thus to the segmentation of the labour market and the structurally uneven general pattern of adult education participation today.

The response from the industry to the growing competition on world market can lead to opposite solutions: external or internal flexibility. External flexibility is based on breaking down production activities into malleable sub-contractible units and on using "lay out – lay in" practices to produce rapid shift in places, techniques and types of production. Internal flexibilisation, on the contrary, puts emphasis on "dynamic flexibility". At micro levels, it centers on expanding learning programmes, negotiating alternatives and creating space for internal initiative in communities of practice. At macro level, it triggers active labour market policies. The required flexibility is seeked not by reinforcing the lay-off arbitrary power of management and, thus, by weakening the right to work, but by supporting, among the personnel, a flexibility of specialisation and the continuous development of employees' hard and soft skills.

This trend towards internal flexibility of production (Piore & Sabel, 1984; Mathews, 1989; Lash & Urry, 1994) is at odds with repetitive work systems of certain industries precisely because it requires more initiative and autonomous competence. In the service sector (Bernier, 1990), the introduction of new technologies and different work arrangements is also introducing more flexibility into the former Taylorist breakdown of tasks between execution and design, leading to multitask job descriptions. In these new information intensive and interactive environments, work has become more abstract, more complex and more "intellectual". It requires new abilities to manage information and an aptitude for interpersonal communication and problem-solving. A sale-person, for example, in retail stores, becomes more of an adviser. Because of digitalisation of his work post increasing the capacity to alter rapidly the fabricating procedures, an operator's activity becomes more multifaceted and the skills required more comprehensive.

The shift in the articulation between modes of production and skill development towards learning-intensive economies carry a further contradiction. It cannot ignore victims of "rationalisation policies" who have lost their jobs due to corporate restructuring. In many countries, even at periods when unemployment goes beyond 8%, the main political and economic discourses promoting lifelong learning still tends to be based on un-nuanced assertion of the twin dogmas, in the current liberal economic context, of full employment combined with unlimited economic growth. The accelerated transformation of production and the predominant "external" mode of managing flexibility, by exploiting, at the global level, the comparative benefits of national labour markets, are leading to a new national, regional and international division of labour and, consequently, to uneven developments in lifelong learning, both nationally and internationally. Economic globalisation, at the same time, is shattering long-established employer-trade union compromises and labour – capital agreement on which economic upturns used to rely. Nevertheless, the most significant social force at work in the current transformation of adult learning policies is, probably, the sharpening contradiction between the production activity and the producer-subject, the actor.

The Social Meanings of the New Requirement of Productivity

The need to avoid the dead-end of Taylorism and have more competent and autonomous staff in the most dynamic economic fields has given rise not only to a real boom, but also to significant shift in learning demand. There is a proliferation of programmes to change enterprises into "learning organisations" (Watkins & Marsick, 1993, Senge, 1990, Wenger, 1998) and adapt organisational structures to "organisational learning" (Cohen & Sproull, 1995). This new reflexive economy (Beck, Giddens & Lash, 1994) not only increases demand for learning, but also tends to modify its character. In the post-Fordist context, work-related learning can no longer be narrowly conceived as a recurrent updating of skills where each technical change leads repeatedly to short-term skill adjustments of operator. This linear Taylorist conception of adult training is outdated in that it reflects and maintains the culture of repetitive piecework based on fragmented specialisation, on sharp social division of labour between execution and conception roles and on recurrent training locking the producing subject into a static definition of his assigned tasks and moulding him to a fixed prescribed definition of his job. Reflexive production demands progressing modes of learning that take into account the inevitable gap between prescribed and real work and task (Teiger, 1993), and refers to the practical knowledge and consciousness individuals use to work out this tension, as well as to the individual and collective intelligence at work in the informal and regulated negotiation of this gap (Dejours, 1993; Brown and Lauder, 2001).

The new emphasis on productivity in public discourses is, indeed, ambiguous, as it simultaneously imparts new meanings and undermines old ones. For example, producing means also taking an active part in production, it means working with others and developing one's capacity through inter-learning in "communities of practice". It also involves influencing production modes and processes, by raising questions and proposing improvements, and thus transforming practical know-how. Through theses processes, the producing subject strives to express himself (De Bandt, Dejours, & Dubar, 1995: Vol. 7, pp. 199–120).

The critique of productivism seeing "economic growth as an end in itself" could prompt a rejection of the very notion of productivity. The notion of carrying out "productively" the production of goods and services is not necessarily linked to the ideology of productivism and economism (Giddens, 1994:

pp. 178, 247–248). This leads us to reconstruct a synthetic vision of the producer and the citizen,[11] and a dialectical view of productive and creative activity. The producer is a subject. He or she reacts to production, observes the problems involved and has to deal with them. The point is, even in repetitive work context, where the intelligence of workers is not recognized, their ingenuity and inventiveness are always at work.

In short, the recent "knowledge-intensive" production tends to develop environments that, although obviously "knowledge-intensive", are also "actor-intensive". Reflexive production creates context potentially conducive to the empowerment and liberation of the actor and, I would add, of the learning actors (Lash & Urry, 1994: p. 119). It requires the individual to be able to acquire and apply knowledge and expertise, and, wherever necessary, to change practical methods. It demands an aptitude for handling written information and communications and an ability to make use of collective knowledge and build on the experience acquired by members of a work team (Brown & Lauder, 2001). The reflexive modernisation sociologists, including Ulrich Beck (1992, 1994, 1999), Anthony Giddens (1990, 1994), Scott Lash and John Urry (1994), provide a more in-depth understanding of the above mentioned contradictions and the significance of this gradual freeing of the actor from the grip of social structures.

This trend can be witnessed in the informal economy, although in a different perspective. Volunteer work, household and caring work (documented in this book by Schugurensky and Eichler) are part of this ignored economy. Production in urban environments outside the "modern" or formal sector (ILO 1991, pp. 42–45), as well as unpaid crafts and agricultural activities, belong also to today's domestic economies; this parallel economy has become important means of survival for many people (Singh, 1998). In France, income from "self-production" is reaching, according to some observers, a level of 56% to 60% of gross domestic product (Sue, 1994, p. 74), a large share of which is produced by voluntary groups.

These individual and collective activities of the informal economy are seldom recognized, either for their contribution to the overall social demand for learning throughout life, or as critical space for subjects to *produce* themselves, to create their "multifaceted self". These efforts to develop an economy of "solidarity", in response to the failure of the late-modern economy to create "primary labour market" jobs, are also undermining old paradigms. For example, the labour sociologist Claus Offe writes about the emergence of production circles and trade co-ops that produce goods and services outside monetary circuits, based on a barter economy. On their own, these micro-strategies do not constitute a full alternative. However, they are questioning the way work is organised today, offering mobilizing "utopias". In doing so, they expose a key contradiction. Given their current structure and orientation, the formal economies cannot ensure full employment and above all cannot bring into play the productive energy and potential activity of all those who seek to work and take part in the economy (Offe & Heinze, 1992, p. 216).

The trend toward reflexive society is not limited to the economic domain. The steady and sustained advances of initial schooling for young people are slowly transforming the cultural aspirations of today's adults both in their social and private life and at work. Life milestones are desynchronised; bases for identity are changing and spatial mobility is increasing. Women are offering different cultural models, creating alternative life-courses, breaking with traditional life-cycle scenarios as well as with gender interaction patterns at work. Men and women, free from conventional biographical landmarks, now face a multitude of unexpected crossroads. They can live out the traditional life stories previously expected of them. All these cross-bordering processes and uncertainties are giving rise to "life choices" that are less predetermined.

Scientific absolutes are being challenged as well. Popular Knowledge and customs and non-institutional practices are no longer rejected readily as mystical or obscure. Prescribed models and customary linear pathways are being questioned at many levels, leading to greater individualisation. Faced with a rising number of increasingly fragmented models and reference points, many individuals have no choice but constantly negotiate and construct their own biography. A key characteristic of reflexive societies is precisely this individualisation. Life courses resemble more an open sea navigation than a train railway. Daily observation of different scenarios embedded in various life's circumstances is opening new pathways (Beck & Beck-Gernsheim, 1990, 1994). Gradual, but sustained reductions in the working week and longer life expectancies in most post-industrial countries are also creating new spaces and time where autonomous non-market activities are becoming sites for liberating productive forces (Piotte, 1990, p. 188f.). In aging societies, a new young-old generation is discovering rooms for the pursuit of creativity and productivity beyond the stricter context of "paid production" (Guillemard, 1995). The very idea of linear and uninterrupted progress is being challenged. Techno-industrial centres are generating environmental hazards that they are unable to control and that eventually call into question the very economic models on which they are based (Beck, 1992). An end to a general absolute belief in the magic touch of scientific and technological "quick-fix" is fuelling scientific doubt and pushing many subjects toward greater intellectual independence. Berman's (1982) prescient analysis of this emergence of a society of incertitude recalls Marx's old phrase: "All that is solid melts into air".[12]

We may very well reach a turning point in late modernity. Strong underlying trends working over decades and micro-changes, at work and outside work, are affecting profoundly the work and out-of-work contexts. A general feeling of malaise and disorientation is pervading the beginning of the 21st century in the world of work and beyond. The last century, which began with unshakeable faith in scientific progress and industrial growth, has ended amidst uncertainty about the future, triggered by the questioning of both the mode of production and the traditional rigid life patterns. We can now see potential for a rediscovery of the actors who have been stigmatized in managerial and marketing discourses as human resources and consumer pockets, in short as passive factors.

All of this is leading to a new historical *momentum* or at least a new historical opportunity. Actors' capacities for action and the fuller development of productive and creative forces take on new recognized economic importance. In this environment, the subject is rediscovered, competent and active participation is demanded and ambiguity and reflexivity are penetrating every field of activity and opening new spaces. Interestingly, our society of incertitude contributes to the "return of the actors" (Touraine, 1984). A key idea, in this new reflexive context of late modernity, is that productivity could very well be subverted by productivism, but, also, that emancipation of the subjects could find spaces and contradictions to move efficiently towards empowerment.

The situation echoes, to some extent, the 19th century, when entrepreneurs recruited extensively from traditional rural society and thus took the unintended risk of liberating the productive forces much beyond short term necessity. The demand for new productive forces is somewhat as important as then. In order to strengthen capacity to produce with flexibility and "for more and more customized products," this time the neo-liberal executives have to enhance the flexible specialisation of their personnel and mobilize the collective intelligence at work in order to reinforce the capacity of organisation to solve its daily problems and meet the new economic challenges. This needed unlocking of the productive forces could not stop at the immediate economic requirement of current corporate managers looking for new expertise, more autonomous manipulation of new tools and capacity to face unforeseen problems. Thus, unintendedly, they are creating conditions for possible much larger empowerment processes, to increase the capacity of subjects to act much beyond the expected immediate increase of productivity. A situation similar to the entrepreneurs of the 19th Century calling for the regrouping of working forces in the new industrial towns. In both cases, the risk associated with the economic demand goes much further. In both cases, unattended social consequences (Giddens, 1984) would surface.

Needed to say, structural inequalities of a now more reflexive modernisation continue to have an impact. In this sense, late modernity is more reflexive in some social and economic sectors than in others. Corporations too often agree to disrupt the historical "give and take" between capital and labour, and find short-term solutions in controlling "human resources" through relocation of production and external flexibility.

Still, a new dynamic is being born through the requirement and recognition of the on-going self-learning of people at work, as well as by a gradual freeing of capacity of initiative in social participation and in intimate life.

This transition towards a "world risk society" (Beck, 1999) or "reflexive modernisation" (Beck, Giddens, & Lash, 1994) gives its full meaning to the recent boom in the social demand for adult learning and the current push for its redefinition.

Adult Learning Policies: The New Issues

Such a demand to increase capacity and possibilities to act more autonomously, to continuously develop human potential and increase competencies, is transforming the debate and societal negotiation on new adult and lifelong learning policies and programmes. Until now, adult learning policies and programs tended to remedial education logic, referring to knowledge updating, recurrent adaptation of the labour force, periodic fixing of knowledge gaps. In the current context, political and economic forces must take the risk of relying more and more on the actors and their creative participation. We are coming to a point where all the new daily necessities such as the act of learning, questioning, redefining and solving problems as well as of taking initiatives, could disrupt traditional *durkheimian* relations between education and work, and between education and society.

The threat of paradigm transformation in adult learning policy and practices is very real. This new ambiguity is unfettering the actors. This is why we have chosen to entitle this chapter: *The Changing Nature of Employment and Adult Learning Policies: Unlocking Creative Forces.* The economic need for a work force that is capable of handling coded information, of operating new digital machinery, of working in interactive small group and of being consulted about production techniques and methods, is leading to a type of informal and organized learning as well as to an individualisation that is very different from the linear adaptation to changes in job positions or job specifications typical of the first modernisation (Lash in Beck, Giddens, & Lash, 1994, p. 113).

The logic of adaptive socialisation typical of "simple modernisation", still prevailing in the current broad gamut of adult learning policies, becomes outmoded! It is not only the expert but also the "secular" and the "floor" employees who are obliged to "put their brains to work," to continually interpret new knowledge, technical information and expertise, to test these through a daily routine of trial-and-error, and to make, on the spot, the best possible decisions (Giddens, 1994, p. 6f.); we are discovering the strategic contribution of informal individual and collective learning practices (Livingston, 1999).

This active participation and, consequently, new reflexive orientation in the development of skills and knowledge does not stop at the door step of industry. "Reflexive society" demands also a higher level of communication abilities and polyvalent qualifications from its citizens, and better synergy among diverse forms and practices of lifelong learning. In a world of intense social reflexivity, democratisation of formal democracy requires active and creative participation of citizens (Giddens, 1994, pp. 7–10). We have documented, through 122 cases in 23 countries (Bélanger & Federighi, 2000), how many recent adult learning policies and programs go much beyond the sole domain of the formal economy and, in many areas, tend to include objectives and element related to the enhancement of adult populations' capacities for initiative, even if this trend is highly uneven and counteracted in various ways.

This is why, instead of opposing the economic demand for intensive learning enterprises and for qualification enhancement of workers in order to raise productivity, some popular education groups and adult learning advocacy networks are piggybacking on the contradictory nature of this work-oriented policy trend, however selective and ambiguous it still is (ICEA, 2001). The programme for the development of human potential in the work place is being taken at its word and pushed further to be made available to everyone in every area of life. This call for the intelligence and creativity of people at work is now extended to all domains: empowering women, improving health conditions, mastering new technology in daily life, taking up environmental matters, creating space for inter-personal dialogue about tolerance and lifestyles, learning second languages and teaching immigrants the first language, and helping senior citizens become more active and autonomous. The efforts to obtain more resources for popular education in South Africa, Spain and Québec, the creative strategies of European non governmental organisations to finance their popular education activities though a panoply of ministerial departments (Bélanger, Bochynek, & Farr, 1999) and the global movement of the annual *Adult Learners Week*, as new practices for the expression and mobilisation of the full social demand for adult learning[13] are good examples of this new trend.

The prevalence of massive layoffs and relocation of factories on which the knowledge-intensive economy built itself through easy use of external flexibility, should not blind us to the conditions it creates for possible emancipatory changes. The emphasis on competencies and empowerment, however segmented, leads to and forms part of a broader dynamic involving the initiative and learning intensive participation of populations, not only in the formal sector of the economy, but also at its boundaries and much beyond. It is increasingly clear that development of the potential for action and communication is cumulative. The acquired capacities to think create and produce fuse over time and transcend spheres of activity and disciplinary boundaries. Adult learning policies, too often confined to technical adaptation and focused on short-term adjustments, cannot prevent the learning demand from being defined ever more sweepingly. The growing investment in education and training in industry does not become pointless just because some corporations are showing less interest in training a more autonomous workforce. The tendency of health care ministries to restrict their effort to therapeutic strategies and neglect health promotion and education could not halt the ongoing profound trend toward public discussion of epidemiological research reports, raise of popular interest for self-learning on health and health conditions. A substantial shift is slowly taking place from curative to preventive, from prophylactic prevention to interactive and education prevention practices.[14]

The reinforcement of various learning experiences in people's educational biographies and transfer of learning and the synergy between the various agents of the fragmented world of adult learning, as well as the reproduction of inequalities in both learning life course and in the current organisation of education provision are central to changing the dynamics of adult learning policy-making. This is likely to lead to a new generation of legislation and programmes, which have already started to take shape in recent policies previously cited as well as, more recently, at the European Commission.[15] Paradoxically, the chaotic development and proliferation of adult learning opportunities in all areas of activities help find a new way for states to regulate and stimulate these emerging trends and regulate them toward a more sustainable and equitable learning societies.

We can already witness emerging patterns of new post-traditional multi-sectorial and multi-ministerial ways to enhance these potential synergies. A look at the increasing number of ministries and public institutions, local authorities and inter or supra governmental organisations involved in various forms of adult learning speaks to the importance of the new inter-sectorial and inter-ministerial communication and linkage strategies that are required on the adult learning scene. In many countries, this process gives rise to new umbrella mechanisms, continuing education council or inter-ministerial adult learning advisory board.[16]

Of course, the paradigm change toward reflexive societies, which has fuelled advances in adult learning, is still blocked in many areas: in the "parking" function of many training programmes imposed on unemployed participants where the training solution is cut off from active employment strategies, in small enterprises and at the bottom of the occupational hierarchy where we observe lower participation in organized learning activities (Dubar 1991; Bélanger & Valdivielso, 1997). The current block comes also from the fact that corporate financial support for education and training goes to regular staff, which tends in majority to be male, that lifelong learning is emerging just when lifelong jobs are disappearing. It comes in addition from hyper-*vocationalisation* of adult learning, uneven development of the different domains of adult learning, and from learning diagnosis based solely on prescribed job requirement ignoring the worker, his informal learning practices and the unpredicted and changing nature of the tasks he undertakes.

Conclusion

The central issue of adult learning policies should not be solely its rapid growth in some sectors at the expense of others. This trend, albeit uneven, helps transform the dynamics. The issue at stake is the limited opportunity for people at work to express their genuine and expanded demand for lifelong learning and lack of space to resist one-dimensional training opportunities completely uprooted from their changing context and their experience (see Lave & Wenger, 1991; Livingstone, 1999). The central issue is the contradiction between the social demand arising from reflexive modernisation and the formal educational responses that often remain reductionist, adaptive and unmediated by the actors and their representatives. This is of critical importance across all adult learning activities, work or non work related.

The new social demand for adult learning is the result of diffuse negotiation between, on the one hand, the external demand on employees and citizens to expand their competencies and capacities for initiative and, on the other, the subjects' aspirations to be recognised as subject, to make individual choices. Here lays a powerful contradiction: to get employees with increased capacity to act autonomously, the corporate management have to take the risk of facilitating the emergence of a reflexive active population, the risk of creating spaces for discovery of meaning by the subject. The demand on individuals to take initiative fuels their search for identity, create environments wherein productive creativity and social creativity can interact (Sainsaulieu, 1995). The rejection of repetitive tasks is not only a productivity and economic issue, it is a question of mental health,[17] and it is definitively a cultural and political issue.

In this chapter, we have tried to show how the dynamics of contemporary reflexive society help understand not only the current proliferation of adult learning policies, but also the necessary shift in the orientation of these policies. Although, this trend stands out most visibly in the formal economy, it is also happening in informal economy and in an increasing number of other fields, sharpening and transforming the dynamics of adult learning policies. For the moment this dynamic tends to be dealt with in discourse on competition and productivity, but this, too, is contradictory. Spurred on by the current deadlock in the world of work, we are only beginning to acknowledge the significance and full extent of the rising movement to unlock people's productive and creative forces.

Notes

1. The data, on which this chapter is based, have been collected through a transnational analysis of adult learning policies, done between 1995 and 2000 in twenty-three countries. The reader will find references related to specific countries in the already published book and article (Bélanger & Federighi, 2000, Haddad 1996).
2. See Belanger &Federighi, op. cit., chapter 1.
3. See bibliography: United Kingdom, 1988, 1990, 1998. In 2002, a new policy was adopted ("Skills Alliance") and the name of the DFEE has been changed to DFES (Department for Education and Skills).
4. See bibliography: Australia 1994.
5. See bibliography: Commission for a Nation of learners, 1983, Hudson Institute, 1987.
6. Canada, 1992, *Roads to Competency.*
7. Finland, 1998, *The Joy of Learning.*
8. Norway, 1998, *New Competence.*
9. CEC, 1993, *Growth, Competitiveness, Employment – The Challenges and Ways Forward into the 21st Century.* Brussels.
10. Athens in June 1994, Dresden in November 1994, Madrid in November 1995, Florence in May 1996 and Manchester in May 1998
11. See the still relevant introduction by Jean-Paul Sartre to the first issue of *Les Temps Modernes* in 1945.
12. The analysis of Marshall Berman (1982) of literary developments in the 19th century forecasts this crisis of modernity. By examining three authors' initial apprehensions and "literary intuitions" about the first traumas of modernisation of that period, he was able to anticipate the heuristic context today and the possibilities of new dialectics.
13. See: http://WWW. unesco.org/education/uie/internationalALW/
http://WWW.adultlearnersweek.org/
http//WWW.niace.org.uk/ALW/
14. http://www.who.int/health_topics/health_promotion/en/. See also in CONFINTEA V Report (UNESCO, 1997), the section of the *Declaration* and the *Agenda for the Future* on health adult learning.
15. *European Memorandum on Lifelong Learning,* see http://europa.eu.int/comm/education/policies/lll/life/index_en.html
16. Botswana, China, Japan and Catalonia in Spain. See Belanger & Federighi, 2000, chapter 9.
17. Work psychiatrists and ergonomists have showed how the refusal to acknowledge the intellectual involvement of workers in repetitive work is hindering mental health (De Bandt, Dejours and Dubar 1995).

References

Aronowitz, S., & Di Fazzio, W. (1994). *The Jobless Future: Sci-Tech and the Dogma of Work.* Minneapolis, MN: University of Minnesota Press.

Australia, 1994, *Working Nation: Policies and Programs*", Canberra: Commonwealth of Australia, Prime ministerial Statement to the House of Representatives.

Beck, U. (1992). *Risk society: Towards a new modernity.* Cambridge: Polity Press.

Beck, U. (1994). *Ecological politics in an age of risk.* Cambridge: Polity Press.

Beck, U. (1999). *World risk society,* London: Sage.

Beck, U., & Beck-Gernsheim, E. (Eds.) (1990). *Das ganz normale Chaos der Liebe.* Frankfurt/Main: Suhrkamp.

Beck, U., & Beck-Gernsheim, E. (Ed.) (1994). *Riskante Freiheiten. Individualisierung in modernen Gesellschaften.* Frankfurt/Main: Suhrkamp.

Beck, U., Giddens, A., & Lash, G. (1994). *Reflexive modernization.* Cambridge: Polity Press.

Bélanger, P., Bochynek, B., & Farr, K. O., (1999). *The financing of adult learning in civil society: A European exploratory study.* Hamburg: UNESCO Institute for Education.

Bélanger, P., & Federighi, P. (2000). *Unlocking people's creative Forces: A transnational study of adult learning policies.* Hamburg: UNESCO Institute for Education.

Bélanger, P., & Valdivielso, S. (Eds.) (1997). *The emergence of learning societies: Who participates in adult learning?* Oxford and New York: Pergamon.

Berman, M. (1982). *All that is solid melts into air.* New York: Verso.

Bernier, C. (1990). *Le travail en mutation.* Montréal: Saint-Martin.

Braverman, H. (1974). *Labor and monopoly capital. The degradation of work in the Twentieth Century.* London and New York: Monthly Review Press.

Brown, P., & H. Lauder. (2001). *Capitalism and social progress: The future of society in a global economy.* New York: Palgrave.

Cohen, M. D., & Sproull, L. S. (Eds.) (1995). *Organizational learning.* Thousand Oaks, London, and New Delhi: Sage.

Economic Council of Canada (1992). *Roads to competency.* Ottawa.

Commission of a Nation of Learners (1997). *A nation learning.* Washington.

De Bandt, S., Dejours, C., & Dubar, C. (1995). *La France malade du travail.* Paris: Fayard.

Dejours, C. (1993). *Travail: Usure mentale. Essai de psychopathologie du travail* (nouvelle édition). Paris: Centurion.

Department of Employment (1998). *Employment in the 1990s.* London: HMSO.

Department of Employment (1990). *Education and Training for the 21st Century.* London: HMSO.

Department of Employment and Education (1998). *The Learning Age.* London.

Doray, P., & Arrowsmith S. (1997). Patterns of participation in adult education: Cross national comparisons. In P. Bélanger & A. Tuijnman (Eds.), *New patterns of adult learning: A six country comparative study.* London: Pergamon.

Dubar, C. (1991). *La socialisation. Construction des identités sociales et professionnelles.* Paris: Armand Colin.

European Commission. (1993). *Growth, competitiveness, employment – The challenges and ways forward into the 21st Century.* Brussels: EC.

European Commission (2001). *Memorandum on lifelong learning.* Brussels: European Commission.

Commission Report to the Government of Finland (1999). *The joy of learning.* Helsinsky.

Giddens, A. (1990). *The consequences of modernity.* Cambridge: Polity Press.

Giddens, A. (1994). *Beyond left and right.* Cambridge: Polity Press.

Guillemard, A. M. (1995). Le cycle de vie en mutation. In F. Dubet & M. Wieviorka (Eds.), *Penser le sujet.* Paris: Fayard.

Haddad, S. (Ed.) (1996) Adult education – The legislative and policy environment. In *International Review of Education* (special issue), *42,* 1–3.

Hudson Institute. (1987). *Work force 2000.* Indianapolis: Hudson Institute.

ICEA (2001). *Investir dans le potentiel des québécoises et québécois pour une politique d'éducation tout au long de la vie.* Montréal, Canada: ICEA.

ILO (1991). *Africa employment report*, Geneva: ILO.

Lash, S., & Urry, J. (1994). *Economics of signs and space*. Thousand Oaks, London and New Delhi: Sage.

Lave, J., & Wenger, E. (1991). *Situated learning. Legitimate peripheral participation*. Cambridge: University of Cambridge Press.

Livingstone, D. W. (1999). *The education-job gap. Underemployment or economic democracy*. Toronto: Garamond Press.

Mathews, J. (1989). *Tools of change*. Sydney: Pluto Press.

National Commission on Excellence in Education (1983). *A Nation at Risk*. Washington: National Commission on Excellence in Education.

Norway (1998). *New Competence*. Oslo: Report to the Norwegian National Assembly.

OCDE (1996). *Lifelong learning for all* (rapport). Paris: OECD.

OECD (1999). *Knowledge society and knowledge management*. Paris: OECD.

OCDE-CERI (1992). *City strategies for lifelong learning*. Paris: OECD – Center for Educational Research and Innovation.

OCDE-CERI (1995). The lifelong learner in the 1990s. In D. Atchoarena (Ed.), *Lifelong education in selected industrialized countries*. Paris: International Institute for Educational Planning, UNESCO.

Offe, K., & Heinze, R. G. (1992). *Beyond employment*. Cambridge: Polity Press.

Piore, M. J., & Sabel, C. F. (1984). *The second industrial divide: Possibilities for posterity*. New York: Basic Books.

Piotte, J. M. (1990). *Sens et politique. Pour en finir avec le grand désarroi*. Outremont/Québec: VLB.

Quebec, 2002, *Government Policy on Adult Education and Continuing Education and Training*, Québec: Ministry of Education.

Reich, R. B. (1991). *The work of nations: Preparing ourselves for 21st Century capitalism*. New York: Knopf.

Sartre, J. P. (1945). Introduction. In *Les temps modernes*, 1(1).

Sainsaulieu, R. (1995). Postface. In B. Ollivier(ed.), *L'acteur et le sujet: Vers un nouvel acteur économique* (pp. 457–464). Paris: Desclée de Brouwer.

Senge, P. M. (1990). *The fifth discipline. The art and practice of the learning organization*. New York: Doubbleday.

Singh. M. (1998). *Adult learning and the changing world of work*. Hamburg: UNESCO Institute for Education.

Statistics Canada (1995). *Literacy, economy and society*. Ottawa: Statistics Canada.

Sue, R. (1994). *Temps et ordre social*, Paris: PUF.

Touraine, A. (1984). *Le retour de l'acteur*. Paris: Arthème Fayard.

Teiger, C. (1993). L'approche ergonomique du travail humain à l'activité des hommes et des femmes au travail. In *Éducation Permanente, 116*, 71–96.

UNESCO (1997). *Declaration and Agenda for the Future, UNESCO 5th International Conference of Adult Education*. Hamburg: UNESCO Institute for Education.

Watkins, K. E., & Marsick, V. J. (1993). *Sculpting the learning organization: Lessons in the art and science of science change*. San Francisco: Jossey-Bass.

Wenger, E. (1998). *Communities of practice. Learning, meaning and identity*. Cambridge: Cambridge University press.

44

CURRENT THEORIES OF WORKPLACE LEARNING: A CRITICAL ASSESSMENT

Paul Hager

University of Technology, Sydney, Australia

This chapter provides a brief outline of selected contributions to the diverse literature on workplace learning from the last thirty years or so. It then examines a series of pertinent ongoing issues that surround this literature and the understanding of workplace learning. Out of this discussion a number of criteria are identified that are considered salient when evaluating understandings of workplace learning. The final section applies these criteria to the categories of workplace learning theories developed in the first section. Throughout the chapter, a recurring theme is the implications of the analysis for policy.

Preliminary Framework of Key Ideas

Before beginning the tasks outlined above, a preliminary framework of key ideas will be established. This framework will underpin much of the discussion throughout the chapter. Firstly, workplace learning theories can be roughly classified in terms of two basic categories of theorising – learning as product and learning as process. Early accounts of workplace learning were strongly influenced by the learning as product view. Here the focus of learning was on learners acquiring novel attributes. More recent accounts are very much in line with the learning as process view. Here the focus is more on learners developing by actively engaging in the processes of workplaces. These two broad categories of workplace learning theories will be characterised in further detail in the next section of this chapter. Secondly, these two basic categories of learning theories fit closely with the two most influential metaphors of learning, *acquisition* and *participation*, that Sfard (1998) argues underpin much educational thought. Learning as product dovetails neatly with the acquisition metaphor, while learning as process accords with the participation metaphor. A third point concerns the links between the two basic categories of learning theories and the notions of human capital and social capital. Here the connections are more complex. As will be argued later in the chapter, it is certainly too simplistic to just align the individual learner acquiring learning as product with human capital theory and

International Handbook of Educational Policy, 829–846
Nina Bascia, Alister Cumming, Amanda Datnow, Kenneth Leithwood and David Livingstone (Eds.)
© 2005 *Springer. Printed in Great Britain.*

to contrast this with group learning as a participatory process based on social capital theory. This is so because some significant learning theories challenge the idea that learning has to be exclusively either individual or social. These theories accept that, while all learning is in some sense social, this is compatible with some instances of learning being learning by individuals, and other instances of learning occurring at the communal level. So at least some of the social learning theories to be discussed later include a place for learning by individuals that is different from pure communal learning. Thus, it is a plausible initial claim that both individual and social learning are different but important dimensions of workplace learning.

As well as this group of initial ideas about learning that will be important for the overall discussion of this chapter, a major overarching theme is: What does it all mean for policy? A central claim of the chapter is that government policies that impact significantly on learning at work commonly treat learning as a product, i.e. as the acquisition of discrete items of knowledge or skill. Thus, as examples discussed below will illustrate, policy makers tend to be anchored firmly in the workplace learning as product view, whereas the most fruitful theoretical developments have long since passed over to the learning as process view. Hence there is often a worrying mismatch between the best available understandings of workplace learning and the assumptions of policies and policy makers. The result is that much policy making actually hinders attempts to develop satisfactory understandings of learning at work.

It should be noted that learning at work, as such, is seldom the central focus of policy. Rather, the typical situation is that policies that are targeted at something else include learning at work within their scope. In the process, learning at work is usually assumed to be, in an uncritical and 'common sense' way, simply the acquisition of discrete items of knowledge and skill. Here are some examples. As nations have sought to respond to globalisation by better recognising and expanding the skills profiles of their labour force, policies to accredit current competence, however it has been attained, have become common. So we have policies that aim to provide big picture detail of national skills attainment. Learning at work is included in these policies as an important, and hitherto underrated, source of skills. However, in the process, the richness and complexity of learning at work is typically reduced to isolated, discrete competencies from a checklist. Work performance is broken down into a series of decontextualised atomic elements or competencies, which novice workers are thought of as needing to gain one by one. It is simply assumed that learning at work is just another option for the serial acquisition of such items. Thus, the policy makers are firmly anchored in learning as product assumptions, at the same time as the best available theoretical accounts suggest that learning at work is not like this at all.

In related policy initiatives, many nations have sought to improve formal vocational education and training (VET) courses by connecting them more closely with workplace practice. However, the vehicles for achieving this desirable integration are usually competence statements, which aim to provide detailed descriptions of proficient work performance. Once again, the typical reality is that they reduce work performance to a series of decontextualised atomic elements – products that learners are supposed to acquire from a planned mixture of off- and on-the-job learning and assessment activities. Such strategies appeal to policy makers as implementing common sense and practical fusions of formal learning with learning at work. Trouble is that they do not accord very well with our the best available understandings of learning at work. Similar criticisms apply to policies adopted by most nations on generic skills (core or basic skills). Putative generic skills, such as communication and problem solving, are presented as discrete, decontextualised elements that, once acquired, can simply be transferred by learners to diverse situations. Certainly, in policy literature emanating from employer groups, this central learning as product assumption is endemic. Yet as the best available theoretical accounts of learning at work suggest, the contextuality of actual work processes severely curtails naïve expectations of unproblematic generic transfer.

In each of these examples, learning at work was not the main focus of the policy initiative. Rather the policies sought to improve something else by connecting it with learning at work. In each case, learning at work was taken to be an unquestioned good, one whose lustre would rub off onto the things that the policies aimed to fix. It is doubly unfortunate, then, that policy makers are still firmly tied to the workplace learning as product view, whereas, as this chapter will demonstrate, contemporary learning theory has long since worked with the learning as process view.

Historical Perspective on Contending Theories

From about the 1970s onwards there has been a continuously growing literature that seeks to understand and improve the learning that occurs in workplaces. This literature falls into two broad categories. This section provides an overview of this literature and its categories. Some of the earliest theorising of workplace learning in this period comes from the fields of organisational psychology and management theory. Key texts are Argyris and Schön (1974, 1978), Schön (1983, 1987), and Marsick and Watkins (1990). The work of Argyris and Schön is best known for some influential distinctions and concepts. They famously distinguished single loop learning (in which the learner exhibits reactive behaviour in order to adapt to changing circumstances) from double loop learning (in which the learner reflectively amends or adds to previous learning in selecting a suitable course of action to deal with a challenging situation). They also pointed out that a worker's theory-in-use (inferred from what they actually do in given circumstances), often differs radically from their espoused theory (the theory that they claim their actions exemplify). From this, Argyris in particular has developed influential work on theories in action. Equally influential has been Schön's subsequent work (1983, 1987) on the 'reflective practitioner'. His rejection of technical rationality and its assumptions has been widely noted and discussed. (Technical rationality is the view that professional practice consists essentially in practitioners using standard disciplinary knowledge to analyse and solve the work problems that their daily practice throws up). In its place Schön (1983) put forward an alternative epistemology of professional workplace performance, albeit one that still focuses on the rational, cognitive aspects of performance. Its central notion is "reflective practitice". The "reflective practitioner" is one who engages in "knowing-in-action" and "reflecting-in-action". For Schön, knowing-in-action is underpinned by "reflecting-in-action" or "reflecting-in-practice". These are underpinned by spontaneous episodes of practitioners "noticing", "seeing" or "feeling" features of their actions and consciously or unconsciously changing their practice for the better. For Schön, this is workplace learning.

Marsick and Watkins are workplace learning theorists who use experience and reflection as major concepts in their well known analysis of "informal learning", and its supposed sub-set "incidental learning". They also openly acknowledge their debt to Dewey (Marsick & Watkins, 1990, pp. 16–17). It is noteworthy that, for Marsick and Watkins, informal and incidental learning include such diverse notions as "learning from experience, learning by doing, continuous learning for continuous improvement, accidental learning, self-managed learning or the learning organization" (Watkins & Marsick, 1992, p. 287). In their influential 1990 book they also describe a series of "characteristics" of informal learning, as well as "conditions that delimit or enhance" it. "Defining characteristics" of informal learning, according to Marsick and Watkins (1990, pp. 15–24) include that it is "experience-based, non-routine and often tacit". Delimiters include problem framing capacity and intellectual ability. Key conditions which enhance the effectiveness of such learning are "proactivity", "critical reflectivity", and "creativity" (Marsick & Watkins, 1990, pp. 24–31). The importance of specific contextual factors (e.g., "the organisation's culture" (1990, p. 29) is also acknowledged. As Marsick and Watkins expand on the factors that they believe underpin the various defining characteristics and key conditions which they claim promote effective informal learning, they provide a fine illustration of the sheer complexity and diversity of this range of factors. Symptomatic perhaps of this complexity difficulty is the fact that seemingly by 1992 Marsick and Watkins had ceased to believe in their earlier "characteristics" vs. "conditions" distinction. Though the various characteristics and conditions are still listed as "elements. ... in theory-building" (1992, p. 293), they are no longer distinguished into these two categories.

The examples of workplace learning theories discussed so far have a range of common features:

1. They centre of individual learners
2. They focus mainly on the rational, cognitive aspects of work performance.
3. Work performance tends to be conceived as thinking or reflection followed by application of the thinking or reflection – this is especially evident in Schön's work.
4. Learning itself is taken for granted and not theorised or problematised. This means in practice that, as Elkjaer (2003) points out, they tend to

assume that workplace learning is akin to formal learning, thereby favouring the acquisition metaphor.

5. They downplay the importance of social, organisational and cultural factors in workplace learning and performance. (In stating that these factors are downplayed, it is accepted that some of the theorists mentioned above do take some account of them. For instance, Marsick and Watkins accept the importance of "organizational context" (1990, p. 210). But they do so in the limited sense that organizational context is the environment in which the individual, the unit of human capital theory, is learning informally and incidentally. As will be argued shortly, in the second main category of accounts of workplace learning, the roles of social, organisational and cultural factors in workplace learning and performance are much stronger than this).

These five common features also apply to influential work in cognitive psychology that sought to explain the development of expertise (Glaser, 1985; Tennant, 1991; Yates & Chandler, 1991). Recent work has reacted against its assumptions that expertise resides in individual rational minds that are remote from arenas of practice (see, e.g., Wertsch, 1998). Likewise, the widely influential Nonaka and Takeuchi (1995) model of knowledge creation exemplifies each of the first four of these five features. Although they claimed to be replacing Western concepts of knowledge with more profound Japanese ones, Bereiter (2002, pp. 175–176) shows convincingly that, in fact, they adhere closely to views akin to the 'folk theory' of learning as product, which will be discussed in section 3 of this chapter. The work outlined so far comprises the first main category of accounts of workplace learning, theories that are influenced by the fields of organisational and cognitive psychology and management theory.

The second main category of accounts of workplace learning broadly includes theories that recognise that workplace learning and performance are embodied phenomena; that they are significantly shaped by social, organisational and cultural factors, thereby extending beyond the individual; and that they seamlessly integrate a range of human attributes that is much wider than just rationality. In doing so, they tend to problematise or seek to re-theorise learning. As such they pose a challenge to mainstream understandings of learning. Various learning theorists such as Dewey and Vygotsky can be seen as major influences in much of this work.

Lave and Wenger (1991) have put into wide currency notions such as workplaces as 'communities of practice' and 'legitimate peripheral participation' as the social learning process that novices go through to become full members of the community of practice. Rather than viewing the learning as acquisition of discrete items, whether propositions or skills, their specifically relational account views the novice as learning how to function appropriately in a particular social, cultural and physical environment. This means that the learning ('situated learning') is something outside of the individual's head, or even body. Rather it occurs in the framework of participation, in a network of relations. As Hodkinson and

Hodkinson (2004) point out, Lave and Wenger (1991) left the key notion of community of practice rather vague, but wished it to have wide applicability as an account of learning. Seeking to remedy this, Wenger (1998) gives a tighter account of what identifies a community of practice, but at the cost of reducing the incidence of such communities. But as Hodkinson and Hodkinson (2004) note, this in turn deflates the Lave and Wenger claim to have developed a general socio-cultural account of learning.

Engestrom (1999, 2001) views workplaces as activity systems that are comprised of a range of components including items such as workplace rules, the division of labour, and mediating artifacts. Engestrom regards learning as occurring as work proceeds within such activity systems, because they continually throw up contradictions and tensions that need to be resolved. Engestrom's account of workplace learning finds places for social, organisational and cultural factors within the activity system. Once again though, it might be questioned whether all learning at work occurs from contradictions and tensions within the system. As well Engestrom posits a dialectical interplay between the learner and the activity system. To what extent is the learner a locus of learning as against the system being the locus? The learner/system locus issue remains unresolved.

Both the Lave and Wenger focus on situated learning and Engestrom's activity systems approach have stimulated a surge of recent research and conceptual innovation on learning at work (e.g., see Rainbird, Fuller and Munro 2004). For instance, Fuller and Unwin (2003, 2004) have developed a new conceptual framework, the *expansive-restrictive continuum*, for analysing the incidence and quality of workplace learning. In particular, the *expansive-restrictive continuum* aims to characterise the key features of different learning environments. It centres on two broad sets of features: those relating to organisational context and culture, and those relating to learning opportunities arising from various forms of participation in workplaces. Their framework is intended specifically to remedy deficiencies that Fuller and Unwin identify in the Lave and Wenger account of learning.

A range of other authors have put forward accounts of learning at work that incorporate main features of this second broad category of accounts of workplace learning. Billett (2001), for example, offers an account of expertise located in the dynamic activities of social practices.

> It proposes how individuals come to know and act by drawing on cognitive, sociocultural and anthropological conceptions, and through an appraisal of the ontological premises of domains of knowledge. The inter-psychological processes for developing expertise are held to be constituted reciprocally between the affordance of the social practice and how individuals act and come to know in the social practice. (p. 432)

In developing his account, Billett casts doubt on whether expertise is a capacity of an individual, locating it instead in particular domains of knowledge and social practice. In contrast, Eraut (2000) wants to retain a place for traditional individual cognitive and tacit knowledges whilst accepting that they are always deployed in a situated way. Eraut can be seen as warning that accounts of workplace learning in the second category should not jettison all of the resources of the first category. Similar remarks apply to the Beckett and Hager (2002) proposal that the development of judgment via experience of practice is a key instance of workplace learning. They argue that some of this learning can be understood at the level of the individual, but some of it is inherently at the level of the group or community of practitioners. These issues are a matter of ongoing debate.

Finally, attention should be drawn to promising work by Hodkinson and Bloomer (2002) and Hodkinson and Hodkinson (in press, 2004). While being in the sociocultural line of accounts of workplace learning, their work seeks to enrich the notion of 'community of practice' by drawing on Bourdieu's concepts of habitus, capital and field. They also stress the importance for workplace learning of individuals' previous learning biographies. This interesting conceptual work is illustrated and supported by a wide range of evidence from a variety of case studies.

Overall, then, there is a growing and diverse range of literature offering accounts of workplace learning. The above is merely a selective overview of main themes in this literature. To make further sense of these matters we need to look more closely at a series of current conceptual issues.

Current Conceptual Issues Surrounding Workplace Learning

How Best to Understand Learning?

As noted already, there is a tendency in the second broad category of theories of workplace learning to reconceptualise the notion of learning itself. The tendency is congruent with trends within the mainstream of educational theorising in which as Schoenfeld (1999) noted

> ... the very definition of learning is contested, and that assumptions that people make regarding its nature and where it takes place also vary widely.

Is the idea of a general theory of learning feasible? According to Winch "... the possibility of giving a *scientific* or even a *systematic* account of human learning is ... mistaken" (1998, p. 2). (p. 6)

His argument is that there are many and diverse cases of learning, each subject to "constraints in a variety of contexts and cultures" which precludes them from being treated in a general way (1998, p. 85). Winch is here thinking of 'contexts and cultures' in the sense of the micro level. Thus while it may be the case that, e.g., the majority of workplaces share a common macro context (e.g., part of a capitalist economy), they each have unique and particular contextual and cultural features at the micro level. Winch concludes that "... grand theories of learning ... are underpinned ... invariably ... by faulty epistemological premises" (Winch, 1998, p. 183). If Winch is correct, not only might it be a mistake to think about workplace learning in the terms that are too closely linked to learning in formal classrooms, it may also be inappropriate to think that all workplace learning is of one kind.

As suggested above, policies that impact on learning at work too often carry with them unreflective assumptions about what such learning is like. Typically, they view it as acquisition of a product of some kind. According to Bereiter (2002) this is also the common-sense or 'folk theory' of learning. This view pictures learning as 'adding more substance' to the learner, preferably as 'bite-sized' chunks. Despite the fact that the educationally sophisticated have long ago moved beyond viewing learning as a product, the pervasiveness of the common-sense or 'folk theory' of learning amongst policy makers and the public at large is still reflected in the *Oxford English Dictionary*. It defines learning as follows: 'To acquire knowledge of (a subject) or skill (an art, etc.) as a result of study, experience or teaching.' Besides clearly portraying learning as a product, the acquisition of discrete bits of substance, this definition limits learning to propositions and skills. It does not take much thought to identify vast areas of learning not covered by this definition. This definition also neatly separates knowing and doing or theory and practice.

While much educational policy and practice, including policies and practices that directly impact on the emerging interest in learning at work, are clearly rooted in the learning as product view, the educational arguments for an alternative view have been persuasive for quite some time now. This alternative view centres on viewing learning as an ongoing process. Dewey (1916) was an early seminal figure in educational thought who saw learning as a process. For Dewey, the overriding principle is that the good life for humans is one in which they live in harmony with their environment. But because the environment is in a state of continuous flux, so humans need to grow and readjust constantly to it so as to remain in harmony with it. Thus, for Dewey, education must instil the lifelong capacity to grow and to readjust constantly to the environment. Since, argued Dewey, reflective thinking as well as inquiry, democracy, problem solving, active learning, experiential learning, etc. are methods that are necessary for humans to learn to readjust effectively to the environment, these are the teaching/learning methods that must feature in education. Dewey argues that reflection is central to effective inquiry and problem solving, but this should not be seen merely in narrowly rational terms. For Dewey, reflective thinking is more holistic, incorporating social, moral and political aspects of the contexts in which it occurs. In his own lifetime, Dewey's ideas were widely noted and discussed. However they can hardly be said to have transformed educational thought, let alone practice, as the ongoing persistence of the dominant metaphor of learning as acquisition shows.

When learning is viewed primarily as a process rather than as a product different features are emphasised. Learning becomes a process that changes both the learner and the environment (with the learner being part of the environment rather than a detached spectator) (Beckett & Hager, 2002, section 7.9). This view of learning underlines its inherently relational character, including its conte-xtuality, and the pervasive influence of cultural and social factors on it. It is a holistic view in that it points to the organic, whole person nature of learning, including the importance of dispositions and abilities. As against the earlier *Oxford English Dictionary* definition of learning that reflected the common-sense idea that it is a product, Schoenfeld (1999, p. 6) offers a definition that captures the more holistic notion of learning as a process: "... coming to understand things and developing increased capacities to do what one wants or needs to do ...". Such an understanding of learning has clearly influenced many of the theories of workplace learning that earlier were placed in the second broad category. Certainly, the two most influential contemporary approaches to under-standing learning centre on viewing it as a process. Firstly, there are sociocultural theorists, such as Lave and Wenger (1991) and Wertsch (1998). Their approach is clearly focused on processes rather than entities or structures, and stresses the inseparability of the individual and the social. Secondly, there are activity theo-rists, an approach originally inspired by the work of Vygotsky and Leont'ev, and developed by Engestrom and others (e.g., Engestrom, Miettinen, & Punamaki, 1999; Engestrom, 2001). This approach produces dynamic process accounts of human activity, including learning, that emphasise its mediation by tools (understood in the broadest sense).

The importance of process considerations for understanding learning at work is further emphasised by some newer developments in educational thought. These developments have been in topics where 'learning as product' was once influential, but increasingly is being questioned. One such area is learning transfer research. Reflecting the learning as product view, it was formerly assumed that the discrete item of learning acquired in one situation would be called up intact ('transferred') to deal with a future situation. Transfer researchers viewed the institution of formal education as being underpinned by the basic assumption that transfer is a ubiquitous phenomenon. However despite increasing power of experimental techniques, transfer "seems to vanish when experimenters try to pin it down" (Schoenfeld, 1999, p. 7). As Bransford and Schwartz (1999) conclude from surveying nearly one hundred years of increasingly sophisticated research, transfer is indeed rare if it is restricted to 'replicative' transfer, which involves assumptions about the stability and replicability of what is transferred. However, they propose that we broaden the notion of 'transfer' by including an emphasis on 'preparation for future learning', the ability to learn in new environments. So the point of transfer is not replication, but further learning. So, learning transfer research has led to recent proposals to reconceptualise not just transfer but, by implication, learning. Yet, earlier in the chapter, we saw that transfer is a crucial concept in much policy that relates to learning at work. It now transpires that naïve notions of transfer that underpin much policy relating to learning at work are flawed. It is more realistic to regard past learning as a basis for further learning in new work situations. Thus learning at work is better viewed as an ongoing process than as acquisition of discrete items from a generic checklist.

Likewise, psychology generally is increasingly moving away from viewing learning as a product, together with its associated assumptions (e.g., Bruner, 1996; Bereiter, 2002). As Bereiter (2002) puts it

> ... everyday cognition makes more sense if we abandon the idea of a mind operating on stored mental content and replace it with the idea of a mind continually and automatically responding to the world and making sense of whatever befalls it. I call this the 'connectionist view of mind' ... (pp. 196–197).

According to Bereiter (1999) we need to understand learning in ways that do not involve products being stored in and retrieved from containers:

> Connectionism provides an alternative metaphor, which enables us to conceive of a mind that can act knowledgeably without containing propositions or other knowledge objects. To gain benefit from the connectionist metaphor, we must find ways to construct mentalistic accounts that do not refer to things residing, being searched for, or undergoing changes in the mind. (p. 179).

Both the connectionist view of mind and the reconceptualisation of transfer are closely linked to the second broad category of accounts of workplace learning. These developments cast further doubt on the assumptions that underpin the educational policies discussed earlier in the chapter.

This sub-section on the nature of learning has been rather lengthy because it is vital for the project of theorising workplace learning to move beyond the systematic misunderstandings of learning that have bedevilled both educational thinking and policy about learning at work. The discussion of the remaining current conceptual issues that impact on the understanding of workplace learning will be briefer, as in various ways they draw on ideas already outlined in this sub-section.

Individual Learning vs Group Learning

The common-sense understanding of learning involves the basic image of an individual human mind steadily being stocked with propositions. This implies that each individual mind can potentially recapitulate the course of human learning. Hence, on this view, in theorising learning, the individual is the appropriate unit of analysis. Thus, when there is some focus on learning processes, it is on circumstances that favour the acquisition of ideas by individual minds. In emphasising learning by minds as the most valuable form on learning, not only does the common-sense story about learning favour a mind/body dualism, it makes learning an essentially solitary process, an individualistic even narcissistic process, where the learner becomes a spectator aloof from the world.

So it is a virtually universal assumption for the common-sense story about learning, reflected in much educational policy, that the individual is the correct unit of analysis. This discounts the possibility, indeed the likelihood, of communal learning, e.g. learning in workplaces by teams and organisations that may not be reducible to learning by individuals. So the assumption that learning is centred on individuals creates the problem of accounting for collective knowledge (Toulmin, 1999, p. 55). The second main category of accounts of workplace learning, outlined earlier, escapes this deficiency by broadly recognising that there are knowledge and skills that reside in shared practices rather than in individuals. However, as noted at the start of the chapter, we should be wary of uncritically adopting a mutually exclusive dualism here. Social accounts of learning, those that comprise the second category, might go too far if they assume that all learning is to be explained by its inherently communal character. A plausible theoretical position, one that should not be dismissed too hastily, views both individual and communal learning as important categories for understanding learning at work. Toulmin, for one, takes this possibility seriously. In arguing that understandings of learning centred on the individuality assumption offer no "convincing account of the relationship between 'knowledge' as the possession of individuals and 'knowledge' as the collective property of communities of 'knowers' ..." (Toulmin, 1999, p. 54), he draws attention to these two dimensions of workplace learning. All of the social accounts of learning recognise "the necessarily *social* nature of learning" (Winch 1998, p. 183). This means that normative learning of all kinds, including the important case of learning rule-following, presupposes the prior existence of social institutions. "No normative activity could exist *ab initio* in the life of a solitary" (Winch, 1998, p. 7). However, none of this rules out the possibility that, in coming to understand learning at work, the focus might be sometimes on the learning by individuals and sometimes on the communal learning that transcends the learning of any individual.

A main conclusion of this section is that, when considering learning at work, the isolated *individual* is often not the appropriate unit of analysis. Yet, shaped no doubt by the power of the learning as product view, educational policies, including those that impact on workplace learning, tend to focus almost exclusively on individual learners. This near universal adoption of the individuality assumption is no doubt reinforced by the popularity of human capital theory. This is evident from a typical definition of human capital: "[T]he knowledge, skills and competences and other attributes embodied in individuals that are relevant to economic activity" (OECD 1998, p. 9). The competencies agenda as implemented in many countries provides an illustration of the powerful attraction of the individuality assumption and human capital thinking. However, recent work suggests a growing interest in social capital (e.g., Winch, 2000; Beckett & Hager, 2002 p. 80ff.).

Tacit vs Explicit Learning

For the common-sense view of learning, to have successfully learnt in the best sense, is to know what it is that you have learnt. Winch (1998) puts this point as follows:

> It is natural for us to talk about learning as if we recognise that we have

both a capacity to learn and a capacity to bring to mind what has been learned. (p. 19)

This second capacity trades on the image of the mind as the home of clear and distinct ideas. If we have really learnt well, we will be able to bring the learning to mind. An inability to do so is a clear indicator that learning has been imperfect or unsuccessful. Once again propositions are the model. If we really understand (have learnt) a proposition then we will be able to 'bring it before the mind'. Inability to do so indicates ineffectual or inferior learning. This also implies that for the common-sense story about learning, non-transparent learning, such as tacit knowledge, informal learning, and the like, is either an aberration or a second rate kind of learning.

The transparency assumption is challenged by the increasing recognition of the importance of non-transparent types of learning, one of which, dispositional learning, is presupposed by other forms of learning (Passmore, 1980). Winch (1998, p. 19) argues that knowledge is largely dispositional, thereby taking the central focus firmly away from transparent propositions in minds. Much dispositional learning is tacit in the sense that we do not know enough about it to be able to verbalise it. This is an important feature of much learning at work. Certainly, as is well-known, workplace learning and performance display a holism that includes tacit components fairly seamlessly with other components that are more amenable to being made explicit. In this sense, workplace learning can be characterised as "organic learning" (Beckett & Hager, 2002, p. 26ff.) in that it often involves the whole person. The competencies agenda illustrates the importance of this point for policy formulation and implementation. It is precisely where competence has been conceptualised in a whole person, holistic way that it has proved most useful and enduring.

Structures Conducive to Workplace Learning

Clearly some workplace arrangements are much more likely to foster workplace learning than others. In thinking about this, it is useful to distinguish between work and labour. According to Standing (1999), work is

rounded activity combining creative, conceptual and analytical thinking and use of manual aptitudes – the *vita activa* of human existence ... Work involves an individual element and a social element, an interaction with objects – raw materials, tools, 'inputs', etc. – and an interaction with people and institutions. (p. 3)

Standing (1999) contrasts labour sharply with work: "Labour is arduous – perhaps *alienated work* – and epistemologically it conveys a sense of 'pain' – *animal laborans*" (p. 4). Thus, for Standing, labour is "activity done under some duress, and some sense of *control* by others or by institutions or by technology, or more likely by a combination of all three."

The economic rationalist labour market policies that have dominated Western countries in recent decades treat individuals as mere economic units ('labour'), rather than as "aspirants with personal and professional goals" (Waterhouse, Wilson, & Ewer, 1999, p. 22). For economists, labour is merely that which is expended in production. The alienation associated with labour reflects an impoverished work context "... that uses only a narrow range of physical or mental attributes, or that restricts the development or renewal of physical, intellectual or psychological capacities ..." (Standing, 1999, p. 7). Whereas the complex set of relationships that characterise work on Standing's account, requires a rich and varying context. Clearly, "... wherever possible, policy should encourage work and not merely labour." (Buchanan et al., 2001, p. 25). Such possibilities are more widespread than previously thought, if Murphy (1993) is correct in his conclusion that economists, including both Adam Smith and Marx, have typically overestimated the technical restrictions that efficiency of production places on work organisation. On Murphy's account, it appears that "[m]any social divisions of labour are compatible with different (but equally technically efficient) configurations of tasks." (Buchanan et al., 2001, p. 25).

It might be objected that all work arrangements will include, inevitably, some degree of labour. What work is under no form of duress or control? However, there is no doubt that some work arrangements encourage learning much more than do others. The point, surely, is to maximise enriching work opportunities. The Fuller and Unwin *expansive-restrictive continuum*, discussed earlier, can provide a useful guide here.

Scope of Workplace Learning Theories

Earlier in this chapter, drawing on Winch's work, it was suggested that the quest for a single preferred theory of learning to cover all cases may be misguided. Rather than seeking universal theories, Winch, influenced by Wittgenstein, recommends that we focus on description and understanding of various instances of learning viewed as distinctive cases: "... we have been obsessed with theory building at the expense of attention to particular cases ..." (Winch, 1998). It might be that 'learning' is a family resemblance concept in that it caters for a rich diversity of cases though there may be no single feature common to all of them. This more inclusive approach is arguably a conceptual advance over the assumption of the common-sense story about learning that cases of learning are to be valued according to how closely they approximate to propositional learning by minds.

Even in the more restricted field of workplace learning it seems likely that the diversity of types of learning will mean that a 'one theory fits all' approach is unlikely to be successful (Hager, 1999). This means, for example, that theories that seek to identify single factors that might underpin all workplace learning are most likely mistaken. Instances of tendencies to single factor explanations have already been cited in this chapter. In the discussion of Engestrom's account of workplace learning, it was questioned whether all learning at work occurs as a result of contradictions and tensions within an activity system. Likewise, doubt was cast on the plausibility of the Lave and Wenger key notion of community of practice as a general account of learning. Finally, it has been suggested that neither the concept of individual learning nor of communal learning might be, by themselves, sufficient to account for learning at work.

Metaphors of Learning and Workplace Learning

As noted at the start of this chapter, Sfard (1998) has argued that there are two basic metaphors – learning as *acquisition* and as *participation* – that have underpinned much educational thought. As the prominence of the learning as product view discussed earlier suggests, the acquisition metaphor has long been influential. It tends to subordinate the process of learning to its products – the something acquired (knowledge, skills, attitudes, values, behaviour, understanding, etc). Sfard contrasts this metaphor with the increasingly influential participation one, claiming that neither metaphor by itself is adequate to understanding of the full complexities of learning. However, I think that Sfard's ideas can usefully be extended. Certainly *acquisition* does emphasise learning as a product and the 'folk theory' of a mind accumulating stable, discrete substances or objects. In contrast, it could be argued that the *participation* metaphor presents learning as either a product or a process. This is because while participation itself is a process, the learner belongs more and more to the community of practice by acquiring the right characteristics (products of learning). However, a metaphor not mentioned by Sfard that better accords with learning as a process is *construction (re-construction)*. This includes the construction of the learning, of the self, and of the environment (world) which includes the self.

Another reason for introducing this third metaphor, is that in my view, participation accounts less well than does construction for change. The notion of the (re)construction of learning, of the self, and of the environment (world) which includes the self, has built into it the idea that change may be unceasing. By contrast, it is quite possible to have successful participation while resisting all change. Some sects and religious orders achieve this. Ancient Sparta was a society that demanded unquestioning participation from its citizens in which they learnt their respective roles within a rigid unchanging system. It was extremely successful for centuries, but succumbed in the end to changes in the wider world. So it seems that the (re)construction metaphor has an extra dimension that the participation one lacks.

Implications for Theories of Workplace Learning

What does the preceding mean for workplace learning? I conclude that workplace learning is poorly understood if it is viewed as a product. There are considerable advantages in viewing it primarily as a process that has important social, cultural, and political dimensions. Both work practices and the learning that accompanies them are processes. This process feature is also best captured by a (re)construction metaphor, given that the use of metaphor seems to be unavoidable when thinking about learning. It also seems that we should be wary of attempts to account for workplace learning in terms of single overriding factors or via universally applicable theories. So I conclude that four major criteria for assessing workplace learning theories are how well they:

1. View such learning as a process
2. Take account of the social, cultural, and political dimensions
3. Reflect (re)construction metaphors
4. Avoid single factor or universally applicable explanations

Returning to the overview of various theories of workplace learning in the first section, we can see that those in the first broad category do not fare well against most of these criteria as they have strong links with the learning as product view and the acquisition metaphor. However, rather than discounting this category entirely, we should note Eraut's warning that just because (say) learning located in the mind is in itself inadequate to account for workplace learning, it does not follow that such learning has no place at all in a satisfactory account.

Turning to the second broad category of theories of workplace learning, the Lave and Wenger theory appears to have some difficulty with the third and fourth criteria. It is open to question how well their work is amenable to interpretation in terms of the (re)construction metaphor (the third criterion). The transition of novices into full participation in the community of practice, might well be seen as a kind of reconstruction of the community. Certainly, according to Lave and Wenger this is a mechanism for change in the community of practice. However, their account has little to say about the learning by the individual learner that underlies the reconstitution of their personal identity from that of novice to full participant. Various writers have noted this deficiency in the Lave and Wenger account (e.g., Elkjaer, 2003; Guile & Young, 1999). As Elkjaer (2003) argues, the Lave and Wenger participation metaphor deals with learning at the organisational level, but ... at the expense of a description of the actual learning process – *how* does learning come about through participation? (p. 488)

Likewise, on the fourth criterion, the wide application of the term 'participation' by Lave and Wenger looks suspiciously like resort to a single factor explanation of learning.

There are also questions about Engestrom's work, at least in relation to third and fourth criteria. In terms of the third criterion, the resolution of contradictions and tensions within activity systems can be viewed, perhaps, as a kind of (re)construction. However, the previously noted unresolved issue between the activity system and the learner as the locus of learning, leaves this matter unclear. Likewise, Engestrom's reliance on contradictions and tensions within activity systems as the drivers of learning, looks to be the type of single factor explanation that the fourth criterion questions. Of the other theorists included in the second broad category of workplace learning theories, it is probably premature to pass judgement. One issue is that the participation metaphor has been extremely influential in this work. Whether the theorising of those who have focused on participation is robust enough to supply the extra edge suggested by (re)construction is a matter for further investigation.

Conclusion

Theorising about workplace learning has come a long way in the last thirty years. This chapter has outlined some main issues that continue to shape this area of investigation. Four criteria have been proposed for assessing current and future theories. As further research continues to clarify this field, it is to hoped that policy makers and implementers will be provided with better conceptual resources than they have had in the past for understanding vocational learning in general and workplace learning in particular. In the meantime, policies that relate to learning at work too often reflect individualistic, learning as product assumptions. They thereby fail to connect in any significant way with the specific activities that they are designed to influence. A reversal of this unsatisfactory situation will require a sea change in the assumptions that policy makers bring to their understanding of workplace learning.

References

Argyris, C., & Schön, D. A. (1974). *Theory in practice: Increasing professional effectiveness.* San Francisco: Jossey Bass.

Argyris, C., & Schön, D. A. (1978). *Organizational learning: A theory of action perspective.* Reading, MA: Addison-Wesley.

Beckett, D., & Hager, P. (2002). *Life, work and learning: Practice in postmodernity.* Routledge International Studies in the Philosophy of Education, Vol. 14, London and New York: Routledge.

Bereiter, C. (2002). *Education and mind in the knowledge age.* Mahwah, NJ and London: Lawrence Erlbaum Associates.

Billett, S. (2001). Knowing in practice: Re-conceptualising vocational expertise. *Learning and Instruction, 11*, 431–452.

Bransford, J. D., & Schwartz, D. L. (1999). Rethinking transfer: A simple proposal with multiple implications. *Review of Research in Education, 24*, 61–100.

Bruner, J. (1996). *The culture of education.* Cambridge, Massachusetts and London: Harvard, University Press.

Buchanan, J., Schofield, K., Briggs, C., Considine, G., Hager, P., Hawke, G., Kitay, J., Meagher, G., McIntyre, J., Mounier, A., & Ryan, S. (2001). *Beyond flexibility: Skills and work in the future.* Sydney: NSW Board of Vocational Education and Training.

Dewey, J. (1916). *Democracy and education.* New York: MacMillan.

Elkjaer, B. (2003). Organizational learning with a pragmatic slant. *International Journal of Lifelong Education, 22*(5), 481–94.

Engestrom, Y. (1999). Activity theory and individual and social transformation. In Y. Engestrom, R. Miettinen & R. Punamaki (Eds.), *Perspectives on activity theory* (pp. 19–38). Cambridge: Cambridge University Press.

Engestrom, Y. (2001). Expansive learning at work: Towards an activity-theoretical reconceptualisation. *Journal of Education and Work, 14*(1), 133–156.

Eraut, M. (2000). Non-formal learning and tacit knowledge in professional work. *British Journal of Educational Psychology, 70*, 113–36.

Fuller, A., & Unwin, L. (2003). Learning as apprentices in the contemporary UK workplace: Creating and managing expansive and restrictive participation. *Journal of Education and Work, 16*(4), 407–426.

Fuller, A., & Unwin, L. (2004). Expansive learning environments: Integrating organisational and personal development. In H. Rainbird, A. Fuller & A. Munro (Eds.), *Workplace Learning in Context* (pp. 126–144). London: Routledge.

Glaser, R. (1985). The nature of expertise. *Occasional Paper No. 107.* Columbus, Ohio: National Center for Research in Vocational Education.

Guile, D., & Young, M. (1999). Beyond the institution of apprenticeship: Towards a social theory of learning as the production of knowledge. In P. Ainley & H. Rainbird (Eds.), *Apprenticeship: Towards a new paradigm of learning* (pp. 111–128) London: Kogan Page.

Hager, P. (1999). Finding a good theory of workplace learning. In D. Boud & J. Garrick (Eds.), *Understanding learning at work* (pp. 65–82). London and New York: Routledge.

Hodkinson, P., & Bloomer, M. (2002). Learning careers: Conceptualizing lifelong work-based learning. In K. Evans, P. Hodkinson & L. Unwin (Eds.), *Working to learn: Transforming learning in the workplace* (pp. 29–43). London: Kogan Page.

Hodkinson, P., & Hodkinson, H. (2004). Rethinking the concept of community of practice in relation to schoolteachers' workplace learning. *International Journal of Training & Development, 8*(1), 21–31.

Hodkinson, P., & Hodkinson, H. (in press). The significance of individuals' dispositions in workplace learning: A case study of two teachers. *Journal of Education and Work.*

Lave, J., & Wenger, E. (1991). *Situated learning.* Cambridge: Cambridge University Press.

Marsick, V., & Watkins, K. (1990). *Informal and incidental learning in the workplace.* London: Routledge.

Murphy, J. B. (1993). *The moral economy of labour – Aristotelian themes in economic theory.* New Haven & London: Yale University Press.

Nonaka, I., & Takeuchi, H. (1995). *The knowledge-creating company: How Japanese companies create the dynamics of innovation.* Oxford and New York: Oxford University Press.

Organisation for Economic Cooperation and Development (OECD) (1998) *Human Capital Investment: An International Comparison.* Paris: OECD.

Passmore, J. (1980). *The Philosophy of Teaching.* London: Duckworth.

Rainbird, H., Fuller, A., & Munro, A. (Eds.) (2004). *Workplace Learning in Context.* London: Routledge.

Schoenfeld, A. H. (1999). Looking toward the 21st Century: Challenges of educational theory and practice. *Educational Researcher, 28*(7), 4–14.

Schön, D. A. (1983). *The reflective practitioner.* New York: Basic Books.

Schön, D. A. (1987). *Educating the reflective practitioner.* San Francisco: Jossey Bass.

Sfard, A. (1998). On two metaphors for learning and the dangers of choosing just one. *Educational Researcher, 27*(2), 4–13.

Standing, G. (1999). *Global labour flexibility: Seeking distributive justice.* London/New York: Macmillan/St. Martin's Press.

Tennant, M. (1991). Expertise as a dimension of adult development: Implications for adult education. *New Education, 13*(1), 49–55.

Toulmin, S. (1999). Knowledge as shared procedures. In Y. Engestrom, R. Miettinen & R. Punamaki (Eds.), *Perspectives on action theory* (pp. 53–64). Cambridge: Cambridge University Press.

Waterhouse, P., Wilson, B., & Ewer, P. (1999). *The changing nature and patterns of work and implications for VET.* Adelaide: National Centre for Vocational Education Research.

Watkins, K., & Marsick, V. (1992). Towards a theory of informal and incidental learning in organizations. *International Journal of Lifelong Education, 11*(4), 287–300.

Wenger, E. (1998). *Communities of practice: Learning, meaning and identity.* Cambridge: Cambridge University Press.

Wertsch, J. W. (1998). *Mind as action.* Oxford and New York: Oxford University Press.

Winch, C. (1998). *The philosophy of human learning.* London and New York: Routledge.

Winch, C. (2000). *Education, work and social capital.* London and New York: Routledge.
Yates, G., & Chandler, M. (1991). The cognitive psychology of knowledge: Basic research findings and educational implications. *Australian Journal of Education, 35*(2), 131–53.

45

LEARNING AND WORK TRANSITION POLICIES IN A COMPARATIVE PERSPECTIVE: CANADA AND GERMANY

Walter R. Heinz* and Alison Taylor[†]
*University of Bremen, Germany; [†]University of Alberta, Canada

It is complicated to compare education and training policies in different countries because their institutional structures are quite different. Comparing participation rates and durations in various transition paths from education to work and the outcomes in North America[1] and Europe directs our attention to multiple causes and different social institutions. Main differences concern the duration of primary and secondary education, and the access to and duration of secondary and postsecondary pathways. Differences also concern the age of entry into post-secondary education, the duration of academic studies, and last but not least, the degree to which linkages between the education system, the labor market and careers are regulated by institutions of the welfare state. Concerning transition policies, for example, in Canada, provincial and territorial governments have jurisdiction over education although the federal government does play a role in youth unemployment programs. Transition issues therefore "lie at the crossroads of several policy jurisdictions" (OECD, 1999, p. 33). As in Germany, Canadian policy-makers share a concern about the need to enhance the skills of workers in a more competitive labor market. The German system has to be analysed at additional levels: There are the policy frameworks developed by the European Union, the training and education-to-work legislation of the Federal Government, the education responsibilities of the state (provincial) governments, and the regional and local education administrations. Thus, school-to-work transitions in Germany are embedded in European federalism, which translates globalization and its effects into an increased competition for maintaining and attracting a highly qualified workforce.

In response to the volatility of market responses to globalization in the last decade, there has been substantial political uncertainty and risk concerning education, training and employment in both countries. This has reinforced the recognition in Germany that the proportion of highly skilled employees in the labor force is an important public good which requires the coordination of business, unions and governments at all levels of decision-making. In Canada,

International Handbook of Educational Policy, 847–864
Nina Bascia, Alister Cumming, Amanda Datnow, Kenneth Leithwood and David Livingstone (Eds.)
© 2005 *Springer. Printed in Great Britain.*

there is also growing realization at federal and provincial levels that organized intervention is required to ensure the responsiveness of education and training systems to changing skill requirements (OECD, 1999). In the following, we document recent developments in transition policies in these two G-7 countries and discuss their implications for young people.

Economic and Labour Market Trends in Canada and Germany

Canada

Different authors (Krahn, 1991; Livingstone, 2002; OECD, 1999) have described economic trends in Canada and in other industrialized countries in recent decades that include the shift from goods-producing to service-sector work, a steady increase in female labor force participation, growth in the proportion of non-standard work forms, an increase in use of computer based technologies in the workplace, the gradual upskilling of work, and increasing polarization between "good" and "bad" jobs in terms of security, working conditions and pay. In 2002, almost three-quarters of workers in Canada were employed in the services-producing sector.[2] Female labour force participation in 2002 was 60.7% for women over 15 years of age (and 81.2% for 25 to 44 year olds) – more than double the 1960 rate. Part time employment accounted for 18.7% of employment, up from 15.6% in 1986.

Some of these changes particularly affect youth, making their transitions more complex and extended (OECD, 2000). For example, the unemployment rate for young Canadians between 15 and 24 years of age has been approximately double the adult rate in recent years (OECD, 1999). In 2002, the adult rate was 7.7% while the rate for 15 to 24 year olds was 13.6%. When employed, young people are disproportionately engaged in non-standard work in the form of part time, short term and self-employment (Felstead, Krahn, & Powell, 1999). As students, they most often find low paid clerical, sales and service positions (Krahn, Lowe, & Lehmann, 2002) and their average earnings have declined since the early 1980s (OECD, 1999). In addition, some of the most highly qualified young graduates have difficulty finding jobs that they believe match their educational credentials and experience (Kelly, Howatson-Leo, & Clark, 2000). Canadian surveys suggest that around 20% of the entire employed workforce and larger proportions of younger, more highly educated workers are underemployed in terms of having a higher credential than their job requires for entry (Livingstone, 1999, p. 75).

More generally, the average duration of youth transitions from the end of high school to work increased by nearly two years across fifteen OECD countries between 1990 and 1996 (OECD, 2000). Young people who experience barriers related to race/ethnicity, region, disability, and poverty have even more difficult transitions (Krahn, 1996; Levin, 1999). For example, while Canadian youth overall were reported to have an unemployment rate of 16% in 1991, the unemployment rate was 25% for First Nations youth, 19% for other visible minorities, 21% for those with disabilities, and 17% for youth in rural areas (OECD, 1999, p. 4). Youth in different regions of the country also face different employment opportunities. For example, while the unemployment rate in Newfoundland was 16.9% in 2002, it was 5.7% in Alberta. The employment situation for youth who had completed high school or less has worsened dramatically over the past twenty years. The unemployment rate for those without a high school diploma in the late 1990s was between two and three times that of university graduates (OECD, 1999).

Educational attainment in North America has also increased significantly in recent decades. For example, while individuals who had not completed high school made up around half of the Ontario workforce in 1978, they made up only a quarter in 1996 (Livingstone, 1999). In addition, enrolment in tertiary education (expressed in relation to the 20 to 24 year old cohort) was the highest in Canada of all the G7 countries. However, governments and employers are concerned about the ability of education and training systems to respond to particular areas of skill shortages and to reduce education-labor market mismatches. The distinctive North American combination of high formal educational attainment, increasing demand for adult education, and employers' reticence to pay for training has resulted in the expansion of general certification and a labor force "without some of the specific technical vocational skills that may be immediately required to do some specific jobs" (Livingstone, 1999, p. 29).

Concerns about Canada's ability to compete within a globalized economy are evident in the analysis of problems and solutions identified recently by federal policy makers in the report "Knowledge Matters" (Government of Canada, 2002). The shift toward a knowledge-based economy is said to require an ever-increasing number of well-educated and skilled workers in all parts of the economy across the country. In particular, people who can combine strong technical skills with "essential skills" such as communication, teamwork, and management skills are said to be in short supply, as are skilled tradespersons in several occupations (Government of Canada, 2000). However, meeting areas of demand may be made difficult by a looming demographic crunch caused by an aging population coupled with slower population growth rates and a smaller cohort of youth workers.

In keeping with human capital ideas, the solution is seen to lie in part in strengthening the "learning system" in order to meet skill and labor force demand in future decades. For example, a report of the Expert Panel on Skills recommended that work experience programs be made more widely available at elementary and secondary school levels, that teachers be prepared to deliver essential skills and monitor their acquisition, and that efforts be made to attract more young people to apprenticeship programs (Government of Canada, 2000, pp. 7–8).

Other necessary actions identified by the federal government to address the education and training of the workforce in Canada include improving academic and computer literacy of young people, assisting youth in labor market entry, increasing access to post-secondary education, upgrading the skills of adults currently in the workplace, and attracting highly-skilled immigrants (Government of Canada, 2002). Difficulties in achieving goals have also been acknowledged, including the lack of recognition of foreign credentials and prior learning, labor market barriers faced by marginalized groups, and a lack of sponsorship of training by employers.

Germany

Germany is experiencing a shift towards an "industrialized service society"[3] too. Data from a longitudinal survey, the socio-economic panel (SOEP-group, 2001) document that the skill structure in Germany has improved in the past 15 years. The proportion of people (age-group 16 to 64) without a vocational training certificate has declined substantially, while the proportion of those with intermediate and higher-level qualifications has increased. Concerning the matching process between qualifications and jobs, there still is a stable link between the occupation a person was trained for and her actual job assignment In 1998, 60% of the respondents in the longitudinal study report that they work in an occupation that they were originally trained for (BIBB, 2002).

These upgrading trends are also reflected in an increase of skill requirements for getting and keeping a job. Nevertheless, 10% of the certified skilled employees worked as semi-skilled workers in 1998, and 25% of so-called "foreign workers" with a German training certificate were in such a form of underemployment. Despite fairly close matches, there is substantial job mobility in Germany: 46% of the adult employed population changed its occupation at least once, out of which 52% left their job category, 28% moved within their job category, 12% from manufacturing to service, and 8% from service to manufacturing (BIBB, 2002).

The higher the level of education and vocational qualification, the less is the risk that a job shift will lead to a de-evaluation of a person's skill profile. Thus, there are more voluntary shifts among the better qualified and more enforced job changes by less qualified employees. Because of its long observation window from 1984 to 1998, the results of the German Socio Economic Panel (SOEP, 2001) document that in Germany job mobility occurs in the context of a relatively stable occupational structure and its feeding institutions in the systems of vocational education and training (VET) and academic (university) education. Job changes occurred mainly in occupations that are linked to organizational, business, and distributive services, while they occur very rarely in the public service occupations.

Having acquired a vocational qualification results in a higher protection against unemployment: In 1999 the unemployment rate for men with a VET-certificate was 6.9%: without VET the rate was 17.7%. These data for West Germany are comparatively low in view of the unemployment rates in East Germany, where 17.3% of men with vocational qualifications were unemployed and 32.8% of those without VET. The situation is even worse for women in East Germany, where for qualified women the unemployment rate was 22.1%

and without vocational qualification it was 39.2%. In the wake of declining economic growth and monetary transfers to East Germany, the unemployment rate for young persons in Germany has reached a hitherto unknown level. Dramatic increases in unemployment with regional variations are reported for the age group 20 to 25: 8.7% are unemployed in West Germany (much higher in Berlin with 20.6%, much less in Bavaria with 6%), and again, we find the highest rate of unemployment in East Germany with 19.6%.

It is mainly young people without VET qualifications who face a high risk of becoming socially marginalized by not getting a chance of employment. Most of the young people under 20 are still in the education system; this is preventing much higher unemployment rates that are found in most other OECD countries, where the obligatory school leaving age is lower than in Germany. Despite changing employment circumstances and job shifts in Germany, specific occupations continue to be the dominant principle for organizing labor markets, industrial relations and vocational education and training curricula (Kocka & Offe, 2000).

Concerning the expenditures for education and training, Germany (with 4.3% of its GNP) ranks below Canada, which spends 5.3% of its GNP. In addition to these state expenditures, we also find private spending for education and training in both countries. In Germany, most of these expenditures concern the company-based part of vocational education and training. This indicates that education policy in Germany is confronted with finding a balance between public and private investment in both its systems of vocational and academic education (OECD, 2001).

Vocational Education and Training Systems in Canada and Germany

Canada

Unlike Germany and certain other European countries, vocational education initiatives in North America have not been institutionalized and Canada lacks a tradition of social partnership comparable to many European countries (Heinz, 2003; OECD, 1999). Employers in North America have underinvested in long-term employee training programs and are less active in education programs compared to those in most other OECD countries (Marquardt, 1998). Canada has historically relied heavily on passive labor market programs, for example, favoring immigration over training to increase the supply of skilled labor (Krahn, 1991).

Historically, provincial governments have given little attention to secondary vocational programs compared to most European OECD countries. Comprehensive schools, which attempted to provide broad opportunities for academic, general, and vocational education without segregating them by program, became predominant in most provinces in Canada in the 1960s and early 70s (Manzer, 1994). These schools were consistent with the North American goal of attempting to provide large numbers of students with a general education and the possibility of studying at the post-secondary level. A credit system with individual timetables and promotion by subject was introduced, making streaming of students more difficult to describe and assess (Gaskell, 1991). The move toward comprehensive schools was partly a response to the recognition that previous vocational programs were class-specific and class-defining and had become a "dumping ground" for students without a place in the educational system (Lazerson & Dunn, 1977).

Across Canada, the current structure of education includes an elementary education of between five and eight years, followed by secondary education which ends at grade 12. In the province of Quebec, secondary education ends after grade 11 and students go to general and vocational colleges (CEGEPs) where they follow a two-year pre-university program or a three-year technical program (OECD, 1999). Most secondary schools offer a mixture of academic and vocational courses although there has been a marked decrease in student enrolments in vocational courses in recent decades (Smaller, 2003). A "market-based model" has developed in the absence of institutions linking schools and the workplace, and there has been limited government spending on secondary school-to-work transition programs (Krahn, 1996).

The community college system, developed in the late 1960s, has been more effective in providing vocational and technical programs in particular areas, and this, combined with the high aspirations of young people in Canada suggests that the future expansion of vocational schooling programs is more likely to occur at the post-secondary level (Livingstone, 1999). However, high youth unemployment rates, an interest in raising high school completion rates, concerns about the effects of an academic bias on the "neglected majority" of students in schools, and perceived demand for intermediate skills (Smith, 2001) have focused policy attention also on vocational programs within secondary schools.

In Canada, there is agreement that the preparation of a skilled labor force requires the state to play a role "which it has not played very efficiently in the past" (Schuetze, 2003, p. 88). The federal government has identified the need for a "Canada-wide skills and learning agenda" (Government of Canada, 2002, p. 4). Efforts have also been made by the federal government and by the Conference Board of Canada (an organization representing some of the largest corporations in the country) to identify essential or employability skills that are required in the workplace and to communicate these to educators. Members of the policy community agree that further developing forms of education that combine practical skill development in the workplace with the acquisition of organized theoretical knowledge in formal education sites is key to more effective school-work pathways (Schuetze & Sweet, 2003). The main focus of recent Canadian education and training policy intended to improve the transition has been on "encouraging high school completion, encouraging participation in post-secondary education, expanding vocational and technical education as well as cooperative education and internship programmes, providing career development courses, orientation and counselling, and in some provinces, developing youth apprenticeship" (OECD, 1999, p. 7).

Policy makers are interested in making career pathways more transparent so that young people can make more informed choices in their initial transitions. Currently most Canadian high school students aspire to middle-class white collar occupations with far less interest in the trades (Krahn, 1996). However, these aspirations do not match available career opportunities, and a national survey of 22,000 young people aged 18 to 20 conducted in 2000 indicates that transitions from secondary school to full-time employment are currently "complex and circuitous" (Bowlby & McMullen, 2002, p. 19). This survey found that many young people aged 18 to 20 were attending post-secondary institutions, some were working full time, others combined school and work, and a small number were still completing high school (Bowlby & McMullen, 2002).

By age 20, 85% of respondents had graduated from high school. Just over a third (37%) were not pursuing further education; of this group, 12% had not graduated from high school. More young men than young women (almost 15% compared to 9%) had dropped out of high school (Bowlby & McMullen, 2002, p. 24). Of those attending post-secondary institutions, about a third were attending university and just over half were attending community colleges, university colleges, or in Quebec, collèges d'enseignment général et professionnel (CEGEPs). This compares to the 7% who attended a technical, trade or vocational school and less than 5% who attended a private business or training school (p. 56). These figures provide a contrast with the German system, where far greater numbers of students pursue a VET certificate and fewer pursue other forms of post-secondary education.

Although the German system has been criticized for promoting the selection of students into a system that reproduces social divisions such as gender, class, and ethnicity, Canadian data also indicate stratification of outcomes. For example, while almost a quarter of the population over 25 year old held a university degree by 1994; nearly half of these degree holders came from professional family origins while only 13% came from families where fathers were industrial workers (Livingstone, 1999, p. 58). Similarly, in comparing Canadian high school dropouts to high school graduates, Bowlby and McMullen (2002, p. 16) found that the proportion of dropouts who had parents who had not completed high school was three times that of graduates. Furthermore, young people from less affluent backgrounds continue to be overrepresented in vocational programs (Krahn, 1996).

Although young women are more likely to graduate from high school, education and career choices are gendered and women continue to be hired into jobs that pay less. As in adult apprenticeship, where women represented 3.6% of persons enrolled in such programs in Canada in 1997/98 (Sharpe, 2003), very few participants in high school apprenticeship programs are female. The numbers of students more generally in high school apprenticeship programs are also very low – less than 5% of eligible students in Ontario and Alberta (Taylor & Lehmann, 2002; Taylor & Spevak, 2003). Dropout rates for Aboriginal youth have been much higher than the national average and very few go on to obtain formal post-secondary credentials. More generally, whites are at least twice as likely as blacks, Hispanics, and Aboriginals to obtain university degrees. Therefore, despite the "openness" of the North American education system, the talents of large numbers of young people continue to be wasted in school systems (Livingstone, 1999, p. 56).

Another presumed advantage of the North American education and training system vis-à-vis more regulated systems in Europe concerns its flexibility and responsiveness to labor market changes. Perhaps for this reason, policy-makers have been reluctant to develop a legislative framework to coordinate secondary school vocational education and training, instead relying on voluntary partnerships with the private sector and devolving responsibility for providing school-to-work transition programs to local communities. Authors examining secondary transition initiatives in Nova Scotia and Quebec suggest that a disadvantage of promoting partnerships involving a multiplicity of players is that it can lead to an uncoordinated maze of initiatives and programs (OECD, 1999). Recent research in Ontario suggested that representatives from organizations involved in secondary school programs also held this perception (Taylor & Spevak, 2003).

Another challenge associated with an unregulated VET system and lack of corporatist partnership is the difficulty in mobilizing employers to provide placements and invest in youth. A "market" system also makes it difficult to ensure that young people who are most at risk of exclusion are assisted. Like other OECD countries, governments in Canada are finding it difficult to reconcile their "public mission of equality of access to education and training for all citizens with increased responsiveness to rapidly changing demands for new skills and knowledge and higher standards for all" (OECD, 1999, p. 30). Finally, secondary and post-secondary vocational programs tend not to be well articulated.

Germany

School-to-work transition is still a "regulated adventure" (Solga, 1998), an adventure that consists of generally successful, but increasingly precarious landings at the shores of the German labor market. Comparing OECD countries, we find on the formal level that there are five main transition routes from school to work: Neither education nor training; episodes of work experience, some education and training; apprenticeship (VET); college and private training providers; and university education (see figure 1.1 in Schuetze & Sweet, 2003, p. 11).

The relative importance of these transition routes varies between OECD countries. In Germany, the main route still is the VET which is travelled by about two thirds of each school-leaving cohort. This distinguishes Germany from Canada, where we find a general lack of public acceptance of apprenticeships as a promising transition to employment. This lack is based on a preference for academic education and a general distaste of vocationalism, which is regarded as the transition context for low achievers (see Schuetze & Sweet, 2003). In contrast to Germany, the institutional gatekeepers in the high schools are less favorably inclined towards vocational education and training, a route which tends to be the most accepted and popular one in the German transition system.

VET in Germany is a training arrangement which consists of a combination of company-based on-the-job training and school-based vocational education. This "dual system" is regulated by the German Vocational Training and Education Act which defines the rights and responsibilities of the social partners: employers, unions, and government, and a federal VET agency for developing, reforming and evaluating guidelines for more than 300 crafts, technical, commercial, and service occupations at present. The occupation-centered transition is built on the traditional German three-tier school system and produces social inequality based on social origin, gender and ethnicity. This inequality begins with the early tracking decisions at school, decisions that predetermine to a large extent the likelihood to enter one of the five transition routes.

There are three thresholds or turning points that characterize the transition from school to work in Germany. Following elementary school, this three-step sequence starts with the tracking of students into lower, middle or higher secondary schools. Upon their completion of 9, 10 or 13 years respectively, the next turning point involves either moving into an apprenticeship or enrolling in a polytechnical college or a university. The last and most important threshold is the entry into the labor market after having acquired a VET certificate or an academic degree. In the 1990s, about 80% of each youth cohort in Germany managed to attain either a vocational certificate or a higher education degree, the vast majority obtaining a VET certificate.

According to the yearly Federal Vocational Training and Education Report (BMBF, 2002), one third of all apprentices in 2000 came from lower secondary schools and mainly entered craft and blue-collar occupations; 40% came from middle secondary schools, most of them will be trained for occupations in commerce, services and technology, and less than 20% came from upper secondary schools which provide university entry exams. Young people with upper secondary exams enter careers after graduation in professions, business and public services. This distribution of transition outcomes has been widely criticized because it reflects the high segmentation between levels of education and access to occupations and training opportunities (Heinz, 2000).

With its roots in the history of industrial Germany and its contemporary embeddedness in the system of social partnership between state, unions and business, the VET system is regarded as a collective good from which not only young people but also employers and civic society will benefit. The training tradition in the crafts and in commerce became a component of the German welfare state and its corporatist labor policy after World War II with the aim of serving not only the economy but also the socialization and social integration of young people. A combination of in-company work experience and theoretical instruction in vocational schools over a regulated period of three to four years has been the trademark of the so-called "dual system" in Germany. This transition arrangement is based on the cooperation of two learning sites: the worksite (craftshop, plant, office or department store) and the vocational school.

Federal training guidelines define the practical and theoretical learning requirements in the firm and in the vocational school. This provides orientation for individual learning processes as well as for examinations that define the core of occupational knowledge and skill profiles.

In summary, the VET system is creating career prospects by providing work-integrated and nationally recognized skill profiles as well as links with the occupational labor market through the training firm. The drawback, however, is that this system still separates the graduates of lower and middle secondary schools from higher education and the professional labor market. The VET system is an example of a transitional arrangement that emphasizes formal qualifications and develops standardized and portable occupational skills, whereas Canada tends to rely on a model that consists mainly of learning-on-the-job which fits the skill requirements and the employability and flexibility demands of the enterprise (Shavit & Müller, 1998).

An increasing number of different pathways in vocational and academic transitions systems have been developed in Germany in response to the lasting labor market crisis of the 1990s. These pathways include young people who finished neither an apprenticeship nor a postsecondary degree. They are offered state-sponsored training and upgrading programs and participate in job-creation schemes. Therefore, the urban underclass of unemployed young people is much smaller in Germany than in other European countries and in North America. The German welfare state still attempts to build bridges or escape routes for youth at risk. Instead of welfare there is the strategy of "trainingfare" programs – for initial and continued VET instead of social assistance.

Because of the embeddedness of the VET in the German system of industrial relations and its supervision by a central Federal administration, time-consuming negotiations are required for introducing and certifying new training occupations. Another point of criticism is that VET in Germany not only separates apprentices from the university-bound students, but that it is also stratified according to gender. Furthermore, this popular transition route still reflects the social dynamics of labor-market segmentation that discriminates against women (Krüger, 1999), lower-class youth and children of immigrant workers.

In contrast to co-op arrangements, consortia and training initiatives in North America, which are initiated to improve the passage from education to employment, the German training system is embedded in a legislative framework that brings together vocational schools and firms in a training partnership. It is important to note that this framework sets universal standards for training companies and apprentices alike by defining the rights and duties of the firms, the content of curricula taught at vocational schools, their duration, the salary levels of apprenticeships (which differ widely by industrial sector) and the form of VET contracts. This institutional fabric leads to much lower proportions of unskilled workers among school leavers in Germany than in North America. The outcome of the unregulated North American transition process is early employment without training or with some on-the-job training for relatively undemanding jobs in youth labor markets – the well-known "McDonald-jobs".

In contrast, the German VET system extends the transition and leads to late entry into the labor force, as skilled blue and white-collar workers.

Implications for Young People's Pathways

Canada

The lack of institutions linking schools and the workplace in North America has meant that young people have been left largely on their own in making career choices and finding employment. The response of many young people to labor market instability has been to stay at school and home longer, combine school and work, and delay marriage and parenthood (Krahn, 1996). Transitions have become longer and more circuitous. Employment opportunities for those with high school or less have deteriorated and "post-secondary education is fast becoming the new educational standard" (Bowlby & McMullen, 2002, p. 19). On the other hand, there is substantial underemployment among young people, suggesting that the technical upgrading of jobs in recent decades may have been exceeded by the formal educational qualifications of the workforce – despite the claims of "knowledge economy" proponents (Livingstone, 1999). Given the generally high level of occupational aspirations, many young people are likely to be disappointed in their labor market outcomes. Still, those who are most at risk of social exclusion are likely to have the least education (e.g., Aboriginal youth), face limited local employment opportunity structures (e.g., rural youth) and face segregation or discrimination in the labor market (e.g., women and some visible minority groups).

Employers in Canada do not have a tradition of providing structured training for new employees. Economic restructuring has exacerbated the tendency for employers to take a short-term view and to expect the formal education system to provide job-ready, flexible entrants. Although there is variation, employers have invested in neither school- nor company-based programs. The range of apprenticeship opportunities is limited and apprenticeship tends to be regarded as very expensive for employers and potential apprentices (Krahn, 1996). Relationships between industrial unions and employers become more adversarial as work is restructured, and few secondary transition programs involve both employers and organized labor as partners. Therefore, local or regional partnerships, as a truncated form of corporatism have developed.

However, there is increased awareness of the need for expanded stakeholder involvement. For example, there have been efforts through sector councils – which bring together representatives from business, labour, education, and other professional groups within particular industries – to address skill requirements through training programs, some of which target youth. In Alberta, leaders from the resource industry have worked in partnership with government since the late 1980s to mobilize employers to provide apprenticeship and work experience opportunities for young people (Taylor & Lehmann, 2002). An industry-driven foundation called CAREERS the Next Generation has worked in partnership with leaders in the health services sector in Alberta to provide summer work experience placements for high school students who are interested in potential careers in this area.

School districts have also developed Tech Prep programs, which attempt to better articulate high school and college curriculum with a focus on particular occupational clusters. Tech Prep was developed in Red Deer, Alberta in 1995 and since then has expanded to other parts of the province. In the US, Tech Prep is usually a tripartite program that includes school-based learning (integrated academic-vocational career education linked to college curriculum), a work based component, and connecting activities (Grubb, 1996). Similarly, in the Alberta model, it is an educational initiative that encourages students to select career pathways and to acquire integrated academic skills and industry based occupational competencies through work-based experiences. In Ontario, the government also recently launched a campaign to mobilize employers to provide career exploration and work experience opportunities for high school students (Taylor & Spevak, 2003). Similar initiatives involving partnerships between governments, employers, and educators are increasingly common in different provinces. However, as mentioned earlier, initiatives tend to be piecemeal and lack coordination across institutions.

There are also contradictions within policy approaches intended to better prepare young people for work. The "forgotten" half of secondary school students is not seen as well-served by the prevailing view that they should be "free to choose whatever education and work they wish" (Gallagher & Kitching, 2003, p. 170). Clearer streaming is desired by policy-makers to better prepare young people for their destinations and to reduce education-skills mismatches. However, in Ontario, the education ministry's recent attempt to articulate school curriculum more clearly to workplace and further education destinations has been highly problematic, since early results indicate that high school graduation is becoming less attainable for many young people and students continue to enroll in courses in numbers disproportionate to their probable destinations. For example, although almost 40% of young people acquire high school education or less, fewer than 10% of students were enrolling in workplace destination courses in senior high school (King, 2002). In addition, over a quarter of students failed at least one component of a literacy test required for high school graduation in October 2002.

If a key goal of public policy is to help ensure that youth are not confronted with a limit on future options and that they have alternative pathways, there is a long way to go. Secondary vocational programs are lacking in terms of their numbers, quality, and integration with other streams (OECD, 1999; Sweet & Schuetze, 2003). The academic bias of schools has been reinforced both by government demands for school accountability and the development of quasi-education markets that promote the ranking of schools based on academic achievement on provincial tests. As a result, there are few incentives for schools to provide vocational programs – particularly when they are associated with low achieving students. Policy responses must therefore involve the integration of academic and vocational subjects. Given the high educational and occupational aspirations of youth, secondary vocational pathways that link to postsecondary destinations are also critical.

Finally, in policy attempts to articulate school curriculum with the workplace, it must be recognized that employers and professional employee groups may inflate credential requirements and that "the problem" may involve the lack of use of employee skills in the workplace as much as a mismatch or actual lack of employee skills (Livingstone, 1999). Therefore, policy must attend to demand-side as well as supply-side issues (Marquardt, 1998). Policy must also attend to differences in opportunity structures for youth based on their region, gender, race/ethnicity, social class, and education level. If the goal is in fact to raise the skill levels of all youth, then more attention must be given in transition policies to ensuring that all youth are supported in high school and have access to postsecondary education. For example, just under half of 18 to 20 year olds in a national survey reported facing barriers to going as far in school as they would like, and the most common barrier mentioned was financial (Bowlby & McMullen, 2002).

Germany

Results from longitudinal studies (Heinz, 1999) suggest that the restructuring of work has made transitions more dependent on the labor market and has intensified the trend towards higher-level credentials and social skills as well as continuing vocational education and training. Research documents an increasing influence of the educational level, work experience and the occupational structure on transition outcomes. Young adults must find out how to use their occupational competencies in their own ways, because they have to respond to the changing opportunity structures which offer far less job openings and career opportunities than a decade ago. Nowadays, the apprenticeship is slowly being transformed from an industrial model of vocational training into a launching pad for different career pathways; it is becoming an outfitter for individual expeditions into the more and more deregulated occupational territories of the labor market. But the VET system still manages to integrate non-college-bound young adults into society by offering them a culturally meaningful and economically rational transition to work – as an institutionalized context for acquiring basic and advanced occupational skills.

In view of the slowdown in economic growth and the rising unemployment rates since the 1990s, there is a growing number of problems which seem to be connected with the VET system. Some commentators even regard it as an obstacle to the modernization of the economy and the re-organization of work because it tends to socialize for occupation-based identities. Such identities tend to resist the flexible and collaborative types of work that are now required in restructured, decentralized and less bureaucratized organizations (cf. Herrigel & Sabel, 1999). This legacy is seen to stem from the German manufacturing industry, which is in decline as far as job growth is concerned. But this criticism of the German crafts and industry tradition ignores the fact that the system of vocational and educational training occurs in all sectors of the German economy and is not just applicable for skilled manual work in small and medium enterprises. The reintegration of mental and manual aspects of work is an obvious solution in view of the increasing intellectual and social demands in the modern workplace.

The modernization of the German industry and the shift from manufacturing to services as well as the restructuring of work has not invalidated the basic structure of VET. It is obvious, however, that employers are becoming more reluctant regarding long-term investments in new training places and in designing new training occupations. This has created labor market mismatches, especially in the balance of demand and supply in new information and technology occupations. In the 1990s, the proportion of German companies which supply training places has declined in spite of the need to recruit and train experts in the fields of modern technology and services.

In response to globalization and intensified economic competition, employers have become more conscious of short term gains and cost-cutting. They demand more deregulation, decentralized bargaining and more flexibility in training, hiring and firing. This gives momentum to a movement from the occupational model of VET to a more flexible organizational model of promoting employability (Shavit & Müller, 1998). These trends accelerated in the late 1990s and tend to undermine not only the structure and continuity of the "dual system," they also have been creating unintended effects. Though the majority of school leavers still enter the apprenticeship route in Germany, many young people are losing trust in this transition arrangement because the number of skilled young workers who do not find employment after graduating from VET is increasing. Overcoming the third threshold has become much more stressful than in earlier school-leaving cohorts. There are fewer job openings after apprenticeship and less job offers from the training firm, a problem that is more pronounced in East Germany, where less than 50% of young skilled workers are able to find employment (BMBF, 2002).

The restructuring of work has led to the creation of a series of newly designed training occupations where young people can acquire enlarged competence to cope with new labor market requirements in a more flexible way. Additional qualifications must be accumulated by participating in continuing education and training which also includes knowledge and skills about other occupations in order to broaden the employability of workers. The state must reclaim its role in education, training and employment policy in order to promote a highly educated and flexible labor force for demanding and competitive workplaces. In order to succeed, this social-democratic strategy depends on an increasing supply of training places for highly skilled occupations. This development poses a threat also to young skilled workers because they lack the work experiences and social skills that are required for succeeding in new work organizations. As the labor market becomes more deregulated and company downsizing continues, part-time, temporary and insecure jobs expand and thus reduce the employment opportunities even of the better qualified job starters.

A good example of innovative policy concerns basic and continuous training in the information and technology sector. A major goal of this training policy is that young skilled workers find bridges to develop their occupational competence in the IT sector by obtaining nationally recognized and certified, as well as internationally comparable competence profiles. For the VET-route, there are now curricula for new IT occupations which have been introduced with much public marketing and a target of 60,000 training places over a period of several years. These demanding VET profiles attract 50 to 60% apprentices with higher secondary level degrees. About 30% of the apprentices are 22 years and older which signals that these young people have already been in other training routes or training occupations. The share of women in IT occupations, however, does not exceed 11% which documents the highly gendered nature of this occupational sector. Another important training route for these new job profiles is flexible retraining and upgrading of adult workers. This strategy is part of the active labor-market policy of the social democratic/green government which covers about 50,000 persons who are unemployed or at risk of becoming unemployed with substantial success in reintegrating them in the labor market (BIBB, 2002).

Conclusion

We can see that deindustrialization, growing unemployment, corporatist or market-driven education and employment policies and the degree of supranational employment and education guidelines are important institutional frames that contribute to a change in the number, shape and duration of school-to-work transition routes and the employment opportunities of each generation of school leavers. As our review has documented, transitions to employment in Canada and Germany mirror the contradictions that are arising from the transformation from an industrial to a service society in the context of a globalized economy. Educational and training policies focus on strengthening human capital by upgrading the skill structure of the population. At the same time, there are skill shortages and a growing credentials-jobs gap due to rising underemployment and non-standard work. While Canada has been responding to the trends by focusing on an expansion of post-secondary education in community colleges and universities, Germany tends to upgrade its skill structure by modernizing its well established vocational education and training system with a focus on new occupations, without fundamentally changing its education-to-employment institutions.

Culture and social institutions seem to prescribe the most convincing (and popular) solutions to the transition issue: In Canada there is a lack of sponsorship of training by employers and little public support for vocational compared to academic education. In Germany, there is an institutionalized social partnership for strengthening the system of vocational education and training and belief that the working life course can be managed with a skill profile acquired through attending vocational school and in-company training. In view of the rising social costs of youth unemployment and in order to reduce the effects of social origin on transition outcomes, there have been provincial initiatives in Canada to curb the unregulated transitions from school to work by establishing local or regional partnerships between schools and employers. The success of these initiatives is limited by institutional and motivational factors: there is little coordination between local, provincial and federal levels of educational decision making concerning the standardization and financing of training and most young people have high expectations concerning post-secondary education with little interest in vocational education.

In Germany, there has been a debate about the effects of the restructuring of work on the VET with an emphasis on employability that focuses on greater flexibility and social competence in combination with vocational skills. This "bounded deregulation" puts more responsibility on the shoulders of young people to manage their transitions by acquiring and changing skill profiles according to labor market opportunities, albeit in the context of a well developed system of curricula and standardized credentials. It remains to be seen whether this policy of institutional flexibilization of the school-to-work transition will continue to succeed in preparing non-college bound youth for a volatile labor market. Therefore, there is some evidence of convergence in policy approaches, with Canada displaying an interest in strengthening social partnerships while Germany is seeking to increase the flexibility of its VET system.

In both countries, the role of the state has become critical in helping young people. In Canada, the market model has spawned concerns about the need for greater coordination and partnership among educators, government, employers, and organized labor. In Germany, the welfare state has played an important role in regulating school-to-work transitions and appears committed to maintaining and expanding the VET system. At the same time, governments face many challenges related to the institutional context and existing values. The German education system streams students early but involves a highly regulated and coordinated VET system. The Canadian school system defers streaming but pays insufficient attention to the group of young people that goes directly to work after high school; its VET system lacks transparency and coordination and is more market-driven. Not surprisingly then, the most popular transition route for young people in Canada is post-secondary education while the main route in Germany is the VET. There are both higher proportions of students attending university and of unskilled workers among school leavers in Canada compared to Germany. The outcomes for young people are therefore tied not only to individual preferences and "choices" but also to cultural and institutional differences that must be addressed in policy deliberations.

Notes

1. Although this paper focuses on Canada, educational policy in the US has taken a similar direction. For example, a series of reports in the 1980s and 90s led to the Carl Perkins Vocational and Applied Technology Education Act (1990), the School to Work Opportunities Act (1994) and Goals, 2000: Education America Act (1994). These Acts were intended to provide more effective forms of vocational education and training for young people.

2. Information about labor force participation, part time work, service sector employment, and unemployment are available from Statistics Canada CANSIM II tables 282-0002 and 282-0008 accessed on June 18, 2003 at: www.statcan/ca/english/Pgdb/labor10a.htm, and www.statcan/ca/english/Pgdb/labor12.htm.
3. Information about labor force participation, employment outlook and VET in Germany are available from www.iab.de and www.bibb.de

References

BIBB (Ed.) (2002). Veränderte Arbeitswelt – veränderte Qualifikationen: Wechselwirkungen zwischen Arbeitsmarkt und Bildungsstrukturen. Bonn: Schriftenreihe des Bundesinstituts für Berufsbildung.

BMBF (2002). Berufsbildungsbericht [Vocational Education and Training Report] Bonn: Federal Ministry for Education and Research.

Bowlby, J., & McMullen, K. (2002). At a crossroads: First results of the 18 to 20-year old cohort of the youth in transition survey. Ottawa: Human Resources Development Canada and Statistics Canada.

Felstead, A., Krahn, H., & Powell, M. (1999). Young and old at risk: Comparative trends in non-standard patterns of employment in Canada and the United Kingdom. *International Journal of Manpower, 20*(5), 277–296.

Gallagher, P., & Kitching, A. (2003). Canada's community colleges and alternation. In H. Schuetze & R. Sweet (Eds.), *Integrating school and workplace learning in Canada* (pp. 156–174). Montreal: McGill-Queen's University Press.

Gaskell, J. (1991). Education as preparation for work in Canada: Structure, policy, and student response. In D. Ashton & G. Lowe (Eds.), *Making their way: Education, training and the labour market in Canada and Britain* (pp. 61–84). Buckingham: Open University Press.

Government of Canada (2002). *Knowledge matters: Skills and learning for Canadians.* Ottawa.

Government of Canada (2000). Stepping up: Skills and opportunities in the knowledge economy (Report of the Expert Panel on Skills). Ottawa: Advisory Council on Science and Technology.

Grubb, N. (1996). The new vocationalism: What it is, what it could be. *Phi Delta Kappan, 77*(8), 535–545.

Heinz, W. R. (2003). The restructuring of work and the modernization of vocational training in Germany. In H. Schuetze & R. Sweet (Eds.), *Integrating school and workplace learning in Canada* (pp. 25–43). Montreal: McGill-Queen's University Press.

Heinz, W. R. (2000): Youth transitions and employment in Germany. *International Social Science Journal, 164*, 161–170.

Heinz, W. R. (Ed.) (1999). From education to work: Cross-national perspectives. New York: Cambridge University Press.

Herrigel, G., & Sabel, C. (1999). Craft production in crisis. In P. C. Culpepper & D. Finegold (Eds.), *The German skills machine: Comparative institutional advantage?* (pp. 77–114). Oxford: Berghahn Books.

Kelly, K., Howatson-Leo, L., & Clark, W. (2000). "I feel overqualified for my job." In Canadian social trends, volume 3 (pp. 182–187). Toronto: Thompson Educational Publishing.

King, A. (2002). *Double cohort study: Phase 2 report.* Prepared for the Ontario Ministry of Education. Kingston: Queen's University.

Kocka, J., & Offe, C. (Eds.) (2000): Geschichte und Zukunft der Arbeit. Frankfurt/New York: Campus.

Krahn, H. (1996). School-Work Transitions: Changing Patterns and Research Needs.

Edmonton: Prepared for *Applied Research Branch, Human Resources Development Canada.*

Krahn, H. (1991). The changing Canadian labour market. In D. Ashton & G. Lowe (Eds.), *Making their way: Education, training and the labour market in Canada and Britain* (pp. 15–37). Buckingham: Open University Press.

Krahn, H., Lowe, G., & Lehmann, W. (2001). Acquisition of employability skills by high school students. *Canadian Public Policy, 28*(2), 275–296.

Krüger, H. (1999). Gender and skills. Distributive ramifications of the German skill system. In P. C. Culpepper & D. Finegold (Eds.), *The German skills machine: Comparative institutional advantage?* (189–227). Oxford: Berghahn Books.

Lazerson, M., & Dunn, T. (1977). Schools and the work crisis. Vocationalism in Canadian education. In H. Stevenson & D. Wilson (Eds.), *Precepts, policy and process: Perspectives on contemporary Canadian education* (pp. 285–303). London: Alexander Blake Associates.

Levin, B. (1999). Schools and work: Towards a research agenda. Paper presented at Western Research Network on Education and Training Conference, Vancouver.

Livingstone, D. (2002). Working and learning in the information age: A profile of Canadians. Canadian Policy Research Networks (Discussion paper W/16). Ottawa.

Livingstone, D. W. (1999): The education–jobs gap: Underemployment or economic democracy. Toronto: Garamond.

Manzer, R. (1994). *Public schools and political ideas: Canadian educational policy in historical perspective*. Toronto: University of Toronto Press.

Marquardt, R. (1998). Labour market policies and programmes affecting youth in Canada. Paper commissioned by OECD Secretariate as background for Thematic Review.

OECD (2001). Education at a glance. OECD indicators. Paris.

OECD (2000). *From initial education to working life: Making transitions work*. Paris: Organization for Economic Cooperation and Development.

OECD (1999). *Thematic review of the transition from initial education to working life*. Paris: Organization for Economic Cooperation and Development.

Schuetze, H. (2003). Alternation education and training in Canada. In H. Schuetze & R. Sweet (Eds.), *Integrating school and workplace learning in Canada* (pp. 66–92). Montreal: McGill-Queen's University Press.

Schuetze, H., & Sweet, R. (Eds.) (2003). *Integrating school and workplace learning in Canada*. Montreal: McGill-Queen's University Press.

Sharpe, A. (2003). Apprenticeship in Canada: A training system under siege? In H. Schuetze & R. Sweet (Eds.), *Integrating school and workplace learning in Canada* (pp. 243–259). Montreal: McGill-Queen's University Press.

Shavit, Y., & Müller, W. (Eds.) (1998). *From school to work*. Oxford: Clarendon Press.

Smaller, H. (2003). Vocational education in Ontario secondary schools. In H. Schuetze & R. Sweet (Eds.), *Integrating school and workplace learning in Canada* (pp. 95–112). Montreal: McGill-Queen's University Press.

Smith, M. (2001). Technological change, the demand for skills, and the adequacy of their supply. *Canadian Public Policy, 27*(1), 1–22.

SOEP Group (2001). The German Socio-Economic Panel (GSOEP) after more than 15 Years – Overview. In E. Holst, D. R. Lillard & T. A. DiPrete (Eds.), Proceedings of the 2000 Fourth International Conference of German Socio-Economic Panel Study Users (GSOEP, 2000). *Vierteljahrshefte zur Wirtschaftsforschung, 70*(1), 7–14.

Solga, H. (1998): Expeditionen ins Berufsleben: Geregelte Abenteuer. Berlin: Max-Planck-Institut für Bildungsforschung.

Sweet, R., & Schuetze, H. (2003). New policy and research directions. In H. Schuetze & R. Sweet (Eds.), *Integrating school and workplace learning in Canada* (pp. 276–286). Montreal: McGill-Queen's University Press.

Taylor, A., & Lehmann, W. (2002). 'Reinventing' Vocational Education Policy: Pitfalls and Possibilities. *Alberta Journal of Educational Research, 48*(2), 139–161.

Taylor, A., & Spevak, A. (2003). Institutionalizing school-work transition in Ontario. Paper presented at the Canadian Society for the Study of Education meeting, Halifax.

46

DISJUNCTIONS IN THE SUPPLY OF AND DEMAND FOR EDUCATION IN THE LABOR FORCE 1930–2003: 'TRAFFICKING IN GAPS'

Ivar Berg

University of Pennsylvania, USA

From the standpoint of a seasoned observer of modern history, the *living* of life is, in many ways, as valuable as encounters with *formal* learning. Indeed, I often find matters to quibble about in younger colleagues' treatments of "contemporary and modern history" based on their distal perceptions of events that I have experienced proximally. My judgment here squares perfectly with Dr. Livingstone's enormously unorthodox and chastening remonstrances, from his own long years of research, that in our discussions of education and work we have attended to laborforce members' so called *informal* learning only with studied negligence. We have been preoccupied with measures of formal education in our efforts to put numbers to propositions about the possible levels of 'mismatching' of the schooling and skills of national workforces on one side, with the quotidian requirements for successful, "productive" performance in millions of jobs, on the other. The facts are that workers, of *all* types, have learned much on their jobs that can be taught to newcomers, for example, and, yes (and perhaps more importantly) to new newly appointed managers who replace the upwardly mobile subalterns in progressive corporate settings. We do know, after all, that "downsizings" have left a very great many survivors very short on knowledgeable peers. About informal learning, more below.

I have spent most of my forty-four 'post-doctoral' years, meantime, joining the conventional issues, studying the ebbs and flows in the matchups and mismatches of job requirements with formal 'learning'; Dr. Livingstone and I crossed paths when he replicated the first of my ongoing studies (Livingstone, 1998) by juxtaposing the methods from an initial U.S. analysis (Berg, 1970) with his U.S. 'update' in the 1990s together with his parallel analysis of "the education-job gap" in Canada in that recent period. He used one version of five specific calculations involving my translations of federal ordinal measures of job require-ments into years of schooling, and augmented these materials with his own instructive and depressing findings based upon a very imaginative analysis of

International Handbook of Educational Policy, 865–883

Nina Bascia, Alister Cumming, Amanda Datnow, Kenneth Leithwood and David Livingstone (Eds.)

© 2005 *Springer. Printed in Great Britain.*

Canadian employers' *additional* "sins of commission", sins that have been compounded by these employers' 'underemployment' of the "informal" as well as the "formal learning" of Canadian workers, a totally neglected issue in my own work.

Mismatching Educational and other Job Relevant Achievements and Attributes in the Pre WWII Era

I will, in these events, review my education-jobs forays (Berg, 1970, 1978, 2003) briefly. But I present first, some historical observations on "mismatching" as a longtime *generic* and longtime problem in American employment practices: the mismatching of America's labor force with the jobs available for these employees began to be serious all the way back in the early 1930s. The types and causes of mismatching have varied but the 'waste' (less often the "surplus") that the notion of mismatching captures has been *very nearly constant*, whatever the directions and precise parameters of mismatching.

The mismatchings that occurred in the later period, 1950–1960, reported in my 1970 effort, were serious enough at the time, but far down in the chronological order of problematical mismatchings we can remember of times past, though the timing of my study's somewhat undeservedly gratifying reception, in 1970, was mistakenly interpreted by a great many – especially young readers – to have been a novelty. Indeed, my study was organized and designed to examine a *secular* change in America's mis-integration of education, but was mistakenly and equally frustratingly taken up by *Fortune, Time, The Readers Digest, The Washington Post, CBS*, the old "Office of Economic Opportunity" and other media and agencies precisely as an explanation for the job problems of the college class of 1970. This group's stricken members were actually suffering only marginally, i.e. less from the result of a downturn in a business cycle, and from a secondary and *short term* paucity of Springtime job offers in that year as most observers urged, than from a *generalized, long term* (i.e., primary) structure-wide upgrading of educational requirements increasingly further above and beyond employers' certifiable needs.

In the ten year-long Depression period, beginning in 1929, we already had a colossal mismatch between *overall* demands in the economy for *all* kinds of labor, involving linkups between the entire labor force's diverse skills, demands that were long-augmented by an array of immigrants' skills, on one side, with employers' demands, on the other side. The totality of disjunctions involved profound underutilization in *general*, i.e. at *all* skill levels/educational levels, but especially of college grads. The underemployment of education mirrored the idle physical capital with which they worked.

The more recent downsizing of American work forces in many settings, 1980s–2003, has been correlated somewhat less robustly with declines in the utilization of physical capacity than during the Great Depression, but it has reportedly been correlated well with the increases in *productivity*, increases that have been happily celebrated, especially by the chairman of the US Federal

Reserve, in the period 1990–2003. Mr. Greenspan and others attribute this increase to an "information revolution" and to computers, more than to employers' successes in eliciting more *work* from *fewer* workers, albeit sometimes with *better* capital equipment, and generally with lower profits. The parameters of profits in the 1990s were, however, quite generally overstated by cavalier accountants and by stock analysts in brokerages and in commercial banking who misrepresented prospective returns to all investors at the behest of their corporate brethren who earned interest for their corporations' money managers from loans to individual banking clients. The celebrated increases in Americans' productivity, I suggest, with Dr. Livingstone's imaginative analyses at hand, may well be more parsimoniously explained by taking full account of employees' work-driven learning experiences in imaginative and successful efforts to cope with what labor leaders, in other days, contemptuously called "speed ups" and "stretch outs". As we will see later, the "human relations" experts, 1930–1970, observed a *great* deal of learning at the hands of "informal groups"! Dr. Livingstone's current work, as we will most assuredly see, will deservedly earn great public attention on this very count!

Back in 1933, in manufacturing, 15% of physical capacity stood idle while (measurable) unemployment reached 25%. All things being equal, in the early days of a new century, we are "underutilizing" or underemploying between 40% and 60% of the work-related skills imputed to college graduates by human capital scholars in our "education-jobs gap" both in the U.S. and Canada (Livingstone, 1998, p. 82). This 'wastage' compares with 15–20% in the '60s (Berg, 1970) and 30% in the mid-'70s (Berg, 1978).

Put bluntly, the U.S. and Canada have suffered periodicities in the losses-of-use of human capacities to work effectively, in different ways, again and again (even ignoring losses from discrimination against women and minorities) over the period 1930–1990s, a loss to workers and their families, to investors and, perforce, to our economies conceived as machines-for-production. I note, in passing, that the *concept* of an economy as a *major segment of a nation's basic structure* (whose levers and sluicegates we now know are operated by unelected teachers and "training agents", i.e. by "managers, professionals and technicians") was only conceptualized, and rather vaguely so, by a small handful of economists – "institutionalists" – led by Richard Ely (1914).

These recollections are apposite: we truly came to see the nation state, itself after all, for what it really was, only in the 18th Century. It was thereafter two centuries before we saw (1) a nation's (arguably) most essential component, its economy-as-a-culture, as a thing unto itself, a macrocosmic "special purpose entity", with both identifiable and consequential attributes; (2) owners, compared with managers, as qualitatively different types of authority figures and producers of goods, services and profits and designers, within a democracy, of a vast system of private governments. We will have cause to return to these topics.

After the Great Depression 1940 to 1946, we had a long and, despite wartime horrors otherwise, happier moments in work settings, as wartime demands for labor rose steeply while the character of supply – its educational attributes, especially -remained fairly constant. The customary U.S. labor force numbers, 1939–1946, were greatly diminished by the mobilization of more than 11 million able bodied military candidates into full time operations; the inflationary potential inherent in such circumstances – limited supplies of labor coupled with limited quantities of both civilian 'consumables' and 'durables' – were substantially contained, on one side, by both wage and price controls, by rationing meat and dairy protein, prepared foods, clothing, footware, gasoline and, on the other side, by the capacities of a very modestly educated workforce to learn *very quickly* (many-hundreds of thousands-of them in only days) to do innumerable, and increasingly high skill and otherwise demanding jobs. Wartime productivity increases owed a little to innovations in technology *but, unquestionably, a great deal to job-related learning*, to able mentoring by experienced employees as well as supervisors' 'upgrades' in their supervisory skills and, in fairness, to wartime patriotism.

Inflation was also blunted well beyond what productivity increases could achieve, by generous corporations' stockholders who continued to pay their chieftains' salaries while a regiment of business leaders, in Washington, and in regional and local agencies, operated our nearly completely planned economy, through public "boards" and commissions, to set prices and wages, plan production, and oversee selective service "draft boards" for staffing our armed forces. No Soviet planning group, under a communist system, ever came even *close* to the efficiency of American executives' five year-long operations of a corporatist state in a meticulously integrated economy which was, in fact, essentially, and at once: (1) a radical extension of the numerous oligopolistic structures of the U.S. economy documented in the 1940s by a Temporary National Congress Committee (TNEC) and the "Pujo Commission's" study of our banking system in the pre-Crash era; (2) a "garrison economy" made up of military planners and a hugh defense sector; and (3) a *"Pax Americana"* consisting of well conceived collaborations among Big Government, Big Labor and Big Business (J. K. Galbraith, 1952).

It is worth pondering the ironies suggested by the proposition that America's leaders, in their entire history, did their very best works as managers only under conditions in which basic capitalist principles in support of competitive market forces were essentially shelved. Note too that the U.S. government and business leaders mobilized and organized a workforce – its top, middle and front line managers, its skilled ranks, its school systems, its officer corps in all our armed forces, its health workers, and forty-nine civil service systems etc. – with a population in which only 24% had high school degrees and in which 4% had college degrees on Dec 7th 1941. And a "high tech" war, and a "high tech" economy it became, and it became so virtually overnight after that fateful date.

Post World War II Developments

In the post war era we laid the ground work for yet another phase in what was now the economic core of the Western world; with Germany's, France's and

England's industrial systems in tatters, ours, Canada's and Australia's systems were the larger industrial world's only surviving children of pre-war capitalism's flirtation with (and wartime marriage) of bigness in business, with bigness in labor, and with big government 'riding shot gun' on this ménage á trois, a tripartite structure that could also "demobilize" a wartime economy by the ends of only days (or a very few months in a few instances) after the war ended in 1945 (Galbraith, 1952).

With the New Deal's "government by commission" in the U.S., and an oligopolized U.S. manufacturing sector, rife with "managed competition", we raced to eliminate rationing, public controls over prices and wages, and substituted oligopolistic controls in manufacturing (of the core economy's wages and most prices) while maintaining Federal regulations only temporarily over all interest rates and taxes, with resultingly highly limited price competition at home and with only negligible competition from Western Europe and what later became the Asian Tigers until the mid-1960s. During our transition, 1945–1955, we also enjoyed our Cold War's encouragement (subsidization) of a hugh "garrison-sector" in our economy, with defense jobs aplenty and even *some* positive civilian fallout from weapons research, including aircraft, and later, from space science, and additional economic stimulus from a brief hot war with China (in North Korea, 1950–53) that further pinched labor supply atop a boom, 1946–73.

During this period of growth and into the early 1970s we suffered only brief cyclical set-backs, principally from "inventory recessions". These novel recessions served to make labor's frequent post-war strikes briefer and less painful simply because our managers could "take" strikes that served them well, indeed, as defacto lay offs in a particular product line's occasional "off seasons"; for example, ample production capacities in steel, among the "big five" US steel makers, satisfied all their customers' requirements in 1959 *before* a 116 days strike that ended when an 80 day "cooling off period" was granted, by the courts, to President Eisenhower, under the Taft Hartly Act (passed in 1947 in popular reaction to a thousand strikes in 1946). The injunction brought workers back to their jobs which, but for a last minute settlement on Dec 28, 1959 (while the injunction would have expired December 31, 1959) would very clearly have seen angry steel workers returning to their picket lines with renewed zeal.

During this long post war boom, the economy was modernizing and expanding with correlatively significant pressures to expand the hiring of 'managers, professionals, and technicians', i.e. college graduates. With only 4% of our labor force with such degrees in pre-Pearl Harbor times, as we have noted, there was a *near term* shortage of college-educated Americans but which was widely regarded as an endlessly long term shortage, making college attendance appear to be ever more "necessary". During the period 1950–1970 we neglected education, "K through 12", especially in large cities.

Measuring Mismatches: The Jobs-Education Gap 1946–1950s

The 'demand' for college grads thus increased gradually, fed by managers who were increasing the numbers of graduates in our substantially oligopolized manufacturing sector with alacrity. These employers wanted very much to believe that their continuingly elevated educational requirements for jobs simply represented their organizations' certifiable needs. Such was the belief inspired by their school-given teachings and assurances, by industry economists, business schools and business apologists, especially, about our managers' putative rationality. Only one of twenty Fortune Five Hundred executives I interviewed doubted, one 'little bit,' that they knew what they were doing in these labor market transactions. These managers also plainly believed, as did the slick business magazines – *Business Week and Fortune* among them – that the vigorous but managed "non-price competition" they actually experienced was absolutely equivalent, *in its strict demands on their business acumen*, to "price competition". This belief was not well founded however; my evidence (Berg, 1970, 1978) showed that not one of twenty "Fortune 500" top-level managers (representing, eighteen industries) even by the late 1960s admitted to having ever seen marginal cost or marginal revenue curves describing the productivity of their human resources (never mind actually crossing these curves, thereby to be guided by them). Indeed, all the executives in these 20 firms questioned *my* judgment, as an educator (in asking about the labor costs of collegians) who appeared to them to be unconscious of *his* own economic interests! The gap between the actual *use* of and empirical *need* for college and high school diplomas, meanwhile, began to widen considerably, until circa 1969–70 (Berg, 1970), and continued to become more widespread in the 90s (Livingstone, 1998).

In the period 1958–64, several major works (Schultz, 1959; Mincer, 1958; Dennison, 1962; Becker, 1964) had appeared offering technical-analytical developments toward a 'theory of human capital' first summarized by Dennison (1962) who correlated measures of economic growth with investments in physical capital, on one side, and in education, on the other, among the most industrialized nations. He attributed the variances in national growth rates left unexplained by these nations' investments in physical capital to investments in education – investments in high school and technical school diplomates, and in college and graduate degrees; the correlations were impressively robust.

The three other of these authors explained the match-up between earnings and education, i.e. high statistical correlations, in the United States labor force after the war, in terms of cause and effect, and reported quite insistently, after allowing for education's non-economic value, that their robust statistical associations between years of formal schooling and earnings were well above the levels that could reasonably be attributed to chance. Like employers, the investigators linked the observed 'demand' for education, represented in workers' returns to education (discounted by costs, over workers' lifetimes) with what they deduced (i.e., postulated), from economists' well established "theory of the firm", to be 'rewards' to workers (and society) for *productivity* engendered by schooling, K-12, plus college. No credit was accorded, for example, to parents for Americans' substantial pre-school 'preparation', or to military training (as aviators, mechanics, electronics repairmen, cooks, bakers, musicians, etc, for example), nor did they control for industry pay differences in order to determine, statistically, what part "imperfect competition", as in our heavily oligopolized sectors, played in the pictures of production and income distribution, on one side, and the education they were studying, on the other side. Beyond all that, there are the vexing problems of conceptualizing costs and benefits; as energy expert S. David Freedman has frequently put it, in lectures and interviews, "on a discounted [cost] basis the earth simply is not worth saving". The point: our conceptions of costs, like those of profits (and unlike cash) are, as Bernard Baruch famously commented "matters of opinion, not facts"; one may ask any ENRON leader about all that, as they currently await their prison sentences for 'cooking' their accounting books, i.e. about one of their company's master business strategies. The fact that inflation was creeping up steadily in the 1960s and continued to move slowly after the early 1980s, meanwhile, made the imputations of higher *productivity* to better educated income earners looked very suspicious to me, especially since "*wage*-push" inflation was consistently identified by all our neo-orthodox colleagues in economics as a national horror story (readily scripted, as critics had it, by merciless union leaders and their political allies in Washington). Nearly all my nearby colleagues suggested I was on a fool's errand in my simpleminded effort to test the human capital thesis by *direct* methods. Most economists, Professor Becker included, and not a little bit self-servingly, blamed inflation on "workers" while simultaneously applauding employers' regularly escalating payments to their *college* grads, without so much as a blush! And, we noted that the decline in the rate of return on education since 1970 has correlated well with the overall decline in inflation rates since the 1980s; silver linings in a cloudburst.

Professor Becker (1964) did acknowledge, in a low key passage, that his analyses and conclusions were rooted entirely in studies of circumstantial evidence: in what was manifestly a tautology he urged that *better educated persons earn more because they are more productive, as indeed their earnings clearly demonstrated!* Their single minded devotion to the sovereignty of price theory made it very difficult for economists to doubt that managers *could conceivably* (they certainly wouldn't do so in willful disregard of efficiency!) hire applicants with educational achievements *beyond* those absolutely needed in a price-competitive environment. The economy was assumed, nearly universally, to be very heavily populated by *economically* rational managers in price competitive markets who meticulously crossed their marginal costs for labor with the marginal revenues generated by each additional increment in the educations of those they hired. Price theory, allegedly *forcing* them to compete, etc., simply exonerates employers of responsibilities-of-initiative, i.e., a 'theodicy of innocence'.

I (and S. M. Miller, in conversations) had doubts about all this, doubts that were soon reinforced by my aforementioned interviews with Fortune 500 leaders who assured me that no such studies were needed; such were their faiths in the received wisdom, specifically, and their subscription to the sapient orthodoxy, fancifully holding that "competition" is as competition does, whether price-driven or not. But workers' earnings were *indirect* not direct evidence in support of human capital students' self evident constructions.

To 'test' the human capital thesis I resolved to use *direct* evidence – concerning "actual" job requirements for educational achievements. The first two prongs: (1) analyses of the "actual" educational requirements of 40,000-odd jobs, representing about 86% of the workforce – that were developed, in condensed (scalar) forms of several different specific vocational skills, by Labor Department jobs analysts, with the 'dedicated' help of employer specialists, and (2) actual rewards (promotions, bonuses, commendations, public recognition, sales records, etc.) accorded employees in a variety of white collar and blue collar settings, including professional, technical, managerial and other white collar and blue collar jobs, and in all wage and salary ranges. These rewards included the rankings of "the best", and "the less valuable personnel" among 620 scientists and engineers divided among the six largest manufacturers of heavy electrical equipment firms surveyed by The Opinion Research Corporation in 1958, all six of which, not so paradoxically, were among 29 companies convicted for pricing conspiracies, under the Sherman Antitrust Act a year later,[1] conspiracies that began as long ago as 1935; massive profits from this gigantic oligopoly could and in fact did support a very great many 'redundant' and 'not so valuable' college graduates.

There was/is no denying that mine were crude measurements, but they were *far less gross* than "earnings", and they were *direct* measures; I found that educational achievements played *no* statistical part, whatever, in explaining how rewards in any of these jobs' settings were accorded (Berg, 1970).

We must emphasize that, while there were few college and high school grads in the early 1950s, it took less than a decade to essentially begin to undo substantially the tremendous *integration* of Americans' *diverse* educational achievements, *especially* in the upper *half* of earners in the American workforce established before and, especially, during the Second World War! The best predictor of income gains among workers, 1930–1955, for example, was age combined with experience, the latter of which workers overall had more, obviously, than they did of education! It was, in the earlier post war period, thus possible (as it is not possible today) to actually compare my estimates of workers' differential productivity by years of education in hundreds of thousands of job settings in which there was *vast heterogeneity* in the education variable. The opportunities for high school grads to enter high-level jobs in both civilian and military skill hierarchies were extraordinarily great in the immediate post war years. Indeed, that most military veterans availed themselves of technical courses or on-the-job-training opportunities, rather than G. I. Bill-funded four year-long college curricula in the 1945–1950 period, reflected the relative (and relatively *very* high) 'opportunity costs', in those early post war years, inherent in deferring earning opportunities for four years, even allowing for federal income support to veterans while studying; a bright and reasonably diligent high school grad, 25 plus years old in 1945, after military 'leave', could go a long way up the income ladder!

Alas for human capital theory, it did not take long for those who chose college to grow in such numbers that, by the early 1960s, this group's growth exceeded the gradually slowing growth in demand for what could have been only *proto-typically college* jobs in the immediately preceding periods; i.e. jobs generated by the post war expansion specifically in the ranks of "managers, professionals and technicians" that were, in fact, heavily populated by high school grads. This 'tailing off' in the growth of truly college jobs[2] showed up in each of five "translations" my colleagues and I rendered of employers' and job analysts' estimates of jobs' actual educational requirements. Even the version that gave the *most* question-begging 'faith and credit' to employers for (putatively) *rational* "up grading" in requirements for college degrees (for jobs *beyond* those so graded as college jobs in our five sets of estimates from the Labor Department/employer analysts' efforts, in the meantime and varying from "excessive" to "rampant") indicated that, by the early 1960s, better than 15% of Americans were in jobs that only slightly earlier had been *essentially* filled, and *perfectly adequately so*, by high school grads! That number went up to nearly 30% in 1978; in Livingstone's (1998) report, using the same 'multiple version' method for estimating 'actual' educational requirements for 86% of America's jobs, about 50% of Americans, both college and high school graduates, were underutilized over these periods, with increases first in underutilized ex-high schoolers and then spreading to the ex-collegians.

In a third prong (1970), I turned to an examination of students' course scores in an enormous variety of military schools' training programs, in all of the U.S. armed forces in 1967. These efforts revealed that high school dropouts and grads, on one side, did substantially better than military personnel with *post* high school exposures, on the other side. The latter group apparently had little interest in military careers and attended only casually to military 'schooling' opportunities. This finding held in all categories of military programs, from truck driving to navigation, radio repair, language learning, pharmaceuticals, ballistics, and meteorology, i.e. from marginally to highly technical subjects. The finding also suggests that learning in very job-linked programs is a function of motivation, a finding that reinforce my interest in Livingstone's and Pankhursts' current research on learning at work! The criteria for success in lower, middle and higher skill military programs, meantime, involved differentially more *learning from applied experience*, and from lectures *about operating methods*, code systems, inductive and deductive reasoning, and the logics of algorithms from problem solving, from lower to higher levels of complexity, than from straight "academic" learning opportunities and from traditional texts. The military has always (and wisely) distinguished "training learning" for "education learning".

Thereafter, I looked at a 5% sample of all federal civil servants. This part of the third prong showed that "progress", i.e. career movements by thousands upon thousands of federal workers to ever-higher level jobs, was closely linked statistically to the number of their bids for job openings *across* agencies, an employee initiative that was far more dispositive of their mobility prospects than upon educational achievements. We should note that both public servants' bids to transfer and their evolving educational achievements were scrupulously logged in civil servants' employment records.[3]

The Decline in Returns to Formal Education, 1970 and Beyond

My results, the consistent 'underutilization' or 'underemployment' of education at all but the lowest levels in each of my prongs, and the anomalous relationships observed between occupational mobility and educational achievements, were also observed later by Livingstone (1998) in his Canadian by data and by Bernhardt et al. (2001) in a recent report based on detailed analyses of the job histories of U.S. workers who entered the labor force, separately in each of two age cohorts, in the late 1960s and in the early 1980s.

Dr. Livingstone, meantime, has added the "informal learning" (including programmatic impartation of knowledge and skill-honing by employers) of Canadian workers to their 'school learning' and the results of his analyses of the education-jobs gap show, sadly, that the gap has thereby widened considerably. His measures for documenting informal learning are both imaginative and compelling. In subsequent studies Livingstone has refined further measures of the underemployment gap (see Livingstone, 2001; Livingstone & Sawchuk, 2003). Such measures offer even more disconcerting evidence of managers' lapses. It is apposite and only a trifle petty, to note, in this context, the comparatively *slow* "informal learning" about *managers' demonstrable underemployment* of their human resources (from their essentially un-examined corporate data) is a matter the reasons for which clearly deserve serious study! The economists will, in theory of course, afford managers no excuse, *in a price-driven economic* world, for such underemployment, but should wonder, in reality at least, as they have not, why employers, by the hundreds of thousands in the two economies, ignored opportunities to gain efficiencies *without* price pressures on oligopolistic profits, 1950–1970s; these long-underutilized people, after all, were the "fat" that was carved away, 1980s–2000, in the movement to be "lean and mean" by downsizing. Why reward these leaders, in the 1990s, with massive stock options when they were simply *undoing* yesteryears' bumblings, during a long period, in the absence of the incentives of price competition, during which they simply 'layered on'.

Some of the most relevant effects of underutilization did indeed become apparent, ironically in the decline in the rates of (personal) returns *on education* in the late 1960s, just as incomes for three fifths of Americans earnings'-after-inflation began to stagnate, a stagnation that continued until about 1995, i.e. in the middle of the decade-long '90s boom; no stock options for them! The stagnation in real earnings, beginning in 1969, then reappeared, marginally, as a new president took office in 2001, but is in full swing as this volume goes to press and may well continue *even if recovery becomes truly robust* in 2004, and beyond. Personally the inflation, complete with wage inflation, simply masked the decline for many of us. We can *impute* a recognition to employers of their earlier misallocations of personnel dollars, meantime, by the onset of the way stagnation intensified in these lines. In fine: the dollar and cents facts of actual *gains*, in the economy deriving from economic growth, post 1969, *barely reached the victims of stagnation* until 1995–6, and, as we have noted, re-stagnated after 2000.

Ironically, the human capital school's belief that workers' educational achievements are 'paid precisely what they're worth' (i.e., for their marginal productivity) does *now* make a great deal more sense than it did in the 1960s (*especially* now that returns to college education, with a long post 90s boom recession) have re-stagnated. The downward adjustments of returns to education occurred gradually but has been systematic for just short of the forty years elapsed after Professor Becker's book appeared – and in perfect alignment with his receipt of a Nobel Medal for Economic Science just two years short of his work's 40th anniversary; the economic *facts* are now all in line with his *then* problematical application of basic price theory: *with price competition now rampant* – at home and abroad, – *college degrees' returns are about on target*, all the more so than they were when the theory *assumed* price competition.

This reduction in return, perhaps 'better later than never', appears to be fully justified (especially by the logics of human capital writer's own theory!) and the decline in *"real" college job* opportunities for college grads, as more of these college grads occupy high school-level jobs, perhaps at the 'high pay ends', at the expense of high school grads who have been 'bumped' down, into the lowest of lower paying high school-level jobs (Bernhardt et al., 2001) And, as these collegians are 'bumped', and just as the upper half of what were once the high schoolers' best paid jobs go to the collegians, the return to *high school diplomates* has fallen off scholars' charts. College grads and some high schoolers are sharing growing numbers of middle level job openings – but, perhaps more devastatingly, the balance of high schoolers have been bequeathed an almost uncontested monopoly on the *least* rewarding of 'blue collar' jobs into which most high schoolers will "skid", their nearest competitors, of course are immigrants and the lesser paid workers in Southeast Asia and, sooner or later, Africa and Latin America.

The Correlates of Declining Returns to Collegians

We can conclude, conservatively, that an investment in a *college* degree of declining value on average, in preparation for entry into the fulltime labor force since the early 1980s, has by now been converted into a variation on an insurance policy for many, many college grads, *for the present at least*, against falling into these lowest paying "high school" jobs (Berg, 2003; Bernhardt et al., 2003, pp. 132, 148). And the college returns, themselves, *have not gone up nearly as fast as high 'schoolers' returns have gone down!* (Berg, & Kalleberg, 2001, Ch 1, 7, 27); it is indeed highly likely that it is the *declines* in high schoolers' *earnings* that explain the collegians' continuing and growing 'advantages', *not* the collegians "higher" *productivity*. This development indeed is assured by human capital theory *given* a long period of increasingly vigorous price competition. The main circumstances generating these declining returns thus are: (1) the collapse of high paying manufacturing jobs and, with this collapse, (2) the declining numbers of old-line oligopolists' opportunities to administer their prices, in favor of robust price competition, in almost every product- and many service precincts in the American economy.

Nowadays many praise our surviving corporations' leaders for 'downsizing', 'offshoring', 'contracting out', 'outsourcing', and for completing economy-targeted mergers and acquisitions (with their emphases on "core" business activities) that make their properties 'lean and mean'. These leaders do not acknowledge their too often misplaced applause, in bygone days however, for mangers' building of higher employment levels, during economic booms, on a pile of extra high payments for education that cannot be readily accounted for by reassuring productivity data. The data on productivity held to be reflections of education were actually inflated in technical measures of productivity, the dollar value of output divided by hours worked. By definition, higher dollar inflation, captured neatly, if only partially, in the exaggerated employers' dollar value of output, actually yields *lower* productivity when the numerator is divided by the denominator (hours worked) and while "temporary" and subcontract works are not even charged, statistically, to their nominal employers but to the outside vendors of these workers' labors.

We routinely provided "asymmetric information" in economists' recent and laudable adoption of other social scientists' findings to investors (and everyone else) long before the wide-spread deceptions in corporate accounting practices discovered in the scandals in America's energy, telecom, and other generally 'hi-tech' industries in 2000–2003, especially. Notoriously, these so-called aggressive practices included exaggerated earnings and wildly understated costs by the attribution of earnings to "parents" from and debts attributed to faux subsidiaries. ENRON, a leading energy corporation, was only the best known of the malefactors in these scandals: facing increasingly vigorous price competition, the company specifically switched accounting practices by simply understating cost while they exaggerated earnings concealed in "special purpose entities" (highly nominal subsidiaries) at the same time the company got "out of assets" – heavy fixed costs – to become brokers; such are the deceptions practiced by the surviving bastard-offspring of the larger institutional American economy's divorce from manufacturing and its oligopolistic structure. While some better educated Americans were quite evidently upper level corporate crooks by 2000, others of this better educated American cohort, were *beginning* to be underutilized by the mid-1960s, at the latest. 'You could look it up', between the lines in our U.S. inflation reports, and palpate the short term effects in "stagflation", 1970 and beyond: inflation *with* unemployment, contrary to traditional "Phillips Curve" – informed analyses (according to which inflation is best countered by high unemployment which can be facilitated by raising interest rates). Today's picture became the 'flip side' of "stagflation", mid-1970s – i.e. a period of high *unemployment* coexisting, anomalously, with *high* inflation, like a rifle rack in a Volvo.

Underutilization and Employee Morale

The other expected consequences of underutilization, as I looked up from my numbers to begin writing in 1970, were captured historically in the compendious term "alienation", a concept in the heritage in the social sciences of Marxian interpretations of the effects of capitalists' "expropriations of the means of production" and of the resulting "surplus value" derived there from. These psychological effects never did appear in the U.S., in significant numbers (and do not look likely now to appear so). In 1967–8, I expected this increasing 'alienation' among all Americans scarred, and soon to be re-scarred, however, by the shattering of whatever specific, positive expectations about education's career-and income-building-capacities they entertained; I was quite wrong, at one level, at least.

The facts of the matter: I was working, in the 1960s, at Columbia University, where widely popular student protests revealed very heated anger, and growing despair as well, over corporate careers in allegedly "big, bloated, corporate bureaucracies" (as Michael Milken famously called them in his mobilization of syndicates funded by junk bonds in the 1980s). These protests were informed and magnified by many students' disappointments with "Cold War multiversities'" putatively wanton, and even evil ways, with their defense-related (and often secret research), with race relations, with the military draft, and on and on. And I anticipated this 'alienation' would grow, and with increasing speed.

Instead, there came Presidents Nixon, Carter, Reagan, Bush, Clinton and a second Bush, all of them with large, strong, and ideologically-lively conservative followings among Americans, a population that found the radicals' protests to be obscene. Mr. Nixon's 1968 election appeals actually won the support of more than half of even 1968's new 18 year old voters! "Alienation" simply could not strike deep roots in America, whatever the economy's declining rewards for nearly all but the top 1% of income earners, for several basic reasons (Berg, 2003). And, or moreover, consider that Mr. Nixon was no retributively angry conservative after taking office: he ended the draft, pursued the Occupational Health and Safety, and the Environmental Protection Acts, and promised withdrawal from Vietnam, in his run for the White House. He also experimented with quotas for a time as a way of moving Affirmative Action forward.

There were at least five reasons for the tempering over alienation: it was muted by a range of "offsetting" phenomena.

First, second incomes in families were a 'growth industry,' as battalions of women (first and foremost among them from inflation-suffering families) went to work. And shrinking families' *sizes*, per se, more often left *families* better, than worse off. Related to earnings "adaptations" to income limitations, Americans experienced a veritable invasion of inflation-neutering cheap foreign imports assuring many, many consumers that their dollars, happily, went further with each "stagnant" income year, as imports kept climbing. These imports combined with the refinancing of home mortgages (and their declining interest rates) have continued to be President Bush's best economic friends.

Second, the '60s' campus lifestyles – including the barely controlled hedonistic impulses of the "asylums' inmates" became the devil's work for many afraid Americans, especially when these styles were coupled with a vital conservative movement's hostilities toward governments, desegregation and affirmative action efforts, as well as America's academics' 'secular humanism'; protestors withal were thus increasingly marginalized and rendered harmless.

Thirdly, the legitimacy of business leaders "private governments", through the rapid maturation of professional managers in the Age of Big Business, was long vetted by the fulsome blessings that the Enlightenments' architects of modern democracy – John Locke, especially – bestowed upon corporate managers, specifically, as agents of the property owners celebrated by Locke. But this mantle of legitimacy has subsequently been vetted (after a flirtation with social Darwinism – the 'survivals' and the 'ascensions' of the "fittest") largely by the axial principles of organization in "rational-legal bureaucracies", especially as conceived by Max Weber and other historians of capitalism's development that have eventuated in widely held popular perceptions of corporate managers' *merits*. The emphases on bureaucratic authority's legitimacy was enlivened by a long history of the acceptance, after ownership, of "managerialism" as entirely legitimate systems of 'private governance'. Thus almost no one doubts today, in keeping with Thomas Jefferson's expectations, that our system would be built upon an "an aristocracy of talent", an aristocracy that is vetted, in parochial and de facto fashion by diplomas and degrees. Best of all: almost any authority thus legitimated draws a welcome bye for managers in a society fairly well given, otherwise, to *egalitarian* values. Thus Chester Barnard, of N. J. Bell urged, in numerous screeds and lectures (and in league with Harvard Business School "human relationists") that managers seek earnestly to broaden workers' "zones of acceptance" and of "zones of indifference" toward managers' authority, by using applied social science techniques; the knowledge of these technologies could assure workers of both managers' professional expertise and their interests in workers. These techniques were the house specialty of the Harvard Business School and their naturally devoted emulators from sea to shining sea. The advent of 'downsizing' calls for a new form of business apologetics for the redemption of managers' authority.

Barnard's dicta about these 'zones' were joined by "managerialists" with Max Weber's emphases on rational-legal bureaucratic structures and the roles of these structures in the screening and development of rigorous selection processes emphasizing formal technical education and training, and the use, further of professional reviews, in legitimating formal "rational-legal bureaucratic authority"; these panacea have left us with formal education playing an ever increasing role in the vetting of professional managers' authority. Education began to figure slowly, in the period 1885–1920s, with the separation of corporate ownership from corporate control, and replaced whatever little has remained, later, of Social Darwinist explanations for the distribution of income, wealth, and power, by the 1940s, among the fittest, the fit and the unfit.

Fourthly, the socio-economic "immiserations" of American workers in the last quarter of the Twentieth Century, counting only those who actually lost their jobs to 'downsizing', 'offshoring' and 'outsourcing' designs have been widely distributed. Managers, in turn, were rewarded by stock options for the allegedly consequent improvements in productivity – improvements that are absolutely nothing more, as already suggested, than the mathematical reciprocals of the dollar value of product sales, (including only current product sales volume!) divided by the hours of work. The increasingly short-term quality of managers' decision making horizons, meanwhile began with blue collar cutbacks in the 1960s and '70s. "Short termism" picked up speed with the decline of manufacturing (especially in the oligopolized industries whose managers' capacities to *manage* prices) simply displacing longer term interest, as 'managed competition' yielded to price wars. The result was to *distribute* increasing increments of un-and underemployment, in successive uses, very widely across the entire economy.

It has clearly been the case that regular epidemic-level lay offs, coupled with the apprehensions of "survivors", have helped to reduce a sense of *relative* deprivation as between small groups of victims and large numbers of "haves". In its place is a growing sense that life is rife with a new kind of coercive comparisons in which unfortunates' envy of those who are still prospering gives way to a very widening sense that one is indeed not truly much *worse* off than a very great many others. Relative deprivation thus becomes a norm, not the basis simply for an *individual's* invidious comparisons. This newer sentiment, of very widely shared difficulties, can easily temper the sense of deprivation, producing a generalized, newly population-wide sense of marginalization, helplessness; "resignation", as Ralph Waldo Emerson once put it, becomes "two thirds of happiness". The refinancing of homes, i.e. our "faiths *in* credit", another theodicy of innocence – has gradually become a new "opium of the people", on which far too many American's are in risk of overdosing, as witnessed by deepening personal bankruptcy rates.

Finally, in our 1978 research, *underemployed* workers who were *better paid* expressed far greater overall job satisfaction than did their *underemployed peers with distinctively lower earnings*. Employers can thus at least 'buy off' 'alienation' with the dollars that are not evidently earning them more education-generated productivity-a kind of perverse 'dividend' to employers from the inflation to which misallocations of education contribute; the *better* paid underemployed were arguably at least, paid to be happy campers not, so palpably, evidently for their productivity (Berg & Freedman, 1978).

There is little evidence currently that we are headed for widespread popular outrages – even in company with radically and increasingly regressive income tax schedules, with rapidly shrinking public and private services, with problematic health policies, with mounting evidence that our business system is rife with overstated earnings, understated liabilities, bizarre accounting practices, offshoring, downsizing, sub-contracting, underutilization and high levels of unpitying assaults on both traditional values about accounting, and veracity of stock analysts' assessments, coupled with hypocritical urgings by conservative publicists about "virtue". And, of course, there is social and political malaise – low key apprehension – attaching to income stagnation for three fifths of us coupled with traces of recession ("stagcession"?).

None of the foregoing discussions take account of the very possible *psychopathological* correlates of 'alienation', or despair in workplaces, however, such as alcoholism, spouse-or child abuse, depression or as we have read about it, in very recent times, aggrieved workers "going postal".

The fact is that we had a burst of dreary reports, in the period well before 1980, on the effects of "automation", for example – and in analyses of earlier series of "stretchouts" and "speedups" affecting blue collar Americans, and highly visible among them during the "rust belt's" gradual corrosion. Later inflictions of "economic capital punishment" on white collar Americans involved more non-invasive studies of despair than those in shops, factories, mills and forges. As it happened, the author assayed a large portion of this mass (as well as the dross) of studies of the mental health of the two classes' with the conclusion that little could be said, dispositively, about the specific effects on the victims' of socio-economic misfortune, though the effects of community upheavals – abandoned towns, inner cities and factory districts – were quite a bit more readily apprehensible. My review (Berg & Hughs, 1979) which some readers may find useful, considered well over 150 discrete studies.[4]

Coda

Graduating classes in Spring 2003, with up to 20% of their members (even in 'Ivy League' colleges) without jobs (and laden with heavy debts from their college expenses) spent late May and June of last year barely cheering their class leaders, their commencement speakers and, many of them, the daily proclamations by America's leaders of our progress against Muslim fundamentalists' worst ambitions (though Sadam Hussein allegedly linked to the terrorists was once an ally precisely because he was *not* a fundamentalist).

There is one additional and likely part of the explanation for so many Americans' apparent sense of equanimity about socio-economic disjunctions. It is quite possible, as several major pundits, Paul Krugman often in *The New York Times* among them, have written that many of us have come to *expect less* than we did in the 1950s–1960s, of each other, of marriage, of guarantees and warrantees, of business leaders, of presidents, and other politicians, accountants, employers, stock analysts, advertisers, even of priests, and, of course, of ourselves; Emerson's resignation, 'one more time', now raised from two-thirds to three quarters of happiness. One cannot but help to see this in undergraduates: whatever views they have in partisan political terms only a small minority of them, nowadays, read a decent daily newspaper, or even *Time* or *Newsweek*.

Notice, too, how much less valuable (or valued) the conditions and benefits we once aspired to enjoy or posses have so often come to seem less than they appeared to be before we earned them – our maturity, seniority, promotions, tenure, earnings, and so on, all have some distinctively hollow qualities, once achieved, compared with the value we invested in them before they were ours; divorce rates, and delayed marriage rates, reduced birth rates, and a troubled Social Security System, all denote a kind of future whose character contributes to a widespread and serious tentativeness in our youths' perspectives about life's prospects.

In the case of college educations we were already in an age of substantial surplus, as clearly connoted by sagging income returns, in the mid-1960s; admiration for the bloom on the education shrub is already shifting away from the blossoms once attaching to college degrees' intrinsic or inherent economic values and are being evermore attached to different institutions' differentiated hierarchical statuses: colleges are consistently and sometimes mercilessly evaluated by rankings and sortings by the editors of 'business slicks', rankings that are unsurprisingly well correlated with their tuition rates, and attended to scrupulously by high school seniors and their families. And, of course, we are currently welcoming hordes of candidates for new fangled terminal masters degrees in an explosion of evening programs, and "distant learning" graduate centers, as university treasurers and deans seek new income sources and as their departments seek enrollments.

Indeed we will likely be obliged to temper, or 'edit', a great many of our disappointments: "we didn't make it to MIT, but with our miss-spent 'teenage ways', we have only ourselves to blame", as with the many unemployed workers in New Haven who, demonstrably, out of pride *and self-blame*, accepted no economic help in the 1930s, as reported by E. Wight Bakke (1934) in his famous study of New Haven's victims of the Depression.

To be sure, there is always *some* mobility in stratification processes and, with that fact, some blunting effects, as well, when we individually 'slip', or skid downhill *less precipitously* than others and, of course, by no means are *all* ex-collegians 'underutilized'. Elite college graduates in the class of 2000 are, on average, somewhat better off, for example, than "second tier" schools' grads, even if they are not earning, after inflation, what their own Ivy League *predecessors* in the class of '55, for example, were earning after their first 8–10 post college years. And there may still be a *little* "relative deprivation", some of which can be rationalized, on both sides, as in 'I had less/more luck', or I really did not work as hard as I could have or, with a shrug, "I guess women and minorities are coming in for a bigger share ...", and again, some resignation.

In any (and most events) the overall levels of protests specifically against inequality, these days, are conspicuously low; half of the African American population is now in middle income groups, a change that may have led more often to resignation than frustration among the members of those 'left behind'; 'self-blame' is not likely restricted to New Haven whites. It is a bit frightening, nevertheless, with what *perhaps* only *appears* to be widespread equanimity, to contemplate an old saw in my own US Marine Corps days: "Griping troops are not bitter troops; the time to worry is when the troops *stop* griping and, as a group becomes sullen".

With proliferation (and increasing stratification) of all types of schools, and with tuition in public institutions rolling up, thus encouraging private colleges not to cut prices, we reduce only slowly the 'price competition' and price-tag pride between 'publics' and "privates", but we will still recognize that we have *two* increasingly important mismatches (and heightened consciousness of them), between what collegians *pay* for their education and the interest rate they pay on loans, on one side, and their initial and *increasingly insecure earnings*, on the other! The high inflation rates of the 1970s, meanwhile, no longer favor these borrowers, (about half of all students, and favored for as long as inflation is under control), posing another range of economic concerns, beyond "mismatching". The Fed has virtually decreed, with its manifestly anti inflation bias, that borrowers will now repay loans with dollars of relatively constant values, and in their February 2004 meeting, indicated that interest rates may well be elevated in the near future.

One fact already outlined must be emphasized: college educations, once the "offensive" vehicles for social mobility, and a versatile offensive weapon in that 'struggle', are now *defensive* weapons of mass deconstruction, for many grads, who are suffering the large declines in income once suffered mostly by high school graduates. *That*, all by itself, is a remarkable change; it is of the order of a tectonic shift like those in the continental-geologic shelf.

Withal, perhaps many Americans' equanimity towards their social and economic is, in empirical terms, a reasonable stance toward a circumstance of such measurably large magnitudes that many 'suffer together' from events that virtually no one can do anything to change. But against the worst implications of this condition, i.e. with only *relatively* higher income generated by one's schooling, many may conclude that at least, they have a welcome, if a slightly porous parachute for a "softer landing" in the mobility stakes.

Notes

1. These six firms were among 29 companies that were convicted, in anti trust proceedings, of rigging prices from 1935 (starting with The National Recovery Act, the so called Blue Eagle Act) to the Fall of 1959!
2. In a related context the honorable George Schultz, asked by the *New York Times* "whether things were getting better or worse" in the economy, as he left Treasury in 1974, a few days before Mr. Nixon resigned, he replied: "They're getting better and better, day by day, but not at a rate fast enough that prevents them from going from bad to worse". So it has been with 'college jobs' vis a vis college grads!
3. Similar data from our 20 Fortune 500 leaders and from others, virtually *anywhere* in the U. S. economy, would not become available until President L. B. Johnson's now notorious Exec. Order 11–246, developed by the Department of Labor pursuant to the Civil Rights Act (of 1964), *required* data on Federal contractors' utilization of education while controlling for race, ethnicity and gender, and compliance reviewers regarding "goals and timetables" for the hiring of "protected group" members.
4. I. Berg and Hughs, M. "Economic Circumstances and The Entangling Webs of Pathologies: An Esquisse" in Ferman, and Gordus, J. P. *Mental Health and the Economy*. Kalamazoo, MI. W. E. Upjohn Institute for Empirical Research, December 1979.

References

Bakke, E. Wight (1934). *The unemployed man: A social study*. New York: Dutton.
Becker, G. (1964). *Human capital*. New York: National Bureau of Economic Research.
Berg, I. (1970). *Education and jobs: The great training robbery*. New York: Praeger.

Berg, I., & Freedman, M. K. (1978). *Managers and work reform: A limited engagement.* New York: Free Press.

Berg, I., & Hughes, M. (1979). Economic circumstances and the entangling web of pathologies: An Esquisse. In L. Ferman & G. J. M. (Eds.), *Mental health and the economy.* Kalamazoo, MI: WE UpJohn Foundation For Employment Research.

Berg, I., & Kalleberg, A. L. (2001). *Sourcebook of labor markets: Evolving structures and processes.* New York:: Kluwer Academic/Plenum.

Berg, I. (Ed.) (2003). *Education and Jobs: The Great Training Robbery (1970) edit. With a New Introduction.* Clinton Corners, New York: Percheron Press.

Berg, I. (2003). *Education and jobs: The great training robbery (1970) edit. New Introduction.* Clinton Corners, New York: Percheron Press.

Bernhardt, A. H., Morris, M., Handcock, M. S., & Scott, M. A. (2001). *Divergent paths: Economic mobility in the new American market.* New York: Russell Sage.

Dennison, E. F. (1962). *Accounting for slower economic growth: The United States in the 1970s.* Washington, D.C: Brookings Institution.

Ely, R. T. (1949). Outlines of economies 1914, passim. In L. H. Haney (Ed.), *History of economic thought* (pp. 883–905). New York: MacMillan.

Galbraith, J. K. (1993). *American capitalism: The concept of countervailing power.* New Brunswick, NJ: Transaction Publishers.

Livingstone, D. W. (1998). *The education-jobs gap: Underemployment or economic democracy.* Boulder, CO: Westview Press.

Livingstone, D. W. (2001). *Basic patterns of work and learning in Canada: Findings of the 1998 NALL survey of Informal learning and related Statistics Canada Surveys,* from www.nall.ca

Livingstone, D. W., & Sawchuk, P. (2003). *Hidden knowledge: Organized labour in the information age.* Lanham, MD: Rowman & Littlefield.

Miller, S. M. (May & August, 1996). Personal conversations.

Mincer, J. (1958). Investment in human capital and personal income. *Journal of Political Economy,* 66, 281–302.

Schultz, T. W. (1959). Investment in man: An economist's view. *Social Service Review, 33,* 109–117.

47

RUNNING FASTER TO STAY IN THE SAME PLACE? THE INTENDED AND UNINTENDED CONSEQUENCES OF GOVERNMENT POLICY FOR WORKPLACE LEARNING IN BRITAIN

Helen Rainbird*, Anne Munro[†], and Peter Senker[‡]
**University College Northampton, UK;* [†]*Napier University, Edinburgh, UK*
[‡]*University of East London, UK*

'Well in *our* country ... you'd generally get to somewhere else – if you ran very fast for a long time, as we've been doing' (Alice, Alice Through the Looking Glass).

Recent policy debates have emphasised the significance of workplace learning to the vision of the 'learning society' and the 'knowledge-based economy'. Whereas these terms trip relatively easily off the tongue, identifying what they mean in terms of a vision of the economy and society is more problematic. We are indebted to Lloyd and Payne (2002) not only for their reflections on the vision of the high skill society, but also for their reference to Lewis Carroll's 'Alice Through the Looking Glass'. The starting point for this paper is the idea that workplace learning ought to be central to any vision of the economy and society which is based on skills and knowledge (cf. Rainbird, 2000). The objective is to examine three major arenas of UK government policy which, it could be assumed, might exemplify the way these connections are made in one form or another. These are policy interventions which are intended to have a direct impact on training and workforce competence, on the one hand, and interventions which affect it indirectly, on the other. The example we have chosen of the former is the development of occupational standards in the care sector. These have been developed and introduced as a means of securing a competent and qualified workforce in a sector which until recently has not been effectively regulated. Our example of the latter is public sector reform in health and local government, where the stated aim of policy is to improve the quality of public services. Following the logic of the argument that the quality of goods and services is linked to the skills and qualifications of the workforce, we might assume that this would involve investment in the training and development of

International Handbook of Educational Policy, 885–901
Nina Bascia, Alister Cumming, Amanda Datnow, Kenneth Leithwood and David Livingstone (Eds.)
© 2005 *Springer. Printed in Great Britain.*

public sector workers. We contrast these major developments with a third, much smaller initiative, the Teaching Company Scheme, which is aimed at supporting innovation in small companies. Here, provisions are made for graduates to be placed in small companies which have previously had little use of qualifications at this level. Each of these interventions is presumed to have consequences for employees' acquisition of skills and knowledge.

The role of social institutions in shaping national patterns in the supply and demand for skills to the economy is well-established. The relatively weak role of the state in regulating vocational training in the UK has been widely debated and will not be discussed here. The British problem has been identified not just in terms of the supply of skills through the education system but also as a question of employers' demand for them (Keep & Mayhew, 1999). Whereas successive governments have sought to intervene in the supply of skills through education and training interventions, since the abolition of the Industrial Training Boards in 1983 and 1988 (see Senker, 1992) they have eschewed direct intervention affecting employers' decisions on investment in training and development. What happens inside the company lies within the domain of employer prerogative. This includes decisions concerning access to training and development, as well as those relating to patterns of job design, team-working and job progression routes which impact on workers' opportunities for informal learning from a range of different sources.[1]

By workplace learning we mean formal training, provided by the employer, both within and outside the workplace, and also a range of informal learning which takes place through on-going practice. In this respect the field we are interested in is learning which is 'not just the acquisition of mental and manual skills but ... also. ... a process of socialisation in work-related values, in a culture and community of work' (Streeck, 1989, p. 98). An understanding of developments in work organisation and in the employment relation is fundamental to our understanding of learning opportunities at work.

The paper draws on the findings of five linked research projects funded under the Economic and Social Research Council's Teaching and Learning Research Programme.[2] It draws specifically on the findings of two of the projects concerning access to workplace learning in cleaning and care services; and on apprenticeship as a model of learning amongst carer support workers and associates of the Teaching Company Scheme. In the latter, apprenticeship was understood as a form of learning through participation in the social relations of the workplace rather than a specific institutional form, following Lave and Wenger (1991). The first of these projects involved conducting semi-structured interviews with care workers and cleaners in the public sector, the private sector and in the private sector under sub-contract to the public sector. The objective was to examine the extent to which differences in ownership and in the employment relationship affected access to formal training, to assessment and to informal learning opportunities at work. The second project involved interviews with carer support workers (CSWs) and their managers working for the non-profit organisation,

Crossroads. This is an organisation which provides respite care for family members caring for relatives in their own homes. It also involved interviews with associates of the Teaching Company Scheme (TCS), their managers in the workplace and mentors in partner universities. The TCS is a government funded programme which aims to encourage small and medium-sized companies to adopt new technologies by employing new graduates. This project also used semi-structured interviews to examine how skills and knowledge were acquired and applied in the workplace, in these two very different contexts.

The paper is divided into four sections. The first section starts with an analysis of the introduction of statutory requirements for workforce competence in the care sector. National Vocational Qualifications (NVQs) are occupational standards, concerned with measuring training outcomes, but in practice the relationship between learning, training and competence assessment is highly problematic. This section explores the extent to which NVQs support or enhance learning in a range of contexts in which care services are provided. It also assesses the relative influence of NVQs compared to other factors in driving access to workplace learning.

The second section examines the impact of reforms in the public services, notably in local government and the National Health Service (NHS), focussing on their intended and unintended consequences for employees' learning at work. We focus on cleaners, an occupational group whose learning needs have often been neglected. Cleaning was also one of the first services to be subject to compulsory competitive tendering in local government and to market testing in the NHS under the Conservative governments (1979–1997). Although the Labour government reforms have the objective of improving public services, there are also pressures to reduce costs, to externalise contracts to the private sector and to meet centrally set targets. These contradictory and sometimes incompatible objectives do not necessarily support workplace learning and, as with NVQs in the care sector, the emphasis on assessment does not necessarily open up learning opportunities.

The third section evaluates a specific policy intervention, the Teaching Company Scheme, which is aimed at creating change in organisations as well as enhancing their appreciation of the value of graduate level skills. We assess the extent to which an initiative, aimed primarily at supporting innovation, can contribute to the learning of the graduate who is on placement and to changes in the learning environment in the organisation. This is followed by a conclusion.

The Capacity of Competence-Based Assessment to Support Workplace Learning: Care Assistant Roles in Health and Social Care

Care services are provided in a number of different locations by direct employees in the NHS and local government, and under contract in the private and voluntary sectors. This is an interesting site to explore training, skills development and workforce competence since the state pays, at least partially, for these services. It therefore has acquired responsibility for the standards of provision and is accountable for public expenditure in this arena. Whereas successive governments have been reluctant to intervene directly in the training decisions of private sector companies, this is not the case where the state provides a service directly or commissions it from a private sector organisation. In this instance, the state can exert some influence over the standards of service provision and these may have implications for the training and competence of the workforce.

Care work has traditionally been seen as unskilled manual work, attracting low pay and with limited opportunities for career progression. It is stereotypically women's work. Workers are employed in caring activities provided as a service to clients and these care-giving activities mirror those performed without payment to family members within the domestic sphere. Because many of the skills are acquired through experience, such as the ability to empathise and communicate with clients whilst attending to their needs, they are undervalued. Nevertheless, it is also the case that some skills and knowledge to perform the job effectively need to be taught. This is particularly the case with techniques for lifting and handling clients, which have important consequences for health and safety. It is also true that increasing specialisation in care services, for example, in the care of the frail elderly and the mentally infirm, require greater knowledge of medical conditions and interactions with healthcare professionals. Increasing requirements for report writing and record keeping have implications for writing skills and access to broader development opportunities. Skill shortages of professional workers in nursing and social work mean that where such opportunities are available, potential career routes may be established into professional work.

Care is provided in a variety of settings, ranging from hospitals and residential homes to peripatetic services provided to people and/or their informal caregivers within the home. Across this range of settings, there are now statutory requirements for induction and foundation training, introduced by the Care Standards Act 2000 (published in 2001). By 2005 all care workers must be registered individually and there are targets for competence assessment so that employers can demonstrate that they have a competent workforce. In the UK competence is certified by occupational standards developed in the form of National Vocational Qualifications (NVQs). In the care sector, this involves the certification of competence at NVQ *level 2* in the care of the elderly and *level 3* in the care of children.[3] The Act also sets environmental standards in care homes concerning room sizes, bathing facilities and clients' access to a single room of their own. The question is, to what extent does the requirement to obtain NVQ competence contribute to care workers' access to learning in relation to their work, given the range of work routines and settings in which they are found? Moreover, what is its relative significance compared to other factors affecting the delivery of care services?

First of all, it is important to set care services in the broader context in which public, private and voluntary sector employers operate in the UK.[4] According to the National Care Homes Association, everything in this sector revolves around the funding of long-term care. Nursing and care home-owners have been faced by a variety of additional costs in recent years which have been created by the introduction of the National Minimum Wage, the Working Time Directive and the need to comply with the Care Standards regulations. Whilst costs have increased, these have not been acknowledged by a commensurate increase in local authority payments for services to clients. These pressures have affected homes of all sizes, but larger organisations probably have greater capacity to absorb additional costs. A study commissioned by the Joseph Rowntree Foundation found that the average weekly cost of running a good quality nursing home was £459 per resident whilst local authority fees were £74 less. As a consequence, fees are no longer enough to provide 'a good service and make a reasonable profit' (*The Guardian*, 19-6-2002).

There are a number of ways in which private residential homes have adapted to these pressures. These include (1) closure; (2) switching to sheltered housing where the standards do not apply; (3) providing specialist care where premium rates apply, although these are still seen as inadequate. A fourth option has been to manage on an inadequate budget in the hope that the government will relax the environmental standards (which it did for existing homes in August 2002) or put more resources into care given the political priority of delivering on the Labour Government's manifesto commitments to improvements to the NHS. Research for the Low Pay Commission shows that in many cases, owners have reduced their takings since there is little scope for reducing staffing levels (Rainbird, Holly, & Leisten, 2002). It is also worth pointing out that although there is still a local authority residential care sector, the process of sub-contracting services to the private sector is continuing. In other words, both the local authority and the private sector are losing rather than increasing their capacity to provide services.

One consequence of the statutory requirements for induction and foundation training is that government funding is available for training and competence assessment for some categories of workers. In some localities regional networks of private, voluntary and public sector employers are emerging, supported by the Training Organisation of the Personal Social Services (TOPSS). So, from one point of view, it would be possible to argue that a statutory requirement to attain NVQs has resulted in the availability of training and development. Ironically, it is the government which has set the requirement for NVQ assessment and which has provided the funding for training and assessment, usually targeted at specific groups (18–25 year olds and workers on Tax Credits).[5] One can not help wonder whether it might have been easier to start with the identification of learning needs and underpinning knowledge, curriculum development for course provision and the setting up of mentoring arrangements.

The general problems with competence assessment and its relationship to underlying knowledge have been debated and will not be explored here (see for example, Wolf, 1995; Senker, 1996; Senker, 2000; Grugulis, 2003). Our focus is on three separate issues: (1) access to assessment; (2) how the process of assessment relates to work-related knowledge, which varies in different care settings;

and (3) the relationship of assessment to access to broader training and development opportunities.

Since there will soon be a statutory requirement for care workers to have an NVQ qualification in order to be registered to work in this sector, access to the process of assessment is a significant issue. Assessment requires an assessor to observe the performance of work routines. In this respect, the ability to be assessed is highly dependent on the work environment, over which the individual worker has limited control. Even so, patterns of work may make this difficult to organise. Although it may be relatively easy for an employer to arrange for an assessor to come into a workplace, it may be more difficult where workers are peripatetic and perform their duties in their clients' homes. Equally, night shift workers may have limited access to assessment because of their hours of work. Whereas progression through an educational route is not dependent on job roles, progression through a system based on competence assessment is and workers on one salary grade may not be able to perform the job roles of workers in more senior positions. A separate issue is the fact that an estimated that 10 per cent of the care workforce in England are agency workers, recruited on short-term contracts to provide cover in a range of health and social care contexts. Where responsibility lies for their assessment is problematic. Agencies are reluctant to provide assessment on the grounds that they have no contact with the workers in the workplace. Equally, the organisations using agency workers usually employ them on a discontinuous basis to provide staff cover. To argue, as some senior agency managers do, that agency workers are responsible for their own assessment places a responsibility which clearly lies with the employer on the individual employee.

The skills and knowledge required by carer support workers differ significantly from those of care workers in residential settings and in peripatetic services. Crossroads carer support workers (CSWs) provide carers with respite from their caring roles. Crucial to this is their ability to offer well founded reassurance to the carer that the person they care for will be well-looked after while the CSW takes over their caring role. CSWs are called on to look after people with a huge range of disabilities, from autistic children to people suffering from the effects of strokes, Alzheimer's, Parkinson's or motor neurone disease. All CSWs receive induction training in basic skills and in moving and handling, food hygiene and first aid. They need to be able to give medication and deal with the medical needs of individual clients. With the Care Standards regulations, induction training will have to comply with the occupational standards set by TOPSS and this does not pose serious problems. However, the requirement for 50% of CSWs to achieve NVQ *level 2* does. A significant proportion of the occupational standards have been derived from skill and knowledge needs in residential care and others from domiciliary care requirements where the focus is on looking after the cared for person and not on respite care for the carers.[6]

An important consideration is the extent to which standards derived from generic care work apply to CSWs. There are at least three dimensions of specialisation of CSWs: by the type of client, by the number and timing of the hours they are prepared to work, and by location. For example, some CSWs prefer to work only with children and looking after autistic children is a significant activity in many Crossroads Schemes. Others specialise in working with old people. In addition, in order to give carers confidence in the service provided, it is important for Scheme Managers to match CSWs to clients with whom they can establish good personal relationships. Workers who may be highly experienced in looking after children may be neither willing nor competent to look after adults. Taking account of considerations relating to certain hours of work, locations and types of client to be looked after, it is questionable whether the generic occupation of CSW actually exists. Moreover, CSWs who work short hours with a specialist range of clients may be unwilling to undergo the process of assessment necessary to secure an NVQ *level 2*, based on a range of different client groups.

TOPSS's willingness to modify existing occupational standards and introduce new standards to meet the full range of domiciliary care needs is not in doubt. In the light of fundamental problems with the NVQ system briefly alluded to above, in the fundamentally different focus of respite care from residential and domiciliary care, and the specialisation of CSWs, it is perhaps reasonable to doubt whether an efficient system of assessment will emerge from the process of continuous improvement and adaptation of national occupational standards.

A further issue is the extent to which the process of NVQ assessment is linked to access to training and development and to the opportunities for learning on-the-job, which vary according to the local settings in which care is provided. Although training needs may be identified in the course of developing the employee's portfolio of evidence, access to training and development is not a requirement. The opportunities for work-related learning may vary enormously according to the environment in which care is provided. This concerns the extent to which workers learn through on-going social practice in daily work routines and whether time can be made available for attendance at formal training sessions and courses. The latter may require arrangements for cover and release from work to be arranged (with all the attendant costs of bringing in additional staff) or may be inserted into natural breaks during working hours. For example, in residential homes for the elderly, there are periods during the day when one shift of workers hands over to the next, during a relatively 'quiet' period in the early afternoon. In many homes this changeover period is used for staff to exchange information about clients' needs. Home managers often use this time to bring in external speakers to talk about specific medical conditions and disabilities, contributing to workers' understanding of clients' needs and ability to empathise with them. Similar practices operate in the health service where there may be quieter periods in the day when there is space for learning activities. However, this may be limited by the size of the unit or ward and the nature of care. In smaller units with fewer staff and in high dependency sectors it is more difficult to create such space. It certainly depends on the willingness of managers to organise work allocation and staffing rosters in such a way as to create space for learning activities.

Independently of the requirement for the individual registration of care staff, the process of regulation of care homes means that what was formally regarded as manual work has increasing demands for report writing and communication skills. Some employers see an increasing need for workers to use communication and written skills which may be achieved through employee development programmes or general education (see Caldwell, 2000). It is in this context that broader development programmes have been put in place, often on the initiative of trade unions, such as the public sector union, UNISON.[7] These programmes can underpin access to broader learning opportunities which are not linked to competence assessment but to educational and vocational progression routes. The provision of such formal learning is independent of the NVQ assessment process and the extent to which these opportunities are created depends on the intervention of 'local enthusiastic actors' on the union and management side (Munro, Rainbird, & Holly, 1997). In other words, access to broader development opportunities is incidental to the statutory requirement for NVQ assessment, although individual manager's perceptions of the extent to which broader education programmes support the achievement of NVQ targets may contribute to their willingness to provide cover to release staff for course attendance.

The limitations of NVQs as a mechanism for raising workforce skills have been well-rehearsed. As Grugulis argues, they certify existing competence in relation to the current organisation of production and are concerned with auditing skills and not with skill development (2003, p. 469). They have been drawn up primarily on the basis of employers' perceived needs rather than the range of workplace interests, and are not concerned with identifying future needs. In the care sector, they can be seen alongside of range of other regulatory pressures as contributing to changes in the way care work is delivered and the skills that are required of the workforce. For some workers, particularly those with few formal qualifications, competence assessment may contribute to their sense of achievement and occupational development. For managers, trainers and trade unionists, the requirement to certify NVQ competence may provide a bargaining tool for creating access to training and development opportunities but they do not, in themselves, require this. Indeed, some managers in specialist care units feel that the emphasis on meeting targets for NVQ *level 2* diverts resources from more challenging specialist courses which would have more relevance to a particular service. The question is, to what extent do the resources committed to the process of NVQ assessment represent a diversion from the provision of training and development more directly linked to workplace learning? Could the spaces that NVQ assessment open up for a range of actors to create learning opportunities for care workers be obtained in a less circuitous way? As far as progression routes are concerned, would an emphasis on training and development rather than assessment be more appropriate? To return to the metaphor at the beginning of the paper, if the starting point had been a clear identification of the ways workers' learning could be supported to develop their occupational knowledge and create progression routes, could less effort have been expended in achieving this?

The Intended and Unintended Consequences of Public Sector Modernisation for Workplace Learning: Case Studies of Cleaning Services

Where the state is effectively the direct employer, there is scope for the organisation to act as a 'good employer', adopting enlightened management practices which improve service delivery as well as contributing to broader social policy objectives on social inclusion and widening participation. Nevertheless, in services provided or commissioned by local government and in the NHS, attempts have been made to reconcile the political need to improve the quality of services with the economic drive to reduce costs. As a consequence, workforce development in these sectors can be seen as a compromise between competing and sometimes contradictory objectives.

Local government and the National Health Service are both subject to processes of modernisation, driven by central government. Under the Conservative government (1979–1997) there was increased central financial control, support for competition with the private sector, the introduction of private sector management techniques and market disciplines (Winchester & Bach, 1999). In local government the requirement to seek 'Best Value' in the provision of public services has replaced compulsory competitive tendering in awarding contracts for services. Whereas CCT emphasised cost as the main criterion for letting contracts, 'Best Value' has introduced quality criteria as well. Theoretically this should mean that factors which contribute to the quality of service delivery (for example, having a competent and well-qualified workforce) might contribute to the training and development strategies of private sector contractors delivering public services. The role of local government is shifting from a direct provider to a commissioner of services, and this has consequences for the way in which workforce competence is regulated and controlled.

However, when local government is compared with the NHS, it could be argued that divergent processes are at work. In local government, the externalisation of services is continuing apace, whereas in the NHS the Labour government removed the purchaser/provider divide established by the Conservatives. There is some evidence of internalisation of formerly sub-contracted services, particularly in relation to cleaning and agency staff. Nevertheless, private sector management methods are encouraged, there is a renewed emphasis on performance targets and some processes of externalisation are continuing through the Private Finance Initiative. As a consequence there are issues concerning the relative advantage of direct managerial control for managing quality, as opposed to the indirect mechanisms available where services are subcontracted (cf. Williamson, 1975).

One consequence of shifting to a sub-contract from the direct provision of services is that the commissioning organisation loses direct control over the labour process. The contract manager therefore needs to seek mechanisms for assuring the quality of the service provided. Mechanisms for 'managing at a distance' might include the requirement for the contractor to have quality assurance mechanisms for its management systems. These include the British quality standard BS5150, the Investors in People award which recognises organisational training systems or having a workforce which has achieved a specified standard of NVQ competence. There is some evidence that where training and competence requirements are specified in contracts, this may restrict rather than open up access to broader development opportunities. Reliance on the contract as a means of standardising the quality of a service may also have the effect of reducing employee discretion to a limited menu of routines (Grugulis et al., 2003).

Even where they are directly employed, cleaners' training is mainly focussed on mandatory health and safety sessions such as 'lifting and handling' or narrow, task-specific training. It could be argued that as well as having limited access to formal training and broader development opportunities, the work environment and its routines provide restricted opportunities for informal learning. Where local government cleaning work has been sub-contracted under the 'Best Value' provisions, training and levels of worker competence may be written into contract specifications. The main focus is on task-specific training at induction stage whilst on-going training is mainly limited to mandatory courses on hygiene and health and safety (although participation even in mandatory courses is uneven). One case study company uses annual 'tests' in which cleaners must demonstrate adequate knowledge of processes and procedures. Here the emphasis is on training records and evidence of training provision to avoid liabilities, but there are few opportunities for employees to access broader development.

The nature of the labour process in cleaning also limits informal learning. Cleaning work has been subject to work intensification over the past twenty years and is frequently organised on a part-time basis (although variations will depend on local labour markets and labour supply) with little down time. The working day is often structured very tightly around key events in the day which cannot be moved, e.g. the arrival of lunch on hospital wards, which means that the work process is in practice almost as fixed as working on a production line. Along with this, work tasks have become more complex and there has been a standardisation of work routines, demanding increased task specific training but resulting in less freedom of activity. The nature of work restricts geographical mobility around the building and staff are tied by time and place. In addition, even in large organisations cleaners tend to work in small isolated groups or as the only cleaner in a particular department or ward. This could be tied to a particular work area in a large building, or in a small workplace which is distant from main sites e.g. a school, clinic or care home.

Job progression is limited in cleaning occupations, even where cleaners are located in a larger organisation. Vertical progression leads into management and supervisory positions, but for large proportion of female workers, horizontal progression into neighbouring occupations is more likely, the classic transition in the NHS being into healthcare assistant roles. Where cleaning contracts are subcontracted to private companies, progression is more difficult than in organisations where cleaning is integrated into other management structures. Under a subcontract, line managers and trainers can be based at distant locations and progression routes with the employer are limited to cleaning only. Organisational boundaries can create barriers to mobility. Even in our private cleaning contractors in the health service, most cleaners seeking career progression were considering moving into care work. In other words, career routes involve changing employer, so there is little incentive for the cleaning company to provide development opportunities.

Even where cleaners are direct employees in a hospital, they are often answerable to both functional line managers and to the senior member of staff where they actually perform the cleaning, e.g. a ward nurse. This all makes participation in learning more difficult. Time off for learning is a major difficulty because it has to be negotiated via two lines of management. There have been attempts to rationalise management structures through the creation of the housekeeper's role or through regular meetings between cleaning supervisors and nursing staff. Nevertheless, the objective of this development is to improve the standards of cleaning not to facilitate learning opportunities. The proposal that cleaners should return to an older model in which the senior nurse acts as line manager is likely limit opportunities for wider learning. This is because nurses are unlikely to be aware of issues facing cleaning staff and developments in lifelong learning. Similarly the formation of Primary Care Trusts, providing integrated services between local authority social services departments and the NHS may transfer cleaners into units where managers have little experience or knowledge of the broader learning opportunities which have been developed in some acute hospital and community NHS trusts. This could also make informal and worker-initiated learning more difficult, as opportunities are reduced for workers to expand their job roles into contiguous areas of work which are more interesting and rewarding, such as basic caring activities in a care home (Munro & Rainbird, 2002).

The presence or not of 'learning champions' within the organisation may make a big difference in terms of the provision of wider development opportunities and in terms of encouragement for staff to take up such opportunities. A training manager, a union activist or the tutor from a course taken could fulfil this role. A commitment by the Chief Executive to learning for all can make a big difference to the overall importance attached to learning for low paid workers like cleaners, yet in large public sector organisations with enormous departmental autonomy, this does not mean that such enthusiasm is mirrored throughout the organisation. Similarly, training managers often have great commitment to employee development, but this does not mean that line managers are enthusiastic about releasing staff for training. In some cases managers responsible for lifelong learning are separated from the training department which is responsible for competence assessment in the form of NVQs. Where this occurs, lifelong learning is more likely to have a limited budget and be marginalised.

In local government and the NHS there are different pressures towards subcontracting, on the one hand, and performance management on the other. Even where 'quality' is supposedly an objective in the management of contracts, workers' training is perceived as a mechanism for standardising task performance and managing risks through quality assurance mechanisms. There was some evidence from the fieldwork of the literacy requirements of jobs being actively reduced to avoid worker error and, as McIntosh and Steedman (2001) have noted, this discourages the use of existing skills, let alone the development of new ones.

In the NHS political considerations are significant. One example of this has been increasing media attention on the issue of dirty wards in hospitals, leading both the Prime Minister and heath ministers to champion the drive toward national standards. Despite this, the imperative for managers to meet targets in the short term has re-emphasised the perceived need for task specific training rather than wider developmental opportunities. The development of an in-house organisation of agency staff, NHS Professionals, is another example of an attempt to increase control of standards, as well as the cost of hiring private agency staff. This has been a site for developing the 'skills escalator' approach to staff development. In this way, agency staff are provided with mandatory training, which is often not provided by agencies, and are also able to access broader training and development opportunities which can provide routes into profes-sional training, to help meet staff shortages.

Although in-house contracts do not guarantee the opening up of training and development, they do not curtail it as effectively as the sub-contract. Unified management structures do not guarantee that all staff gain access to training and development, but the presence of a training function and collective actors – trade unions – which can make connections within a larger organisation, can facilitate this.

At the beginning of the paper, we referred to the argument that employer demand for skills and qualifications is linked to the strategy an organisation develops towards the quality of goods and services it produces. In other words, if the objective is to provide high quality public services, we would expect to see this reflected in the priority attached to investment in workers' skills. In the public sector, the government is effectively the employer, so we would expect to see policies towards training and development which exemplify model practices. When we compare local government and the NHS we can see not only the different political priorities attached to the services, but also to the training and development of the workforce. Although additional resources are being directed into both areas, higher priority is attached to the NHS. This is reflected in pressures to bring contracts in-house, where greater control is possible, and greater emphasis not just on training for staff, even on the lowest salary grades, but on broader development opportunities as well. In contrast, in local govern-ment, there has been a shift from the letting of contracts solely on the basis of price competition to one where quality is also a criterion. The problem is that 'quality' has been interpreted as standardisation and has been introduced after years of undermining baseline budgets for essential services through price-based competition. The conflict between providing a quality service and controlling costs has been resolved in different ways in the two services, and this is reflected in different emphases on the training and development of staff and their capacity to progress educationally and occupationally within the service. Therefore, in this instance, it is a question of how quality is defined in the looking glass world, as well as the mechanisms which have been put in place to achieve it.

Promoting Innovation Through Change: The Contribution of the Teaching Company Scheme to Workplace Learning

The extent to which the learning environment in an organisation promotes or discourages learning is the result of attitudes and practices established over a long period and may be very difficult to change. One of the explicit aims of Teaching Company Schemes (TCS schemes) is to facilitate the transfer of technology and the diffusion of technical and management skills to companies. TCS schemes operate through programmes in which academics in universities join with companies to contribute to the implementation of strategies for technical or managerial change. TCS programmes are designed to stimulate innovation in SMEs through a range of mechanisms. These include ensuring that products meet more stringent quality requirements, developing new product ranges to meet the needs of changing markets, and developing and using suitable technologies. It can also involve implementing more efficient methods for controlling production by shortening lead-times and reducing work-in-progress and inventories, thereby lowering the costs involved in carrying them.

The principle behind the Teaching Company Scheme (TCS) is to identify new skills and knowledge which a company needs but does not yet have. The company and a university department work together with a consultant appointed by the Teaching Company Directorate (TCD) to submit proposals for a programme of work. This involves the recruitment of a graduate, known as Teaching Company Scheme Associate to carry out the programme in the company under the joint supervision of nominated supervisors in the company and the university department. The aim is to recruit an Associate with the knowledge needed by the company. Associates are selected because they have a degree in a scientific, technical or management subject. The Associate learns about the company and its practices and, at the same time, acquires more abstract knowledge through the mentoring role of the academic supervisor and attendance at courses. Successful performance by a TCS Associate involves becoming accepted in the company and, at the same time, being instrumental in getting the company to change its practices through the application of knowledge. The changes necessary to achieve this may conflict with existing company practice in several often quite fundamental ways. This may also involve the need for extensive learning on the part of managers and employees in the company.

A restrictive learning environment in a company can act as a major barrier to employees' learning and to the organisation's capacity for innovation. Research findings indicate that TCS Associates, supported by the infrastructure of company and academic supervisors, consultants and Local Management Committees provided by TCS, can sometimes be successful in increasing the expansiveness of learning environments. TCS Schemes can be conceptualised as aiming to achieve major transformations in what Engestrom (2001) calls activity systems. For Engestrom, contradictions are structural tensions within and between activity systems and represent a potential source of innovation. He points out that innovation requires risky learning processes, which cannot be explained by 'mere participation and gradual acquisition of mastery'. Engestrom's fifth principle of activity systems 'proclaims the possibility of expansive transformations in activity systems ... As the contradictions of an activity system are aggravated, some individual participants begin to question and deviate from its established norms. In some cases this escalates into collaborative envisioning and a deliberative collective change effort. An expansive transformation is accomplished when the object and motive of the activity are re-conceptualised to embrace a radically wider horizon of possibilities than in the previous mode of the activity' (2001, p. 137). These are extremely ambitious objectives and inherently embody considerable risks. Indeed, both this and previous research on TCS schemes (e.g., Senker & Senker, 1994) have included examples of failures. On the other hand, when TCS schemes are largely successful in their aims, the end result may be described as 'cultural change' (Senker & Senker, 1994) or, to use Engestrom's term, 'expansive transformation'. As he suggests '(e)xpansive learning activity produces culturally new patterns of activity. Expansive learning at work produces new forms of work activity' (2001, p. 137).

Conclusion

In this paper we have explored three different arenas in which government policy has a direct or indirect impact on workplace learning. In the first section we examined the role of competence assessment in the form of NVQs in developing a more professionalised workforce in the care sector. Although for some staff this may have been experienced as a positive experience which has boosted their self-confidence, this has not always been the case. As argued earlier, competence assessment is primarily about auditing skills and averting risk for the commissioners and providers of care services. Assessment is problematic for the workforce, who may gain little from having their competence certified. It is also problematic for employers, who are obliged to expend resources on assessment without necessarily enhancing workforce skills and organisational competence. We have argued that a different starting point could have been taken, entailing a more effective identification and provision of learning opportunities, with resources directed towards skill development rather than the auditing of competence. As Senker has pointed out, prior to the introduction of NVQs, the education, training and qualifications of toolmakers, carpenters or architects were based on traditional 'bottom-up' analysis. This followed a general pattern: let us consider what knowledge and skills are required in each individual occupation; let us consider how the occupation is likely to change in the future and how the organisation of work is changing, the growing use of Information

Technology, new materials, new production processes. More importantly, let us consider how people learn, and then let us decide how people can best be helped to learn. Let us then design education and training syllabuses, qualification and assessment methodologies on a pragmatic basis in accordance with the needs of each set of occupations, not in accordance with a centrally dictated methodology (Senker, 2000, p. 9). Competence assessment, in focussing on narrow definitions of performance and observed behaviour, focuses on present rather than future occupational skill needs and has been disarticulated from the process of learning.

As far as the objective of providing quality in public services is concerned, developing a well-trained workforce is only one of a number of competing priorities for service providers. 'Quality' can be interpreted in a number of different ways, but only some of these require a significant investment in workers' skills. Where sub-contracting continues, even if it is not based on price-competition, training is a control mechanism for delivering a standardised service rather than a developmental one. This is certainly the case in services delivered and commissioned by local government in the UK. Where there are greater pressures to improve the quality of services by recruiting more staff and bringing services in-house, this is reflected not just in mandatory training, but also in the provision of broader development opportunities and the establishment of internal educational and occupational pathways. These pressures are more in evidence in the NHS.

In contrast, the starting point for the TCS scheme is to promote innovation, by explicitly introducing new types of higher level skills into companies. This is a risky activity, but where it succeeds, it can lead to cultural change and managers' reassessment of their need for skills. It is a telling observation that the intervention which does address innovation in the workplace and has the potential to transform organisational competence and the workplace as a learning environment, is miniscule compared to the resources put into NVQ assessment in the social care sector, on the one hand, and training and development in local government and the NHS, on the other.

We started this paper with a quote from 'Alice through the Looking Glass'. The Red Queen's reply is: 'Now *here*, you see, it takes all the running *you* can do to stay in the same place. If you want to get somewhere else, you must run at least twice as fast as that!' We would like to suggest that rather than adopting this solution from the world of the looking glass, a more appropriate starting point would be to focus on workplace learning and the mechanisms for enhancing it. This would involve identifying workers' needs for skills and knowledge which are not restricted to training for their current job roles and their employers' current business needs, as we have outlined above. It would also involve curriculum development and tools for supporting learning in the broadest sense in the workplace, including the capacity to innovate. These observations raise questions concerning the status of the quest for the learning society and the knowledge economy and whether they are are no more than reflections in the looking glass world.

Notes

1. See Munro and Rainbird (2002) for a discussion of the implications of job expansion, job contraction and work intensification for workers' learning.
2. The Research Network 'Improving incentives to learning at work' (ESRC ref. L13925 1005) ran from April 2000 until June 2003 and involved research teams at University College Northampton, the Institute of Education, London, Leeds and Leicester universities and Napier University, Edinburgh. For further details of the Teaching and Learning Research Programme see http://www.TLRP.org.
3. NVQs are awarded at five levels, level 1 being the simplest and level 5 the most advanced. Level 3 is an intermediate level qualification, equivalent to an apprenticeship. See Grugulis, 2003 for an up-to-date critique.
4. Some of the material follows was part of a research project commissioned by the Low Pay Commission on the National Minimum Wage and Training (see Rainbird et al., 2002).
5. Due to the restrictions on under 18s conducting intimate care tasks, Modern Apprenticeships in England are only available for 18 to 21 year olds.
6. This latter consideration has been brought to the attention of TOPSS by the researcher and, in response to this, TOPSS will develop a national occupational standard for respite carers.
7. See Munro et al., 1997 and Munro and Rainbird, 2000, for analysis of the UNISON programmes.

References

Caldwell, P. (2000). Adult learning and the workplace. In H. Rainbird (Ed.), *Training in the workplace* (pp. 244–263). Basingstoke: Macmillan.

Engestrom, Y. (2001). Expansive learning at work: toward an activity theoretical reconceptualization. *Journal of Education and Work, 14*(1), 133–156.

Grugulis, I. (2003). National Vocational Qualifications: A research-based critique. *British Journal of Industrial Relations, 41*(3), 457–475.

Grugulis, I., Vincent, S., & Hebson, G. (2003). The rise of the "network form" and the decline of discretion. *Human Resource Management Journal, 13*(2), 45–59.

Keep, E., & Mayhew, K. (1999). The assessment: knowledge, skills and competitiveness. *Oxford Review of Economic Policy, 15*(1), 1–15.

Lave, J., & Wenger, E. (1991). *Situated learning: Legitimate peripheral participation.* Cambridge: Cambridge University Press.

Lloyd, C., & Payne, J. (2002). *Through the looking glass: Images, reflections and visions of the high skill society.* Paper presented at the Training, Employability and Employment Conference, Monash University Centre, London.

McIntosh, S., & Steedman, H. (2001). Learning in the workplace: some international comparisons. In F. Coffield (Ed.), *What progress are we making with lifelong learning? The evidence from research*: Department of Education, University of Newcastle.

Munro, A., Rainbird, H., & Holly, L. (1997). *Partners in workplace learning: The UNISON/employer employee development programme.* London: UNISON.

Munro, A., & Rainbird, H. (2000). The new unionism and the new bargaining agenda: UNISON/ employer partnerships on workplace learning in Britain. *British Journal of Industrial Relations, 38*(2), 223–240.

Munro, A., & Rainbird, H. (2002). Job change and workplace learning in the public sector: The significance of new technology for unskilled work. *New Technology, Work and Employment, 17*(3), 224–235.

Rainbird, H. (2000). The contribution of workplace learning to a learning society. In W. Richardson & L. Unwin (Eds.), *The Learning Society and the Knowledge Economy NACETT sponsored lecture series.* Coventry: Learning and Skills Council.

Rainbird, H., Holly, L., & Leisten, R. (2002). *The national minimum wage and training. Report prepared for the Low Pay Commission.* Northampton: University College Northampton.

Senker, P. (1992). *Industrial training in a cold climate: An assessment of Britain's training policies.* Aldershot: Avebury.

Senker, P., & Senker, J. (1994). Transferring technology and expertise from universities to industry: Britain's Teaching Company Scheme. *New Technology, Work and Employment, 9*(2), 81–92.

Senker, P. (1996). The development and implementation of National Vocational Qualifications: An engineering case study. *New Technology, Work and Employment, 11*(2), 83–95.

Senker, P. (2000). *The relationship of the NVQ system to learning in the workplace.* Paper presented at the CEREQ seminar The Certification of Vocational Qualifications in France and the United Kingdom, Marseilles.

Williamson, O. E., (1975). *Markets and hierarchies.* New York: Free Press.

Winchester, D., & Bach, S. (1999). Britain: the transformation of public service employment relations. In S. Bach, L. Bordogna, G. della Rocca & D. Winchester (Eds.), *Public service employment relations in Europe: Transformation, modernization or inertia?* London and New York: Routledge.

Wolf, A. (1995). *Competence-based assessment.* Buckingham: Open University Press.

48

IMPROVING GENDER EQUALITY IN WORK ORGANISATIONS BY ACTION RESEARCH[1]

Tapio Rissanen and Sirpa Kolehmainen
Work Research Centre, University of Tampere, Finland

Feminisation of the labour force has been one of the major changes in the labour market during the past three decades. Nowadays women constitute over 40% of the labour force in the OECD countries with only few exceptions (OECD Statistics Portal). At the same time a relatively extensive legislative framework concerning equality between women and men has been adopted in nearly all OECD countries. Nevertheless, differentiation and hierarchy in the labour market and unequal opportunities in working life between women and men still prevail. Year after year, employment statistics describe the continuing gap between women and men in labour force participation; permanence of gender segregation within labour markets; atypical forms of working such as part-time work and fixed-term contracts, for example, accumulating to women; gender wage gaps and glass ceiling hindering women's career advancement. These structural patterns of inequalities result from interactions between institutionalised activities and concrete actions in everyday working life (Women and structural change, 1994; Dex & Sewell, 1995; Rubery, Smith, & Fagan, 1999).

Gender equality in working life can be defined as equal opportunities for women and men to develop their competencies, to make their choices and realise their ambitions in working life without constrictions caused by their gender. Furthermore, equality entails that women's and men's different activities, attributes and needs are acknowledged and equally valued (Lehto, 1999; Horelli, & Saari, 2002). Equal opportunity policy concerning labour markets includes mainly legislation on employment equity and active measures through labour market programmes. Legislative policies developed by the International Labour Organization (ILO), the United Nations (UN) and the European Union (EU) encompass two main aspects of equality: equal pay and equal opportunities. The principle of equal pay for work of comparable worth prevails in pay legislation. Equal opportunity legislation aims at eliminating all forms of discrimination, direct, indirect and systemic in recruitment, access to training, promotion, working conditions, dismissals and retirement, and thus is directed towards employers

International Handbook of Educational Policy, 903–922
Nina Bascia, Alister Cumming, Amanda Datnow, Kenneth Leithwood and David Livingstone (Eds.)
© 2005 *Springer. Printed in Great Britain.*

and personnel management. Specific measures included in labour market programmes of almost every OECD country have been designed specifically for
women; integrating women into non-traditional education and occupations,
promoting women's entrepreneurship and promoting women's re-entering the
labour market after having children. While the equality policy has developed
from the notion of forbidding (anti-discrimination) to obliging (affirmative
action), it has also become more complex and difficult to implement in practice
(Women and structural change, 1994). For example, within work organisations
the present equality policy may succeed in having effect on reducing gender
inequalities on the open level of formal and informal organisation, but by means
of it the interaction and practices on the hidden level and especially within the
area of informal organisation are difficult to achieve (see Figure 1).

Gender mainstreaming is a new strategy for the equality policy. It was officially
launched by the UN at the Beijing Conference on Women in 1995
(Mückenberger, 2001). According to the Council of Europe (EC) definition
(1998, see Mückenberger, 2001) gender mainstreaming *"consists of re-organising,
improving, developing and evaluating of decision-making processes – with the
explicit objectives that the actors involved in political decision-making take the
perspective of equality between men and women in all areas and on all levels."*
Gender mainstreaming aims at dynamic, positive activities and interventions on
many levels to eliminate inequalities and to promote equality. It can be understood as a developmental strategy for breaking ostensibly gender-neutral culture
by challenging the existing gendered structures and often invisible everyday life
practices.

The EC directive on implementation of the principle of equal treatment for
men and women in access to employment, vocational training and promotion,
and working conditions (Directive 2002/73/EC) states that member states should
encourage employers to promote equal treatment for men and women in the

Figure 1.   The arenas of gender inequality in work organisations

	Formal organisation	Informal organisation
Open level	Gender pay gap Vertical and horizontal gender segregation Difference in hierarchical positions	Sexistic language, jokes etc. Sexual harassment, insinuation, pressure, intimidation
Hidden level	Determination of wages Division of extra rewards Division of work tasks	Passing over in informal networks Deficit in getting information Poor possibilities to participate in decision making

Source: Kauppinen & Veikkola 1997.

workplace in a planned and systematic way. Furthermore, employers should also provide employees with appropriate information about equal treatment within the work organisation at appropriate regular intervals. In the Nordic countries, equality legislation has since the 1980s included the obligation for equality planning in public and private work organisations (Tasa-arvolaki, 1998; Jämställdhetslagen, 1991).

The question of gender equality is nowadays seen, not only as a basic human right, but also as a premise for the survival of the workplace in many ways. Globalisation of the economy provokes intensification of work processes. In many countries there will be a remarkable reduction of aged labour through pension schemes during the next decade. Employers have to tangle with the problems of recruiting new skilled personnel, of utilising more effectively and in more flexible ways the existing labour, of increasing creativity and productivity at work and of creating an encouraging working atmosphere and a positive public image of the workplace. This calls for the alleviation of strict and unequal gendered divisions in working life.

Gender equality is an aspired value to be pursued in society, but the promotion of gender equality often conflicts with the attitudes and prejudices on the organisational level. Päivi Korvajärvi (2002a) has pointed out that gender is often accounted as a personal issue, not a part of the realm of work. Women and men recognize gender inequality and subordination of women in the working life as social problems in general, but they generally consider their own workplaces to be equal (Melkas, 1999). The meaning of gender as a source of inequality within everyday practices seems to be difficult to identify. Gendered structures in concrete and symbolic differences and distinctions between women's and men's activities at work are usually visible, but they are taken for granted. A closer focus on individual activities and interaction between people seems to make gender more invisible. Gender-neutrality often prevails in workplaces (Korvajärvi, 2002b).

Research on career mobility (Scott & Burchell, 1994; Granqvist & Persson, 1997; Hakim, 1996; Kolehmainen, 1999) has shown that women's and men's careers in education and in the labour market are highly segregated. Women and men choose and are selected into education that is "typical" to their sex and, regardless of education, they choose occupations that are "typical" to their sex. It is also rather seldom that they advance in their work careers to occupations of the opposite sex. Instead, if they start their career in an occupation typical to the opposite sex, both women and men tend to change quickly to occupations of their own sex. Work cultures tend to be firmly gendered and thus they define occupations and related behavior as male or female (Cockburn, 1988; Bradley, 1989; Reskin & Padavic, 1994; Hakim, 1996). Promoting equality in working life is a complex task that demands collective actions of legislators, education and labour policy authorities and concrete activities on the workplace level.

The starting point of this chapter is the idea that the gendered practices in work organisations and gendered work cultures hold the key position in promoting or inhibiting women's and men's equal opportunities in working life. The challenge for equality policy is to make gender visible in work organisations, to concretise the significance of gender functioning as a precondition, an inhibitor and a facilitator of equal opportunities. By making gender visible it is also possible to identify the actual targets for change in gendered work culture and to develop concrete actions for equal opportunities diffusion through the work organisation. In this chapter we discuss theoretical and methodological tools needed in mainstreaming gender equality within work organisations, present an action research approach to addressing mainstreaming, and discuss the implications and challenges of methodological choices from the standpoint of equality policy.

In the first section, different ways of conceptualising gender and gender equality will be introduced. These conceptualisations include the possible ways of promoting gender equality and also the possible pitfalls in the promotion. The second section discusses the experiences of action research (AR) methodology in studying gender and organisations. The third section introduces AR strategies and methods through the phases of an ongoing research project. In the concluding section, the implications of conceptualising gender and AR for improving gender equality from the standpoint of workplace learning will be considered.

Gender and Equality

Conceptualisations of gender and gender equality have developed hand in hand in feminist approaches and women's studies over the past three decades. In broad terms the scientific conception of gender has developed up from theories of sex roles and socialisation, through the dichotomy of biological sex versus social gender, to the understanding of gender as a relation and process. Gender is nowadays understood as a socially constructed relation including biological, cultural and social aspects. As a relation, gender contains the duality of woman/man and feminine/masculine, the hierarchical power relation in which the man and the masculine are more highly valued, and finally a contextuality of both duality and power relations. The concepts of woman/man or feminine/masculine find different meaning depending on the specific historical time and place (Scott, 1986; Hirdman, 1988; Flax, 1990; Silius, 1992).

Gender is a central category that organises, restructures, creates and interprets the meanings of our social life. It is embedded in all other social relations, practices, attributes and structures thus pervading all social processes and relationships. Gender is produced in complex and comprehensive processes within and between the following three interrelated levels: cultural symbols (norms, values, conceptions of the meanings of feminine/masculine), social structures and organisations (an institutionalised division of labour and power between women and men within labour market, work, economy, politics, family, etc.), and individual identities (socialisation processes taking advantage of gendered symbols and structures). The manifestation of gender converts dynamically along with the economic, political and socio-cultural changes. People always have before them some set, even though naturalised, gendering practices and structures within which they as women and men, mostly subconsciously, reproduce gender in their own activities (Harding, 1986; Scott, 1986; Hirdman, 1988; Flax, 1990; Silius, 1992).

Intertwining with the concept of gender, the understanding of gender equality has shifted from the idea of similarity to that of difference and equal worth of feminine and masculine, and to an emphasis on the significance of gendering processes (Calás & Smircich, 1996; Lehto, 1999; Horelli & Saari, 2002). In the area of working life research, the above-mentioned perspectives on gender and equality linked with feminist theories have produced at least three different approaches. All of these approaches are used simultaneously and they do not exclude each other (Meyerson & Kolb, 2000; Korvajärvi, 1998; Calás & Smircich, 1996).

Equality Research Approach

The equality research approach is basically concerned with the similarity or difference of women and men in society because of their sex role socialisation (to biological sex). The most common line of this approach (e.g., Hakim, 1981; Blau & Ferber, 1986; Dex, 1987; OECD, 1988) seeks to demonstrate how the position of women is poorer than that of men in the distribution of occupations and hierarchical positions, career advancement and pay, for example. The goal of the approach is to support women in achieving as good positions as men in the workplace and in the labour market. Another variant of equality research focuses on structural barriers in working life (see Reskin, 1984; Reskin & Hartman, 1986; Cockburn, 1988). According to this view, gender inequalities are the result of prejudiced hiring and evaluation practices and promotion processes, which result in the gender segregation of occupations and workplaces. The goal of this approach is to eliminate structural and procedural barriers to women's advancement, by means of legislation and organisational policies, for example. Equality approach is closely linked with liberal feminist theory.

Research Approaches Focusing on Women's Own Activities

Research approaches focusing on women's own activities shift from similarity to difference between women and men by valuing the difference and especially women's activity. Radical feminist theories are avowedly women-centred. According to this approach, women are disadvantaged in working life because the attributes and skills associated with women are devalued in relation to the attributes of men. This research has made feminine activities and styles of working, women's work, skills and orientations in employment visible (e.g., Harding, 1991; Smith, 1992; Fletcher, 1999). Along with this approach, new demands for pay policy were also generated, i.e. equal pay for work of comparable worth (Robinson, 2001; Heide, 2001). The main problem with this view is that recognition of differences does not necessarily ensure an equal value. On the contrary, women-centred research may confirm gender differences and stereo-types, and thus fails to question the practices producing the differences and hierarchies.

Gendering Approach

The gendering (doing gender) approach starts from the premise that social structures are inherently gendered and that gender differences are created and sustained through formal and informal institutionalised social processes. Reskin and Padavic (1994), for example, consider gendered work as an institution which has three distinctive features: division of labour between women and men, devaluation of women's work and the construction of gender on the job. Key actors of gendering are the employers and workers who bring gender into the workplace through sex stereotypes that exaggerate actual sex differences and through policies and behaviours that highlight irrelevant sex differences. Gender is understood in terms of active production and reproduction, a general process of continuous re-organisation of gender, shaped by social structures, identities and knowledge. The gendering approach focuses on researching how gender is presented or how it is produced in different places and discourses at different times. Along with the focus on places, spaces and activities of women and men, and of feminine and masculine attributes, the focus is especially on activities and practices producing and reproducing all of these aspects in particular local contexts such as work organisations (Korvajärvi, 1998).

Although there are many gendering processes in working life that create contextual knowledge, relations and identities, there are generalisable types of gendering processes. Joan Acker (1990) has identified five such processes: 1) production of gendered divisions; 2) construction of symbols and images that explain, express and reinforce or oppose the gendered divisions; 3) everyday social interaction that enacts patterns of dominance and submission between women and men; 4) production of gendered components in individual identity; and finally, 5) gender is intertwined in the fundamental continuing processes of creating and conceptualising social structures (formal and informal 'gender neut-ral' practices and policies, which are still gender differentiated). Kinnunen and Korvajärvi (1996) have suggested that doing gender consists of talking and writing, images and symbols, experiences and feelings. It involves a constant flow of interactions in everyday life. In Acker's (1998) view, there is a gender substructure (or gender contract) that continuously operates to help reproduce gender divisions and inequalities in organisations.

Though we are supposed to live in a gender-neutral world, gender is a central but largely unconscious organising aspect of our organisational life and society at large. The first two perspectives on gender and equality treats and compares women and men as similar or different groups. The third gendering approach highlights the gendered structures and practices in different fields of social life which points the focus to women and men in their everyday life working practices. Gendering is constructed simultaneously on the levels of structures, social interaction, symbols and thoughts. In order to understand the significance of gender in promoting equality at the workplace level, it is necessary to look for concrete social actors and practices. According to Rantalaiho, Heiskanen, Korvajärvi, and Vehviläinen (1997, p. 10). *"Practice is what people do, again and again. With the concept of practice, we can ask about who is doing, and how, where, when, in what circumstances. [...] Practices are local, situational – and alterable"*. The concept of gendering practices can be understood as a methodological tool that can help to find the most significant actual barriers but also identify opportunities for promoting gender equality in the organisations. Korvajärvi (1998) argues that subordination and empowerment are closely interwoven with one another. By identifying the gendering processes, the particular ways in which concrete formal and informal organisational practices produce structural gender inequalities, we may find the potential arenas for change in these practices. All three approaches on gender and equality, e.g. structural barriers, women's and men's skills and attributes and gendering organisational practices, are needed to make the gender substructure or gender contract visible in the organisations.

Surfacing Gender in Action Research

Gendered divisions at the workplace can be easily detected, but they often are taken as unproblematic intrinsic aspects of work organisations (Korvajärvi, 2002b). These aspects consist of dominant organisational structures and practices, valued and devalued skills, work styles and activities, relation between the public sphere of work and private sphere of family and home, and the hegemonic ideology of individualism and competition which undermines forms of collaboration and feminine values of caring and compassion (Meyerson & Kolb, 2000; Fletcher, 1999). The implicit organisational aspects tend to silence, marginalise and trivialise women and feminine activities at work (Maguire, 2001). The starting point for developmental work aiming at improving gender equality must thus be to make the gendered hierarchies and practices visible and to question their taken-for-granted existence. This is possible by creating new kind of spaces of learning, in which these kinds of taken-for-granted premises can be detected and analysed (Filander, 2003).

We argue that gendered structures, practices and power relations can best be captured and challenged for change by an action research (AR) approach based on participation, communication and collaboration (Ely & Meyerson, 2000). AR can be described as a process that opens communicative space for the researchers and the participants of workplaces to share ideas and experiences, reflect on them and learn from them to develop practical knowledge and to pursue practical solutions to help them to conduct their everyday lives and to improve the functioning of the organisation. The open communicative space can only be created by promotion of participation and democratic collaboration between all members of the work community and the researchers. It is essential to involve all stakeholders in questioning, sensemaking and theorising and in creating new forms of understanding and knowing which all inform the research (Reason & Bradbury, 2001). The demand for participation in AR also gives right for all members to express their point of view, which – by itself – can contest the existing power structures and facilitate liberation from the often hidden or invisible structures and practices (Maguire, 2001; Fals Borda, 2001). Björn Gustavsen has argued that a participative process is not the core issue to be pursued in AR. Instead the promotion of communication is the spearhead of the whole process of change. Participation can bring in the multiple voices of the work organisation in AR, but developing new knowledge and viable practical solutions still needs a dialogue of these voices and creation of shared understanding. This calls for establishing democratic systems for collaboration and learning in the work organisation (Gustavsen, 1996).

Bringing in gender to the development agenda calls for questioning the existing everyday practices in the workplaces, unsettling taken-for-granted assumptions of gender and encouraging women and men in different hierarchical positions to reflect and make sense of their everyday life in the work organisation. Giving women and men the right to speak and promoting dialogue and shared theorising of gender AR can contest the existing gendered power relations and practices and offer new grounds for promoting gender equality.

Only rarely has action research been used to promote gender equality (Maguire, 2001). AR can also be seen as a deconstruction and construction process of established discourses of gender. This process makes visible the social architecture of action and creates at the same time preconditions for change (Filander, 2003; Jyrkämä, 1996). However there are some recent studies which have produced new methods to study and develop gender equality on the organisational level. Joyce K. Fletcher (1999) studied the relational practices in work projects of a high-technology company with a feminist standpoint approach. Using the concept of relational practices, Fletcher referred to different kinds of invisible female work tasks that are essential for the work organisation, but that often are not recognised as work at all. The practices were preserving the work project through task accomplishment, workers' mutual empowering to enhance project effectiveness, self-achieving and team creating by sustaining group life. The participant women in her study produced strategies to make the relational practices more visible and more highly valued in the work organisation.

A group of British and American researchers used AR methods to move from academic 'armchair feminism' into real-life work organisations to create more gender-equitable workplaces (See Meyerson & Kolb, 2000; Coleman & Rippin, 2000; Ely & Meyerson, 2000). Their understanding of gender was based on Acker's gendering processes in organisations. The research group developed two methodological tools to contest the prevailing gender-neutrality in work organisations: dual agenda and gender lenses. With the concept of gender lenses they refer to a systematic way of probing the underlying assumptions, values and practices that hold gender inequalities in place in organisations. Their systematic approach focused beyond activities like hiring and promotion which are the most visible in organisations. The approach concerned also the dominant organisational structures, practices and ideologies, the valuation of different forms of work, work styles and activities and the relation between work and family life (Meyerson & Kolb, 2000).

Dual agenda means the strategy of linking improving gender equality and increasing organisational effectiveness together in AR aims. The researchers took these aims as two sides of the same coin. Their intervention aimed to enhance both equity and business goals. Dual agenda was thought to decrease resistance, to increase political viability and to ensure that the development efforts were aligned with the mission of the organisation (Meyerson & Kolb, 2000).

Unfortunately these methodological tools did not work as expected in the AR processes. The implementation of gender lenses into the communication of the workplaces failed in problems of understanding the term gender. For most of the participants, gender meant just women, and thus the whole gender problem became a dichotomy and even a conflict of men versus women (Meyerson & Kolb, 2000). A serious problem arose with the systematic approach and its deeper critique of how gender operates in organisations. The connections of gender and existing structures and practices presented by the researchers, were difficult for participants to understand not only because of their complexity, but also because the connections penetrated deep into many long-held gender-neutral beliefs and assumptions. The critique extended to questions how participants performed the work tasks, what they valued in their work, how they oriented to work and even how they lived their lives. This was too disturbing for many (Ely & Meyerson, 2000).

Researchers also faced problems with the dual agenda tool. The use of dual agenda blurred the focus of the developmental work. As the other aim of the project – questioning gender and promoting gender equality – was misunderstood, the concepts of gender and gender equality tended to edge out from the agenda of the development process. Instead the participating organisation concentrated on waiting for the results of the business aims of the project, e.g. increased organisational efficiency. Still the success of the development work was designed to be embedded in the promotion of both gender equality and change in the gendered working processes and business goals of the organisation (Coleman & Rippin, 2000; Ely & Meyerson, 2000).

On the whole, the AR that has been conducted to promote gender equality in work organisations has faced several problems. The composition of research could have awoken gender conflict in the organisation or at least strong resistance for change. It has also been hard to engage the whole work organisation to the research aims (Brooker, Smeal, Ehrich, Daws, & Bannock, 1998; Meyerson & Kolb, 2000; Ely & Meyerson, 2000). The most crucial problem has still been that the main conceptual tools in the development, gender and gender equality, tend to fade away during the research process and the development process of workplace learning never crosses its starting line. Thus it can only end up in failure (Coleman & Rippin, 2000; Ely & Meyerson, 2000; Hearn, 2000).

Still AR, understood as a process of transformative learning in making basic value assumptions visible (Mezirow et al., 1990; Filander, 2003), can open up a powerful tool to promote gender equality in working life. The tool needs to be modified to overcome the encountered problems. Modification should include creating stronger collaborative relationships between researchers and participants, taking time to create shared spaces for understanding and commitment. The participants in the work organisations, both women and men in different hierarchical positions, should also be better equipped with knowledge and empowered to theorise gender themselves, to build narratives about their own gendered organisational experience and to increase their capacity to exceed roles and power relationships at work. In this way the AR process is fundamentally a process of workplace learning and learning of transformative character. A development project cannot succeed without distributing responsibility for the success of the project as well as distributing necessary power to all the participants to strive for changes in the organisation (Coleman & Rippin, 2000; Ely & Meyerson, 2000; Hearn, 2000). The next section presents an attempt to overcome these problems.

Anchoring Gender in Organisation Development

Finland is often regarded as one of the leading countries in gender equality. The Equality Act 1987, reformed in the 1995, prohibits discrimination by gender, demands the improvement of the status of women in working life and orders all authorities and employers who employ more than 30 employees to promote gender equality in systematic and target-oriented ways. According to the Act, promoting gender equality has special importance to work organisations that are highly gender segregated. As a tool for promoting equality within the work organisations the Act introduces an equality plan, which can be either a discrete plan of action or part of other personnel strategies. Equality plans can consist of strategies for more equal recruitment and division of labour, career development, working conditions, training and payroll system, for example.

However, according to the European Employment Strategy and the Finnish National Action Plans for Employment Policy, persisting gender segregation is still the major equality problem in the Finnish labour market (Council Recommendation 2002; Employment Action Plan 1999). The work tasks, occupations, lines of industry, as well as hierarchies of authority are actually more segregated by gender in Finland than in most of the other EU countries (Melkas & Anker, 1997; Joint Employment Report, 1999; Supporting document to the Joint Employment Report, 2002). Substantial gender pay gaps, unequal career advancement and different treatment of women and men in working life persist as consequences of segregation.

This contrast between legislation and practice is quite exceptional, considering that Finnish women are better educated than men, that they have participated in the labour market as full-time wage-earners equally with men for the past three decades, and that the policies for promoting gender equality have been in effect since the 1960s. In this period, equality policy has been developed with the national social and employment policies in co-operation with international organisations (UN, ILO). The Finnish equality policies include equal status in the labour force for women and men, statutory requirements for the employers to promote equal opportunities in the workplace, prohibition of gender discrimination, and social policy systems to help to reconcile work and family responsibilities. In Finland gender equality exists *de jure*, but equality *de facto* is still to be accomplished. Both explicit and hidden equality obstacles can be found in both formal and informal work organisations. It can be said that gender-neutral or even gender-blind culture still prevails in Finland, which emphasises the need for more visible policy measures for ensuring equal opportunities for both women and men.

In this context, the Finnish research and development project, *Equality Promoting Surplus Value – Equality Planning in Practice: Experiences from Workplaces with Female, Male or Equal Representation (EPSUVA)*, was launched in August 2002. The aims of the project are to investigate the state of equality planning at workplaces in Tampere Region, to study gendered structures and practices, to develop gender equality in a group of work organisations by AR methods, and to produce and distribute knowledge of concrete interplay of equality policy and experienced practices of equality. The project lasts three years and it is funded by the European Social Fund and the Finnish Ministry of Social Affairs and Health.

The understanding of gender in the project has especially been inspired by theories and research defining gender as a socially and culturally constructed relation and as gendering processes produced in everyday working life practices of individual actors. Gender is seen both as an analytical category and an activity that is anchored to the local context and social practices. In researching gendered work organisations the three approaches of gender and equality reviewed above – the equality perspective, feminist standpoint and gendering perspective – together can be considered as a methodological tool for step-by-step advancement in implementing the central concepts into the development process. The strategy of using these approaches in the EPSUVA project is the following.

According to the equality perspective, the first task of our research is to reveal, for example by surveys, the gendered divisions and their impact for the positions of women and men in the formal arenas of organisation. These offer firm evidence of the existence and meaning of gendering. Especial stress here should be given to demonstrate how women and men can be subordinated or how they have faced discrimination in different fields of working life. The feminist standpoint approach could be applied to shift to focus on gender equality towards more informal level of the organisation, e.g. how female and male competencies and skills differ and how they could be better utilised in the organisation. Finally the gendering processes are brought under scrutiny to reveal to the participants how the gendered divisions are created and maintained. The purpose of making visible women and men as genders is to anchor the concept of gender into the communication of the development and workplace learning processes and to justify the need for promoting gender equality for sake of both femininities and masculinities. This way we are trying to avoid the gender dichotomisation, contradiction and also conflict and promote participants' commitment to the processes of learning and collaboration.

In addition to the feminist researches' contribution, we will apply the strategies developed in the extensive Swedish action research programme LOM (leadership, organisation and co-operation). The LOM programme affirmed the collaboration in AR by using the bipartite organs of employers and workers/unions in the organisations (Gustavsen, 1996). All the Nordic countries have high labour unionising rates and the activity of the elected workers' representatives, like shop stewards and industrial safety delegates, is well established in the work organisation. Operating through the bipartite system the workers' views are taken better into account in the Nordic ARs already from the first contact to the workplaces, which promotes their commitment to the development process.

The LOM programme has also developed methods to support democratic communication, collaboration and learning in AR. *Work conference* is an advanced group work method, which aims at creating open space for communication for all participants from all levels of the organisation. *Democratic dialogue* is a set of rules regulating communication in the work conferences. The principals of these methods will be explained later in this section.

The LOM programme offers also another complement for the EPSUVA project: network-based strategy. Commonly the AR aiming at improving gender equality has operated only in one organisation or in a part of an organisation. According to the network-based strategy, several workplaces are collected to develop their organisation and practices in an AR project. The experiences in the LOM programme have shown that networking and possibilities to compare development processes in different workplaces creates firmer grounds for learning and change in the participating organisations, especially if the workplaces represent various kinds of organisations, e.g. in their line of industry (Gustavsen, 1991, 1996, 2001).

Finally the EPSUVA project will use the statutory equality planning as an enhanced method to promote equality. The Equality Act urges workplaces to make their equality plans consisting among other things schedules to improve gender equality by concrete actions, the success of which should be monitored. An equality plan sketched by an AR could be understood as an agreement between the employer and the employees on how they want the gender equality to be promoted. The project is especially interested in examining whether the equality planning processes could be the concrete tool for changing gendered work cultures and mainstreaming gender equality in everyday practices in work organisations.

The EPSUVA project started in autumn 2002 with a survey. The aim of the survey was to map the status of equality planning in the workplaces of Tampere Region. The questionnaire was sent to all workplaces with over 30 employees in the area. About 30% of the workplaces answered the survey. Small workplaces especially in the service sector are underpresented in the data. The results show that although the employer's statutory obligation to make plans to promote gender equality has been effective for eight years, equality planning is still lacking in over half of the workplaces.

Along with the questionnaire, the workplaces received a short introduction to the aims of the project and an invitation to participate as a co-operating organisation in the project's developmental work. The project offered to arrange training and assistance in making and implementing an equality plan, as well as to help in building networks with other working organisations, local authorities, etc., in the region. The project used dual agenda (Myerson & Kolb, 2000) in encouraging the workplaces to join the project. According to dual agenda, the promotion of gender equality was presented in the light of other possible contributions of equality: recruitment of new staff, better utilisation of personnel skills, creation of more inspiring and innovative working atmosphere, increase in productivity and generation of a positive public image of the workplace.

Some 30 workplaces (16% of the respondents) expressed their interest in registering as a collaborative organisation in the project. The majority of the registering workplaces indicated that they did not have any equality problems, but merely lacked the statutory equality plan. Their motivation to participate the project was obviously alone to acquire a plan. The project chose six workplaces that volunteered to participate in the project. The reasons for enlisting as a collaborative organisation varied in the chosen workplaces. Some of them did not have an equality plan or the plan was out of date. Some were worried about recruitment of new staff in the future. Some had a poor working atmosphere and wanted to improve it and cut down the number of sick leaves caused by it. Some were eager developers of their organisation and had participated in similar projects earlier. These six organisations represent female- and male-dominated as well as equally gender-divided organisations in both the public and the private sector. This choice makes it possible to compare detailed and individual differences, variations and alternatives of gendering processes and practices within feminine and masculine work cultures.

During spring and summer 2003, the project started the developmental work with the selected project partners. In the first phase (see Figure 2), the main task was to bring the invisible gendering processes and gendered practices in the organisation onto the agenda of the development work and construct shared understanding of the project's aims. This was achieved by using varying methods to demonstrate how gender is involved in different formal and informal relations, practices and structures in the organisations' everyday life. A sample survey on the personnel's experiences of fairness and equality and the quality of working life in the workplace was conducted in each participating organisation. The survey data were augmented by interviews of women and men on different levels in the organisation hierarchy, and by visits to the workplaces.

On the basis of the collected data the researchers wrote equality reports for each workplace. In these reports, the structural and hierarchical differences of women's and men's positioning in the organisation, the distinctions in their experiences of equality, and the gendered practices in each organisation were represented. Particular weight was given to breaking down the misconception

Figure 2.   Stages of developmental work in EPSUVA project

Aim of the stage	Tools/Spaces for learning
Exposing the hidden gender Bringing the male gender on the agenda ↓	Surveys, interviews
Creating shared understanding of gender and equality ↓	First general work conference Development days in the workplaces
Visioning for future ↓	Work conference and development days
Defining equality problems Planning for actions ↓	Working parties for making the plans
Functionalising the plan Mainstreaming the actions with other activities ↓	Working parties Collaboration with working party, management and personnel
Executing the plan ↓	Working party and management
Monitoring the plan ↓	Working party
Disseminating planning experiences Updating the understanding of gender and the definition of problems	Last general work conference Reports, articles, etc.

that "gender equals women". Men and women in different positions and performing varying work tasks were found to have faced inequality or discrimination in various areas of working life and for diverse reasons. Characteristically, it was almost solely women who mentioned gender as a reason for discrimination against them. In the conclusion of each report, the major inequality problems for women and men were collected and simple ways were suggested to solve them.

After distributing the reports to the collaborating organisations, the project arranged a two-day conference for all the participating organisations in autumn 2003 to start their own equality planning and development process. The conference was arranged according to the LOM programme AR methods: *work conference* and *democratic dialogue* (Gustavsen, 1991).

The work conference method is based on the idea of creating an open and democratic space for exchanging and learning from ideas and experiences of the participants representing various hierarchical positions in different work organisations. The method consists typically of a three-phase working schedule. In the first phase, the participants are organised in little groups to create a shared vision of a desired good work organisation. In the second phase, groups concentrate on defining the major problems in reaching the vision and the ways to solve the problems. In the final phase, groups compose an action plan to implement the solutions in everyday activities in the work organisation.

The composition of the work groups changes in each phase. In the visioning phase, groups are made up homogeneously. Every group consists of participants with similar hierarchical positions in different work organisations. In our work conference we divided groups also according to gender. Six groups were made, separate male and female groups for those performing managerial tasks, white-collar tasks and blue-collar tasks, respectively. The grouping aimed at bringing in the different voices and future visions from the diverse levels of organisation according to gender to be heard in the general discussions.

In the problem-defining and solution phase, groups are put together diago-nally, so that in every group there is a representative from every hierarchical position, but from different work organisations. This group composition is targeted at contributing experience exchange and detachment from the very concrete everyday problems in work organisations to a more conceptual level. In the final phase, each group consists of the representatives of all hierarchical positions in a single organisation aiming at utilising what they have learned in the previous group works to improve their own work organisation. In our work conference, the groups in the last phase concentrated on sketching their own equality plan.

The communication in the groups was regulated by the rules of democratic dialogue. The dialogue is understood as a process of exchanging ideas and arguments, which must continuously produce agreements of different views to provide platforms for workplace learning and practical actions. The basic idea of a democratic system is the ability to combine pluralism with efficient decision making. All participants have an equal position in the group. Everyone has valuable knowledge for the development work in the groups based on their work experience. All arguments must be heard and discussed. Everyone is obliged to participate to the discussions in groups and also help others to contribute the discussion (Gustavsen, 1991). In each group of our work conference there was a researcher present as a 'resource person' to guarantee the democracy in the discussions and to help the groups to complete their work. The democratic dialogue seemed to function well in bringing in the voices from the different levels of the organisational hierarchy, but not satisfactorily the voices of women and men separately.

The EPSUVA project's solution to overcome the problems of the previous AR on work-based gender inequalities has been to expose the hidden gender, and also men as gender, by demonstrating their existence in figures and examples in the equality reports. The reports performed as a concrete starting point for the developmental work in the first work conference. The work conference, as a space for transformative learning (Filander, 2003; Mezirow et al., 1990; Argyris & Schön, 1978), also offered the participants a platform to detach from everyday activities and experiences in their own work organisation and reflect them from a distance in comparison with others' experiences from other organisations. The first work conference produced sketches for the equality plans.

In the next phase of the ongoing project, we will arrange development days in the work organisations to disseminate the present results of the development work through the work organisations and to give a chance for as many members of each organisation as possible to take part in the organisation development process. This way we are aiming at creating shared understanding of gender and equality in the organisations and to promote wide participation, involvement and engagement in the developmental objectives. For example, one of the participating work organisations will hold nearly ten development days so that all of its 550 employees will have a chance to participate in the process of transformative workplace learning.

All these research, training and developing actions will provide a solid ground for the next major step in the development work, which is accomplishing a practical and viable equality plan and implementing it in each organisation. At this stage of the project, the workplaces are gathering bipartite working parties to continue to make the plans. The researchers of the project will participate in the working parties' meetings to help and support the parties. The project's aim is to solidify the equality plans' position and viability in the organisations, by encouraging organisations to mainstream their equality plan and its actions with other administrative activities in the workplaces, and by creating a continuous system of reflecting, retargeting and revising the plans at intervals in the future. The key point for the future equality planning depends on shared understanding on gender and equality within the organisation will develop. How our AR strategies will succeed in improving gender equality in working life still remains to be seen.

The Implications for Gender Equality

The main argument in this chapter is that gendering practices in work organisations and gendered work cultures hold the key position in promoting or inhibiting women's and men's equal opportunities in working life. So far equal opportunity policy and legislation have had only marginal effects on working conditions and the gender equality in paid work organisations. The policy challenge is thus how to get the formal (*de jure*) equality policy to function (*de facto*) on the concrete level of structures, practices and everyday interaction between people in these work organisations. To make equality policy effective in practice necessitates theoretical and practical understanding of the meaning of gender, various collaborative methods to make gender visible on the organisational level and methods to change gender-neutral or gender-blind work cultures as well. The major challenge is how to match gender theory with the gendering practices and promotion of gender equality in the work organisations, especially while these practices are highly contextual and local in their nature.

The equality approach emphasises similarity of women and men. Its strategy is to guarantee equity, equal treatment and prohibition of gender discrimination by legislation. The strategy integrates women into the labour market and promotes formal and quantitative equality. It does not challenge gender-neutrality;

on the contrary, it reproduces and maintains sex stereotypes and gender dichotomy. Typically this approach describes trends in women's and men's employment and division of labour in the wider labour market context. However, in the organisational context, by drawing on gender statistics, surveys and interviews directed at women's and men's experiences on gender equality it is possible to produce basic knowledge of the general structural barriers and gendered practices that set boundaries for women and men as groups and as individuals within particular organisations.

Women's standpoint approach focuses on the differences between women and men and especially the specificity of women's abilities, skills and innovativeness. Its strategy is the empowerment of women and the implementation of actions targeted at promoting women's position in working life. While women's attributes and skills are often invisible or undervalued, this approach is also needed in promoting gender equality within working life. The main problem with the women's standpoint approach is that it may foster gender conflict. However, gender defines and constrains both women's and men's opportunities in working life, and gender equality should be seen in a wider perspective. The promotion of equality is important for women and men and for the better functioning of work organisations.

The gendering approach emphasises diversity and the process of gendering embedded in individual identities, social and structural institutions, organisations and culture as well. Its strategy is to break the gender-neutral work cultures and mainstream equality into all the activities in the work organisation. On the workplace level, a useful tool for mainstreaming is offered by the equality planning process built on the experiences, commitment and collaboration of the whole personnel of the organisation. Unfortunately the planning process has not yet been able to challenge the gendered structures and gendering processes.

Action research can support the equality planning process by providing it with spaces to learn the meaning of gendering structures and practices, and thereby enabling change in work organisations and their gendered cultures. But so far the efforts in AR have only partly succeeded in this. Network-based AR and its method, the work conference, can be of great help in completing these efforts. The work conference method aims at empowering the employees and promoting their participation in the development work. Network-based AR utilises networks of developing work organisations and offers possibilities for inter-organisational learning. The equality planning with its continued processes of context mapping, practical short-term and innovative long-term visioning and reflection can be considered as a model of transformative learning in the organisation.

The AR method also offers another supportive strategy to strengthen equality planning. As AR increases the visibility of gender and the gendering practices in both open and hidden levels of the formal and informal organisation, it also opens the gate to intervene in these practices by designing targeted actions for the process of changing gendered work cultures. Equality plan could become a new visible, conscious and continuously evaluated gender contract for the work organisation. Such implementation of statutory equality planning is the next step to improve gender equality in everyday practices in work organisations.

Note

1. The article is based the research done in the project *Equality Promoting Surplus Value – Equality Planning in Practice: Experiences from Workplaces with Female, Male or Equal Representation (EPSUVA)* Tapio Rissanen is a researcher and Sirpa Kolehmainen the leader of the project. The other researchers in the project are Riitta Lavikka, Katja Uosukainen, Minna Leinonen and Hanna Ylöstalo.

References

Acker, J. (1990). Hierarchies, jobs, bodies: A theory of gendered organizations. *Gender & Society,* 4(2), 139–158.

Acker, J. (1998). The future of gender and organizations: Connections and boundaries. *Gender, Work and Organizations,* 5(4) 199–206.

Argyris, C., & Schön, D. (1978). *Organizational learning: A theory of action perspective.* Massachusetts: Addison-Wesley.

Bradley, H. (1989). *Men's work, women's work: A sociological history of the sexual divisions of labour in employment.* Cambridge: Polity Press.

Brooker, R., Smeal, G., Ehrich, L., Daws, L., & Brannock, J. (1998). Action research for professional development on gender issues. In B. Atweh, S. Kemmis & P. Weeks (Eds.), *Action research in practice: Partnership for social justice in education* (pp. 189–211). London and New York: Routledge.

Blau, F., & Ferber, M. (1986). *The economics of women, men and work.* New Jersey: Prentice-Hall.

Fals Borda, O. (2001). Participatory (action) research in social theory: Origins and challenges. In P. Reason & H. Bradbury (Eds.), *Handbook of action research: Participative inquiry and practice* (pp. 27–37). London: Thousand Oaks/New Delhi: Sage Publications.

Calás, M. B., & Smircich, L. (1996). From 'The women's' point of view: Feminist approaches to organization studies. In S. R. Glegg, C. Hardy & W. R. Nord (Eds.), *Handbook of organization studies* (pp. 218–258). London: Sage Publications.

Cockburn, C. (1988). The gendering of jobs: Workplace relations and the reproduction of sex segregation. In S. Walby (Ed.), *Gender segregation at work* (pp. 29–42). Milton Keynes: Open University Press.

Coleman, G., & Rippin, A. (2000). Putting feminist theory to work: Collaboration as a means towards organisational change. *Organization,* 7(4), 573–588.

Council Recommendation (2002) on the implementation of Member States' employment policies. The Council of European Union 2002/178/EC. Retrieved January 19, 2004 from http://europa.eu.int/comm/employment_social/employment_strategy/recomm_en.htm.

Dex, S. (1987). *Women's occupational mobility: A lifetime perspective.* London: MacMillan Press.

Dex, S., & Sewell, R. (1995). Equal opportunities policies and women's labour market status in industrialised countries. In J. Humphries & J. Rubery (Eds.), *The economics of equal opportunities* (pp. 367–392). Manchester: Equal Opportunities Commission.

Ely, R. J., & Meyerson, D. E. (2000). Advancing gender equity in organizations: The challenge and importance of maintaining a gender narrative. *Organization,* 7(4), 589–608.

Employment action plan, Finland Ministry of Labour (1999). Labour Administration Publication 227. Helsinki.

Filander, K. (2003). *Vocabularies of change – Analysing talk on change and agency in development work.* Roskilde: Roskilde University Press.

Flax, J. (1990). Postmodernism and gender relations in feminist theory. In L. J. Nicholson (Ed.), *Feminism/postmodernism* (pp. 39–62). New York: Routledge.

Fletcher, J. K. (1999). *Disappearing acts: Gender, power and relational practice at work.* Cambridge & London: The MIT Press.

Granqvist, L., & Persson H. (1998). *Career mobility in the private service sector – are women trapped in "bad" jobs?* Stockholm University. Swedish Institute for Social Research, Working Paper 1.

Gustavsen, B. (1991). The LOM program: A network-based strategy for organisation development in Sweden. *Research in organisational change and development, 5,* 285–315.

Gustavsen, B. (1996). Development and the Social Sciences: An uneasy relationship. In S. Toulmin & B. Gustavsen (Eds.), *Beyond theory. Changing organizations through participation* (pp. 5–30). Amsterdam/Philadelphia: John Benjamins Publishing Company.

Gustavsen, B. (2001). Theory and practice: The mediating discourse. In P. Reason & H. Bradbury (Eds.), *Handbook of action research: Participative inquiry and practice* (pp. 17–26), London: Thousand Oaks/New Delhi: Sage Publications.

Hakim, C. (1981). Job segregation: trends in the 1970s. *Employment Gazette,* 521–529.

Hakim, C. (1996). *Key issues in women's work.* London: Athlone Press.

Harding, S. (1986). *The science question in feminism.* Ithaca: Cornell University Press.

Harding, S. (1991). *Whose science? Whose knowledge? Thinking from women's lives.* Ithaca: Cornell University Press.

Hearn, J. (2000). On the complexity of feminist intervention in organizations. *Organization, 7*(4), 609–624.

Heide, I. (2001). Supranational action against sex discrimination: Equal pay and equal treatment in the European Union. In M. Fetherolf Loutfi (Ed.), *Women, work, what is equality and how do we get there?* Geneva: ILO.

Hirdman, Y. (1988). Genussystemet – reflexioner kring kvinnors sociala underordning. *Kvinnovetenskaplig tidskrift, 3,* 49–63.

Horelli, L., & Saari, M. (2002). *Tasa-arvoa valtavirtaan. Tasa-arvon valtavirtaistamisen menetelmiä ja käytäntöjä.* Helsinki: Sosiaali- ja terveysministeriön selvityksiä 11.

Joint Employment Report (1999) Part I: the European Union. Retrieved January 19, 2004, from http://europa.eu.int/comm/employment_social/employment_strategy/employ_en.htm.

Jyrkämä, J. (1996). Action research and social practices – new remarks on an old approach. Nordiske Udkast. *Journal of Critical Social Science, 24,* 33–44.

Jämställdhetslagen (1991: 433). Jämställdhetsombudsmannen. Retrieved from http://www.jamombud.se/en/generalinformat.asp.

Kauppinen, K., & Veikkola, H.-K. (1997). *Tasa-arvoistuvat työyhteisöt.* Helsinki: Työterveyslaitos, työsuojeluhallinto.

Kinnunen, M., & Korvajärvi, P. (1996). Johdanto: Naiset ja miehet työelämässä. In M. Kinnunen & P. Korvajärvi (Eds.), *Työelämän sukupuolistavat käytännöt.* Tampere: Vastapaino.

Kolehmainen, S (1999). *Naisten ja Miesten työt. Työmarkkinoiden segregoituminen Suomessa 1970–1990.* Helsinki: Tilastokeskus, Tutkimuksia 227.

Korvajärvi, P. (1998). *Gendering Dynamics in White-Collar Work Organisations,* Acta Universitas Tamperensis 600. Tampere: University of Tampere.

Korvajärvi, P. (2002a). Locating gender neutrality in formal and informal aspects of organisational cultures. *Culture and organisation, 8*(2), 101–115.

Korvajärvi, P. (2002b). Gender-neutral gender and denial of the difference. In B. Czarniawska & H. Höpfl (Eds.), *Casting the other. The production and maintenance of inequalities in work organisations.* London & New York: Routledge.

Lehto, A.-M. (1999). Towards equality in working life? In A.-M. Lehto & H. Sutela (Eds.), *Gender equality in working life.* Helsinki: Labour Market 1999:22, Statistics Finland.

Maguire P. (2001). Uneven ground: Feminisms and action research. In P. Reason & H. Bradbury (Eds.), *Handbook of action research: Participative inquiry and practice* (pp. 59–69). London: Thousand Oaks, New Delhi: Sage Publications.

Melkas, H., & Anker, R. (1997). Occupational segregation by sex in Nordic countries: An empirical investigation. *International Labour Review, 136*(3), 341–363.

Melkas, T. (1999). *The Gender barometer 1998. Equality between Men and Women in Finland.* Helsinki: Statistics Finland – Council of Equality, SVT Living conditions 1999:1. Gender Statistics.

Meyerson, D. E., & Kolb, D. M. (2000). Moving out the 'Armchair': Developing a framework to bridge the gap between feminist theory and practice. *Organization, 7*(4), 553–571.

Mezirow, J., & Associates (1990). *Fostering critical reflection in adulthood. A guide to transformative and emancipatory learning.* San Francisco: Jossey-Bass.

Mückenberger, U. (2001). Gender mainstreaming – from traditional anti-discrimination policies to an integrated gender equality approach. In Mückenberger, U. (Ed.), *Manifesto social Europe* (pp. 269–287). Brussels: ETUI.

OECD Employment Outlook (1988) September. Paris: OECD.

OECD Statistics Portal. Retrieved on December 15, 2003, from http://www.oecd.org/statsportal/ 0,2639,en_2825_293564_1_1_1_1_1,00.html

Rantalaiho, L., Heiskanen, T., Korvajärvi, P., & Vehviläinen, M. (1997). Studying gendered practices. In L. Rantalaiho & T. Heiskanen (Eds.), *Gendered practices in working life.* London: Macmillan.

Reason, P., & Bradbury, H. (2001). Introduction: Inquiry and participation in search of a world worthy of human aspiration. In P. Reason & H. Bradbury (Eds.), *Handbook of action research: Participative inquiry and practice* (pp. 1–14). London: Thousand Oaks, New Delhi: Sage Publications.

Reskin, B. (1984). *Sex segregation in the workplace. Trends, explanations, remedies.* Washington: National Academy Press.

Reskin, B., & Hartman, H. (Eds.) (1986) *Women's work, men's work. Sex segregation on the job.* Washington: National Academy Press.

Reskin, B., & Padavic, I. (1994). *Women and men at work.* Thousand Oaks: Pine Forge Press.

Robinson, D. (2001). Differences in occupational earnings by sex. In M. Fetherolf Loutfi (Ed.), *Women, work, what is equality and how do we get there?* Geneva: ILO.

Rubery, J., Smith, M., & Fagan C. (1999). *Women's employment in Europe.* Routledge, London.

Scott, J. W. (1986). Gender: A useful category of historical analysis. *The American Historical Review, 91*(5), 1053–1075.

Scott MacEwen, A., & Burchell, B. (1994). 'And never the twain shall meet'? Gender segregation and work histories. In A. Scott MacEwen (Ed.), *Gender segregation and social change* (pp. 121–156). New York: Oxford University Press.

Silius, H. (1992). *Den kringgärdade kvinligheten. Att vara kvinliga jurist i Finland.* Åbo: Åbo Akademis Förlag.

Smith, D. (1992). Sociology from women's experience: A reaffirmation. *Sociological Theory, 10*(1), 88–98.

Supporting document to the Joint Employment Report 2002. Commission staff working paper. Assessment of the implementation of the 2002 employment guidelines. COM 621 final. Retrieved on January 19 2004, from http://europa.eu.int/comm/employment_social/employment_strategy/ employ_en.htm

Tasa-arvolaki. Tasa-arvoesitteitä 1998:2 fin. Tasa-arvotoimisto. Helsinki: Sosiaali- ja tervey-sministeriö.

Women and Structural Change. New Perspectives (1994) Paris: OECD.

49

INFORMATION AND COMMUNICATION TECHNOLOGIES AND WORKPLACE LEARNING: THE CONTESTED TERRAIN OF LEGISLATION, POLICIES, PROGRAMS AND PRACTICES

Peter H. Sawchuk

Ontario Institute for Studies in Education of the University of Toronto, Canada

> Governments everywhere try to formulate productivity-enhancing policies ... [E]conomists have found that technological change is a principal source of economic growth and rising per capita income. Students of business identify it as basic cause of the growth of the corporation. Its effects on employment, the distribution of income and regional differences in growth are carefully scrutinized. (Thomson, 1993, p. 1)

At the turn of the new millennium, national expenditures on Information and Communication Technology (ICT) have approached double digits as a percentage of GDP within the USA, Japan and the European Union countries breaking the 7.5 percent mark. In the USA alone, these expenditures represent over 1.5 trillion dollars per year. Despite this, OECD policy analysts (1999) and an enormous array of others (e.g., Reich, 1991; Thomson, 1993; Castells, 1996; Archibugi & Lundvall, 2001) suggest this isn't enough. For them, it is clear that economic success is dependent on further development of ICT: investment in it, its application, and its diffusion. However, what are we to make of this policy orthodoxy? How is 'technology' itself understood in this context? What are the presumptions made about the relationship between ICT development, implementation, learning and use?

A corollary of this orthodoxy is of course that the invention of new technologies have defined the path of economic progress. However, economic history teaches us that the claims of links between technology, productivity and the emergence of past and future phases in the economy are far from straightforward. The key technologies of modernity, those that are said to have defined the first, second and third industrial revolutions (steam, electricity, and ICT respectively), have in fact seen fascinating, contentious and complex pathways

International Handbook of Educational Policy, 923–941

Nina Bascia, Alister Cumming, Amanda Datnow, Kenneth Leithwood and David Livingstone (Eds.)

© 2005 *Springer. Printed in Great Britain.*

toward application in the workplace (e.g., Von Tunzelmann, 1978; Devine, 1983; Gospel, 1991; Thomson, 1993; Lipsey, Bekar, & Carlaw, 1998). Indeed, the major 'General Purpose Technologies' (GPT's) including electricity (e.g., Hughes, 1983), ICT (e.g., Noble, 1979, 1984), and in particular steam (e.g., Devine, 1983) have been shown to be the subject of political and economic struggle. In fact, in this chapter I argue that the details of the emergence, diffusion and transfer of GPT's provide important clues as to the actual nature of technology as a phenomenon that run counter to conventional wisdom. I begin by asking, is technology a 'thing' or is it a social process? Lazonick (1993) suggests the latter in his discussion of the meaning of 'technological transfer':

> Insofar as the utilization of technology requires complementary human inputs with specific cognitive capabilities and behavioural responses, the transferred technology will have to be developed in the new national environment before it can be utilized there. As a result, when 'transferred' technology is ultimately developed so that it can be productively utilized in a new national environment, it is in effect a new technology (Lazonick, 1993, p. 194).

Lazonick's perspective is in fact aligned with a broad and interactional view of technology represented in the concept that Fleck refers to as 'configurations' (1993). Technology, understood as 'configuration', is defined as a complex mix of standardized and locally customized elements that are always highly specific to specific historical, national, regional or organizational settings. Building on this we can say that those who have been most insightful in considering the nature of technology have defined the term quite broadly to reflect this broad complex. Technology is not this or that tool, artifact or machine, nor is it a 'GPT' such as steam, electricity or ICT. Rather, it is 'the way we do things around here' (Franklin, 1990); the 'organization of resources' (Hacker, 1991; Mumford, 1964); or, 'society made durable' (Latour, 2000). The suggestion here is that any genuinely useful approach to the issue of ICT, work and learning must, then, expand its perspective on technology in order to make it 'social'.

In the context of ICT defined as a social process, it becomes clear that traditional policy research on work and technological innovation has arrived at something of a cross-road: how, in times in which the combination of ICT and knowledge work appear to be pivotal (e.g., Castells, 1996; Reich, 1991), can such policy research credibly proceed without a robust theory of ICT as a broad, interactive phenomenon encapsulating design, implementation, practice and, perhaps most importantly of all, learning?

The most practical outcome of the realization that technologies are really 'social processes' rather than 'devices' is that we are forced to conclude that ICT-based policy cannot be understood in isolation from either industrial relations and training policy on the one hand, or analyses of actual labour and learning processes on the other. However, even this important step in our thinking is not enough. The question remains 'What kind of social phenomenon are we talking about?' I have mentioned already that steam, electricity and ICT all emerged from, and in fact can be defined through, the push and pull of economic and political struggle. As Feenberg (1991) has said, 'technology is a scene of struggle ... a parliament of things'. Historically, as now, the intersection of work, learning and technological change has occasioned conflict: from the Luddite revolts of early 19th century to the countless industrial conflicts caused by the imposition of technological change and, more recently, the transformation of occupations including printers (e.g., Zimbalist, 1979; Wallace & Kalleberg, 1982; Cockburn, 1985; Smith, 1988), engineering (e.g., Jones, 1988), textile work (e.g., Lazonick, 1979), postal work (e.g., Louli & Bickerton, 1995), and computer programming (e.g., Kraft, 1977). Wallace and Kalleberg (1982), working from the US context, summarize:

> We have argued that while technology is the proximate cause of this trans-formation, the underlying and fundamental sources for these changes are found in historically developed social relations of production ... The stated goal of automation in printing, as in other industries, is the rationalization of the labor process: the streamlining of production and elimination of costly sources of human error ... However, efficiency is not a value-neutral goal in capitalist economies (pp. 321–322).

Thus, it is the core point of departure in this chapter that our conceptions of ICT, and, in turn, the intersection of ICT, work and learning, must be 'de-reified' if we're to move beyond mere appearances toward substantial, critical analysis. ICT as an isolated device, tool or machine is an abstraction; in reality however, it is an elaborate, historical process. It is fundamentally both a social and highly conflictual phenomenon.

In this chapter I explore a selection of policies and practice at the intersection of ICT, work and learning. I use a broad definition of policy that encompasses formal legislation, regulation and programs at various international, national, as well as regional, sectoral and organizational levels. Defined in this way, policy involves the efforts of national governments and inter-governmental bodies as well as sectoral bodies, firms, research institutes and labour unions. My discus-sions of practice in this chapter deal with the processes of technological design and implementation as well as the full range of work activity involved in the development of skill and knowledge necessary to diffuse, transfer and actually put to use ICT at the point of production.

The examples I draw on respect this broad, integrative approach to policy and practice. National and international policy and programs are examined with reference to USA, Canada, the European Union, as well as Sweden and Norway. I then look at important types of policy and practice at the level of the firm with a focus first on 'Technology Agreements' and second, on research concerning the practice of ICT innovation and use in the labour process, with an emphasis on what is known in the sociology of work field as the 'de-skilling/en-skilling' debates. I begin, however, with a brief discussion of the central ideological approaches to technological thought: an indispensable resource for assessing the meanings, the biases and the trajectories of recent policies and practice at the intersection of ICT, work and learning.

Historical and Philosophical Contexts of ICT, Work and Learning

In North America, according to Theodore Roszak (1994), the word 'computer' entered the public vocabulary in the 1950's at a time when the most advanced models were still room-sized beasts that burned enough electricity to present a serious cooling problem. Building on the principle of ICT, work and learning as a conflictual social phenomenon as explained above, we can note that computerization was not simply 'discovered' in the conventional sense of the term. Rather, its was brought into being by specific historical and political economic processes of politics, policy and practice. Noble (1984) provides the definitive analysis in these terms by noting how contemporary computerization emerged through a series of concerted and contested activities through which companies like General Electric, Westinghouse, RCA, AT&T and IBM, relying upon private control over public funds vis-a-vis what could be called the 'university-industrial-military' complex of the post World War II era in America, led the development of specific forms of technology: Numerical Control, Computerized Numerical Control (CNC) and automated robotics. Importantly, Noble makes it clear that, in fact, alternatives to CNC could have been developed that were just as efficient, and that strategic choices by dominant groups revolved around issues of power and control over the organization of production. Just as the Luddites of 19th century Britain were in favour of technologies that supplemented rather than displaced human skills (Sale, 1995), the key alternative with regard to CNC technology was 'Record/Playback' (R/P) technology; a system that was actively ignored largely because, as Noble (1984, p. 190) puts it, "to the software engineer, this places far too many cards in the hands of the lowly machinist".

While this historical background is important, if we are to understand the current intersection of ICT, work and learning as a contested social phenomenon, it is equally important to have a basic understanding of the competing ideologies or philosophical approaches that inform the policy and practice of ICT development and use. Williams and Edge (1996, p. 2) reminds us, "these debates are not merely 'academic': they relate to policy claims and objectives". Extending the analysis of Feenberg (1991), we can categorize the different approaches into four basic categories: instrumental/technocratic; substantive; constructivist; and, what Feenberg refers to as a 'critical theory' of technology.

Instrumentalist or technocratic approaches tend to be the source of either the positive or neutral characterizations of ICT's in the workplace. This is the dominant approach amongst government, business and mainstream policy sciences. Here the transfer of technology is inhibited only by cost; what works in one context can be expected to work equally well, more or less, in another; and, "the only rational stance is an unreserved commitment to its employment" (Feenberg, 1991, p. 6). Influential original formulations of this approach as it involves work can be found in the work of Dahrendorf (1959), Kerr (1962) and Bell (1973) who wrote at length on the issues of technology and evolutionary industrial progression. More often than not under this approach, technology comes to take on a kind of autonomous, creative and deterministic role (and thus it makes sense that Time Magazine, in 1982, could award 'person of the year' to the computer). This autonomous casting, in turn, gives rise to exaggerated tales of the emergence of 'knowledge workers' (Bell, 1973; further popularized in Naisbitt, 1982) and 'symbolic analysts' (Reich, 1991).

A competitor to technocratic thought is the *substantive approach*, represented best in the writings of Jacques Ellul (1964) or Martin Heidegger (1977). This approach presumes a technology which necessarily crystallizes and expresses a type of destructive, alienating, environmentally degrading, instrumental rationality. Like the technocratic approach the substantive approach is largely determinist. It attributes an autonomous force to technology, with an emphasis on its role in our 'cultural systems', and orients the world as an 'object of control'. An intensely dark trajectory is pre-figured from the substantive approach (e.g., as Heidegger said, 'Only God can save us now'); a return to simplicity or primitivism, according to this approach, offers the only viable alternative.

Standing in many ways separate from either of these first two perspectives is the *constructivist approach*, exemplified (though quite differently) by the likes of Latour (2000), Callon (1992), and Suchman (1987). Taken as a whole, we can say that these works emphasize how technology is rooted in human interaction and the local activation or use of mediating objects or artifacts. The meaning and effects of technology are determined in their use by actors and not necessarily in any straight-forward, *a priori* way by designers. Among all the approaches to ICT, it is the constructivist approach that most clearly articulates how users implement and appropriate ICT; sometimes in keeping with the intentions of the designers (and those who have contracted them), sometimes not. Others (see contributors to Rip, Misa, & Schot, 1995; Suchman, 2002) have echoed the importance of this approach for technological development, emphasizing reciprocal relations between moments of design, implementation, and use in such a way as to open up new ground in conventional understandings of 'choice' within the course of technological development. There is at the heart of this approach a sensibility that suggests that the ways and contexts in which users interact with devices is definitive of the technology as a whole.

Finally there is the *critical approach*. Its roots are largely, although not exclusively, in the Frankfurt School of critical social theory (e.g., Feenberg, 1991). I say not exclusively because a variety of other work, such as that of Lewis Mumford (e.g., 1964), have relevant connections to this approach as well. In general, the critical approach rejects the presumptions of both the technocratic and the substantive perspectives, charting a course, as Feenberg says, between the poles of resignation and utopian visions of efficiency. With its emphasis on power relations, to some degree the critical and constructivist approach can overlap as when authors such as Latour (2000) and Callon (1992) recognize the inherent political dimensions of technological development (e.g., 'Technologies are politics pursued by other means' – Latour). Nevertheless, central to the critical approach may be what Feenberg calls the 'democratic advance'; that is, the democratic participation of citizens in the establishment of both the goals and means of technological development, implementation and diffusion. Echoing this concern in terms of policy analysis, Gärtner and Wagner (1996) have noted, drawing on case studies in Europe, the difficulties faced by design efforts situated within 'fragmented political cultures'. Likewise, Mumford's (1964) pan-historic discussions stress what he calls 'authoritarian and democratic technics', the former being 'system-centred,' immensely powerful and yet inherently unstable due to its centralization of control. Indeed, he goes on to say that to cope with increasingly powerful technologies of the modern era, "if democracy did not exist, we would have to invent it" (p. 21).

I suggest that these four basic approaches to technological thought will be useful as a type of philosophical compass for analysing policy and practice. In other words, they orient us to the more general directions and purposes that, all too often, remain hidden beneath the surface of legislation, policy, programs and practice that express them.

ICT and Workplace Learning Legislation, Policy and Programs

If we commit to understanding the intersection of ICT, work and learning as a broad, conflictual social phenomenon, then, as I suggested from the outset, we must look at a variety of types of policies that relate to ICT training. We must also regard work-based learning – whether it is organized as a training program or undertaken informally in everyday participation within the labour process – as a phenomenon that sits atop, gives meaning to, reacts upon and affects legislation, policy and programs regarding ICT.

Research and development (R&D) is central to the efforts of core capitalist countries (Archibugi & Lundvall, 2001) though there is considerable variation internationally (e.g., see Mani, 2002 for how developed and developing countries compare). In terms of recognition within formal policy of the linkages between technological development and the broader regulation of industrial relations, we see that Northern European governments are most advanced with other European governments such as France and Germany (as well as Japan) moderately so, and the governments of countries such as the UK, USA, Southern Europe, Australia and Canada least likely to recognize, in the form of regulatory policy, these linkages. Clearly, the most 'interventionist' responses of government are to be found in countries like Norway and Sweden where issues of ICT R&D application as well as industrial relations more broadly speaking are shaped by general policy commitments toward 'co-determination'. However, in general, the power of national or international governmental bodies to influence the introduction and application of ICT in actual work processes and workplaces through regulation is quite limited. In the USA, for example, while Carnoy, Pollack and Wong (1993) have noted that labour relations structures, policies and practices are coming to the center of the debate over the design and adoption of new technologies, the most common model of employer/employee negotiation on ICT adoption is adversarial, antagonistic as well as fragmented.

It is relevant to briefly note, however, that a parallel system of coordinated private-sector policy and (corporate-based) governance has blossomed. There have been, for example, a growing number of international agreements between large corporations in terms of various forms of ICT development and application. According to Archibugi and Coco (2000), between the periods of 1981–86 and 1993–98 international, firm-to-firm technological development agreements have doubled. In particular, strategic technology partnerships (R&D) between Europe and the USA have rocketed in the last 10 years. These partnerships sometimes involve collaborations with public research institutions and universities who play an important role in the international dissemination of knowledge and ICT development, but, conspicuously absent, is the involvement of either unions or the public at large. While this layer of ICT, work and learning policy is important, a solid grasp of the range of governmental legislation, policy and programs in the area remains most relevant for our discussion here. To review these, I rely on several selected examples involving different countries as well as different political levels of enactment.

An examination of the US system of training, ICT development and implementation – increasingly set as an ideal in the policy world in terms of leading edge practices of ICT innovation – on closer look reveals a fragmented, chaotic and, in light of the trade-offs it produces for the population as a whole (Audretsch & Thurik, 2001), possibly ineffective overall mix of federal, state and regional efforts. Audretsch and Thurik (2001) suggest this goes hand-in-hand with economic growth associated with the entrepreneurial (versus the managed) economy as policies become most effective at the regional rather than the national level. However, at the more localized level of the firm and sector, the USA system of industrial relations places decisions on technological change and work organization firmly under the 'management rights clause' of any collective agreement (Kelley, 1990). This context includes a corporate culture hostile to unions and comparatively high levels of involvement in 'inter-firm' technological development agreements, both of which decrease the likelihood of genuine 'co-determination'. In slightly broader terms, vocational and work-based training policy in the USA has also been recognized to be a patch-work of state and federal programs, beginning in 1962 with the Manpower Development Training Act, to the Comprehensive Employment and Training Act of 1973, through to the Job Training Partnership Act (1983) and the School-to-Work Opportunities Act (1994–2001) (see Grubb, 1996). Likewise, host of authors have lamented the general lack of industrial policy in the USA historically, which is also reflected in the arena of ICT R&D policy (see contributors to *Industrial Policy: Investing in America*, Volume 5, Number 1). At the same time however, Herman (2001) has documented some important examples of multi-lateral partnership agreements over ICT implementation and training in the USA that would appear to hold a good deal of promise for the future. Based on 14 case studies of 'high-road' partnerships between employers, government as well as unions and local communities, Herman concludes that, in the USA, ICT/work/learning policy that is most successful tends to be found at the sectoral rather than the state or federal level which tends to support the types of claims economists such as Audretsch and Thurik (2001), cited earlier, make around the effects of globalization.

As something of an alternative to the type of de-centralized, largely corporate-controlled policy models seen in the USA, in Canada there has been more innovative experimentation with governmental policy. 'Sector Skills Councils' in Canada offer a unique model not seen elsewhere in the world. At the federal level, these councils have their roots in the Industrial Adjustment Services established in 1963, and saw a height of 22 councils in the mid-1990's (17 with union participation) following establishment of the Sectoral Partnership Initiative by the federal government earlier in the decade. Related initiatives also emerged at the provincial level in Canada. In general, the Skills Council built on pioneering examples such as the Canadian Steel Trade and Employment Congress (Sharpe, 1997). Both federally and provincially, sectoral skills councils had their origins in the inability of the private sector to develop workable options for high levels of training and adjustment on their own.

An important example at the provincial level was established in Canada's most industrialized province (Ontario). It represented a mixed governmental/firm/corporate model that, as in the USA, seemed most effective at the sectoral level. The 'Technology Adjustment Research Programme' (TARP) was first envisioned by the Premier's Council of Ontario in the late 1980's, and was later funded by Ontario Federation of Labour and the provincial government's Ministry of Economic Development and Trade (Schenk & Anderson, 1995). It involved the participation of 16 unions. Connected to this program, the government established sectoral strategic initiatives in areas including aerospace, steel, biotechnology, plastics, automotive parts. 'Sectoral Skills Councils' emerged, a variety of sectoral initiatives were established, and a variety of innovative, multi-lateral research efforts were undertaken. However, the results were mixed in terms of outcomes at the level of the workplace, ICT implementation and learning. With the withdrawal of the government, only remnants remain today. Without both broader legislative support as well as ongoing resources for developing this multi-lateral model (inclusive of a genuinely multi-lateral industrial policy), even the best efforts were hampered. Frequently, those at the center of policy implementation and program research lamented a lack of a broader 'European' approach (and funds to match).

One of the most comprehensive sets of studies of ICT, work and learning was conducted in western Europe in the early 1990's. This research was entitled "Participation in Technological Change" and was undertaken by the European Foundation for the Improvement of Living and Working Conditions. Based on 64 case studies and a large ($n = 7,326$) survey, the study showed technological change dependent on national industrial relation regimes as well as, in broader terms, "historical and cultural factors" associated with particular nations and sectors (Carnoy, Pollack, & Wong, 1993). In keeping with our prior discussion, two key factors for success were unionization and skill level of workers. The European Union (EU) represents the key example of how inter-national policy and programs are created and carried out, and provides important information on the current status of the intersection of ICT, work and learning in advanced capitalism. In general terms, this model of policy development contrasts starkly with the de-centralized model in the USA. The EU's policies on technology and training revolved around the principle that the circulation of knowledge is as important as a common currency; even more starkly put, "that economic growth, employment and welfare in the old continent are strictly associated to its capability to generate and diffuse new technologies" (Archibugi & Coco, 2000, p. 1).

Perhaps as important as the centralized organization of ICT, work and learning policy, however, is the willingness and ability of the EU to carry out combined R&D, training and implementation research programs that link corporations, research institutions and governmental resources. The most relevant example in this regard is the European Commission's Information Technology program entitled 'European Strategic Programme of Research on Information Technology' (ESPRIT, 1994–1998) (see Cressey & Di Martino, 1991). ESPRIT represents an international attempt, at the policy/programmatic level, to organize R&D, ICT based innovation as well as work and learning outcomes to respond to the needs of the workplace. The ESPRIT outcomes, however, have remained ambiguous from a critical approach perspective, partially due to the phenomenon that Gärtner and Wagner (1996) describe as narrow forms of 'agenda setting'; that is,

> What is politically and ethically legitimate and desirable cannot be simply solved by establishing participatory structures. The kind of close partnership between designers and users at which, e.g. situated design, aspires is not a sufficient answer to the core question of what makes a 'good system'. Our case analysis points at the importance of understanding agenda setting. Each arena has its own set of legitimate agenda, from questions of user interface design to quality of working life and privacy issues. (p. 203)

The ESPRIT program and associated European Commission policies on which it is built is largely democratic, but at the same time its agenda is largely pre-defined along technocratic lines. At the point of learning and ICT use, for example, its' motive is tied, mostly to serving markets, and relatively narrow interests of profitability rather than issues of quality of working life, sustainability, equity and so forth (Gärtner & Wagner, 1996).

In Northern Europe, however, there is yet another different tradition at the intersection between ICT, work and learning. Again, Gärtner and Wagner's (1996) work is instructive. Their work looked closely at the role of formal national legislative frameworks, such as the Norwegian Work Environment Act (NWEA), which detail the relations between the various industrial partners and the norms of work, technological development and ICT use. The NWEA defines participation in work-related areas using ICT systems and suggests a much deeper form of participation in policy formation.

Specifically, the 1970's was a water-shed decade for progressive policy and legislation around ICT design, implementation, work and learning in Northern Europe. In 1977, the Norwegians put the NWEA into place giving workers formal participation in 'company assemblies' and the right to appoint specific trade union representatives in the area of technological change. Co-determination procedures were established and a system of penalties was set in place. Likewise, in the late 1970's, Sweden enacted a series of 'work democracy' regulations, including establishing a legal framework for 'Labor Representatives' on company boards, disclosure acts, and other items under the 'Work Environment Act' (1978). This set of acts, described by some as the most important reform in Swedish society since the universal right to vote, also included the 'Joint Regulation Act' of 1977 which guaranteed co-determination around issues of design and use of new technology specifically. While management did retain certain rights of ownership, articles in these acts stipulated that employers must negotiate with local unions before making any major changes to work processes; that the workers can initiate such negotiations as well; and that all parties had the rights to relevant documentation (financial and technical). Significantly, in Sweden these legislative and policy frameworks were complemented by specific ICT development research programs, namely DEMOS and UTOPIA (see Ehn, 1988) which had as their central goal to investigate how technical design could, in fact, respond to this radical new legislative environment. Complementing these legislative frameworks were innovative experiments in user-based design: Scandinavia's UTOPIA program (Bjerknes, Ehn, & Kyng, 1987) as well as the Effective Technical and Human Implementation of Computer-based Systems (ETHICS – Beirne & Ramsay, 1992), made the network of policies, programs and legislation particular thick with ideas and potential. The conclusions from this exciting period in Northern Europe were that local participants must be deeply involved in the process, but also that participatory design was necessary but not sufficient for genuinely progressive socio-economic outcomes surrounding technology design, implementation, learning and use (Gärtner & Wagner, 1996). They discovered that often trade unions were not prepared to adequately take advantage of their new powers and responsibilities; notably, that they did not have the resources or the organizational structure to produce levels of expertise comparable to business.

Across these international examples of legislation and policy, we see that technocratic ideologies have tended to prevail in the USA. These ideologies appear slightly less powerful in Canada and in Europe where experiments in the democratization of industrial and technological development policy (at sectoral and EU level respectively) have seen the light of day. Technocratic ideologies are least powerful in the Nordic countries where 'co-determination' opens up the apparently autonomous force of technological development to the scrutiny of workers and citizen's to a much greater extent. As one might expect, this break in technocratic hegemony allows additional experimentation with constructivist approaches to ICT which have traditionally been most developed in the Nordic countries as well (e.g., the 'Collective Resource Approach'; see Bansler, 1989).

Linkages Between Policy and Practice

I have explored the historical and philosophical context of ICT and reviewed key legislative, policy and programmatic initiatives. However, I have also emphasized that policy takes on its meaning within the cycle of social processes that includes practice and learning. With this in mind, in this section I want to review existing literature on workplace ICT, skill and learning to fill in an important gap in of our discussion thus far. In terms of the philosophical framework I established above, we now look toward issues of application and use, and thus more closely implicate the critical and constructivist approaches.

We can begin by noting that one of the ways that policy and practice intersect in the workplace is through what are known as 'Technology Agreements'. These agreements, often though not exclusively seen in unionized firms, establish a form of co-determination relationship in regard to ICT adoption, learning and use. In some ways, these agreements mirror, on a smaller scale, the kinds of national legislative frameworks seen in Norway and Sweden. However, these agreements have appeared in a much wider range of countries.

Although not quite as prevalent as when they were first introduced in the 1970's and 1980's, the basic Technology Agreement remains an important form of workplace-based policy concerning ICT and learning. According to Evans (1983; see also Small & Yasin, 2000), writing in the early days of their emergence, these agreements typically include two basic components: first, 'procedural' elements which include broad statements on the need for new technologies, but also, more importantly, statements on timely disclosure of information by employers inclusive of the likely affects of the changes and possible options. This category often includes procedures for the development of joint union/ management committees and change monitoring practices; the establishment of worker 'technology representatives'; arrangements for union and management to draw on outside experts/consultants, etc. Occasionally, unions establish 'veto' powers if clear violation of procedures are evident. A second component to Technology Agreements involves what are called 'substantive' elements – including specific statements on how things such as job security, re-training and adjustment, methods of sharing economic benefits, health and safety, and surveillance issues are to be handled. Small and Yasin (2000) have noted the varied affects that Technology Agreements had on practice in the workplace, and they note the importance of related industrial relations infra-structure in a firm (i.e., unionization). Though many factors impact on the overall success of Technology Agreements, evidence suggests they tend to lead to better firm performance, a broader and more productive labour process, and a collective learning feedback loop which leads to better choice and implementation surrounding new technologies (Small & Yasin, 2000).

However, the preceding discussion of workplace-based Technology

Agreements does not entirely exhaust our description of the 'cycle' of social processes that define policy and practice. To complete the picture, we must look carefully at discussions of ICT and workplace skill and learning specifically, and for this we turn to adult education, industrial relations and sociology of work scholarship. At the same time, generally speaking (and with a variety of notable exceptions), it has been unusual to see work-based learning talked about as an interactive, social practice. That is, most often learning has been discussed as a sort of passive 'by-product' of work: a skill, a credential, an increase (*n.b.* rarely as a decrease) in productivity, and so forth.

Nevertheless, skill/knowledge development in the workplace has regularly been associated with both the introduction of new technologies, often in conjunction with the different historical phases of the labour process (e.g., 'craft production', 'Taylorism', 'Fordism', 'neo-Fordism', 'flexible specialization', etc.). Approaches to work, learning and policy (e.g., Reich, 1991; Archibugi and Lundvall, 2001) associated with the technocratic approach, for example, largely presume that ICT requires advanced skills. However, among those that have looked closely at skill and learning practice associated with workplace technological change, many have questioned this assumption (e.g., Hyman, 1991; Gee, Hull, & Lankshear, 1996). Poster (2002), for example, suggests that levels of learning may be reduced in some ways by the introduction ICT, and that, in any case, accurate assessments of performance and skill change remain elusive. Important empirical analyses in North America (e.g., Berg, 1970; Livingstone, 1999; Sawchuk, 2003) seem to support Poster's claim, with some suggesting there may in fact be a "surplus" in computer literacy given the inadequacy of actual opportunities that workers have to actually apply their skills at work. For example, referring to computer literacy in the Canadian context, Lowe (2000) notes this specifically, stating that typically "job structures deprive workers of opportunities to use their education and talents" (p. 170). Comparative North American research (Livingstone, 1999, p. 50) shows that, despite calls from the corporate and government sectors to increase computer literacy, "empirical evidence certainly suggests that there are now more people with basic computer literacy than there are jobs which need it". By all estimates, North American workplaces are not alone in this paradoxical situation of, on the one hand, the relatively wide-spread availability of ICT, and, on the other, apparent barriers to effective diffusion, implementation, learning and use.

Kelley (1990) provides a useful review of literature on the work-based skills use issues (as well as empirical analysis of her own) which focuses on technology and work practices at the level of the firm. She concludes that translating a firm's adoption of ICT into increased skill and learning is dependent on a host of organizational as well as broader industrial relations policy and practice issues. According to Kelley, the 'least complex' firms are most effective; that is, open participation of workers in all facets of production, including management operations, appears to be vital. In some sense, the conditions that Kelley describes represent the spirit of 'co-determination' legislation, policy and programs discussed earlier. Nevertheless, how any organization achieves this type of open participation remains an open question. Small firms seem to offer hope for translating ICT adoption into effective learning and production outcomes, but typically lack the levels of capital for significant ICT investment. Large firms have the capital but may not have the ability to generate accountable, shared decision-making across all levels of the organization; unionized firms offer an infrastructure for shared decision-making, but, given that in most countries workers must actively fight to obtain union representation, these firms can be host to bitter management/labour relations. It is worth noting here, however, in terms of unions and learning, that for some time it has been a demonstrated fact that the forms of representation offered through unions often provide the best chance for achieving effective work/learning outcomes (e.g., Doeringer & Piore, 1971; Mishel & Voos, 1992; Livingstone & Sawchuk, 2003).

Another way of understanding questions surrounding learning, technology and work can be seen in research related to what is known as the 'de-skilling/en-skilling'? debate. This 'debate' was initiated in the work of Harry Braverman (1974; see Penn & Scattergood, 1985) and his ground-breaking research based on an elaboration of Marxist theory through a critique of Frederick Taylor's 'Scientific Management' (i.e., Taylorism). Along with Braverman himself, other advocates of the 'de-skilling thesis' (e.g., Glenn & Feldberg, 1979; Zimbalist, 1979; Noble, 1979; Shaiken, Herzenberg, & Kuhn, 1986) note that the goal of the labour process under capitalism is to generate managerial control for maximization of efficiency and profitability.

> The focus on the labour process points also to the irremediable necessity of a coercive system of control and surveillance, leading to a critical perspective towards the role of 'management'. Of crucial importance, such a focus also helps deflate the ideology of 'technology' as a neutral, autonomous and irresistible force ... (Hyman, 1982, p. 93)

In Taylorist, Fordist and neo-Fordist models of production the de-skilling argument points toward the stark division of mental and manual labour and the breaking up of complex tasks into smaller more discrete ones often with the aid of new technologies. As Hyman (1982) suggests, in these situations there is often a significant growth in worker surveillance as well (see also Sewell & Wilkinson, 1992). The classic assembly line, and the myriad of similar work design principles we see today across manufacturing as well as many service sector workplaces, attempts to generate profit and managerial control by breaking up knowledge/skill forms 'owned' (for lack of a better word) by individual workers or groups of workers, thus converting these skills into a feature of the work system itself (owned by owners; and under the control of managers).

While this classic form of de-skilling still occurs widely, the introduction of new forms of advanced ICT has re-defined the de-skilling process for a small number of occupational groups (see Burris, 1999; Rothman, 2000). The classic separation of mental and manual has evolved into something more complex (though it is difficult to argue that it is fundamentally distinct). Within some firms and amongst certain occupational groups, we now see a more nuanced form of mental/manual skill division associated with the struggle over macro-design (or, 'agenda setting') and creative micro- or local-design and use of ICT. Hosts of workers are now being asked to use the tools provided for them in creative and responsive ways but in processes which are set within pre-established boundaries beyond their control. It bears mentioning that this is entirely within the range of commentators such as Marx (e.g., 1973) who, more than a century ago, noted that the capitalist labour process does not necessarily seek to eliminate the mental capacities of labour but rather seeks to appropriate and control these capacities. The so-called 'en-skilling' thesis advocates are quick to seize upon these complexities, pointing to niches in the economy (often involving small firms) where the stark divisions of mental/manual labour are less often seen. Friedmann (1961), Blauner (1964) and Bell (1973) are, in a sense, the forefathers of the 'en-skilling thesis', collectively suggesting that unskilled jobs will simply be 'automated away', while Reich (1991) and Castells (1996) and a host of technocratic analysts can be viewed as more contemporary advocates.

Between these two camps are writers such as Kelley (1990), Piore and Sabel (1984), Sorge and Streeck (1988), Form, Kaufman, Parcel and Wallace (1988) and others who emphasize a range of organizational, institutional and market factors that shape the de-skilling/en-skilling learning outcomes of the introduction of new technology, and by extension ICT policy. Burris (1999), however, sums things up nicely by noting that a commonly held corollary of technocratic restructuring is,

> 'skill restructuring' (Cockburn, 1983), 'skill disruption' (Hodson, 1988) and new types of alienation, stress and occupational hazards (see Hirschhorn, 1984). Both de-skilling and re-skilling occur, and the balance between the two depends upon both the design of the technology and the way in which it is implemented (Burris, 1999, pp. 40–41)

Still, de-skilling/en-skilling debates, invaluable as they are, can't help but gloss over the actual learning processes that spring from the organization of work, industrial relations and ICT development policies. The 'how' of ICT skill and knowledge development remains obscure, and thus an important role is left to workplace learning scholars who analyze the learning process (as opposed to the learning outcomes) specifically. In terms of comparative international analyses, Lam (2002) provides a good example of how institutions, legislation and policy in different countries (i.e., Japan, UK, USA and Denmark) actually supports/inhibits ICT innovation and learning. At the center of this analysis is the concept of 'tacit knowledge', rooted in the relations of discretionary communities of practice (established among either organizations or a specific occupational group). In the USA, anthropologist Charles Darrah (1994, 1996) has extensively described workers' learning processes, and specifically analyzed these processes in advanced ICT settings (Darrah, 1999). A host of detailed empirical studies of exactly how ICT and learning practice relate are available in Luff,

Hindmarsh and Heath (2000; see also selected contributors to Engeström and Middleton, 1992). Each of these studies shows that ICT is not merely 'adopted' by a workplace, but rather is activated and, in some sense, re-configured by users in the course of (learning) practice.

A particularly relevant piece of work in this area is found in Livingstone and Sawchuk (2003). This collection of case studies provides an important complement to the sociology of work and de-skilling/en-skilling debates based on comparative examination of workplaces across five sectors (auto assembly, garment, light manufacturing, chemical and public service) in the Canadian economy. Drawing on in depth 'learning life-history' interviews, what these case studies demonstrate, among other things, is how ICT use and learning at work is shaped by the industrial relations climate and the dynamics of a specific sector, as well as the struggle by workers for greater participation in the labour process. Moreover, the analysis makes it clear that issues of race, gender, and age as well as occupational type are also significant indicators of skill and knowledge development. Related work on computer literacy development among manufacturing workers in Canada (Sawchuk, 2003) delves even more deeply into the types of linkages (cultural, economic, and political) between ICT and learning. It shows how learning is rooted in collective, informal groupings of workers and operates interactively across workplace, home and community spheres. This learning is carried out in order to cooperate with the needs of industry and labour markets as well as in order to satisfy needs that may diverge from the interests of business. Overall, in both Livingstone and Sawchuk (2003) and Sawchuk (2003), we see computer literacy skills among workers that far outstrip the actual needs of their workplaces. Thus, as we saw in the previous sections, important assumptions informing mainstream, technocratic approaches to policy surrounding ICT, work and learning are questioned.

Conclusions and Future Directions

Comparative, international analyses of legislation, policy and programs provide an important basis for understanding ICT-based learning practices in the workplace. In terms of integrative research studies of policy and practice involving ICT, work and learning, I have suggested a broad, multi-leveled approach. Such an approach requires robust theories of learning and cognition such as those discussed in Latour (2000), Engeström and Middleton (1992), Luff, Hindmarsh and Heath (2000) and Billett (2001) to name only a few. It also requires critical scholarship on adult education (e.g., Foley, 1998), philosophy (e.g., Feenberg, 1991) and histories of technology (e.g., Noble, 1984) and of ICT development (e.g., Ehn, 1988; Asaro, 1996).

In reviewing the most relevant examples of legislation, policy, programs and analyses of learning and skill development, we are, to my mind, aided by a general understanding of the ideological approaches to technological thought which I took time to summarize early on. How do specific policies relate to either technocratic or critical approaches to technology? At several points above

I've left some indications. What role, for example, do the substantive critiques of Heidegger or Ellul play in attenuating the messages offered by the likes of Negroponte (1995), Castells (1996) or Reich (1991)? What can the constructivist approach of Suchman, Latour or Callon add to the de-skilling/en-skilling debates surrounding ICT, work and learning, and how might policy benefit from such research? After reading this chapter, a variety of answers to these and other questions should begin to emerge, but perhaps more importantly one should be in a better position to understand, evaluate and perhaps even affect the current landscape and trajectory of ICT, work and learning policy and practice. Clearly, technocratic approaches continue to (and perhaps increasingly) hold sway in the policy efforts across most countries, though this is not absolute as recent attempts in the USA discussed above (see Herman, 2001) indicate. Substantive approaches appear to offer few work-able paths forward for policy as it relates to our present conditions, and thus tend to be excluded from mainstream debate. Under appreciated and with a great deal of potential for positive economic and social outcomes are the constructivist and critical approaches, though they remain a minority in policy circles. However, just as clearly as technocratic approaches continue to hold sway in these circles, so it is that democratization of technological design, policy, work and learning processes, potentially drawing on both critical and constructivist approaches, offer the most relevant and progressive means to move forward into a future with increasingly powerful technological forces at play.

References

Archibugi, D., & Coco, A. (2000). *The globalisation of technology and the European innovation system.* Rome: Italian National Research Council.

Archibugi, D., & Lundvall, B. (Eds.) (2001). *The globalising learning economy.* Oxford: Oxford University Press.

Asaro, P. (1996). Transforming society by transforming technology: The science and politics of participatory design. *CMS Conference Stream: Information Technology and Critical Theory.* Urbana, IL: University of Illinois at Urbana-Champaign.

Audretsch, D., & Thurik, A. R. (2001). *What's New about the New Economy? Sources of growth in the managed and entrepreneurial economies.* (ISSN 01-1). Institute for Developmental Strategies, Indiana University, USA.

Bansler, J. (1989). Systems development in Scandinavia: Three theoretical schools. *Office: Technology and People,* 4(2), 117–133.

Beirne, M., & Ramsay, H. (Ed.) (1992). Information technology and workplace democracy. London: Routledge & Kegan Paul.

Bell, D. (1973). *The coming of the post-industrial society.* New York: Basic Books.

Berg, I. (1970). *Education and jobs: The great training robbery.* New York: Praeger.

Billett, S. (2001). Co-Participation: Affordance and engagement at work. *New Directions For Adult And Continuing Education,* 92, 63–72.

Bjerknes, G., Ehn, P., & Kyng M. (Eds.) (1987). Computers and democracy: A Scandinavian challenge, Aldershot, UK: Avebury.

Blauner, R. (1964). *Alienation and freedom: The factory worker and his industry.* Chicago: University of Chicago Press.

Braverman, H. (1974). *Labor and monopoly capitalism: The degradation of work in the twentieth century.* New York: Monthly Review Press.

Burris, B. (1999). Braverman, Taylorism and Technocracy. In M. Wardell, T. Steiger & P. Meiksins (Eds.), *Rethinking the labor process.* New York: SUNY.

Callon, M. (1992). The dynamics of techno-economic networks. In R. Carnoy, S. Pollack & P. L. Wong (Eds.) (1993). *Labour Institutions and Technological Change: A Framework for Analysis and a Review of the Literature* (pp. 72–102). Stanford University/International Labour Organization.

Castells, M. (1996). *The Rise of the Network Society,* Vol. 1. Oxford: Blackwell.

Cockburn, C. (1985). Machinery of dominance: Men, women and technical know-how. London: Pluto.

Cressey, P., & Di Martino, V. (1991). Agreement and innovation: The international dimension of technological change. New York: Prentice Hall.

Dahrendorf, R. (1959). *Class and class conflict in an industrial society.* London: Routledge & Kegan Paul.

Darrah, C. (1994). Skill Requirements at work: Rhetoric versus reality. *Work and Occupations, 21*(1), 64–84.

Darrah, C. (1996). *Learning and work: An exploration in industrial ethnography.* New York: Garland Publishing.

Darrah, C. (1999). *Learning Tools Within a Context: History and Scope.* Washington, DC: U.S. Department of Education, National Institute on Postsecondary Education, Libraries, and Lifelong Learning (PLLI) of the U.S. Department of Education.

Devine, W. (1983). From shafts to wires: Historical perspective on electrification. *Journal of Economic History, 43,* 347–372.

Doeringer, P. B., & Piore, M. (1971). *Internal labor markets and manpower analysis.* Lexington, MA: D.C. Heath.

Ehn, P. (1988). *Work-oriented design of computer artifacts.* Arbetslivscentrum: Stockholm.

Ellul, J. (1964). *The technological society.* New York: Vintage Books.

Engeström, Y., & Middleton, D. (1992). *Cognition and communication at work.* New York: Cambridge University Press.

Evans, J. (1983). Negotiating Technological Change. In H. J. Otway & M. Pletu (Eds.), *New Office Technology: Human and Organizational Aspects* (pp. 152–168). London: Francis Pinter.

Feenberg, A. (1991). *Critical theory of technology.* New York: Oxford University Press.

Fleck, J. (1993). Configurations: Crystallizing contingency. *International Journal of Human Factors in Manufacturing, 3*(1), 15–36.

Foley, G. (1998). *Learning in social action: A contribution to understanding informal education.* London: Zed Books.

Form, W., Kaufman, R., Parcel, T., & Wallace, M. (1988). The impact of technology on work organization and work outcomes. In G. Farkas & P. England (Eds.), *Industries, firms and jobs: Sociology and economic approaches* (pp. 303–328). New York: Plenum.

Franklin, U. (1990). *The real world of technology.* Toronto: CBC Enterprises.

Friedmann, G. (1961). *The anatomy of work.* Glencoe, IL: Free Press.

Gärtner, J., & Wagner, I. (1996). Mapping actors and agendas: Political frameworks of systems design and participation. *Human-Computer Interaction, 11,* 187–214.

Gee, J., Hull G., & Lankshear, C. (1996). *The new work order: Behind the language of the new capitalism.* Boulder, CO: Westview.

Glenn, E., & Feldberg, R. (1979). Proletarianizing clerical work: Technology and organizational control in the office. In A. Zimbalist (Ed.), *Case Studies on the Labor Process* (pp. 51–72). New York: Monthly Review Press.

Gospel, H. (Ed.) (1991). *Industrial training and technological innovation: A comparative and Historical Perspective.* London: Routledge & Kegan Paul.

Grubb, N. (1996). *Learning to work: The case for reintegrating job training and education.* New York: Russell Sage Foundation.

Hacker, S. (1991). Doing it the hard way: Investigations of gender and technology. Winchester, MA: Unwin Hyman.

Heidegger, M. (1977). *The question concerning technology.* New York: Harper and Row.

Herman, B. (2001). How high-road partnerships work. *Social Policy, 31*(3), 11–19.

Hughes, T. (1983). *Networks of power.* Baltimore, MD: Johns Hopkins University Press.

Hyman, R. (1982). What ever happened to industrial sociology? In D. Dunkerley & G. Salaman (Eds.), *The international yearbook of organisation studies 1981.* London: Routledge and Kegan Paul.

Hyman, R. (1991). Plus ca charge? The theory of production and the production of theory. In A. Pollert (Ed.), *Farewell to flexibility?* (pp. 259–283). Oxford: Blackwell.

Jones, B. (1988). Work and flexible automation in Britain: A review of developments and possibilities. *Work, Employment and Society, 2*(4), 451–486.

Kelley, M. R. (1990). New process technology, job design and work organization: A contingency mode. *American Sociological Review, 55,* 191–208.

Kerr, C. et al. (1962). *Industrialism and Industrial Man.* London: Heinemann.

Kraft, P. (1977). *Programmers and Managers: The Routinisation of Computer Programming in the United States.* New York: Springer-Verlag.

Lam, A. (2002). Alternative societal models of learning and innovation in the knowledge economy. *International Social Science Journal,* March, 67–82.

Latour, B. (2000). Technology is society made durable. In K. Grint (Ed.), *Work and society: A reader* (pp. 41–53). Cambridge, UK: Polity.

Lazonick, W. (1979). Industrial relations and technical change: The case of the self-acting mule. *Cambridge Journal of Economics, 3,* 231–262.

Lazonick, W. (1993). Learning and the dynamics of international competitive advantage. In R. Thomson (Ed.), *Learning and technological change* (pp. 172–197). New York: St. Martin's Press.

Lipsey, R. G., Bekar, C., & Carlaw, K. (1998). What requires explanation? In E. Helpman (Ed.), *General purpose technologies and economic growth.* Cambridge, MA: MIT Press.

Livingstone, D. W. (1999). *The education jobs gap.* Toronto: Garamond Press.

Livingstone, D. W., & Sawchuk, P. (2003). *Hidden knowledge: Organized labour in the information age.* Toronto: Garamond Press/Washington, DC: Rowman & Littlefield.

Louli, C., & Bickerton, G. (1995). Decades of Change, Decades of Struggle: Postal Workers and Technological Change. In C. Schenk & J. Anderson (Eds.), *Re-shaping work: union responses to technological change* (pp. 216–232). Toronto: Our Times Publishing.

Lowe, G. (2000). *The quality of work: A people-centred agenda.* New York: Oxford University Press.

Luff, P., Hindmarsh, J., & Heath, C. (2000). *Workplace studies: Recovering work practice and informing system design.* New York: Cambridge University Press.

Mani, S. (2002). *Government, innovation and technology policy: An international comparative analysis.* Cheltenham, UK: Edward Elgar.

Marx, K. (1973). *Grundrisse.* Baltimore: Penguin.

Mishel, L., & Voos, P. (Eds.) (1992). *Unions and economic competitiveness.* New York: M.E. Sharpe Inc.

Mumford, L. (1964). Authoritarian and Democratic Technics. *Technology and Culture, 5*(1), 1–8.

Naisbitt, J. (1982). *Megatrends: Ten new directions transforming our lives.* New York: Warner.

Negroponte, N. (1995). *Being digital.* New York: Knopf.

Noble, D. (1979). Social Choice in Machine Design: The Case of Automatically Controlled Machine Tools. In A. Zimbalist (Ed.), *Case studies on the labour process* (pp. 18–50). New York: Monthly Review Press.

Noble, D. (1984). *The forces of production: A social history of industrial automation.* New York: Alfred A. Knopf Inc.

OECD (1999). *The knowledge-based economy: A set of facts and figures.* Paris: OECD.

Penn, R., & Scattergood, H. (1985). Deskilling or enskilling?: An empirical investigation of recent theories of the labour process. *British Journal of Sociology, 36*(4), 611–630.

Piore, M., & Sabel C. (1984). The second industrial divide. New York: Basic Books.

Poster, M. (2002). Workers as cyborgs: Labor and networked computers. *Journal of Labor Research, 23*(3), 339–354.

Reich, R. (1991). *The work of nations: Preparing ourselves for 21st Century capitalism.* New York: Knopf.

Rip, A., Misa, T., & Schot, J. (Eds.) (1995). *Managing technology in society: The approach of constructive technology assessment*. London: Pinter.

Roszak, T. (1994). *The cult of information: A Neo-Luddite treatise on high tech, artificial intelligence and the true art of thinking*. Berkeley: University of California Press.

Rothman, H. K. (2000). What has work become? *Journal of Labor Research, 21*(3), 379–392.

Sale, K. (1995). *Rebels against the future: The Luddites and their War on the industrial revolution – lessons for the computer age*. London: Addison Wesley.

Sawchuk, P. (2003). *Adult learning and technology in working-class life*. New York: Cambridge University Press.

Schenk, C., & Anderson, J. (Eds.) (1995). *Re-shaping work: Union responses to technological change*. Toronto: Our Times Publishing.

Sewell, G., & Wilkinson, B. (1992). Someone to Watch over me – Surveillance, Discipline and the Just-in-Time Labor Process. *Sociology, 26*(2), 271–289.

Shaiken, H., Herzenberg, S., & Kuhn, S. (1986). The work process under more flexible production. *Industrial Relations, 25*, 167–183.

Sharpe, A. (1997). *Sectoral skills councils in Canada: Future challenges*. Ottawa: Human Resources Development Canada.

Small, M., & Yasin, M. (2000). Human factors in the adoption and performance of advanced manufacturing technology in unionized firms. *Industrial Management & Data Systems, 100*(8–9), 389–401.

Smith, P. (1988). The impact of trade unionism and the market in a regional newspaper. *Industrial Relations Journal, 19*, 214–221.

Sorge, A., & Streeck, W. (1988). Industrial relation and technical change: The case for an extended perspective. In R. Hyman & W. Streeck (Eds.), *New technology and industrial relations* (pp. 19–47). Oxford: Blackwell.

Suchman, L. (1987). *Plans and situated action: The problem of human-computer communication*. New York: Cambridge University Press.

Suchman, L. (2002). Practice-based design of information systems: Notes from the hyperdeveloped world. *The Information Society, 18*, 139–144.

Thomson, R. (Ed.) (1993). *Learning and technological change*. New York: St. Martin's Press.

Von Tunzelmann, G. N. (1982). *Steam power and British industrialization to 1860*. Oxford: Wallace and Kalleberg.

Wallace, M., & Kalleberg, A. (1982). Industrial transformation and the decline of craft: The decomposition of skill in the printing industry, 1931–1978. *American Sociological Review, 47*, 307–324.

Williams, R., & Edge, D. (1996). The social shaping of technology. *Research Policy, 25*, 856–899.

Zimbalist, A. (Ed.) (1979). *Case studies on the labor process*. New York: Monthly Review Press.

50

RECOGNITION OF LEARNING THROUGH WORK

Stephen Billett
Griffith University, Australia

The recognition of skills is important for individuals. The acquisition of qualifi-cations, their level and standing is correlated to levels of remuneration (Groot, Hartog, & Oosterbeek, 1994; Grubb, 1996; Lengerman, 1999; O'Connell, 1999), associated with occupational identity (e.g., Noon & Blyton, 1997, Pusey, 2003) and, likely, the standing of the work individuals are permitted to engage in (e.g., Darrah, 1996). Those whose work is low paid and least valued (e.g., women, migrants, non-native speakers) often have the greatest need for skill recognition. Yet, for many workers there exists no bases or mechanism for their skills to be recognised, because of a lack of courses or other means of recognition. Given that workplaces are key sites for learning and demonstrating the knowledge required for work, they present an option for the recognition and certification of work skills that can assist overcome disadvantage and also be used to maintain the recognition of skills throughout working life. Yet, currently, the practice of the recognition and certification of skills learnt through work is underdeveloped and constrained by complexities in its organisation and enactment that have particular and significant policy implications. It follows that understanding further how the recognition of workplace learnt knowledge might be best enacted and identifying policies and practices to support its enactment are worthy and timely goals.

The recognition of skills is achieved mainly through successful participation in courses. Workers able to access to these courses can secure national certifica-tion (e.g., qualifications), internationally recognised qualifications (e.g., City and Guilds) or vendor-specific authorisation (e.g., Microsoft certification). There are, however, alternative processes for the recognition of skills. These include the recognition of prior learning, accreditation of prior and experiential learning and licensing arrangements (e.g., fork lift driving, aircraft engineering) and the assessment of competence for occupational certification purposes (e.g., Tradesperson's rights in Australia). In common, these alternative recognition processes require some kind of occupational benchmarks for judgements to be made about the level and scope of individuals' skills. Typically, statements of

International Handbook of Educational Policy, 943–962
Nina Bascia, Alister Cumming, Amanda Datnow, Kenneth Leithwood and David Livingstone (Eds.)
© 2005 Springer. *Printed in Great Britain.*

course outcomes (e.g., objectives, competency statements) are used in processes such as the recognition of prior learning. Yet, if individuals' work is not reflected in or closely aligned to any available benchmarks, these alternatives will not be available. Therefore, workers whose occupational practice sits outside provisions of courses and easy certification are structurally and doubly disadvantaged. Moreover, the kinds of occupational practice denied courses and certification are often low paid and characterised as being 'low skill', and occupied by disadvantaged groups, such as women (Bierema, 2001) and migrants (Hull, 1997). Finding means to legitimately and authoratively recognise skills acquired through work holds the prospect of providing just arrangements for these other-wise disadvantaged workers as well as those requiring recognition throughout their working life.

However, commensurate with the worthiness of this goal are complexities hindering its achievement. These include identifying and selecting appropriate focuses for skill recognition, how it might be undertaken fairly (i.e., with validity and reliability) and how these arrangements should be administered and moni-tored. For instance, should that recognition be based on individuals' develop-ment, the specific requirements of a workplace or on occupational-wide criteria? Such alternatives have sometimes-conflicting purposes. Workplace assessment and certification processes will also require some transformation from current practices. Vocational educational institutions commonly use statements of out-comes (e.g., objectives, performance criteria) provided in documents (e.g., sylla-buses) and tasks that are usually substitute for or remote from actual workplace performance (Raizen, 1991). These are used to predict individuals' performance in occupational activities in another environment – the workplace where individ-uals will exercise their skills. In contrast, skills assessment and recognition in workplaces will almost inevitably be premised on individuals' performance in activities in the particular workplace setting. This is because their performance will provide compelling and authentic bases for those judgements. Yet, while being authentic, workplace environments also foster conditions that counter the fairness of assessment processes. Workplaces are contested environments (Bierema, 2001; Billett, 2001c; Solomon, 1999). Expectations of increased remu-neration or enhanced status likely accompany the recognition of workers' skills. Such rewards may be unreasonably pursued by or denied to some individuals and deliberately thwarted or unreasonably supported by interests within the workplace. Assessments of and judgments about performance are likely to be subject to the interests and influences of workplace affiliations, cliques, demarc-ations and management that can render them unfair (Billett, 2001c). As a consequence, securing bases for and enacting fairness in the recognition of individuals' skills needs to circumvent workplace factors and practices that may attempt to thwart its validity and reliability. So individuals' workplace perfor-mance provides bases for making judgments about their occupational compe-tence and recognition. To provide fairness in the assessment and buttress the standing of that certification, agencies and individuals from outside the work-place may be required to conduct assessments and legitimise certification. This could assist making the processes and outcomes fair to both individuals seeking recognition and those already certified. Yet, in many countries this will require identifying and supporting host organisations to administer and monitor the recognition of skills acquired in workplaces, and i.e. the enactment of processes that are legitimate and provide confidence in the paid workforce and employers.

This chapter advances policy options for the recognition of learning through work by discussing how it might be enacted in ways that reflect the contributions of workplace and workplace practices, yet are taken and sustained as being fair, legitimate and worthy. The case is made through, firstly, elaborating the justification for the worth of recognising skills in the workplace. The purposes for and processes of workplace assessment and recognition of skills are then discussed to identify appropriate focuses and procedures for recognition. It is proposed that, except for some large or particularly prestigious enterprises, currently there is initially a need for the administration, monitoring and certification of skills recognition to be hosted outside of workplaces. This is to assist establishing the legitimacy of the recognition of workplace learnt knowledge and because the conditions for fair and valid recognition will not always be present in workplaces. Some options for these hosting arrangements (i.e., industry or professional associations, vocational education systems and local organisations) are advanced through a consideration of workplace goals and assessment and certification practices located outside workplaces.

Legitimacy of Workplaces as Sites for the Recognition of Skills

Workplaces are increasingly being acknowledged as rich and accessible learning environments (Boud & Garrick, 1999; Fenwick, 2001; Inman & Vernon, 1997; Livingstone, 2001). They offer a range of potential contributions to learning the knowledge required for paid work. These include access to authentic work activities in which to engage and learn, opportunities to practice and refine what has been learnt, and interactions with more experienced co-workers to guide learning and assist the kinds of learning that would not be possible without that guidance (Billett, 2001b). The physical setting and ordering of activities in workplace can also contribute to learning through the authenticity of experiences that are distinct from those in educational settings. The worth of workplace experiences in developing occupational practice has been long acknowledged (Boud, Solomon & Symes, 2001) with extensive periods of workplace experience being required before individuals are accepted into trades or professions. There is also growing acceptance of learning environments outside education institutions perhaps supported by their long held acceptance within adult education (Kasworm & Marienau, 1997; Livingstone, 2001).

Yet, despite all this, the standing of workplace learning experiences and its contributions are often viewed with ambivalence, being described erroneously as informal, ad hoc and concrete (Billett, 2002). So, on the one hand, workplace experiences are valued, but, on the other, they are denied legitimacy as effective learning environments, seemingly because they occur outside of educational programs. True, there are potential shortcomings of learning through work. These include the variability of experiences and support, the problem of accessing and engaging with hard-to-learn knowledge and the contested nature of workplace life that distribute workplace learning experiences in particular ways. Yet, despite evidence to the contrary, generally the view persists that learning experiences in workplaces and their outcomes are sometimes less legitimate and robust than those of educational institutions, particularly in relation to prized learning (i.e., that which provides status and high levels of remuneration). Such premises have direct implications for the recognition of learning secured through work and present tangible goals for policy.

It seems that the legitimacy of learning environments and their certification remains largely founded in the often-unquestioned acceptance of an irreducible relationship between teaching and learning. The absence of teachers or teaching-type facilities, processes of moderation and verifying assessments appear to lead to a characterisation of workplaces as 'informal' or 'unstructured' learning environments with assumptions that their learning outcomes are necessarily weak and ad hoc. Yet, the kinds of learning secured in workplace-type settings has been shown to be as robust (i.e., transferable and adaptable) as that arising from educational institutions (Raizen, 1991; Rogoff & Lave, 1984; Scribner, 1985). Standing outside of educational institutions means that learning through work typically remains either un-credentialled or its credentials have limited standing (Livingstone, 2001). While programs of learning organised through educational institutions that sometimes include workplace experiences enjoy certification, often at the highest level (e.g., in law, medicine, nurse and teacher education and the trades), the basis for their certification tends to be largely premised on experiences in educational institutions. Recently, some university programs are providing direct credit for workplace based learning and accrediting prior (Boud et al., 2001; Evans, 2001). This also occurs in vocational education courses through the recognition of prior learning. Yet, overall, there is little evidence of learning through work systematically being recognised and certified on its own terms and merits. Nor is workplace learnt knowledge granted the legitimacy through certification that is warranted by its widely acknowledged contributions to learning and development (see Billett, 2001b). This situation stands to perpetuate existing inequities in the distribution of opportunities for the development and recognition of adults' skills, because for many workers there are no courses to provide for certification. It also amplifies the need for workplaces to be seen as legitimate environments for the learning and recognition of occupational skills. This is no more urgent than at a time when many governments are emphasising learning throughout working life as a means to maintain and improve national productivity levels (Organisation of Economic Cooperation and Development (OECD), 1996).

Need for Recognition of Workplace Learning Experiences

A key rationale for recognising learning through work is to assist workers denied this recognition because of historical or institutional precedents. Overall, it seems that workers without certification are likely paid less, their employment is more tenuous and their prospects for advancement more limited than those with qualifications (Groot et al., 1994; Grubb, 1996; Leuven & Oosterbeek, 1999; O'Connell, 1999). In many countries, the provision of initial preparation and certification of skills does not extend to all occupational practice or locations. For instance, small business workers, who constitute a substantial portion of private sector workforces, are less likely to participate in vocational programs than those in larger enterprises (O'Connell, 1999) and often report a dissonance between their needs and educational programs (Coopers & Lybrand, 1994). With tight labour markets, the constant churning of the workforce through restructuring and the reorganisation of work, those workers without certification of their skills may be rendered less employable and less able to secure career goals. Moreover, for probably most in the workforce, workplaces are the key site to develop further their occupational skills throughout their working lives. Yet, Giraud (2002) notes that even where there are systems in place to fund the certified training within workplaces, employers tend to sponsor the further training of already qualified employees over those who are not qualified.

There are also cultural impediments. The premises for the certification of skills are not necessarily exercised on objective assessments of the complexity or demands of the occupation. Instead, historical precedents often determined which occupations warranted certification and at what level. For instance, by tradition, trade apprenticeships form the core of the vocational education system and the certification of prized vocational skills in many countries. These occupations enjoy significant publicly funded educational provisions and certification processes. However, other occupations, for instance those without apprenticeships, are often less well represented and sponsored. Some countries have a far wider range of trade callings than others, thereby leading to distinct patterns of skill recognition, which illustrates the disparity in recognition across countries. Retail workers in Germany are apprenticed and receive formal certification on completion, whereas their counterparts in other countries would generally not enjoy structured training or such high status certification. Darrah (1996) notes how, despite similarity in the complexity of requirements for effective work performance, qualified design engineers in a computer manufacturing plant enjoyed higher status, acknowledgement and remuneration than workers in the production area. This kind of distinction leads to those workers unable to secure credentials being relatively under-qualified in labour markets that value qualifications (Brunello & Medio, 2001). All this is exacerbated when there appears to be a surfeit of qualified workers in some labour markets (Livingstone, 2001). Those without certification of their skills are potentially disadvantaged in securing work and advancing careers.

The need for recognition extends beyond the initial preparation of occupational skills, as there is a growing demand for the development and acknowledgement of currency of skills throughout working lives (OECD, 1996). Within recent policies of lifelong learning, workers are increasingly being expected to maintain their skill currency and its utility to their employers throughout their working lives (OECD, 1996, 2000). However, not only is the provision of support for this ongoing learning underdeveloped, the means of recognising that on-going learning is also relatively absent. Although recognition of prior learning initiatives are promoted on equity grounds, the practice can be quite different. Central to these processes is the need for benchmarks against which individuals' knowledge can be assessed and certified. In practice, statements of intended outcomes within curriculum documents are used often for these purposes. However, the greatest need for the recognition of learning through work is for those workers for whom there are no courses and, hence, no benchmarks. At least one large industry sector in Australia raised workers' expectations about recognising their learning through work only to be unable to fulfil these expectations because of an absence of agreed benchmarks. Significantly, governments' promotion of the recognition of prior learning in Australia was not accompanied by the development of occupational benchmarks for those industry sectors that lack them. Moreover, these recognition processes are usually individual, time intensive and costly. So, opportunities for individuals seeking recognition of their skills are not always available and individuals usually have to carry the cost, thereby jeopardising equity goals. Therefore, enacting accessible arrangements for the recognition of learning through workplace activities and using the workplace as sites for and bases for appraisal holds the promise of greater fairness and standing for individuals' a skill recognition throughout their working lives.

The standing of occupational activities also shapes at what level certification is available (Lengerman, 1999). Yet, the level of certification appears not always premised on objective analyses of work. For instance, on what bases is nurses' preparation recognised at degree level, whereas electricians work, is at trade certificate level. Quite different benefits and status are associated with these levels of certification (e.g., ease of access to further education). These anomalies and shortcomings in how the recognition of skill is acknowledged and variably enacted suggest that the bases for the recognition of learning through work and the processes of certification warrant urgent, but careful consideration and policy action.

Workplaces as Sites of Assessment and Certification

Workplaces present novel challenges for the assessment and certification of vocational knowledge. These challenges are central to issues of securing fair assessment and legitimated recognition. They include issues associated with what should constitute the focus for assessment and certification, the validity – the worth of judgments made against some criteria – and reliability – the consistency of judgments across time and location. However, firstly it is useful to consider some orientations for the assessment and recognition of individuals' skills.

Orientations of Workplace Assessment and Recognition

There are at least three distinct foci for the recognition of workplace learnt knowledge. These are: (i) *individual development* – an individualistic, humanistic, and potentially critical approach focused on individuals' development; (ii) *work-place practice* – focused on the performance requirements of the particular workplace in which individuals are employed and (iii) *occupational practice* – the focus on the capacities expected to be deployed effectively by somebody working in the particular occupational field (e.g., cooks, production work, teachers).

Individual development. An individual focus is consistent with a view of adult learning that provides opportunities for individuals to explore and extend their knowledge according to their personal goals, in this case, within their working lives. As is central to contemporary concepts of adult learning, this assessment can have a humanistic or critical orientation (Kasworm & Marienau, 1997). Here, the purpose would be to identify individual workers' needs and aspirations, and determine the degree by which their learning meets these goals. If adopted, a critical perspective requires the individual to demonstrate a capacity to criti- cally appraise, identify contradictions and alternatives within their work and work practices (Brookfield, 1997). Assessment and recognition of these kinds provide a vehicle for recognising the individual's development and capacities in ways not constrained by the requirements of particular workplace. The strengths of this orientation are in its capacity to reflect emancipatory and transformative goals for adult learners who have exercised their agency in addressing the particular demands that their adult role or societal expectation are making of them (e.g., their working life). A limitation of this focus is that it may not attract the sympathy of or recognition within the workplace or the broader occupational practice. The recognition of actual performance is central to the enterprise and most valued and rewarded by employers (Smith & Billett, 2003), whereas pre- dicted performance against occupational standards will be the focus of occupa- tional licensing. For instance, current policy goals in most Western countries are associated with adults learning to maintain their skill currency and workplace effectiveness throughout their working lives (OECD, 2000), rather than indivi- dual goals.

Workplace practice. A focus on a particular workplace practice for the recogni- tion of skills emphasizes the situatedness of performance, and the need for it to be appraised and acknowledged in actual practice. This includes relations between individuals' requirement for performance and their acknowledgement (e.g., status, pay, promotion) in a particular workplace. Recognition focused in this way privileges the validity of current performance and can assist in making predictions about future performance in this or similar work practices. The validity and reliability of judgments leading to certification can be apprehended through accounts of individuals' performance in that workplace. Overtime, these accounts can provide bases for high validity when judgments are closely linked to a history of individual applicants' performance (i.e., supporting valid judg- ments) and supporting reliability through comparisons with others in the work- place over time. An approach that acknowledges actual performance is compelling and almost inescapable in a workplace setting. That is, current workplace activities and preferences offer bases for decision-making about individuals' performance, and for those decisions to be appraised by others, thereby shaping their standing. Moreover, comparisons across individuals might be easier to exercise when the focus for performance has some commonality (e.g., performance in the same workplace tasks), thereby likely aiding the reliability of such judgments. So focussing on workplace practice has the advantage of acknowledging performance associated with individuals' current employment and on that basis can potentially be conducted with high degrees of reliability and validity. Its weaknesses include a highly situational basis for recognition, and potential constraints on the ability to predict performance in other workplaces (e.g., changing employment, promotion, capacity to change) or in the changed circumstances in the workplace. Also, individuals can only practice, perfect and demonstrate those skills that they can access in their work activities. This access may be constrained by workplace factors.

This approach to recognition is likely to be highly valued by some employers, particularly those cautious about sponsoring workplace training. The evidence internationally suggests that enterprises value the development and acknowledgement of skills that are enterprise specific (Smith & Billett, 2003). Some enterprises have created their own enterprise specific qualifications to meet their particular needs. Software companies have been at the forefront of the organisation of these arrangements from product specific purposes across national boundaries (Adelman, 2001) and fast food companies within those boundaries (e.g., McDonalds).

Occupational practice. The requirements for occupational practice, such as those stated in national curriculum documents and competency standards, describe the capacities demanded of a practitioner in a particular occupation. They offer a premise for judgments that can transcend the requirements of a particular workplace, because their purpose is to determine whether the individual possesses the capacities to practice the occupation more widely. Here, the focus is on the capacity for adaptability within the occupation and competence with than recognition of performance in a particular workplace. Complicating such a purpose are the difficulties to apprehend bases for the validity and reliability of such recognition. As the requirement for occupational practice can be quite distinct across different workplaces (i.e., different versions of the occupational activity occur, in different ways and different standards) (Billett 2001a), benchmarks that describe idealised statements of occupational practice may or may not reflect the actual performance requirements of specific workplaces. Moreover, there can be significant variations in the requirements for work across industry sub-sectors. For instance, in the food processing sector, the skills required in vegetable processing are quite distinct from those in fish processing, viticulture, cannery or dairy work. The same can be said for secondary processing and some primary production work, such as agriculture. These differences complicate making reliable judgements about occupational performance, thereby undermining their utility. So, although national competency standards, statements of occupational requirement or even professional standards might be available as benchmarks, the consonance between the occupational practice in a particular workplace and these benchmarks will shape their usefulness as bases for reliable assessment. Moreover, inferences from observation or a history of individuals' performance are really needed for judgements to be made against such standards. Industry spokespersons and the government often favour the recognition of skills at the occupational or industry level because it offers the promise of a basis for administering standards and courses. Individuals also favour this kind of recognition, as it grants options beyond their particular workplace. Yet, the problem is how this recognition can best address variability of occupational practice and also predict adaptability to changing circumstances within enterprises and across the sector. Hence, the provision and organisation of occupational benchmarks needs to be open and flexible enough to accommodate variations in occupational practice across workplaces and industry sub-sectors.

These three focuses represent different perspectives or orientation for recognising learning through work. The assumption of assessment within vocational education using occupational standards is that it provides judgments about capacities to perform within the occupation, regardless of the particular workplace performance requirements. This claim seems very ambitious. Moreover, increasingly the capacity to transfer or adapt knowledge (i.e., robust workplace performance) is not a wholly individual quality, being premised on variations in the social practice (e.g., requirements for performance in particular workplaces) (e.g., Pea, 1997). Therefore, assessment of individuals' capacities alone will be insufficient to predict adaptability across occupational practice. More likely, evidence of understanding something of the different contexts in which the occupation is enacted (e.g., variations in requirements for mechanics', electricians', chefs' work) will be more predictive of adaptability across the occupation practice. In so far as evidence is required about performance, actual performance stands as compelling bases for judgements about individuals' workplace competence. The desirable goal would be to incorporate and integrate the three purposes (i.e., individual, enterprise and occupation). Yet, finding a balance among these purposes may not be easy. Moreover, employers' preference for specific performance and for broader requirements to secure occupational certification will predominate when issues of remuneration and occupational certification are addressed.

Procedures for the Recognition of Workplace Skills

There are also significant procedural issues for the recognition of learning through work, as foreshadowed. These include: (i) the bases for assessment (i.e., benchmarks, performance indicators or situational requirements); (ii) workplace factors influencing the fairness of assessment and certification processes (e.g., contested workplace practices and conflicting goals); and (iii) the standing or credibility of these processes' outcomes. These issues go beyond mere procedural matters for assessment. They also reflect concerns about the bases upon which judgments about the recognition of occupational competence should be made, conflicts and consequences of the acknowledgement of individuals' performance and the different status of social institutions that host the certification process and qualifications.

Premises of workplace recognition. Workplace assessment and skills recognition will likely proceed on different bases than in educational institutions. In workplaces, assessment will likely focus on the actual practices being enacted in the workplace. In education institutions, statements within curriculum documents that predict performance or address specific criteria will likely be used. These documents are usually syllabuses, national competency standards or industry standards, comprising disembedded statements about occupational competence (Billett, 2003). Curriculum documents in vocational education often comprise an aggregation of employers' and practitioners' beliefs about what comprises the skills and practices constituting an occupation. What they describe is not always consonant with the actual requirements in particular workplaces. This is because requirements for workplace performance are not uniform or a version of the occupation practice; they can have distinct qualities (Billett, 2001a). Compare the work of a motor mechanic in a inner-city dealership with that of a mechanic a garage in a non-metropolitan community; an electrician installing and maintaining elevators with that of an electrical contractor engaged in domestic installation work, chefs working in a five-star hotels with those who preparing precooked meals for airlines, hospitals, or for supermarkets, etc. Regardless of where they are practised, when considering the performance of mechanics, electricians and chefs, it will be their capacities to be effective in the workplace in which they are employed that stands as the compelling basis for the assessment and recognition of work performance, rather than some abstracted statement of occupational performance.

So a different focus for assessment and certification exists in workplaces than education institutions. In the former, the focus will be on specific workplace requirements, and for the latter on predictions of performance in workplaces that are based on statements of occupational competence. As foreshadowed, judgments of specific workplace performance may be more situationally valid and possibly reliable, because they are embedded in and can be moderated through available evidence (i.e., other workers' performance). However, this assessment and any certification may be too specific, and not predictive of wider occupational competence or future performance in even that workplace, when conditions change. Conversely, assessment against statements of occupational competence may be quite spurious (i.e., of low validity and reliability) because workplaces have quite diverse requirements for occupational performance.

So, it may be more difficult to assess individuals' capacity to practice occupational skills in work situations that are different from those at that workplace. Consequently, a key concern is about the kind of benchmarks against which assessment and accreditation in workplaces will be exercised. Will it be sufficient to utilise enterprise-specific benchmarks or should some occupational standard be used? Perhaps some occupational statements that acknowledge difference in its enactment of the practice may be a useful compromise.

Factors influencing the fairness of workplace assessment processes. There are inherent difficulties in securing fair assessment in workplaces. Workplaces are often contested environments and, potentially, the assessment of individuals' skills and provision of certification will be enmeshed in workplace relations, including the standing of individuals and cohorts of workers. In all, the evidence suggests that workplaces are far from benign and that opportunities to access training, support and therefore recognition are not equally distributed (Leuven & Oosterbeek, 1999). Old-timers may inhibit the progress of newcomers to avoid displacement (Lave & Wenger, 1991), part-time workers' activities and opportunities may be constrained by full-time workers (Hughes & Bernhardt, 1999) to avoid being replaced. Differences in opportunities and acknowledgement may be afforded on the basis of gender (Bierema, 2001; Solomon, 1999), language and ethnicity (Hull, 1997). Workplace affiliations of different kinds will serve to overtly support some individuals' aspirations and actively inhibit others (Billett, 2001b). Given the legitimacy and status that potentially arises from the certification of skills, it is likely that processes granting recognition to individuals or cohorts of workers could become highly contested. Moreover, contested workplaces may act to test the validity of the workplace assessment and accreditation processes. That is, the recognition of skills sits within environments where the recognition of skills may serve to reinforce or challenge particular interests, advantage individuals or groups of individuals and in ways that displace other individuals or reposition interests within the workplace. For instance, trade workers might enjoy higher status and be paid more than, un-credentialled production workers. The provision of certification for production workers, may ultimately lead to contestation between two groups of workers because of challenges to the standing of the trade workers. In a workplace, where peer assessment was trialed, workers had great difficulty in gaining promotion to higher classifications because peers had unreasonable expectations of their performance. Eventually, management had to intercede to ensure that at least some workers were promoted (Billett 2001b).

A graphic account of how workplace affiliations and relationships can subvert and render workplace assessments unfair and invalid was demonstrated in a study within in the coal mining industry. In the coalmines investigated, assessment of competence was linked to levels of remuneration. The very high rates of successful workplace assessments identified in the study were achieved through the subversion of the assessment process and even coercion of assessors (Billett, 1995). Trade workers were given the assessment tasks and selected segments of training modules days before the tests. These workers focussed their efforts only on those materials and rehearsed responses to the selected assessment items. Despite the use of external assessors, the briefing and provision of assessment items by workplace delegates largely invalidated the assessment process. These trade workers generally secured higher remuneration as a result. Beyond this direct subversion, were instances of coercion of workplace assessors that invalidated the assessment of production workers' competence. Mine site production workers had their skills assessed by other, but more senior or staff workers.

Some of these assessors reported often feeling obliged to record successful outcomes. The assessors worked in the same workplaces as those whom they assessed, lived with their families in the same remote mining communities, their children went to the same school as those of the parents they would be assessing, they shopped in the same shops, socialised in the same clubs etc. To record unsuccessful assessments might come at a high personal price for them or their family members. There were also tests and testing reported whose validity could be questioned. If operators could start and move a bulldozer a short distance, lift and lower its blade and push a small amount of dirt they would be deemed to be competent in its operation. There were also reports of assessments being hurriedly and successfully completed when they coincided with meal breaks of the end of shifts.

Although many trade and production workers were successful in a range of workplace assessments, and enjoyed increased remuneration as a result, there was consensus by the miners, union delegates and managers that the workplace was less safe and possibly less productive and viable (i.e., because of increased labour cost) as a result of these assessments. Many workers became authorised to use equipment that they were not competent to operate and potentially were risks to themselves and other workers. For instance, those certified to operate a bulldozer, as described above, could be expected to shift dirt or coal, on a coal wall under lights at night and in the rain. So the actions of workplace affiliations (i.e., union delegates), the concern about reprisals and ineptness of the assessment processes invalidated many of the assessments and subverted their purposes. The salient point here was that ultimately the assessment and certification process was undermined and lacked legitimacy in the minds of those who had benefited from it, sponsored and enacted it.

Beyond co-workers either facilitating or inhibiting the fairness of the assessment process, workplace managers or owners may well seek to limit the recognition of skills. This might be done to maintain the viability of the enterprise, or the management or owners' control of it. Employers are usually keen to constrain the level of remuneration and the numbers of employees trained in order to limit the percentage of highly paid workers (Leuven & Oosterbeek, 1999) or to avoid their portability. For instance, many workers in the Australian food processing industry are enrolled in modules of the Certificate of Food Production. However, the completion rate of the Certificate is relatively low. Because the modules need to be sponsored by employers, the range of modules are accessible for workers are often constrained by employers. It seems few enterprises are willing to sponsor the range of modules required for workers to complete the Certificate (Billett, 2000). Employers claim to be sponsoring only those modules pertinent to their enterprises' needs. However, too frequently the scope of this sponsorship also coincidentally fails to extend to that required for individuals' to secure certification.

In sum, arrangements for the recognition of skills in the workplace needs to be enacted to counter the: (i) negative effects of the interests of workplace cliques and affiliations; (ii) the interests of management; and (iii) can secure assessment procedures. These kind of obstacles need to be addressed by policies and practices in order for fair and accessible recognition of skills to proceed. This includes removing instances of coercion, the prospect for fairness in the recognition workplace skills and the legitimacy of that certification may otherwise be jeopardised.

The standing and credibility of workplace recognition. Because of the kind of issues raised above, and the standing of particular social institutions, there is a residual concern that assessment and credentials administered through work-places will remain of low status. The exceptions are where workplaces enjoy particularly high status or are large enough to offer quality assessment and recognition (e.g., Buckingham Palace, national airlines). In addressing the impor-tant equity goals of assessing and recognising skills in workplaces, it may be too difficult to initially achieve (a) the legitimisation of learning in the workplace and (b) their credibility as institutions able to provide certifications in ways that would have the legitimacy and authority enjoyed by education institutions. If workplaces gain a greater legitimacy as sites for learning, then it may be timely to consider offering credentials. Yet, even then, there remains pervasive problems associated with assessing and credentialling workers in workplaces, as outlined above. So while workplaces offer bases for highly valid assessment against individuals' enactment of practice, there are concerns about the inevitable enter-prise-specific focus for assessing workers and offering credentials; the undermin-ing of the assessment processes by contested workplace practices; and a concern about the standing or acceptability of credentials issued from the workplace. In order to address the important goal of recognising workplace learning, it is necessary to consider options for occupational assessment and certification, and advance mechanisms that can assist with fair and valid assessment, thereby establishing and maintaining the legitimacy and standing of the certification of workplace learning.

Options for the Recognition of Learning Through Work

Ideally, approaches to recognise learning through work need to be conceptuali-sed, their development premised, directed towards and evaluated on the basis of how they meet three kinds of outcomes outlined earlier. These are: (i) individ-uals' goals; (ii) the requirements of their workplaces; and (iii) recognition for their occupation. While meeting all three of these needs represents the ideal goal for recognising learning through work, addressing individuals' performance in the workplace within the context of an occupational practice is proposed here as providing a useful starting point. In meeting both workplace and occupational requirements, many individuals' vocational aspirations will also be met.

It is unlikely that a single or uniform approach to the recognition of learning through work will be sufficient or feasible. The diversity of occupational practices, including its multifold manifestations within some subsections of industry (e.g., secondary processing, food production), the structuring of industry sectors (e.g., those predominantly comprising large or small enterprises), their professional and affiliations arrangements, and the levels of readiness to proceed down a track of recognition (e.g., those with existing courses, benchmarks) militate a unitary process. Instead, because of differences in the requirements, structures, affiliations and readiness of industry or occupational sectors, options for processes of recognition will need to be enacted. The utility of these various options will be shaped by the existence or otherwise of professional associations and trade unions, the geographical distribution of workplaces and any requirements for occupational licensing. However, across these options there is a common goal of securing the legitimate and authoritative recognition of individuals' skills, in relation to their enactment in a particular workplace setting and the wider potential of their application across instances of the occupational practice.

Hosting the Recognition of Learning Through Work

Some form of agency external to workplaces may best assist the standing of the recognition of workplace-learnt knowledge (i.e., through certification, licensing, and qualifications). High standards for the conduct of workplace assessment processes will be required, to establish the legitimacy of certification. While some large and prestigious enterprises may have the standing and resources to conduct assessment fairly and to be recognized as legitimate, most enterprises will not. The use of external agents and agencies will not always be welcomed by enterprises or their management, who might be concerned about the undermining of their capacity to control levels of remuneration and reward. There are also problems associated with the focus of and funding of such arrangements. Yet, what seems essential, at this stage, is some separation between the workplace and the organisation that is assessing and providing recognition. However, a rich interaction is also necessary to assist understanding the full worth of the enterprises' activities and individuals' performance in those activities. This includes building both the employers' and employees' confidence in the fairness of the assessment processes. Moreover, because each workplace's particular requirements need to be accounted for as it constitutes a version of the enactment of the occupational practice. There is no ideal or archetypal instance of occupational practice (Billett, 2003), just a range of variations of practice dependent upon the particular circumstances of the particular workplace. A key role for external agencies will be to identify what constitutes effective performance in a workplace and, perhaps, make judgements about how this relates to performance in other workplaces where similar performance is required. So benchmarking will be a key concern and well as assessment and certification.

The following represent some options for achieving this common goal organised on the basis of their hosting within different kinds of organisations and agencies. What will be required, however, are policy frameworks to support coherent and legitimate practices across the different kinds of hosting organisations in the administration of assessment and recognition of occupational skills.

Large enterprises. Although using major enterprises to host the recognition of employees' learning is problematic in terms of ensuring the fairness of assessment for all employees (Giraud, 2002), it may be a useful option in some instances. This is particularly likely when the industry sector and, hence, occupational practice, is dominated by a few large enterprises or even a single employer. For instance, national railway systems, automotive manufacturers, aeroplane manufacturers, may virtually represent industry sectors or large parts of them. Hence, enterprise certification may have currency and be quite appropriate in industry sectors where employees can only seek employment in a small number of large enterprises. Such large enterprises may also have the capacities (e.g., resources, expertise, procedures) for the legitimate and authoritative recognition of learning through work. Policy considerations here include identifying industry-wide statements of occupational competence, negotiating around enterprise sensitivities about codifying patent or specific skills and enacting processes to assist the ability and reliability of assessment processes and recognition (Adelman, 2001). In these large enterprises, issues associated with validity are likely to focus on the enterprises' work practices, as much as a wider occupational applications, because these enterprises' practices may represent occupational benchmarks. Issues of reliability would be premised on the conduct of the assessment processes within the enterprise. However, it needs to be acknowledged that management of many workplaces would be reluctant to lose control of processes that linked the recognition of workers' skills to increases in remuneration. There is also the question of who pays for these processes of and maintenance of certification. Policy intervention that supports and promotes good practice, yet avoids external intervention might be the most appropriate approach.

Industry or professional associations. Industry and professional associations in some countries are the centre of the development and recognition of occupational skills. For instance, in Germany local trade and professional organisations play a mature and active role in shaping what is required for occupational practice of how best it can be learnt and the arrangements for its recognition (Giraud, 2002; Koch & Reuling, 1994). These arrangements are, however, not widespread outside of northern Europe. Elsewhere, there are active industry or professional associations that could play a significant role in the establishment of occupational benchmarks and the recognition of workplace learning. For instance, they may generate industry or occupational statements that have standing within the sector. Also, because of relatively small workforces of individual enterprises, their specializations and geographical dispersal, local industry or professional organisations may be appropriate to host assessment and recognition arrangements, as in Germany (Koch & Reuling, 1994). Similarly, there are associations that promote the occupational concerns of their members (e.g., Master Builders' Association) and industry training associations might also lend themselves as hosting organizations in some countries.

There is, however, a particular need to be sensitive to and accommodate specific sector arrangements that might be overlooked or swamped by larger industry or professional associations and affiliations. Emerging sectors (e.g., natural therapy, software development) or those with low status (e.g., production work, service work) all might struggle to have their interests well represented within larger affiliations. For instance, the diverse needs within the food-processing sector, as noted, may be unable to secure appropriate space or place within a sector where its practices are viewed as being of low order. Equally, the specific requirements of small businesses or those engaged in highly specialised activity may well warrant particular support and attention within policy frameworks to ensure that these interests are well represented.

Policy considerations here include the identification and selection of an association or associations that could best represent the needs of an industry sector, or its sub sectors. The degree of institutional maturity or organisational capacity to undertake such a role will need to be appraised in order to determine if it requires support from government to achieve this goal. In Germany, these capacities were developed over time and now operate with high levels of autonomy from government (Giraud, 2002). This includes the capacity to be representative of the occupation or sector, and developing its competence to conduct or licence assessments and also to administer certification that would be seen by the occupation or industry sector as legitimate and authoritative. A starting point would be to determine whether an occupational, industry or industry sector focus is the most salient. Some occupational activity sits well within a particular industry or even sub sectors (e.g., pilots in aviation and marine, train drivers within rail, military work within defence, hairdressers within the service sector, nurses within health) yet many others transcend industry sector boundaries (e.g., clerical work, electricians, metal fabricators, construction workers). Following this, some identification of those areas where there are no bases for the recognition of skills and certification establish themselves as priorities for government action. In all of this, the need to be sensitive to: (i) situational variation; (ii) developing (further) the capacity for fair assessment; and (iii) arrangements that authorise and legitimise certification are important policy goals, as these will underpin the standing of the bodies such as trade, industry and professional associations.

Vocational education systems. Vocational education systems can likely provide at least two kinds of hosting arrangements for the recognition of learning. Firstly, where there exists certification and benchmarks in the form of course outcomes and qualifications, these constitute bases for vocational education systems to engage with workplaces in providing assessment and the recognition of learning acquired through work. The task would be to understand what these occupational benchmarks mean in terms of the requirements of particular workplaces and the deployment of assessment processes that are fair and authoritative. The second role is for vocational education systems to conduct assessment and recognition processes on behalf of industry sectors, large enterprises and regional bodies who may lack the resources to effectively provide fair assessment, and legitimate and prestigious certification. Both the validity and reliability of assessment and certification may also benefit from some form of external monitoring or evaluation. As enterprises, particular large enterprises, are increasingly subject to external monitoring of their activities (e.g., quality assurance, occupational health and safety) there exist models for monitoring and auditing that might be readily adaptable to the recognition of skills. Policy considerations here include using benchmarks for assessment that are flexible enough to address diverse instances of occupational practice and ensuring that those assessing are able to translate their assessment and certification practices to adapt to the exigencies of workplace settings.

Local-regional arrangements. The assessment and recognition of learning through work, if not its certification, will sometimes need to be sensitive to the geographical distribution of workers and workplaces. This includes localising an understanding of the requirements for performance (e.g., what a mechanic, builder, nurse, teacher has to do in rural, isolated or remote communities in contrast to their metropolitan counterparts), making accessible assessment process and facilitating the kinds of support required to secure certification and its administration. In particular, the skill recognition needs of those in small business will often require localised responses, and in ways that may be remote from metropolitan and regional centres. Existing agencies in these communities (e.g., regional development boards, local learning networks) might be encouraged and supported to act as the occupational assessment groups. Such localised arrangements are likely to need the support of local employers and enterprises, as other policy initiatives suggests (e.g., Smith & Billett, 2003).

These hosting options are not exhaustive or mutually exclusive. They represent a set of options for organising the recognition of learning in the workplace. In particular ways, these options might be best able to address the: (i) diversity of occupational practice; (ii) readiness of enterprises to conduct assessment; and certification; (iii) and a concern for buttressing the legitimacy of workplace assessment and recognition. As they utilise existing institutions and associations they may not make overwhelming demands upon governmental resources. However, in extending and separating some of their existing roles, the focus and means for recognising learning through work will often sit in highly contested relations. These relations include teachers assessing knowledge not acquired through teaching processes, enterprises supporting the assessment of workers' skills which may precipitate claims for higher remuneration, and workers cooperating with peers in ways that will fairly recognise the breadth and depth of co-workers' skills; as opposed to their own. So the policy task goes beyond enacting arrangements for identifying what counts as occupational practice in particular workplaces, mere ordering of assessment processes, making them valid and reliable, and maintaining the standards of certification. It also comprises changing views about what kinds of work is worth certifying, understanding the disadvantage experienced by those without certification, inviting enterprises to support and engage in such processes, particularly where there is little history of such engagement, and directing priorities to areas of need rather than ease of recognition. It follows that government policy needs to:

- identify and support the development of agencies (e.g., professional, union, local) that are best placed to administer and monitor workplace-based assessments;
- identify and trial methods for benchmarking workplace performance;
- enact arrangements that changed the existing views about the lack of legitimacy of work learnt knowledge and elevate the standing of learning arising outside of educational institutions or programs;
- develop procedures for the hosting arrangements identified above; and
- ensure those arrangements are monitored to maintain fair and accessible skill recognition through work.

These organisations enacting the assessment and certification of workplace learnt knowledge will need to build confidence in their capacity to provide fair and valid assessments and in the administration of those arrangements. This will include:

- linking specific workplace performances to occupational requirements;
- developing or adapting benchmarks for the assessment of workplace skills;
- enacting assessments that are valid in terms of workplace performance and reliable in terms of relative levels of performance across industry sectors;
- identifying how best different kinds of occupational practice might be recognised; and
- managing consistency in decision-making across sectors, workforces or workplaces.

It will ultimately be the quality of the enactment of such arrangements that will shape the standing and legitimacy of these the recognition of the workplace learnt knowledge.

Recognising Learning Through Work

In summary, despite the complexities and difficulties in the provision of the authorative and legitimate recognition of learning through work, it remains a worthy goal for policy deliberations and actions by government, professional associations, unions and other agencies. For all workers, the ongoing maintenance of their individual skills throughout working lives is becoming increasingly salient to the continuity of their employment (OECD, 1996). Given this, and the increasingly transitory nature of contemporary employment, the need for recognition of those skills is compelling. For those marginalised by existing education provisions or workplace practices, there is an even more compelling case for the recognition of learning through work. It has been proposed that except for some large or particularly prestigious enterprises, there is currently a need for the administration, monitoring and certification of workplace skills recognition to be hosted outside of workplaces. This is to assist establishing the legitimacy of the recognition of workplaces learnt knowledge and because the conditions for fair and valid recognition will not always be present in workplaces. Underpinning these processes is the ongoing task for government, professional associations and unions of championing the richness and diversity of vocational knowledge, the sources of its complexities in different workplaces and the need for this richness and complexity to be fully valued. The key policy goals are necessary to identify the focus for the recognition of skills (i.e., occupational, workplace, personal), enacting procedures to recognise learning, selecting and supporting hosting organisations and institutions and developing those procedures, so that the recognition of skills through work becomes as legitimate that provided by educational institutions.

References

Adelman, C. (2001). The medieval guild in cyberclothes: International dimensions of industry certification in information technology. *Tertiary Education and Management, 7*, 277–291.

Bierema, L. L. (2001). Women, work, and learning. In T. Fenwick (Ed.), *Sociocultural perspectives on learning through work*. New Directions in Adult and Continuing Education (Vol. 92, pp. 53–62). San Francisco: Jossey Bass/Wiley.

Billett, S. (1995). *Skill formation in three central Queensland coalmines: Reflections on implementation and prospects for the future*. Brisbane: Centre for Research into Employment and Work, Griffith University.

Billett, S. (2000). Defining the demand side of VET: Industry, enterprises, individuals and regions. *Journal of Vocational Education and Training, 50*(1), 5–30.

Billett, S. (2001a). Knowing in practice: Re-conceptualising vocational expertise. *Learning and Instruction, 11*(6), 431–452.

Billett, S. (2001b). *Learning in the workplace: Strategies for effective practice*. Sydney: Allen and Unwin.

Billett S (2001c) Coparticipation at work: Affordance and engagement. In T. Fenwick (Ed.), *Sociocultural perspectives on learning through work*. New Directions in Adult and Continuing Education (Vol. 92, pp. 63–72). San Francisco: Jossey Bass/Wiley.

Billett, S. (2002). Critiquing workplace learning discourses: Participation and continuity at work. *Studies in the Education of Adults, 34*(1), 56–67.

Billett, S. (2003). Vocational curriculum and pedagogy: An activity theory perspective. *European Journal of Educational Research, 2*(1), 6–21.

Boud, D., & Garrick, J. E. (Eds.) (1999). *Understanding Learning at Work*. London: Routledge.

Boud, D., Solomon, N., & Symes, C. (2001). New practices for new times. In N. Solomon (Ed.), *Work-based Learning: A New Higher Education?* (pp. 3–17). Buckingham: Open University Press.

Brookfield, S. (1997). Assessing Critical Thinking. In M. A. Leahy (Ed.), *Assessing Adult Learning Settings: Current Issues and Approaches* (pp. 17–30). San Francisco: Jossey-Bass.

Brunello, G., & Medio, A. (2001). An explanation of international differences in education and workplace training. *European Economic Review, 45*(2), 307–322.

Coopers and Lybrand. (1994). *Training practices and preferences of small business in Australia: A report for vocational education and training providers,*. Brisbane: Australian National Training Authority.

Danford, A. (1998). Teamworking and labour regulation in the autocomponents industry. *Work, Employment & Society, 12*(3), 409–431.

Darrah, C. N. (1996). *Learning and Work: An Exploration in Industrial Ethnography*. New York: Garland Publishing.

Evans, N. (2001). From once upon a time to happily ever after: The story of work-based learning in the UK Higher Education sector. In N. Solomon (Ed.), *Work-based Learning: A new Higher Education* (pp. 61–73). Buckingham: Open University Press.

Fenwick, T. (2001). *Sociocultural Perspectives on Learning through Work*. San Francisco: Jossey Bass.

Giraud, O. (2002). Firms' further training practices and social exclusion: Can industrial relations systems provide greater equality? Theoretical and empirical evidence from Germany and France. In P. J. Connell (Ed.), *Education, training and employment dynamics: transitional labour markets in the European Union*. Cheltenham: Edward Elgar.

Groot, W., Hartog, J., & Oosterbeek, H. (1994). Costs and revenues of investment in Enterprise-Related Schooling. *Oxford Economic Papers, 46*(4).

Grubb, W. N. (1996). *Working in the middle: Strengthening education and training for the mid-skilled labor force*. San Francisco: Jossey Bass.

Hughes, K., & Bernhardt, A. (1999). *Market segmentation and the restructuring of banking jobs* (IEE Brief number 24). New York: Institute on Education and the Economy.

Hull, G. (1997). Preface and Introduction. In G. Hull (Ed.), *Changing work, changing workers: Critical perspectives on language, literacy and skills*. New York: State University of New York Press.

Inman, P., & Vernon, S. (1997). Assessing Workplace Learning: New Trends and Possibilities. In A. D. Rose & M. A. Leahy (Eds.), *Assessing Adult Learning in Diverse Settings: Current Issues and Approaches* (pp. 75–86). San Francisco: Jossey Bass Publishers.

Kasworm, C. E., & Marienau, C. A. (1997). Principles for assessment of adult learning. In M. A. Leahy (Ed.), *Assessing adult learning in diverse settings: Current issues and approaches* (pp. 5–16). San Francisco: Jossey-Bass.

Koch, R., & Reuling, J. (1994). The responsiveness and regulation of training capacity and quality. In Organisation for Economic Cooperation and Development (Ed.), *Vocational Training in Germany: Modernisation and Responsiveness*. Paris: Organisation for Economic Cooperation and Development.

Lave, J., & Wenger, E. (1991). *Situated learning – legitimate peripheral participation*. Cambridge, UK: Cambridge University Press.

Lengerman, P. A. (1999). How long do the benefits of training last? Evidence of long term effects across current and previous employers. *Research in Labour Economics, 18*, 439–461.

Leuven, E., & Oosterbeek, H. (1999). The demand and supply of work related training: Evidence from four countries. *Research in Labour Economics, 18*, 303–330.

Livingstone, D. (2001). Expanding notions of work and learning. In T. Fenwick (Ed.), *Sociocultural Perspectives on Learning through Work* (pp. 19–30). San Francisco: Jossey Bass.

Noon, M., & Blyton P. (1997). *The Realities of Work*. Basingstoke, Hants, Macmillan.

O'Connell, P. J. (1999). *Adults in training: An international Comparison of Continuing Education and Training*. Paris: OECD.

Organisation of Economic Cooperation and Development (1996). *Lifelong learning for all*. Paris: OECD.

Organisation of Economic Cooperation and Development (2000). *Economics and Finance of Lifelong Learning*. Paris: OECD.

Pea, R. D. (1997). Practices of distributed intelligence and designs for education. In G. Salomon (Ed.), *Distributed cognitions: Psychological and educational considerations* (pp. 47–87). Cambridge: Cambridge University Press.

Pusey, M. (2003). *The Experience of Middle Australia*. Cambridge, UK: Cambridge University Press.

Raizen, S. A. (1991). *Learning and work: The research base. Vocational Education and Training for youth: Towards coherent policy and practice*. Paris: OECD.

Rogoff, B., & Lave, J. (Eds.) (1984). *Everyday cognition: Its development in social context*. Cambridge, Mass: Harvard University Press.

Scribner, S. (1985). Knowledge at work. *Anthropology and Education Quarterly, 16*, 199–206.

Smith, A., & Billett, S. (2003). *Enhancing Employers' Expenditure on Training*. Adelaide: National Centre for Vocational Education Research.

Solomon, N. (1999). Culture and difference in workplace learning. In D. Boud & D. J. Garrick (Eds.), *Understanding learning at work* (pp. 119–131). London: Routledge.

51

TRADE UNIONS AND CHANGING PRACTICES OF WORKERS' EDUCATION

Keith Forrester
University of Leeds, UK

For millions of workers throughout the world today, the trade union often remains the primary, and sometimes the only vehicle of their adult learning. For some trade unionists, worker education today involves engaging with the knowledge, skills and capabilities seen as necessary to economically survive within a late capitalist environment. Elsewhere, such as in post-colonial Africa, worker education has recently involved or currently involves the learning necessary to challenge apartheid regimes (South Africa), forms of political injustice and dictatorship (Zambia, Malawi and Zimbabwe) or in the case of post-communist countries, union members learning once again, to create workers' organisations that defend workers' interests within the workplace.

This chapter provides a brief overview of changing patterns of worker education. However, the 'worker' aspect of worker education continues to pose conceptual problems. Different academic perspectives will provide different understandings. Different cultural or, even, country/regional perspectives will provide different 'standpoints' or understandings (see Spencer's (2002) edited text on 'unions and learning' for further discussion and examples on this matter). Although it is common to distinguish between 'worker' and 'union' learning-especially in studies from a historical perspective,-this chapter will conflate the two categories. In the main, worker learning in this chapter will be discussed in relationship to union activity. Adopting such an approach risks ignoring important 'worker' learning experiences existing outside trade unions. Historically, struggles around civil rights, racial bigotry or gender issues for example, have often taken place outside unions (and sometimes, against unions). Despite such risks, focussing on the trade union element can be justified perhaps in that unions remain important agencies in characterising understandings and practises of the 'worker' element in worker education. Moreover, although arising from different and often contradictory processes, the 'revitalised' attention to union membership development in recent decades is likely to be of considerable importance to any understanding of 'worker' education. This chapter then, will selectively comment on the changing patterns of learning opportunities available to

International Handbook of Educational Policy, 963–975
Nina Bascia, Alister Cumming, Amanda Datnow, Kenneth Leithwood and David Livingstone (Eds.)
© 2005 *Springer. Printed in Great Britain.*

union members that have been organised through their trade union or indirectly, have been associated with trade unions. The use of 'learning' in this chapter incorporates both an informal and formal dimension. Rather than insisting on too rigid a distinction between these types of learning as is often the case within the literature, this chapter prefers to see learning as often involving both these overlapping dimensions. It is the 'curriculum' of the workplace, characterised by particular and unequal social and productive relationships, that provides the impetus and source for much worker learning (Billett, 2002). This learning will usually be of an 'informal' nature but will sometimes involve participation in courses, discussion groups, forms of industrial action or distributing bulletins. Cultural and artistic activities are less frequently discussed as forms of worker learning. But, as Bratton and his colleagues (2003, p. 31) demonstrate, 'labour arts, broadly conceived, provides some of the most engaging sources of worker learning'.

Learning in this chapter then, will be broadly understood as that 'knowing' arising from participation in particular social and productive activities occurring within particular contexts and shaped by particular relationships of a socio-economic character. The first section of the chapter will suggest a conception of trade unionism that provides the distinctive character of 'union learning' and, secondly, helps to situate the often acrimonious debates and contested nature of such learning. The following section illustrates these debates. Historical examples are drawn from the early formative period of unions in the West together with more recent examples of educational provision associated with unions recently emerging from political repression. The third part of this chapter will examine the assumptions and practises of workers' education associated with recent moves by unions towards a greater professionalism in their educational provision. Examples from a number of countries will be used to illustrate such developments in the latter decades of the twentieth century. The final and longest section of the chapter will discuss current initiatives. Two interrelated objectives can be seen as informing recent policy developments and practises; namely, a determination to contribute towards 'lifelong learning' measures and, secondly, the possible contribution of union learning initiatives towards union renewal and revitalisation strategies.

The educational activities historically and currently associated with labour organisations remains a neglected area of study. While an extensive trade union literature can be located within academic areas such as industrial relations, sociology and labour history, systematic study of labour education continues to be of marginal significance. To an important extent, this reflects until recently, the lack of attention, resources and importance attached to union education by unions themselves. This neglect among unions throughout the world, it will be demonstrated, is fast changing.

Situating Union Learning

Whether through participation in the mobilizing activities of unions or through formal course provision, worker education historically associated with unions has tended to be shaped by the peculiar and distinctive character and nature of unions themselves. Although less explicitly recognised today within the developed economies, trade unions remain the historical products of the relationship between wage labour and capital. Whether viewed as servicing, organising or social movement organisations, trade unions exist within a particular societal context whereby work -equated with employment- is organised on the basis of a deeply unequal market relationship. Given the centrality of contested political perspectives, values and objectives to any form of policy analysis, it is not surprising that any understanding of labour organisations exist within a continuing engagement with the wider policy context. In contrast to the 'de-politised' rationalist view of policy analysis, trade union formation can be seen as a study of 'deciding how to decide' at a societal and increasingly, wider regional policy level. Unions are a particular organisational form for collective action. In seeking to defend and develop the interests of the membership, relationships with employers and the wider state regulatory framework, trade unions are characterised simultaneously by conflict (over terms and conditions of this employment as well as aspects of the labour process) and by cooperation (in maintaining an 'orderly' and negotiated employment relationship).As Hyman (1989, p. 230) points out:

> The central contradiction of trade unionism is that, at the same time as it makes possible the consolidation and increased effectiveness of worker's resistance to capitalism, it also makes this resistance more manageable and predictable and can even serve to suppress struggle.

As will be argued in the sections below, these ambiguities in the nature and character of trade unions have continually shaped discussions and interpretations of worker education.

Radical Learning

Given the nature and origins of trade unions, it is not surprising that much of the early history of worker education can be seen as a contested battle, often of a bitter character, for the allegiance and loyalty of the rapidly growing ranks of the 'labouring population'. The dislocation, bewilderment and underlying violence accompanying the birth of industrial capitalism from the middle of the eighteenth century through to the first decades of the twentieth century was associated with a series of struggles and imaginative initiatives by (or on behalf of) the emerging working class (Harrison, 1961). Often conceived of as a form of moral regulation, self-education and as a vehicle of social mobility, early worker education in Britain, for example, was based on nonconformist religious movements such as Methodism or on early socialist movements, such as Chartism. Arising from the early waves of (largely unsuccessful) unionism in the first decades of the nineteenth century, a distinguishing feature of socialist education towards the end of the nineteenth century was its unambiguously political character; education was a means of changing the world. Directly or indirectly influenced by Marxism as a 'way of knowing', this strand within worker education was to reappear, with a vengeance, in the first decades of the twentieth century. Alongside numerous small embryonic communist parties and in response to a set of severe economic and political problems facing the working class, there emerged in many parts of Europe, the USA, Latin America and Australia a distinctive group of social movements called 'revolutionary syndicalist', 'anarcho-syndicalist' and 'industrial unionist' (Holton, 1976; Kornbluh, 1965). Unlike many radicals who looked to political parties within state institutions to initiate socialism, these social movements sought to create a new society free from economic and political oppression through industrial class struggle in alliance with the trade unions. Amongst those nascent unions influenced by such ideas were the French Confederation Generale du Travail founded in 1895, the American Industrial Workers of the World set up in 1905, the Spanish Confederacion Nacional de Trabajo established in 1910 and the Italian Unione Syndicale Italiano formed in 1912. Australia, Sweden, Britain and Latin America were other countries with significant syndicalist groupings. Understanding capitalism so as to change it via revolutionary action was a strong feature. Educational classes in trade union centres, in IWW halls in the USA or through the Plebs League in Britain, were accompanied by a variety of informal discussion circles, journals and propaganda groups.

In contrast to such examples of autonomous 'independent working class' education, there continued the strand of self- improvement education such as, in Britain the Mechanics Institutes and Working Men's Colleges. In Scandinavia, the Folk High Schools had close links with the labour movement and were one of the influences in establishing a Working People's College in 1907 in Minnesota, which in turn, was an important influence on the radical Labour College movement which blossomed in the USA in the 1920s. Although the college eventually closed as a result of pressure from conservative trade unions and from government pressure, the Highlander Folk School established in the 1930s in Tennessee by Myles Horton continues today (Adams & Horton, 1975).

The early birth of trade unionism, then, was associated, at particular times and in particular countries with a rapid expansion of learning through participation in trade unions and through involvement in classes and discussion groups. Arguably, all serious educational movements from this period have been also social movements. To a lesser extent and in very different circumstances, the more recent birth or rebirth of trade unions that have emerged in the post-Soviet countries, in post-colonial Africa or in countries of severe political oppression exhibit aspects of this 'social movement learning'.

The Confederation, Central Unica dos Trabalhadores (CUT) in Brazil, for example, was formed in 1983 and emerged after decades of campaigning against labour regulations inspired by Mussolini and,secondly, against the military coup of 1964 through to 1985 with its suppression of trade unionism. Originating around struggles within the manufacturing sector, CUT has grown to include rural and public sector unions. This growing confidence among the urban working class throughout the 1980s led to the creation of the Workers' Party. From an educational perspective, 'CUT's socialist objectives permeate its education programme' argues Hannah (1992, p. 8). The interrelationship of training and education, she suggests, encourages a cadre-building capacity situated within a broad 'emancipatory' framework.

A similar social-movement model of trade unionism can be found in South Africa; a model of unionism that significantly relies on the informal learning among great swathes of members and participants. The strongest confederation, the Confederation of South African Trade Unions (COSATU), can be traced back to the 1970s. Mass strikes by unorganised workers led to the formation of 'independent trade unions' as distinct from those unions -dominated by white workers and the state. Similar to the educational practice of the CUT in Brazil, worker education in the 1970s and 1980s in South Africa incorporated an organisation-building capacity within a 'militant, action-orientated and oppositional political character' (Cooper, 1997, p. 121) Valuing 'everyday' knowledge and the workers 'own experiences, the learning strongly reflected local context-embedded forms of knowledge arrived at through trade union activity and political struggle. 'There was a self-conscious blurring of boundaries between 'mental' and 'manual' labour (every worker had some form of 'expertise' and knowledge about life and struggle) and between education, culture and struggle' (*ibid.*, p. 121).

Social movement unionism then, with its stress on involvement, participation and mobilisation in the workplace, but within a framework of broader socio-economic change, has continued to provide a rich environment for worker learning. Although 'acquisition' based ways of knowing (formal courses) were developed, of greater significance was the 'participatory' (informal) based form of 'popular education' with its emphasis of local experiential forms of knowledge, inclusivity and equality.

However, the case of the emerging independent trade unions within post-communist societies suggest a number of cautionary caveats to such generalisations. As Ost (2002) points out, in a number of countries, the new eastern-European unions energetically campaigned for the creation of a capitalist system and played an important role in 'educating' workers about their responsibilities and obligations as wage employees. The early years of Solidarity in Poland in the 1980s, for example, were almost exclusively concerned with large successful mobilisations around societal issues to the exclusion of workplace concerns. The success of these Solidarity activities in Poland led to other unions, for example in Bulgaria and Hungary, seeking to replicate this model. However, the lack of attention given to the workplace by Solidarity resulted in dramatic membership losses in the 1990s. Withdrawal by Solidarity from the governing coalition in 2001 together with a greater emphasis on old-fashioned workplace unionism (recruitment, education courses, employer agreements, workplace representation) was expected to reverse the period of decline experienced in the 1990s.

The search for really useful knowledge in periods before the creation of the unions' own institutional programmes, then, was a contested search for a way of knowing that was integral to the unions' social, economic and political activities. There can be little doubt that the socially-purposeful nature of this largely ephemeral, informal learning attracted and influenced large numbers of working people. As will be noted later in the chapter, many of the concerns and debates associated with 'early union learning' were to reappear in later times.

The Institutionalisation of Trade Union Education

Common to many of the earlier forms and understandings of 'worker education' has been a disputed search for distinctiveness ('workers' as opposed to state or 'bosses' education) and self-identity. In the case of trade unions, for much of their history worker education was seen as happening largely through participation in, and membership of, the unions themselves. However, as mentioned above, there have always been a variety of non-union organisations that, in relationships of co-operation, indifference or political hostility, have sought to involve trade unionists in their educational activities. University-provided labour colleges in the USA for example, have been an important location for worker education throughout most of the past century. It was mainly in the period after World War 11 that universities significantly expanded their links with the trade unions. Forty years later, some 46 state supported universities were involved with labour education (Brown, 1981). Elsewhere, although not as extensive as in the USA, university involvement in labour education can be found in numerous countries such as South Africa, Australia, Canada, Britain, Germany and in Scandinavian countries. In the case of Britain, the universities worked in partnership with the Workers' Education Association and for much of the first half of the last century acrimoniously competed over understandings of 'worker education' with the more socialistically orientated independent providers, such as the National Council for Labour Colleges (McIlroy, 1996).

Trade unions themselves, throughout the last century, were beginning to focus greater attention on education. Issues of control, curriculum, costs and participation were to be of increasing importance. The International Ladies Garment Workers Union, with a largely female membership, created the first education department of an American trade union in 1918. This was soon followed by the Amalgamated Clothing Workers and then the United Cloth and Cap Makers. In Britain, the large Transport and General Workers Union created an education department in 1938 based around a curriculum that included the history and organisation of the union, rights and duties of members, negotiating procedures and industrial legislation (McIlroy, 2002, p. 278). The Trades Union Congress (TUC), with which most trade unions are affiliated, appointed a Director of Studies in 1946 to ensure that members are 'trained in the concrete application of the policy and principles of our movement' (as quoted in McIlroy, 2002).

Today many unions from different parts of the world have their own educational programmes and facilities. Even in those countries with weaker economies and fragile trade union structures, financial and personnel support for educational activities is often provided by the larger union confederations from outside the country, by the respective international trade union secretariats or through other international agencies. The Commonwealth Trade Union Council in 2002, for example, was involved in supporting Sierra Leone trade unionists in a civil society programme (with a strong focus on HIV/AIDS), campaigning against child labour in collaboration with trade unions in Botswana, Mozambique, Namibia, Tanzania, Malawi, Zambia and Zimbabwe, encouraging women's participation in Bangladesh unions and in strengthening the voice of unorganised workers in Zimbabwe. In Ghana, the Trades Union Congress has prioritised the education of members as an important part of its difficult struggle against structural adjustment policies. Training at the Ghanain TUC's Labour College covers three broad areas; union organisational issues including health and safety, trade union history and finally, special programmes. Funding support for such union educational initiatives is provided from the Netherlands, the Commonwealth TUC and from the International Confederation of Free Trade Unions (ICFTU). In Niger, the International Labour Organisation since 1999, has been supporting the two national union confederations in the provision of worker's education in the informal sector and the French trade unions are involved in the development of a health insurance project.

Whether in late capitalist economies, the transitional economies of post-communist countries or those societies emerging from political oppression, worker education today is increasingly characterised by its uniformity in curriculum and purpose. Part of the reason for this convergence has been the growth, over the last thirty or so years, of international neo-liberal policies and measures. But these same economic and political pressures and processes are currently behind widespread rethinking of trade union objectives and strategies.

'Modernised' Worker Education

For trade unions, an essential element of worker education will always be the training and enculturation processes necessary to provide future organisational leadership. For most unions, supported where necessary by national, regional and global labour agencies, leadership training is the minimum required of its often scarce educational resources and capabilities. The educational focus on these organisational requirements has been accompanied by an increasingly professional emphasis on the industrial relations agenda. Although often couched within an implicitly oppositional context, the development of alternative economic strategies situated within an historically informed wider socio-economic framework has been of less importance. Labour organisations have always been more than economic actors. While intimately involved with economic systems of production and distribution, labour organisations are also a large grouping within civil society. The aggregation and representation of a wide variety of interests, including often the most vulnerable, has been an important democratic contribution in and out of the workplace. In many parts of the world, trade unions currently play a leading role in struggles against political repression and dictatorships.

Today, however, trade unions almost everywhere are seen to be in crisis. Whether measured by membership loss, declining effectiveness at the workplace level, problems of representation, declining mobilising capacities or curtailment of political choice, there is a widespread global recognition of union decline (Jose, 2002). Whether as a result of internationally imposed structural adjustment policies or as a result of new production regimes within an increasingly hostile or indifferent political environment, trade unions appear to be in difficulties. New forms of capital accumulation and neo-liberal economic policy measures have resulted in unions struggling to adapt to the new disorder in the world economy. Although impacting in different ways in different contexts, the consequences for trade unions have been severe. As Hyman (2001, p. 4) points out,

> The crisis of traditional trade unionism is reflected not only in the more obvious indicators of loss of strength and efficacy, but also in the exhaustion of a traditional discourse and a failure to respond to new ideological challenges – unions have to recapture the ideological initiative.

Much of the debate around experiences and measures of union decline has centred on the necessity of movement away from the traditional uncritical conception of professional unionism encompassed by a 'servicing' model to one which stresses the importance of local innovative organisation (the 'organising' model) or towards 'social movement unionism' with its emphasis on ensuring that unions are part of a broader struggle for social justice. Business or servicing unionism with its narrow focus on the immediate economic interests of workers, in other words, is no longer seen as an adequate strategy in the engagement of a changed political, economic and global environment. Although the specific structural and ideological context will shape what model of unionism works best, the present period is characterised by an unusually wide-ranging discussion on the possibilities, practises and urgency of union reform.

Although rarely discussed, underpinning the debate and reforms already underway are the implications for worker education. The much-heralded moves in late capitalist economies to a 'post-industrial' society with its emphasis on 'knowledge workers', 'smart working' and 'the informational economy' (Castells, 1996), have resulted in an explosion of interest in learning, work and employee subjectivity. Moderised conceptions of work stress the centrality of commitment (to the enterprise), emotional engagement and trust relationships. Capturing the hearts of employees as opposed to the fatigued and exhausted 'physicality' of worker performance, is at the centre of the managerial thinking (Thompson & Warhurst, 1998). Worker experience and knowledge is seen to be the vital new capital resource. In the moves towards a post-Taylorist environment, successfully exploiting this 'human resource' is seen as requiring a variety of workplace organisational reforms such as flattened hierarchies, flexibility, team-working and shifting divisions of labour. Worker motivation, engagement and identification with the workplace are the crucial ingredients of the new production regimes. The collapse of boundaries within the traditionalist Tayloristic distinction between thinking and doing is key to involving the 'whole' employee and enhancing the sense of belonging (Casey, 1995).

The interest in worker knowledge and learning from academics, the state, employers and even trade unions is not new; it has always been an essential element within the labour process. What is new is the lifelong learning policy discourse that is being developed to frame the emphasis on worker skills, knowledge, creativity and 'hidden' knowledge. It is lifelong learning that has emerged as the cement in a strategy that interrelates learning, competitiveness, with inclusiveness within the enterprise and throughout society. Not surprisingly, employee empowerment, experiential learning, informal learning, self-directed learning and the "learning organisation" have suddenly appeared as the de-politicised, official language of the new workplaces. For those long involved with adult learning, such developments have provided a legitimacy and pedagogical space for critically inquiring into previously ignored or marginalised understandings of learning. For trade unions, the new emphasis on worker skill formation and workplace knowledge has returned vocational learning to the industrial relations agenda. For many trade unions in many different countries, union education today is of greater significance than has been the case for most of the last century.

This significance stems from the growing visibility of knowledge and knowing within the production process and, secondly, from the acknowledged need for union reform. Worker knowledge and skills in other words, are an important part of union renewal strategies. The increased significance of 'knowledgeability in work' (as opposed to the largely rhetorical and uncritical notion of 'knowledge workers') has forced unions to encompass a more extensive notion of union learning. While a professional training emphasis continues to be a necessary component of any union educational programme, it is no longer adequate as a means of engaging with the lifelong learning agenda or in responding to the changing 'globalised' environment. Although at an early stage, there are nevertheless indications of change underway. In the case of the American labour movement for example, much attention has focused on the revitalisation currently underway. This is seen to stem, in part, from the new national leadership which has provided resources and institutional support for local efforts to organise, build coalitions and expand the scope of grass-roots politics (Bronfenbrenner et al., 1998). Other commentators, such as Ferge and Kelly (2003) suggest a number of strategies that can be seen as contributing to union revitalisation in general; these include coalition building, labour management partnerships, mergers and internal restructuring and finally, international solidarity. In the USA, campaigning coalitions which are seen as a central component of the revitalisation in American unionism, include the Seattle Coalition, Justice for Janitors in Los Angeles and in several other cities, the nation-wide living wage movement, the anti-sweatshop movement of the late 1990s and the sustainability alliances (Bronfenbrenner, 1998). Coalition building seeks to move beyond 'the special interest group' mentality of business unionism and so broaden the unions' community base while expanding their political influence. While the moves towards an organising and social movement unionism are at an early stage, there are indications in many cases of lasting reform efforts and strategic union successes.

Baccaro and his colleagues (2003) similarly are interested in union revitalisation strategies. They argue, from a mainly European perspective, that 'unions are everywhere re-launching themselves as 'political subjects', as actors not just in collective bargaining and workplace regulation but also in the broader aggregation of political and social interests' (*ibid.*, p. 119). Changing economic activities are forcing unions into expanded political participation. Irrespective of the institutional, historical or cultural variables, unions everywhere are responding to the pressures of global capitalism by recasting themselves and deepening their efforts as political actors beyond their more limited traditional roles as labour market intermediaries. However, the precise nature of this political activism will differ. In the case of the Italian and German unions, the primary strategic development is through institutional involvement or social partnership. In Spain and Britain, there is a greater emphasis on social movement unionism with political engagement underpinning renewal strategies.

Irrespective of which strategy is best suited to national and regional circumstances, it is likely that a parallel rethinking of union education and training will be required. Situating workplace concerns within a broader community and political and global context requires a different order of learning and acting to business unionism; one that is characterised by a critical reflexive quality that begins to acknowledge and address the concerns of 'others'. It will also need to involve as many members in the learning as is possible rather than the earlier focus on those already active within the union. Union learning needs to reflect not the typical 'mass worker' but instead the diverse and fragmented cultural and social groupings that today increasingly make up the labour force. Worker education will be one of the principal vehicles for addressing the decline of traditional union identities and semi-automatic appeal of transformational ideals. The dilution of the communal networks of everyday life that encouraged the formation of collective solidarities is requiring unions to initiate imaginative activities that move beyond the old model of mechanical solidarity to a new model of organic solidarity (Hyman 2002, p. 11). From the evidence available, it seems that an important learning element in the new forms of organic solidarity will be greater attention to the wider socio-economic global environment, to the essentially contested nature of what passes as 'workplace learning' and to the recognition of the disputed claims over worker allegiance that are increasingly part of the 'new workplace'. Much of this worker learning will be of a situated nature; that is, the development of knowing and skills through participation in the concrete everyday activities of unionism. This situational learning is likely to be supported through learning of a more formal nature, involving residential courses, learning materials and campaigning newsletters.

A good example of how unions are expanding their learning activities as an integral part of their renewal efforts is the case of the British unions. For the unions in general and the Trades Union Congress (TUC) in particular, the promotion of learning opportunities for their 7–8 million members has emerged as an important recent success story. Developing learning opportunities for trade union members and non-members is cited as an illustration of 'the modern role for unions' and is seen as 'representing an ambitious and innovative agenda for future union activity' (TUC, 1998, p. 22) Regional networks of Learning Advisors have been established by the TUC and by some affiliated unions to strengthen the vertical and horizontal support for local workplace learning activity. There is some evidence to suggest significant developments towards the 1998 aspiration to 'locate unions at the centre of the learning agenda, raise expectations and encourage members to recognise that unions seriously are key players in the learning world' (TUC, 1998, p. 22). The 'quiet revolution', as the TUC describes this development, has resulted in some 4,500 workplace union learning representatives already trained. By 2010, it is estimated that this figure will have risen to 22,000. Survey evidence suggests that 14,000 people have taken part in some aspect of workplace learning initiated by the unions and over 25,000 people have been involved in awareness-raising activities (Antill et al., 2001). Healy and Engel (2003, p. 4) argue 'that skills and raising productivity are now trade union issues but, first and foremost, unions must re-focus their own organisations to become centres of learning if the trade union movement is to assert its relevance in today's world of work'.

There seems little doubt that British unions have positioned education and training as an important element in their attempt to grapple with the legacy of the hostile political environment characterising the last twenty years or so. However, a dominant perspective of 'employability' frames the nature and content of what is to be understood as 'learning'. Within such a narrow vocational training and skills perspective, often in partnership with the employer; any development of learning initiatives related to a concern with social alliances or community partnerships is much less likely. This emphasis on a narrow economic skills strategy by British trade unions, often at the expense of wider societal concerns, perhaps reflects an overly strong influence by the current 'New Labour' government.

Such tensions resulting from the embedded institutional pathways of political representation within a particular country are not particular to late capitalist environments. As Linda Cooper (1997, p. 121) points out in discussing the situation facing South African trade unions,

> COSATU's policies on worker education and training have been dictated by the perception that for the time being at least, the labour movement has no choice but to defer its long-term goal of socialist transformation and accept some of the consequences of South Africa's new form of insertion into the global capitalist economy.

The trade unions' historically close association with the ruling African National Congress (ANC) is today posing particular and fundamental issues of a strategic nature. The unions' difficulties in successfully dealing with the new global agenda of work intensification and casualisation are straining the links with the ANC and forcing the unions to become more outward looking and to link with unions and social movements globally. Although union education remains a contradictory and incomplete process, the meanings and understandings involved are subject to massive pressures of adaptation and incorporation. The immediate years ahead will reveal the success of South African unions in attempting to bridge the transformational ideals of union education in earlier times with 'modernised' demands for 'relevance' and labour market value.

Conclusions

Worker education strongly reflects the wider socio-economic environment within which labour organisations are situated and seek to change. Trade unions' continuing negotiating is of an unequal character; labour is structurally 'always on the defensive in a capitalist economy, where ownership and economic decision-making lie largely beyond the reach of workers and unions' (Baccaro et al., 2003, p. 119). The distinctive identity of worker education – its view of the world – is thus subject to unrelenting assaults on such issues as autonomy, control and relevance. The beginning of this century is one such period of intensified pressure as unions seek to address the consequences of the political and economic turmoil resulting from the collapse of the planned economies, the fall of racist regimes, the rise of nationalist passions and the insertion of new markets into the 'globalising' environment. The particular strategies adopted by unions will to some extent depend on how close they are to the centre as opposed to the periphery, of this global economic and political disorder. The terrains of union engagement have changed in diverse ways. At another level however, it can be argued that the problems facing unions are not that dissimilar. These problems can be summarised as: a need for greater organisational coherence that integrates support for local activity into the union mainstream; the need for wider societal forms of representation around issues of freedom, democratisation and social justice; the development of alternative agendas and institutions that interrelate local workplace issues to the wider socio-economic environment; and finally, greater attention to international activities and policies. Trade unions today remain on the defensive but have recognised that 'more of the same' is no longer an option. In the experimenting and exploration of possible avenues out of this defensiveness by the trade unions, worker education has emerged as a key vehicle for assisting attempts at addressing recent and current shortcomings. As the authors of a recent text on labour education entitled '*Educating for Change*' note: 'this book celebrates the unions that are using education as a strategy for change and offers tools to further their work' (Burke et al., 2002, p. 1). As unions struggle in different countries and within different institutional arrangements and traditions to cope with the challenges of the global economy, a small measure of their success will depend on the learning initiatives, involvement and breadth of 'knowing' promoted by their educational change strategies.

References

Adams, F. (1975). Unearthing Seeds of Fire: The Idea of Highlander. J. F. Blair, North Carolina: Winston-Salem.

Antil, M., Cutler, J., Brass, J., Mortimore, C., Roder, J., & Shaw, N. (2001). Evaluation of the union learning fund in year 3, Department for Education and Skills, Research Report RR282, Nottingham.

Baccaro, L., Harman, K., & Turner, L. (2003). The politics of labour movement revitalization: The need for a revitalized perspective. *European Journal of Industrial Relations, 9*(1), 119–133.

Billett, S. (2002). Critiquing workplace learning discourses: Participation and continuity at work. *Studies in the Education of Adults, 34*(1), 56–67.

Bratton, J., Helms-Mills, J., Pyrch, T., & Sawchuk, P. H. (2003). *Workplace learning: A critical introduction.* Toronto: Garamond Press.

Bronfenbrenner, K., Fredman, F., Hurd, R., Oswald, R., & Saver, R. (Eds.) (1998). *Organising to win: New research on union strategies.* Ithaca: New York.

Brown, J. (1981). Trade union education in the USA. A comparative note. *The Industrial Tutor, 3*(4), 28–35.

Burke, B., Geronimo, J., D'Arcy, M., Thomas, B., & Wall, C. (2002). *Educating for Changing Unions.* Toronto: Between The Lines.

Casey, C. (1995). *Work, self and society. After industrialisation.* London: Routledge.

Castells, M. (1996). *The rise of the network society.* Oxford: Blackwell.

Congress. T. U. (1998). *TUC 'Learning Services' Task Group Report to Congress 1998.* London: Congress House.

Cooper, L. (1997). *New education policy directions in South Africa: Shifting the boundaries of worker education.* Paper presented at the 27th Annual SCUTREA conference, Birkbeck College, University of London.

Ferge, C. M., & Kelly, J. (2003). Union revitalisation strategies in comparative perspective. *European Journal of Industrial Relations, 9*(1), 7–24.

Hannah, J. (1992). 'Radical' trade union education in Brazil. *The Industrial Tutor, 5*(5), 5–10.

Harrison, J. F. C. (1961). *Learning and living, 1760–1960.* London: Routledge and Keegan Paul.

Healy, J., & Engel, N. (2003). *Learning to organise.* London: Congress House.

Holton, B. (1976). *British Syndicalism 1900–1914.* London: Pluto Press.

Hyman, R. (1989). *The Political Economy of Industrial Relations. Theory and Practice in a Cold Climate.* London: Macmillan Press.

Hyman, R. (2001). *Understanding European Trade Unionism: Between Market, Class and Society.* London: Sage.

Jose, A. V. (Ed.) (2002). *Organized labour in the 21st century.* Geneva: International Institute for Labour Studies.

Kornbluh, J. (1965). *Rebel voices; An IWW anthology.* Ann Arbor: University of Michigan.

McIlroy, J. (1996). Independent working class education and trade union education and training. In R. Fieldhouse (Ed.), *A History of Modern British Adult Education* (pp. 264–289). Leicester: National Institute of Adult Continuing Education.

Ost, D. (2002). The weakness of strong social movements; Models of unionism in the East European context. *European Journal of Industrial Relations, 8*(1), 33–51.

Spencer, B. (2002). *Unions and learning in a global economy. International and comparative perspectives.* Canada: Thompson Educational Publishing.

Thompson, P., & Warhurst, C. (Eds.) (1998). *Workplaces of the Future.* London: Macmillan Press.

Trades Union Congress (1998). TUC 'Learning Services' Task Group Report to Congress 1998. London, Congress House.

52

EXPANDING CONCEPTION OF WORK AND LEARNING: RECENT RESEARCH AND POLICY IMPLICATIONS

David W. Livingstone
Ontario Institute for Studies in Education of the University of Toronto, Canada

A few generations ago, research and policy thinking about learning and work in the advanced capitalist world focussed on education and employment issues. It still does, but not quite so exclusively. The significance of other forms of learning and work are entering social consciousness.

The main reason for the change in thinking about "work" is that with the expansion of commodity production and wage labour into more and more service areas of life, it becomes harder to ignore or deny that those still performing similar domestic and community services without pay are doing important work. The increasing participation of married women in paid employment puts pressure on them to do less domestic labour, on their partners to do more and on both of them to recognized and renegotiate divisions of this labour. Declining time for and interest in volunteer work beyond the household has also accentuated the centrality of this sort of labour for sustaining community life. So discussions about work now at least sometimes take domestic labour and community volunteer work as well as paid employment into explicit account.

In the post WWII expansionary era, capital intensification in extractive and manufacturing industries has put increasing emphasis on human mediation of expensive machinery. The rise of the service sector has been contingent on the selling of labour-intensive services rather than material goods. During this era, school systems were greatly expanded as presumed determinants of economic growth, while learning was often equated with formal schooling. But in the 1960s, de-schooling critics challenged this assumption as did adult educators who documented substantial adult participation in further education courses, training programs and "self-directed" learning projects. As schooling became more pervasive, its limitations in terms of inclusive forms of knowing became more evident. The more recent proliferation of information technologies has made a wider array of work tasks dependent on the self-monitoring use of workers' minds. The motives and learning capacities of the workforce now play a more strategic role in the capitalist labour process. The dominant discourse

International Handbook of Educational Policy, 977–995
Nina Bascia, Alister Cumming, Amanda Datnow, Kenneth Leithwood and David Livingstone (Eds.)
© 2005 *Springer. Printed in Great Britain.*

of management theory has shifted from extrinsic rewards for investment in schooling to promotion of "learning organizations" designed to enable continuing learning and enhance worker motivation to share their knowledge (see Boud & Garrick, 1999). While actual working conditions in most paid workplaces at the turn of the century may seriously diverge from idealized versions of such learning organizations, there is little doubt that employers, employees and researchers alike are paying more concerted conscious attention to workplace learning activities beyond schooling (e.g., Garrick, 1998).

Two related assumptions pervade current discourses about work and learning. First, a "knowledge-based economy" which requires a much higher proportion of highly skilled workers is widely presumed to be rapidly emerging. Secondly, increased emphasis on lifelong learning, the creation of a "learning society", is generally seen as imperative in order for people to acquire the additional knowledge and skills needed to survive in this new economy (e.g., OECD, 1998, p. 10) But a great deal of recent empirical evidence suggests that the converse conditions may actually be prevalent. Careful assessments of the changing occupational composition of the employed labour force and of specific vocational preparation requirements for the aggregate array of jobs in countries like Canada and the U.S. have found only gradual net upgrading of the actual skill requirements of jobs over the past few generations (Lavoie & Roy, 1998; Leckie, 1996; Barton, 2000; Handel, 2000). On the other hand, rates of completion of post-compulsory schooling and participation in further education courses have grown exponentially during the same period (Livingstone, 2002). The underutilization or underemployment of the knowledge and skill of the labour force has also grown significantly during this period (Livingstone, 2004). We may already live in a learning society, but not yet in a knowledge-based economy. In any case, neither the forms of work and learning nor their correspondence should be taken for granted in current policy studies in this field.

Forms and Extent of Work

Over the past two generations, most advanced capitalist economies have experienced a substantial shift from goods-producing jobs to service sector jobs, greatly increased female labour force participation, major increases in the polarization of wealth and poverty, growth in the proportion of temporary and part-time jobs, an increasing use of computer-based technologies in work processes and movement away from the traditional linear school-to-employment model to multiple transitions between school and jobs. All of these trends have undergone uneven rather than consistent trends in response to the intensity of enterprise competition, the supply and organizational strength of labour, and the persistent quest for labour-saving work techniques. These persistent tendencies continue to make capitalism far more dynamic and prolific than any prior mode of production. The recent compositional shifts have not led to a radical change in the organizing principles of industrial societies, but rather only to a greater range and intensity of their applications, what I have elsewhere terms the

"accelerated continuity thesis" (Livingstone, 2004). Recent changes in employment conditions have been exceptionally disruptive and challenging for those
currently in the labour force. While these changes may not have led to very
rapid aggregate increases in required skill levels, they have been associated with
extensive modifications of job types and restructuring of job tasks (see Advisory
Committee on the Changing Workplace, 1997; Betcherman & Lowe, 1997;
Statistics Canada, 1998).

Household work includes such activities as cooking/cleaning, housekeeping,
maintenance and repair, shopping for goods and services, and child and elder
care. The growing recognition of the value of household work corresponds
closely with the entry of married women into the paid labour force. Between
1961 and 1986, one-earner couples dropped extremely rapidly from 65 percent
to 12 percent of all Canadian families (Myles, 1991). According to time use
surveys by the General Social Survey (GSS) in Canada, the amount of time
devoted to household work and paid work are now almost equal (Fredericks,
1993; Status of Women Canada, 1997). Statistics Canada (Jackson, 1996) has
estimated that the monetarized value of household work in 1992 was between
31 and 46 percent of Canada's gross domestic product (GDP). But women still
do most of the household work while men have marginally increased their
"helping out" activities in the home.

Volunteer community work includes participating in community organizations
(through such activities as supervising events, fundraising, serving on a board,
or providing numerous other support services) as well as helping and supporting
non-household relatives and other people on one's own (through driving to
appointments, babysitting, finding information or assisting sick or elderly
people). Recent surveys indicate that while around 70 percent are involved
generally in helping others, most people spend little or no time in organized
volunteer activities. Around one third of Canadian adults now participate in
community organizations and the average time they devote is a few hours per
week (Hall, Knighton, Reed, Bussiere, McRae, & Bowen, 1998). This appears
to be less time than in past generations and the growing scarcity of this volunteer
work has stimulated a burgeoning literature on its centrality for the community
sustainability and generation of "social capital" (Putnam, 2001).

The 1998 GSS survey provides the best recent comparative estimates of the
time Canadians devote to paid work, household work and volunteer community
work. The basic findings for men and women are summarized in Table 1.

Both men and women in Canada today estimate that they put in an average
of nearly 50 hours per week of paid and unpaid work. This is very close to
current estimates in a U.S. time series survey, which found significant increases
from 40 hours in 1973 to 50 hours in 1993, and little change since then in self-
reported hours of work (Harris Poll, 1999). In spite of likely underestimates of
unpaid work, the GSS survey generally finds that Canadian women work for a
slightly greater total of hours than their male counterparts: 3 percent more in
1998 (Status of Women Canada, 1997; Statistics Canada 1999). Similar general

Table 1.   Household Work and Community Volunteer Work Time by Sex, Canada, 1998

	Men (hrs/wk)	Women (hrs/wk)	Both (hrs/wk)
Type of work			
Paid work	28.7	17.5	23.1
Household work	16.8	28.7	22.4
Volunteer work	2.1	2.8	2.8
Total work	47.6	49.0	48.3
Total N	4,856	5,893	10,749

Source: 1998 General Social Survey special tabulation (1998) [population 15 +].

patterns of time use have been found in recent European surveys (Aliaga & Winqvist, 2003).

In sum, while a knowledge-based economy may be emerging gradually, there have been more rapid changes in the distribution of both paid and unpaid work. Unpaid work certainly warrants some consideration in relation to understanding current efforts to acquire more skill and knowledge.

Forms and Extent of Learning

Learning is a continual process and any identification of forms of learning is a somewhat arbitrary exercise. But several basic forms of learning may be roughly distinguished in terms of the primacy of teachers and the type of organization of the body of knowledge to be learned. The basic forms of learning are formal schooling and further education courses as well as informal education and self-directed learning. *Education*, which derives from the Latin verb (educere) meaning "to lead forth", encompasses the first three forms of learning characterized by the presence of a teacher, someone presumed to have greater knowledge, and a learner or learners presumed to have lesser knowledge and expected to be instructed or led by said teacher.

When a teacher has the authority to determine that people designated as requiring knowledge effectively learn a curriculum taken from a pre-established body of knowledge, the form of learning is *formal education*, whether in the form of age-graded and bureaucratic modern school systems or elders initiating youths into traditional bodies of knowledge.

When learners opt to acquire further knowledge or skill by studying voluntarily with a teacher who assists their self-determined interests by using an organized curriculum, as is the case in many adult education courses and workshops, the form of learning is *non-formal education* or *further education*.

When teachers or mentors take responsibility for instructing others without sustained reference to an intentionally-organized body of knowledge in more incidental and spontaneous learning situations, such as guiding them in acquiring job skills or in community development activities, the form of learning is *informal education* or *informal training*.

Finally, all other forms of intentional or tacit learning in which we engage either individually or collectively without direct reliance on a teacher or an externally-organized curriculum can be termed *self-directed* or *collective informal learning*. In the most expansive conceptions of human learning, self-directed learning may be seen as coterminous with life experience itself. Figure 1 portrays these different forms of learning in terms of primary agency and extent of institutionalization of knowledge.

Participation rates in formal schooling have grown very rapidly in the past two generations in all advanced capitalist societies. The vast majority now complete high school and university or college certification is rapidly approaching a majority status in younger age cohorts. Canadian post-secondary completion rates have increased about sixfold since 1960 and now lead the world with around 60 percent of the 25 to 29 population attaining a diploma or degree (Statistics Canada, 2000). Similarly, over 40 percent of the 25 to 64 Canadian population had completed post-secondary education by 2000, followed closely by the United States, Ireland and Japan (Statistics Canada, 2003).

Adult course participation has also expanded rapidly in most OECD countries, coinciding quite closely with increasing post-secondary completion. The more schooling people have, the more further education the appear to seek. In Canada, the increase has been from 4 percent in 1960 to 35 percent in the early 1990s (Livingstone, 2002). In some European countries with stronger and longer traditions of adult education, trends are less pronounced (OECD, 2003).

Informal learning is now widely declared to be an important dimension of lifelong learning. But empirical studies of the extent of informal education and self-directed learning are less frequent and fraught with methodological problems (see Livingstone, 2001). In particular, these two forms of learning are often conflated. Researchers of "learning organizations" increasingly recognize that continued informal training and untaught learning are important for success in the context of paid workplaces (e.g., Matthews & Candy, 1999). Recent survey

		Primary Agency	
		Learner(s)	*Teacher(s)*
	Pre-established	Non-formal education Further education	Formal schooling Elders' teachings
Knowledge Structure			
	Situational	Self-directed learning Collective untaught learning	Informal education Informal training

studies have confirmed that most job-related training is done informally (see Betcherman, Leckie, McMullen, 1997; Center for Workforce Development, 1998). But informal training is not distinguished from non-taught learning in such studies. Conversely, most other studies of informal learning have assumed a learner-centred focus and paid little attention to mentoring activities.

Case studies of the time invested in self-directed learning activities have found that in most social groups – whether distinguished by gender, age, class, race, ableism or nationality – the distribution of the basic amount of time that people were spending on self-directed learning projects was very similar. During the 1970s, the average number of hours devoted to informal learning was generally found to be around 10 hours a week or 500 hours a year in most of these case studies (Tough, 1978). Since the extensive character of informal learning was first indicated by these case studies, there have been very few larger scale surveys to verify and further explore the social relations of informal learning with representative samples (e.g., Johnstone & Rivera, 1965; Penland, 1977). Most of the sample surveys conducted in North America and Europe since the early 1970s on the general frequency of informal learning are summarized in Table 2.

Most of the recent surveys of informal learning (i.e., the Finnish, U.K. and 1998 GSS surveys) very likely produce *serious underestimates* of the actual current extent of intentional informal learning. The questions on informal learning are typically posed immediately after a series of questions about initial schooling, adult credit courses and non-credit courses. This initial emphasis may serve to predispose respondents to think of learning in terms of organized education, especially when only cryptic definitions of informal learning are provided, and no opportunity is usually offered to consider informal learning activities in relation to any other specific learning context besides educational institutions. These survey questions also tend to dichotomize courses and learning on your own, suggesting – explicitly in the case of the GSS survey – that you normally only do one or the other. Virtually all the earlier studies, informed by Tough's case study research, demonstrated this is clearly false. Most course participants also engage in substantial informal learning activities. It is likely that these recent surveys have merely rediscovered the "iceberg" of intentional informal learning rather than plumbing its depths.

The most expansive recent surveys of informal learning have been conducted in Canada. Four surveys conducted in Ontario, Canada between 1996 and 2002 on public attitudes to educational policies have included a few questions which used a similar format to the original Tough studies and the Penland survey. These surveys have found that the vast majority of adults indicate involvement in some form of informal learning during the past year. Estimated time commitments have fluctuated between averages of about 12 and 15 hours per week during this six year period (Livingstone, Hart, & Davie, 2003). In 1998, the research network on New Approaches to Lifelong Learning (NALL) conducted the first national survey in Canada focussed on adults' informal learning practices (NALL, 1998; Livingstone, 1999).[1] The NALL survey respondents were asked

Table 2. Estimated Incidence of Informal Learning Activities, Selected Countries, 1975–2000

Survey*	Sample size	Total hours per year	Informal learners (%)
Hiemstra (1975) [Nebraskans over 55]	256	325	84
Penland (1976) [U.S. national adult population]	1,501	514	76
Tough (1971–78) [Estimate based on 1970s case studies]	N/A	500	98
Leean & Sisco (1981) [Rural Vermont school dropouts]	93	425	98
Blomqvist, Niemi & Ruuskanen (1995) [Finnish adult population]	4,107	20+	22
Livingstone, Hart & Davie (1996) [Ontario adult population]	1,000	600	86
Beinhart & Smith (1994–97) [United Kingdom adult population]	5,653	N/A	57
Statistics Canada (1998) [Canadian national adult population]	10,749	230	30
NALL (1998) [Canadian national adult population]	1,562	750	95
Livingstone, Hart & Davie (1998) [Ontario adult population]	1,007	750	88
Livingstone, Hart & Davie (2000) [Ontario adult population]	1,002	650	86
Livingstone, Hart & David (2002) [Ontario adult population]	1032	600	85

*Years cited refer to period of learning surveyed rather than time of publication.

Sources: Livingstone (2001); Livingstone, Hart and Davie (2003).

to indicate their participation in four aspects of informal learning: employment-related; community volunteer work-related; household work-related; and other general interest-related. In each aspect, respondents were asked about informal learning activities on several specific themes. The most relevant NALL findings are that:

- currently employed respondents (over 60%) estimated that they spent about 6 hours per week in informal learning activities related to their current or future employment during the past year;
- those involved in household work (over 80%) averaged about 5 hours per week in informal learning related to their household work. Given the greater proportion of adults involved in housework than in paid employment and the only slightly higher average hours devoted to informal learning related to employment, it appears that Canadians are now devoting about as much aggregate time to informal learning related to housework as to paid employment.

- those who have been involved in organized community work (around 40%) devote about 3 hours a week on average to community-related informal learning.
- those who engage in some other types of informal learning related to their general interests (around 90%) spend on average about 6 hours a week on these learning activities. These interests range widely from hobbies to religion.
- overall, according to the NALL survey, nearly all Canadian adults (over 95%) are involved in some form of informal learning activities that they can identify as significant. The estimated average number of hours devoted to all forms of informal learning activities by all Canadian adults during 1998 was around 15 hours per person per week. There is considerable variation from the less than 5 percent who insist they are doing no informal learning, to the 25 percent who say they are doing over 20 hours per week. About three-quarters of Canadian adults are now spending 6 hours or more each week in some kind of self-reported intentional informal learning activities, most of this related to paid or unpaid work.

The NALL survey estimate for the amount of time that Canadian adults are spending in organized courses (including time in class and doing homework and class assignments) is about 3 hours per week averaged over the entire adult population, or about 12 hours per week among those who actually participated in courses. The most recent national survey of further education, which focussed in more detail on different types of non-formal course participation but only asked about hours participants took the course rather than explicitly asking them to consider homework time, generated an average of about 1 hour a week for the entire adult population or 4 hours a week per participant (Arrowsmith & Oikawa, 2001, p. 35). Even if the focus is restricted to those who participated in courses, they appear to devote slightly more time to intentional informal learning activities than to course-based learning. If we consider the entire adult population, *Canadian adults are clearly spending vastly more time in intentional informal learning activities than in non-formal education courses, a ratio of about five to one.* The use of the metaphor of the submerged part of an "iceberg" to describe the informal portion of adult learning is fairly apt.

In summary, the few inclusive and directly comparable surveys on adult informal learning suggest that North Americans were spending around 10 hours per week in intentional informal learning activities in the 1970s, and that the incidence may have been greater in the past decade (see also Candy, 1993). Clearly, the overwhelming majority of Canadian adults are now spending a substantial amount of time regularly in these pursuits and are able to recognize this intentional informal learning as a significant aspect of their daily lives. The recent proliferation of information technologies and exponential increases in the production of information may have created greater opportunities for informal learning beyond their own direct experience for people in all walks of life. Whatever the actual extent and trends over time are found to be through further, more refined studies, virtually all empirical studies to date that have estimated the extent of adults' intentional informal learning have confirmed that it is a very extensive activity. When the incidence of informal learning is considered in conjunction with the greatly increased participation in advanced schooling and further education, it is reasonable to conclude that the "learning society" has arrived, both in Canada and in other advanced capitalist societies. Given the finite amount of time available for all forms of learning, we might also expect some substitution effects between formal and informal learning activities. It may be that the incidence of informal learning is greater in less credentialed societies. It may also be that informal learning decreases when adult education course participation increases in highly credentialed societies. In any case, informal learning in paid workplaces is now of major strategic interest in the major capitalist societies, as many of the chapters in this section indicate.

Theories of Work and Learning Relations

There is much theoretical dispute about the changing nature of work, adult learning processes, and learning-work relations.

Scientific debate about the changing nature of paid work has become polarized into approaches that emphasize more flexible employment structures which are typically driven by increased global competition as well as new information technologies to more fully engage the skills of employees (e.g., Sabel, 1982; Hirst & Zeitlin, 1991; Dastmalchian & Blyton, 2001), and opposed perspectives that stress the continuities of mass production and persistent tendencies to routinizing de-skilling in the labour process (e.g., Braverman, 1974; Kumar, 1995). A potentially more fruitful approach is suggested by flexible accumulation theory (Harvey, 1989; Rubin, 1995) which posits that integrated internal organizational structures are becoming increasingly destabilized and that the structures of work and employment relations are being refashioned in more complex and contradictory ways. Dominant predicted tendencies include sharpening divisions between core and peripheral employees, expanded centrality of the formal knowledge of professional employees, further standardization and quantification of work methods of other employees, and growing reliance on subcontracting by core organizations, all of which have been tentatively confirmed by the most thorough empirical assessments to date (Commission on Behavioral and Social Sciences and Education, 1999; Vallas, 1999).

Much learning theory continues to be preoccupied with individual cognition and maturation as reflected in school testing programs. The general literature on adult learning has increasingly emphasized independent and self-directed learning under the impetus of accumulated experience (Knowles, 1980; Cyr, 1999) but these studies have not led to any distinctive theory of adult learning (Brookfield, 1995). Learning is increasingly understood as an interactive process through which learners socially construct their own understanding of the world they live in, for example by reflecting on their experiences in relation to a variety of mentors, peers and other sources for learning. Studies of learning have generally become increasingly sensitive to the effects of contextual factors on learning processes and outcomes as indicated by research on distinctive modes of thought in different socio-historical settings (e.g., Luria, 1981) and on the hidden curriculum of schooling (Rosenthal & Jacobson, 1992). Vygotsky's (1986) socio-cultural theory of learning argues that learning is inescapably a historically specific process, whereby learners are socialized into using appropriate cognitive and communicative tools by more capable caretakers, teachers and peers, extend their competencies with the help of others (the zone of proximal development), and become increasingly capable of independent learning. Developments of this perspective in activity theory (Engestrom, Miettinen, & Punamaki, 1999) and situated learning theory (Lave & Wenger, 1991) have generated a corpus of case studies on work-based learning. However, to date, researchers using this approach have only begun to offer specific arguments about adult learning in relation to the changing nature of work (e.g., Livingstone & Sawchuk, 2004). A fruitful approach to further empirical studies of adult learning may be guided by a general notion of the flexible accumulation of knowledge and skills in relation to a widening array of contextual factors within and beyond workplaces.

Theorists also differ widely about the relations between learning activities and paid work requirements in the new economy. Most theories of the relationship between learning and work can be identified as *supply-side determined, demand-side determined or supply-demand interactive* (see Livingstone, 2004). *Supply-side theories* basically suggest that the pursuit of more advanced education generates more productive workers and that their "intellectual capital" investment leads to a more prosperous economy. Human capital theories which assume that investment in education necessarily results in increased economic growth are the leading examples (Becker, 1964, 1993). Invest in education and good jobs will follow. *Demand-side theories* are more diverse. On the one hand, the increasingly dominant advocates of either a "post-industrial society" or a "knowledge-based economy" assume that modern information-based production systems generally require workers with substantially more complex analytic and design skills to operate them, and that education systems must increasingly respond to the need to produce such knowledge workers (Machlup, 1980; Marshall & Tucker, 1994). On the other hand, the prophets of the degradation of paid work argue that inherent tendencies within modern production systems are leading either to a profound deskilling of job requirements or widespread automation, with consequent proliferation of underemployment and unemployment (Braverman, 1974; Rifkin, 1995). In both optimistic and pessimistic varieties of demand-side theories, the labour force as well as employers are generally regarded as reactive to secular trends rather than influencing these trends through increased learning or other activities. *Supply-demand interactive theories* emphasize the relational character of education and job connections in terms of the bargaining processes between employers and current or prospective employees as well as state agencies A real or anticipated oversupply of highly qualified job seekers may lead employers and/or well-organized groups of professional or skilled employees to try either directly or through legislative means to raise entry criteria substantially beyond what is actually required to perform the work. Screening theories suggest that greater formal education serves as an admission ticket to better jobs but is not necessarily related to greater productivity (Stiglitz, 1975). Credential society theories explain job entry processes in terms of the power of these groups to construct restrictive qualification regimes (Collins, 1979). Conversely, either an undersupply of qualified applicants or the prospect of greater productivity from an underutilized workforce could provoke redesign of job performance demands.

Generally speaking, supply-demand interaction theories have been better able to explain observable patterns of education-employment relations than simpler supply-side or demand-side theories. The most notable evidence is the now substantial occurrence of underemployment and under-qualification mismatches between the educational qualifications among the available labour force and aggregate job requirements. The particular version of a supply-demand interaction theory of education-employment relations espoused by the current author posits specific patterns of the degree of matching of knowledge attainments and job requirements determined by continuing negotiations between specific groups of class, gender, generation, imputed ability and ethnically-based agents with differential power (see Livingstone, 2004). We expect to find highest levels of underutilization of working knowledge in the jobs held by those in lower occupational class positions, as well as among those job holders whose general subordination in society has put them at a disadvantage in negotiations over working conditions, especially women, younger people, ethnic and racial minorities, recent immigrants and those labelled as "disabled. Similarly, this knowledge-power model predicts single mothers, who are among the most powerless, will tend to have very high levels of underemployment regardless of their prior level of formal education. These negotiations are mediated through previously institutionalized forms of work and learning. We continue to make our own work and learning histories but in constrained contexts not of our own choosing. This interactive theory posits that inter-firm competition, technological innovation, and conflicts between employers and employees over working conditions, benefits and knowledge requirements all lead to incessant shifts in the numbers and types of jobs available. Population growth cycles, modified household needs and new legislative regulations also frequently serve to alter the supply of labour. At the same time, popular demand for general education and specialized training increases cumulatively as people generally seek more knowledge, different skills and added credentials in order to live and work in such a changing society. So, there are always some "mismatches" between employers' aggregate demand and requirements for employees on the one hand, and the aggregate supply and qualifications of job seekers on the other. The accelerating productivity of private enterprises regularly throws workers into unemployment, reproducing the most evident part of a reserve army of labour. In societies like Canada, with liberal democratic state regimes that acclaim the right to equal educational opportunity and with labour markets in which both employers and job seekers make mainly individual employment choices, the dominant historical tendency is posited to have been an excess of supply of educationally qualified job seekers over the demand for any given type of job. These same dynamics are also posited to generate formal underqualification of some workers, particularly older employees who are experienced in their jobs and have had few incentives to upgrade their credentialed skills. In addition to unemployment and credential gaps, other dimensions of underemployment (i.e., involuntary temporary employment, performance gaps and subjective underemployment) are also posited to differentially effect subordinated workers (see Livingstone, 2004).

This interactive theory of education and employment should be extended to the spheres of unpaid work and informal learning that conventional theoretical perspectives on employment and organized education usually ignore. Across all three spheres of work, the correspondence between knowledge attainments and work requirements is posited to differ markedly by social position, with the greatest discrepancies experienced by those with the least economic or political power to define the appropriate requirements for their work. Greater levels of learning-work correspondence should generally be found between unpaid work and informal learning because of less pronounced power hierarchies in these spheres of activity. Household labour is just as necessary as paid employment labour for social reproduction, but the more economically and politically powerful tend to do less of it. Women who lack or have relatively little employment-based bargaining power still do most of the unpaid household labour with little recognition, but they have somewhat greater discretionary control over both the extent and intensity of this work and the related learning activities. Since people are not generally compelled to do community volunteer work, we posit that relevant informal learning activities may be more closely associated with involvement in this sort of work than either hierarchically structured employment or necessary domestic labour.

Empirical Research on Work and Learning Relations

This more inclusive and dynamic perspective on work and learning relations has informed some of the most recently completed empirical research in this field (see www.nall.ca). This ongoing corpus of survey, case study and secondary analyses (see www.wall.utoronto.oise.ca) has found preliminary support for the main posited learning and work relations. First, aggregate educational attainments are generally outpacing skill upgrading of the job structure (Livingstone, 2001, 2004). That is, growing proportions of both the currently employed and unemployed appear to have greater knowledge and skill than current jobs require. More specifically, the majority of the labour force who are industrial and service workers are found to have the highest underemployment rates.

Secondly, the possibility of substitution effects between formal education and informal learning is supported by survey evidence which suggests that the levels of participation in adult education courses declined during the mid-1990s (Arrowsmith & Oikawa, 2001; Livingstone, Hart, & Davie, 1999), while perceived material barriers to adult education course participation and the incidence of informal learning both increased (Livingstone, Raykov, & Stowe, 2001; Livingstone, Hart, & Davie, 1999). More recent evidence suggests that adult course participation may have again increased and that the incidence of informal learning may have declined somewhat (Livingstone, Hart, & Davie, 2001, 2003). The possibility of such an inverse relationship, with increased incidence of informal learning substituting for diminished access to further education courses and vice versa, should be examined by additional longitudinal surveys. But any examination of such an inverse relationship should not lose sight of the dominant trend of increasing formal course participation in the post WWII era, the fact that informal self-directed learning and informal training remain far more pervasive than course participation and the practical complementarity of all four types of learning through the life course. With further reliable estimates of informal learning over time and in different jurisdictions, it should be possible to estimate effectively the relationships between organized schooling and non-formal education on the one hand and informal learning and training on the other.

Thirdly, nearly all prior studies of employment-related further education have found that managerial and professional employees receive more of it than lower level employees (e.g., Statistics Canada, 2001). But there has been virtually no prior systematic research beyond scattered ethnographic studies on the relations between informal learning and training and different types of paid and unpaid work. Correlation analysis of the association between the time devoted to different types of work (employment, housework and community volunteer work) and informal learning specifically-related to these three types of work in the 1998 NALL survey found that association is highest between community volunteer work and community-based informal learning and lowest between paid employment and job-related informal learning (Livingstone, 2002). This supports the prediction that the greater discretion one has to engage in the work, the stronger the association between the hours of such work and the related incidence of informal learning. Prior research on relations between degrees of autonomy in paid employment and personality characteristics is of some relevance (e.g., Kohn & Schooler, 1983), but no other empirical studies have addressed these relations between types of informal learning and work inclusively to date.

Fourthly, all empirical studies of informal learning that have included different social groups have found few significant differences in the distribution of time devoted to this learning across groups, and consequently no strong relations with success in formal schooling. Two aspects are most notable. Prior research on aging and learning has focussed on declining speed and efficiency of skill acquisition. No comparable decline has been found in the incidence of informal learning. Case studies and experimental research examining the actual informal learning practices, topical foci and skill outcomes of older adults are much needed to get beyond stereotypes of decline and to understand the interaction of cumulative experience and new skill acquisition. Similarly, youth in the transition to adulthood appear to devote somewhat more time to informal learning than all older adults. This includes school dropouts; discouraged students are not discouraged learners. More attention needs to be paid to the distinctively high incidence of both organized education activities and informal learning among those making the transition to adulthood. The general finding of no significant differences in incidence of informal learning activity between most socio-demographic groups also needs to be tested much more thoroughly against reliable measures of informal learning over time. Further more sensitive case studies may also discover significant content differences in the informal learning practices of socially disadvantaged groups.

The further development and testing of more inclusive, interactive supply-demand models of knowledge-power relations in learning and work is likely to provide a better understanding of the distinctiveness of actual learning practices and a more effective guide to social policy making in current capitalist economies than simpler assumptions of human capital theory or a knowledge-based economy perspective.

Policy Implications and Concluding Remarks

More comprehensive documentation of organized and informal learning activities in relation to the existing job structure and patterns of unpaid work should provide a more adequate basis for developing employment policies that are more responsive to the actual employability of the current and prospective labour force. For example, the issues of whether there are skill surpluses or shortages in specific sectors and whether training or economic policy priorities are most appropriate really require such intelligence to aid effective, sustained government decision-making. There is mounting evidence, based on measures of occupational structures and organized education and training, that there is now no general skill shortage in many advanced industrial societies (see Lavoie & Roy, 1998). This is in addition to the large body of empirical evidence indicating that aggregate educational attainments have increased much quicker than aggregate educational requirements to perform existing jobs, particularly in Canada and the U.S. (see Livingstone, 2004). The increasing documentation of informal self-learning and training relevant to actual job performance and to unpaid work activities tends to accentuate the growing gap. Aside from the small but important proportion of adults with low literacy and increasing marginalization from the credential-based labour market, the most basic problem now may not be skill supply shortages but underemployment of people's available skills and knowledge in our current job structure. In any event, neither researchers nor public policy makers can afford to ignore the growing problem of training-employment gaps. More comprehensive ongoing surveys of adult learning are clearly needed to inform employment and training policies. As the OECD (1997) *Manual for Better Training Statistics* suggest, the temptation to focus narrowly on the most easily identifiable and immediately applicable aspects of vocational learning in such research and ignore more extensive informal workplace learning activities should be resisted.

Efforts to measure returns to informal learning and training should proceed very cautiously given the elusive character of these activities, and the differential interests of employers and employees and other citizens in controlling access to working knowledge. Further case studies and comparative sectoral studies should address the relative and complementary effectiveness of informal learning and training and organized education programs/courses in relation to a wide range of indicators of social benefit, including productivity and sustainable employment. But future rate of return estimates should beware of the "most immediately tangible measures bias". A pragmatic fixation on monetary rates of return for the employed labour force alone excludes consideration of benefits of education and training for the unemployed and non-employed (about 40% of adult population in most countries), other non-monetary benefits for all people including the employed (consumption effectiveness, informed citizenship, familial health), and macro-societal benefits (besides Gross Domestic Product, these should include Quality of Life measures). While both the extent and rates of return to informal learning and training are much less well documented than either schooling or non-formal training, informal learning and training could well turn out to be the most productive investments in terms of a more inclusive cost-benefit analysis of lifelong learning.

While there are continuing conceptual difficulties in distinguishing informal self-directed learning, informal training, non-formal education and formal education, as well as methodological challenges in generating reliable readings of informal learning and training, the empirical research to date has at least established that adults' intentional informal learning activities are very extensive and warrant continuing documentation and assessment in relation to other economic and social activities. The insights generated by the early adult education research on self-directed learning should be taken into fuller account in future large-scale surveys of informal learning activities. Most pertinent in social justice terms is the consistent finding of virtually all prior studies that the basic incidence of adult informal learning is not closely related to either prior formal educational participation or most socio-demographic differences. This suggests that the more effective recognition of prior informal learning in both work settings and educational institutions – through further research and fuller use of prior learning recognition mechanisms – could stimulate greater educational accessibility and enhanced workplace utilization of knowledge. Enhanced policies and programs to recognize and reward relevant prior informal learning should be developed for most educational institutions and places of employment.

The recognition of the extent and economic value of household work and community volunteer work should also lead to fuller understanding and appreciation of the relevance of related informal learning and to policies and programs to facilitate the lateral transfer of acquired knowledge and skills into the sphere of employment (see the Eichler and Schugurensky and Mundel papers in this section).

Perhaps the exposure of the large and increasing extent of underemployment, a gap which is only increased by inclusion of informal learning, has the most significant policy implication of all the recent research on learning and work relations. Given the irreversibility of knowledge acquisition, the most plausible conclusion is that current job structures should be reformed to accommodate such cumulative knowledge through measures including further democratization of many paid workplaces, creation of new environmentally sustainable forms of paid work ("green jobs"), and redistribution of paid work through reduced normal work weeks (see Livingstone, 2004).

Those committed to the principles of lifelong learning and the democratic provision of work in these changing times (see OECD, 1998) should seriously consider incorporating three largely ignored dimensions into their current studies and policy formation on learning and work issues. These dimensions are the still largely hidden informal mass of the iceberg of adult learning, the still widely underestimated import of essential unpaid work, as well as the growing social problem of underemployment.

Notes

1. In addition to the first national survey of informal learning practices, NALL also conducted a parallel national survey of teachers' informal learning practices, and completed follow-up surveys, as well as over 30 related case studies. Most of these studies examine the relations between informal learning, schooling and further education, as well as their relations with paid and unpaid work and other socio-demographic characteristics. For further information, see the NALL website: www.nall.ca. This research is continuing under a new national research network on "The Changing Nature of Work and Lifelong Learning" (WALL). The WALL website is: www.wall.oise.utoronto.ca. Both of these research networks have been funded by the Social Sciences and Humanities Research Council of Canada.

References

Advisory Committee on the Changing Workplace (1997). *Collective Reflection on the Changing Workplace.* Ottawa: Human Resources Development Canada.

Aliaga, C., & Winqvist. K. (2003). How women and men spend their time: Results from 13 European countries. *Eurostat Statistics in Focus: Population and Social Conditions, 3,* 1–7.

Arrowsmith, S., & Oikawa, C. (2001). Trends in Canadian adult learning. In Statistics Canada. *A Report on Adult Education and Training in Canada: Learning a Living.* Ottawa: Statistics Canada and Human Resources Development Canada.

Barton, P. E. (2000). *What jobs require: Literacy, education and training, 1940–2006.* Princeton, NJ: Educational Testing Service.

Becker, G. S. (1964). *Human capital: A theoretical and empirical analysis, with special reference to education.* New York: National Bureau of Economic Research.

Becker, G. (1993). *Human capital* (3rd ed.). Chicago: University of Chicago Press.

Beinhart, S., & Smith, P. (1998). *National adult learning survey 1997.* Sudbury, Suffolk: Department for Education and Employment. Research Report No. 49.

Betcherman, G., & Lowe, G. (1997). *Canadian policy research networks: The future of work in Canada.* Ottawa, ON: Renouf Publishing Company, Ltd.

Betcherman, G., Leckie, N., & McMullen, K. E. (1997). *Developing skills in the Canadian workplace: The results of the Ekos workplace training survey* (CPRN Study #W 92). Ottawa: Canadian Policy Research Networks.

Blomqvist, I., Niemi, H., & Ruuskanen, T. (1998). *Participation in adult education and training in Finland 1995*. Helsinki: Statistics Finland.

Boud, D., & Garrick, J. (Eds.) (1999). *Understanding learning at work*. London: Routledge.

Braverman, H. (1974). *Labor and monopoly capital*. New York: New York Monthly Review Press.

Brookfield, S. (1995). *Becoming a critically reflective teacher*. San Francisco: San Francisco: Jossey-Bass.

Candy, P. (1993). *Self-direction for lifelong learning: A comprehensive guide to theory and practice*. San Francisco: Jossey-Bass.

Center for Workforce Development (1998). *The teaching firm: Where productive work and learning converge*. Newton, Mass.: Education Development Center.

Collins, R. (1979). *The credential society: An historical sociology of education and stratification*. New York: Academic Press.

Commission on Behavioral and Social Sciences and Education (1999). *The changing nature of work: Implications for occupational analysis*. Washington, DC. National Academy Press.

Cyr, A. V. (1999). *Overview of theories and principles relating to characteristics of adult learners: 1970s–1999*. Cyr Consultant Service.

Dastmalchian A, & Blyton, P. (2001). Workplace flexibility and the changing nature of work: An introduction. *Canadian Journal of Administrative Sciences, 18*(1), 1–4.

Engestrom, Y., Miettinen, R., & Punamaki, R-L. (Eds.) (1999). *Perspectives on activity theory*. Cambridge: Cambridge University Press.

Fredericks, J. (1993). *A comparison of results from the general social survey on time use-1986 and 1992*. Ottawa: Statistics Canada.

Garrick, J. (1998). *Informal learning in the workplace: Unmasking human resource development*. New York: Routledge.

Hall, M., Knighton, T., Reed, P., Bussiere, P., McRae, D., & Bowen, P. (1998). *Caring Canadians, involved Canadians: Highlights from the 1997 national survey of giving, volunteering and participating*. Ottawa: Minister of Industry.

Handel, M. (2000). *Trends in direct measures of job skill requirements*. Working Paper No. 301, Jerome Levy Economics Institute. Retrieved on March 10, 2004 from www.levy.org/does/wrkpap/papers.

Harris Poll. (1999, June). *Time at work and play*. Press release of June 10–15, 1999 survey.

Harvey, D. (1989). *The condition of postmodernity*. London: Blackwell.

Hiemstra, R. (1976). *Lifelong learning*. Lincoln: Professional Educators Publications.

Hirst, P., & Zeitlin, J. (1991). Flexible specialization versus post-Fordism: Theory, evidence and policy implications. *Economy and Society, 20*(1), 1–56.

Jackson, C. (1996). Measuring and valuing households' unpaid work. *Canadian Social Trends* (Autumn), 25–29.

Johnstone, J., & Rivera, R. (1965). *Volunteers for learning: A study of the educational pursuits of American adults*. Chicago: Aldine.

Knowles, M. (1980). *The modern practice of adult education: From pedagogy to andragogy* (2nd ed.). Cambridge, The Adult Education Co., New York.

Kohn, M., & Schooler, C. (1983). *Work and personality: An inquiry into the impact of social stratification*. Norwood, NJ.: Ablex.

Kumar, K. (1995). *From post-industrial to post-modern society: New theories of the contemporary world*. Oxford: Blackwell.

Lave, J., & Wenger, M. (1991). *Situated learning: Legitimate peripheral participation*. Cambridge: Cambridge University Press.

Lavoie, M., & Roy, R. (1998). *Employment in the knowledge-based economy: A growth accounting exercise for Canada*. Ottawa: Applied Research Branch, Strategic Policy, HRDC.

Leckie, N. (1996). *On skill requirements trends in Canada, 1971–1991*. Research Report for Human Resources Development Canada and Canadian Policy Research Networks.

Leean, C., & Sisco, B. (1981). *Learning projects and self-planned learning efforts among undereducated adults in rural Vermont*. Washington, D.C.: National Institute of Education.

Livingstone, D. W. (1999). Exploring the icebergs of adult learning: Findings of the first Canadian survey of informal learning practices. *Canadian Journal for the Study of Adult Education, 13*(2), 49–72.

Livingstone, D. W. (2001). *Adults' informal learning: Definitions, findings, gaps and future research.* Position paper for the Advisory Panel of Experts on Adult Learning, Applied Research Branch, Human Resources Development Canada.

Livingstone, D. W. (2002). *Working and learning in the information age: A profile of Canadians.* Ottawa: Canadian Policy Research Networks. [free download from www.cprn.org].

Livingstone, D. W. (2004). *The education-jobs gap: Underemployment or economic democracy.* Toronto: Garamond Press (2nd ed.).

Livingstone, D. W., Hart, D., & Davie, L. E. (1997). *Public attitudes toward education in Ontario 1996: Eleventh OISE/UT survey.* Toronto: University of Toronto Press.

Livingstone, D. W., Hart, D., & Davie, L. E. (1999). *Public attitudes toward education in Ontario 1998: Twelfth OISE/UT Survey.* Toronto: University of Toronto Press.

Livingstone, D. W., Hart, D., & Davie, L. E. (2001). *Public attitudes toward education in Ontario 2000: Thirteenth OISE/UT survey.* Toronto: OISE Press.

Livingstone, D. W., Hart, D., & Davie, L. E. (2003). *Public attitudes toward education in Ontario 2002: Fourteenth OISE/UT Survey.* Toronto: OISE Press.

Livingstone, D. W., Raykov, M., & Stowe, S. (2001). *Interest in and factors related to participation in adult learning and informal learning.* Ottawa: Human Resources Development Canada. Research Paper R-01-9-3E.

Livingstone, D. W., & Sawchuk, Peter H. (2004). *Hidden knowledge: Organized labour in the information age.* Toronto: Garamond Press and New York: Rowman and Littlefield.

Luria, A. R. (1981). *Cognitive development: It is cultural and social foundations.* Cambridge. Harvard University Press.

Machlup, F. (1980). *Knowledge, its creation, distribution and economic significance.* Princeton: Princeton University Press.

Marshall, R., & Tucker. M. (1994). *Thinking for a living: Education and the wealth of nations.* New York: Basic Books.

Matthews, J. H., & Candy, P. C. (1999). New dimensions in the dynamics of learning and knowledge. In D. Boud & J/ Garrick (Eds.), *Understanding learning at work.* Routledge, London.

Myles, J. (1991). Women, the welfare state and care giving. *Canadian Journal on Aging, 10*(2), 82–85.

NALL (1998). *Lifelong learning profiles: General summary of findings from the first Canadian survey of informal learning* (www.nall.ca).

OECD Documents (1997). *Manual for better training statistics: Conceptual, measurement and survey issues.* Paris: OCED.

OECD (1998). Lifelong learning: A monitoring framework and trends in participation. in centre for educational research and innovation. *Education Policy Analysis 1998* (pp. 7–24), Paris: OECD, .

OECD (2003). *Education at a glance: OECD indicators.* Paris: OECD.

Penland, P. (1977). *Self-planned learning in America.* Pittsburgh: University of Pittsburgh.

Putnam, R. (2001). *Bowling alone: The collapse and revival of American community.* New York: Simon and Schuster.

Rifkin, J. (1995). *The end of work: The decline of the global labor force and the dawn of the post-market era.* New York: Tarcher/Putnam.

Rosenthal, R., & Jacobson, L. (1992). *Pygmalion in the classroom: Teacher expectation and pupils' intellectual development.* Irvington Publishers: New York.

Rubin, Beth A. (1995). Flexible accumulation: The decline of contract and social transformation. *Research in Social Stratification and Mobility, 14,* 297–323.

Sabel, C. (1982). *Work and politics: The division of labor in industry.* New York: Cambridge University Press.

Statistics Canada (1997). *Adult education and training in Canada: Report of the 1994 adult education and training survey.* Ottawa: Statistics Canada.

Statistics Canada (1998). *The evolving workplace: Findings from the pilot workplace and employee survey.* Ottawa: Statistics Canada.

Statistics Canada (1999). *Public use tape for the general social survey 1998.* Available for the University of Toronto Data Archive.

Statistics Canada (2000). *Education indicators in Canada: Report of the pan-Canadian education indicators program 1999.* Ottawa: Statistics Canada.

Statistics Canada (2001). *Learning and living: A report on adult education and training in Canada.* Ottawa: Statistics Canada. Catalogue no. 81–586-XPE.

Statistics Canada (2003). *Education in Canada: Raising the standard. 2001 census: 2001: Analysis series.* Ottawa: Statistics Canada. Catalogue no. 960030XIE2001012.

Status of Women Canada (1997). *Economic gender equality indicators.* Ottawa: Federal-Provincial/Territorial Ministers Responsible for the Status of Women.

Stiglitz, J. (1975). The theory of screening, education, and the distribution of income. *American Economic Review, 65,* 283–300.

Tough, A. (1971). *The adult's learning projects.* Toronto: OISE Press.

Tough, A. (1978). Major learning efforts: Recent research and future directions. *Adult Education Quarterly, 28*(4), 250–263.

Vallas, S. P. (1999). Rethinking post-Fordism: The meaning of workplace flexibility. *Sociological Theory, 17*(1), 68–101.

Vygotsky, L. (1986). *Mind in society.* Cambridge: Harvard University Press.

53

VOLUNTEER WORK AND LEARNING: HIDDEN DIMENSIONS OF LABOUR FORCE TRAINING

Daniel Schugurensky and Karsten Mündel
Ontario Institute for Studies in Education of the University of Toronto, Canada

This chapter explores the links between learning and voluntary work, a topic that is usually absent both in the academic literature and in policy debates. Two reasons may account for the scant attention paid to this issue. First, unpaid work (such as household work and volunteer work) is seldom considered as 'real' work, and therefore the literature on labour force training tends to focus on paid labour, often within the formal sector of the economy. Second, most of the learning connected to volunteer work falls into the category of informal learning, a field that only recently has captured the attention of educational researchers, who traditionally have focussed their efforts on the formal education system. In the late nineties, however, this situation began to change, as the interest of researchers in both areas grew.

In relation to unpaid work, only a few years ago researchers began to document the economic contribution of volunteer work, and the emerging findings are not trivial. A recent study of 22 OECD countries estimates that volunteer contributions (made by approximately 28% of the population) were equivalent to 10.6 million full-time jobs and their value added amounted to $840 billion, representing 3.5% of the Gross Domestic Product (GDP) of those countries (Salamon et al., 1999). In Canada, volunteer work contributes the equivalent of close to 550,000 full-time jobs per year, which represents 11% of the total labour contribution, and an addition of about $13 billion to the national economy – about 1.4% of the Canadian GDP. Moreover, volunteers contribute significant amounts to the economy in out-of-pocket expenses ($841 million in the late 1980s) that are not reimbursed (Hall, McKeown, & Roberts, 2001; Statistics Canada, 2001; Ross & Shillington, 1990; Duchesne, 1989; Quarter, Mook, & Richmond, 2003). The recognition of the economic and social contribution of volunteer work, compounded with the new awareness of the impressive nature and scope of this contribution, are leading to an understanding that volunteer work is indeed 'real work'.

Regarding informal learning, a few years ago, after a quarter century of relative oblivion, educational researchers began to explore systematically this field once

International Handbook of Educational Policy, 997–1022
Nina Bascia, Alister Cumming, Amanda Datnow, Kenneth Leithwood and David Livingstone (Eds.)
© 2005 Springer. Printed in Great Britain.

again. One of the most serious initiatives in this regard was conducted between 1996 and 2001 by the New Approaches to Lifelong Learning research network (NALL), led by David Livingstone, a professor at the Ontario Institute for Studies in Education of the University of Toronto (OISE/UT). Building on the pioneering efforts carried out by Alan Tough in the early 1970s at the same institution (Tough, 1971), NALL completed the first extensive national survey of informal learning practices ever conducted in Canada. Five main findings arose from this survey and related exploratory case studies carried out by NALL associates. First, it was found that Canadian adults were engaging in a vast array of informal learning activities in relation to their paid employment, house-work, community volunteer work and general interests. This is learning that people reported doing on their own outside any educational institutions or organized courses. Second, it was found that work-related informal learning was much more extensive than participation in adult education courses and pro-grams. Third, the general incidence of informal learning appears to have increased over the past quarter century, from an average of 10 hours per week in the early seventies (as reported by Tough) to 15 hours in the late nineties. Fourth, NALL researchers did not find any strong correlation between informal learning and either formal schooling or participation in adult education courses. Indeed, adults with little formal schooling or adult course participation were just as likely to devote time to informal learning as are the highly schooled. Finally, and this is particularly relevant for this chapter, NALL researchers found a much stronger association between community volunteer work time and com-munity-related informal learning than there is between paid employment time and job-related informal learning. This finding supports the hypothesis that greater discretionary control or self-management can lead to fuller use of work-related skills and knowledge (Livingstone, 1999).

Although these two bodies of literature (on informal learning and on volunteer work) have been growing significantly lately, connections between them do not abound. While there is an extensive literature on volunteer training programs, as well as on the recruiting and training of volunteers, such literature focuses almost exclusively on the non-formal learning of volunteers. In this chapter, we make an attempt to expand this body of knowledge by bringing to the fore selected issues and policy implications related to informal learning. We will illustrate some of our conceptual discussions with preliminary data arising from our current study on the informal learning of volunteer workers. At the end of the chapter we include a few notes for a research agenda on this topic.

Our discussion is framed in the context of our current study on volunteer learning in three different contexts: community development, housing coopera-tives, and the labour market. Our first case study, in conjunction with the Ontario Health Communities Coalition (OHCC), deals with volunteers whose work aims to benefit their communities in some way. The second case study, in conjunction with A Commitment to Training and Employment for Women (ACTEW), explores the learning of immigrants who volunteer in order to gain entry into the labour market.[1] The third case study, in conjunction with the

Cooperative Housing Federation of Toronto, is about the learning of housing cooperative board and committee members whose volunteer work is central to the maintenance and survival of the cooperatives. This study is part of a larger project coordinated by the Work and Lifelong Learning Research Network.

Informal Learning

The concept of informal learning and how is it is distinguished from formal and nonformal education has already been sufficiently discussed in the opening chapter of this collection. We will only discuss here two issues with this three-part taxonomy. First, as most taxonomies, it is to a certain extent arbitrary, and by using one main criterion to distinguish the categories (the setting in which learning takes place), it may not provide a full account of the complex reality of learning. For instance, if we look at the process of learning, and not only at the setting, we note that schools and universities are not only sites of formal learning, but also sites of nonformal and informal learning. Nonformal learning can take place through practica, student clubs and a variety of extracurricular activities. Likewise, significant informal learning can occur (in most cases, does occur) among students through the hidden curriculum and through a variety of interactions with classmates and with other actors of the educational system (authorities, staff, etc.). Differentiating between learning location and learning process helps to recognize that a given learning experience may incorporate more than one of the three categories at the same time. That is, informal and non-formal learning can occur at the same time as formal learning in a school setting just as formal learning can occur outside of a classroom through distance education.

Secondly, the implicit meaning conveyed in the concepts of formal, nonformal and informal learning implies a hierarchy of learning experiences. In this regard, Billett (2001, p. 14) points out that "although unintended, this labelling [of formal, non-formal, and informal] has fostered a view that learning experiences in the workplace are incoherent as being 'informal' and 'incidental', and as failing to furnish critical insights". While Billett is writing from the context of paid workplace learning, the critique is still relevant to other contexts, including volunteer work. As Illich (1970) and other educational critics have commented, informal learning from experience is seldom given the same prestige as learning that is acquired (and accredited) through either formal or non-formal systems. A contributing factor to this phenomenon is that informal learning has been under-theorized and under-researched, largely because it is more difficult to uncover and analyse than formal or non-formal educational activities that have a set curriculum and objectives whose attainment can be identified and evaluated. Indeed, most of informal learning is incorporated as tacit knowledge, which was characterized by Polanyi (1966) as "that which we know but cannot tell." This explains why informal learning has been for a long time a sort of 'black box' about which not much was known.

More recently, however, attempts have been made to explore the internal dynamics of informal learning. For instance, considering the criteria of intentionality and awareness, Schugurensky (2000) identified three types of informal learning: self-directed learning (intentional and conscious), incidental learning (unintentional but conscious) and socialization (unintentional and unconscious). Likewise, Livingstone (forthcoming) divides informal learning into two main types. The first type of informal training, which occurs "when teachers or mentors take responsibility for instructing others without sustained reference to an intentionally-organized body of knowledge in more incidental and spontaneous learning situations, such as guiding them in acquiring job skills or in community development activities" (p. 2). The second type is self-directed or collective informal learning, a residual category for "all other forms of intentional or tacit learning in which we engage either individually or collectively without direct reliance on a teacher or an externally-organized curriculum" (p. 2). Both attempts recognize that within informal learning there is continuum of experiences that can be more or less structured and organized, and that can occur at the individual and at the collective level.

Whereas the taxonomy of learning are not without problems they can be useful to understanding how and what people learn as long as we recognize the fluidity of the boundaries between and the potential simultaneity of the different learning types.

Volunteer Work

Volunteer work includes a wide range of activities. Among them are organising and supervising events; coaching children and youth; delivering food and clothes to the needy; serving on boards, councils and committees; providing support and healthcare; driving; taking part in canvassing, campaigning and fundraising; protecting the environment and wildlife; teaching and tutoring; raising awareness and advocating on important issues; greeting visitors; doing office work; leading tours and other recreational activities; ushering in religious institutions; assisting the elderly; researching and disseminating information; fighting fires, and doing repairs, maintenance and construction work (Hall, McKeown, & Roberts, 2001; Ilsley, 1990). Although these examples illustrate what volunteers do, they do not suggest a universal definition of volunteer work. In common usage, volunteer work is understood as work that is freely chosen, unremunerated, and of some benefit to community or society. This understanding provides a good working definition, but two considerations regarding the diversity and complexity of volunteer work (both at the organizational and at the individual level) are pertinent at this point.

First, volunteering tends to be conflated with the voluntary sector, as if they were the same thing, or as if volunteering only occurs through voluntary organizations. While a great deal of volunteer work is indeed done through voluntary organizations, it is important to recognize that there is also widespread volunteer activity in the public sector, in the private sector and in the community at large (Brudney, 1990; Sheard, 1995). Secondly, volunteer work can take different forms, and volunteers are motivated (and sometimes coerced) by different circumstances. Let's consider, for instance, teaching literacy on a regular basis, helping a disabled neighbour with certain chores on occasional basis, undertaking an internship in a corporation in order to gain job experience, working outside of regular hours in a non-governmental organization (NGO) in order to complete tasks, participating in a governing board, doing community work as mandated by a government agency, or participating in a social movement against child labour. All these activities can be considered volunteer work according to the general definition, but clearly they are of very different nature. Some of them, like working beyond regular hours or doing long-term internships with negligible educational impact are even borderline cases, and some may consider them unpaid work rather than volunteer work.

While there is an abundance of literature on volunteering and on voluntary organizations, most authors take the definition of volunteer work for granted. Indeed, after reviewing more than 300 articles and reports, Cnaan, Handy, and Wadsworth (1996, p. 369) reported that the term volunteer was seldom defined. Therefore, they undertook a comprehensive study that included a review of 11 widely used definitions. They found four dimensions that were present in those definitions of volunteer work: the voluntary nature of the act, the nature of the reward, the context or auspices under which the volunteering is performed, and who benefits. Within each dimension, two to three categories were identified:

Dimension	Categories
Free Choice	1. Free will (the ability to voluntarily choose)
	2. Relatively uncoerced
	3. Obligation to volunteer
Remuneration	1. None at all
	2. None expected
	3. Expenses reimbursed
	4. Stipend/low pay
Structure	1. Formal
	2. Informal
Intended beneficiaries	1. Benefit/help others/strangers
	2. Benefit/help friends or relatives
	3. Benefit oneself (as well)

From Cnaan, Handy, & Wadsworth (1996, p. 371)

In any given context, different profiles of volunteers can be identified, depending on the specific combination of these four dimensions and their categories. In the last instance, claim the authors, the perception of who is a volunteer and who is not boils down to the net cost of the undertaking: "concept of net cost best accounted for the perception of who is a volunteer" (Cnaan et al., 1996, p. 381).

In their follow-up study that included over 3000 questionnaires administered in Canada, the Netherlands, India, Italy, and the United States, Handy et al. (2000) further developed that thesis. They found that the public perception is that the greater the self-sacrifice the more altruistic the action. Likewise, the more the work benefits strangers (rather than oneself or friends), the more it is totally unpaid, and the more uncoerced it is, the more it will considered a 'true' volunteer activity. The coercion factor also calls into question whether we can even consider an activity as a voluntary one if it is not chosen in total freedom. Indeed, historically the concept of volunteer has been negatively associated with coercion. In the past, a volunteer was one who voluntarily offered to serve in the military, in contrast to those who were under obligation to do so, or were part of a regular army of military force (Oxford English Dictionary, 2003). However, certain degree of coercion is often present in some volunteer activities, sometimes expressed through legal requirements, social and religious mandates, workplace commitments, community expectations and the like. Where to draw the line between 'genuine' and 'coerced' volunteer work is not easy, and the decision probably varies vary from context to context.

In relation to the formal and informal structures in the volunteer experience, Ilsley (1990) makes the following distinction:

> Formal voluntarism can be defined as service that is addressed to a social need or needs defined by an organization, performed in a coordinated way in an organizational context, and rewarded by psychological or other benefits. Informal voluntarism is spontaneous expression of service in response to a personally perceived social need, performed freely (without organizational constraints) and often without any thought of reward (p. 5).

The National Survey on Giving, Volunteering and Participating (NSGVP)[2] makes a simpler distinction in this regard: formal volunteering is unremunerated and freely chosen work done through an organization whereas informal volunteering is done outside the confines of an organization (Hall, McKeown, & Roberts, 2001). While we recognize the relevance of informal volunteering, in this chapter we focus on formal volunteering.

Previous research into volunteer work and volunteers has also used many other categorizations and distinctions alternately focusing on the nature of the voluntary organization, the role of the voluntary organization in society, and the role volunteering fills in volunteers' lives (e.g., Hustinx & Lammertyn, 2003; Salamon & Sokolowski, 2002; Abdennur, 1987; Elsdon, 1995; Elsdon, Reynolds, & Stewart, 1995; Isley, 1990) In our research in progress on the learning of volunteers, we identified six profiles of volunteers that may correlate with different learning experiences. These six profiles relate to some elements of the definitional and conceptual frameworks mentioned above, and imply different degrees of passion, social pressure and self-interest. Before we delve into them, it is pertinent to note that a given organization may encompass a variety of volunteer profiles, and that a given volunteer may change their profile over time.

The first profile is the *altruistic volunteer*. That is the volunteer who is compelled only by a desire to help others, devotes high levels of time and energy to the volunteer work, and gains no personal benefit (other than satisfaction) from the outcomes of the activities undertaken. The more unlikely that the project undertaken benefits the volunteers themselves, as well as their families, friends and communities, the more altruistic is it considered. Altruistic volunteers may be found in international organisations like Amnesty International, Habitat for Humanity, Greenpeace, Doctors without Borders, the Red Cross, Wildlife Fund, Save the Children, Oxfam, the World Coalition Against the Death Penalty, and also in a wide range of national and local organisations.

A second type is the *semi-altruistic volunteer*. Unlike the fully altruistic type, the semi-altruistic volunteers combine in different ways a desire to help others with an interest for helping themselves and their communities. While fully altruistic volunteers may engage without hesitation in emergency relief efforts and in projects aiming at protecting exotic animals or the rainforest, eliminating hunger or denouncing human rights abuses in places far from home, semi-altruistic volunteers are more likely to engage in projects of local community development (from neighbourhood revitalization projects to community gardening to music festivals), in groups advocating for a cause to which they have a personal or family connection (e.g., special education programs, bicycle routes, seniors' rights, etc.), or in recreation/educational activities that involve their own family members or neighbours (e.g., coaching a sport team, teaching ceramics in the local community centre, helping in the school library, etc.).

A third type is the *socially-coerced volunteer*. In this case, volunteering is to some extent freely chosen, but also done because it is highly expected by others (family, community, workplace, religious institution, the labour market, society at large, etc.). Unlike the altruistic volunteers (who are motivated only by their inner conscience), in this case group identity, social pressure, and the ethos and informal rules of a given community play a central role in the motivation and in the nature of the volunteer experience.

A fourth type is the *compulsory volunteer*. Perhaps a contradiction in terms, this volunteer work is mandated by legislation or a policy and often supervised by an institution. Some educational institutions require students to do volunteer work in order to graduate. For example, Mexican university students must complete a *social service* in order to have their degree formally conferred, and Ontario high school students are required to complete at least 40 hours of community service before graduation (Ontario Ministry of Education and Training, 1999, pp. 9–10). Other state agencies can also require people to volunteer in order to receive social assistance such as the Ontario Works program (Government of Ontario, 1997). The justice system is another state agency that mandates volunteer work in the form of community service for those who have committed a small infraction and for inmates in correctional institutions, usually for rehabilitation purposes or in exchange for paying a fine. While the idea of a compulsory volunteer is conceptually an oxymoron (and perhaps should be called unpaid work rather than volunteer work), in the real world it is a category that exists, because even though the work is mandated, it is often construed as volunteer work by the institutions, by the volunteers themselves and by the community. Moreover, the fact that it is mandatory does not preclude that the experience could be a good one for the volunteer and/or the community, and that significant learning can occur through the experience. In 2000, over 7% of Canada's volunteers were mandated to do so by their school, government, or employer (Hall et al., 2001, p. 39).

A fifth type is the *overtime volunteer*. This type of volunteer activity is likely most prevalent in voluntary organisations themselves, and in general in the nonprofit sector. In this sector employees put in significant additional work time during the evenings and weekends (or during the rest of the week if they are hired as part-time workers) to fulfil organizational objectives which are not part of their job description or are not expected of them. They do it partly because of their commitment to organisational goals, and partly because the job needs to be done, and it is in this confusing double role of volunteer and employee where the boundary between volunteer work and plain unpaid work is blurred. A possible criterion to distinguish whether overtime unpaid work falls into the category of volunteer work or not is to consider if the worker can be penalised (financial penalties, suspension, termination) or reprimanded for not doing that particular job. The problem is that in real life many employees in the nonprofit sector have a high level of commitment towards their work and the mission of their organization, and it is difficult even for themselves to determine whether they are freely contributing to the work of their organization or whether the are being exploited.

A sixth category is the *intern volunteer*, who works in an unpaid or poorly paid capacity in order to gain entry into a particular segment of the labour market. At least two variations of this category can be identified: juniors and seniors. The former volunteer because they have no experience in a given field due to age or a career change. The latter volunteer because their experience and/or diplomas are not recognised by potential employers or by a professional association. This is the case for many immigrants whose training and experience in their country of origin are not recognised in the country they have moved to. In both cases, there is no overt coercion for people to volunteer, but the structures and pressures of the labour market make it very difficult to find a paid job without a volunteer experience. Theoretically, the major beneficiaries of the internship are the volunteers themselves, who aimed at increasing their opportunities in the labour market.[3] In this sense, this category could be understood more as 'unpaid work for self-benefit' than as volunteer work. However, personal benefit and social benefit are not necessarily excluding of each other, especially if the unpaid work performed has a great social and community impact. Moreover, if the intern does not obtain a paid job as a result of the internship, the real self-benefit will be very low even if the motivation to volunteer was based on self-benefit.

It is probably true that these six profiles do not provide a full account of volunteer work, and that they need to be further refined in order to reduce overlaps. In any case, the point we are trying to make here is that the world of volunteer work is diverse and complex, and that volunteers are motivated by a variety of reasons that are not necessarily exclusive. For instance, in the most recent Canadian National Survey on Giving, Volunteering, and Participation (NSGVP), the 27% of citizens of reported to do formal volunteer work were asked about the different reasons that led them to volunteer. Almost all of them (95%) reported that they volunteer to help a cause they believe in. More than 8 in 10 (81%) volunteer because they want to put their skills and experience to use. Over two-thirds (69%) volunteered because they had been personally affected by the cause the organisation supports. More than half (57%) saw volunteering as an opportunity to explore their strengths. Finally, 30% volunteered because their friends did, 26% were also fulfilling religious obligations, and 23% wanted to improve their job opportunities (Hall et al., 2001, p. 43). The existence of a diversity of motivating factors for doing volunteer work presupposes, at least as a hypothesis, a diversity of learning experiences. Available research evidence suggests that volunteers' choice of learning experiences is strongly related to their choice of objects for commitment (Isley 1990, p. 64). In other words, what volunteers learn is closely connected to the type of activities they undertake, and this is largely connected to why they decided to volunteer in the first place.

Learning, Work and Volunteering: Exploring the Connections

If we look again at the reasons for volunteering reported by the NSGVP, we would notice that learning was not mentioned at all. This is due to the fact that the survey did not included learning in the list of possible responses, so respondents were not given a chance to name learning as a reason for volunteering. It may also be the case that, with the exception of internships, learning is not perceived as an important motivation for volunteering. This hypothesis is supported by recent research on the accreditation and rewarding of volunteer activities (Percy et al., 1998; Cox, 2002). Cox found that "explicitly educational motives are rarely cited as the reason, people engaged in voluntary activity perceive their activities as 'doing' rather than learning" (Cox, 2002, p. 166). Likewise, Percy, Barnes, Graddon, and Machell (1988) found that "an adult may speak about 'learning' as a motive for attending a voluntary organization, but is most likely not to do so" (p. 58). The NSGVP suggests that volunteers are more likely to perceive the opposite connection: 81% of respondents felt that the volunteering experience let them apply previous learning to a concrete situation. For reasons probably related to the invisibility and the tacit character of informal learning, the connection between learning and volunteering is mostly perceived as a one-way street. The dominant perception is that we learn in school and to some extent in our professional work, and then we can put our acquired knowledge and skills to social use through volunteering.

The learning dimension of volunteer work is not only often ignored by volunteers themselves; it is also outside the radar of researchers and voluntary organisations. Eldson et al. (1995), after reviewing the literature on the connection between learning and volunteering (pp. 24–26), concluded that very few studies exist that directly explore the learning that results from volunteering. Ilsley (1990) found that voluntary organisations do not pay much attention to the learning of their volunteer members:

> Although most formal volunteer organizations offer training programs, we found that much of the actual learning in volunteer organizations is unplanned. Perhaps relatedly, learning – especially forms of learning other than instrumental/didactic – appears to be undervalued in most volunteer programs. This is highly unfortunate.

One possible way to explore the connections between learning, volunteer work and labour force training is the relationship between volunteer work and paid work. In this regard, in our fieldwork we identified three main different routes taken by volunteers: sequential, simultaneous and intermittent.

The sequential route refers to volunteering either to gain entry into the labour market or after leaving the labour market. There is a clear demographic factor at play here, as young people are more likely to volunteer before joining the formal labour market, and older people are more likely to volunteer after retirement. Having said that, in the movement from unpaid to paid work, we are not only speaking of newcomers to the labour market (who tend to be predominantly youth) but also of more mature people making a career change or needing to gain experience in a new context. The 'training' rationale for volunteering is well understood by youth and newcomers. The National Survey on Giving, Volunteering and Participating found that only 23% of volunteers agreed that improving job opportunities was a reason for volunteering. However, when we look at the responses given by younger volunteers (15–24) the percentage increases to 55% (Hall et al., 2001, p. 35). In other words, young volunteers are twice as likely to see a causal connection between volunteering and paid work.

In the sequential mode, people generally volunteer in an organization related to a field they are interested in, either because they want to be working in it or because they have accumulated a great deal of expertise and passion for it. In the first case, the hope is that they will gain new skills (of social or technical nature) or add to their existing repertoire of skills which will make them more attractive to potential employers. In the second case, the expectation is usually to continue the activity in the field, be it to apply their skills to a social purpose, to keep themselves updated and connected to the field, to fill their time, to feel useful or to repay society with good deeds. In sum, in the sequential mode the link between learning and volunteering is quite clear. For the person hoping to enter the labour market, volunteering is an opportunity to learn skills and make connections to facilitate entry into the labour market. For the person leaving the labour market, learning from the workplace is applied to the volunteer context.

The simultaneous route is where volunteering and paid employment – in the same or different fields – take place at the same time. This could be a lawyer doing pro bono work, a dentist volunteering in a poor area, an electrician helping to build houses in Habitat for Humanity, a businessperson coaching a basketball team, or a teacher spending time as Big Sister or Brother mentoring a child. In this mode, learning could take place in either setting with learning being transferred from setting to setting as appropriate. The interaction between volunteering and learning is not as clear as in the sequential mode, and particularly nebulous are the ways in which learning acquired through volunteering informs activities in the paid job.

The intermittent route occurs when a person performs similar jobs in the same field for a significant amount of time, sometimes with remuneration and sometimes without. In this mode there is little distinction between paid employment and volunteer work except whether payment is received or not. A typical example of this route is a person who believes strongly in a cause and works for many years raising awareness about such cause. At a certain point the person becomes employed by an expanding non-profit organisation related to that cause, and so the person begins receiving money for doing essentially the same work. This same organization may succeed in getting their cause reflected in legislation and so financial support for the organization wanes leaving the person out of a job. Even without the job, the person continues to be active researching, advocating and raising public awareness for her cause, and eventually may be hired again to do more research, advocacy and education. In this route, it is very difficult to distinguish what learning comes from volunteer work and what from paid employment, and the specific transfer mechanisms from one setting to the other. While this is an interesting route that we identified through our interviews with volunteers in the areas of health promotion and community development, the majority of volunteers use one or both of the first two routes. Several interviewees also reported instances in which the knowledge, skills and/or values acquired through one type of volunteer work were transferred to another type of volunteer work. Like in the volunteer work/paid work relation, this pattern of transference can also follow the sequential, simultaneous or intermittent routes.

A more explicit link between learning and volunteering can be found in service learning, that is, volunteer work mandated by an educational institution. One of the objectives of mandating volunteer service is to encourage students to develop awareness and understanding of civic responsibility and of the role they can play in supporting and strengthening their communities. Although it is recognised that students' volunteer work will benefit communities, its primary purpose is to contribute to students' development (Ontario Ministry of Education and Training, 1999, p. 9). However, it is also assumed that the learning of individual students in turn will be of benefit to society in the future. Furthermore, another objective of service learning is to socialize youth into volunteering roles. The assumption behind this strategy is that by becoming volunteers at a young age, participants will be more likely to volunteer throughout their lives. Indeed, in many service learning programs it is expected that the learning acquired through volunteer work relates not only to occupational skills and to the economic realm, but also to the social arena (Andersen, 1999). It is also expected that as volunteers become socialized in a culture of social service and community participation, they can also develop – at least in certain types of programs – democratic values and practices.

In this regard, connections between volunteer work, civic learning and civic engagement have been identified in the literature on political participation and citizenship learning (Merrifield, 2001; Pateman, 1970; Roker, Player, & Coleman, 1999; Westheimer & Kahne, 2002; Schugurensky, 2002). One of the central arguments of participatory democracy advocates like Rousseau, Dewey and Pateman is that the most effective way to learn democracy is by doing it, and that citizens have to be involved in the practice of democracy and not just the theory. This involvement requires a high level of commitment in time and energy devoted to local democratic processes, and this sustained effort can be considered volunteer work. According to some recent studies, participatory democracy has the potential to contribute significantly to the development of an engaged and informed citizenship, as well as to the democratization of the state and other institutions (Abers, 2000; Baiocchi, 1999; Schugurensky, 2001).

In closing, the connections between learning and volunteer work, and between them and paid work, can be explored through a variety of avenues. In the analysis of those connections, it is pertinent to examine the dynamics between structure and agency in the reproduction of social inequality. For instance, volunteers with higher levels of cultural and social capital (Bourdieu, 1986) are more likely to be placed in more intellectually demanding roles and functions. This experience, in turn, can have positive effect in the expansion of their social and cultural capital, and eventually their transferability to economic capital (e.g., higher employability). In some experiments of local democracy, for instance, participants with higher levels of schooling and connections tend to be elected to take a more active role in councils and committees. This experience may be useful to get into paid positions in legislative or executive government offices, in the leadership of political parties, in nonprofits, etc, even if this was not their rationale for joining the process. At the same time, participants who enter the process with lower levels of cultural and social capital, tend to remain at the lower levels of the decision-making structures. Hence the participatory democracy model, although it provides great learning opportunities to all participants, is seldom sufficient to counteract existing inequalities, and sometimes ends up reproducing them by allowing the development of an internal pyramid.[4] Having said that, anecdotal information also reveals that some organisations do not pay much attention to match the tasks assigned to volunteers with their talents and possibilities, and missing opportunities for benefiting both the organisation and the volunteer are not uncommon.

Informal Learning through Volunteering: What and How do Volunteers Learn?

The discussion of the previous sections suggests that the diversity and complexity of volunteer experiences make it very difficult to generalise about volunteer learning. However, it is safe to point out that that in most cases volunteer learning is particularly significant, probably because of the high degree of relevance and motivation implicated in the learning process. This was one of the key findings of the 1998 NALL survey. The survey also found that people who have been involved in community work over past year (over 40%) devoted about 4 hours a week on average to community-related informal learning. About two thirds reported learning interpersonal skills, almost 60% learned communication skills, over half learned about social issues; and over 40% were learned about organizational/managerial skills (Livingstone, 1999, 2001a, 2001b).

These findings were confirmed by the 2000 Canadian Survey on Giving, Volunteering and Participating (NSGVP), in which the large majority of volunteers (79%) reported an increase in interpersonal skills as a result of their volunteering activities. Other skills mentioned, in decreasing order, were communication skills (68%), specific knowledge on a particular subject (63%) and organizational/managerial skills (57%). Among the interpersonal skills identified were understanding people better, learning how to motivate others, and learning how to deal with difficult situations. The most frequently mentioned communication skills were public speaking, writing, conducting meetings, and doing public relations. Knowledge was most often acquired in areas such as health, women's issues, political affairs, criminal justice and the environment, all items that correspond with the category 'social issues' of the NALL survey (Hall et al., 2001, p. 45). While this survey did not ask questions about the mode through which the learning was acquired, preliminary data from our own research in progress suggest that most of these skills are the result of incidental informal learning.

Along the same lines were the findings of a large research project with 31 case studies conducted in Britain by Eldson et al. (1995). They reported the existence of significant changes in areas such as personal confidence, empowerment, making constructive relationships, organizational learning, or the ability and willingness to shoulder responsibility. Changes in these five areas were consistently mentioned as the most important learning by an overwhelming majority of interview respondents, regardless of what kind of voluntary organization they belonged to. Moreover, most of this learning was unpremeditated. In their own words:

> a trawl of the interviews shows that the great majority of the respondents attached a high value to these unpremeditated learnings and resulting personal change *after experiencing them*, and indicated that they considered them even more important than the deliberate learning content of their membership (Elsdon et al., 1995, p. 49 original emphasis).

This unpremeditated learning, which corresponds with our category of 'incidental learning' and was referred to by one of our research participants as "accidental learning," is typical informal learning. In our interviews, many volunteers commented that they had seldom made connections before between the different volunteer activities and the learning acquired through them, and that they had never realized the amount and quality of the learning until the interview elicited that.

Back to Polanyi's (1966) characterization ("that which we know but cannot tell") this indicates that much of the informal learning from volunteer work results in tacit knowledge that can only be uncovered after some type of introspective exercise – if at all.

Most of informal learning, both in volunteer work and paid work, is acquired 'by doing'. However, the structuring of learning experiences can extend and supplement the contributions of everyday activities. The structuring involves the development of a curriculum and the provision of guided learning by experienced or expert workers (Billet, 2001, p. 175). Sometimes, these structured teaching/ learning processes may have a greater impact than the informal processes. For example, in a study on social movement learning of a Community Shared Agriculture project in Canada, Clover and Hall (2000) found that although the informal learning was extremely important, it was the 'nonformal' education activities organized by GJOBS/CSA [Growing Jobs for Living Coalition/ Community Shared Agriculture] which were the most valuable sources of learning and contributed the most to personal and social transformation.

This finding reminds us of the need to distinguish, at least for research purposes, between non-formal and informal learning processes in voluntary work. In their study of learning in 800 voluntary organizations in England, Percy et al. (1998) grouped learning in voluntary organizations into two groups. Under the first type, which corresponds to our category of non-formal learning, they found teaching, discussion, training, assessment and certification. In the second type, which relates to our category of informal learning, they identified practise learning, apprenticeship learning,[5] learning from experience, and learning through social interaction. The prevalence of one type of learning over the other in a given voluntary organization may be associated with the availability of non-formal programs, but also with the learning preferences of volunteers, which in turn may be related to their institutional affiliation. For instance, Ilsley (1990, p. 65), in a four-year study of volunteering in the United States, found out that in contrast to organization-centred volunteers, client-centred volunteers often reject formal training programs and learn primarily from the work itself.

In that study, Ilsley proposed three categories of volunteer learning (instrumental/didactic, social/expressive, and critical reflection) and noted an affinity between each type of learning and the ways of acquiring it. Instrumental/ didactic learning is often aimed at increasing the professional profile of volunteers; it is usually generated through standardized training programs to instill minimum levels of competence so volunteers can feel assured that they will have the intellectual tools they need for their assignments. Social/expressive learning refers to communication, trust, respect, compassion, and openness, which usually result from the volunteer experience rather than from courses or workshops. Critical reflection means turning inward, and deliberately analysing one's own politics, values, and priorities as well as those of society. This learning, also known in the literature as 'transformative learning' (Mezirow et al., 2001) is especially evident in volunteers involved in social and political movements and in those "who have made great sacrifices for the sake of a cause" (Ilsley 1990, p. 65). These volunteers tend to place value on learning political and social issues that are perceived as enhancing their social consciousness and their social vision, and as important to pursue their mission.

In Ilsley's typology of learning through volunteering, the first category is the easiest to identify and research (Ferguson, 2000; Kuhn, 1990; McCoy, 1996; Ojanlatva, 1991; Payne, 2001; Rayner & Marshall, 2003; South Carolina State Department of Health and Environmental Control, 1991; Stenzel & Feeney, 1968; Tedesco, 1991; Wilson, Steele, Thompson, & D'Heron, 2002; Wisconsin Public Television, 1995). Generally, this instrumental/didactic learning is achieved through non-formal means, as it can be observed through the many manuals, textbooks, courses and workshops which are in place for the training and retention of volunteers and for ensuring that the volunteers have the necessary skills to do their work. It is the other two forms (social/expressive and critical reflection) that have a greater link to informal learning.

This does not mean, however, that instrumental skills cannot be acquired through informal learning. In a study on informal learning of front-line workers in the fast-food sector, and using a different typology, Grolnic (2001) identified three types of skills learned informally in the workplace: contextual (e.g., knowing the organization's values), intrapersonal and technical (e.g., making decisions, problem solving, improving job performance), and interpersonal (e.g., working with others). Grolnic concludes that there is much for schools to learn from examining how workers learn on the job. This examination should be broadened to include volunteer work given the importance of motivation to choice of volunteer work and to learning. Moreover, a better understanding of motivation can also help to further explore the links between what volunteers learn and why they volunteer. For example, if their main motivation for volunteering is normative (e.g., a concern for a certain cause like the environment, human rights, or homelessness) they are more likely to learn more about issues related to that particular cause and to strategies to advocate for it. However, if their motivation is primarily social (e.g., to interact with others, to become more confident in public speaking, to develop leadership capacities) then they are more likely to improve their social skills (Ilsley, 1990, p. 64). Interestingly enough, these two areas (social and normative) are the most cited ones by volunteers when asked about the benefits derived from volunteering in community organizations. For instance, Chinman and Wandersman (1999) found that the most important benefits reported by volunteers are socializing with others (e.g., gaining personal recognition and respect from others) and the rewards of striving to reach the goals of the organization (e.g., make the community a safer place to live). Likewise, the two most frequent benefits reported by volunteers in the NSGVP were improvement of interpersonal skills (79%) and communication skills (68%) (Hall et al., 2001, p. 45).

Thus far, we have looked at the individual learning of volunteer workers. In their own attempt to categorize the seamless web of adult learning and change, Elsdon et al. (1995, p. 52) developed the following categories: Social and Group, Content, Occupational, Political, and Personal. From these categories, the first one is particularly interesting because Elsdon et al. argue that voluntary organizations learn as a group as well. In order to analyse such collective learning, they categorised the organizations as dynamic, static, or divergent.

> The dynamic are those which, at the time we studied them, were observably learning and developing. Another set appeared to be static in the sense that they were not undergoing any notable changes. The divergent were those which appeared to be in some kind of [contradictory] position in relation to their declared objectives (Elsdon et al., 1995, p. 97).

These three concepts were only applied to the group learning aspect of the voluntary organizations. Interestingly, in spite of splitting out collective from individual learning, they found that the groups that saw the most individual learning also saw the most group learning. This was the case for both the more mature static groups and the dynamic ones. This led them to conclude that "high levels of individual learning and development, and of group learning and development, go together with an organization's commitment to learning and social or caring objectives" (Elsdon et al., 1995, p. 120). They also observed that two major ways of learning for voluntary organizations were through processes of internal reflection on group experience (a source for both individual and collective learning), and through networks.

Policy Considerations

Seven policy considerations arise from the previous sections. The first four appeal directly to volunteer organizations and communities that rely heavily on volunteers, and have to do with their own internal strategies for capacity building as well as with their connections with other organizations and agencies. The next two policy considerations deal with public agencies that mandate volunteer work. This includes the implementation of service learning programs in schools and other government agencies that mandate community service in order to receive social assistance. Although this troubles the notion of the freely chosen nature of a volunteer activity – consider that the term compulsory volunteer is an oxymoron – these developments are on the rise and should not be ignored in a discussion of voluntary work. The final policy consideration deals with the recognition of learning achieved through volunteer work either by educational institutions and/or by the labour market. A common theme permeating the seven policy considerations is the need for organizations to create enabling structures that maximize the individual and collective learning from the volunteer experience.

The first policy consideration relates to creating an ethos of volunteer participation within an organization. There are several ways in which this can happen:

First, by having structures that encourage continuous volunteering through matching tasks to volunteer ability and interests. For instance, in our study on volunteer learning in housing co-ops, we noted that in those co-ops that offer a broader range of activities, responsibilities and possibilities for growth through committees, boards and other means, members tend to report greater satisfaction, continuity and repertoire of learning skills. Through our interviews, we have identified more than 30 specific areas of learning and change in relation to knowledge, skills, values and attitudes, and behaviours, ranging from a better understanding of the co-operative movement to leadership, managerial and clerical skills, from respecting diversity to facilitating democratic processes, from gardening to self-confidence, from finances and budgeting to conflict resolution, from civic engagement to concern for the common good. Similar findings were reported by Richmond and Mook (2001) in their study on the skills acquired by resident members in a student housing cooperative.

As a policy guideline for volunteer organizations, it becomes clear that the narrower the repertoire of volunteer experiences offered by the organization, and the scarcer the opportunities for reflecting on those experiences, the weaker the likelihood of significant learning and growth among volunteer participants. Providing enabling structures for volunteering and for learning implies the development of mechanisms and processes for identifying the talents, the needs and the interests of volunteers, linking these talents, needs and interests to meaningful volunteer experiences, creating new areas as required. It also implies providing opportunities for regular collective reflection, opening spaces for volunteer contributions to the wellbeing of the organization and for providing input for the improvement of processes, and encouraging volunteer participation in decision-making about matters that directly affect them.

A second way to create an ethos of volunteering is by including a social and caring element in the organization. As Elsdon et al. (1995) found, more individual and collective learning of volunteers took place in organizations that had not only learning objectives, but also social and caring ones. In terms of internal policy, if organizations focus at least some of their energy on the social element and on caring for volunteers, they are more likely to create conditions through which the tacit learning of volunteers can become explicit. That is, while non-formal training sessions or group reflections can lead to significant learning – especially instrumental or didactic learning – a supportive organizational culture can contribute significantly to the informal learning of its volunteers.

A second policy consideration, which stems from the first one, relates to the continuous offering of non-formal educational experiences that are relevant, meaningful, innovative and enjoyable. This could include workshops, seminars, short courses, external or internal mentorship programs, and the like. While much of the learning in our lives takes place in informal ways, that does not mean that more formalised structures or systems do not also influence the learning potential. Designers and facilitators of these non-formal experiences should aim at linking both content and method to the informal and to the formal learning already acquired by volunteers. If an organization lacks the resources to offer what its members need at a given time, a pool of organizations with similar needs can be formed to develop initiatives together in a cost-effective way. By creating enabling structures for learning, even if they are just creating a chance for informal discussion between organization members, there is a directed nature to the learning experience. Simply planning to have coffee together as a group on a regular basis may not be considered non-formal learning – or at least not at the same level as a workshop – yet that simple structure may create conditions in which volunteers can reflect, articulate, and make explicit their tacit knowledge.

A third policy consideration has to do with the development of equalization mechanisms that provide relevant learning opportunities for the least disadvantaged members of a given community. If the quality of the volunteer experience and the responsibility for learning are left entirely to the individual volunteer, organizations are potentially obfuscating the role that systemic barriers may play in the process. In many organizations, the quality of the volunteer experience and the inherent level of decision-making are influenced by factors such as gender, race, class, age, professional and educational background, or physical disability. This tends to create an internal pyramid of 'high level volunteers' who lead and 'low level volunteers' who are assigned the more menial jobs and have the least opportunities for learning and growth. A labour distribution is often justified, as the functioning of an organization requires a great variety of tasks. However, to permanently confine certain members to certain roles is not only unfair but also inefficient for the improvement of the collective, as all members have actual and potential talents that can benefit the organization. This should not be left to random initiatives of goodwill but to clear policies of human development. If informal learning is going to challenge systems of oppression, enabling structures should be explicitly put in place to equalize opportunity (see for example Foley, 1999; Freire, 1970/2000).

A fourth policy consideration has to do with organizational learning. If the focus remains on the learning of individual volunteers, it is possible to miss some of the systemic factors that may be at play both within the organization and in its relationship with other social groups. Organizations can develop activities to put both individual and collective learning into social context. In what ways is a given organization mirroring or perpetuating systemic injustices and in what way is it challenging them? How is it learning from its interactions in society? The policy consideration here is the importance for groups to build opportunities to collectively reflect, both within their organization and with other groups, about their experiences. An example would be a voluntary organization that does service provision for a state agency. If there is not an opportunity for members to proactively reflect on what the organization is doing through its work as an agent of the state, then they will be less likely to consciously support or challenge given state policies related to their service provision.

A fifth policy consideration relates to the inclusion of community service in the school curriculum, an overlapping area between voluntary and mandatory work. In a school context, volunteer service policies can be found on a continuum from volunteer service opportunities to service-learning courses integral to a school's mission. As Andersen (1999, p. 2), observes, many schools or districts start with a policy that mandates service hours, and then move towards more service-learning. This type of evolution occurs because these policies are easier to plan and implement in terms of logistics (e.g., track hours, fill out forms, little to no formal assessment, little monitoring, etc). The two most contested policy issues in these initiatives are: a) the level of integration of the volunteer work experience into the curriculum and, b) whether participation in the program should be mandatory or not.

In relation to the integration issue, it seems that the greater the volunteer experience is integrated into the students' curriculum, the greater the learning potential (Westheimer & Kahne, 1999). In their study about the impact of mandated 40 hours of volunteer service in Ontario for high school graduation, Foster & Meinhard (2000) concluded that significant learning was

> more likely to occur in programs in which students were obliged to keep a journal, in which time was set aside during class to talk about the experience and in which students designed the program for themselves as opposed to having it assigned.

That is not to say that any volunteer activity that is not integrated into the curriculum will not facilitate students' learning, but rather that the reliability of the results is less assured. Back to Andersen's point, it is clear why integrating the experience into the curriculum, even if it is seen as desirable, is not always carried out because of the extra work it creates.

In relation to the second issue, emerging studies suggest that mandatory community programs result in lower learning outcome than voluntary programs (Andersen, 1999; Foster & Meinhard, 2000). These studies found that student autonomy was important to learning. If the students felt that they had some control over where and how they volunteered, they were likely to do so more willingly and to learn more from the experience. This research suggests that keeping the experience voluntary will reap greater rewards. In fact, Andersen found that schools without a mandatory component of volunteer service often have higher rates of participation in volunteer activities than those with mandatory components. What is important is making different volunteer opportunities available to students. Again, this means more work for the schools themselves, but if there is commitment to outcomes of an ethic of volunteering and helping society, then it seems that simply mandating volunteering without support in the form of finding placements and reflecting on learning, will not achieve the desired results (see also Loupe, 2000; Stukas, Snyder, & Clary, 1999).

A sixth policy consideration relates to mandatory "volunteer" work or community service as part of social assistance plans, also referred to as workfare plans. It is beyond the scope of this piece to discuss all of the relevant literature on this topic (for a recent comprehensive review of research on workfare, see Steger, 2002). The reasons for mandating community service are generally two-fold. First, to provide the social assistance recipient a chance to practice some new skills, brush up on some old ones, gain some recent experience and current references to build a résumé (Ontario Ministry of Community Family and Children's Services, 2003). Second, to give community organizations extra help. Regardless of the motivation behind them, at the level of policy implementation these policies may have a more punitive than educative effect. That is, unless there is sufficient support – as in the case above with schools – to reflect deliberately on the "volunteer" experience, the effect of a program can be more to punish people for needing social assistance rather than helping them to acquire skills, knowledge, and attitudes that would facilitate re-entry to the labour market. Again, and this connects to other policy considerations already mentioned, if the program is to meet educative rather than punitive objectives, it should include structures that enable reflections on the 'volunteer' experience.

Last but not least, a policy consideration relevant to the link between informal learning and volunteering work relates to issues of assessment and recognition. One of the most developed policy instruments in this regard is probably PLAR (Prior Learning Assessment and Recognition (PLAR), a technique for recognizing learning that has taken place outside of the formal educational system. It is in use by different educational institutions to give people without formal accreditation entry into programs or to give them advanced placement in their program. It is also in use in the workplace to recognize learning that workers do outside of the workplace that is relevant to their jobs (see Thomas, 1998 and www.nall.ca for a more complete review of PLAR). While each institution is ultimately responsible for their own PLAR system making it hard to generalize, policies need to recognize especially the tacit knowledge that is acquired through volunteering and find ways to encourage a reflective process. As mentioned above, the most significant learning for many volunteers is unpremeditated. It is important for PLAR policies to find ways to tease out such tacit learning so that they can be recognized. Additionally, portfolios prepared for a PLAR process can show the different activities and campaigns that a learner has completed through their volunteering.

Summary and Conclusions

After writing this chapter, it became clear to us that the great diversity of realities at both the individual and organization level, makes it very difficult to generalize about volunteer work, particularly about the learning that results from the activity. Having said that, prior studies on volunteer work suggest that learners are often unaware of the knowledge, skills and values acquired through the volunteer experience. Additionally, learners are often unaware of the ways and processes by which they learned. In our own research in progress, often the tacit knowledge of volunteers becomes explicit through the interview itself. Many interviewees comment: "I've never thought about that before, but I really did learn something from that experience", or "I didn't know how much I have learned; I am impressed!" Then, when we ask volunteers how they have learned, many reply that they don't know or say that they learned "just by doing it."

Learning from experience in this way generally would fit into the category of informal learning.

Livingstone's (forthcoming) distinction between the different types of learning is useful because it gives more clarity to how things are being learned. It allows us to identify whether there is a more senior member of an organization acting as a mentor, or a deliberate attempt to reflect on past experiences, or whether the learning is more tacit in nature.

In terms of policy recommendations, we suggest that the amount, quality and diversity of volunteer learning experiences is more likely to increase if the organization creates an ethos of volunteer participation and provides enabling structures for a variety of volunteer opportunities that match the interests and needs of members. The quality of the learning experiences is also likely to increase if the organization combines non-formal educational initiatives with continuous reflective processes during and after each volunteer experience. These recommendations also apply to community service mandated by schools and other public agencies, whose programs are more likely to succeed if the volunteer dimension is stronger than the mandatory one and hence if volunteer motivation is higher.

There is also a need to further develop and refine policies and programs for assessment and recognition of informal learning acquired through volunteer work by educational institutions and employers. In this regard, it is pertinent to note that some skills learned through volunteer work can be directly applied to careers (like in the case of computer software as discussed above), but other, more generic skills, are also important for formal workplaces. Indeed, certain social, interpersonal and organisational skills, critical reasoning and decision-making abilities, understanding a problem from someone else's perspective, developing a work ethic, working in groups, or examining one's values in relation to other people's values, are important ones, although they are difficult to measure and even more difficult to put a monetary value on them.

Finally, we suggest that the study of learning through volunteer work can inform educational initiatives in schools and training initiatives in the paid work sector. By uncovering the hidden world of informal learning, particularly in unpaid work, we can improve the pedagogical potential of non-educational agencies that nonetheless educate, and transfer important lessons to the world of formal educational institutions and paid workplaces. If the 21st century is going to become the century of a learning society we will have to generate a greater synergy among educational and non-educational institutions, creating an archipelago of learning communities that maximize our learning potential.

Epilogue: Notes for a Research Agenda on Learning and Voluntary Work

Because research on the connections between informal learning and volunteering is still in its infancy, more studies are needed in several areas. Two area for further research, suggested by Handy et al. (2000) has to do with public perceptions of voluntary work, and with measuring the net cost and benefit of a given volunteer activity. In future studies on these issues we suggest to include the notion of learning. For instance, what is the public perception on the nature of volunteering if learning is closely associated with the activity? Would people who learn a great deal from their volunteer work be seen as 'lesser volunteers' in the sense that they benefit from it) than those who do not? How to predict the individual and social impact of the future application of that learning to a particular purpose, and how would that be included in a cost/benefit analysis?

Another area for further research is exploring the connections between the type of volunteer work experience and the intensity and quality of the learning experience. If, as NALL suggests, informal learning tends to be more intense in voluntary work than in paid work, it is important to further explore whether this is a fact across the board or only in some types of voluntary work, and to determine the implications of this for training policies and programs, and for the assessment and recognition of informal learning as well. Although there are many studies on voluntary work in Canada, little is known yet about the extent, modes and effectiveness of volunteers' acquisition of new skills, knowledge, attitudes and values, and the relationship between formal, nonformal and informal learning in this process.

A related theme, which we just touched on in this chapter, deals with the degree of coercion in a given volunteer job and its impact on learning. A test of our six ideal types of volunteers, focusing on variables such as passion, social pressure and self-interest, might be an interesting place to explore the impact of mandatory volunteering on learning. What are the political and ethical ramifications of some mandating others to do volunteer work? What is the long-term impact of forced volunteering on the volunteer ethic? What do people learn about volunteering if they do not freely choose to volunteer? What happens when volunteer service is mandated by the state leaving individual schools and communities no choice but to implement the programs? What impact does this have on the learning opportunities that can be created for participants?

Further work needs to be done to understand the type of learning acquired through volunteer work. We are exploring this by looking at three different types of learning: cumulative, new, and transformative. Using this kind of lens hopefully gives a more nuanced understanding of what processes volunteers are using to learn. It would also be interesting to explore ways in which the tacit knowledge gained through volunteering is made explicit through enabling structures for informal learning and non-formal opportunities for reflection in different organizations. How can this be fostered within the day-to-day operations of voluntary organizations and how can the knowledge be made explicit for recognition by employers, educational institutions and society in general?

Another interesting question to explore in further research is whether voluntary organizations that have educational objectives (be it through direct services to students, like adult literacy, or through public education on broad issues such as environment, health and the like) are more likely to support the learning needs of volunteers than those organisations which do not focus on education. In other words, are educational organisations more sensitive to the educational needs of their volunteers and more committed to provide them with learning opportunities than non-educational organisations?

This preliminary list suggests that the field of volunteer learning still has more questions than answers, which is good news for researchers. Hopefully, this chapter is making a modest contribution to this collective inquiry, and helps to call public attention to the significance of the informal learning acquired by volunteers and to its potential role in the construction of a more inclusive learning society.

Notes

1. Many newcomers are unable to find work in Canada in spite of meeting the job qualifications and professional licensing requirements; often they have to volunteer in order to get Canadian experience which they hope will help them find work in their profession.
2. This survey was conducted by Statistics Canada in 1997 and 2000 and will be conducted again in 2003. It is the only survey of its kind in Canada that explores the philanthropy, volunteering and participation of Canadians.
3. We are well aware that especially in the case of immigrants, the major beneficiary is the organization/corporation employing the volunteer but conceptually, the beneficiary can be construed as the individual.
4. To take a different example related to more instrumental learning, one participant in our study noted that had the opportunity to volunteer in a nonprofit agency organising a conference. Because he already had a certain level of computer knowledge, he was given the task of organising the computer database to track conference registrations. Other volunteers without the same cultural capital would be given tasks such as collecting tickets at the door at the day of the conference. This participant was later able to transfer the new addition to his cultural capital to a paid position for another organisation, which he found thanks to his connections (social capital). Meanwhile, volunteers who worked as ushers and other low skilled tasks for the conference would have had much greater difficulty translating their learning into paid employment.
5. We acknowledge that sometimes apprenticeship training can be implemented through formal and nonformal methods.

References

Abdennur, A. (1987). *The conflict resolution syndrome: Volunteerism, violence and beyond.* Ottawa: University of Ottawa Press.

Abers, R. (2000). *Inventing local democracy: Grassroots politics in Brazil.* Boulder, Co.: Lynne Rienner Publishers.

Andersen, S. M. (1999). *Mandatory community service: Citizenship education or involuntary servitude? Issue Paper.* Denver, CO: Education Commission of the State.

Baiocchi, G. (1999). Participation, activism, and politics: The Porto Alegre experiment and deliberative democratic Theory. Retrieved April 28, 2001, from http://www.ssc.wisc.edu/~wright/Baiocchi.PDF

Billett, S. (2001). *Learning in the workplace: strategies for effective practice.* Crows Nest, Australia: Allen & Unwin.

Bourdieu, P. (1986). The forms of capital (R. Nice, Trans.). In J. Richardson (Ed.), *Handbook of theory and research for the sociology of education* (pp. 241–258). New York: Greenwood Press.

Brudney, J. (1990). *Fostering volunteer programs in the public sector*. San Francisco: Jossey-Bass.

Chinman, M., & Wandersman, A. (1999). The benefits and costs of volunteering in community organizations: Review and practical implications. *Nonprofit and Voluntary Sector Quarterly, 28*(1), 46–63.

Clover, D. E., & Hall, B. L. (2000). *In search of social movement learning: The growing jobs for living project. NALL Working Paper*. Retrieved December 5, 2002, from http://www.oise.utoronto.ca/depts/sese/csew/nall/res/18insearchof.htm

Cnaan, R. A., Handy, F., & Wadsworth, M. (1996). Defining who is a volunteer: Conceptual and empirical considerations. *Nonprofit and Voluntary Sector Quarterly, 25*(3), 364–383.

Cox, E. (2002). Rewarding volunteers: A study of participant responses to the assessment and accreditation of volunteer learning. *Studies in the Education of Adults, 34*(2), 156–170.

Elsdon, K. T. (1995). Values and learning in voluntary organizations. *International Journal of Lifelong Education, 14*(1), 75–82.

Elsdon, K. T., Reynolds, J., & Stewart, S. (1995). *Voluntary organisations: Citizenship, learning and change*. Leicester, England: NIACE (National Organization for Adult Learning) & Department of Adult Education University of Nottingham.

Ferguson, R. M. (2000). *An evaluation of the Carbondale Women's Center volunteer training program (Illinois)*. Unpublished PhD thesis, Southern Illinois University, Carbondale.

Foley, G. (1999). *Learning in social action:Aa contribution to understanding informal education*. New York: Zed.

Foster, M. K., & Meinhard, A. G. (2000). *"Structuring Student Volunteering Programs to the Benefit of Students and the Community: The Ontario Experience"* presented at the International Society for Third-Sector Research Fourth International Conference: Dublin, July 5–8, 2000. Retrieved June 13, 2003, from http://www.jhu.edu/~istr/conferences/dublin/abstracts/foster-meinhard.html

Freire, P. (1970/2000). *Pedagogy of the oppressed: 30th anniversary edition*. New York: Continuum.

Government of Ontario. (1997). *Ontario Works Act, 1997*. Retrieved June 13, 2003, from http://192.75.156.68/DBLaws/Statutes/English/97o25a_e.htm

Grolnic, S. (2001). Informal learning in the workplace: What can be learned doing a McJob? Unpublished PhD Thesis, Harvard University.

Hall, M., McKeown, L. E., Roberts, K., Canadian Centre for Philanthropy, & Statistics Canada. (2001). *Caring Canadians, involved Canadians: highlights from the 2000 National Survey of Giving, Volunteering and Participating*. Ottawa: Statistics Canada.

Handy, F., Cnaan, R. A., Brudney, J. L., Ascoli, U., Meijs, L. C. M. P., & Ranade, S. (2000). Public perception of "Who is a volunteer": An examination of the net-cost approach from a cross-cultural perspective. *Voluntas: International Journal of Voluntary and Nonprofit Organizations, 11*(1), 45–65.

Hustinx, L., & Lammertyn, F. (2003). Collective and reflexive styles of volunteering: A sociological modernization perspective. *Voluntas: International Journal of Voluntary and Nonprofit Organizations, 14*(2), 167–187.

Illich, I. (1970). *Deschooling society*. NY: Longman.

Ilsley, P. J. (1990). *Enhancing the volunteer experience: New insights on strengthening volunteer participation, learning, and commitment*. San Francisco: Jossey-Bass.

Kuhn, A. (1990). *A handbook for volunteer coordinators in Head Start* (ERIC Document: ED396828). District of Columbia.

Livingstone, D. W. (1999). Exploring the icebergs of adult learning: Findings of the First Canadian Survey of Informal Learning Practices. *Canadian Journal for the Study of Adult Education, 13*(2), 49–72.

Livingstone, D. W. (2001a). Adults' Informal Learning: Definitions, Findings, Gaps and Future Research. NALL Website, www.nall.ca

Livingstone, D. W. (2001b). *Basic patterns of work and learning in Canada: Findings of the 1998 NALL survey of informal learning and related Statistics Canada surveys*. http://www.oise.utoronto.ca/depts/sese/csew/nall/res/33working&learning.htm

Livingstone, D. W. (forthcoming). Learning in Places: The informal education reader. In Z. Bekerman, N. Burbules & D. Silberman (Eds.), *Learning in hidden places: The informal education reader*. New York: Peter Lang.

Loupe, D. (2000). Community Service: Mandatory or Voluntary? *School Administrator, 57*(7), 32–34, 36–39.

McCoy, M. (1996). *Planning community-wide study circle programs. A step-by-step guide* (ERIC Document: ED391940). Connecticut: Study Circles Resource Center.

Merrifield, J. (2001). *Learning citizenship:Learning from experience and trust.* Retrieved May 27, 2003, from http://www.commonwealthfoundation.com/documents/learning.pdf

Mezirow, J., & Associates (2001). *Learning as transformation. Critical perspectives on a theory in progress.* San Francisco: Jossey-Bass.

Ojanlatva, A. (1991). *Training volunteers for an AIDS buddy program.* (ERIC Document Reproduction Service No. ED336378).

Ontario Ministry of Community Family and Children's Services (2003). *Employment assistance.* Retrieved June 14, 2003, from http://www.cfcs.gov.on.ca/CFCS/en/programs/IES/OntarioWorks/ employmentAssistance/default.htm

Ontario Ministry of Education and Training (1999). *Ontario Secondary Schools Grades 9–12, Program and Diploma Requirements 1999.* Retrieved June 13, 2003, from http://mettowas21.edu.gov.on.ca/ eng/document/curricul/secondary/oss/oss.pdf

Oxford English Dictionary (2003). *Oxford English Dictionary: volunteer.* Retrieved April 21, 2003, from http://www.chass.utoronto.ca/patbin/new/oed-idx?fmt = entry&type = entry&byte = 543111921

Pateman, C. (1970). *Participation and democratic theory.* Cambridge: University Press.

Payne, S. (2001). The role of volunteers in hospice bereavement support in New Zealand. *Palliative Medicine, 15*(2), 107–115.

Percy, K., Barnes, B., Graddon, A., & Machell, J. (1988). *Learning in voluntary organisations* (ERIC Document: ED318890): National Institute of Adult Continuing Education, Leicester, England.

Polanyi, M. (1966). *The tacit dimension.* New York: Doubleday.

Quarter, J., Mook, L., & Richmond, B. J. (2003). *What counts: Social accounting for nonprofits and cooperatives.* Upper Saddle River, NJ: Prentice Hall.

Rayner, H., & Marshall, J. (2003). Training volunteers as conversation partners for people with aphasia. *International Journal of Language & Communication Disorders, 38*(2), 149–164.

Richmond, B. J., & Mook L. (2001). Social audit report for Waterloo Co-operative Residence Incorporated (WCRI). Toronto: Author.

Roker, D., Player, K., & Coleman, J. (1999). Young people's voluntary and campaigning activities as sources of political education. *Oxford Review of Education, 25*(1–2), 185–198.

Salamon, L. M., Anheier, H. K., List, R., Toepler, S., Sokolowski, S. W., & Associates. (1999). *Global civil society: Dimensions of the nonprofit sector.* Baltimore: The Johns Hopkins Centre for Civil Society Studies.

Salamon, L., & Sokolowski, W. (2002). Institutional roots of volunteering: Towards a macro-structural theory of individual voluntary action. Paper presented at ARNOVA Conference. Montreal, Canada, November 14–16.

Schugurensky, D. (2000). The forms of informal learning: Towards a conceptualization of the field. *NALL working paper #19–2000.* Retrieved August 28, 2003, from http://www.oise.utoronto.ca/ depts/sese/csew/nall/res/19formsofinformal.htm

Schugurensky, D. (2001). Grassroots democracy: The participatory budget of Porto Alegre. *Canadian Dimension, 35*(1), 30–32.

Schugurensky, D. (2002). Transformative learning and transformative politics: The pedagogical dimension of participatory democracy and social action. In E. O'Sullivan, A. Morrell & M. A. O'Connor (Eds.), *Expanding the boundaries of transformative learning: essays on theory and praxis* (pp. 59–76). New York: Palgrave.

Sheard, J. (1995). From lady bountiful to active citizen: Volunteering and the voluntary sector. In J. D. Smith, C. Rochester & R. Hedley (Eds.), *An introduction to the voluntary sector.* New York: Routledge.

South Carolina State Department of Health and Environmental Control. (1991). *Volunteer training manual.* Bureau of Home Health and Long Term Care. Columbia, SC.

Steger, M. A. E. (2002). Welfare reform: Process, participation, discourse, and implications. *The Journal of Politics, 64*(3), 914–918.

Stenzel, A. K., & Feeney, H. M. (1968). *Volunteer training and development; A manual for community groups.* New York: Seabury Press.

Stukas, A. A., Snyder, M., & Clary, E. G. (1999). The effects of "mandatory volunteerism" in intentions to volunteer. *Educational Horizons, 77*(4), 194–201.

Tedesco, J. E. (1991). *Catholic schools and volunteers: A planned involvement.* Washington: National Catholic Educational Association.

Thomas, A. M. (1998). The tolerable contradictions of prior learning assessment. In S. M. Scott, B. Spencer & A. M. Thomas (Eds.), *Learning for life: Canadian readings in adult education* (pp. 330–342). Toronto: Thompson Educational Publishing.

Tough, A. (1971). *The adult's learning projects.* Toronto: OISE Press.

Westheimer, J., & Kahne, J. (1999). Service learning as democratic action. *Educational Horizons, 77*(4), 186–193.

Westheimer, J., & Kahne, J. (2002). *What kind of citizen? The politics of educating for democracy.* Paper presented at the Annual Meeting of the American Educational Research Association, New Orleans, LA.

Wilson, L., Steele, J., Thompson, E., & D'Heron, C. (2002). The leadership institute for active aging: A volunteer recruitment and retention model. *Journal of Volunteer Administration, 20*(2), 28–36.

Wisconsin Public Television and Wisconsin State Department of Public Instruction. (1995). *School volunteer resource guide.* Madison, WI.

54

THE OTHER HALF (OR MORE) OF THE STORY: UNPAID HOUSEHOLD AND CARE WORK AND LIFELONG LEARNING

Margrit Eichler

Ontario Institute for Studies in Education of the University of Toronto, Canada

Looking at how adult educators see adult learning, we would expect to see family and housework front and center as an area of utmost importance. Consider the following: Informal learning is the truly lifelong process whereby every individual acquires attitudes, values, skills and knowledge from daily experience and the educative influences and resources in his or her environment – from family and neighbours, from work and play, from the market place, the library and the mass media (Garrick, 1996).

It involves "[l]earning to love the world and make it more human; learning to develop in and through creative work" (Williams as quoted in Collins, 1998).

Indeed, adult educators agree that civil society itself depends critically on lifelong learning.

> In sociological language, we can speak of the cultural, social and personal reproductive tasks of civil society. This rather flat language does not fully communicate what is at stake. If the reproductive tasks are interfered with, or cannot be carried out for systematically rooted reasons, then the spiritual, moral and social infrastructure of the economy and state will be imperiled. (Welton, 1998)

In considering various perspectives on informal learning, Garrick (1996) sums up the overall understanding as follows: "... people engaged in day to day situations and interventions; people trying to make sense of their lives." Much of contemporary adult education is influenced by Habermas' notion of a life-world, who himself derived the concept from Alfred Schutz (Williamson, 1998). Collins (1998) notes that "The concept also accounts for how in social relations we blend our individual experiences with the life-world of others. Thus, the lifeworld incorporates community-forming processes that actively and passively shape it into a social world."

One would expect that such a conception of lifelong learning has generated a

International Handbook of Educational Policy, 1023–1042
Nina Bascia, Alister Cumming, Amanda Datnow, Kenneth Leithwood and David Livingstone (Eds.)
© *2005 Springer. Printed in Great Britain.*

great wealth of information about what is learned in the family and the home. After all, this is the generally acknowledged place where biological and social reproduction occurs, where "attitudes, values, skills and knowledge" are acquired from daily experience of interacting in a social context, where people's character and citizenship are shaped, an essential part of our lifeworld.

Canadian adult education, in particular, has a "historic commitment to helping Canadians 'live a life' and 'earn a living' (Coady's metaphor of the 'good and abundant life'" (Welton, 1998). However, it seems that only the second part of this commitment is actually undertaken: a concern with earning a living, and definitely *not* with living a life if the work involved is carried out within the home and is unpaid. When I was invited to write this chapter on unpaid housework and lifelong learning, I eagerly went to the literature to enjoy and learn from the surely abundant reflections of adult educators on this important topic. Three computer searches, conducted by three different people, using a variety of synonyms such as housework, domestic labour, caring work, etc., resulted in zero references. In some panic, I asked knowledgeable colleagues: what had I done wrong? Would they guide me to the important works in this area? At the end of this process I still had only two references. There are, of course, two huge literatures on lifelong learning and on housework but it seems that they almost never cross paths. The two exceptions are Livingstone's 1999 NALL survey, which did ask questions about housework and learning and at least demonstrated that this is an area in which much learning occurs, and the other a set of German studies on worker-self-managers that will be discussed below (Frey, 2003).

The first question that arises, then, is why is there such a monumental oversight of this topic within adult education? The second issue that follows is: what are some of the questions that we might profitably investigate with respect to lifelong learning and unpaid housework, and of what relevance might they be to the larger understanding of adult education? I will address both of these questions in the following, and in the second section draw on some preliminary findings of an empirical study on lifelong learning and unpaid housework. I will here briefly introduce the study to set the context.

Study on Lifelong Learning and Unpaid Housework

This study is one of a series of studies of the WALL project (Work and Lifelong Learning, see http://wall.oise.utoronto.ca/ for a description of the complete project). The housework study consists of four phases, and at the time of writing this we are at phase 2. The first phase involved sending questionnaires to members of various women's groups, asking about the nature of their unpaid housework as well as community work and the learning attached to it. The second phase involves focus groups that follow up on some of the findings of the questionnaires. To date, four focus groups have been held. The intent is not to determine how much housework individuals perform. Instead, our intent is to discover what category of work is mentioned when questions are posed in an open-ended manner, and, equally important, what category of work is *not* mentioned although we know that it is performed in many households. It is this latter question that we probe in the focus groups, since it allows us tap into some of the invisible work that is performed within households and the tacit learning that accompanies it.

The Monumental Oversight: Why the Overwhelming Neglect of Lifelong Learning through Unpaid Housework?

Due to the fact that lifelong learning has largely been the domain of adult education, the enormous amount of informal learning that children acquire in the home is generally omitted in this context. I shall here conform to this practice.

(a) Sexism in Adult Education

I define sexism in research as a tripartite problem of a) maintaining a gender hierarchy, (b) gender insensitivity, and c) double standards based on sex (Eichler, 1988b, 2002). Several authors have remarked on a prevailing androcentric tradition within adult education, part of maintaining a gender hierarchy. Stalker (1998) puts this argument in a most forceful manner.

Welton (1998) notes that the contributions of women in adult education are routinely ignored in the literature – another aspect of maintaining a gender hierarchy:

> Women's associations and movements were important oppositional learning sites in Canada's time of great transformation. Why have references to Women's Institutes, the YWCA, the Women's League for Peace and Freedom, the Home and School associations been so marginal in Canadian adult education history? ... These sites enabled women to school themselves for active citizenship. It was in these lifeworld institutions that women entered public debate and began to transform Canadian society.

This point is echoed by Selman (1998). There are, of course, feminist adult educators who have vigorously challenged such androcentric tradition, and many educators do make formal bows in their direction. Miles (1988), e.g., argues that the women's movement provides possibilities for important linkages between adult education and a new paradigm of looking at the world. Scott (1998) looks at feminist theory as one of the radical orientations in adult education. Hart (1992) probably comes the closest to looking at housework. She uses the concept of subsistence work (following Mies & Shiva, 1993) in order to argue that the ultimate purpose of subsistence work is "to maintain and improve *life*" (Hart, 1992). Others argue that lifelong learning would have a different focus if the emphasis was on the homeplace rather than the marketplace (Gouthro & Plumb, 2003). In a useful summary of feminist research, Merriam and Caffarella (1999) discuss feminist contributions, which center around a feminist pedagogy that is liberatory and promotes personal emancipation and public action. In spite of such potential openings, I did not find any empirical investigation of how people might learn through housework, besides Livingstone's statistical data.

Unpaid housework is seen as an activity engaged in by women. It is true internationally that women do perform significantly more unpaid housework (Benéria & Roldán, 1987; Ross, 1987; Coverman, 1989; South & Spitze, 1994; Massey, Hahn et al., 1995; Kiger & Riley, 1996; Perkins & DeMeis, 1996; Baxter, 1997; John & Shelton, 1997; Sanchez & Thomson, 1997; Sullivan, 1997; Kamo & Cohen, 1998; Speakman & Marchington, 1999; Beaujot, Haddad et al., 2000; Bond & Sales, 2001; Leonard, 2001; Pittman, Kerpelman et al., 2001; Windebank, 2001) than men although most men probably do *some* housework. The strong empirical connection of housework with women has led to a strong theoretical connection as well (see Doucet 2000). This goes some distance to explain why a discipline with a historic androcentric bent would have overlooked this area.

(b) Unpaid Housework is Not Seen as Real Work

Beyond its association with women, for the longest time housework was not only not seen as work, it was explicitly excluded from the concept of work. Hence, the home was not seen has a workplace, and if housework was not work, then obviously adult education did not need to consider the relationship between unpaid housework and adult learning.

By now, most researchers would acknowledge that work comes in two versions – paid and unpaid – and that the unpaid work performed within the home is of tremendous economic importance. Just how enormous the economic importance of housework is depends on the way it is conceptualized (cf. Eichler, 2003). Chandler estimates the gross value of unpaid housework in Canada as either 46.3% of the Gross Domestic Product (GDP) if calculating the opportunity cost, or as 41.4% of the GDP if calculating the replacement cost (Chandler, 1994).

The Australian economist Ironmonger has argued that in order to make meaningful comparisons between the value of market work and unpaid housework, we need to calculate the gross values in comparable ways, by including both capital and labour in both instances. We thus need to include the capital goods used in household production (housing, vehicles and domestic appliances) along with the value of unpaid labour to arrive at a figure that is comparable to the GDP. He calculates the Gross Household Product (GHP) in this manner at about 98% of the Gross Market Product (GMP). "In other words, the aggregate value of the goods and services produced in the household sector of the economy is almost equivalent to the entire output of the market economy" (Ironmonger, 1996). Whatever method we use, clearly the economic importance of unpaid household work is very large and very important.

Furthermore, paid work and unpaid housework intersect in a number of significant ways. Macroeconomic theory usually excludes unpaid household labour from consideration, in spite of its massive value. This, in turn, distorts policies (Bakker, 1998) with particularly important consequences for women (see below for some examples). Some of the ways in which paid work and unpaid household labour intersect include the following:

1. The money economy rests squarely on the basis of unpaid household labour. Without the social and biological production and reproduction of the labour force, there would be no paid labour force (Boserup, 1970; Benéria & Roldán, 1987; Waring, 1988; Ironmonger, 1996; Bakker, 1998).
2. Household work maintains the human capital that the market economy requires (Ironmonger, 1996). Changes in the money economy result in changes in unpaid labour. For instance, if hospital downsizing results in patients being released earlier into their families, this intensifies the work conducted at home. What is claimed as a cost reduction in public accounting thus becomes a cost increase for family carers (Aronson & Neysmith, 1997) This might even take the extreme form that a person, usually a woman, has to give up her paid work in order to look after an adult in need of care –with lifelong negative consequences in terms of seniority and entitlement to pension benefits. If we considered the value of unpaid work for policy formation, such cost-cuttings might therefore possibly be shown to be economically inefficient.
3. Workplace organization and regulations influence the division of labour within the household. For instance, Arrighi and Maume found that men's contributions to household work decreased as their subordination in the workplace increased (Arrighi & Maume, 2000). Women's household work decreases as they engage in more paid work (Baxter, 1997).
4. Higher earnings of women result in their purchasing more household services, thus reducing their household labour and affecting the market through increased consumption of services, although this is mediated by race and the husband's education (Cohen, 1998).
5. The amount and type of household work for which people are responsible affects their earnings on the labour market (Noonan, 2001). Some authors suggest that "The subordination of women in the family leads to their subordination in the labour market" (Leonard, 2001). However, it is probably more appropriate to postulate a two-way interaction than a one-way effect.

Family life events influence the nature and amount of household work performed which in turn influences the labour force participation of women and to a lesser extent that of men. For example, marriage, separation, divorce, arrival and departure of children, chronic illness or disability of oneself or family members can all affect patterns of labour force participation. They are also major occasions for learning new skills.

In other words – housework is real work in terms of the time and energy it requires, in terms of the goods and services it produces, and in terms of its economic impact, but it tends not be regarded as such because it is unpaid, and because it tends to be devalued. People spend about the same amount of time on unpaid work as on paid work, although this varies by sex: men spend more time on paid work, and women on unpaid work. (See Livingstone chapter, table 1, and Ironmonger, 1996.)

(c) Adult Education has Become a Corporate Enterprise

There is an on-going critique of adult education that charges that it has become too much of a corporate enterprise. Collins (1998, p. 56) notes that modern adult education practice "has become effectively commodified and given over largely to the ethos of bureaucratic control and corporate enterprise". This compromises the notion of the adult as an autonomous participant who learns voluntarily. In a review of the adult education literature, Solar (1998) found that by far the greatest attention is now oriented towards the labour market.

While many adult educators critique this trend, it certainly does not help put unpaid housework onto the research agenda. On the other hand, it is worth serious study to examine to what degree and in what way corporations actually do try to educate housewives and other consumers in order to increase consumption of items they wish to sell. The supermarket at which I shop at present routinely lists information on how to choose and utilize the exotic fruits and vegetables it offers for sale, and it also offers an astonishing array of classes. In June of 2003, there were 34 seminars offered just in that month, ranging from cooking classes – for kids and speciality cooking for adults – to seminars about computing, various health issues and pregnancy and labour. While the health courses are free, the cooking courses (the vast majority) charge a modest fee (Loblaws, 2003).

(d) Adult Education Tends to Focus on the Educator, Not the Learner

There is a prevailing concern with what is an appropriate pedagogy for today's world – in other words: how and what should I teach? rather than: how and what should I learn? For instance, in exploring the difference between lifelong learning and lifelong education, Collins suggests that

> ... it is useful to think of lifelong learning as referring to the actual experience of the individual or of groups of learners. The focus, then, is on how psychological factors, social contexts, teaching practices, curriculum formation and educational management techniques come to bear on the shaping of learning experiences in their immediacy. (Collins, 1998)

This is clearly a notion of lifelong learning that is structured, planned, and organized by adult educators – not informal self-directed learning that is self-initiated and undertaken by an individual in her home – which is likely a particularly important form of learning that occurs through the performance of housework. (See Livingstone's chapter in this volume for a clarification of the concepts of formal, informal and non-formal learning and education.) In her review of the adult education literature, Solar (1998) noted the relative unimportance of the adult learner in the literature.

Overcoming the Monumental Oversight

In order to deal effectively with learning through household work, adult education will need to overcome its sexist bias, accept housework as real work and shift the focus to include informal learning that occurs through housework and care work and that is self-initiated and self-managed by the learner.

If we were to engage in this endeavour – what might be the benefits? In the next section I will first look at some preliminary findings from our study. I will then consider some of the questions directed to lifelong learning and paid work, and speculate on what might be some of the insights we would derive if we were to expand our notion of work to include unpaid housework.

Asking Questions Concerning Housework and Lifelong Learning

I will draw here on some preliminary findings from our questionnaire and the first four focus groups. Our first wave of 254 respondents to the questionnaire were all drawn through a number of women's groups. In one of our groups we asked the women to hand the questionnaire to their partners. Therefore, 38 of the respondents are men. The respondents are not representative of the general Canadian population, being mostly middle class, white, and very socially active. Our intent was to examine how housework is conceptualized by a group of women who mostly define themselves as feminists and who are likely more alert to some of the invisible work performed under the rubric of housework and care work than most other people. This, we reasoned, would enable the women to recognize the learning that takes place through this work. If people are unaware of the actual work they perform, they are likely to be "competence-blind" (Butler, 1993) with respect to the skills required.

Of the questionnaire group, then, 46.5% did not identify anything they had learned through their housework/care work, while 53.5% indicated that they had learned something. At the more formal end, people learn by taking courses, attending lectures, seminars, workshops, conferences or tutorials, although it is not clear from the data just how formal or informal these courses are. They range from university courses to training for specific activities, such as learning to breastfeed through the La Leche League or by attending a once only seminar on bladder control.

Most learn more informally, by discussing issues, talking and sharing information with friends and neighbours, or by learning from professionals in informal ways, as well as participating in e-mail lists, on-line help lists, internet searches and through meetings. Reading is of course of major importance, and some use tapes, mention TV, or participate in study groups. Finally, learning by doing is a major aspect, in other words, experiential learning. Many people state that they learn both on their own as well as together with others.

In our focus groups (consisting so far only of women) we asked people again what housework/care work they had done during the last year, and we received mostly (but not entirely) the standard list of specific tasks that are the concern of most of the studies on housework – namely housekeeping functions such as cleaning, doing the laundry, preparing meals, transporting children, etc. We then provided a list of six activities drawn from the critical literature: providing emotional support; organizing, planning, managing or arranging matters; dealing with crises; maintaining contact with family members or friends; self care; and conflict resolution and asked whether they engaged in this work, and uniformly respondents all agreed they did. This is my life! one of them exclaimed to the nodding of heads around the table.

Even in this group of mostly feminist women, then, much of the work they did was not perceived as work at the conscious level, although there were some exceptions to this. If people do not know that they are performing work, clearly they will not realize what they may learn through it. The task in recognizing learning through housework, then, is a double one: first, to bring to consciousness what work is actually done, and then to get people to think about what they learned through it.

The exceptions to the rule were women who had to reflect very carefully about their unpaid work, for instance, because they had chosen to become full-time mothers and felt considerable pressure from other people to take up paid work, or because they had lost their paid job due to disability and had to re-think the value and meaning of their work in a world which discriminates against people with disabilities.

We approached the learning issue by asking the women how their work had changed over the past five years, and following this, what they had to learn in order to be able to manage these changes. Most of the women – although not all – had experienced some dramatic changes within the last five years, although for some others the most important changes were farther back in their lives. Some of the examples include the death of their children's father, losing one's job, retiring, having another baby, children growing older, finding out one's child is autistic:

> My son, 5 years ago, I didn't even know he was autistic. You know, he was, just seemed a little slow in his speech development. I didn't have a 14-year-old son 5 years ago. This is like, over night this kid just goes from child from heaven to child from hell. And I have very little support at home in terms of my partner helping out, because he's had a year of 18 hours in bed. So you know, I've been it. And it's just been devastating.[1]

Still more changes include the death of a husband who required constant care, grandchildren grown up, a son "who fried his brain on drugs, adult children moved away, living alone, turning blind, going back to school, caring for a husband who has become less self-reliant, an adult child moving back home, both husband and wife losing their jobs, their house and having to move into a dump" in a different city, becoming the care-giver of elderly parents, and much more.

The women talked about what they learned primarily in terms of self-growth, rather than in terms of learning to perform specific skills (e.g., learning new recipes, learning how to do home repairs, etc.). They mentioned having to learn discipline, acquiring a different attitude towards time, learning to cope with depression, and becoming self-aware. The disabled women, in particular, talked about having to find the inner strength to value themselves when all external props are gone and in the face of rampant external de-valuation.

Naomi, a mother of two young children had spontaneously said self-awareness when I asked what they had learned through the changes they had experienced. She explained:

Naomi: I wasn't sure if I wanted to have another child, because it's a lot of work, and it hurts. And, my first daughter, I had a lot of health problems related to having a baby. And so, I had to learn literally about my body. When I say self-awareness', I mean every aspect, because I had to learn.

ME: And how did you do that? Did you read? Did you go to classes? Did you see something on TV? Did you talk with people?

Naomi: I just got used to myself. In terms of what changes my body went through. I had sudden allergies that were death-related allergies, and so, I had to figure out what I was allergic to. I went to an allergist for that. But other things, you know, like, you eat and you get a different reaction. So, it's more self-observation, I guess.

She, like others, also mentioned interest courses, such as learning how to ski, reading, traveling, counseling, talking with other women, talking with her doctor, and using the internet.

Another mother of two young children, Barbara, also said that self-awareness was the most important thing she learned, along with the capacity to change – a theme that was repeated over and over again.

I maybe talk to peers my own age group, or in similar situations, and go, 'Nah, that's not me.' I very much know who I am, and am at the point were there's growing to be done. It's understanding that we go through phases in our life. For a long time, I always thought it was going to be one way, and then it hits you, no, you're going through a phase. This is the phase – welcoming that, 'accepting' it. I hear you guys saying accepting', right? And not anticipating, but knowing that it's not a static state – it will change. And, I will be required to change with it, whether I'm ready or not. And again, right now, that direct link goes to my children.

In contrast to the answers to the questionnaire, *all* of the women in the focus groups realized that they had learned significant skills. When we asked them *how* they acquired these skills, the answers were complex and defy simple categorization. Self-observation and awareness emerged as two important ways of learning, as well as "just doing it", and unexpectedly therapy played such a strong role in the first focus group that we included a probe about it in the subsequent groups. It was important for the women in two of the other groups, but not for the group of disabled women, who were too poor to pay for therapy, but who mentioned group support instead.

As became clear in the focus groups, change, sometimes very dramatic changes, are part of most people's life cycle. While some women, particularly the disabled women, but also some of the others had gone through traumatic changes, everyone had experienced changes that required new skills from them. What happens if people fail to acquire the necessary skills to cope with new situations? The next segment provides an example.

Dorothy talked about having to cope with her adult son moving back with her. She realized that she had to learn to say no to him, and mused that she might sell her house and move into a condo if he was not going to move. This led another participant to recount the following about people she knew:

> I know people who've done that. 'I am going to move into a condo.' Or I know one family that moved to Vancouver (laughs). Their son was separating from his wife, and he had quit his job in another city and he was moving back to Toronto, he was going to move in with them. Well it was amazing. They had been talking about moving out to the West coast for a long time, but I mean it was just done (laughter). 'Gee I'm sorry for going to Vancouver!'

Another participant replied:

> That would be a bit sad, though. Because when I lived on the West coast, there were 3 or 4 families I met who said they had moved out West because they were tired of babysitting, they were tired of being put upon. And they didn't really like it. There they were, hundreds, thousands of miles away from their family, because they wouldn't put their foot down and stay put and live their lives as they really wanted to.

We could identify the latter families as people who did *not* learn how to set the appropriate boundaries and hence they disrupted family ties very severely. Clearly, the learning that takes place in the home is of the most profound importance.

Now, turning back to the literature on learning and paid work, let us see how themes from lifelong learning and paid work might or might not apply to unpaid housework.

(a) The Interplay Between Motivation and Incentives to Learn

I will here consider an edited book that claims that it "looks at what makes adults participate in education and training, particularly in relation to work"

(Hirsch & Wagner, 1995). The book explores the nature and effectiveness of various types of incentives.

Ryan (1995) defines training as incorporating both "vocationally relevant education and learning by experience", which means that it should be relevant to housework. The major "incentive for adults to undertake training is an expectation of gains in job rewards, supplemented sometimes by consumption and developmental benefits." He then focusses on pecuniary gains (p. 14), which may take the form of wages or bonuses for workers who engage in training (Hirsch & Wagner, 1995; Mikulecky, 1995; Ryan, 1995). Some countries have legally mandated access to training programs (Luttringer, 1995; Noyelle & Hirsch, 1995) and employer incentives to provide training (Bishop, 1995; Mikulecky, 1995).

At first look, this seems completely inapplicable to housework. There are no wages or bonuses, since the work is unpaid, and no employers who require incentives to provide training.

However, the basic assumption that adults engage in learning primarily in expectation of job rewards may no longer be tenable once we start to include unpaid housework and care work. There may be some pecuniary gain, such as when people research major purchases, and achieve significant savings, which is an activity that was mentioned by some of our respondents on the questionnaire. Other savings may be effected by producing items at home that would otherwise have to be purchased. Nevertheless, willingness to learn is likely mostly of intrinsic value to unpaid houseworkers. Exploring this might shed important light on understanding motivations for learning not only where externally financed incentives are missing, but also in situations where financial incentives are present. Educators in the humanistic tradition hold that "the individual may be most productive when she feels that work is personally meaningful and not simply an instrumental means to another end" (Garrick, 1996).

(b) Benefits to Civil Society

There is some recognition that On-the-Job-Training has social benefits, besides benefits to the individual workers who take/receive the training and the employer. Bishop, for instance, notes that

> ... private benefits account for only part of the total benefits to society of education and training, however. People who have received more or better education and training or who achieved more during the experience benefit others in society by paying higher taxes, by making discoveries or artistic contributions that benefit others in society, by being more likely to give time and money to charity, by being less likely to experience long periods of hospitalization that are paid for by insurance or government, and in many other ways ... (Bishop, 1995).

Similarly, Sticht argues that "not only may companies influence the productivity of their current workplace, but the intergenerational transfer of educational outcomes from parents to their children may also improve the productivity of schools and a more competent future workforce will be available ..." (Sticht, 1995).

How might society profit if people were encouraged to learn more about household and care work? Part of care work directly saves money for governments, hospitals, etc., particularly when we are dealing with preventive actions. More importantly, however, it creates healthier and stronger people. Health maintenance is one of the most important activities that are fostered (or neglected) within the home. In our study, we found that health maintenance is a very important activity undertaken by people – and not just for their immediate family, but also for extended kin and unrelated people.

Various countries provide some modest legal access for workers to vocational training (Luttringer, 1995; Noyelle & Hirsch, 1995). Garrick (1996) argues that "[t]here is scope for the extension of a public subsidy beyond its traditional associations with unemployment and formal schooling in order to provide more loans and grants to individuals sponsoring their own learning" (p. 36). Should we have legally mandated access to training for unpaid household and care work occurring within private households? Implementing such a scheme would *not* present a theoretically insurmountable problem. There might be some very concrete benefits along with some very real dangers. The benefits are potential better care and health maintenance of people. The dangers include its possible misuse for political reasons. If such training was provided within a neo-conservative climate, it might lead to further downloading of services onto the family – meaning primarily onto individual women – and a subsequent potential deterioration, rather than improvement of care, together with a substantial danger to the health of the care provider.

Home economics used to teach a range of housekeeping skills, but tended to so in a very gendered manner, thus reinforcing the separate spheres of women and men – not a result most of us would wish to see today.

With respect to democracy, Okin (1989) has mounted a strong argument that gender equality in society is dependent on gender equality within the family. She suggests "Until there is justice within the family, women will not be able to gain equality in politics, at work, or in any other sphere" (Okin, 1989). While I disagree with the monocausal nature of the statement, there is nevertheless clearly a strong interdependence between the status of women in various social spheres. Children will learn – or fail to learn – within the family to accord equal dignity to all, and to deal with conflicts in a constructive (or destructive) manner. They will also pick up attitudes towards environmental issues, social responsibility, and much more. Parent training could potentially have a great impact on civil society, depending on how it is undertaken.

(c) Has Housework Become More Kowledge Based?

One of the much discussed shifts in paid work is the move towards a knowledge-based economy (Livingstone, 1999), and its corresponding needs for skills, training and education.

In asking what shifts have occurred within housework, and what knowledge is therefore needed for competently performing unpaid housework, we are at the disadvantage that there is no clear evidence how the nature of housework has shifted. There are a number of studies which allow us to point to some of the very broad changes that have occurred. For instance, the change from an agricultural to an industrial and post-industrial society has had significant impacts on the housework of women (Cohen, 1988) and children (Rollings-Magnusson, 2003). The influx of machines into the home has to some degree industrialized housework and child care has to some degree been professionalized (Eichler, 1988). We have some notion of the differences in housework performed by women of three generations (Luxton, 1980). However, we are missing detailed studies of how housework and care work have changed and continue to change over the life course and with the introduction of new appliances and products. When new practices appear, we need to learn new things – most of us have learned how to operate a computer, a microwave oven, various other appliances and a car, for instance – but we are likely to also forget old skills when they are no longer as necessary or functional as they used to be, such as baking our own bread, sewing, darning socks, making jam and preserves, etc.

The disappearance of certain knowledges seems to me to be a missing puzzle piece when looking at "the knowledge-based economy" – there is a suggestion that knowledge is added, not that knowledge may also be lost. Both in housework as well as in paid work it would seem to be valuable to ask "What new knowledges have people acquired? What old knowledges and skills have people lost?" In immigrant countries such as Canada, Australia and the United States, but also increasingly in Europe, it would be interesting to examine what new ways of running households and caring for people are learned by immigrants – and what old ways are forgotten? For instance, is the new way of running households more or less ecologically damaging?

To answer such questions for housework requires, first, an assessment of the changes that have taken place, and second, an assessment how the necessary (or desirable) skills are acquired. I would guess that there has been a significant loss of skills with respect to some of the household tasks, but a gain in care for chronically disabled or sick children and adults – because of changes in medical knowledge and technology that keep children as well as adults alive who would in earlier times have simply died, coupled with de-institutionalization, which sends people back into their homes. One of our questionnaire respondents stated something along these lines: "I think hospital should give guidance to relative when a person leaves hospital after a very short stay and serious surgery".

This said, we need to look at disabled people not just as care recipients, but also as workers (for pay as well as with respect to unpaid housework) and as care providers – particularly as care providers. We found in our focus group that all of the disabled women provided very significant care to family members as well as friends and others. It would be very worthwhile to study the particular learning required of a disabled person in order to understand how she is able to perform the regular daily tasks of living while often providing care for others. As Marlene recounted:

> ME: Marlene, you were talking about that you actually took a course on how to learn to navigate with much less sight than you used to have, right?
>
> Marlene: Oh, yes. Well, CNIB gave these courses. For instance, it took me an hour's course, ... not lecture, seminar or something, to learn how to use my walking stick so that you don't ram everybody with it, and so on.

Likewise, those who live with disabled people need to learn how to behave appropriately. One of our questionnaire respondents, for instance, wrote: I have learned, am learning, how to support and accommodate the work methods of a woman labeled mentally handicapped in order to be able to provide weekly work for her (paid work) as our housekeeper (an agency helps me).

The disabled women, in particular, as well as the other women, needed to learn how to spend their energy, how much they can do, deciding what is too much.

(d) Looking at Prior Learning Assessment in a More Radical Way

Thomas (1998, p. 330) considers PLAR (Prior Learning Assessment and Recognition)[2] the "potentially most radical innovation in education since the development of mass formal education during the last century". Even a cursory look over the literature demonstrates, however, that it is still oriented either towards recognizing formal education obtained in a context different from the one within which it is to be recognized, or looking at experiential learning in terms of what has been learned through (and for) paid work. A more radical approach would be to recognize knowledge that has been acquired in whatever manner – completely outside a formal structure, for instance, thus opening the door to credit people with learning they may have acquired through household and care work.

Michelson (1996, p. 649) has argued for the need of a feminist intervention in the retheorizing of assessment practice based on epistemologies that do not reify the university as the unitary arbiter of knowledge claims or reinscribe the universal and disembodied knower of abstract masculinities. However, she also suggests that "skills such as 'parenting' and 'family management' are unlikely to be accredited, although some sporadic attempts to do so have been made" (Michelson, 1996, p. 647) However, a very interesting study by Butler (1993) lays the groundwork for assessing the skills acquired through housework by utilizing a systematic functional analysis of housework that makes visible the competencies involved in successfully running a household. She therefore demonstrates implicitly that the problem in recognizing learning through housework is neither a theoretical nor a practical one, but instead one of ideology and power differentials.

(e) Transferability of Knowledge Acquired Through Housework

"The key to the transferability of work-based learning, suggests Stevenson (1994), resides in the rich base of higher order procedural knowledge. The optimum path to these higher order cognitive functions is, argues Pea (1987), through engagement with authentic (workplace) activities within a 'purposeful' cultural and social context" (Garrick, 1996, p. 24).

There can be little doubt that the household is an authentic workplace with a purposeful cultural and social context – most people see raising their children, and caring for family members as highly authentic and purposeful, in terms of household and caring work.

However, whether or not we consider skills acquired through housework as transferable depends to a large degree on how we define housework. If the work is defined solely as a set of discrete specific skills, such as cooking, cleaning, etc., then we will see only the learning that attaches to these specific skills. Such skills would have a very limited applicability for paid work. Unfortunately, most of the operationalizations that are employed in research on housework are composed of just such specific sets of tasks. Hence, if we ask for the learning attached to these tasks, we will *not* be informed about higher order skills, such as the capacity to organize, administrate, communicate, establish lasting and positive human relations, time management, crisis management, adaptability to change, dealing with difficult personalities in a tactful and effective manner, kin-keeping, emotion work (cf. Hochschild, 1983), etc.

In fact, "[r]esponsibility for the household involves performing work that is largely mental" (Hessing, 1994, p. 613), because the planning and management aspects determine how well a household and a family will function.

In our questionnaire we found that women do a lot of managerial work, e.g., co-ordinating complicated family events, arranging moves for self or family members, co-ordinating family schedules, handling the business affairs of a disabled sibling, and so on. Nevertheless, when it came to learning, people tended to mention lower-order skills – e.g., learning about pet care, gardening related issues, renovations, etc. Remarkably few respondents actually listed higher-order skills, except when related to parenting.

When we probed on these issues in the focus groups, it became obvious that beyond these lower-order skills, women learn tremendous amounts about planning, time management, conflict resolution, health maintenance, avoiding crises and handling them when they arrived, dealing constructively with their own and other people's emotions, and much more. In particular, women learned how to deal with changes, expecting them, and adapting creatively to them. As Betty said: "I learned how to deal with change".

These findings resonate with a set of recent studies that have been carried out in Germany. In Germany, as elsewhere, the structure of the labour force has changed significantly in the past decade. To a much higher degree than before, workers must organize their own labour, paid work has lost its clear limits (*Entgrenzung der Arbeit*), requirements are more diffuse, only the bottom line counts, the workplace has lost its physical stability due to project work or for other reasons, and the boundary between management and workers has become blurred. The workplace is less secure than it used to be. This has led to the thesis that the modern worker needs to be a "worker-self-manager" *(Arbeitskraftunternehmer)* in the sense that s/he needs to manage his or her own work, although s/he is an employee. It is thus different from being an independent entrepreneur.

To the surprise of the researchers, a set of studies demonstrated that women cope much better with these new requirements than men. First this was attributed only to women who had lived in the former GDR, but a new set of studies found that this was also true for women from the west. In both cases, it is particularly mothers who combined paid work with unpaid work who have acquired the skills demanded by the new labour market. This is explained by the gender division of labour within the home. The conditions that are now starting to dominate the labour market are similar to those experienced by women in their work at home. Women who are doing much of the housework and care work are therefore more adept at dealing with the changed labour market conditions (Frey, unpublished).

Fenwick (2002, p. 15) studied the learning involved in Canadian women who became entrepreneurs, and noted that "In the stories of transition from an organizational job to self-employment ... [w]omen seemed more conscious of learning instrumental or 'technical' knowledge of their new role, than of developing the communicative or personal changes they said they experienced" – although these changes must have been unfolding simultaneously. One possible interpretation of this finding might be that the women had less to learn in this area, due to their prior life experiences, than in the technical area. Fenwick notes that "most seemed to have internalized an expectation that they be self-reliant, autonomous architects of their own economic fates" (Fenwick, 2002, p. 21).

Conclusion

There is a barely a glimmer of a dawning realization in the literature on lifelong learning that by focusing on paid work only, some important paths have remained unexplored. Rather than regarding the home as a site of non-traditional learning that is "not **yet** as fully accredited by the world of organized institutional education" (Whitman, 2003, p. 4, emphasis in the original), it seems to me more appropriate to recognize the home – and the unpaid work performed within the home – as a traditional but not yet fully acknowledged site of learning. Yet unpaid housework is of tremendous social and economic value, and studying it is likely to open up new vistas on understanding lifelong learning.

Housework and housework-based learning also have important policy implications. For instance, some of the disabled women in the focus group who all had university education talked indignantly about the fact that some government programs are oriented towards teaching them basic skills which they emphatically do not need, but that they cannot access the services they do need.

If we were to recognize the value of unpaid care work, we would have a public pension for people who spend their time looking after others who cannot look after themselves (Eichler, 1988a, 1997). They would have access to holidays, replacement help when they were sick, etc. Recognizing the home as a very important work place would mean that health and safety measures would have to be developed and implemented, and that education for greater safety would be provided, to mention just a few issues.

It is clear that studying lifelong learning through unpaid housework is both an interesting and important topic. It will also shed new light on our understanding of lifelong learning in the paid labour force, by providing a test site for the generalizations that have been made in that setting. For instance, we need to reconsider how incentives interact with motivations to learn given the vast amount of learning that happens without subsequent job advancement. We can explore the benefits to civil society if we were to provide non-formal training on housework-related issues (oriented to members of both sexes, of course!). We can investigate what knowledge has been gained and lost with respect to both paid and unpaid work. Drawing on Butler's (1993) work, we can test for and recognize knowledge that has been acquired through running a household, both for credit at educational institutions and for paid work. We need to explore the capacity to adapt to changes that is generated through involvement in housework and caring work, and utilize it in the paid labour force. This could become a potent argument for fostering the advancement of women into managerial positions.

Clearly, then, extending the investigation of lifelong learning to include unpaid housework and care work is not only valuable for understanding for its own sake, but also for understanding the whole process of lifelong learning better.

Notes

1. All quotes have been slightly edited to make them more readable, and all names, when used, are fictitious to protect anonymity.
2. The acronyms are sometimes difficult to follow. Other, comparable terms are PLA (Prior Learning Assessment), PLV (Prior Learning Validation) and RPL (Recognition of Prior Learning) – see Thomas, 1998: 330 & 342 – as well as APL (Assessment of Prior Learning) and APEL (Assessment of Prior Experiential Learning) see Evans, N. (1994). *Experiential Learning for All*. London, Cassell.

References

Aronson, J., & Neysmith, S. M. (1997). The retreat of the state and long-term care provision: Implications for frail elderly people, unpaid family careers, and paid home care workers. *Studies in Political Economy, 53*, 37–66.

Arrighi, B. A., & Maume, D. J. (2000). Workplace subordination and men's avoidance of housework. *Journal of Family Issues, 21*(4), 464–487.

Bakker, I. (1998). *Unpaid work and macroeconomics: New discussions, new tools for action.* Ottawa, Status of Women Canada.

Baxter, J. (1997). Gender equality and participation in housework: A cross-national perspective. *Journal of Comparative Family Studies, 220–247.*

Beaujot, R., Haddad, T. et al. (2000). Time constraints and relative resources as determinants of the sexual division of domestic work. *Canadian Journal of Sociology, 25*(1), 61–82.

Benéria, L., & Roldán, M. (1987). *The crossroads of class and gender: Industrial homework, subcontracting, and household dynamics in Mexico City.* Chicago: University of Chicago Press.

Bishop, J. H. (1995). Do most employers and workers under-invest in training and learning on the job? In D. Hirsch & D.A. Wagner (Eds.), *What Makes Workers Learn? The role of incentives in workplace education and training* (pp. 37–48). Cresskill, N.J.: Hampton Press.

Bond, S., & Sales, J. (2001). Household work in the UK: An analysis of the British household panel survey, 1994. *Work, Employment, & Society, 15*(2), 233–250.

Boserup, E. (1970). *Women's role in economic development.* New York: St. Martin's Press.

Butler, L. (1993). Unpaid work in the home and accreditation. In M. Thorpe, R. Edwards & A. Hanson (Eds.), *Culture and processes of adult learning: A reader* (pp. 66–86). New York: Routledge (in assoc. with the open university).

Chandler, W. (1994). The value of household work in Canada, 1992. *Canadian Economic Observer,* 3.1–3.9.

Cohen, M. G. (1988). *Women's work, markets, and economic development in nineteenth-century Ontario.* Toronto: University of Toronto Press.

Cohen, P. N. (1998). Replacing housework in the service economy: Gender, class, and race-ethnicity in service spending. *Gender and Society, 12*(2), 219–231.

Collins, M. (1998). Critical returns: From andragogy to lifelong education. In S. M. Scott, B. Spencer & A. M. Thomas (Eds.), *Learning for life. Canadian readings in adult education* (pp. 46–58). Toronto: Thompson Educational Publishing.

Coverman, S. (1989). Women's work is never done: The division of domestic labor. In J. Freeman (Ed.), *Women: A feminist perspective* (pp. 356–367). Palo Alto, CA: Mayfield.

Doucet, A. (2000). 'There's a huge gulf between me as a male carer and women': Gender, domestic responsibility, and the community as an institutional area. *Community, Work, & Family, 3*(2), 163–184.

Eichler, M. (1988). *Families in Canada today: Recent changes and their policy implications.* Toronto: Gage.

Eichler, M. (1988). *Non-sexist research methods. A practical guide.* Boston: Allen & Unwin.

Eichler, M. (2002). *Measuring gender bias and more.* Gender Based Analysis (GBA) in Public Health Research, Policy and Practice. (Documentation of the International Workshop in Berlin). Berlin: Landesvereinigung fuer Gesundheit Niedersachsen.

Eichler, M. (2003). "Faire mon lit: est-ce un travail socialement utile? Un nouveau regard sur le travail ménager vu dans le context de l'amélioration de la sécurité économique des femmes". La securite economique des femmes: Les critiques feministes du discours economique dominant et les nouvelles avenues de politiques sociales, Universite Laval, Institut de recherches et d'etudes feministes UQAM.

Evans, N. (1994). *Experiential learning for all.* London: Cassell.

Frey, M. (2003). Ist der "Arbeitskraftunternehmer" weiblich? "Subjektivierte" Erwerbsorientierungen von Frauen in prozessen betreiblicher Diskontinuitaet. Berlin: Humboldt University.

Garrick, J. (1996). Informal learning: Some underlying philosophies. *CJSA/RCEEA, 10*(1), 21–46.

Gouthro, P. A., & Plumb, D. (2003). *Remapping the tripartite register: Moving beyond forma, non-formal, and informal learning.* Toronto: Canadian Association for the Study of Adult Education (CASAE).

Hart, M. U. (1992). *Working and educating for life: Feminist and international perspectives on adult education.* London: Routledge.

Hirsch, D., & Wagner, D. A. (1995). Introduction. In D. Hirsch & D. A. Wagner (Eds.), *What makes workers learn? The role of incentives in workplace education and training* (pp. 1–10). Cresskill, N.J.: Hampton Press.

Hirsch, D., & Wagner, D. A. (Eds.) (1995). *What makes workers learn? The role of incentives in workplace education and training.* Cresskill, N.J.: Hampton Press.

Ironmonger, D. (1996). Counting outputs, capital inputs, and caring labour: Estimating gross household product. *Feminist Economics*, 2(3), 37–64.

John, D., & Shelton, B. A. (1997). The production of gender among black and white women and men: The case of household labor. *Sex Roles*, 36(3/4).

Kamo, Y., & Cohen, E. L. (1998). Division of household work between partners: A comparison of black and white couples. *Journal of Comparative Family Studies*, 131–145.

Kiger, G., & Riley, P. J. (1996). Gender differences in perceptions of household labor. *The Journal of Psychology*, 130(4), 357–370.

Leonard, M. (2001). Old wine in new bottles? Women working inside and outside the household. *Women's Studies International Forum*, 24(1), 67–78.

Loblaws (2003). What's coooking in your community? Toronto: Loblaws.

Luttringer, J. M. (1995). Worker access to vocational training: A legal appraoch. What Makes Workers Learn. In D. Hirsch & D. A. Wagner (Eds.), *The role of incentives in workplace education and training* (pp. 51–64). Cresskill, N.J.: Hampton Press.

Luxton, M. (1980). *More than a labour of love: Three generations of women's work in the home*. Toronto: Women's Press.

Massey, G., Hahn, K. et al. (1995). Women, men, and the 'second shift' in socialist Yugoslavia. *Gender and Society*, 9(3), 359–379.

Merriam, S. B., & Caffarella, R. S. (1999). *Learning in adulthood. A comprehensive guide*. San Francisco: Jossey-Bass.

Mies, M., & Shiva, V. (1993). *Ecofeminism*. London: Zed Books.

Mikulecky, L. (1995). Workplace literacy programs: Organization and incentives. In D. Hirsch & D. A. Wagner (Eds.), *What makes workers learn? The role of incentives in workplace education and training* (pp. 129–148). Cresskill, N.J.: Hampton Press.

Miles, A. (1998). Learning from the women's movement in the neo-liberal period. In S. M. Scott, B. Spencer & A. M. Thomas (Eds.), *Learning for life. Canadian readings in adult education* (pp. 250–258). Toronto: Thompson Educational Publishing.

Noonan, M. C. (2001). The impact of domestic work on men's and women's wages. *Journal of Marriage and Family*, 63, 1134–1145.

Noyelle, T., & Hirsch, D. (1995). Legal incentives and the new workforce. In D. Hirsch & D. A. Wagner (Eds.), *What makes workers learn? The role of incentives in workplace education and training* (pp. 65–69). Cresskill, N.J.: Hampton Press.

Okin, S. M. (1989). *Justice, gender, and the family*. USA: Basic Books.

Perkins, H. W., & DeMeis, D. K. (1996). Gender and family effects on the 'second shift' domestic activity of college-educated young adults. *Gender and Society*, 10(1), 78–93.

Pittman, J. F., Kerpelman, J. L. et al. (2001). Stress and performance standards: A dynamic approach to time spent in housework. *Journal of Marriage and Family*, 63, 1111–1121.

Rollings-Magnusson, S. (2003). Heavy burdens on small shoulders: The invisible labour of pioneer children of the western Canadian prairies 1871–1913. *Sociology*. Edmonton: University of Alberta.

Ross, C. E. (1987). The division of labor at home. *Social Forces*, 65(3), 816–833.

Ryan, P. (1995). Adult learning and work: Finance, incentives, and certification. *What Makes Workers Learn*. In D. Hirsch & D. A. Wagner (Eds.), *The role of incentives in workplace education and training* (pp. 11–36). Cresskill, N.J.: Hampton Press.

Sanchez, L., & Thomson, E. (1997). Becoming mothers and fathers: Parenthood, gender, and the division of labor. *Gender and Society*, 11(6), 747–772.

Scott, S. M. (1998). Philosophies in action. In S. M. Scott, B. Spencer & A. M. Thomas (Eds.), *Learning for life. Canadian readings in adult education* (pp. 98–106). Toronto: Thompson Educational Publishing.

Selman, G. (1998). The imaginative training for citizenship. In S. M. Scott, B. Spencer & A. M. Thomas (Eds.), *Learning for life. Canadian readings in adult education* (pp. 24–34). Toronto: Thompson Educational Publishing.

Solar, C. (1998). Trends in adult education in the 1990s. In S. M. Scott, B. Spencer & A. M. Thomas (Eds.), *Learning for life. Canadian readings in adult education* (pp. 71–84). Toronto: Thompson Educational Publishing.

South, S. J., & Spitze, G. (1994). Housework in marital and non-marital households. *American Sociological Review, 59*(3), 327–347.

Speakman, S., & Marchington, M. (1999). Ambivalent patriarchs: Shift-workers, 'breadwinners' and housework. *Work, Employment, & Society, 13*(1), 83–105.

Stalker, J. (1998). Women in the history of adult education: Misogynist responses to our participation. In S. M. Scott, B. Spencer & A. M. Thomas (Eds.), *Learning for life. Canadian readings in adult education* (pp. 238–249). Toronto: Thompson Educational Publishing.

Sticht, T. G. (1995). Functional context education for schoolplaces and workplaces. In D. Hirsch & D. A. Wagner (Eds.), *What makes workers learn. The role of incentives in workplace education and training* (pp. 117–126). New Jersey: Hampton Press.

Sullivan, O. (1997). The division of housework among 'remarried' couples. *Journal of Family Issues, 18*(2), 205–223.

Waring, M. (1988). *If women counted. A new feminist economics.* New York: Harper & Row.

Welton, M. R. (1998). The struggle of memory against forgetting. In S. M. Scott, B. Spencer & A. M. Thomas (Eds.), *Learning for life. Canadian readings in adult education* (pp. 35–45). Toronto: Thompson Educational Publishing.

Williamson, B. (1998). *Lifeworlds and learning. Essays in the theory, philosophy, and practice of lifelong learning.* Leicester: National Institute of Adult Continuing Education.

Windebank, J. (2001). Dual-earner couples in Britain and France: Gender divisions of domestic labour and parenting work in different welfare states. *Work, Employment, & Society, 15*(2), 269–290.

55

NEW FORMS OF LEARNING AND WORK ORGANIZATION IN THE IT INDUSTRY: A GERMAN PERSPECTIVE ON INFORMAL LEARNING

Peter Dehnbostel*, Gabriele Molzberger*, and Bernd Overwien**

*University of the Armed Forces, Institute of Vocational Education, Hamburg, Germany
**Technical University of Berlin, Centre for Global and International Cooperation, Germany

Initial and Further Vocational Education and Training in the IT-Sector

According to the German Federal Association of Information Economy, Telecommunication, and New Media (Bitkom) information technology includes both the production of office machinery and data processing equipment and the domain of software and IT services while the production of communication engineering equipment and facilities as well as communications services belong to the division of telecommunication. Accordingly, production and work structures differ greatly within the IT industry as documented by the industrial sociological study by Baukrowitz and Boes (2002). The segment of software development and IT services, with which the following study was concerned, is characterized by work processes which do not correspond to a traditional tayloristic work organization and division of labor but are mostly carried out in the form of project work. This has consequences for the high staff qualification requirements and for the shaping of the qualification development.

In Germany during the boom of the IT industry in the 1990s, four new dual occupations (apprenticeships combining practical learning in the enterprise and theoretical learning in vocational schools) in the IT industry were developed under the lead management of the Federal Institute for Vocational Education (BIBB) and promulgated by the Federal Ministry of Economics as of August 1, 1997. What is new about this IT initial vocational education and about the structure of the job description is that 50% of the occupations consist of key qualifications which include both technical business and management competencies. While a high proportion of key qualifications are scheduled for the first year of apprenticeship, this will continuously decrease in favor of specialty

International Handbook of Educational Policy, 1043–1064
Nina Bascia, Alister Cumming, Amanda Datnow, Kenneth Leithwood and David Livingstone (Eds.)
© 2005 *Springer. Printed in Great Britain.*

qualifications during the additional two years of training. The concept is advantageous for the training enterprises since the training is geared to a greater extent towards business requirements. Common key qualifications facilitate a later change to one of the adjoining lines of work for the trained specialists.

The four new dual occupations have had a positive echo in the expert public and are very popular with the adolescents and are also accepted by the enterprises. The total number of training relationships of all years of apprenticeship in the four IT occupations increased continuously since their introduction. Meanwhile in the field of IT-related advanced training the range diversified more and more in accordance with the great demand for skilled personnel, and a bewildering variety of different vocational designations emerged for the development, application, and maintenance of advanced information and telecommunication systems in the 1990s.

Especially at the higher qualification levels primarily occupied by university graduates the demand for skilled IT personnel is great. However, most first-year students do not behave anticyclically to the economic development in the choice of their field of study. In the last years probably because of the economic downswing of the IT industry, the subject of computer science has lost its attractiveness for first-year students. The still existing shortage of skilled personnel in the IT industry is opposed by a relatively high number of unemployed skilled IT personnel which has continuously increased since the year 2000 (Dostal, 2002). Despite this availability of skilled IT personnel, jobs offered can frequently not be filled immediately as IAB has found (Dostal, 2002, p. 145). Evidently skilled IT personnel, once they are out of a job, are not readily reintegrated into the job market.

Within this situation in Germany an advanced IT training system is being developed since the end of the 1990s which shall essentially take place on the job and lead to recognized occupations requiring advanced training (BMBF, 2002; Rohs, 2002). With this, a modern advanced training concept shall be implemented which will apply to the entire Federal Republic. Upon successful implementation, it would not only change vocational and on-the-job training, but initial and further education and training as a whole in its historically evolved structure. The advanced IT training system is characterized by the direct combination of working and learning in the work process which, at the same time, stands for a change of perspective with respect to advanced on-the-job training. Improvement and optimization processes, task integration, quality assurance, and other modern forms and methods of working require this combination of working and learning. It is a constitutive element of new models and concepts of work-based learning. Advanced on-the-job training is becoming more important than training courses and classes which for the most part still predominate today. Future-oriented, competence-based advanced training is characterized by process orientation, reference to subjects, self-direction, demand orientation, revaluation of experiential learning, and the combination of formal and informal learning.

The system is based on the apprenticeship; so-called lateral and re-entries are admitted to this system, thus it also addresses those seeking work and do not have yet a formal qualification. The aim of this system is to provide "key qualifications that equip employees to cope with the rapid pace of change." (Ehrke & Müller, 2002, p. 9). It also enquires to provide a training system which is not organised exclusively for the development of product specific skills, but provides long-lived relevance. The basic idea of the professional system is to enable a "diagonal career development in the workplace" (*ibid.*, p. 12).

The qualification process itself is conducted mainly in the workplace as a work-process-oriented learning concept which is based on the assumption that, "the work process defines the relevant actions from which the learning goals and contents are derived" (Rohs & Büchele, 2002, p. 69). To identify relevant work processes reference projects, which are abstract descriptions for all typical work processes for an occupational profile, had been developed.

It is decisive for the advanced training policy that advanced IT training is primarily provided by on-the-job learning in a graded system of different occupations requiring advanced training, thus making it possible to climb to the highest professional levels and academic qualifications. The so far more than 300 job names related to information technology will be replaced by six occupations requiring advanced training and 29 specialist profiles. This advanced training system provides reliable career development paths for the currently 800,000 employees in the information and communication economy in Germany and is characterized by flexibility, transparency, and adaptability. The manufacturers' certificates predominating in advanced training up to now and the offers supported by the chambers could thereby be guided by a system that is recognized throughout the industry and the Federal Republic of Germany, and could be utilized internationally by determining equivalencies, even in the sector of academic professions.To ascertain quality standards the qualification process of operative and strategic professionals falls into an area regulated by law and certified consistent with the provisions of the Federal Education Act.

Informal Learning, Experiential Learning, and Implicit Learning

From the point of view of the enterprises it already became apparent in the 1980s that new enterprise and work concepts require comprehensive competence development of the staff and increased learning on the job. In the progressing knowledge and service society and the associated propagation of new information and communication technologies, the decrease of manual and increase of knowledge-based activities, knowledge resources and on-the-job learning play a more and more important role. Continuous learning in and from organizations shall make innovations possible, build up and extend knowledge, and enhance efficiency and competitiveness. It has turned out that the increasing outsourcing of learning away from the job is widening the gap between seminar-oriented vocational training and real professional action competence that it leads to learning and motivation problems. Action and experience-oriented learning is only conditionally possible in educational establishments; situation and process-determined

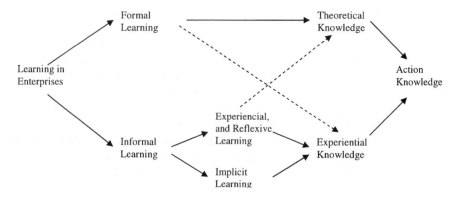

Figure 1.   Kinds of Learning and Knowledge in Enterprises

modern work requirements can be anticipated and simulated less and less. Without any links to real work contents and real working conditions, vocational on-the-job learning will remain rooted in a formal understanding of education and will not lead to comprehensive professional action competence and reflexive capacity for action.

With the renaissance of learning on the job, a countertrend to the systematization and centralization prevailing until then developed for vocational training. The increasing importance of learning on the job is reflected in nearly all areas of vocational training: In advanced on-the-job training, learning on the job has been intensified, varied forms of learning have been developed, and self-directed learning has been revalued (Dehnbostel, 2002). For small enterprises, learning on the job by means of order-oriented learning and learning in networks has considerably increased in quality and scope. In large-scale and medium-sized enterprises, on-the-job qualification times have been increased, and forms of learning integrating work and learning such as quality circles and training workshops have been created. In the enterprises, the trend of centralizing vocational learning, which has prevailed for decades, has given way to decentralization which attributes decisive importance to experiential learning and informal learning on the job.

In this context, the business concepts and projects which emerged in vocational training at the end of the 1980s have been extensively discussed, among others under the heading "Dezentrales und erfahrungsorientiertes Lernen im Betrieb" (decentralized and experiential learning on the job) (Dehnbostel & Peters, 1991). Decentralization and increased learning on the job were the focus of the model test program "decentralized learning" also beginning at the end of the 1980s in which 12 individual model tests participated (Dehnbostel, Holz, & Novak, 1992). The program started out from the guiding thesis that in modern, technologically sophisticated work processes integrative forms of combining work and learning have become necessary and possible. The central issue for this combination of work and learning in modern work processes was: "When selecting and developing workplaces as educational settings, it must be asked as to what extent systematic learning processes will be possible and how closely these can be combined with informal learning processes and learning processes guided by experience" (Dehnbostel, 1992, p. 19 *et seq.*). This combination of organized learning and informal learning is characteristic of the forms of learning "learning bay", "learning station", and "work and learning tasks" which were developed in this program and are spreading increasingly.

Informal learning is to be understood as unorganized and not formally defined learning at home and at work. According to Dohmen (1999), it is the basic "natural" self-learning of human beings, characterized as follows:

It does not take place in special educational establishments standing out from normal life and professional practice;

- it has no curriculum and is not professionally organized but rather originates accidentally, sporadically, in association with certain occasions, from changing practical requirement situations;
- it is not planned pedagogically conscious, systematically according to subjects, test and qualification-oriented, but rather unconsciously incidental, holistically problem-related, and related to situation management and fitness for life;
- It is not unrealistic stockpile-learning, but is experienced directly in its "natural" function as a tool for living and survival.

In international discussions, the concept of informal learning, already used by Dewey at an early stage and later on by Knowles, experienced a renaissance, especially in the context of development policy (Overwien, 2000, 2004). At first, informal learning was only delimited from formal school learning and nonformal learning in courses (Coombs & Achmed, 1974). Basically, this just created a residual category of learning which takes place outside of organized education. Marsick and Watkins take up this approach and go one step further in their definition. They, too, begin with the organizational form of learning and call those learning processes informal which are nonformal or not formally organized and are not financed by institutions (Watkins & Marsick, 1990, p. 12 *et seq.*). At the center of learning is the individual in a process of action and reflection. An example for a wider approach is Livingstone's definition which is oriented towards autodidactic and self-directed learning and places special emphasis on the self-definition of the learning process by the learner (Livingstone, 1999, p. 68 *et seq.*).

If one considers informal learning within the context of vocational learning, it has to be regarded as an important type of learning among all the types of on-the-job learning and knowledge. One must generally differentiate between organized and informal learning. Organized or formal learning is geared towards imparting specified learning contents and learning objectives. From the outset, it aims at a specified learning result while, with informal learning, learning is achieved without endeavoring it pedagogically.

Informal learning can be in turn subdivided into two types of learning: experiential learning, and implicit learning. To roughly distinguish between the concepts – which can only be separated analytically anyway – it can be stated that experiential learning is achieved by reflectively processing experience while with implicit learning the process is more likely unreflected and unconscious. In experiential learning, experiences are integrated into reflection and lead to cognition. This presupposes that the actions are not repetitive, but are integrated in problems, challenges, and uncertainties and thus affect the actor accordingly. This is usually the case in dynamic work processes and environments. Compared with experiential learning, implicit learning generates a learning process where the learner is not conscious of and does not reflect its progress and result. Pertinent examples for this are the learning processes which enable the learner to swim or ride a bicycle. But the skills of a chess champion and experienced physician or motor mechanic are also essentially learned through implicit learning processes. Learning is a rather unconscious process; it is experienced directly in the situation, without rules and regularities being recognized or even turned into the basis for structured learning processes.

The experiential knowledge accumulated through informal learning and the theoretical knowledge accumulated through organized learning is pooled in action knowledge. Experiential knowledge is not only accumulated through experiential learning and implicit learning, but also through organized learning provided this takes place. For in almost any situation in life, and thus also in the situation of organized learning, informal learning is going on – even though incidentally. Theoretical knowledge, on the other hand, is enriched through experiential learning inasmuch as theoretical discoveries can be made by reflecting on experience.

Research Studies about Informal Learning Related to Work in Germany

In the German context, there have been comparatively few studies so far which explicitly use the concept of informal learning. Already in 1994, the German Youth Institute (Deutsches Jugendinstitut) conducted a study on "informal education for adolescents by use of computers and media" (Tully, 1994). As a basis for the then following analysis of the media and courses provided, the author developed his own concept of "computer competence". This study is important because of the interaction addressed here between different educational settings and ways of learning for the mostly informal acquisition of the bundle of competencies important for the use of computers. Tully emphasized the role of informal forms of acquisition. He was brought to this by the obvious realization that the handling of programs could only be learned in practice. In addition, he discussed the dynamization of software knowledge, the speed of change which could not be anticipated, and, against this background, thought about which of the competencies acquired would later on be of application relevance for the adolescents in the professional context. According to this, computer knowledge, unlike general knowledge, can hardly be imparted by school training. Here, "informal education" is prominent which is characterized especially by an individualization of learning and acquisition strategies. He attributed not only importance to it for directly computer-related learning processes, but also a special relevance for using computers as tools in learning processes going beyond this. "Informal learning" is particularly characterized by "... individual learning speed, own planning of learning progress, reinforcement and practice as required and not according to schedule as at school" (Tully, 1994, p. 183).

A qualitative study by Kirchhöfer dealt with informal learning in the daily conduct of life with direct reference to professional competence development (Kirchhöfer, 2000). Informal learning processes in everyday life were identified by means of recorded daily routine. From the record analyses, learner typing and learning strategies were derived. These were based on an increasing debordering of many people's situation at home and at work. Again and again, learning situations develop in the social environment where the results influence the process of professional competence development. The author thus directed special attention to questions of competence transfer from the social environment to the professional sphere. Kirchhöfer based this on a concept of informal learning which is closely related to the concept of self-directed learning and Livingstone's concept. According to this, informal learning has a "concrete goal anticipation". It is a conscious, reflected, and problem-oriented learning within a self-determined learning process. Formal learning is problem-independent and characterized by externally determined objectives and learning processes. Kirchhöfer also identified an incidental learning similar to implicit learning.

The particular importance of Kirchhöfer's study lies in its meticulous reconstruction of everyday learning situations and their analysis. Thus, it is established that learning situations are determined by work contents, organization of work, and the social context within the learning environment. Closed routine activities provide less learning content then relatively open work processes where the sequence is not yet predetermined. An externally provided structuring of the learning environment conducive to learning supports the individual learning performance, but at the same time the individual also structures the learning process by changing the learning situation (*ibid.*, p. 80). In other words, the learning situation contains externally determined portions and, at the same time, it is also changed by the learning individual with respect to learning. The exploitation of learning opportunities will depend on the self-learning competence acquired in the course of the individual's life and an his/her motivation to learn. Kirchhöfer identified many learning strategies. He found observation, imitation, and experiential learning as well as mental trial actions. "Social-communicative strategies" play an important role: Talks and consultations make it necessary "to formulate action programs". It is also important to specifically use written resources such as instructions, technical literature, or internet inputs. Critical system analysis is also counted among the strategies (*ibid.*, p. 81).

At work, a direct competence transfer will always occur if the learning situation is directly transferable, if the developed learning strategies are usable, and/or if knowledge acquired in the everyday environment can be used. An indirect transfer will occur if a more general competence enhancement and identity growth, combined with improved self-esteem, positively affect the professional competencies. Since Kirchhöfer also analyzed case examples where unemployment or job-creating measures played a role, he realized that a professional transfer is also connected with employment prospects. With respect to his case studies and the transfer in professional activities, he regarded a "stockpile" acquisition of competencies as unrealistic (*ibid.*, p. 85). The typing of learning and the identification of learning situations, learning strategies, and transfer processes permit a number of suggestions for the shaping of learning environments and for combining informal learning with various forms of formal learning.

Stieler-Lorenz described a study conducted in the "New Länder" (former GDR) in 2000 (Stieler-Lorenz, 2002). It centered on the acquisition of job and occupation-related competencies which also consider references to learning in the social and political environment. The questionnaire for the 30 to 45 minute telephone interviews with 1012 persons was based on Livingstone's definition of informal learning. Only the learner him-/herself could evaluate his/her learning "by him/herself and reflexively" (Stieler-Lorenz, Frister, Jakob, Liljeberg, & Steinborn, 2001, p. 281). Experts would only be able to evaluate explicit learning, but not the individual's learning process. The study of the group around Stieler-Lorenz went one step beyond the Canadian study (see above) in that it combined the quantitative survey with qualitative parts of the study. 24 employees and 6 managers of three enterprises from "traditional industries" and "knowledge-based services" were additionally questioned within the framework of focused interviews since it was assumed that the enterprises were interested in the results of informal learning (*ibid.*, p. 302 *et seq.*). The results of the study emphasize the great importance of informal learning, especially in fields of learning relating to the general conditions of work (labor protection, labor law, organization of work, etc.), work with computers, customization, or work using new technologies and products (*ibid.*, p. 286).

On the basis of criteria generated by means of bipolar estimation scales and hypotheses based on the evaluations provided by those interviewed, the qualitative part of the study established that the work contents found in knowledge-based activities in "traditional enterprises" as well as in "knowledge-based enterprises" from the sector of software applications particularly encourage learning (*ibid.*, p. 306). In the latter enterprises, formal advanced training played a relatively minor role and was often limited to certificates from software producers. Those interviewed were of the opinion that organized advanced training could no longer keep up with the learning requirements of the job. Especially communication skills and social competence as prerequisites for market domination, handling of customers, and teamwork were acquired through informal learning. The "traditional enterprises" interviewed which evidently were larger enterprises (no details given), rather complained that their staff was too much orientated towards organized advanced training and had not yet learned to continue their training informally (*ibid.*, p. 311). All in all, one was faced with a situation where informal learning was expected, but not stimulated and promoted by the enterprises. As a consequence of the study, it was noted as an unsettled issue that it would be necessary to find out how precisely informal learning processes took place, under what conditions, and how this type of learning could be promoted (*ibid.*, p. 213).

New Forms of Learning and the Organization of Work

Apart from the primarily analytical examination of competence development and different types of learning, the important question to be asked with regard to the practical side of on-the-job learning concerns the form of organization in which this will take place. Compared to functional adaptive learning for which traditional craft and industrial work processes at best provided instruction methods as a form of organization, a great number of different forms of learning organizations – briefly: forms of learning – have developed in the enterprises with the debordering and pluralization of educational settings and types of learning; namely, coaching, e-learning, quality circle, work and learning tasks, learning bays, and communities of practice, among others.

With respect to on-the-job learning, the question is, however, whether it is organized at all in special forms of learning such as those mentioned, or simply integrated into the normal work process. Especially the forms of work such as teamwork and job rotation associated with new business and organizational concepts are characterized by the fact that they combine working and learning to a high degree. The relative autonomy, unrestricted objectives, disposition diversity, and totality of reorganized work processes require this. Against this background, the new forms of learning and new forms of working shall be considered in more detail in the following, with the form of learning "qualification network" being dealt with separately because of its special significance to small and medium-sized enterprises.

New Forms of Learning and Working

If one considers the new forms of on-the-job learning, then the most important feature they have in common is that they purposefully combine informal learning with organized or formal learning. Even if these forms of learning clearly differ in their structures, objectives, and degrees of distribution, they have in common that work tasks and work processes are extended and enriched with learning systematic and work pedagogy in mind. Or, in other words: Working and learning are combined; informal learning incorporated into work-related actions is interleaved with organized learning by means of experience.

The new forms of on-the-job learning are also called decentralized forms of learning. They are characterized by a dual infrastructure: on the one hand, a work infrastructure appropriate to the respective work environment with respect to work tasks, technology, work organization, and qualification requirements; on the other hand, a learning infrastructure providing additional space, time,

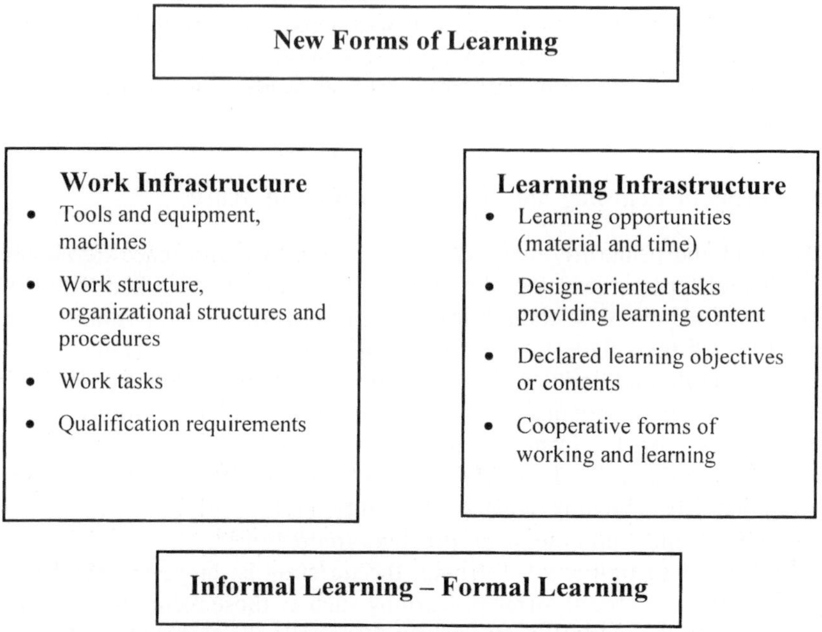

```
┌─────────────────────────────────────────────────┐
│              New Forms of Learning                │
└─────────────────────────────────────────────────┘
```

```
┌──────────────────────────────┐   ┌──────────────────────────────┐
│      Work Infrastructure     │   │    Learning Infrastructure   │
│  • Tools and equipment,      │   │  • Learning opportunities    │
│    machines                  │   │    (material and time)       │
│                              │   │                              │
│  • Work structure,           │   │  • Design-oriented tasks     │
│    organizational structures │   │    providing learning content│
│    and procedures            │   │                              │
│                              │   │  • Declared learning         │
│  • Work tasks                │   │    objectives or contents    │
│                              │   │                              │
│  • Qualification requirements│   │  • Cooperative forms of      │
│                              │   │    working and learning      │
└──────────────────────────────┘   └──────────────────────────────┘
```

```
┌─────────────────────────────────────────────────┐
│      Informal Learning – Formal Learning          │
└─────────────────────────────────────────────────┘
```

Figure 2. Dual Infrastructure of New Forms of Learning

material, and personnel resources. The learning is work-based, but not limited to experience-related learning processes during work. Work-related actions and reflections related to them are interrelated with the declared objectives and contents of on-the-job training activities. As the following illustration shows, informal learning and organized learning are systematically combined on the basis of the work infrastructure interleaved with a learning infrastructure.

Decentralized forms of learning play an important role in both qualification and the initiation and establishment of innovations and improvement processes. They are geared towards the acquisition or extension of professional action competence and professional capacity for action and at the same time meet the qualification requirements on the job. The form of learning "learning bay" which has, in the meantime, become more and more common in on-the-job initial and advanced training is described in the following as an example.

In the early 1990s, learning bays were introduced within the framework of the model test program "decentralized learning" and have become conceptually and practically established within a few years (compare Dehnbostel, Holz, & Novak, 1992; Dehnbostel and Molzberger, 2001). Learning bays mostly originated in connection with business reorganization and restructuring measures, first in industrial-technical vocational training. They then gained increasing importance in advanced on-the-job training and were also adopted in the commercial domain. All in all, learning bays have proliferated greatly and become more varied since their introduction a few years ago. Different forms of the learning bay concept have been developed in business use, such as the "learning and working bays", "temporary learning bays", and "learning centers". Their high acceptance must surely be attributed to both the qualification quality and cost-effectiveness.

Learning bays are a form of qualification and learning on the job. In learning bays, real work tasks are processed largely autonomously by teamwork, this being the same work tasks as those performed in the learning bay environment. As opposed to the surrounding workplaces, however, more time is available to carry out the desired qualification and learning processes. Summarily, learning bays are characterized by the following overlapping features:

- Learning bays are workplaces with added learning equipment where real work orders are processes and qualification takes place;
- the work orders meet the criteria of all-inclusive-type work and provide good opportunities and stimulation for learning through complexity, problem content, and a wealth of variants;
- in the learning bay, work is carried out in teams, with this form of organization being structured according to the principles of partly autonomous teamwork;
- a qualified person of the respective operating division who primarily plays the role of process advisor and development tutor of the learning bay team and has qualified in work and vocational pedagogy is in charge of the learning bay;
- learning bays can also be places of innovation in the work process, primarily for organizational, social, and methodological areas of work.

Although learning bays and other forms of decentralized learning have become established in individual enterprises, their distribution and growth will essentially depend on the extent to which learning for business requirements is not covered by new forms of work such as teamwork, project work, and job rotation because it is characteristic for these forms of work that they systematically fall back on learning during task processing in order to find problem solutions and decide on possible dispositions. As an objective of the development of business competencies, the "reflexive capacity for action" discussed above is essentially based on this.

These forms of business work must be considered as a special type of on-the-job learning. Learning is primarily carried out as informal learning and experiential learning; organized and intentional learning do usually not take place. Experiential learning is intensified especially in task processing, group meetings, or in continuous improvement and optimization processes; i.e. it is promoted by measures conducive to learning and by appropriate working methods. It is an informal, not organized, learning, but for all that its effects are taken into account because experiential learning essentially makes it possible to stick to the agreed objectives and establish integrated quality assurance processes and participative improvement processes. Learning time is integrated into working time; the workplace thus also functions as an educational setting.

Qualification Networks as Modern Form of On-the-Job Learning

Traditional forms of learning and cooperation in vocational education such as the dual system as well as initial and advanced training networks are based on firm, mostly contractually fixed arrangements and offer traditionally oriented qualification measures and education. Most cooperation models have clear hierarchies and high commitments in organizational, legal, and financial matters. The didactic-curricular orientation is also mostly fixed and, at the most, provides the learner with opportunities for self-direction and co organization at the methodological level. This is contrasted by more flexible and open network approaches developed primarily in the industrial sphere, but also in the IT sector, during the past years.

Compared to traditional forms of advanced education and organization, including networks, vocational education networks are characterized by new control and cooperation principles. It must be pointed out in particular that there are no specified and hierarchically supported curriculum and qualification schedule, and competencies are developed on the basis of learning in interconnected structures and jointly supported agreements on objectives.

In vocational education, qualification networks seem to be most suitable for ensuring the cooperation and coordination of educational settings under self-direction and self-qualification aspects. It is a matter of promoting competence development processes as well as planning, organizing, executing, assessing, and evaluating qualification and vocational education measures (Benzenberg, 1999; Kremer, 1998). If one defines the concept of network more precisely semantically, it must be pointed out that networks comprises interactions and co operations between persons, groups, and organizations.

The Study "Informal Learning in Modern Work Processes"

Research Design, Methods and Description of the Field

The empirical research project, discussed in the following section, is based on a multi-methodical approach encompassing a survey of 110 written questionnaires of 500 SME in the IT-sector in Berlin, document analyses and three case studies. The case studies were at the heart of the study. All together 13 guide-oriented interviews with employees and management were conducted. The aim of the interviews was to induce the reflection of own learning processes in those interviewed without committing them to certain strategies, concepts, and learning routes. Consequently the interviewed persons could ex-post emphasise, retell or caricature specific facts on their learning and working routines. Since informal learning is tied to the subject, methods of data collection are required in any case which are open and thus permit research into individual, frequently incidental, learning processes.

There are various classifications of enterprises according to their size. In this study, the EU definition is used as a measure for determining the size of an enterprise. It results from the strength of the staff of an enterprise and its annual turnover (compare Bulletin EU 1996). Following the definition of the European commission SMEs engage less than 249 persons. Especially micro (1–9) and small enterprises (10–49 persons) usually don't have structural personnel development or formalized structures for learning as they can be found in large enterprises. They develop forms of learning through their own practice. In the past SME have not been in the focus of German vocational and educational research projects, although most of the employees are work in SMEs.

Summary and Key Findings

In the following the results of the study will be discussed along the lines of the main topics of, which are:

- Enterprise data and gender aspect
- Informal learning during the hours of work
- Formal learning and organized advanced training
- Competence development
- Work conductive to learning and new forms of learning

Under the last of the topics listed above, "work conductive to learning and new forms of learning", learning organization forms – in short learning forms – that were developed by the case enterprises are described. In those forms work is purposefully linked to formal learning. Thus they meet the requirements of modern enterprises by creating a purposeful framework that structurally and lastingly supports, requires and promotes learning. Additionally, some variants of different work organization forms are described, which are practiced in case enterprises and which also include learning components, so that they are conductive to learning.

Enterprise data. Initially the survey by questionnaire was used to register the structural characteristics such as size, areas of business and qualification of the employees of small and medium-size enterprises in the Berlin IT industry. It can be said that the majority of the small and medium-size enterprises are small and micro enterprises with less than 50 employees. The enterprises are relatively young; more than half of them were founded in the nineties. Their areas of business also show industry-specific structures, from consulting and the sale of systems over the administration and maintenance of these products to software development and the development of data bases. Enterprises of the telecommunications industry are not part of this study.

The three enterprises that were studied in more detail in our case studies represent in their variety the spectrum of the economic sector of the IT industry. A first, smaller enterprise developed an astonishingly broad offering of IT services that are connected with the sale of corresponding products. Most of the employees do not have completed a formal IT qualification. Some joined the enterprise while studying computer science at the university and since then have not had a chance to complete their university education. The second enterprise works for a permanent customer and orients its business areas exclusively towards the needs of this customer. In contrast to the enterprise of the first case study, in this enterprise many employees have several qualifications and all have completed a university degree. Both enterprises have short communications channels and display an almost informal working climate. Finally, the third enterprise is larger and evidently about to develop a division of labor that is differentiated in more detail for a better handling of its business areas in the field of system support. The employees of this enterprise include lateral entries as well as formally qualified and certified personnel. Common to all three enterprises is that they strive to achieve "flat hierarchies". This goal, however, sometimes clashes with the requirements of smooth working processes. Thus the enterprises have a very heterogeneous staff structure with regard to the formal qualification of their employees, which is also confirmed by the survey by questionnaire.

Informal learning on the job. Both the case studies and the questionnaire survey give evidence of the great importance of informal learning processes in IT enterprises. The quantitative interviews show that the overwhelming majority of the enterprises assume that business knowledge is obtained informally. When on-the-job learning is considered as a whole, there is a different importance of different types of learning. The importance of communication-focused approaches for on-the-job learning, such as inquiries on the phone or direct consultation with colleagues, becomes evident.

> "And there is of course also a distributed knowledge here in the company. You can ask your colleague, who may not be able to solve the exact problem, because he is new, but who sees the problem from a different point of view or who has a different competence. Thus you are lead on a different track and you may then find a solution yourself." (GZ § 88)

The reason why the forms of e-learning play a comparatively subordinate role in the enterprises is probably also the great importance of direct communication among colleagues. Even if working with new media and technologies is a matter of course in IT enterprises, the proximity of the colleagues for learning processes is obviously an important basic requirement for successful work-related actions. The internet is usually used as a knowledge and information storage device that supplements the distributed knowledge of the employees within the enterprise. People resort to the internet, if a new work task cannot be performed with routine, in order to meet the learning requirement and if no colleague is able to help. In this process for example knowledge bases from product manufacturers are used, which serve as a replacement for on-the-job experience. A similar function is performed also by chats and newsgroups whose use varies greatly. As a learning strategy people resort to such platforms in particular if even an approach for the solution to the problem is lacking.

In practice informal learning appears generally as part of a problem-oriented approach to work tasks. In the center is the problem that has to be solved. Strategies to solve this problem are to a large extent identical with learning strategies. In addition to discussing the problem with colleagues, actual approaches include making phone calls to personally known specialists or resorting to the internet, books or journals, though those are read mainly to update the knowledge about new products in general and more selectively. One employee ironically gets to the heart of the issue of learning and work by saying that learning must be "some kind of disease" that accompanies him all his life.

If the employees are approached with a new topic, at first it is important to isolate the relevant issues. In the case studies the employees describe the subsequent course of informal learning processes approximately as follows: A new work task, such as the installation of a new product, is supported by personal basic skills and basic experience concerning the behavior of computer systems. There may be situations, however, in which no more progress is made. People then consult help files or books or resort to the internet, where they visit newsgroups or certain forums. This involves experience from former work tasks. It is approximately known how a program was made to run and how a complex system reacts if individual components are changed. The employees that were interviewed also said that people should be capable of making good guesses. If concrete, sensory experience and trial and error on the acute problem are required to achieve sustained learning successes in the cognitively highly demanding field of information technology, this indicates a new form of tacit knowledge. Implicit learning and reflected learning experience complement each other.

All employees know the necessity to learn in the course of work projects – sometimes they feel that this is a pressure, sometimes they feel that this is a stimulus. If they are left alone with the informal learning during work, they get in a dilemma. This dilemma will become clear especially in the different assessment of advanced training and learning issues from the point of view of the management of the company and from that of the employees. This different perspective or the conflict of interest will become evident mainly in the handling of time and pressure of time with regard to project work as well as with regard to learning and learning needs. This results in the necessary balancing of business requirements and learning requirements within the enterprise that can be highlighted in the following fundamental question: At what time is learning useful? In the sense of our second thesis this "conflict" may be interpreted in such way that in the long term those enterprises will prevail that will support the informal learning of their employees in a way that it has its own legitimacy as an integral component of work.

Some enterprises have installed e-mail accounts for certain groups of employees or established their own documentation to record and transfer business knowledge and to permit communication between colleagues at different work locations. However, the handling of such data bases, guidelines, work process and project descriptions with established routine knowledge is still in the experimental stage. The aim is to make experiential learning of the employees a permanent process.

As a whole the studies show that qualification and business innovation are supported essentially by and through informal learning. The emphasis on and the extension of these learning processes in "natural" work-learning environments corresponds with the new appreciation of self-organization processes as well as with the orientation in everyday life and at work. Or, from a different point of view, this indicates that goal-oriented and largely organized learning is abandoned. The workplace as an educational setting is thus upgraded in its original form, which was oriented towards functional learning. At the same time this tendency involves considerable dangers, at least if the structure and intention of the learning were narrowed to the business function and if external educational settings were excluded. In this case personnel development and advanced training could not be performed systematically and in connection with inter-company and social standards. The studies have shown the intensity of informal learning. At the same time, however, they have shown that it depends to a large extent on the workplace and the specific order, and that it does not promote the general acquisition of competences on a broad basis.

Formal learning and organized advanced training. For the enterprises that were interviewed advanced training plays an important role; at least, it enjoys a high esteem. In particular in-house workshops, but also external seminars are considered the preferred forms of advanced training. The systematical development of their employees, of which two thirds of the interviewed enterprises say that they support it, includes for at least almost half of them also the release from duty.

However, in the case studies also a certain skepticism concerning concrete issues with regard to advanced training is encountered. Stockpile-learning is mostly not considered practical. In particular certification courses conducted by software manufacturers have a dubious reputation. Although they are considered necessary, this is justified by their publicity value. With regard to the contents and didactic organization of the courses, the statements of the people that were interviewed are rather reserved.

"For some time we also attended their demonstrations. However, I must say that I was not very much convinced by the results. Half of the demonstration is always a promotion event for beautiful new products. (...) Judged by the content, it is really not of much use, you rather have the feeling of having wasted your time. At any rate, this has been my experience to date" (BK § 246).

The advantage of product-oriented certifications is that with them a marketable qualification system has been established, which in certain market segments has also become a standard for quality control and order placement.

Nevertheless, there is a necessity for small and medium-size enterprises to design their own career development paths, because they usually cannot compete with large enterprises for highly specialized experts. However, the enterprises did hardly develop their own ideas in this respect, which is evident, among other things; in their reserved to skeptical view concerning a system for advanced IT training. In the opinion of the management of the enterprises company-specific competence requirements cannot be imparted within the framework of a "system" because of the dynamics of the development in the field of IT. The employees, on the other hand, are interested in a systematic advanced IT training, because the chances for their professional development are better on the basis of qualifications that are also valid outside the company. It seems that presently the organized advanced training of the employees in the enterprises is limited to contractual provisions, the right to advanced training measures and the participation in courses of the product manufacturers. These marketable qualifications of the employees, however, are connected with dependencies of the corresponding employees and enterprises on the product manufacturers, leading to a orientation of the courses with regard to learning theory and methodology that is questionable.

Competence. In the case studies we asked in detail about the importance of human, social and functional competence in the business context. The answers given to these questions show that, although these competences are attributed an equal role compared to functional competences, subconsciously functional competences are considered to be more important. In case studies it is always stressed that although human and social competences matter too, these competences cannot be seen without the functional competences. Because they solve problems in record time, even "eccentrics" or "IT freaks" are valued with their functional competence in such a way that they can have their place in the enterprise as long as the other employees compensate for their lack of communication skills. The special emphasis on functional competence also corresponds with the repeatedly voiced comment that in the case of IT experts the important things are their fundamental attitude, talent, special approach and personality. In their self-conception as IT experts the interviewed persons have a certain "affinity" or a "potential". They see themselves as "persons doing their job out of conviction" or as "curious nursery children". Thus they consider their individual talents and their individual educational and professional biography particularly important to the development of their competences.

The empirical analysis of the functional, social and human competences, which jointly form the professional action competence, deals primarily with the interplay between these competences. According to our studies, one capability that integrates these three competence forms is the communication competence. In the case studies all interview partners mention the communication with colleagues in the work process as a central capability.

"In principle, this was in a purely autodidactic manner: by learning in various projects, which I initiated myself. (...) For me, this is the interesting thing about the IT sector (...), that I can define a learning path for myself wherever I want to go, whatever I want to learn next. You can realize this rather openly – in contrast to a large-scale enterprise or a government agency. There are those who also have an appropriate formal qualification" (UT § 53).

What is striking is that in particular lateral entries stress their non-functional knowledge and capabilities, emphasizing their self-learning capability and their communicative competences.

Organization of work so as to promote learning and new forms of learning. In the enterprises included in our study there are in some cases forms of learning of the type discussed in Chapter 4. The great learning demands at work have obviously leaded to the development of new forms of learning. Only part of these learning forms, however, has been specifically developed for this purpose. Characteristic of such new forms of learning, such as quality circle, learning bays, coaching or e-learning, which appeared in large and medium-size enterprises, is the systematic linking of a work infrastructure with a learning infrastructure. In most of the enterprises of our case study, however, only the beginnings of the development of such structures, which are to ensure a continuous learning process in the enterprise and contribute to an increase in efficiency, exist.

The results of the case studies cannot be generally brought into correspondence with the information obtained from the enterprises that participated in the quantitative study. In the case study there are for example no clues for a purposeful coaching or for structured team discussions that, according to the questionnaire survey, are both performed by more than half of the enterprises. Nevertheless it can be said that the enterprises strive to support the communicative exchange about in-house work processes systematically and with the intention to achieve gains from learning. There are forms such as meeting day, team meetings for the discussion of problems that have to be dealt with or project manager circles for the discussion of current projects. These are mostly intended to provide for a smooth work process, but on the other hand provide time and space for learning. They can be called forms of work organization that are conductive to learning and that, in this function, are definitely comparable to semi-autonomous team work and other team meetings in reorganized enterprises.

A substantial characteristic of the work in the IT industry is that jobs are performed in the form of projects. In such projects, which may be oriented towards a complete business process, routine actions are again and again brought together with new experience, because they always lead to new situations.

> "Usually I will not go somewhere and do my routine job. Only once in a time. It is always a new situation. If I have here a permanent position, I know my stuff. But in project-related work and when workings at the customer's, things are always different." (BS § 95)

Beyond these project form of the work, the enterprises of our case study fulfill the criteria of a work that is conductive to learning that are presented in Chapter 4 to a varying extent and have also developed elaborated company-owned forms of learning.

For example the larger enterprise studied in the case studies has developed an individual form of learning by establishing so-called specialist working groups. In this groups employees of all fields that deal with specific problems meet. By the employees it is considered a distinction to be a member of a specialist working group. Interested colleagues may take the initiative if they want to become a member of a specialist working group. Each of the specialist working groups, whose job is the further development of the know-how of the enterprise, has a chairman who structures the work. Some topics may also be brought into the monthly meetings by the executive board. The chairmen of the specialist working groups discuss matters regularly and form technical management levels. At the same time the specialist working group structure show the employees an opportunity for an individual development and career path.

Another variant to promote on-the-job learning that was tested in an enterprise of the case study included the setup of a model computer system in order to practice the installation of an operating system in the form of a game. When taking into account the working time allocated to this purpose, this measure was considered expensive, but on the other hand a workshop-like initial indoctrination and a follow-on coaching on such a system were considered more important than formal weekend seminars.

> "In this case we try to learn from each other and to learn by trial-and-error. Currently we are thinking how we can push that a little. We are thinking about whether it makes more sense to have people try out the new operating system and play with it on five computers for four weeks. This is pretty expensive. But on the other hand we do not think that it is useful to send people to a weekend seminar which is equally expensive (...). We rather consider providing a one- or two-day workshop-like initial indoctrination with technicians from partner organizations or even real lecturers and then a workshop-like coaching, so that there will be somebody around whom people can ask from time to time. But this trial-and-error process is important." (LK § 105)

This approach includes in turn linking the work infrastructure with the learning infrastructure. This is, however, more a work-associated learning, i.e. it is not directly integrated in the real work, but associated with it. It is also obvious that in this learning form the method of simulation can be directly connected with workplace-related learning. Additionally, this indicates that coaching as a learning form should follow the workshops.

In the three qualitatively studied enterprises organized workshops are the most distinct learning form that exhibits signs of the formalization of informal learning. In these workshops for example an employee with special knowledge or an external person presents his knowledge about specific business topics and if necessary demonstrates the required skills. Also personal networks are used to invite known personalities to lecture on business matters or an up-to-date operating system. The choice of words of the interviewed persons ("indoctrination" etc.) indicates that these workshops are demand-oriented, but nevertheless formal. A didactic approach is explicitly expected ("viewgraphs and documents"). The different forms and arrangement variants of in-house workshops range from casual meetings with friendly experts to indoctrination-like "events" extending over several days. The use of the things that have been learned ranges from direct application to additional background knowledge. Common to these different variants is common that a defined learning space is created that is relieved from acute work requirements and in which expert knowledge is presented systematically. In these work-related and mostly work-associated workshops working and learning are brought together. They also perform the function of reflection discussions as they are planned in the new advanced IT training in accordance with the APO concept.

"Another thing we did, and where the result was not bad, was to invite two friends who talked to us about various topics for one or two days. We paid them for this, to be sure. And they gave us lectures on some ideas and technologies we already knew well. These lectures were worked out in detail with viewgraphs and documents and all, which was very nice. The drawback was that although we needed this knowledge we did not directly have the opportunity to use it at that time. If I remember well that since then half to three quarters of a year has passed, and now we are beginning to work with it, but you find that you have already forgotten approximately 90 percent of it." (BK § 185)

Workshops are thus an important form of in-house support for the learning of the employees and they fulfill this function in the sense of our initial theses by combining informal learning and formal learning. For a more detailed understanding of the processes it is necessary to find out in each case whether it is an workshop with the primary aim of learning and qualification. In this case this is a form of learning. If it is, however, a workshop with the aim of working on a job, then this is a form of work that includes informal, if necessary also formal learning. Both forms can be encountered and the transitions are fluid. Also these working-learning forms are quite obviously just being developed and shaped.

To summarize it can be stated, that the SME of the IT-sector have recognized the need to systematically support their employees and that at the same time they are testing various forms of such support. This is substantiated by the results obtained by the questionnaires as well as by the case study. The organization of work by including criteria concerning the promotion of learning is done more intuitively and based on slogans like "we can manage it", "to pull oneself out of the mud" or "to make a virtue of necessity". This situative handling of learning and advanced training of the employees does hardly exhibit any structural and sustained enterprise-specific concepts. The thesis that we placed at the beginning of our study, i.e. that a professional education management is required to support learning at work, is thus convincingly proven.

References

Baukrowitz, A., & Boes, A. (2002). Weiterbildung in der IT-Industrie. In WSI-Mitteilungen 1/2002, pp. 10–18.

Benzenberg, I. (1999). Netzwerke als Regulations- und Aktionsfeld der beruflichen Weiterbildung. Bochum: Winkler.

Bundesministerium für Bildung und Forschung (2002). (Ed.), IT-Professional Education System. (IT-Weiterbildung mit System. Neue Perspektiven für Fachkräfte und Unternehmen.) Bonn: BMBF, Referat Öffentlichkeitsarbeit.

Bulletin EU 1/2–1996; Retrieved March 9th, 2004 from http://europa.eu.int/abc/doc/off/bull/en/9601/p103082.htm

Coombs, Ph., & Ahmed, H. (1974). Attacking rural poverty. How nonformal education can help. Baltimore: John Hopkins University Press.

Dehnbostel, P. (1992). Ziele und Inhalte dezentraler Berufsbildungskonzepte. In P. Dehnbostel, H. Holz & H. Novak (Eds.), Lernen für die Zukunft durch verstärktes Lernen am Arbeitsplatz – Dezentrale Aus- und Weiterbildungskonzepte in der Praxis (pp. 9–24). Berlin: BIBB.

Dehnbostel, P. (2002). Bringing work-related learning back to authentic work contexts. In P. Kämäräinen et al. (Eds.), *Transformation of learning in education and training: Key qualifications revisited* (pp. 190–202). Luxemburg: Office for Publications of the European Communities.

Dehnbostel, P., Holz, H., & Novak, H. (Eds.) (1992). Lernen für die Zukunft durch verstärktes Lernen am Arbeitsplatz – Dezentrale Aus- und Weiterbildungskonzepte in der Praxis. Berlin: BIBB.

Dehnbostel, P., & Molzberger, G. (2001). Combination of Formal Learning and Learning by Experience in Industrial Enterprises. In J. N. Streumer (Ed.), *Perspectives on learning at the Workplace: Theoretical positions, organizational factors, learning processes and effects* (pp. 77–85). Enschede: Universiteit Twente.

Dehnbostel, P., & Peters, S. (Ed.) (1991). Dezentrales und erfahrungsorientiertes Lernen im Betrieb. Alsbach/Bergstr.

Dohmen, G. (1999). Informelles Lernen. Karteikarte. In Berufsbildung, Vol. 57, pp. 25–26.

Dostal, W. (2002). IT-Arbeitsmarkt und erkennbare Qualifikationsstrategien. In Bundesinstitut für Berufsbildung (Ed.), Veränderte Arbeitswelt – veränderte Qualifikationen: Wechselwirkungen zwischen Arbeitsmarkt und Bildungsstrukturen. Bonn: BIBB.

Ehrke, M., & Müller, Kh. (2002). Design, development and implementation of the new continuing IT training system. (Begründung, Entwicklung und Umsetzung des neuen IT-Weiterbildungssystems.) In BMBF (Ed.), IT-Professional education system. (IT-Weiterbildung mit System. Neue Perspektiven für Fachkräfte und Unternehmen.) (pp. 7–18). Bonn.

Kirchhöfer, D. (2000): Informelles Lernen in alltäglichen Lebensführungen. Chance für berufliche Kompetenzentwicklung. (Quem-Report No. 66). Berlin.

Kremer, J. (1998): Qualifizierungsnetzwerke beruflicher Weiterbildung – dargestellt an der Wirtschaftsregion Aachen. Alsbach/Bergstraße: LTV-Verlag.

Livingstone, D. W. (1999). Informelles Lernen in der Wissensgesellschaft. In Arbeitsgemeinschaft Qualifikations-Entwicklungs-Management (QUEM): Kompetenz für Europa – Wandel durch Lernen – Lernen im Wandel. Referate auf dem internationalen Fachkongress (pp. 65–92). Berlin.

Overwien, B. (2000). Informal learning and the role of social movements. *International Review of Education, 46*(6), 621–640.

Overwien, Bernd: Informelles Lernen. In: Otto, Hansuwe; Coelen, Thomas (Hrsg.) Grundbegriffe der Ganztagsbildung. Zur Integration von formeller und informeller Bildung. Opladen 2004 (in Press)

Rohs, M. (2002). Arbeitsprozessorientierte Weiterbildung in der IT-Branche: Ein Gesamtkonzept zur Verbindung formeller und informeller Lernprozesse. In M. Rohs (Ed.), Arbeitsprozessintegriertes Lernen. Neue Ansätze für die berufliche Bildung. (pp. 75–94). Münster: Waxmann.

Rohs, M., & Büchele, U. (2002). Work process-oriented competence development. (Arbeitsprozessorientierte Kompetenzentwicklung.) In Bundesministerium für Bildung und Forschung (Ed.), IT-Professional Education System. (IT-Weiterbildung mit System. Neue Perspektiven für Fachkräfte und Unternehmen.) (pp. 69–76). Bonn: BMBF, Referat Öffentlichkeitsarbeit.

Stieler-Lorenz, B. (2002). Informelles Lernen nach der Wende in den neuen Bundesländern. In M. Rohs (Ed.), Arbeitsprozessintegriertes Lernen. Neue Ansätze für die berufliche Bildung (pp. 127–142). Münster.

Stieler-Lorenz, B., Frister, S., Jakob, K., Liljeberg, H., & Steinborn, D. (2001). Untersuchung zum informellen Lernen in den neuen Bundesländern. In Arbeitsgemeinschaft Betriebliche Weiterbildungsforschung (Ed.), Berufliche Kompetenzentwicklung in formellen und informellen Strukturen, (pp. 277–318). Berlin (Quem-Report No. 69): ABWF.

Tully, C. J. (1994). Lernen in der Informationsgesellschaft. Informelle Bildung durch Computer und Medien. Opladen: Westdeutscher Verlag.

Watkins, K., & Marsick, V. (1990). Informal and incidental learning in the workplace. London: Routledge.

INDEX

community (*continued*)
  learning 299
  literacy practices 715–34
  media education 743
  MicroSociety 213
  parent and community involvement 295,
    297, 298, 300–2, 310, 312–15, 321–3
  policy makers separation from 680
  professional 534, 537
  school-community partnerships 430, 431,
    600
  social ecology models 304
  standards-based reform 144
  volunteer work 1003, 1007, 1008, 1012
  see also learning communities
community colleges 363, 852, 853, 861
community service programs 431–2, 1003,
  1007–8, 1012, 1014–16, 1017
community work 977, 979, 984, 988, 989,
  991, 998, 1009
comparative studies 75–99, 509
  challenges for 94–6
  functions and purposes of 76–8
  impact of 84–91
  literacy assessment 707–9
  policy relevance 91–4, 96
compensatory education 421
competencies
  adult learning 816–17, 821, 823
  business 1053
  communicative 1059
  competency-based curriculum 768
  computer use 1048
  functional 1059
  human capital theory 839
  informal learning 1049, 1050, 1058
  literacy 781, 782, 783, 784
  occupational 858, 859, 951–2, 1050
  public preoccupation with 736
  qualification networks 1054
  teacher regulation 573, 575, 584, 587–8
  whole person conceptualization 840
  see also skills
competition
  adult learning 815, 816
  charter schools 268
  economic 297, 816, 860
  financial incentives 789
  hegemonic ideology of 909
  higher education diversity 388
  inter-school 9, 47
  limitation of access to education 340
  market approaches to
    accountability 442–4, 445
  neo-liberal ideology 31
  price 869, 870, 871, 874, 875–6, 881, 896
  school choice 38, 183, 190, 266
  school-to-work transition policies 847
competitiveness
  continuous learning 1045

economic 284, 394, 395, 509
  marketization 19
  reforms 9–12
comprehension 123, 657
  assessment of 700, 707
  National Reading Panel report 654
  National Reporting System 125–6
  Reading First program 654, 655
  technology 752–3
  see also reading
comprehensive community initiatives
  (CCIs) 315–16
comprehensive school reform
  (CSR) 195–215, 246, 312–15, 322
Comprehensive School Reform Demonstration
  Program (CSRD) 196–8, 201, 203,
  204–5, 206–7, 209–10, 243
comprehensive schools 26, 851–2
compulsory education 351, 544
computers
  comprehension strategy instruction 752–3
  contexts for literacy 754
  historical context 926
  informal learning 550, 551, 555, 558–9,
    1048–9
  phonics instruction 751–2
  special needs students 701
  work productivity 867
  work-based skills 934, 937
  writing assessment 703–4
  see also information and communication
    technology; Internet; software;
    technology
Computers in Education Study 79, 81
conceptual change research 529–30
Confederation of South African Trade Unions
  (COSATU) 967, 973
connectionism 838
consensualism 341
conservatism
  Canada 68, 69
  choice 344
  France 515
  literacy 745
  opposition to multicultural
    education 65–6
  United States 29, 877
Consortium for Policy Research in Education
  (CPRE) 137, 138, 139
constructivism
  assessment 695, 696, 697–8, 709
  literacy 739
  technology 926, 932–3, 938
  see also social constructivism
Continua Model of Biliteracy 724–7
Continuing Professional Development
  (CPD) 394
contracting out 269–70, 274, 275, 889
  see also subcontracting
control-oriented approach 533

Springer International Handbooks of Education

Volume 1

International Handbook of Educational Leadership and Administration
Edited by Kenneth Leithwood, Judith Chapman, David Corson,
Philip Hallinger, and Ann Hart
ISBN 0-7923-3530-9

Volume 2

International Handbook of Science Education
Edited by Barry J. Fraser and Kenneth G. Tobin
ISBN 0-7923-3531-7

Volume 3

International Handbook of Teachers and Teaching
Edited by Bruce J. Biddle, Thomas L. Good, and Ivor L. Goodson
ISBN 0-7923-3532-5

Volume 4

International Handbook of Mathematics Education
Edited by Alan J. Bishop, Ken Clements, Christine Keitel, Jeremy Kilpatrick,
and Collette Laborde
ISBN 0-7923-3533-3

Volume 5

International Handbook of Educational Change
Edited by Andy Hargreaves, Ann Leiberman, Michael Fullan,
and David Hopkins
ISBN 0-7923-3534-1

Volume 6

International Handbook of Lifelong Learning
Edited by David Aspin, Judith Chapman, Micheal Hatton,
and Yukiko Sawano
ISBN 0-7923-6815-0

Volume 7

International Handbook of Research in Medical Education
Edited by Geoff R. Norman, Cees P.M. van der Vleuten, and David I. Newble
ISBN 1-4020-0466-4

Volume 8

Second International Handbook of Educational Leadership and
Administration
Edited by Kenneth Leithwood and Philip Hallinger
ISBN 1-4020-0690-X

Volume 9

International Handbook of Educational Evaluation
Edited by Thomas Kellaghan and Daniel L. Stufflebeam
ISBN 1-4020-0849-X

Volume 10

Second International Handbook of Mathematics Education
Edited by Alan J. Bishop, M.A. (Ken) Clements, Christine Keitel,
Jeremy Kilpatrick, and Frederick K.S. Leung
ISBN 1-4020-1008-7

Volume 11

International Handbook of Educational Research in the Asia-Pacific Region
Edited by John P. Keeves and Ryo Watanabe
ISBN 1-4020-1007-9

Volume 12

International Handbook of Self-Study of Teaching and Teacher Education
Practices
Edited by J. John Loughran, Mary Lynn Hamilton, Vicki Kubler LaBoskey
and Tom Russell
ISBN 1-4020-1812-6

Volume 13

International Handbook of Educational Policy
Edited by Nina Bascia, Alister Cumming, Amanda Datnow, Kenneth
Leithwood and David Livingstone
ISBN 1-4020-3189-0